T0130672

Get the eBooks FREE!
(PDF, ePub, Kindle, and liveBook all included)

We believe that once you buy a book from us, you should be able to read it in any format we have available. To get electronic versions of this book at no additional cost to you, purchase and then register this book at the Manning website.

Go to https://www.manning.com/freebook and follow the instructions to complete your pBook registration.

That's it!
Thanks from Manning!

Dependency Injection Principles, Practices, and Patterns

Dependency Injection
Principles, Practices, and Patterns

STEVEN VAN DEURSEN
MARK SEEMANN

MANNING
SHELTER ISLAND

For online information and ordering of this and other Manning books, please visit
www.manning.com. The publisher offers discounts on this book when ordered in quantity.
For more information, please contact

    Special Sales Department
    Manning Publications Co.
    20 Baldwin Road
    PO Box 761
    Shelter Island, NY 11964
    Email: orders@manning.com

Manning Publications Co.
20 Baldwin Road
PO Box 761
Shelter Island, NY 11964

Acquisitions editor:	Mike Stephens
Development editors:	Marina Michaels and
	Dan Maharry
Technical development editor:	Karsten Strøbæk
Review editor:	Ivan Martinović
Production editor:	Anthony Calcara
Copy editor:	Frances Buran
Proofreader:	Katie Tennant
Technical proofreader:	Chris Heneghan
Typesetter:	Happenstance Type-O-Rama
Cover designer:	Marija Tudor

ISBN 9781617294730
Printed in the United States of America

brief contents

PART 1 PUTTING DEPENDENCY INJECTION ON THE MAP............1

 1 ▪ The basics of Dependency Injection: What, why, and how   3
 2 ▪ Writing tightly coupled code   34
 3 ▪ Writing loosely coupled code   52

PART 2 CATALOG 81

 4 ▪ DI patterns   83
 5 ▪ DI anti-patterns   124
 6 ▪ Code smells   163

PART 3 PURE DI..209

 7 ▪ Application composition   211
 8 ▪ Object lifetime   236
 9 ▪ Interception   281
 10 ▪ Aspect-Oriented Programming by design   301
 11 ▪ Tool-based Aspect-Oriented Programming   341

PART 4 DI CONTAINERS 357

 12 ▪ DI Container introduction   359
 13 ▪ The Autofac DI Container   393
 14 ▪ The Simple Injector DI Container   427
 15 ▪ The Microsoft.Extensions.DependencyInjection DI Container   466

v

contents

preface xv
acknowledgments xvii
about this book xix
about the authors xxiii
about the cover illustration xxiv

PART 1 PUTTING DEPENDENCY INJECTION ON THE MAP ... 1

1 The basics of Dependency Injection: What, why, and how 3

1.1 Writing maintainable code 5
   Common myths about DI 5 • *Understanding the purpose of DI* 8

1.2 A simple example: Hello DI! 14
   Hello DI! code 15 • *Benefits of DI* 17

1.3 What to inject and what not to inject 24
   STABLE DEPENDENCIES 26 • VOLATILE DEPENDENCIES 26

1.4 DI scope 27
   OBJECT COMPOSITION 29 • OBJECT LIFETIME 30
   INTERCEPTION 30 • *DI in three dimensions* 31

1.5 Conclusion 32

2 *Writing tightly coupled code 34*

  2.1 Building a tightly coupled application 35
        *Meet Mary Rowan 35 ▪ Creating the data layer 36
        Creating the domain layer 39 ▪ Creating the UI layer 42*

  2.2 Evaluating the tightly coupled application 44
        *Evaluating the dependency graph 44
        Evaluating composability 45*

  2.3 Analysis of missing composability 47
        *Dependency graph analysis 47 ▪ Data access interface
        analysis 48 ▪ Miscellaneous other issues 50*

  2.4 Conclusion 50

3 *Writing loosely coupled code 52*

  3.1 Rebuilding the e-commerce application 53
        *Building a more maintainable UI 56 ▪ Building an
        independent domain model 61 ▪ Building a new data
        access layer 70 ▪ Implementing an ASP.NET Core–specific
        IUserContext Adapter 71 ▪ Composing the application
        in the COMPOSITION ROOT 73*

  3.2 Analyzing the loosely coupled implementation 74
        *Understanding the interaction between components 74
        Analyzing the new dependency graph 75*

PART 2   CATALOG...81

4 *DI patterns 83*

  4.1 COMPOSITION ROOT 85
        *How COMPOSITION ROOT works 87 ▪ Using a DI CONTAINER
        in a COMPOSITION ROOT 88 ▪ Example: Implementing
        a COMPOSITION ROOT using PURE DI 89 ▪ The apparent
        dependency explosion 92*

  4.2 CONSTRUCTOR INJECTION 95
        *How CONSTRUCTOR INJECTION works 95 ▪ When to use
        CONSTRUCTOR INJECTION 97 ▪ Known use of CONSTRUCTOR
        INJECTION 99 ▪ Example: Adding currency conversions to
        the featured products 100 ▪ Wrap-up 102*

4.3   METHOD INJECTION   104
          *How METHOD INJECTION works   104 ▪ When to use METHOD
          INJECTION   105 ▪ Known use of METHOD INJECTION   111
          Example: Adding currency conversions to the* Product
          ENTITY   112

4.4   PROPERTY INJECTION   114
          *How PROPERTY INJECTION works   114 ▪ When to use
          PROPERTY INJECTION   115 ▪ Known uses of PROPERTY
          INJECTION   118 ▪ Example: PROPERTY INJECTION as an
          extensibility model of a reusable library   118*

4.5   Choosing which pattern to use   120

5   *DI anti-patterns   124*

5.1   CONTROL FREAK   127
          *Example: CONTROL FREAK through newing up DEPENDENCIES   128
          Example: CONTROL FREAK through factories   129 ▪ Example:
          CONTROL FREAK through overloaded constructors   134
          Analysis of CONTROL FREAK   135*

5.2   SERVICE LOCATOR   138
          Example: ProductService *using a SERVICE LOCATOR   140
          Analysis of SERVICE LOCATOR   142*

5.3   AMBIENT CONTEXT   146
          *Example: Accessing time through AMBIENT CONTEXT   147
          Example: Logging through AMBIENT CONTEXT   149
          Analysis of AMBIENT CONTEXT   150*

5.4   CONSTRAINED CONSTRUCTION   154
          *Example: Late binding a ProductRepository   154
          Analysis of CONSTRAINED CONSTRUCTION   156*

6   *Code smells   163*

6.1   Dealing with the Constructor Over-injection code smell   164
          *Recognizing Constructor Over-injection   165 ▪ Refactoring from
          Constructor Over-injection to Facade Services   168 ▪ Refactoring
          from Constructor Over-injection to domain events   173*

6.2   Abuse of Abstract Factories   180
          *Abusing Abstract Factories to overcome lifetime
          problems   180 ▪ Abusing Abstract Factories to select
          DEPENDENCIES based on runtime data   187*

6.3   Fixing cyclic DEPENDENCIES   194

*Example: DEPENDENCY cycle caused by an SRP
violation   195 • Analysis of Mary's DEPENDENCY
cycle   199 • Refactoring from SRP violations to resolve
the DEPENDENCY cycle   200 • Common strategies for
breaking DEPENDENCY cycles   204 • Last resort: Breaking
the cycle with PROPERTY INJECTION   204*

PART 3   PURE DI 209

7   *Application composition   211*

7.1   Composing console applications   213

*Example: Updating currencies using the UpdateCurrency
program   214 • Building the COMPOSITION ROOT of the
UpdateCurrency program   215 • Composing object graphs
in CreateCurrencyParser   216 • A closer look at
UpdateCurrency's layering   217*

7.2   Composing UWP applications   218

*UWP composition   218 • Example: Wiring up a product-management
rich client   219 • Implementing the COMPOSITION ROOT in the
UWP application   226*

7.3   Composing ASP.NET Core MVC applications   228

*Creating a custom controller activator   230 • Constructing
custom middleware components using PURE DI   233*

8   *Object lifetime   236*

8.1   Managing DEPENDENCY LIFETIME   238

*Introducing LIFETIME MANAGEMENT   238 • Managing
lifetime with PURE DI   242*

8.2   Working with disposable DEPENDENCIES   245

*Consuming disposable DEPENDENCIES   246 • Managing
disposable DEPENDENCIES   250*

8.3   LIFESTYLE catalog   255

*The SINGLETON LIFESTYLE   256 • The TRANSIENT
LIFESTYLE   259 • The SCOPED LIFESTYLE   260*

8.4   Bad LIFESTYLE choices   266

*CAPTIVE DEPENDENCIES   266 • Using LEAKY ABSTRACTIONS to
leak LIFESTYLE choices to consumers   269 • Causing concurrency
bugs by tying instances to the lifetime of a thread   275*

9 *Interception* 281

9.1 Introducing INTERCEPTION 283

Decorator design pattern 284 • Example: Implementing auditing using a Decorator 287

9.2 Implementing CROSS-CUTTING CONCERNS 290

Intercepting with a Circuit Breaker 292 • Reporting exceptions using the Decorator pattern 297 • Preventing unauthorized access to sensitive functionality using a Decorator 298

10 *Aspect-Oriented Programming by design* 301

10.1 Introducing AOP 302

10.2 The SOLID principles 305

SINGLE RESPONSIBILITY PRINCIPLE (SRP) 306 • OPEN/CLOSED PRINCIPLE (OCP) 306 • LISKOV SUBSTITUTION PRINCIPLE (LSP) 307 • INTERFACE SEGREGATION PRINCIPLE (ISP) 307 DEPENDENCY INVERSION PRINCIPLE (DIP) 308 • SOLID principles and INTERCEPTION 308

10.3 SOLID as a driver for AOP 308

Example: Implementing product-related features using IProductService 309 • Analysis of IProductService from the perspective of SOLID 311 • Improving design by applying SOLID principles 314 • Adding more CROSS-CUTTING CONCERNS 327 • Conclusion 336

11 *Tool-based Aspect-Oriented Programming* 341

11.1 Dynamic INTERCEPTION 342

Example: INTERCEPTION with Castle Dynamic Proxy 344 Analysis of dynamic INTERCEPTION 346

11.2 Compile-time weaving 348

Example: Applying a transaction aspect using compile-time weaving 349 • Analysis of compile-time weaving 351

PART 4 DI CONTAINERS 357

12 *DI Container introduction* 359

12.1 Introducing DI CONTAINERS 361

Exploring containers' Resolve API 361 • AUTO-WIRING 363 Example: Implementing a simplistic DI CONTAINER that supports AUTO-WIRING 364

12.2   Configuring DI CONTAINERS   372

Configuring containers with configuration files   373
Configuring containers using CONFIGURATION AS
CODE   377 ▪ Configuring containers by convention using
AUTO-REGISTRATION   379 ▪ Mixing and matching configuration
approaches   385

12.3   When to use a DI CONTAINER   385

Using third-party libraries involves costs and risks   386 ▪ PURE DI
gives a shorter feedback cycle   388 ▪ The verdict: When to use a DI
CONTAINER   389

13   The Autofac DI Container   393

13.1   Introducing Autofac   394

Resolving objects   395
Configuring the ContainerBuilder   398

13.2   Managing lifetime   404

Configuring instance scopes   405 ▪ Releasing components   406

13.3   Registering difficult APIs   409

Configuring primitive DEPENDENCIES   409 ▪ Registering
objects with code blocks   411

13.4   Working with multiple components   412

Selecting among multiple candidates   413
Wiring sequences   417 ▪ Wiring Decorators   420
Wiring Composites   422

14   The Simple Injector DI Container   427

14.1   Introducing Simple Injector   428

Resolving objects   429 ▪ Configuring the container   432

14.2   Managing lifetime   438

Configuring LIFESTYLES   439 ▪ Releasing components   440
Ambient scopes   443 ▪ Diagnosing the container for common
lifetime problems   444

14.3   Registering difficult APIs   447

Configuring primitive DEPENDENCIES   448 ▪ Extracting primitive
DEPENDENCIES to Parameter Objects   449 ▪ Registering objects with
code blocks   450

14.4 Working with multiple components 451

Selecting among multiple candidates 452
Wiring sequences 454 ▪ *Wiring Decorators 457*
Wiring Composites 459 ▪ *Sequences are streams 462*

15 **The Microsoft.Extensions.DependencyInjection DI Container 466**

15.1 Introducing Microsoft.Extensions.DependencyInjection 467

Resolving objects 468
Configuring the ServiceCollection *471*

15.2 Managing lifetime 476

Configuring LIFESTYLES 477 ▪ *Releasing components 477*

15.3 Registering difficult APIs 480

Configuring primitive DEPENDENCIES 480 ▪ *Extracting primitive*
DEPENDENCIES to Parameter Objects 481 ▪ *Registering objects with*
code blocks 482

15.4 Working with multiple components 483

Selecting among multiple candidates 483 ▪ *Wiring*
sequences 486 ▪ *Wiring Decorators 489* ▪ *Wiring*
Composites 492

glossary 499

resources 504

index 507

preface

There's a peculiar phenomenon related to Microsoft called the *Microsoft Echo Chamber*. Microsoft is a huge organization, and the surrounding ecosystem of Microsoft Certified Partners multiplies that size by orders of magnitude. If you're sufficiently embedded in this ecosystem, it can be hard to see past its boundaries. Whenever you look for a solution to a problem with a Microsoft product or technology, you're likely to find an answer that involves throwing even more Microsoft products at it. No matter what you yell within the echo chamber, the answer is *Microsoft!*

When Microsoft hired me (Mark) in 2003, I was already firmly embedded in the echo chamber, having worked for Microsoft Certified Partners for years—and I loved it! They soon shipped me off to an internal tech conference in New Orleans to learn about the latest and greatest Microsoft technology.

Today, I can't recall any of the Microsoft product sessions I attended—but I do remember the last day. On that day, having failed to experience any sessions that could satisfy my hunger for cool tech, I was mostly looking forward to flying home to Denmark. My top priority was to find a place to sit so I could attend to my email, so I chose a session that seemed marginally relevant for me and fired up my laptop.

The session was loosely structured and featured several presenters. One was a bearded guy named Martin Fowler, who talked about Test-Driven Development (TDD) and dynamic mocks. I had never heard of him, and I didn't listen very closely, but something must have stuck in my mind.

Soon after returning to Denmark, I was tasked with rewriting a big ETL (extract, transform, load) system from scratch, and I decided to give TDD a try (it turned out to be a very good decision). The use of dynamic mocks followed naturally, but also introduced the need to manage dependencies. I found that to be a very difficult but very captivating problem, and I couldn't stop thinking about it.

What started as a side effect of my interest in TDD became a passion in itself. I did a lot of research, read lots of blog posts about the matter, wrote quite a few blogs myself, experimented with code, and discussed the topic with anyone who cared to listen. Increasingly, I had to look outside the Microsoft Echo Chamber for inspiration and guidance. Along the way, people associated me with the ALT.NET movement even though I was never very active in it. I made all the mistakes it was possible to make, but I was gradually able to develop a coherent understanding of Dependency Injection (DI).

When Manning approached me with the idea for a book about Dependency Injection in .NET, my first reaction was, "Is this even necessary?" I felt that all the concepts a developer needs to understand DI were already described in numerous blog posts. Was there anything to add? Honestly, I thought DI in .NET was a topic that had been done to death already.

Upon reflection, however, it dawned on me that while the knowledge is definitely out there, it's very scattered and uses a lot of conflicting terminology. Before the first edition of this book, there were no titles about DI that attempted to present a coherent description of it. After thinking about it further, I realized that Manning was offering me a tremendous challenge and a great opportunity to collect and systematize all that I knew about DI.

The result is this book and its predecessor—the first edition. It uses .NET Core and C# to introduce and describe a comprehensive terminology and guidance for DI, but I hope the value of this book will reach well beyond the platform. I think the pattern language articulated here is universal. Whether you're a .NET developer or use another object-oriented platform, I hope this book will help you be a better software engineer.

acknowledgments

Gratitude may seem like a cliché, but this is only because it's such a fundamental part of human nature. While we were writing the book, many people gave us good reasons to be grateful, and we would like to thank them all.

First of all, writing a book in our spare time has given us a new understanding of just how taxing such a project is on marriage and family life. Mark's wife Cecilie stayed with him and actively supported him during the whole process. Most significantly, she understood just how important this project was to him. They're still together, and Mark looks forward to being able to spend more time with her and their kids Linea and Jarl. Steven's wife Judith gave him the space needed to complete this immense undertaking, but she certainly is glad that the project is *finally* finished.

On a more professional level, we want to thank Manning for giving us this opportunity. Michael Stephens initiated the project. Dan Maharry, Marina Michaels, and Christina Taylor served as our development editors and kept a keen eye on the quality of the text. They helped us identify weak spots in the manuscript and provided extensive constructive criticism.

Karsten Strøbæk served as our technical development editor, read through numerous early drafts, and provided much helpful feedback. Karsten was there when Mark wrote the first edition and served as the technical proofreader during production at that time. In this edition, technical proofreading was done by Chris Heneghan, who caught many subtle bugs and inconsistencies throughout the manuscript.

After we were done writing the manuscript, we entered the production process. This was managed by Anthony Calcara. During that process, Frances Buran was our copyeditor, while Nichole Beard held a close watch on the book's graphics and diagrams.

The following reviewers read the manuscript at various stages of development, and we're grateful for their comments and insight: Ajay Bhosale, Björn Nordblom, Cemre Mengu, Dennis Sellinger, Emanuele Origgi, Ernesto Cardenas Cangahuala, Gustavo Gomes, Igor Kochetov, Jeremy Caney, Justin Coulston, Mikkel Arentoft, Pasquale Zirpoli, Robert Morrison, Sergio Romero, Shawn Lam, and Stephen Byrne. Reviewing was made possible by Ivan Martinovic, the book's review editor.

Many of the participants in the Manning Early Access Program (MEAP) also provided feedback and asked difficult questions that exposed the weak parts of the text.

Special thanks go out to Jeremy Caney, who started out as a MEAP participant but was promoted to reviewer. He supplied us with an immense amount of feedback, both linguistic and contextual. His deep understanding of DI and software design was invaluable.

Also special thanks to Ric Slappendel. Ric advised us on how to compose UWP applications using DI. His knowledge about WPF, UWP, and XAML saved us countless hours and sleepless nights, and completely shaped section 7.2 and its companion code examples. Without Ric's help, we likely would've ended up with a book that didn't discuss UWP at all.

Alex Meyer-Gleaves and Travis Illig reviewed early versions of chapter 13 and provided us with feedback on using the new Autofac configuration and Decorator support. We're grateful for their participation.

And finally, Mogens Heller Grabe courteously allowed us to use his picture of a hair dryer wired directly into a wall outlet.

about this book

This is a book about Dependency Injection (DI), first and foremost. It's also a book about .NET, but that's much less important. Although C# is used for code examples, much of the discussion in this book can be easily applied to other languages and platforms. In fact, we learned a lot of the underlying principles and patterns from reading books where Java or C++ was used in examples.

DI is a set of related patterns and principles. It's a way to think about and design code, more than it is a specific technology. The ultimate purpose of using DI is to create maintainable software within the object-oriented paradigm.

The concepts used throughout this book all relate to object-oriented programming. The problem that DI addresses (code maintainability) is universal, but the proposed solution is given within the scope of object-oriented programming in statically typed languages: C#, Java, Visual Basic .NET, C++, and so on. You can't apply DI to procedural programming, and it may not be the best solution in functional or dynamic languages.

DI in isolation is just a small thing, but it's closely interwoven with a large complex of principles and patterns for object-oriented software design. Whereas the book focuses consistently on DI from start to finish, it also discusses many of these other topics in the light of the specific perspective that DI can give. The goal of the book is more than just teaching you about DI specifics: the goal is to make you a better object-oriented programmer.

Who should read this book?

It would be tempting to state that this is a book for all .NET developers. But the .NET community today is vast and spans developers working with web applications, desktop applications, smartphones, RIA, integration, office automation, content management systems, and even games. Although .NET is object oriented, not all of those developers write object-oriented code.

This is a book about object-oriented programming, so at a minimum readers should be interested in object orientation and understand what an interface is. A few years of professional experience and knowledge of design patterns or SOLID principles will certainly be of benefit as well. In fact, we don't expect beginners to get much out of the book; it's mostly targeted toward experienced developers and software architects.

The examples are all written in C#, so readers working with other .NET languages must be able to read and understand C#. Readers familiar with non-.NET object-oriented languages like Java and C++ may also find the book valuable, because the .NET platform-specific content is relatively light. Personally, we read a lot of pattern books with examples in Java and still get a lot out of them, so we hope the converse is true as well.

Roadmap

The contents of this book are divided into four parts. Ideally, we'd like you to first read it from cover to cover and then subsequently use it as a reference, but we understand if you have other priorities. For that reason, a majority of the chapters are written so that you can dive right in and start reading from that point.

The first part is the major exception. It contains a general introduction to DI and is probably best read sequentially. The second part is a catalog of patterns and the like, whereas the third and largest part is an examination of DI from three different angles. The fourth part of the book is a catalog of three DI CONTAINER libraries.

There are a lot of interconnected concepts, and, because we introduce them the first time it feels natural, this means we often mention concepts before we've formally introduced them. To distinguish these universal concepts from more local terms, we consistently use SMALL CAPS to make them stand out. All these terms are briefly defined in the glossary, which also contains references to a more extensive description.

Part 1 is a general introduction to DI. If you don't know what DI is, this is the place to start; but even if you do, you may want to familiarize yourself with the contents of part 1, as it establishes a lot of the context and terminology used in the rest of the book. Chapter 1 discusses the purpose and benefits of DI and provides a general outline. Chapter 2 contains a big and rather comprehensive example of tightly coupled code, and chapter 3 explains how to reimplement the same example using DI. Compared to the other parts, part 1 has a more linear progression of its content. You'll need to read each chapter from the beginning to gain the most from it.

Part 2 is a catalog of patterns, anti-patterns, and code smells. This is where you'll find prescriptive guidance on how to implement DI and the dangers to look out for. Chapter 4 is a catalog of DI design patterns, and, conversely, chapter 5 is a catalog of anti-patterns. Chapter 6 contains generalized solutions to commonly occurring issues. As a catalog, each chapter contains a set of loosely related sections that are designed to be read in isolation as well as in sequence.

Part 3 examines DI from three different angles: OBJECT COMPOSITION, LIFETIME MANAGEMENT, and INTERCEPTION. In chapter 7, we discuss how to implement DI on top of existing application frameworks—ASP.NET Core and UWP—and how to implement DI using a console application. Chapter 8 describes how to manage DEPENDENCY lifetimes to avoid resources leaks. Whereas the structure is a little less stringent than previous chapters, a large part of that chapter can be used as a catalog of well-known LIFESTYLES. The remaining three chapters describe how to compose applications with CROSS-CUTTING CONCERNS. Chapter 9 goes into the basics of INTERCEPTION using Decorators, whereas chapters 10 and 11 dive deep into the concept of ASPECT-ORIENTED PROGRAMMING. This is where you harvest the benefits of all the work that came before, so, in many ways, we consider this to be the climax of the book.

Part 4 is a catalog of DI CONTAINER libraries. It starts with a discussion on what DI CONTAINERS are and how they fit into the overall picture. The remaining three chapters each cover a specific container in a fair amount of detail: Autofac, Simple Injector, and Microsoft.Extensions.DependencyInjection. Each chapter covers its container in a rather condensed form to save space, so you may want to read about only the one or two containers that interest you the most. In many ways, we regard these three chapters as a very big set of appendixes.

To keep the discussion of DI principles and patterns free of any specific container APIs, most of the book, with the exception of part 4, is written without referencing a particular container. This is also why the containers appear with such force in part 4. It's our hope that by keeping the discussion general, the book will be useful for a longer period of time.

You can also take the concepts from parts 1 through 3 and apply them to container libraries not covered in part 4. There are good containers available that, unfortunately, we couldn't cover. But even for users of these libraries, we hope that this book has a lot to offer.

Code conventions and downloads

There are many code examples in this book. Most of those are in C#, but there's also a bit of XML and JSON here and there. Source code in listings and text is in a `fixed-width font like this` to separate it from ordinary text.

All the source code for the book is written in C# and Visual Studio 2017. The ASP.NET Core applications are written against ASP.NET Core v2.1.

Only a few of the techniques described in this book hinge on modern language features. We wanted to strike a reasonable balance between conservative and modern coding styles. When we write code professionally, we use modern language features to a far greater degree, but, for the most part, the most advanced features are generics and LINQ. The last thing we want is for you to get the idea that DI can only be applied with ultra-modern languages.

Writing code examples for a book presents its own set of challenges. Compared to a modern computer monitor, a book only allows for very short lines of code. It was very tempting to write code in a terse style with short but cryptic names for methods and variables. Such code is already difficult to understand as real code even when you have an IDE and a debugger nearby, but it becomes really difficult to follow in a book. We found it very important to keep names as readable as possible. To make it all fit, we've sometimes had to resort to some unorthodox line breaks. All the code compiles, but sometimes the formatting looks a bit funny.

The code also makes use of the C# var keyword. In our professional code, where line width isn't limited by the size of a book's page, we often use a different coding style when applying var. Here, to save space, we use var whenever we judge that an explicit declaration makes the code less readable.

The word *class* is often used as a synonym for a type. In .NET, classes, structs, interfaces, enums, and so on are all types, but because the word *type* is also a word with a lot of overloaded meaning in ordinary language, it would often make the text less clear if used.

Most of the code in this book relates to an overarching example running through the book: an online store complete with supporting internal management applications. This is about the least exciting example you can expect to see in any software text, but we chose it for a few reasons:

- It's a well-known problem domain for most readers. Although it may seem boring, we think this is an advantage, because it doesn't steal focus from DI.
- We also have to admit that we couldn't really think of any other domain that was rich enough to support all the different scenarios we had in mind.

We wrote a lot of code to support the code examples, and most of that code isn't in this book. In fact, we wrote almost all of it using Test-Driven Development (TDD), but as this isn't a TDD book, we generally don't show the unit tests in the book.

The source code for all examples in this book is available from Manning's website: www.manning.com/books/dependency-injection-principles-practices-patterns. The README.md in the root of the download contains instructions for compiling and running the code.

liveBook discussion forum

The purchase of *Dependency Injection Principles, Practices, and Patterns*, includes free access to a private web forum run by Manning Publications, where you can make comments about the book, ask technical questions, and receive help from the authors and from other users. To access the forum and subscribe to it, point your web browser to https://livebook.manning.com/#!/book/dependency-injection-principles-practices-patterns/discussion. You can also learn more about Manning's forums and the rules of conduct at https://livebook.manning.com/#!/discussion.

Manning's commitment to our readers is to provide a venue where a meaningful dialogue between individual readers and between readers and the authors can take place. It isn't a commitment to any specific amount of participation on the part of the authors, whose contribution to the forum remains voluntary (and unpaid). We suggest that you ask them some challenging questions lest their interest stray! The book forum and the archives of previous discussions will be accessible from the publisher's website as long as the book is in print.

about the authors

Steven van Deursen is a Dutch freelance .NET developer and architect with experience in the field since 2002. He lives in Nijmegen and enjoys writing code for fun and profit. Besides writing code, Steven trains in martial arts, likes to go out for food, and certainly fancies a good whiskey.

Mark Seemann is a programmer, software architect, and speaker living in Copenhagen, Denmark. He has been working with software since 1995 and TDD since 2003, including six years with Microsoft as a consultant, developer, and architect. Mark is currently professionally engaged with software development and is working out of Copenhagen. He enjoys reading, painting, playing the guitar, good wine, and gourmet food.

about the cover illustration

On the cover of *Dependency Injection Principles, Practices, and Patterns* is "A woman from Vodnjan," a small town in the interior of the peninsula of Istria in the Adriatic Sea, off Croatia. The illustration is taken from a reproduction of an album of Croatian traditional costumes from the mid-nineteenth century by Nikola Arsenovic, published by the Ethnographic Museum in Split, Croatia, in 2003. The illustrations were obtained from a helpful librarian at the Ethnographic Museum in Split, itself situated in the Roman core of the medieval center of the town: the ruins of Emperor Diocletian's retirement palace from around AD 304. The book includes finely colored illustrations of figures from different regions of Croatia, accompanied by descriptions of the costumes and of everyday life. Vodnjan is a culturally and historically significant town, situated on a hilltop with a beautiful view of the Adriatic and known for its many churches and treasures of sacral art. The woman on the cover wears a long, black linen skirt and a short, black jacket over a white linen shirt. The jacket is trimmed with blue embroidery, and a blue linen apron completes the costume. The woman is also wearing a large-brimmed black hat, a flowered scarf, and big hoop earrings. Her elegant costume indicates that she is an inhabitant of the town, rather than a village. Folk costumes in the surrounding countryside are more colorful, made of wool, and decorated with rich embroidery.

Dress codes and lifestyles have changed over the last 200 years, and the diversity by region, so rich at the time, has faded away. It is now hard to tell apart the inhabitants of different continents, let alone of different hamlets or towns separated by only a few miles. Perhaps we have traded cultural diversity for a more varied personal life—certainly for a more varied and fast-paced technological life.

Manning celebrates the inventiveness and initiative of the computer business with book covers based on the rich diversity of regional life of two centuries ago, brought back to life by illustrations from old books and collections like this one.

Part 1

Putting Dependency Injection
on the map

Dependency Injection (DI) is one of the most misunderstood concepts of object-oriented programming. The confusion is abundant and spans terminology, purpose, and mechanics. Should it be called Dependency Injection, Dependency Inversion, Inversion of Control, or even Third-Party Connect? Is the purpose of DI only to support unit testing, or is there a broader purpose? Is DI the same as SERVICE LOCATION? Do we need DI CONTAINERS to apply DI?

There are plenty of blog posts, magazine articles, conference presentations, and so on that discuss DI, but, unfortunately, many of them use conflicting terminology or give bad advice. This is true across the board, and even big and influential actors like Microsoft add to the confusion.

It doesn't have to be this way. In this book, we present and use a consistent terminology. For the most part, we've adopted and clarified existing terminology defined by others, but, occasionally, we add a bit of terminology where none existed previously. This has helped us tremendously in evolving a specification of the scope or boundaries of DI.

One of the underlying reasons behind all the inconsistency and bad advice is that the boundaries of DI are quite blurry. Where does DI end, and where do other object-oriented concepts begin? We think that it's impossible to draw a distinct line between DI and other aspects of writing good object-oriented code. To talk about DI, we have to pull in other concepts such as SOLID, Clean Code, and even ASPECT-ORIENTED PROGRAMMING. We don't feel that we can credibly write about DI without also touching on some of these other topics.

The first part of the book helps you understand the place of DI in relation to other facets of software engineering—putting it on the map, so to speak. Chapter 1 gives you a quick tour of DI, covering its purpose, principles, and benefits, as well as providing an outline of the scope for the rest of the book. It's focused on the big picture and doesn't go into a lot of details. If you want to learn what DI is and why you should be interested in it, this is the place to start. This chapter assumes you have no prior knowledge of DI. Even if you already know about DI, you may still want to read it—it may turn out to be something other than what you expected.

Chapters 2 and 3, on the other hand, are completely reserved for one big example. This example is intended to give you a much more concrete feel for DI. To contrast DI with a more traditional style of programming, chapter 2 showcases a typical, tightly coupled implementation of a sample e-commerce application. Chapter 3 then subsequently reimplements it with DI.

In this part, we'll discuss DI in general terms. This means we won't use any so-called DI CONTAINER. It's entirely possible to apply DI without using a DI CONTAINER. A DI CONTAINER is a helpful, but optional, tool. So parts 1, 2, and 3 more or less ignore DI CONTAINERS completely, and instead discuss DI in a container-agnostic way. Then, in part 4, we return to DI CONTAINERS to dissect three specific libraries.

Part 1 establishes the context for the rest of the book. It's aimed at readers who don't have any prior knowledge of DI, but experienced DI practitioners can also benefit from skimming the chapters to get a feeling for the terminology used throughout the book. By the end of part 1, you should have a firm grasp of the vocabulary and overall concepts, even if some of the concrete details are still a little fuzzy. That's OK—the book becomes more concrete as you read on, so parts 2, 3, and 4 should answer the questions you're likely to have after reading part 1.

The basics of Dependency Injection: What, why, and how

In this chapter

- Dispelling common myths about Dependency Injection
- Understanding the purpose of Dependency Injection
- Evaluating the benefits of Dependency Injection
- Knowing when to apply Dependency Injection

You may have heard that making a *sauce béarnaise* is difficult. Even among people who regularly cook, many have never attempted to make one. This is a shame, because the sauce is delicious. (It's traditionally paired with steak, but it's also an excellent accompaniment to white asparagus, poached eggs, and other dishes.) Some resort to substitutes like ready-made sauces or instant mixes, but these aren't nearly as satisfying as the real thing.

A sauce béarnaise is an emulsified sauce made from egg yolk and butter, that's flavored with tarragon, chervil, shallots, and vinegar. It contains no water. The biggest challenge to making it is that its preparation can fail. The sauce can curdle or separate, and, if either happens, you can't resurrect it. It takes about 45 minutes to prepare, so a failed attempt means that you may not have time for a second try. On the other hand, any chef can prepare a sauce béarnaise. It's part of their training and, as they'll tell you, it's not difficult.

You don't have to be a professional cook to make sauce béarnaise. Anyone learning to make it will fail at least once, but after you get the hang of it, you'll succeed every time. We think *Dependency Injection* (DI) is like sauce béarnaise. It's assumed to be difficult, and, if you try to use it and fail, it's likely there won't be time for a second attempt.

> **DEFINITION**   *Dependency Injection* is a set of software design principles and patterns that enables you to develop loosely coupled code.

Despite the fear, uncertainty, and doubt (FUD) surrounding DI, it's as easy to learn as making a sauce béarnaise. You may make mistakes while you learn, but once you've mastered the technique, you'll never again fail to apply it successfully.

Stack Overflow, the software development Q&A website, features an answer to the question, "How to explain Dependency Injection to a 5-year old?" The most highly rated answer, by John Munsch, provides a surprisingly accurate analogy targeted at the (imaginary) five-year-old inquisitor:[1]

> *When you go and get things out of the refrigerator for yourself, you can cause problems. You might leave the door open, you might get something Mommy or Daddy doesn't want you to have. You might even be looking for something we don't even have or which has expired.*
>
> *What you should be doing is stating a need, "I need something to drink with lunch," and then we will make sure you have something when you sit down to eat.*

What this means in terms of object-oriented software development is this: collaborating classes (the five-year-old) should rely on infrastructure (the parents) to provide necessary services.

> **NOTE**   In DI terminology, we often talk about services and components. A *service* is typically an ABSTRACTION, a definition for something that provides a service. An implementation of an ABSTRACTION is often called a *component*, a class that contains behavior. Because both *service* and *component* are such overloaded terms, throughout this book, you'll typically see us use the terms "ABSTRACTION" and "class" instead.

This chapter is fairly linear in structure. First, we introduce DI, including its purpose and benefits. Although we include examples, overall, this chapter has less code than any other chapter in the book. Before we introduce DI, we discuss the basic purpose of DI—maintainability. This is important because it's easy to misunderstand DI if you aren't properly prepared. Next, after an example (Hello DI!), we discuss benefits and scope, laying out a road map for the book. When you're done with this chapter, you should be prepared for the more advanced concepts in the rest of the book.

To most developers, DI may seem like a rather backward way of creating source code, and, like sauce béarnaise, there's much FUD involved. To learn about DI, you must first understand its purpose.

---

[1]   See "How to explain Dependency Injection to a 5-year old?" by John Munsch et al. (2009), https://stackoverflow.com/questions/1638919/.

1.1 *Writing maintainable code*

What purpose does DI serve? DI isn't a goal in itself; rather, it's a means to an end. Ultimately, the purpose of most programming techniques is to deliver working software as efficiently as possible. One aspect of that is to write maintainable code.

Unless you only write prototypes, or applications that never make it past their first release, you find yourself maintaining and extending existing code bases. To work effectively with such code bases, in general, the more maintainable they are, the better.

An excellent way to make code more maintainable is through *loose coupling*. As far back as 1994, when the Gang of Four wrote *Design Patterns*, this was already common knowledge:[2]

> *Program to an interface, not an implementation.*

This important piece of advice isn't the conclusion, but, rather, the premise of *Design Patterns*. Loose coupling makes code extensible, and extensibility makes it maintainable. DI is nothing more than a technique that enables loose coupling. Moreover, there are many misconceptions about DI, and sometimes they get in the way of proper understanding. Before you can learn, you must *unlearn* what (you think) you already know.

1.1.1 *Common myths about DI*

You may never have come across or heard of DI before, and that's great. Skip this section and go straight to section 1.1.2. But, if you're reading this book, it's likely you've at least come across it in conversation, in a code base you inherited, or in blog posts. You may also have noticed that it comes with a fair amount of heavy opinions. In this section, we're going to look at four of the most common misconceptions about DI that have appeared over the years and why they aren't true. These myths include the following:

- DI is only relevant for late binding.
- DI is only relevant for unit testing.
- DI is a sort of *Abstract Factory* on steroids.
- DI requires a DI CONTAINER.

Although none of these myths are true, they're prevalent nonetheless. We need to dispel them before you can start to learn about DI.

LATE BINDING

In this context, *late binding* refers to the ability to replace parts of an application without recompiling the code. An application that enables third-party add-ins (such as Visual Studio) is one example. Another example is the standard software that supports different runtime environments.

Suppose you have an application that runs on more than one database engine (for example, one that supports both Oracle and SQL Server). To support this feature,

---

[2] Erich Gamma et al., *Design Patterns: Elements of Reusable Object-Oriented Software* (Addison-Wesley, 1994), 18.

the rest of the application talks to the database through an interface. The code base provides different implementations of this interface to access Oracle and SQL Server, respectively. In this case, you can use a configuration option to control which implementation should be used for a given installation.

It's a common misconception that DI is only relevant for this sort of scenario. That's understandable, because DI enables this scenario. But the fallacy is to think that the relationship is symmetric. The fact that DI enables late binding doesn't mean that it's only relevant in late-binding scenarios. As figure 1.1 illustrates, late binding is only one of the many aspects of DI.

If you thought that DI was only relevant for late-binding scenarios, this is something you need to unlearn. DI does much more than enable late binding.

UNIT TESTING

Some people think that DI is only relevant for supporting unit testing. This isn't true, either, although DI is certainly an important part of support for unit testing. To tell you the truth, our original introduction to DI came from struggling with certain aspects of *Test-Driven Development* (TDD). During that time, we discovered DI and learned that other people had used it to support some of the same scenarios we were addressing.

Even if you don't write unit tests (if you don't, you should start now), DI is still relevant because of all the other benefits it offers. Claiming that DI is only relevant for supporting unit testing is like claiming that it's only relevant for supporting late binding. Figure 1.2 shows that although this is a different view, it's a view as narrow as figure 1.1. In this book, we'll do our best to show you the whole picture.

If you thought that DI was only relevant for unit testing, unlearn this assumption. DI does much more than enable unit testing.

Late binding

Figure 1.1   Late binding is enabled by DI, but to assume that it's only applicable in late-binding scenarios is to adopt a narrow view of a much broader vista.

Late binding   Unit testing

Figure 1.2   Perhaps you've been assuming that unit testing is the sole purpose of DI. Although that assumption is a different view than the late-binding assumption, it, too, is a narrow view of a much broader vista.

AN ABSTRACT FACTORY ON STEROIDS

Perhaps the most dangerous fallacy is that DI involves some sort of general-purpose Abstract Factory that you can use to create instances of the DEPENDENCIES needed in your applications.

> ### Abstract Factory
>
> An Abstract Factory is typically an ABSTRACTION that contains multiple methods, where each method allows the creation of an object of a certain kind.[3]
>
> A typical use case for the Abstract Factory pattern is for user interface (UI) toolkits or client applications that must be run on multiple platforms. To achieve a high degree of code reusability on all platforms, you could, for example, define an IUIControlFactory ABSTRACTION that allows the creation of certain kinds of controls like text boxes and buttons for consumers:
>
> ```
> public interface IUIControlFactory
> {
>     IButton CreateButton();
>     ITextBox CreateTextBox();
> }
> ```
>
> For each operating system (OS), you could have a different implementation of this IUIControlFactory. In this case, there are only two factory methods, but depending on the application or toolkit, there could be many more. An important point to note is that an Abstract Factory specifies a predefined list of factory methods.

In the introduction to this chapter, we wrote that "collaborating classes *should rely on infrastructure* to provide necessary services." What were your initial thoughts about this sentence? Did you think about infrastructure as some sort of service you could query to get the DEPENDENCIES you need? If so, you aren't alone. Many developers and architects think about DI as a service that can be used to locate other services. This is called a SERVICE LOCATOR, but it's the exact opposite of DI.

A SERVICE LOCATOR is often called an Abstract Factory on steroids because, compared to a normal Abstract Factory, the list of resolvable types is unspecified and possibly endless. It typically has one method allowing the creation of all sorts of types, much like in the following:

```
public interface IServiceLocator
{
    object GetService(Type serviceType);
}
```

> **IMPORTANT** If you thought of DI as a SERVICE LOCATOR (that is, a general-purpose factory), then this is something you need to unlearn. DI is the opposite of a SERVICE LOCATOR; it's a way to structure code so that you never have to imperatively ask for DEPENDENCIES. Rather, you require consumers to supply them.

---

[3] Erich Gamma et al., *Design Patterns*, 87.

DI CONTAINERS

Closely associated with the previous misconception is the notion that DI requires a DI CONTAINER. If you held the previous, mistaken belief that DI involves a SERVICE LOCATOR, then it's easy to conclude that a DI CONTAINER can take on the responsibility of the SERVICE LOCATOR. This might be the case, but it's not at all how you should use a DI CONTAINER.

A DI CONTAINER is an optional library that makes it easier to compose classes when you wire up an application, but it's in no way required. When you compose applications without a DI CONTAINER, it's called PURE DI. It might take a little more work, but other than that, you don't have to compromise on any DI principles.

DEFINITION PURE DI is the practice of applying DI without a DI CONTAINER.[4]

IMPORTANT If you thought that DI requires a DI CONTAINER, this is another notion you need to unlearn. DI is a set of principles and patterns, and a DI CONTAINER is a useful, but optional tool.

We have yet to explain exactly what a DI CONTAINER is, and how and when you should use it. We'll go into more detail on this at the end of chapter 3; part 4 is completely dedicated to it.

You may think that, although we've exposed four myths about DI, we have yet to make a compelling case against any of them. That's true. In a sense, this book is one big argument against these common misconceptions, so we'll certainly return to these topics later. For example, in chapter 5, section 5.2 discusses why SERVICE LOCATOR is an anti-pattern.

In our experience, unlearning is vital because people often try to retrofit what we tell them about DI and align it with what they think they already know. When this happens, it takes time before it finally dawns on them that some of their most basic assumptions are wrong. We want to spare you that experience. If you can, read this book as though you know nothing about DI.

1.1.2 *Understanding the purpose of DI*

DI isn't an end goal—it's a means to an end. DI enables loose coupling, and loose coupling makes code more maintainable. That's quite a claim, and although we could refer you to well-established authorities like the Gang of Four for details, we find it only fair to explain why this is true.

To get this message across, the next section compares software design and several software design patterns with electrical wiring. We've found this to be a powerful analogy. We even use it to explain software design to non-technical people.

We use four specific design patterns in this analogy because they occur frequently in relation to DI. You'll see many examples of three of these patterns—Decorator, Composite, and Adapter—throughout this book. (We cover the fourth, the Null Object pattern, in chapter 4.) Don't worry if you're not that familiar with these patterns: you will be by the end of the book.

---

4 The first edition of this book, *Dependency Injection in .NET*, uses the term *Poor Man's DI*. PURE DI replaces this term, but don't be surprised to see the old terminology on the internet. To learn more about why we changed this terminology, see Mark Seemann, "Pure DI" (2014), https://blog.ploeh.dk/2014/06/10/pure-di/.

Software development is still a rather new profession, so in many ways we're still figuring out how to implement good architecture. But individuals with expertise in more traditional professions (such as construction) figured it out a long time ago.

CHECKING INTO A CHEAP HOTEL

If you're staying at a cheap hotel, you might encounter a sight like the one in figure 1.3. Here, the hotel has kindly provided a hair dryer for your convenience, but apparently they don't trust you to leave the hair dryer for the next guest: the appliance is directly attached to the wall outlet. The hotel management decided that the cost of replacing stolen hair dryers is high enough to justify what's otherwise an obviously inferior implementation.

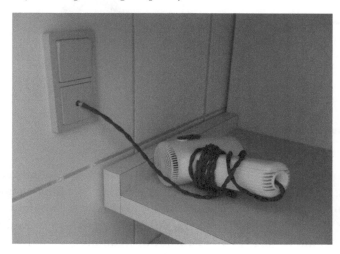

Figure 1.3   In a cheap hotel room, you might find a hair dryer wired directly into the wall outlet. This is equivalent to using the common practice of writing tightly coupled code.

What happens when the hair dryer stops working? The hotel has to call in a skilled professional. To fix the hardwired hair dryer, the power to the room will have to be cut, rendering it temporarily useless. Then, the technician must use special tools to disconnect the hair dryer and replace it with a new one. If you're lucky, the technician will remember to turn the power to the room back on and go back to test whether the new hair dryer works—if you're lucky. Does this procedure sound at all familiar?

This is how you would approach working with tightly coupled code. In this scenario, the hair dryer is tightly coupled to the wall, and you can't easily modify one without impacting the other.

COMPARING ELECTRICAL WIRING TO DESIGN PATTERNS

Usually, we don't wire electrical appliances together by attaching the cable directly to the wall. Instead, as in figure 1.4, we use plugs and sockets. A socket defines a shape that the plug must match.

In an analogy to software design, the socket is an interface, and the plug with its appliance is an implementation. This means that the room (the application) has one or (hopefully) more sockets, and the users of the room (the developers) can plug in appliances as they please, potentially even a customer-supplied hair dryer.

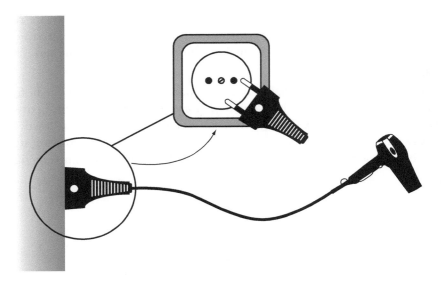

**Figure 1.4   Through the use of sockets and plugs, a hair dryer can be loosely coupled
to a wall outlet.**

In contrast to the hardwired hair dryer, plugs and sockets define a loosely coupled
model for connecting electrical appliances. As long as the plug (the implementation)
fits into the socket (implements the interface), and it can handle the amount of volts
and hertz (obeys the interface contract), we can combine appliances in a variety of
ways. What's particularly interesting is that many of these common combinations can
be compared to well-known software design principles and patterns.

First, we're no longer constrained to hair dryers. If you're an average reader, we
would guess that you need power for a computer much more than you do for a hair
dryer. That's not a problem: you unplug the hair dryer and plug a computer into the
same socket (figure 1.5).

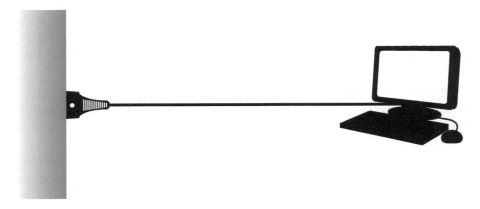

**Figure 1.5   Using a socket and a plug, you can replace the original hair dryer from figure 1.4
with a computer. This corresponds to the LISKOV SUBSTITUTION PRINCIPLE.**

LISKOV SUBSTITUTION PRINCIPLE

It's amazing that the concept of a socket predates computers by decades, and yet it provides an essential service to computers. The original designers of sockets couldn't possibly have foreseen personal computers, but because the design is so versatile, needs that were originally unanticipated can be met.

The ability to switch plugs, or implementations, without requiring a change to the socket, or interface, is similar to a central software design principle called the LISKOV SUBSTITUTION PRINCIPLE. This principle states that we should be able to replace one implementation of an interface with another without breaking either the client or the implementation.

When it comes to DI, the LISKOV SUBSTITUTION PRINCIPLE is one of the most important software design principles. It's this principle that enables us to address requirements that occur in the future, even if we can't foresee them today.

You can unplug the computer if you don't need to use it at the moment. Even though nothing is plugged in, the room doesn't explode. That is to say, if you unplug the computer from the wall, neither the wall outlet nor the computer breaks down.

With software, however, a client often expects a service to be available. If you remove the service, you get a `NullReferenceException`. To deal with this type of situation, you can create an implementation of an interface that does nothing. This design pattern, known as *Null Object*, corresponds to having a children's safety outlet plug (a plug without a wire or appliance that still fits into the socket). And because you're using loose coupling, you can replace a real implementation with something that does nothing without causing trouble. This is illustrated in figure 1.6.

There are many other things you can do, as well. If you live in a neighborhood with intermittent power failures, you may want to keep the computer running by plugging in into an uninterrupted power supply (UPS). As shown in figure 1.7, you connect the UPS to the wall outlet and the computer to the UPS.

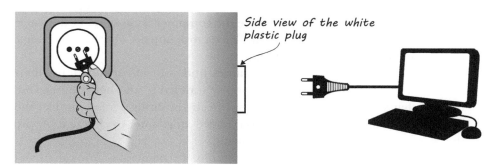

Side view of the white plastic plug

Figure 1.6 Unplugging the computer causes neither room nor computer to explode when replaced with a children's safety outlet plug. This can be roughly likened to the Null Object pattern.

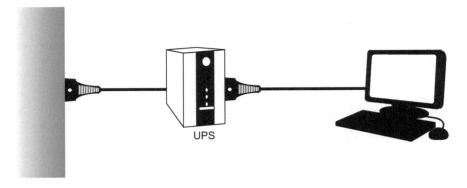

Figure 1.7   A UPS can be introduced to keep the computer running in case of power failure. This corresponds to the Decorator design pattern.

The computer and the UPS serve separate purposes. Each has a SINGLE RESPONSIBILITY that doesn't infringe on the other unit. The UPS and computer are likely to be produced by two different manufacturers, bought at different times, and plugged in separately. As figure 1.5 demonstrated, you can run the computer without a UPS, and you could also conceivably use the hair dryer during blackouts by plugging it into the UPS.

In software design, this way of intercepting one implementation with another implementation of the same interface is known as the *Decorator* design pattern.[5] It gives you the ability to incrementally introduce new features and CROSS-CUTTING CONCERNS without having to rewrite or change a lot of existing code.

Another way to add new functionality to an existing code base is to refactor an existing implementation of an interface with a new implementation. When you aggregate several implementations into one, you use the *Composite* design pattern.[6] Figure 1.8 illustrates how this corresponds to plugging diverse appliances into a power strip.

The power strip has a single plug that you can insert into a single socket, and the power strip itself provides several sockets for a variety of appliances. This enables you to add and remove the hair dryer while the computer is running. In the same way, the Composite pattern makes it easy to add or remove functionality by modifying the set of composed interface implementations.

Here's a final example. You sometimes find yourself in situations where a plug doesn't fit into a particular socket. If you've traveled to another country, you've likely noticed that sockets differ across the world. If you bring something like the camera in figure 1.9 along when traveling, you'll need an adapter to charge it. Appropriately, there's a design pattern with the same name.

The *Adapter* design pattern works like its physical namesake.[7] You can use it to match two related, yet separate, interfaces to each other. This is particularly useful when you

---

[5]   Erich Gamma et al., *Design Patterns*, 175.

[6]   Erich Gamma et al., *Design Patterns*, 163.

[7]   Erich Gamma et al., *Design Patterns*, 139.

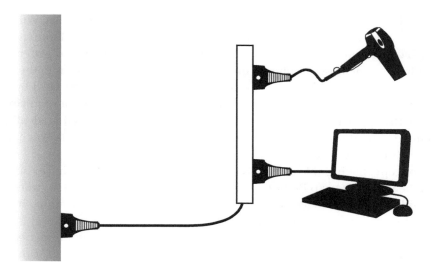

Figure 1.8   A power strip makes it possible to plug several appliances into a single wall outlet. This corresponds to the Composite design pattern.

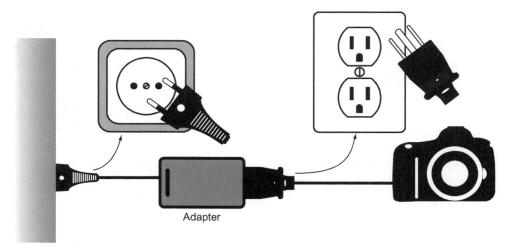

Adapter

Figure 1.9   When traveling, you often need to use an adapter to plug an appliance into a foreign socket (for example, to recharge a camera). This corresponds to the *Adapter design pattern*. Sometimes, translation is as simple as changing the shape of the plug, or as complex as changing the electric current from alternating current (AC) to direct current (DC).

have an existing third-party API that you want to expose as an instance of an interface your application consumes. As with the physical adapter, implementations of the Adapter design pattern can range from simple to extremely complex.

What's amazing about the socket and plug model is that, over decades, it's proven to be an easy and versatile model. Once the infrastructure is in place, it can be used by anyone and adapted to changing needs and unanticipated requirements. What's even more interesting is that, when we relate this model to software development, all the building blocks are already in place in the form of design principles and patterns.

The advantage of loose coupling is the same in software design as it is in the physical socket and plug model: Once the infrastructure is in place, it can be used by anyone and adapted to changing needs and unforeseen requirements without requiring large changes to the application code base and infrastructure. This means that ideally, a new requirement should only necessitate the addition of a new class, with no changes to other already-existing classes of the system.

This concept of being able to extend an application without modifying existing code is called the OPEN/CLOSED PRINCIPLE. It's impossible to get to a situation where 100% of your code will always be *open* for extensibility and *closed* for modification. Still, loose coupling does bring you closer to that goal.

And, with every step, it gets easier to add new features and requirements to your system. Being able to add new features without touching existing parts of the system means that problems are isolated. This leads to code that's easier to understand and test, allowing you to manage the complexity of your system. That's what loose coupling can help you with, and that's why it can make a code base much more maintainable. We'll discuss the OPEN/CLOSED PRINCIPLE in more detail in chapter 4.

By now you might be wondering how these patterns will look when implemented in code. Don't worry about that. As we stated before, we'll show you plenty of examples of those patterns throughout this book. In fact, later in this chapter, we'll show you an implementation of both the Decorator and Adapter patterns.

The easy part of loose coupling is programming to an interface instead of an implementation. The question is, "Where do the instances come from?" In a sense, this is what this entire book is about: it's the core question that DI seeks to answer.

You can't create a new instance of an interface the same way that you create a new instance of a concrete type. Code like this doesn't compile:

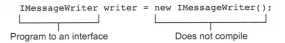

```
IMessageWriter writer = new IMessageWriter();
```
Program to an interface   Does not compile

An interface contains no implementation, so this isn't possible. The `writer` instance must be created using a different mechanism. DI solves this problem. With this outline of the purpose of DI, we think you're ready for an example.

1.2   *A simple example: Hello DI!*

In the tradition of innumerable programming textbooks, let's take a look at a simple console application that writes "Hello DI!" to the screen. Note that the full code is available as part of the download for this book, as mentioned in the section "Code conventions and downloads" at the beginning of this book.

In this section, we'll show you what the code looks like and briefly outline some key benefits without going into details. In the rest of the book, we'll get more specific.

1.2.1 Hello DI! code

You're probably used to seeing Hello World examples that are written with a single line of code. Here, we'll take something that's extremely simple and make it more complicated. Why? We'll get to that shortly, but let's first see what Hello World would look like with DI.

COLLABORATORS

To get a sense of the structure of the program, we'll start by looking at the `Main` method of the console application. Then we'll show you the collaborating classes; but first, here's the `Main` method of the Hello DI! application:

```
private static void Main()
{
    IMessageWriter writer = new ConsoleMessageWriter();
    var salutation = new Salutation(writer);
    salutation.Exclaim();
}
```

Because the program needs to write to the console, it creates a new instance of `ConsoleMessageWriter` that encapsulates that functionality. It passes that message writer to the `Salutation` class so that the salutation instance knows where to write its messages. Because everything is now wired up properly, you can execute the logic via the `Exclaim` method, which results in the message being written to the screen.

The construction of objects inside the `Main` method is a basic example of PURE DI. No DI CONTAINER is used to compose the `Salutation` and its `ConsoleMessageWriter` DEPENDENCY. Figure 1.10 shows the relationship between the collaborators.

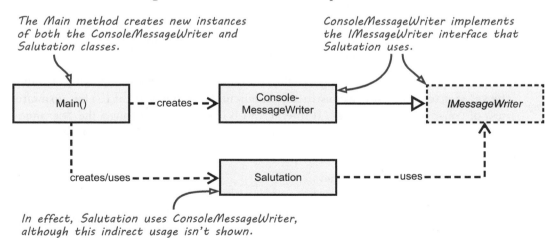

Figure 1.10 Relationship between the collaborators of the Hello DI! application

IMPLEMENTING THE APPLICATION LOGIC

The main logic of the application is encapsulated in the `Salutation` class, shown in listing 1.1.

Listing 1.1   Salutation class encapsulates the main application logic

```
public class Salutation
{
    private readonly IMessageWriter writer;

    public Salutation(IMessageWriter writer)
    {
        if (writer == null)
            throw new ArgumentNullException("writer");

        this.writer = writer;
    }

    public void Exclaim()
    {
        this.writer.Write("Hello DI!");
    }
}
```

Provides the Salutation class with the IMessageWriter DEPENDENCY using CONSTRUCTOR INJECTION

Guard Clause verifies that the supplied IMessageWriter isn't null

Sends the Hello DI! message to the IMessageWriter DEPENDENCY

The Salutation class depends on a custom interface called IMessageWriter (defined next). It requests an instance of it through its constructor. This practice is called CONSTRUCTOR INJECTION. A *Guard Clause* verifies that the supplied IMessageWriter isn't null by throwing an exception if it is.[8] And, finally, you use the previously injected IMessageWriter instance inside the implementation of the Exclaim method by calling its Write method. This sends the Hello DI! message to the IMessageWriter DEPENDENCY.

> **DEFINITION**   CONSTRUCTOR INJECTION is the act of statically defining the list of required DEPENDENCIES by specifying them as parameters to the class's constructor. (CONSTRUCTOR INJECTION is described in detail in chapter 4, which also contains a more detailed walk-through of a similar code example.)

To speak in DI terminology, we say that the IMessageWriter DEPENDENCY is injected into the Salutation class using a constructor argument. Note that Salutation has no awareness of ConsoleMessageWriter. It interacts with it exclusively through the IMessageWriter interface. IMessageWriter is a simple interface defined for the occasion:

```
public interface IMessageWriter
{
    void Write(string message);
}
```

It could have had other members, but in this simple example, you only need the Write method. It's implemented by the ConsoleMessageWriter class that the Main method passes to the Salutation class:

```
public class ConsoleMessageWriter : IMessageWriter
{
    public void Write(string message)
    {
        Console.WriteLine(message);
    }
}
```

---

[8]   Martin Fowler et al., *Refactoring: Improving the Design of Existing Code* (Addison-Wesley, 1999), 250.

The `ConsoleMessageWriter` class implements `IMessageWriter` by wrapping the `Console` class of the .NET Base Class Library (BCL). This is a simple application of the Adapter design pattern that we talked about in section 1.1.2.

1.2.2 *Benefits of DI*

You may be wondering about the benefit of replacing a single line of code with two classes and an interface, resulting in 28 lines total. You could easily solve the same problem as shown here:

```
private static void Main()
{
    Console.WriteLine("Hello DI!");
}
```

DI might seem like overkill, but there are several benefits to be harvested from using it. How is the previous example better than the usual single line of code you normally use to implement Hello World in C#? In this example, DI adds an overhead of 2800%, but, as complexity increases from one line of code to tens of thousands, this overhead diminishes and all but disappears. Chapter 3 provides a more complex example of applied DI. Although that example is still overly simplistic compared to real-life applications, you should notice that DI is far less intrusive.

We don't blame you if you find the previous DI example to be over-engineered, but consider this: by its nature, the classic Hello World example is a simple problem with well-specified and constrained requirements. In the real world, software development is never like this. Requirements change and are often fuzzy. The features you must implement also tend to be much more complex. DI helps address such issues by enabling loose coupling. Specifically, you gain the benefits listed in table 1.1.

Table 1.1 Benefits gained from loose coupling. Each benefit is always available but will be valued differently depending on circumstances.

Benefit	Description	When is it valuable?
Late binding	Services can be swapped with other services without recompiling code.	Valuable in standard software, but perhaps less so in enterprise applications where the runtime environment tends to be well defined.
Extensibility	Code can be extended and reused in ways not explicitly planned for.	Always valuable.
Parallel development	Code can be developed in parallel.	Valuable in large, complex applications; not so much in small, simple applications.
Maintainability	Classes with clearly defined responsibilities are easier to maintain.	Always valuable.
TESTABILITY	Classes can be unit tested.	Always valuable.

We listed the late-binding benefit first because, in our experience, this is the one that's foremost in most people's minds. When architects and developers fail to understand the benefits of loose coupling, it's most likely because they never consider the other benefits.

LATE BINDING

When we explain the benefits of programming to interfaces and DI, the ability to swap out one service with another is the most conspicuous benefit for most people, so they tend to weigh the advantages against the disadvantages with only this benefit in mind. Remember when we suggested that you may need to unlearn before you can learn? You may say that you know your requirements so well that you know you'll never have to replace, say, your SQL Server database with anything else. But requirements change.

NoSQL, Microsoft Azure, and the argument for composability

Years ago, I (Mark) was often met with a blank expression when I tried to convince developers and architects of the benefits of DI. "Okay, so you can swap out your relational data access component for something else. For what? Is there any alternative to relational databases?"

XML files never seemed like a convincing alternative in highly scalable enterprise scenarios. This has changed significantly in the last couple of years.

Azure was announced at PDC 2008 and has done much to convince even die-hard Microsoft-only organizations to reevaluate their position when it comes to data storage. There's now a real alternative to relational databases, and I only have to ask if people want their application to be cloud ready. The replacement argument has now become much stronger.

A related movement can be found in the whole NoSQL concept that models applications around denormalized data—often document databases. But concepts such as Event Sourcing are also becoming increasingly important.[9]

In section 1.2.1, you didn't use late binding because you explicitly created a new instance of `IMessageWriter` by hard coding the creation of a new `ConsoleMessageWriter` instance. You can, however, introduce late binding by changing this single line of code:

```
IMessageWriter writer = new ConsoleMessageWriter();
```

To enable late binding, you might replace that line of code with something like the following.

Listing 1.2   Late binding an `IMessageWriter` implementation

```
IConfigurationRoot configuration = new ConfigurationBuilder()
    .SetBasePath(Directory.GetCurrentDirectory())
    .AddJsonFile("appsettings.json")
    .Build();
```

---

[9] Martin Fowler, "Event Sourcing" (2005), https://martinfowler.com/eaaDev/EventSourcing.html.

```
string typeName = configuration["messageWriter"];
Type type = Type.GetType(typeName, throwOnError: true);

IMessageWriter writer = (IMessageWriter)Activator.CreateInstance(type);
```

> **NOTE** Listing 1.2 takes some shortcuts to make a point. In fact, it suffers from the CONSTRAINED CONSTRUCTION anti-pattern covered in detail in chapter 5.

By pulling the type name from the application configuration file and creating a Type instance from it, you can use reflection to create an instance of IMessageWriter without knowing the concrete type at compile time. To make this work, you specify the type name in the messageWriter application setting in the application configuration file:

```
{
  "messageWriter":
    "Ploeh.Samples.HelloDI.Console.ConsoleMessageWriter, HelloDI.Console"
}
```

Loose coupling enables late binding because there's only a single place where you create the instance of IMessageWriter. Because the Salutation class works exclusively against the IMessageWriter interface, it never notices the difference. In the Hello DI! example, late binding would enable you to write the message to a different destination than the console; for example, a database or a file. It's possible to add such features—even though you didn't explicitly plan ahead for them.

EXTENSIBILITY

Successful software must be able to change. You'll need to add new features and extend existing features. Loose coupling lets you efficiently recompose the application, similar to the way you have flexibility when working with electrical plugs and sockets.

Let's say that you want to make the Hello DI! example more secure by only allowing authenticated users to write the message. Listing 1.3 shows how you can add that feature without changing any of the existing features—you simply add a new implementation of the IMessageWriter interface.

Listing 1.3 Extending the Hello DI! application with a security feature

```
public class SecureMessageWriter : IMessageWriter        ◀─── Implements the
{                                                               IMessageWriter interface
    private readonly IMessageWriter writer;                     while also consuming it
    private readonly IIdentity identity;

    public SecureMessageWriter(
        IMessageWriter writer,              ◀─── CONSTRUCTOR INJECTION that requests an
        IIdentity identity)                      instance of IMessageWriter
    {
        if (writer == null)
            throw new ArgumentNullException("writer");
        if (identity == null)
            throw new ArgumentNullException("identity");

        this.writer = writer;
```

```
        this.identity = identity;
    }

    public void Write(string message)
    {
        if (this.identity.IsAuthenticated)     ◄─────┤ Verifies whether the user is authenticated
        {
            this.writer.Write(message);     ◄──────┐ If authenticated, writes the message
        }                                          │ using the injected message writer
    }
}
```

NOTE   This is a standard application of the Decorator design pattern that we mentioned in section 1.1.2. We'll talk much more about Decorators in chapter 9.

Besides an instance of `IMessageWriter`, the `SecureMessageWriter` constructor requires an instance of `IIdentity`. The `Write` method is implemented by first checking whether the current user is authenticated, using the injected `IIdentity`. If this is the case, it allows the decorated writer field to `Write` the message. The only place where you need to change existing code is in the `Main` method, because you need to compose the available classes differently than before:

```
IMessageWriter writer =
    new SecureMessageWriter(     ◄──────────┐ The ConsoleMessageWriter is intercepted
        new ConsoleMessageWriter(),         │ with the SecureMessageWriter Decorator.
        WindowsIdentity.GetCurrent());
```

NOTE   Compared to listing 1.2, you now use a hard-coded `ConsoleMessageWriter`.

Notice that you wrap or *decorate* the old `ConsoleMessageWriter` instance with the new `SecureMessageWriter` class. Once more, the `Salutation` class is unmodified because it only consumes the `IMessageWriter` interface. Similarly, there's no need to either modify or duplicate the functionality in the `ConsoleWriter` class, either. You use the `System.Security.Principal.WindowsIdentity` class to retrieve the identity of the user on whose behalf this code is being executed.[10]

As we've stated before, loose coupling enables you to write code that's *open for extensibility, but closed for modification.* The only place where you need to modify the code is at the application entry point. `SecureMessageWriter` implements the security features of the application, whereas `ConsoleMessageWriter` addresses the user interface. This enables you to vary these aspects independently of each other and compose them as needed. Each class has its own SINGLE RESPONSIBILITY.

PARALLEL DEVELOPMENT

Separation of concerns makes it possible to develop code in parallel. When a software development project grows to a certain size, it becomes necessary to have multiple

---

[10] The `System.Security.Principal.WindowsIdentity` class is located in the System.Security. Principal.Windows NuGet package, which is part of .NET Core.

developers work in parallel on the same code base. At a larger scale, it's even necessary to separate the development team into multiple teams of manageable sizes. Each team is often assigned responsibility for an area of the overall application. To demarcate responsibilities, each team develops one or more modules that will need to be integrated into the finished application. Unless the areas of each team are truly independent, some teams are likely to depend on functionality developed by other teams.

> **DEFINITION** In object-oriented software design, a *module* is a group of logically related classes (or components), where a module is independent of and interchangeable with other modules. Typically, you'll see that a *layer* consists of one or more modules.

In the previous example, because the `SecureMessageWriter` and `ConsoleMessage-Writer` classes don't depend directly on each other, they could've been developed by parallel teams. All they would have needed to agree on was the shared interface `IMessageWriter`.

MAINTAINABILITY

As the responsibility of each class becomes clearly defined and constrained, maintenance of the overall application becomes easier. This is a consequence of the SINGLE RESPONSIBILITY PRINCIPLE, which states that each class should have only a single responsibility. We'll discuss the SINGLE RESPONSIBILITY PRINCIPLE in more detail in chapter 2.

Adding new features to an application becomes simpler because it's clear where changes should be applied. More often than not, you don't need to change existing code, but can instead add new classes and recompose the application. This is the OPEN/CLOSED PRINCIPLE in action again.

Troubleshooting also tends to become less grueling, because the scope of likely culprits narrows. With clearly defined responsibilities, you'll often have a good idea of where to start looking for the root cause of a problem.

TESTABILITY

An application is considered TESTABLE when it can be unit tested. For some, TESTABILITY is the least of their worries; for others, it's an absolute requirement. Personally, we belong in the latter category. In Mark's career, he's declined several job offers because they involved working with certain products that weren't TESTABLE.

TESTABILITY

The term TESTABLE is horribly imprecise, yet it's widely used in the software development community, chiefly by those who practice unit testing. In principle, any application can be tested by trying it out. Tests can be performed by people using the application via its UI or whatever other interface it provides. Such manual tests are time consuming and expensive to perform, so automated testing is preferred.

You'll find different types of automated testing—unit testing, integration testing, performance testing, stress testing, and so on. Because unit testing has fewer requirements on runtime environments, it tends to be the most efficient and robust type of test. It's often in this context that TESTABILITY is evaluated.

(continued)

Unit tests provide rapid feedback on the state of an application, but it's only possible to write unit tests when the unit in question can be properly isolated from its DEPENDENCIES. There's some ambiguity about how granular a unit really is, but everyone agrees that it's certainly not something that spans multiple modules. The ability to test modules in isolation is crucial in unit testing.

It's only when an application is susceptible to unit testing that it's considered TESTABLE. The safest way to ensure TESTABILITY is to develop it using TDD.

It should be noted that unit tests alone don't ensure a working application. Full system tests or other in-between types of tests are still necessary to validate whether an application works as intended.

The benefit of TESTABILITY is perhaps the most controversial of those we've listed. Some developers and architects still don't practice unit testing, so they consider this benefit irrelevant at best. We, however, see it as an essential part of software development, which is why we marked it as "Always valuable" in table 1.1. Michael Feathers even defines the term *legacy application* as any application that isn't covered by unit tests.[11]

Almost by accident, loose coupling enables unit testing because consumers follow the LISKOV SUBSTITUTION PRINCIPLE: they don't care about the concrete types of their DEPENDENCIES. This means that you can inject Test Doubles into the System Under Test (SUT), as you'll see in listing 1.4.

Test Doubles

It's a common technique to create implementations of DEPENDENCIES that act as stand-ins for real or intended implementations. Such implementations are called *Test Doubles*, and they'll never be used in the final application. Instead, they serve as placeholders for real DEPENDENCIES when these are unavailable or undesirable to use.

A Test Double is useful when the real DEPENDENCY is slow, expensive, destructive, or simply outside the scope of the current test. There's a complete pattern language around Test Doubles and many subtypes, such as Stubs, Mocks, and Fakes.[12]

The ability to replace intended DEPENDENCIES with test-specific replacements is a by-product of loose coupling, but we chose to list it as a separate benefit because the derived value is different. Our personal experience is that DI is beneficial even during integration testing. Although integration tests typically communicate with real external systems (like a database), you still need to have a certain degree of isolation. In other words, there are still reasons to replace, INTERCEPT, or mock certain DEPENDENCIES in the application being tested.

---

[11] Michael C. Feathers, *Working Effectively with Legacy Code* (Prentice Hall, 2004), xvi.

[12] Gerard Meszaros, *xUnit Test Patterns: Refactoring Test Code* (Addison-Wesley, 2007), 522.

> ## Intercepting text messages
>
> I (Steven) worked on multiple applications that sent SMS messages through a third-party service. I didn't want our test environment to send those text messages to the real gateway because there was a per-message cost, and I certainly didn't want to accidentally spam mobile phones with those test messages.
>
> During manual testing, on the other hand, text messages were sent to mobile phones. But, in this case, a Decorator was applied that changed the phone number sent to the gateway to one that the tester could supply. This way the tester was able to get all messages on his own phone and verify the system under test.

Depending on the type of application you're developing, you may or may not care about the ability to do late binding, but we always care about TESTABILITY. Some developers don't care about TESTABILITY but find late binding important for the application they're developing. Regardless, DI provides options in the future with minimal additional overhead today.

EXAMPLE: UNIT TESTING HELLODI LOGIC

In section 1.2.1, you saw the Hello DI! example. Although we showed you the final code first, we developed it using TDD. Listing 1.4 shows the most important unit test.

NOTE Don't worry if you don't have experience with unit tests. They'll occasionally pop up throughout this book but are in no way a prerequisite for reading it.[13]

Listing 1.4   Unit testing the `Salutation` class

```
[Fact]
public void ExclaimWillWriteCorrectMessageToMessageWriter()
{
    var writer = new SpyMessageWriter();
    var sut = new Salutation(writer);          ◄─── The IMessageWriter DEPENDENCY is stubbed
    sut.Exclaim();                                   using the SpyMessageWriter Test Spy.
    Assert.Equal(
        expected: "Hello DI!",
        actual: writer.WrittenMessage);
}

public class SpyMessageWriter : IMessageWriter
{
    public string WrittenMessage { get; private set; }

    public void Write(string message)
    {
        this.WrittenMessage += message;
    }
}
```

---

[13] You may, however, want to read Roy Osherove's *The Art of Unit Testing*, 2nd Ed. (Manning, 2013), followed by Gerard Meszaros' *xUnit Test Patterns* (Addison-Wesley, 2007).

The `Salutation` class needs an instance of the `IMessageWriter` interface, so you need to create one. You could use any implementation, but in unit tests, a Test Double can be useful—in this case, you roll your own Test Spy implementation.[14]

In this case, the Test Double is as involved as the production implementation. This is an artifact of how simple our example is. In most applications, a Test Double is significantly simpler than the concrete, production implementations it stands in for. The important part is to supply a test-specific implementation of `IMessageWriter` to ensure that you test only one thing at a time. Right now, you're testing the `Exclaim` method of the `Salutation` class, so you don't want a production implementation of `IMessage-Writer` to pollute the test. To create the `Salutation` class, you pass in the Test Spy instance of `IMessageWriter` using CONSTRUCTOR INJECTION.

After exercising the SUT, you can call `Assert.Equal` to verify whether the expected outcome equals the actual outcome. If the `IMessageWriter.Write` method was invoked with the `"Hello DI!"` string, `SpyMessageWriter` would have stored this in its `Written-Message` property, and the `Equal` method completes. But if the `Write` method wasn't called, or was called with a different value, the `Equal` method would throw an exception, and the test would fail.

Loose coupling provides many benefits: code becomes easier to develop, maintain, and extend, and it becomes more TESTABLE. It's not even particularly difficult. We program against interfaces, not concrete implementations. The only major obstacle is to figure out how to get hold of instances of those interfaces. DI surmounts this obstacle by injecting the DEPENDENCIES from the outside. CONSTRUCTOR INJECTION is the preferred method of doing that, though we'll also explore a few additional options in chapter 4.

1.3   *What to inject and what not to inject*

In the previous section, we described the motivational forces that makes one think about DI in the first place. If you're convinced that loose coupling is a benefit, you may want to make everything loosely coupled. Overall, that's a good idea. When you need to decide how to package modules, loose coupling proves especially useful. But you don't have to abstract everything away and make it pluggable. In this section, we'll provide some decision tools to help you decide how to model your DEPENDENCIES.

The .NET BCL consists of many assemblies. Every time you write code that uses a type from a BCL assembly, you add a dependency to your module. In the previous section, we discussed how loose coupling is important and how programming to an interface is the cornerstone. Does this imply that you can't reference any BCL assemblies and use their types directly in your application? What if you'd like to use an `XmlWriter` that's defined in the System.Xml assembly?

---

[14] A Test Spy is "a Test Double that captures the indirect output calls made to another component by the SUT for later verification by the test." See Gerard Meszaros' *xUnit Test Patterns*, 538.

You don't have to treat all DEPENDENCIES equally. Many types in the BCL can be used without jeopardizing an application's degree of coupling—but not all of them. It's important to know how to distinguish between types that pose no danger and types that may tighten an application's degree of coupling. Focus mainly on the latter.

As you learn DI, it can be helpful to categorize your DEPENDENCIES into STABLE DEPENDENCIES and VOLATILE DEPENDENCIES. Deciding where to put your SEAMS will soon become second nature to you. The next sections discuss these concepts in more detail.

SEAMS

Everywhere you decide to program against an ABSTRACTION instead of a concrete type, you introduce a SEAM into the application. A SEAM is a place where an application is assembled from its constituent parts, similar to the way a piece of clothing is sewn together at its seams.[15] It's also a place where you can disassemble the application and work with the modules in isolation.

The Hello DI! example we built in section 1.2 contains a SEAM between `Salutation` and `ConsoleMessageWriter`, as illustrated in the following figure. The `Salutation` class doesn't directly depend on the `ConsoleMessageWriter` class; rather, it uses the `IMessageWriter` interface to write the message. You can take the application apart at this SEAM and reassemble it with a different message writer.

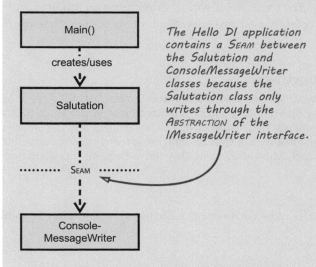

The Hello DI application contains a SEAM between the Salutation and ConsoleMessageWriter classes because the Salutation class only writes through the ABSTRACTION of the IMessageWriter interface.

The SEAM in the Hello DI! application from section 1.2

---

[15] Michael C. Feathers, *Working Effectively with Legacy Code*, 29–44.

1.3.1   STABLE DEPENDENCIES

Many of the modules in the BCL and beyond pose no threat to an application's degree of modularity. They contain reusable functionality that you can use to make your own code more succinct. The BCL modules are always available to your application, because it needs the .NET Framework to run, and, because they already exist, the concern about parallel development doesn't apply to these modules. You can always reuse a BCL library in another application.

By default, you can consider most (but not all) types defined in the BCL as safe, or STABLE DEPENDENCIES. We call them *stable* because they're already there, they tend to be backward compatible, and invoking them has deterministic outcomes. Most STABLE DEPENDENCIES are BCL types, but other DEPENDENCIES can be stable too. The important criteria for STABLE DEPENDENCIES include the following:

- The class or module already exists.
- You expect that new versions won't contain breaking changes.
- The types in question contain deterministic algorithms.
- You never expect to have to replace, wrap, decorate, or INTERCEPT the class or module with another.

Other examples may include specialized libraries that encapsulate algorithms relevant to your application. For example, if you're developing an application that deals with chemistry, you can reference a third-party library that contains chemistry-specific functionality.

> **Referencing the DI CONTAINER**
>
> DI CONTAINERS themselves might be considered either STABLE DEPENDENCIES or VOLATILE DEPENDENCIES, depending on whether you want to replace them. When you decide to base your application on a particular DI CONTAINER, you risk being stuck with this choice for the entire lifetime of the application. That's yet another reason why you should limit the use of the container to the application entry point. Only the entry point should reference the DI CONTAINER.

In general, DEPENDENCIES can be considered stable by exclusion. They're stable if they aren't volatile.

1.3.2   VOLATILE DEPENDENCIES

Introducing SEAMS into an application is extra work, so you should only do it when it's necessary. There can be more than one reason it's necessary to isolate a DEPENDENCY behind a SEAM, but those reasons are closely related to the benefits of loose coupling (discussed in section 1.2.2).

Such DEPENDENCIES can be recognized by their tendency to interfere with one or more of these benefits. They aren't stable because they don't provide a sufficient foundation for applications, and we call them VOLATILE DEPENDENCIES for that reason. A DEPENDENCY should be considered volatile if any of the following criteria are true:

- *The DEPENDENCY introduces a requirement to set up and configure a runtime environment for the application.* It isn't so much the concrete .NET types that are volatile, but rather what they imply about the runtime environment.

  Databases are good examples of BCL types that are VOLATILE DEPENDENCIES, and relational databases are the archetypical example. If you don't hide a relational database behind a SEAM, you can never replace it by any other technology. It also makes it hard to set up and run automated unit tests. (Even though the Microsoft SQL Server client library is a technology contained in the BCL, its usage implies a relational database.) Other out-of-process resources like message queues, web services, and even the filesystem fall into this category. The symptoms of this type of DEPENDENCY are lack of late binding and extensibility, as well as disabled TESTABILITY.

- *The DEPENDENCY doesn't yet exist, or is still in development.*

- *The DEPENDENCY isn't installed on all machines in the development organization.* This may be the case for expensive third-party libraries or DEPENDENCIES that can't be installed on all operating systems. The most common symptom is disabled TESTABILITY.

- *The DEPENDENCY contains nondeterministic behavior.* This is particularly important in unit tests because all tests must be deterministic. Typical sources of nondeterminism are random numbers and algorithms that depend on the current date or time.

  Because the BCL defines common sources of nondeterminism, such as `System` `.Random`, `System.Security.Cryptography.RandomNumberGenerator`, or `System` `.DateTime.Now`, you can't avoid having a reference to the assembly in which they're defined. Nevertheless, you should treat them as VOLATILE DEPENDENCIES because they tend to destroy TESTABILITY.

> **IMPORTANT**   VOLATILE DEPENDENCIES are the focal point of DI. It's for VOLATILE DEPENDENCIES rather than STABLE DEPENDENCIES that you introduce SEAMS into your application. Again, this obligates you to compose them using DI.

Now that you understand the differences between STABLE and VOLATILE DEPENDENCIES, you can begin to see the contours of the scope of DI. Loose coupling is a pervasive design principle, so DI (as an enabler) should be everywhere in your code base. There's no hard line between the topic of DI and good software design, but to define the scope of the rest of the book, we'll quickly describe what it covers.

1.4   DI scope

As we discussed before, an important element of DI is to break up various responsibilities into separate classes. One responsibility that we take away from classes is the task of creating instances of DEPENDENCIES. The task of creating instances of DEPENDENCIES is referred to as OBJECT COMPOSITION.

We discussed this in our Hello DI! example where our `Salutation` class was released of the responsibility of creating its DEPENDENCY. Instead, this responsibility was moved to the application's `Main` method. The UML diagram is shown again in figure 1.11.

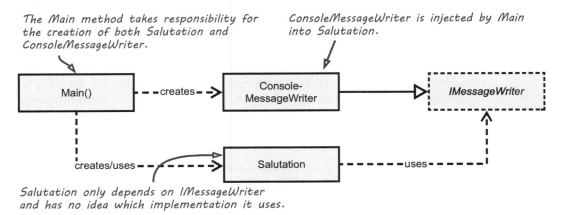

The Main method takes responsibility for the creation of both Salutation and ConsoleMessageWriter.

ConsoleMessageWriter is injected by Main into Salutation.

Salutation only depends on IMessageWriter and has no idea which implementation it uses.

Figure 1.11   Relationship between the collaborators of the Hello DI! application (repeated)

As a class relinquishes control of DEPENDENCIES, it gives up more than the decision to select particular implementations. By doing this, we, as developers, gain some advantages. At first, it may seem like a disadvantage to let a class surrender control over which objects are created, but we don't lose that control—we only move it to another place.

> **NOTE**   As developers, we gain control by removing a class's control over its DEPENDENCIES. This is an application of the SINGLE RESPONSIBILITY PRINCIPLE. Classes shouldn't have to deal with the creation of their DEPENDENCIES.

OBJECT COMPOSITION isn't the only dimension of control that we remove: a class also loses the ability to control the *lifetime* of the object. When a DEPENDENCY instance is injected into a class, the consumer doesn't know when it was created, or when it'll go out of scope. This should be of no concern to the consumer. Making the consumer oblivious to the lifetime of its DEPENDENCIES simplifies the consumer.

DI gives you an opportunity to manage DEPENDENCIES in a uniform way. When consumers directly create and set up instances of DEPENDENCIES, each may do so in its own way. This can be inconsistent with how other consumers do it. You have no way to centrally manage DEPENDENCIES and no easy way to address CROSS-CUTTING CONCERNS. With DI, you gain the ability to INTERCEPT each DEPENDENCY instance and act on it before it's passed to the consumer. This provides extensibility in applications.

With DI, you can compose applications while intercepting DEPENDENCIES and controlling their lifetimes. OBJECT COMPOSITION, INTERCEPTION, and LIFETIME MANAGEMENT are three dimensions of DI. Next, we'll cover each of these briefly; a more detailed treatment follows in part 3 of the book.

1.4.1 OBJECT COMPOSITION

To harvest the benefits of extensibility, late binding, and parallel development, you must be able to compose classes into applications. This means that you'll want to create an application out of individual classes by putting them together, much like plugging electrical appliances together. And, as with electrical appliances, you'll want to easily rearrange those classes when new requirements are introduced, ideally, without having to make changes to existing classes.

OBJECT COMPOSITION is often the primary motivation for introducing DI into an application. In fact, initially, DI was synonymous with OBJECT COMPOSITION; it's the only aspect discussed in Martin Fowler's original article on the subject.[16]

You can compose classes into an application in several ways. When we discussed late binding, we used a configuration file and a bit of dynamic object instantiation to manually compose the application from the available modules. We could also have used CONFIGURATION AS CODE using a DI CONTAINER. We'll return to these in chapter 12.

Many people refer to DI as INVERSION OF CONTROL (IoC). These two terms are sometimes used interchangeably, but DI is a subset of IoC. Throughout the book, we consistently use the most specific term—DI. If we mean IoC, we refer to it specifically.

Dependency Injection or INVERSION OF CONTROL?

The term INVERSION OF CONTROL originally meant any sort of programming style where an overall framework or runtime controlled the program flow.[17] According to that definition, most software developed on the .NET Framework uses IoC. When you write an ASP.NET Core MVC application, for instance, you create controller classes with action methods, but it's ASP.NET Core that will be calling your action methods. This means you aren't in control—the framework is.

These days, we're so used to working with frameworks that we don't consider this to be special, but it's a different model from being in full control of your code. This can still happen for a .NET application, most notably for command-line executables. As soon as `Main` is invoked, your code is in full control. It controls program flow, lifetime—everything. No special events are being raised and no overridden members are being invoked.

Before DI had a name, people started to refer to libraries that manage DEPENDENCIES as INVERSION OF CONTROL CONTAINERS, and soon, the meaning of IoC gradually drifted towards that particular meaning: INVERSION OF CONTROL over DEPENDENCIES. Always the taxonomist, Martin Fowler introduced the term *Dependency Injection* to specifically refer to IoC in the context of dependency management. Dependency Injection has since been widely accepted as the most correct terminology. In short, IoC is a much broader term that includes, but isn't limited to, DI.

---

[16] See Martin Fowler's "Inversion of Control Containers and the Dependency Injection pattern," 2004, https://martinfowler.com/articles/injection.html.

[17] See Martin Fowler's "InversionOfControl," 2005, https://martinfowler.com/bliki/InversionOfControl.html.

1.4.2   OBJECT LIFETIME

A class that has surrendered control of its DEPENDENCIES gives up more than the power to select particular implementations of an ABSTRACTION. It also gives up the power to control when instances are created and when they go out of scope.

In .NET, the garbage collector takes care of these things for us. A consumer can have its DEPENDENCIES injected into it and use them for as long as it wants. When it's done, the DEPENDENCIES go out of scope. If no other classes reference them, they're eligible for garbage collection.

What if two consumers share the same type of DEPENDENCY? Listing 1.5 illustrates that you can choose to inject a separate instance into each consumer, whereas listing 1.6 shows that you can alternatively choose to share a single instance across several consumers. But from the perspective of the consumer, there's no difference. According to the LISKOV SUBSTITUTION PRINCIPLE, the consumer must treat all instances of a given interface equally.

> **Listing 1.5   Consumers getting their own instance of the same type of DEPENDENCY**

```
IMessageWriter writer1 = new ConsoleMessageWriter();
IMessageWriter writer2 = new ConsoleMessageWriter();

var salutation = new Salutation(writer1);
var valediction = new Valediction(writer2);
```

Two instances of the same IMessageWriter DEPENDENCY are created.

Each consumer gets its own private instance.

> **Listing 1.6   Consumers sharing an instance of the same type of DEPENDENCY**

```
IMessageWriter writer = new ConsoleMessageWriter();

var salutation = new Salutation(writer);
var valediction = new Valediction(writer);
```

One instance is created.

That same instance is injected into two consumers.

Because DEPENDENCIES can be shared, a single consumer can't possibly control its lifetime. As long as a managed object can go out of scope and be garbage collected, this isn't much of an issue. But when DEPENDENCIES implement the IDisposable interface, things become much more complicated as we'll discuss in section 8.2. As a whole, LIFETIME MANAGEMENT is a separate dimension of DI and important enough that we've set aside all of chapter 8 for it.

1.4.3   INTERCEPTION

When we delegate control over DEPENDENCIES to a third party, as figure 1.12 shows, we also provide the power to modify them before we pass them on to the classes consuming them.

In the Hello DI! example, we initially injected a `ConsoleMessageWriter` instance into a `Salutation` instance. Then, modifying the example, we added a security feature by creating a new `SecureMessageWriter` that only delegates further work to the `ConsoleMessageWriter` when the user is authenticated. This allows you to maintain

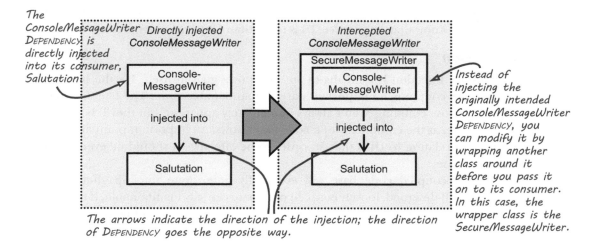

Figure 1.12 Intercepting a `ConsoleMessageWriter`

the SINGLE RESPONSIBILITY PRINCIPLE. It's possible to do this because you always program to interfaces; recall that DEPENDENCIES must always be ABSTRACTIONS. In the case of the `Salutation`, it doesn't care whether the supplied `IMessageWriter` is a `ConsoleMessageWriter` or a `SecureMessageWriter`. The `SecureMessageWriter` can wrap a `ConsoleMessageWriter` that still performs the real work.

> **NOTE** INTERCEPTION is an application of the Decorator design pattern. Don't worry if you aren't familiar with the Decorator design pattern. We'll provide a refresher in chapter 9, which is entirely devoted to INTERCEPTION.

Such abilities of INTERCEPTION move us along the path towards ASPECT-ORIENTED PROGRAMMING (AOP), a closely related topic that we'll cover in chapters 10 and 11. With INTERCEPTION and AOP, you can apply CROSS-CUTTING CONCERNS such as logging, auditing, access control, validation, and so forth in a well-structured manner that lets you maintain Separation of Concerns.

1.4.4 DI in three dimensions

Although DI started out as a series of patterns aimed at solving the problem of OBJECT COMPOSITION, the term has subsequently expanded to also cover OBJECT LIFETIME and INTERCEPTION. Today, we think of DI as encompassing all three in a consistent way.

OBJECT COMPOSITION tends to dominate the picture because, without flexible OBJECT COMPOSITION, there'd be no INTERCEPTION and no need to manage OBJECT LIFETIME. OBJECT COMPOSITION has dominated most of this chapter and will continue to dominate this book, but you shouldn't forget the other aspects. OBJECT COMPOSITION provides the foundation, and LIFETIME MANAGEMENT addresses some important side effects. But it's mainly when it comes to INTERCEPTION that you start to reap the benefits.

In part 3, we've devoted a chapter to each dimension briefly mentioned here. But it's important to know that, in practice, DI is more than OBJECT COMPOSITION.

1.5   Conclusion

Dependency Injection is a means to an end, not a goal in itself. It's the best way to enable loose coupling, an important part of maintainable code. The benefits you can reap from loose coupling aren't always immediately apparent, but they'll become visible over time, as the complexity of a code base grows. An important point about loose coupling in relation to DI is that, in order to be effective, it should be everywhere in your code base.

A tightly coupled code base will eventually deteriorate into Spaghetti Code;[18] whereas a well-designed, loosely coupled code base can stay maintainable. It takes more than loose coupling to reach a truly supple design,[19] but programming to interfaces is a prerequisite.

> **TIP**   DI must be pervasive. You can't easily retrofit loose coupling onto an existing code base.

DI is nothing more than a collection of design principles and patterns. It's more about a way of thinking and designing code than it is about tools and techniques. The purpose of DI is to make code maintainable. Small code bases, like a classic Hello World example, are inherently maintainable because of their size. This is why DI tends to look like overengineering in simple examples. The larger the code base becomes, the more visible the benefits. We've dedicated the next two chapters to a larger and more complex example to showcase these benefits.

Summary

- Dependency Injection is a set of software design principles and patterns that enables you to develop loosely coupled code. Loose coupling makes code more maintainable.
- When you have a loosely coupled infrastructure in place, it can be used by anyone and adapted to changing needs and unanticipated requirements without having to make large changes to the application's code base and its infrastructure.
- Troubleshooting tends to become less taxing because the scope of likely culprits narrows.
- DI enables late binding, which is the ability to replace classes or modules with different ones without the need for the original code to be recompiled.
- DI makes it easier for code to be extended and reused in ways not explicitly planned for, similar to the way you have flexibility when working with electrical plugs and sockets.

---

[18] William J. Brown et al., *AntiPatterns: Refactoring Software, Architectures, and Projects in Crisis* (Wiley Computer Publishing, 1998), 119.

[19] Eric Evans, *Domain-Driven Design: Tackling Complexity in the Heart of Software*, 243.

- DI simplifies parallel development on the same code base because the Separation of Concerns allows each team member or even entire teams to work more easily on isolated parts.

- DI makes software more TESTABLE because you can replace DEPENDENCIES with test implementations when writing unit tests.

- When you practice DI, collaborating classes should rely on infrastructure to provide the necessary services. You do this by letting your classes depend on interfaces, instead of concrete implementations.

- Classes shouldn't ask a third party for their DEPENDENCIES. This is an anti-pattern called SERVICE LOCATOR. Instead, classes should specify their required DEPENDENCIES statically using constructor parameters, a practice called CONSTRUCTOR INJECTION.

- Many developers think that DI requires specialized tooling, a so-called DI CONTAINER. This is a myth. A DI CONTAINER is a useful, but optional, tool.

- One of the most important software design principles that enables DI is the LISKOV SUBSTITUTION PRINCIPLE. It allows replacing one implementation of an interface with another without breaking either the client or the implementation.

- DEPENDENCIES are considered STABLE in the case that they're already available, have deterministic behavior, don't require a setup runtime environment (such as a relational database), and don't need to be replaced, wrapped, or intercepted.

- DEPENDENCIES are considered VOLATILE when they are under development, aren't always available on all development machines, contain nondeterministic behavior, or need to be replaced, wrapped, or intercepted.

- VOLATILE DEPENDENCIES are the focal point of DI. We inject VOLATILE DEPENDENCIES into a class's constructor.

- By removing control over DEPENDENCIES from their consumers, and moving that control into the application entry point, you gain the ability to apply CROSS-CUTTING CONCERNS more easily and can manage the lifetime of DEPENDENCIES more effectively.

- To succeed, you need to apply DI pervasively. All *classes* should get their required VOLATILE DEPENDENCIES using CONSTRUCTOR INJECTION. It's hard to retrofit loose coupling and DI onto an existing code base.

Writing tightly coupled code

In this chapter

- Writing a tightly coupled application
- Evaluating the composability of that application
- Analyzing the lack of composability in that application

As we mentioned in chapter 1, a *sauce béarnaise* is an emulsified sauce made from egg yolk and butter, but this doesn't magically instill in you the ability to make one. The best way to learn is to practice, but an example can often bridge the gap between theory and practice. Watching a professional cook making a sauce béarnaise is helpful before you try it out yourself.

When we introduced Dependency Injection (DI) in the last chapter, we presented a high-level tour to help you understand its purpose and general principles. But that simple explanation doesn't do justice to DI. DI is a way to enable loose coupling, and loose coupling is first and foremost an efficient way to deal with complexity.

Most software is complex in the sense that it must address many issues simultaneously. Besides the business concerns, which may be complex in their own right, software must also address matters related to security, diagnostics, operations, performance, and extensibility. Instead of addressing all of these concerns in one big ball of mud, loose coupling encourages you to address each concern separately. It's easier to address each in isolation, but ultimately, you must still compose this complex set of issues into a single application.

In this chapter, we'll take a look at a more complex example. You'll see how easy it is to write tightly coupled code. You'll also join us in an analysis of why tightly coupled code is problematic from a maintainability perspective. In chapter 3, we'll use DI to completely rewrite this tightly coupled code base to one that's loosely coupled. If you want to see loosely coupled code right away, you may want to skip this chapter. If not, when you're done with this chapter, you should begin to understand what it is that makes tightly coupled code so problematic.

2.1 Building a tightly coupled application

The idea of building loosely coupled code isn't particularly controversial, but there's a huge gap between theory and practice. Before we show you in the next chapter how to use DI to build a loosely coupled application, we want to show you how easily it can go wrong. A common attempt at loosely coupled code is building a layered application. Anyone can draw a three-layer application diagram, and figure 2.1 proves that we can too.

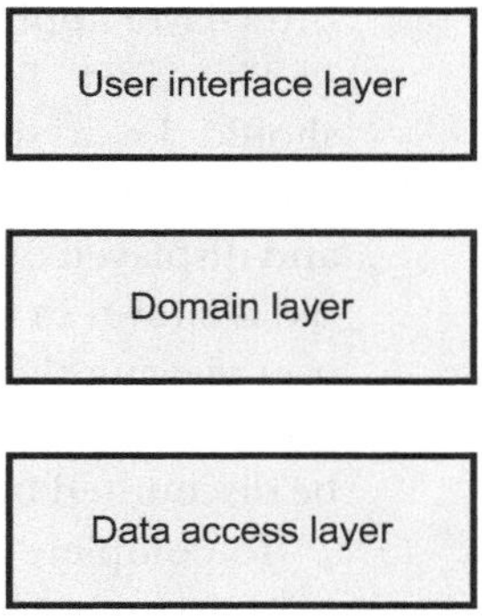

Drawing a three-layer diagram is deceptively simple, but the act of drawing the diagram is akin to stating that you'll have sauce béarnaise with your steak: it's a declaration of intent that carries no guarantee with regard to the final result. You can end up with something else, as you shall soon see.

There's more than one way to view and design a flexible and maintainable complex application, but the *n*-layer application architecture constitutes a well-known, tried-and-tested approach. The challenge is to implement it correctly. Armed with a three-layer diagram like the one in figure 2.1, you can start building an application.

Figure 2.1 Standard three-layer application architecture. This is the simplest and most common variation of the *n*-layer application architecture, whereby an application is composed of *n* distinct layers.

2.1.1 Meet Mary Rowan

Mary Rowan is a professional .NET developer working for a local Certified Microsoft Partner that mainly develops web applications. She's 34 years old and has been working with software for 11 years. This makes her one of the more experienced developers in the company. In addition to performing her regular duties as a senior developer, she often acts as a mentor for junior developers. In general, Mary is happy about the work that she's doing, but it frustrates her that milestones are often missed, forcing her and her colleagues to work long hours and weekends to meet deadlines.

She suspects that there must be more efficient ways to build software. In an effort to learn about efficiency, she buys a lot of programming books, but she rarely has time to read them, as much of her spare time is spent with her husband and two girls. Mary likes to go hiking in the mountains. She's also an enthusiastic cook, and she definitely knows how to make a real sauce béarnaise.

Mary has been asked to create a new e-commerce application on ASP. NET Core MVC and Entity Framework Core with SQL Server as the data store. To maximize modularity, it must be a three-layer application.

The first feature to implement should be a simple list of featured products, pulled from a database table and displayed on a web page (an example is shown in figure 2.2). And, if the user viewing the list is a preferred customer, the price on all products should be discounted by 5%.

To complete her first feature, Mary will have to implement the following:

Featured Products

Criollo Chocolate ($34.95)
Gruyère ($48.50)
White Asparagus ($39.80)
Anchovies ($18.75)
Arborio Rice ($22.75)

Figure 2.2   Screen capture of the e-commerce web application Mary has been asked to develop. It features a simple list of featured products and their prices.

- *A data layer*—Includes a Products table in the database, which represents all database rows, and a `Product` class, which represents a single database row
- *A domain layer*—Contains the logic for retrieving the featured products
- *A UI Layer with an MVC controller*—Handles incoming requests, retrieves the relevant data from the domain layer, and sends it to the Razor view, which eventually renders the list of featured products

Let's look over Mary's shoulder as she implements the application's first feature.

2.1.2   *Creating the data layer*

Because Mary will need to pull data from a database table, she has decided to begin by implementing the data layer. The first step is to define the database table itself. Mary uses SQL Server Management Studio to create the table shown in table 2.1.

Table 2.1 Mary creates the Products table with the following columns.

Column Name	Data Type	Allow Nulls	Primary Key
Id	uniqueidentifier	No	Yes
Name	nvarchar(50)	No	No
Description	nvarchar(max)	No	No
UnitPrice	money	No	No
IsFeatured	bit	No	No

To implement the data access layer, Mary adds a new library to her solution. The following listing shows her `Product` class.

Listing 2.1 Mary's `Product` class

```
public class Product
{
    public Guid Id { get; set; }
    public string Name { get; set; }
    public string Description { get; set; }
    public decimal UnitPrice { get; set; }
    public bool IsFeatured { get; set; }
}
```

Mary uses Entity Framework for her data access needs. She adds a dependency to the Microsoft.EntityFrameworkCore.SqlServer NuGet package to her project, and implements an application-specific `DbContext` class that allows her application to access the Products table via the `CommerceContext` class. The following listing shows her `CommerceContext` class.

Listing 2.2 Mary's `CommerceContext` class

Enables queries on the underlying database's Products table

Called for each instance of the context that's created, allowing it to be configured

```
public class CommerceContext : Microsoft.EntityFrameworkCore.DbContext
{
    public DbSet<Product> Products { get; set; }

    protected override void OnConfiguring(
        DbContextOptionsBuilder builder)
    {
        var config = new ConfigurationBuilder()
            .SetBasePath(
                Directory.GetCurrentDirectory())
            .AddJsonFile("appsettings.json")
            .Build();
```

Loads a configuration file (similar to what you saw in listing 1.2)

```
    string connectionString =
        config.GetConnectionString(
            "CommerceConnectionString");

    builder.UseSqlServer(connectionString);
    }
}
```

Reads a connection string from the configuration file and applies it to DbContextOptionsBuilder. This effectively configures the application's CommerceContext using the configured connection string.

Because CommerceContext loads a connection string from a configuration file, that file needs to be created. Mary adds a file named appsettings.json to her web project, with the following content:

```
{
  "ConnectionStrings": {
    "CommerceConnectionString":
      "Server=.;Database=MaryCommerce;Trusted_Connection=True;"
  }
}
```

Entity Framework Core crash course

Entity Framework Core is Microsoft's Object/Relational Mapper, or ORM for short. It bridges the gap between relational database models and object-oriented code like C#. It allows developers to work at a higher level of abstraction because we don't have write SQL queries ourselves: Entity Framework Core will do the transformation from C# to SQL for us.

Entity Framework's central class is DbContext. The DbContext class is a Unit of Work.[1] A *Unit of Work* consists of a local cache of the objects required for a single business transaction. DbContext allows access to the data in the database like the example with the Products table.

Don't worry if you aren't familiar with Microsoft Entity Framework. The details of the data access implementation aren't that important in this context, so you should be able to follow the example even if you're more familiar with a different data access technology.[2]

WARNING CommerceContext loads the connection string from a configuration file—this is a trap. It causes every new CommerceContext to read the configuration file, even though the configuration file typically doesn't change while an application is running. A CommerceContext shouldn't contain a hard-coded connection string, but neither should it load a configuration value from the configuration system. This is discussed in section 2.3.3.

---

[1] Martin Fowler, *Patterns of Enterprise Application Architecture* (Addison-Wesley, 2002), 184.

[2] There's a whole book about Entity Framework Core: *Entity Framework Core in Action*, by Jon Smith (Manning, 2018).

CommerceContext and Product are public types contained within the same assembly. Mary knows that she'll later need to add more features to her application, but the data access component required to implement the first feature is now completed (figure 2.3).

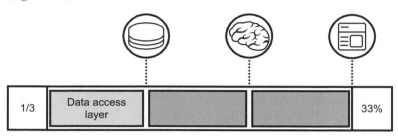

Figure 2.3   How far Mary has come in implementing the layered architecture envisioned in figure 2.1.

Now that the data access layer has been implemented, the next logical step is the domain layer. The *domain layer* is also referred to as the domain logic layer, business layer, or business logic layer. Domain logic is all the behavior that the application needs to have, specific to the domain the application is built for.

2.1.3   Creating the domain layer

With the exception of pure data-reporting applications, there's always domain logic. You may not realize it at first, but as you get to know the domain, its embedded and implicit rules and assumptions will gradually emerge. In the absence of any domain logic, the list of products exposed by CommerceContext could technically have been used directly from the UI layer.

> **WARNING**   Implementing domain logic in either the UI or data access layers will lead to pain and suffering. Do yourself a favor and create a domain layer from the beginning.

The requirements for Mary's application state that preferred customers should be shown the product list prices with a 5% discount. Mary has yet to figure out how to identify a preferred customer, so she asks her coworker Jens for advice:

MARY: I need to implement this business logic so that a preferred customer gets a 5% discount.

JENS: Sounds easy. Just multiply by .95.

MARY: Thanks, but that's not what I wanted to ask you about. What I wanted to ask you is, how should I identify a preferred customer?

JENS: I see. Is this a web application or a desktop application?

MARY: It's a web app.

JENS: Okay, then you can use the User property of the HttpContext to check if the current user is in the role PreferredCustomer.

MARY: Slow down, Jens. This code must be in the domain layer. It's a library. There's no HttpContext.

JENS: Oh. [Thinks for a while] I still think you should use the `HttpContext` of ASP.NET to look up the value for the user. You can then pass the value to your domain logic as a boolean.

MARY: I don't know...

JENS: That'll also ensure that you have good Separation of Concerns because your domain logic doesn't have to deal with security. You know, the SINGLE RESPONSIBILITY PRINCIPLE! It's the Agile way to do it!

MARY: I guess you've got a point.

Jens is basing his advice on his technical knowledge of ASP.NET. As the discussion takes him away from his comfort zone, he steamrolls Mary with a triple combo of buzzwords. Be aware that Jens doesn't know what he's talking about:

- *He misuses the concept of Separation of Concerns.* Although it's important to separate security concerns from the domain logic, moving this to the presentation layer doesn't help in separating concerns.
- *He only mentions Agile because he recently heard someone else talk enthusiastically about it.*
- *He completely misses the point of the SINGLE RESPONSIBILITY PRINCIPLE.* Although the quick feedback cycle that Agile methodologies provide can help you improve your software design accordingly, by itself, the SINGLE RESPONSIBILITY PRINCIPLE as a software design principle is independent of the chosen software development methodology.

SINGLE RESPONSIBILITY PRINCIPLE

As discussed in chapter 1, the SINGLE RESPONSIBILITY PRINCIPLE (SRP) states that each class should only have a single responsibility, or, better put, a class should have only one reason to change.[3]

If we put SQL statements in a view that contains HTML markup, we'd all quickly agree that changes to the markup will happen at different times, at different rates, and for different reasons than changes to SQL statements. Our SQL statements change when we're changing our data model or need to do performance tuning. Our markup, on the other hand, changes when we need to change the look and feel of the web application. These are different concerns that change for different reasons. Putting SQL statements directly into a view is, therefore, an *SRP violation*.

More often than not, however, it can be more challenging to see whether a class has multiple reasons to change. What often helps is to look at the SRP from the perspective of code cohesion. *Cohesion* is defined as the functional relatedness of the elements of a class or module. The lower the relatedness, the lower the cohesion, and the higher the risk a class violates the SRP.

---

[3]   Robert C. Martin, *Agile Principles, Patterns, and Practices in C#* (Pearson Education, 2007), 115.

> Being able to detect SRP violations is one thing, but determining whether a violation should be fixed is yet another. It isn't wise to apply the SRP if there are no symptoms. Needlessly splitting up classes that cause no maintainability problems can add extra complexity. The trick in software design is to manage complexity.

Armed with Jens' unfortunately poor advice, Mary creates a new C# library project and adds a class called `ProductService`, shown in listing 2.3. To make the `ProductService` class compile, she must add a reference to her data access layer, because the `Commerce-Context` class is defined there.

Listing 2.3 Mary's `ProductService` class

```
public class ProductService
{
    private readonly CommerceContext dbContext;

    public ProductService()
    {
        this.dbContext = new CommerceContext();      // Creates a new CommerceContext
    }                                                 // instance for later use

    public IEnumerable<Product> GetFeaturedProducts(
        bool isCustomerPreferred)
    {
        decimal discount =
            isCustomerPreferred ? .95m : 1;

        var featuredProducts =                        // Gets all products from
            from product in this.dbContext.Products   // the database, filtered by
            where product.IsFeatured                  // featured products
            select product;

        return                                        // Creates a list of discounted
            from product in                           // products based on the
                featuredProducts.AsEnumerable()       // discount percentage for
            select new Product                        // the given customer
            {
                Id = product.Id,
                Name = product.Name,
                Description = product.Description,
                IsFeatured = product.IsFeatured,
                UnitPrice =
                    product.UnitPrice * discount
            };
    }
}
```

Mary's happy that she has encapsulated the data access technology (Entity Framework Core), configuration, and domain logic in the `ProductService` class. She has delegated the knowledge of the user to the caller by passing in the `isCustomerPreferred` parameter, and she uses this value to calculate the discount for all the products.

Further refinement could include replacing the hard-coded discount value (.95) with a configurable number, but, for now, this implementation will suffice. Mary's almost done. The only thing still left is the UI layer. Mary decides that it can wait until tomorrow. Figure 2.4 shows how far Mary has come with implementing the architecture envisioned in figure 2.1.

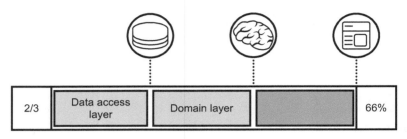

Figure 2.4 Compared to figure 2.3, Mary has now implemented the data access layer and the domain layer. The UI layer still remains to be implemented.

What Mary doesn't realize is that by letting the `ProductService` depend on the data access layer's `CommerceContext` class, she tightly coupled her domain layer to the data access layer. We'll explain what's wrong with that in section 2.2.

2.1.4 *Creating the UI layer*

The next day, Mary resumes her work with the e-commerce application, adding a new ASP.NET Core MVC application to her solution. Don't worry if you aren't familiar with the ASP.NET Core MVC framework. The intricate details of how the MVC framework operates aren't the focus of this discussion. The important part is how DEPENDENCIES are consumed, and that's a relatively platform-neutral subject.

> ### An ASP.NET Core MVC crash course
>
> ASP.NET Core MVC takes its name from the Model View Controller design pattern.[4] In this context, the most important thing to understand is that when a web request arrives, a controller handles the request, potentially using a (domain) model to deal with it, and forms a response that's finally rendered by a view.
>
> A *controller* is normally a class that derives from the abstract `Controller` class. It has one or more action methods that handle requests; for example, a `HomeController` class typically has a method named `Index` that handles the request for the default page. When an action method returns, it passes on the resulting model to the view through a `ViewResult` instance.

The next listing shows how Mary implements an `Index` method on her `HomeController` class to extract the featured products from the database and pass them to the view. To make this code compile, she must add references to both the data access layer and the domain layer. This is because the `ProductService` class is defined in the domain layer, but the `Product` class is defined in the data access layer.

---

[4] Martin Fowler et al., *Patterns of Enterprise Application Architecture*, 330.

Listing 2.4 Index method on the default controller class

Determines whether a customer is a preferred customer

```
public ViewResult Index()
{
    bool isPreferredCustomer =
        this.User.IsInRole("PreferredCustomer");

    var service = new ProductService();          ◄── Creates ProductService
                                                     from the domain layer

    var products = service.GetFeaturedProducts(
        isPreferredCustomer);

    this.ViewData["Products"] = products;        ◄── Stores the list of products in the
                                                     controller's generic ViewData
    return this.View();                              dictionary for later use by the view
}
```

Gets the list of featured products (defined in the data access layer) from the ProductService

As part of the ASP.NET Core MVC lifecycle, the User property on the HomeController class is automatically populated with the correct user object, so Mary uses it to determine if the current user is a preferred customer. Armed with this information, she can invoke the domain logic to get the list of featured products.

NOTE When Mary created her domain layer, she again created tightly coupled code. In this case, HomeController is tightly coupled to ProductService. This wouldn't be that bad if ProductService was a STABLE DEPENDENCY but, as you learned in chapter 1, ProductService is a VOLATILE DEPENDENCY. It's VOLATILE because it introduces a requirement to set up and configure a relational database.

In Mary's application, the list of products must be rendered by the Index view. The following listing shows the markup for the view.

Listing 2.5 Index view markup

```
<h2>Featured Products</h2>                    Gets the products
<div>                                         populated by the controller
@{
    var products =
        (IEnumerable<Product>)this.ViewData["Products"];

    foreach (Product product in products)     ◄──
    {
        <div>@product.Name (@product.UnitPrice.ToString("C"))</div>
    }
}                                    Loops through the products, formats their
</div>                                UnitPrice, and renders them as HTML
```

ASP.NET Core MVC lets you write standard HTML with bits of imperative code embedded to access objects created and assigned by the controller that created the view. In this case, the HomeController's Index method assigned the list of featured products to a key called Products that Mary uses in the view to render the list of products. Figure 2.5 shows how Mary has now implemented the architecture envisioned in figure 2.1.

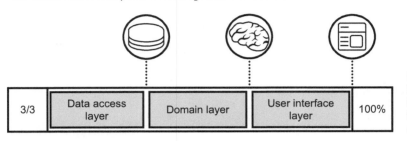

Figure 2.5   Mary has now implemented all three layers in the application.

With all three layers in place, the applications should theoretically work. But only by running the application can she verify whether that's the case.

2.2   Evaluating the tightly coupled application

Mary has now implemented all three layers, so it's time to see if the application works. She presses F5 and the web page shown in figure 2.2 appears. The Featured Products feature is now done, and Mary feels confident and ready to implement the next feature in the application. After all, she followed established best practices and created a three-layer application ... or did she?

Did Mary succeed in developing a proper, layered application? No, she didn't, although she certainly had the best of intentions. She created three Visual Studio projects that correspond to the three layers in the planned architecture. To the casual observer, this looks like the coveted layered architecture, but, as you'll see, the code is tightly coupled.

Visual Studio makes it easy and natural to work with solutions and projects in this way. If you need functionality from a different library, you can easily add a reference to it and write code that creates new instances of the types defined in the other libraries. Every time you add a reference, though, you take on a DEPENDENCY.

2.2.1   Evaluating the dependency graph

When working with solutions in Visual Studio, it's easy to lose track of the important DEPENDENCIES. This is because Visual Studio displays them together with all the other project references that may point to assemblies in the .NET Base Class Library (BCL). To understand how the modules in Mary's application relate to each other, we can draw a graph of the dependencies (see figure 2.6).

The most remarkable insight to be gained from figure 2.6 is that the UI layer depends on both domain and data access layers. It seems as though the UI could bypass the domain layer in certain cases. This requires further investigation.

2.2.2 *Evaluating composability*

A major goal of building a three-layer application is to separate concerns. We'd like to separate our domain model from the data access and UI layers so that none of these concerns pollute the domain model. In large applications, it's essential to be able to work with each area of the application in isolation. To evaluate Mary's implementation, we can ask a simple question: Is it possible to use each module in isolation?

In theory, we should be able to compose modules any way we like. We may need to write new modules to bind existing modules together in new and unanticipated ways, but, ideally, we should be able to do so without having to modify the existing modules. Can we use the modules in Mary's application in new and exciting ways? Let's look at some likely scenarios.

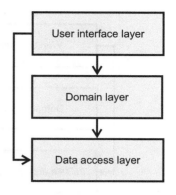

Figure 2.6   The dependency graph for Mary's application, showing how the modules depend on each other. The arrows point towards a module's dependency.

> **NOTE**   The following analyses discuss whether modules can be replaced, but be aware that this is a technique we use to evaluate composability. Even if we never want to swap modules, this sort of analysis uncovers potential issues regarding coupling. If we find that the code is tightly coupled, all the benefits of loose coupling are lost.

BUILDING A NEW UI

If Mary's application becomes a success, the project stakeholders would like her to develop a rich client version in Windows Presentation Foundation (WPF). Is this possible to do while reusing the domain and data access layers?

When we examine the dependency graph in figure 2.6, we can quickly ascertain that no modules are depending on the web UI, so it's possible to remove it and replace it with a WPF UI. Creating a rich client based on WPF is a new application that shares most of its implementation with the original web application. Figure 2.7 illustrates how a WPF application would need to take the same dependencies as the web application. The original web application can remain unchanged.

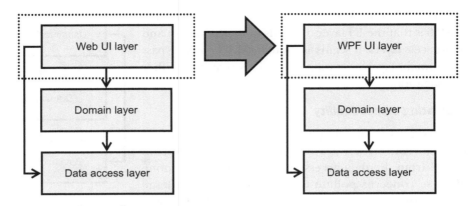

Figure 2.7   Replacing a web UI with a WPF UI is possible because no module depends on the web UI. The dashed box signals the part that we want to replace.

Replacing the UI layer is certainly possible with Mary's implementation. Let's examine another interesting decomposition.

BUILDING A NEW DATA ACCESS LAYER

Mary's market analysts figure out that, to optimize profits, her application should be available as a cloud application hosted on Microsoft Azure. In Azure, data can be stored in the highly scalable Azure Table Storage Service. This storage mechanism is based on flexible data containers that contain unconstrained data. The service enforces no particular database schema, and there's no referential integrity.

Although the most common data access technology on .NET is based on ADO.NET Data Services, the protocol used to communicate with the Table Storage Service is HTTP. This type of database is sometimes known as a *key-value database*, and it's a different beast than a relational database accessed through Entity Framework Core.

To enable the e-commerce application as a cloud application, the data access layer must be replaced with a module that uses the Table Storage Service. Is this possible?

From the dependency graph in figure 2.6, we already know that both the UI and domain layers depend on the Entity Framework–based data access layer. If we try to remove the data access layer, the solution will no longer compile without refactoring all other projects because a required DEPENDENCY is missing. In a big application with dozens of modules, we could also try to remove the modules that don't compile to see what would be left. In the case of Mary's application, it's evident that we'd have to remove all modules, leaving nothing behind, as figure 2.8 shows.

Although it would be possible to develop an Azure Table data access layer that mimics the API exposed by the original data access layer, there's no way we could apply that to the application without touching other parts of the application. The application isn't nearly as composable as the project stakeholders would have liked. Enabling the profit-maximizing cloud abilities requires a major rewrite of the application because none of the existing modules can be reused.

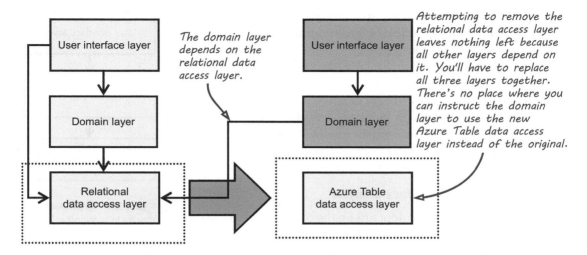

Figure 2.8 **An attempt to replace the relational data access layer**

EVALUATING OTHER COMBINATIONS

We could analyze the application for other combinations of modules, but this would be a moot point because we already know that it fails to support an important scenario. Besides, not all combinations make sense.

For instance, we could ask whether it would be possible to replace the domain model with a different implementation. But, in most cases, this would be an odd question to ask because the domain model encapsulates the heart of the application. Without the domain model, most applications have no reason to exist.

2.3 Analysis of missing composability

Why did Mary's implementation fail to achieve the desired degree of composability? Is it because the UI has a direct dependency on the data access layer? Let's examine this possibility in greater detail.

2.3.1 Dependency graph analysis

Why does the UI depend on the data access library? The culprit is this domain model's method signature:

```
public IEnumerable<Product> GetFeaturedProducts(bool isCustomerPreferred)
```
Exposes to clients a type defined in the data access library

The GetFeaturedProducts method of the ProductService class returns a sequence of products, but the Product class is defined in the data access layer. Any client consuming the GetFeaturedProducts method must reference the data access layer to be able to compile. It's possible to change the signature of the method to return a type defined within the domain model. It'd also be more correct, but it doesn't solve the problem.

Let's assume that we break the dependency between the UI and data access library. The modified dependency graph would now look like figure 2.9.

Would such a change enable Mary to replace the relational data access layer with one that encapsulates access to the Azure Table service? Unfortunately, no, because the domain layer still depends on the data access layer. The UI, in turn, still depends on the domain model. If we try to remove the original data access layer, there'd be nothing left of the application. The root cause of the problem lies somewhere else.

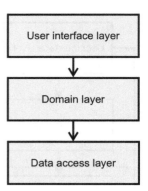

Figure 2.9   Dependency graph of the hypothetical situation where the UI's dependency on the data access layer is removed

2.3.2   *Data access interface analysis*

The domain model depends on the data access layer because the entire data model is defined there. Using Entity Framework to implement a data access layer may be a reasonable decision. But, from the perspective of loose coupling, consuming it directly in the domain model isn't.

The offending code can be found spread out in the ProductService class. The constructor creates a new instance of the CommerceContext class and assigns it to a private member variable:

```
this.dbContext = new CommerceContext();
```

This tightly couples the ProductService class to the data access layer. There's no reasonable way you can INTERCEPT this piece of code and replace it with something else. The reference to the data access layer is hard-coded into the ProductService class!

The implementation of the GetFeaturedProducts method uses CommerceContext to pull Product objects from the database:

```
var featuredProducts =
    from product in this.dbContext.Products
    where product.IsFeatured
    select product;
```

The reference to CommerceContext within GetFeaturedProducts reinforces the hard-coded dependency, but, at this point, the damage is already done. What we need is a better way to compose modules without such tight coupling. If you look back at the benefits of DI as discussed in chapter 1, you'll see that Mary's application fails to have the following:

- *Late binding*—Because the domain layer is tightly coupled with the data access layer, it becomes impossible to deploy two versions of the same application, where one connects to a local SQL Server database and the other is hosted on Microsoft Azure using Azure Table Storage. In other words, it's impossible to load the correct data access layer using late binding.
- *Extensibility*—Because all classes in the application are tightly coupled to one another, it becomes costly to plug in CROSS-CUTTING CONCERNS like the security feature in chapter 1. Doing so requires many classes in the system to be changed. This tightly coupled design is, therefore, not particularly extensible.

- *Maintainability* — Not only would adding CROSS-CUTTING CONCERNS require sweeping changes throughout the application, but every newly added CROSS-CUTTING CONCERN would likely make each class touched even more complex. Every addition would make a class harder to read. This means that the application isn't as maintainable as Mary would like.

- *Parallel development* — If we stick with the previous example of applying CROSS-CUTTING CONCERNS, it's quite easy to understand that having to make sweeping changes throughout your code base hinders the ability to work with multiple developers in parallel on a single application. Like us, you've likely dealt with painful merge conflicts in the past when committing your work to a version control system. A well-designed, loosely coupled system will, among other things, reduce the amount of merge conflicts that you'll have. When more developers start working on Mary's application, it'll become harder and harder to work effectively without stepping on each other's toes.

- *Testability* — We already established that swapping out the data access layer is currently impossible. Testing code without a database, however, is a prerequisite for doing unit testing. But even with integration testing, Mary will likely need some parts of the code to be swapped out, and the current design makes this hard. Mary's application is, therefore, not TESTABLE.

At this point, you may ask yourself what the desired dependency graph should look like. For the highest degree of reuse, the lowest amount of dependencies is desirable. On the other hand, the application would become rather useless if there were no dependencies at all.

Which dependencies you need and in what direction they should point depends on the requirements. But because we've already established that we have no intention of replacing the domain layer with a completely different implementation, it's safe to assume that other layers can safely depend on it. Figure 2.10 contains a big spoiler for the loosely coupled application you'll write in the next chapter, but it does show the desired dependency graph.

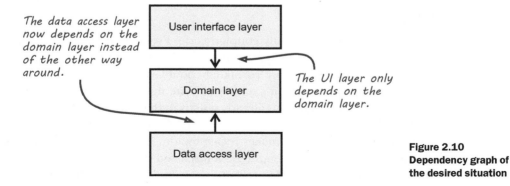

The data access layer now depends on the domain layer instead of the other way around.

The UI layer only depends on the domain layer.

**Figure 2.10
Dependency graph of
the desired situation**

The figure shows how we inverted the dependency between the domain and data access layers. We'll go into more detail on how to do this in the next chapter.

2.3.3   *Miscellaneous other issues*

We'd like to point out a few other issues with Mary's code that ought to be addressed.

- *Most of the domain model seems to be implemented in the data access layer.* Whereas it's a technical problem that the domain layer references the data access layer, it's a conceptual problem that the data access layer defines such a class as the Product class. A public Product class belongs in the domain model.

- *On Jens' advice, Mary decided to implement in the UI the code that determines whether a user is a preferred customer.* But how a customer is identified as a preferred customer is a piece of business logic, so it should be implemented in the domain model. Jens' argument about Separation of Concerns and the SINGLE RESPONSIBILITY PRINCIPLE is no excuse for putting code in the wrong place. Following the SINGLE RESPONSIBILITY PRINCIPLE within a single library is entirely possible — that's the expected approach.

- *Mary loaded the connection string from the configuration file from within the* Commerce-Context *class (shown in listing 2.2).* From the perspective of its consumers, the dependency on this configuration value is completely hidden. As we alluded to when discussing listing 2.2, this implicitness contains a trap.

  Although the ability to configure a compiled application is important, only the finished application should rely on configuration files. It's more flexible for reusable libraries to be imperatively configurable by their callers, instead of reading configuration files themselves. In the end, the ultimate caller is the application's entry point. At that point, all relevant configuration data can be read from a configuration file directly at startup and fed to the underlying libraries as needed. We want the configuration that CommerceContext requires to be explicit.

- *The view (as shown in listing 2.5) seems to contain too much functionality.* It performs casts and specific string formatting. Such functionality should be moved to the underlying model.

2.4   *Conclusion*

It's surprisingly easy to write tightly coupled code. Even when Mary set out with the express intent of writing a three-layer application, it turned into a largely monolithic piece of Spaghetti Code.[5] (When we're talking about layering, we call this Lasagna.)

One of the many reasons that it's so easy to write tightly coupled code is that both the language features and our tools already pull us in that direction. If you need a new instance of an object, you can use the new keyword. If you don't have a reference to the required assembly, Visual Studio makes it easy to add. But every time you use the new keyword, you introduce a tight coupling. As discussed in chapter 1, not all tight coupling is bad, but you should strive to prevent tight coupling to VOLATILE DEPENDENCIES.

---

[5]   William J. Brown et al., *AntiPatterns: Refactoring Software, Architectures, and Projects in Crisis* (Wiley Computer Publishing, 1998), 119.

By now you should begin to understand what it is that makes tightly coupled code so problematic, but we've yet to show you how to fix these problems. In the next chapter, we'll show you a more composable way of building an application with the same features as the one Mary built. We'll also address those other issues discussed in section 2.3.3 at the same time.

Summary

- Complex software must address lots of different concerns, such as security, diagnostics, operations, performance, and extensibility.
- Loose coupling encourages you to address all application concerns in isolation, but ultimately you must still compose this complex set of concerns.
- It's easy to create tightly coupled code. Although not all tight coupling is bad, tight coupling to VOLATILE DEPENDENCIES is and should be avoided.
- In Mary's application, because the domain layer depended on the data access layer, there was no way to replace the data access layer with a different one. The tight coupling in her application caused Mary to lose the benefits that loose coupling provides: late binding, extensibility, maintainability, TESTABILITY, and parallel development.
- Only the finished application should rely on configuration files. Other parts of the application shouldn't request values from a configuration file, but should instead be configurable by their callers.
- The SINGLE RESPONSIBILITY PRINCIPLE states that each class should only have one reason to change.
- The SINGLE RESPONSIBILITY PRINCIPLE can be viewed from the perspective of cohesion. *Cohesion* is defined as the functional relatedness of the elements of a class or module. The lower the amount of relatedness, the lower the cohesion; and the lower the cohesion, the greater the chance a class violates the SINGLE RESPONSIBILITY PRINCIPLE.

Writing loosely coupled code

3

In this chapter

- Redesigning Mary's e-commerce application to become loosely coupled
- Analyzing that loosely coupled application
- Evaluating that loosely coupled application

When it comes to grilling steak, an important practice is to let the meat rest before you cut it into slices. When resting, the juices redistribute, and the results get juicier. If, on the other hand, you cut it too soon, all the juice runs out, and your meat gets drier and less tasty. It'd be a terrible shame to let this happen, because you'd like to give your guests the best tasting experience you can deliver. Although it's important to know the best practices for any profession, it's just as important to know the bad practices and to understand why those lead to unsatisfactory results.

Knowing the difference between good and bad practices is essential to learning. This is why the previous chapter was completely devoted to an example and analysis of tightly coupled code: the analysis provided you with the *why*.

To summarize, loose coupling provides a number of benefits—late binding, extensibility, maintainability, TESTABILITY, and parallel development. With tight coupling, you lose those benefits. Although not all tight coupling is undesirable, you should strive to avoid tight coupling to Volatile Dependencies. Moreover, you can use Dependency Injection (DI) to solve the issues that were discovered during that analysis. Because DI is a radical departure from the way Mary created her application, we're not going to modify her existing code. Rather, we're going to re-create it from scratch.

NOTE You shouldn't infer from this decision that it's impossible to refactor an existing application towards DI or that we encourage you to rewrite existing applications completely from scratch. Big rewrites are costly and high risk. Preferred are slow, step-by-step refactorings. That's not to say that refactoring is easy, because it's not. It's hard. In our experience, it takes a lot of work to get there.[1]

Let's start with a short recap of Mary's application. We'll also discuss how we'll approach the rewrite and what the desired result will look like when we've finished.

3.1 Rebuilding the e-commerce application

The analysis of Mary's application in chapter 2 concluded that Volatile Dependencies were tightly coupled across the different layers. As the dependency graph of Mary's application in figure 3.1 shows, both the domain layer and the UI layer depend on the data access layer.

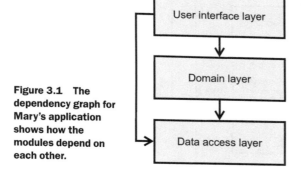

What we'll aim to achieve in this chapter is to invert the dependency between the domain layer and the data access layer. This means that instead of the domain layer depending on the data access layer, the data access layer will depend on the domain layer, as shown in figure 3.2.

Figure 3.1   The dependency graph for Mary's application shows how the modules depend on each other.

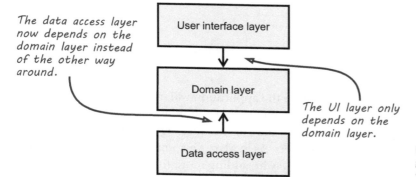

The data access layer now depends on the domain layer instead of the other way around.

The UI layer only depends on the domain layer.

Figure 3.2   Dependency graph of the desired inversion for Mary's application

---

[1]   There's a whole book about refactoring. See Michael C. Feathers, *Working Effectively with Legacy Code* (Prentice Hall, 2004).

By creating this inversion, we allow the data access layer to be replaced without having to completely rewrite the application. (This is a radical departure from the way Mary developed her application.) We'll also apply several patterns along the way. Then we'll apply CONSTRUCTOR INJECTION, which we discussed in chapter 1. And finally, we'll also use METHOD INJECTION and COMPOSITION ROOT, which we'll discuss as we go.

This approach will lead to quite a few more classes as we focus on separating the application concerns. Where Mary defined four classes, we'll define nine classes and three interfaces. Figure 3.3 drills a little deeper into the application and shows the classes and interfaces we'll create throughout this chapter.

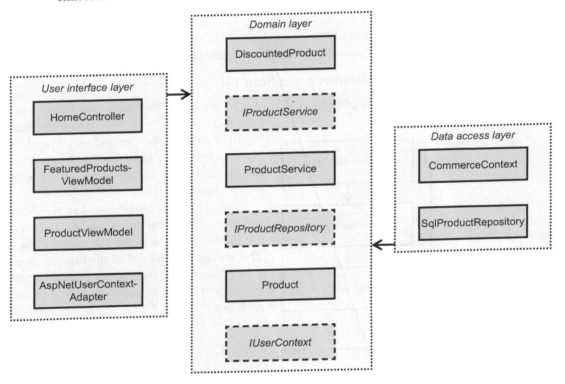

Figure 3.3 The classes and interfaces that we'll have at the end of this chapter. Interfaces are marked with dashed lines.

Figure 3.4 shows how the main classes in the application will interact. At the end of this chapter, we'll take a look at a slightly more detailed version of this diagram again.

When we write software, we prefer to start in the most significant place—the part that has most visibility to our stakeholders. As in Mary's e-commerce application, this is often the UI. From there, we work our way in, adding more functionality until one feature is done; then we move on to the next. This *outside-in* technique helps us to focus on the requested functionality without overengineering the solution.

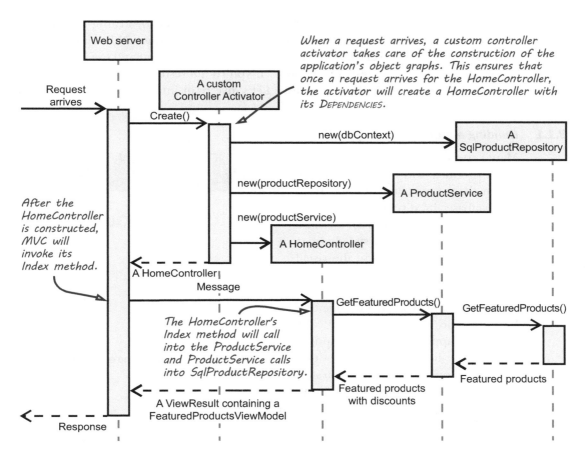

Figure 3.4 Sequence diagram showing the interaction between elements involved in DI in the e-commerce application that we build in this chapter

In chapter 2, Mary used the opposite approach. She started with the data access layer and worked her way out, working *inside-out*. It would be harsh for us to say that working inside-out is bad, but as you'll see later, the outside-in approach gives you quicker feedback on what you're building. We'll therefore build the application in the opposite order, starting with the UI layer, continuing with the domain layer, and then building the data access layer last.

NOTE The outside-in technique is closely related to the YAGNI principle — "You Aren't Gonna Need It." This principle emphasizes that only required features should be implemented, and that the implementation should be as simple as possible.

Because we practice Test-Driven Development (TDD), we start by writing unit tests as soon as our outside-in approach prompts us to create a new class. Although we wrote unit tests to create this example, TDD isn't required to implement and use DI, so we're not going to show these tests in the book. If you're interested, the source code that accompanies this book includes the tests. Let's dive right into our project and begin with the UI.

3.1.1   Building a more maintainable UI

Mary's specification for the list of featured products was to write an application that extracts those items from the database and displays them in a list (shown again in figure 3.5). Because we know that the project stakeholders will mainly be interested in the visual result, the UI seems like a good place to start.

The first thing you do after opening Visual Studio is add a new ASP.NET Core MVC application to the solution. Because the list of featured products needs to go on the front page, you start by modifying the Index.cshtml file to include the markup shown in the following listing.[2]

Figure 3.5   Screen capture of the e-commerce web application

---

Listing 3.1   Index.cshtml view markup

```
@model FeaturedProductsViewModel

<h2>Featured Products</h2>
<div>
    @foreach (ProductViewModel product in this.Model.Products)
    {
        <div>@product.SummaryText</div>
    }
</div>
```

Notice how much cleaner listing 3.1 is compared to Mary's original markup.

Listing 3.2   Mary's original Index view markup from chapter 2

```
<h2>Featured Products</h2>
<div>
@{
```

---

[2]   The view for the Index action of HomeController is typically located in the web application project at /Views/Home/Index.cshtml.

```
    var products = (IEnumerable<Product>)this.ViewData["Products"];

    foreach (Product product in products)
    {
        <div>@product.Name (@product.UnitPrice.ToString("C"))</div>
    }
}
</div>
```

The first improvement is that you no longer cast a dictionary item to a sequence of products before iteration is possible. You accomplished this easily by using MVC's special @model directive. This means that the Model property of the page is of the FeaturedProducts-ViewModel type. Using the @model directive, MVC will ensure that the value returned from the controller will be cast to the FeaturedProductsViewModel type. Secondly, the entire product display string is pulled directly from the SummaryText property of ProductViewModel.

Both improvements are related to the introduction of view-specific models that encapsulate the behavior of the view. These models are Plain Old CLR Objects (POCO).[3] The following listing provides an outline of their structure.

> **Listing 3.3 FeaturedProductsViewModel and ProductViewModel classes**

```
public class FeaturedProductsViewModel
{
    public FeaturedProductsViewModel(
        IEnumerable<ProductViewModel> products)
    {
        this.Products = products;
    }

    public IEnumerable<ProductViewModel> Products
        { get; }                                  ◄───────────────────────┐
}                                                                          │
                                            The FeaturedProductsViewModel contains a list of
public class ProductViewModel               ProductViewModel instances. Both are POCOs,
{                                           which makes them amenable to unit testing.
    private static CultureInfo PriceCulture = new CultureInfo("en-US");

    public ProductViewModel(string name, decimal unitPrice)
    {
        this.SummaryText = string.Format(PriceCulture,
            "{0} ({1:C})", name, unitPrice);
    }

    public string SummaryText { get; }  ◄──────┐ The SummaryText property is derived
}                                               │ from two values — name and unitPrice —
                                                │ to encapsulate rendering logic.
```

---

[3] A Plain Old CLR Object (POCO), or Plain Old C# Object as it's sometimes referred to, is a simple class created in C# or another language for the Common Language Runtime (CLR), which is free from dependencies on an external framework.

The use of view models simplifies the view, which is good because views are harder to test. It also makes it easier for a UI designer to work on the application.

> **NOTE** Did you happen to notice a bug in Mary's original markup? Although the call to UnitPrice.ToString("C") formats decimal as a currency, it does so based on the user's cultural preferences as supplied to the application by their browser. This means that a visitor from the USA sees a dollar symbol, whereas someone from Denmark sees the Danish krone symbol. This wouldn't be bad if both currencies had the same value, but they don't. This would lead to Danish visitors getting the products for a fraction of the intended price. That's why ProductViewModel states the culture information explicitly.

HomeController must return a view with an instance of FeaturedProductsViewModel for the code in listing 3.1 to work. As a first step, this can be implemented inside Home Controller like this:

```
public ViewResult Index()
{
    var vm = new FeaturedProductsViewModel(new[]          Creates a view model with a
    {                                                      hard-coded list of discounted
        new ProductViewModel("Chocolate", 34.95m),         products
        new ProductViewModel("Asparagus", 39.80m)
    });

    return this.View(vm);          Wraps the view model in an MVC ViewResult
}                                  object using MVC's helper method, View
```

We hard-coded the list of discounted products inside the Index method. This isn't the desired end result, but it enables the web application to execute without error and allows us to show the stakeholders an incomplete, but running example of the application (a stub) for them to comment on.

> **IMPORTANT** From a DI point of view, POCOs, DTOs, and view models like FeaturedProductsViewModel and ProductViewModel aren't really interesting.[4] They don't contain any behavior you might want to INTERCEPT, replace, or mock. They are mere data objects. This makes them safe to create in your code, so there's no risk in tightly coupling your code to these data objects. These objects contain the application's runtime data that flows through the system after classes like HomeController and ProductService have long been created.

At this stage, only a stub of the UI layer has been implemented; a full implementation of the domain layer and data access layer still remains. One advantage of starting with the UI is that we already have software we can run and test. Contrast this with Mary's

---

[4] A Data Transfer Object (DTO) is an object that carries data between processes.

progress at a comparable stage. Only
at a much later stage does Mary arrive
at a point where she can run the application. Figure 3.6 shows the stubbed
web application.

For our `HomeController` to fulfill
its obligations, and to do anything of
interest, it requests a list of featured
products from the domain layer.
These products need to have discounts
applied. In chapter 2, Mary wrapped
this logic in her `ProductService` class,
and we'll do that too.

The `Index` method on `Home-`
`Controller` should use the `Product-`
`Service` instance to retrieve the list of featured products, convert those to `ProductViewModel`
instances, and then add those to `FeaturedProductsViewModel`. From the perspective of
`HomeController`, however, `ProductService` is a VOLATILE DEPENDENCY because it's a
DEPENDENCY that doesn't yet exist and is still in development. If we want to test `Home-`
`Controller` in isolation, develop `ProductService` in parallel, or replace or INTERCEPT it
in the future, we need to introduce a SEAM.

Recall from the analysis of Mary's implementation that depending on VOLATILE
DEPENDENCIES is a cardinal sin. As soon as you do that, you're tightly coupled with the
type just used. To avoid this tight coupling, we'll introduce an interface and use a technique called CONSTRUCTOR INJECTION; how the instance is created, and by whom, is of
no concern to `HomeController`.

Featured Products

Chocolate ($34.95)
Asparagus ($39.80)

Figure 3.6   Screen capture of the stubbed e-commerce web application. Here the product list is hard-coded.

Listing 3.4   `HomeController` class

```
public class HomeController : Controller
{
    private readonly IProductService productService;

    public HomeController(
        IProductService productService)
    {
        if (productService == null)
            throw new ArgumentNullException(
                "productService");

        this.productService = productService;
    }
```

**The constructor specifies that
anyone wanting to use the class
must provide an instance of an
IProductService interface.**

**A Guard Clause prevents the
supplied instance from being
null by throwing an exception.**

**The injected DEPENDENCY can be stored
for later and safely used by other
members of the HomeController class.**

```
public ViewResult Index()
{
    IEnumerable<DiscountedProduct> products =
        this.productService.GetFeaturedProducts();

    var vm = new FeaturedProductsViewModel(
        from product in products
        select new ProductViewModel(product));

    return this.View(vm);
}
}
```

A view model is constructed out of the list of featured products.

We changed ProductViewModel to accept a DiscountedProduct instead of a string and decimal.

The stored productService DEPENDENCY. Notice how GetFeaturedProducts returns a collection of DiscountedProduct rather than Product. The DiscountedProduct class is defined in the domain layer.

As we stated in chapter 1, CONSTRUCTOR INJECTION is the act of statically defining the list of required DEPENDENCIES by specifying them as parameters to the class's constructor. This is exactly what `HomeController` does. In its public constructor, it defines what DEPENDENCIES it requires for it to function correctly.

The first time we heard about CONSTRUCTOR INJECTION, we had a hard time understanding the real benefit. Doesn't it push the burden of controlling the DEPENDENCY onto some other class? Yes, it does—and that's the whole point. In an *n*-layer application, you can push that burden all the way to the top of the application into a COMPOSITION ROOT.

> ### COMPOSITION ROOT
>
> As we discussed in section 1.4.1, we'd like to be able to compose our classes into applications in a way similar to how we plug electrical appliances together. This level of modularity can be achieved by centralizing the creation of our classes into a single place. We call this location the COMPOSITION ROOT.
>
> The COMPOSITION ROOT is located as close as possible to the application's entry point. In most .NET Core application types, the entry point is the `Main` method. Inside the COMPOSITION ROOT, you can decide to compose your application manually—that's using PURE DI—or to delegate it to a DI CONTAINER. We'll discuss COMPOSITION ROOT in more detail in chapter 4.

Because we added a constructor with an argument to `HomeController`, it'll be impossible to create a `HomeController` without that DEPENDENCY, and that's exactly why we did that. But that does mean that the application's home screen is broken, because MVC has no idea how our `HomeController` must be created—unless you instruct MVC otherwise.

In fact, the creation of `HomeController` isn't a concern of the UI layer; it's the responsibility of the COMPOSITION ROOT.[5] Because of this, we consider the UI layer completed, and we'll come back to the creation of `HomeController` later on. Figure 3.7 shows the current state of implementing the architecture envisioned in figure 3.2.

---

[5] As we explain in more detail in chapter 4, the COMPOSITION ROOT isn't part of the UI layer, even though it might be placed in the same assembly.

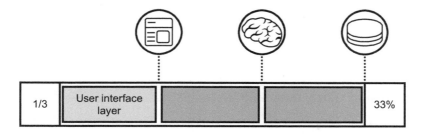

Figure 3.7   At this stage, only the UI layer has been implemented; the domain and data access layers have yet to be addressed.

This leads us to the next stage in the re-creation of our e-commerce application, the domain model.

3.1.2   *Building an independent domain model*

The domain model is a plain, vanilla C# library that we add to the solution. This library will contain POCOs and interfaces. The POCOs will model the domain while the interfaces provide ABSTRACTIONS that will serve as our main external entry points into the domain model. They'll provide the contract through which the domain model interacts with the forthcoming data access layer.

The `HomeController` delivered in the previous section doesn't compile yet because we haven't defined the `IProductService` ABSTRACTION. In this section, we'll add a new domain layer project to the e-commerce application and a reference to the domain layer project from the MVC project, like Mary did. That will turn out OK, but we'll postpone doing a dependency graph analysis until section 3.2 so that we can provide you with the full picture. The following listing shows the `IProductService` ABSTRACTION.

Listing 3.5   `IProductService` interface

```
public interface IProductService
{
    IEnumerable<DiscountedProduct> GetFeaturedProducts();
}
```

`IProductService` represents the heart of our current domain layer in that it bridges the UI layer with the data access layer. It's the glue that binds our initial application together.

The sole member of the `IProductService` ABSTRACTION is the `GetFeatured-Products` method. It returns a collection of `DiscountedProduct` instances. Each `DiscountedProduct` contains a `Name` and a `UnitPrice`. It's a simple POCO class, as can be seen in the next listing, and this definition gives us enough to compile our Visual Studio solution.

Listing 3.6 `DiscountedProduct` **POCO class**

```
public class DiscountedProduct
{
    public DiscountedProduct(string name, decimal unitPrice)
    {
        if (name == null) throw new ArgumentNullException("name");

        this.Name = name;
        this.UnitPrice = unitPrice;
    }

    public string Name { get; }
    public decimal UnitPrice { get; }
}
```

The principle of programming to interfaces instead of concrete classes is a cornerstone of DI. It's this principle that lets you replace one concrete implementation with another. Before continuing, we should take a quick moment to recognize the role of interfaces in this discussion.

> **IMPORTANT** Programming to interfaces doesn't mean that all classes should implement an interface. It typically makes little sense to hide POCOs, DTOs, and view models behind an interface, because they contain no behavior that requires mocking, INTERCEPTION, or replacement. Because `Discounted-Product`, `FeaturedProductsViewModel`, and `ProductViewModel` are (view) models, they implement no interface. We'll take another look at whether to use interfaces or abstract classes later in this section.

Next we'll write our `ProductService` implementation. The `GetFeaturedProducts` method of this `ProductService` class should use an `IProductRepository` instance to retrieve the list of featured products, apply any discounts, and return a list of `Discounted-Product` instances.

A common abstraction over data access is provided by the Repository pattern, so we'll define an `IProductRepository` abstraction in the domain model library.[6]

Listing 3.7 `IProductRepository`

```
public interface IProductRepository
{
    IEnumerable<Product> GetFeaturedProducts();
}
```

`IProductRepository` is the interface to the data access layer, returning "raw" ENTITIES from the persistence store. By contrast, `IProductService` applies business logic, such as the discount in this case, and converts the ENTITIES to a narrower-focused object. A full-blown Repository would have more methods to find and modify products, but,

---

[6] The Repository design pattern is described in Fowler's *Patterns of Enterprise Application Architecture* on pages 322-327, but the way people typically use it has little to do with the original pattern description. In this example, we follow the typical usage rather than Fowler's description, as the typical usage is better known and easier to understand.

following the outside-in principle, we only define the classes and members needed for the task at hand. It's easier to add functionality to code than it is to remove anything.

> **ENTITY**
>
> An ENTITY is a term from Domain-Driven Design that covers a domain object that has a long-term identity unrelated to a particular object instance.[7] This may sound abstract and theoretical, but it means that an ENTITY represents an object that lives beyond arbitrary bits in memory. Any .NET object instance has an in-memory address (identity), but an ENTITY has an identity that lives across process lifetimes.
>
> We often use databases and primary keys to identify ENTITIES and ensure that we can persist and read them even if the host computer reboots. The domain object `Product` is an ENTITY because the concept of a product has a longer lifetime than a single process, and we use a product ID to identify it in `IProductRepository`.

Because our goal is to invert the dependency between the domain layer and the data access layer, `IProductRepository` is defined in the domain layer. In the next section, we'll create an implementation of `IProductRepository` as part of the data access layer. This allows our dependency to point at the domain layer.

NOTE By letting `ProductService` depend on `IProductRepository`, we allow behavior to be replaced or INTERCEPTED. By placing that behavior in a different library, we allow a whole library to be replaced.

The `Product` class is also implemented with the bare minimum of members, as shown in the following listing.

Listing 3.8 Product ENTITY

```
public class Product
{
    public string Name { get; set; }
    public decimal UnitPrice { get; set; }
    public bool IsFeatured { get; set; }

    public DiscountedProduct ApplyDiscountFor(
        IUserContext user)
    {
        bool preferred =
            user.IsInRole(Role.PreferredCustomer);

        decimal discount = preferred ? .95m : 1.00m;

        return new DiscountedProduct(
            name: this.Name,
            unitPrice: this.UnitPrice * discount);
    }
}
```

The Product class only contains the Name, UnitPrice, and IsFeatured properties, because those are the only properties needed to implement the desired application feature.

This method requires IUserContext as an argument. IUserContext is part of the domain layer, and we'll define it shortly.

The ApplyDiscountFor method applies the discount (if any) based on the user's role, and returns an instance of the DiscountedProduct class.

Figure 3.8 illustrates the relationship between `ProductService` and its DEPENDENCIES.

---

[7] Eric Evans, *Domain-Driven Design: Tackling Complexity in the Heart of Software* (Addison-Wesley, 2004), 89.

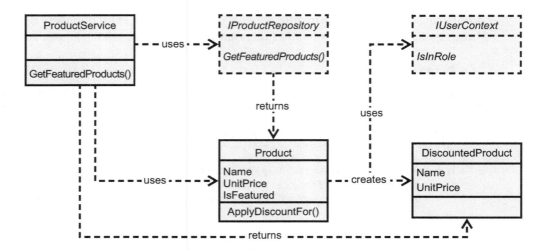

Figure 3.8   `ProductService` **and its DEPENDENCIES**

The `GetFeaturedProducts` method of the `ProductService` class should use an `IProductRepository` instance to retrieve the list of featured products, apply any discounts, and return a list of `DiscountedProduct` instances. The `ProductService` class corresponds to Mary's class of the same name, but is now a pure domain model class because it doesn't have a hard-coded reference to the data access layer. As with our `HomeController`, we're again going to relinquish control of its VOLATILE DEPENDENCIES using CONSTRUCTOR INJECTION, as shown next.

Listing 3.9   `ProductService` with CONSTRUCTOR INJECTION

```
public class ProductService : IProductService
{
    private readonly IProductRepository repository;
    private readonly IUserContext userContext;

    public ProductService(
        IProductRepository repository,          ⎤ CONSTRUCTOR INJECTION
        IUserContext userContext)               ⎦
    {
        if (repository == null)
            throw new ArgumentNullException("repository");
        if (userContext == null)
            throw new ArgumentNullException("userContext");

        this.repository = repository;
        this.userContext = userContext;
    }

    public IEnumerable<DiscountedProduct> GetFeaturedProducts()
    {
        return                              ⎤ The repository and userContext DEPENDENCIES
            from product in this.repository ⎥ pull a list of products and apply a discount
                .GetFeaturedProducts()      ⎦ for each featured product, respectively.
            select product
```

```
            .ApplyDiscountFor(this.userContext);
    }
}
```

**Supplies the userContext DEPENDENCY to the
ApplyDiscountFor method using METHOD INJECTION**

Besides an `IProductRepository`, the `ProductService` constructor requires an instance of `IUserContext`:

```
public interface IUserContext
{
    bool IsInRole(Role role);
}

public enum Role { PreferredCustomer }
```

This is another departure from Mary's implementation, which only took a boolean value as argument to the `GetFeaturedProducts` method, indicating whether the user is a preferred customer. Because deciding whether a user is a preferred customer is a piece of the domain layer, it's more correct to explicitly model this as a DEPENDENCY. Besides that, information about the user on whose behalf the request is running is contextual. We don't want every controller to be responsible for gathering this information. That would be repetitive and error prone, and might lead to accidental security bugs.

Instead of letting the UI layer provide this information to the domain layer, we allow the retrieval of this information to become an implementation detail of `Product-Service`. The `IUserContext` interface allows `ProductService` to retrieve information about the current user without `HomeController` needing to provide this. `HomeController` doesn't need to know which role(s) are authorized for a discount price, nor is it easy for `HomeController` to inadvertently enable the discount by passing, for example, `true` instead of `false`. This reduces the overall complexity of the UI layer.

> **TIP** To reduce the overall complexity of a system, runtime data that describes contextual information is best hidden behind an ABSTRACTION and injected into a consumer that requires it to function. *Contextual information* is metadata about the current request. This is typically information that the user shouldn't be allowed to influence directly. Examples are the user's identity (which was established on login) and the system's current time.

Although the .NET Base Class Library (BCL) includes an `IPrincipal` interface, which represents a standard way of modeling application users, that interface is generic in nature and isn't tailored for our application's special needs. Instead, we let the application define the ABSTRACTION.

The `ProductService.GetFeaturedProducts` method passes the `IUserContext` DEPENDENCY on to the `Product.ApplyDiscountFor` method. This technique is known as METHOD INJECTION. METHOD INJECTION is particularly useful in cases where short-lived objects like ENTITIES (such as the `Product` ENTITY, in our case) need DEPENDENCIES. Although the details vary, the main technique remains the same. We'll discuss this pattern in more detail in chapter 4. At this stage, the application doesn't work at all. That's because three problems remain:

- *There's no concrete implementation of `IProductRepository`.* This is easily solved. In the next section, we'll implement a concrete `SqlProductRepository` that reads the featured products from the database.
- *There's no concrete implementation of `IUserContext`.* We'll take a look at this in the next section too.
- *The MVC framework doesn't know which concrete type to use.* This is because we introduced an abstract parameter of type `IProductService` to the constructor of `HomeController`. This issue can be solved in various ways, but our preference is to develop a custom `Microsoft.AspNetCore.Mvc.Controllers.IController-Activator`. How this is done is outside the scope of this chapter, but it's a subject that we'll discuss in chapter 7. Suffice it to say that this custom factory will create an instance of the concrete `ProductService` and supply it to the constructor of `HomeController`.

In the domain layer, we work only with types defined within the domain layer and STABLE DEPENDENCIES of the .NET BCL. The concepts of the domain layer are implemented as POCOs. At this stage, there's only a single concept represented, namely, a `Product`. The domain layer must be able to communicate with the outside world (such as databases). This need is modeled as ABSTRACTIONS (such as Repositories) that we must replace with concrete implementations before the domain layer becomes useful. Figure 3.9 shows the current state of implementing the architecture envisioned in figure 3.2.

We succeeded in making our domain model compile. This means that we created a domain model that's independent of the data access layer, which we still need to create. But before we get to that, there are a few points we'd like to explain in more detail.

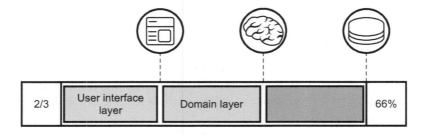

Figure 3.9   The UI and domain layer are now both in place, whereas the data access layer remains to be implemented.

DEPENDENCY INVERSION PRINCIPLE

Much of what we're trying to accomplish with DI is related to the DEPENDENCY INVERSION PRINCIPLE.[8] This principle states that higher-level modules in our applications shouldn't depend on lower-level modules; instead, modules of both levels should depend on ABSTRACTIONS.

This is exactly what we did when we defined our `IProductRepository`. The `ProductService` component is part of the higher-level domain layer module, whereas the `IProductRepository` implementation—let's call it `SqlProductRepository`—is part of the lower-level data access module. Instead of letting our `ProductService` depend on `SqlProductRepository`, we let both `ProductService` and `SqlProductRepository` depend on the `IProductRepository` ABSTRACTION. `SqlProductRepository` implements the ABSTRACTION, while `ProductService` uses it. Figure 3.10 illustrates this.

The relationship between the DEPENDENCY INVERSION PRINCIPLE and DI is that the DEPENDENCY INVERSION PRINCIPLE prescribes what we would like to accomplish, and DI states how we would like to accomplish it. The principle doesn't describe how a consumer should get ahold of its DEPENDENCIES. Many developers, however, aren't aware of another interesting part of the DEPENDENCY INVERSION PRINCIPLE.

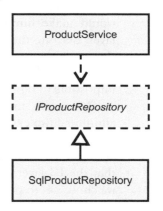

Not only does the principle prescribe loose coupling, it states that ABSTRACTIONS should be owned by the module using the ABSTRACTION. In this context, "owned" means that the consuming module has control over the shape of the ABSTRACTION, and it's distributed with that module, rather than with the module that implements it. The consuming module should be able to define the ABSTRACTION in a way that benefits itself the most.

Figure 3.10 Instead of `ProductService` depending on `SqlProductRepository`, both classes depend on an ABSTRACTION.

You already saw us do this twice: both `IUserContext` and `IProductRepository` are defined this way. They're designed in a way that works best for the domain layer, even though their implementations are the responsibility of the UI and data access layers, respectively, as shown in figure 3.11.

Letting a higher-level module or layer define its own ABSTRACTIONS not only prevents it from having to take a dependency on a lower-level module, it allows the higher-level module to be simplified, because the ABSTRACTIONS are tailored for its specific needs. This brings us back to the BCL's `IPrincipal` interface.

As we described, `IPrincipal` is generic in nature. The DEPENDENCY INVERSION PRINCIPLE instead guides us towards defining ABSTRACTIONS tailored for our application's special needs. That's why we define our own `IUserContext` ABSTRACTION instead of letting the domain layer depend on `IPrincipal`. This does mean, however, that we

---

[8] Robert Martin, *Agile Principles, Patterns, and Practices in C#* (Pearson Education, 2007).

have to create an Adapter implementation that allows translating calls from this application-specific `IUserContext` ABSTRACTION to calls to the application framework.

If the DEPENDENCY INVERSION PRINCIPLE dictates that ABSTRACTIONS should be distributed with their owning modules, doesn't the domain layer `IProductService` interface violate this principle? After all, `IProductService` is consumed by the UI layer, but implemented by the domain layer, as figure 3.12 shows. The answer is yes, this does violate the DEPENDENCY INVERSION PRINCIPLE.

If we were keen on fixing this violation, we should move `IProductService` out of the domain layer. Moving `IProductService` into the UI layer, however, would make our domain layer dependent on that layer. Because the domain layer is the central part of the application, we don't want it to depend on anything else. Besides, this dependency would make it impossible to replace the UI later on.

This means that to fix the violation, we need an additional two extra projects in our solution—one for the isolated UI layer without the COMPOSITION ROOT and another for the `IProductService` ABSTRACTION that the UI layer owns. Out of pragmatism, however, we chose not to pursue this path for this example and, therefore, leave the violation in place. We hope you can appreciate that we don't want to overcomplicate things.

INTERFACES OR ABSTRACT CLASSES?

Many guides to object-oriented design focus on interfaces as the main abstraction mechanism, whereas the .NET Framework Design Guidelines endorse abstract classes over interfaces.[9] Should you use interfaces or abstract classes? With relation to DI, the reassuring answer is that it doesn't matter. The important part is that you program against some sort of abstraction.

Choosing between interfaces and abstract classes is important in other contexts, but not here. You'll notice that we use these words interchangeably; we often use the term ABSTRACTION to encompass both interfaces and abstract classes. This doesn't mean that

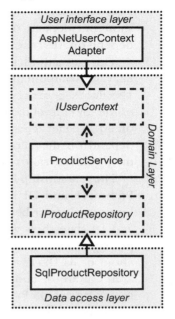

Figure 3.11   Both `IUserContext` and `IProductRepository` are part of the domain layer, because `ProductService` "owns" them.

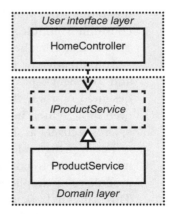

Figure 3.12   By making `IProductService` part of the domain layer, we violate the DEPENDENCY INVERSION PRINCIPLE.

---

[9] Krzysztof Cwalina and Brad Abrams, *Framework Design Guidelines: Conventions, Idioms, and Patterns for Reusable .NET Libraries,* 2nd Ed. (Addison-Wesley, 2009), 88-95.

we, as authors, don't have a preference for one over the other. We do, in fact. When it comes to writing applications, we typically prefer interfaces over abstract classes for these reasons:

- *Abstract classes can easily be abused as base classes.* Base classes can easily turn into ever-changing, ever-growing God Objects.[10] The derivatives are tightly coupled to its base class, which can become a problem when the base class contains VOLATILE behavior. Interfaces, on the other hand, force us into the "Composition over Inheritance" mantra.[11]
- *Concrete classes can implement several interfaces, although in .NET, those can only derive from a single base class.* Using interfaces as the vehicle of ABSTRACTION is more flexible.
- *Interface definitions in C# are less clumsy compared to abstract classes.* With interfaces, we can omit the `abstract` and `public` keywords from their members. This makes an interface a more succinct definition.

When writing reusable libraries, however, the subject is becoming less clear-cut, due to the need to deal with backward compatibility. In that light, an abstract class might make more sense because non-abstract members can be added later, whereas adding members to an interface is a breaking change. That's why the .NET Framework Design Guidelines prefer abstract classes.

Reusable libraries

Reusable libraries within the .NET ecosystem are typically distributed through NuGet. An important characteristic is that their clients aren't known at compile time. This is different from a project that's reused by other projects in the same Visual Studio solution. Although your Visual Studio solutions might contain projects that are reused by multiple projects within that same solution, such projects aren't considered to be reusable libraries. The domain layer project, for instance, might be reused by multiple projects, but that still doesn't make it a reusable library.

External libraries are harder to change because they might have thousands of consuming code bases, none of which the library designer has access to. Such a reusable library can't be tested against its consuming code bases.

Now let's move on to the data access layer. We'll create an implementation for the previously defined `IProductRepository` interface.

---

[10] A *God Object* is an object that knows too much or does too much, and it's an anti-pattern.

[11] The Composition over Inheritance principle states that classes in object-oriented programming should achieve polymorphic behavior and code reuse by containing instances of other classes that implement the desired functionality (composition), rather than inheritance from a base or parent class.

3.1.3   *Building a new data access layer*

Like Mary, we'd like to implement our data access layer using Entity Framework Core, so we follow the same steps she did in chapter 2 to create the ENTITY model. The main difference is that CommerceContext is now only an implementation detail of the data access layer, as opposed to being the entirety of the data access layer.

In this model, nothing outside of the data access layer will have any awareness of, or dependency on, Entity Framework. It can be swapped out without any upstream effects. With that in mind, we can create an implementation of IProductRepository.

Listing 3.10   Implementing IProductRepository using Entity Framework Core

```
public class SqlProductRepository : IProductRepository
{
    private readonly CommerceContext context;

    public SqlProductRepository(CommerceContext context)
    {
        if (context == null) throw new ArgumentNullException("context");

        this.context = context;
    }

    public IEnumerable<Product> GetFeaturedProducts()
    {
        return
            from product in this.context.Products
            where product.IsFeatured
            select product;
    }
}
```

In Mary's application, the Product ENTITY was also used as a domain object, although it was defined in the data access layer. This is no longer the case. The Product class is now defined in our domain layer. Our data access layer reuses the Product class from that layer.

For simplicity, we chose to let the data access layer reuse our domain object instead of defining its own implementation. We were able to do so because Entity Framework Core allows us to write ENTITIES that are persistence ignorant.[12] Whether this is a reasonable practice depends a lot on the structure and complexity of your domain objects. If we later conclude that this shared model is enforcing unwanted constraints on our model, we can change our data access layer by introducing internal persistence objects, without touching the rest of the application. In that case, we'd need the data access layer to convert those internal persistence objects into domain objects.

---

[12] *Persistence ignorance* means that ENTITIES are plain POCOs with no dependency on any persistence framework.

In the previous chapter, we discussed how the implicit dependency of Mary's `CommerceContext` on the connection string caused her problems along the way. Our new `CommerceContext` will make this dependency explicit, which is another deviation from Mary's implementation. The next listing shows our new `CommerceContext`.

Listing 3.11 A better `CommerceContext` class

```
public class CommerceContext : DbContext
{
    private readonly string connectionString;

    public CommerceContext(string connectionString)
    {
        if (string.IsNullOrWhiteSpace(connectionString))
            throw new ArgumentException(
                "connectionString should not be empty.",
                "connectionString");

        this.connectionString = connectionString;
    }

    public DbSet<Product> Products { get; set; }

    protected override void OnConfiguring(DbContextOptionsBuilder builder)
    {
        builder.UseSqlServer(this.connectionString);
    }
}
```

> Uses CONSTRUCTOR INJECTION on the required DEPENDENCIES; in this case, connectionString

> The DEPENDENCY is stored and used later in the OnConfiguring method to set up the CommerceContext for use.

This almost brings us to the end of our re-implementation of the e-commerce application. The only implementation still missing is that of `IUserContext`.

3.1.4 Implementing an ASP.NET Core–specific `IUserContext` Adapter

The last concrete implementation missing is that of `IUserContext`. In web applications, information about a user who issues a request is usually passed on to the server with each request. This information is relayed using cookies or HTTP headers. How we retrieve the identity of the current user is highly dependent on the framework we use. This means that we'll need a completely different implementation when building an ASP.NET Core application compared with, for instance, a Windows service.

The implementation of our `IUserContext` is framework specific. We want neither our domain layer nor our data layer to know anything about the application framework. That would make it impossible to use those layers in a different context. We need to implement this elsewhere. The UI layer, therefore, is an ideal place for our `IUserContext` implementation.

The following listing shows a possible `IUserContext` implementation for an ASP.NET Core application.

Listing 3.12   `IUserContext` implementation for ASP.NET Core

```
public class AspNetUserContextAdapter : IUserContext
{
    private static HttpContextAccessor Accessor = new HttpContextAccessor();

    public bool IsInRole(Role role)
    {
        return Accessor.HttpContext.User.IsInRole(role.ToString());
    }
}
```

`AspNetUserContextAdapter` requires an `HttpContextAccessor` to work. `HttpContext-Accessor`, a component specified by the ASP.NET Core framework, allows access to the `HttpContext` of the current request, like we were able to in ASP.NET "classic" using `HttpContext.Current`. We use `HttpContext` to access the request's information about the current user.

`AspNetUserContextAdapter` adapts our application-specific `IUserContext` ABSTRACTION to the ASP.NET Core API. This class is an implementation of the Adapter design pattern that we discussed in chapter 1.[13]

The Adapter design pattern

As a reminder, the Adapter design pattern falls into the category of structural patterns. This group is concerned with how classes and objects are composed to form larger structures. Other patterns in this category are Composite, Decorator, Facade, and Proxy. Like an adapter for an electrical appliance, the Adapter design pattern converts the interface into one that clients expect. This allows classes (or plugs and sockets) to work together that wouldn't otherwise because of their incompatible interfaces.

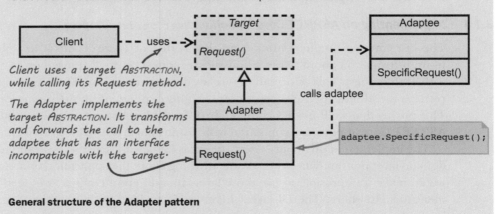

General structure of the Adapter pattern

---

[13] For this Adapter to work, it requires the `HttpContextAccessor` to be registered in ASP.NET Core's `IServiceCollection`. This is demonstrated in the next chapter in listing 4.3.

Implementations of the Adapter pattern are typically quite straightforward, but don't be surprised if the Adapter contains complex conversions. The idea is that this complexity is hidden from the client.

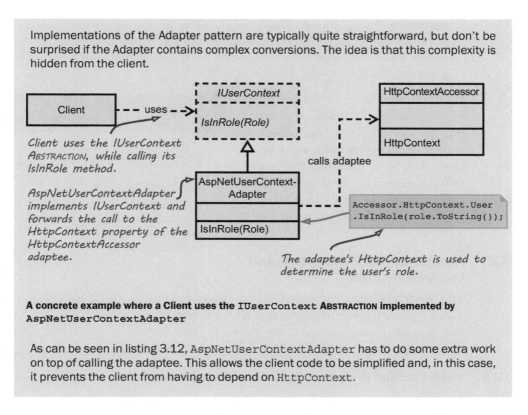

A concrete example where a Client uses the `IUserContext` ABSTRACTION implemented by `AspNetUserContextAdapter`

As can be seen in listing 3.12, `AspNetUserContextAdapter` has to do some extra work on top of calling the adaptee. This allows the client code to be simplified and, in this case, it prevents the client from having to depend on `HttpContext`.

With `AspNetUserContextAdapter` implemented, our reimplementation of the e-commerce application is finished. This brings us to our COMPOSITION ROOT.

3.1.5 Composing the application in the COMPOSITION ROOT

With `ProductService`, `SqlProductRepository` and `AspNetUserContextAdapter` implemented, we can now set up ASP.NET Core MVC to construct an instance of `Home-Controller`, where `HomeController` is fed by a `ProductService` instance, which itself is constructed using a `SqlProductRepository` and an `AspNetUserContextAdapter`. This eventually results in an object graph that would look as follows.

Listing 3.13   The application's object graph

```
new HomeController(
    new ProductService(
        new SqlProductRepository(
            new CommerceContext(connectionString)),
        new AspNetUserContextAdapter()));
```

DEFINITION   In an object-oriented application, groups of objects form a network through their relationships with each other, either through a direct reference to another object or through a chain of intermediate references. These groups of objects are referred to as *object graphs*.

We'll discuss how the construction of such an object graph is plugged into the ASP.NET Core framework in greater detail in chapter 7, so we won't show that here. But now that everything is correctly wired together, we can browse to the application's homepage and get the page shown in figure 3.13.

Featured Products

Criollo Chocolate ($34.95)
Gruyère ($48.50)
White Asparagus ($39.80)
Anchovies ($18.75)
Arborio Rice ($22.75)

Figure 3.13   Screen capture of the finished application

3.2   Analyzing the loosely coupled implementation

The previous section contained lots of details, so it's hardly surprising if you lost sight of the big picture along the way. In this section, we'll try to explain what happened in broader terms.

3.2.1   Understanding the interaction between components

The classes in each layer interact with each other either directly or in abstract form. They do so across module boundaries, so it can be difficult to follow how they interact. Figure 3.14 shows how the different DEPENDENCIES interact, giving a more detailed overview to the original outline described in figure 3.4.

When the application starts, the code in Startup creates a new custom controller activator and looks up the connection string from the application's configuration file. When a page request comes in, the application invokes Create on the controller activator.

The activator supplies the stored connection string to a new instance of Commerce-Context (not shown in the diagram). It injects CommerceContext into a new instance of SqlProductRepository. In turn, the SqlProductRepository instance together with an instance of AspNetUserContextAdapter (not shown in the diagram) are injected into a new instance of ProductService. Similarly, ProductService is injected into a new instance of HomeController, which is then returned from the Create method.

The ASP.NET Core MVC framework then invokes the Index method on the Home-Controller instance, causing it to invoke the GetFeaturedProducts method on the ProductService instance. This in turn calls the GetFeaturedProducts method on

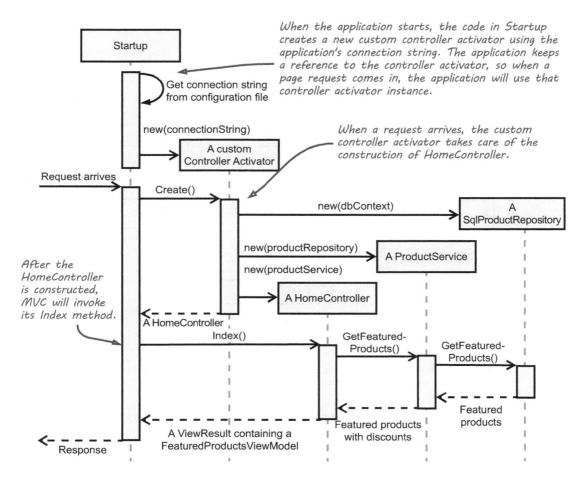

Figure 3.14 Interaction between elements involved in DI in the e-commerce application

the SqlProductRepository instance. Finally, the ViewResult with the populated FeaturedProductsViewModel is returned, and MVC finds and renders the correct view.

3.2.2 Analyzing the new dependency graph

In section 2.2, you saw how a dependency graph can help you analyze and understand the degree of flexibility provided by the architectural implementation. Has DI changed the dependency graph for the application?

Figure 3.15 shows that the dependency graph has indeed changed. The domain model no longer has any dependencies and can act as a standalone module. On the other hand, the data access layer now has a dependency; in Mary's application, it had none.

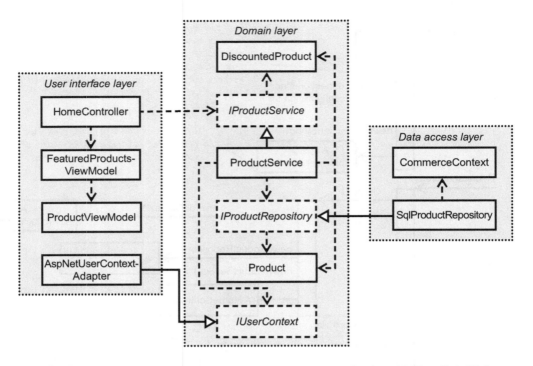

Figure 3.15   Dependency graph showing the sample e-commerce application with DI applied. All classes and interfaces are shown, as well as their relationships to one another.

The most important thing to note in figure 3.15 is that the domain layer no longer has any dependencies. This should raise our hopes that we can answer the original questions about composability (see section 2.2) more favorably this time:

- *Can we replace the web-based UI with a WPF-based UI?* That was possible before and is still possible with the new design. Neither the domain model library nor the data access library depends on the web-based UI, so we can easily put something else in its place.
- *Can we replace the relational data access layer with one that works with the Azure Table Service?* In a later chapter, we'll describe how the application locates and instantiates the correct IProductRepository, so, for now, take the following at face value: the data access layer is being loaded by late binding, and the type name is defined as an application setting in the application's configuration file. It's possible to throw the current data access layer away and inject a new one, as long as it also provides an implementation of IProductRepository.

About DI CONTAINERS

A DI CONTAINER is a software library that provides DI functionality and automates many of the tasks involved in OBJECT COMPOSITION, INTERCEPTION, and LIFETIME MANAGEMENT. DI CONTAINERS are also known as INVERSION OF CONTROL (IoC) containers. Up until this point, we touched on the subject of DI CONTAINERS only gently. This is deliberate because, as we explained in chapter 1, a DI CONTAINER is a useful, but optional, tool. We postpone a detailed discussion about DI CONTAINERS until part 4 because we feel that teaching you about the set of principles and patterns that DI consists of, as well as the existing code smells and anti-patterns, is more important.

We build applications both with and without DI CONTAINERS, and you should be able to do so too. And yet, we feel that it would be counterproductive if you started using a DI CON-TAINER without the knowledge presented in parts 2 and 3. On the other hand, after you understand the principles and practices, using a DI CONTAINER primarily consists of getting acquainted with its API. At this point, it's only important to get a broad sense of what a DI CONTAINER is and how it can help you.

When the first edition of this book came out, we used DI CONTAINERS exclusively in all the applications we built. Although we knew that applying DI without a DI CONTAINER was possible, we thought that it was never practical. Our ideas about this have changed, and that's why we now focus even more on the patterns and techniques behind DI.

Although you need to address the application's infrastructure, doing so doesn't in itself add business value; sometimes, using a general-purpose library can make sense. It's no different than implementing logging or data access. Logging application data is the kind of problem that's best addressed by a general-purpose logging library. The same is true for composing object graphs. In part 4, we'll go into a more detailed discussion of when a DI CONTAINER might be useful and when it isn't.

Don't expect a DI CONTAINER to magically change tightly coupled code into loosely coupled code. A DI CONTAINER can make your COMPOSITION ROOT more maintainable, but for an application to become maintainable, it must first be designed with DI patterns and techniques in mind. Using a DI CONTAINER neither guarantees nor necessitates the correct usage of DI.

The sample e-commerce application described in this chapter only presents us with a limited level of complexity: there's only a single Repository involved in a read-only scenario. Until now, we've kept the application as simple and small as possible to gently introduce some core concepts and principles. Because one of the main purposes of DI is to manage complexity, we need a complex application to fully appreciate its power. During the course of the book, we'll expand the sample e-commerce application to fully demonstrate different aspects of DI.

Does DI make me lose the bigger picture?

A common complaint from developers starting with DI is that they feel they lose sight of the structure of the application; it's not immediately clear who is calling whom. Although it's absolutely true that with DI, we move this knowledge away from individual classes, listing 3.13 proves that we don't have to lose this information at all. Listing 3.13 is an example of PURE DI. When practicing PURE DI, the COMPOSITION ROOT typically contains this information in a coherent way. Even better, it gives you a view of the complete object graph, not just the direct DEPENDENCIES of a class, which is what you get with tightly coupled code.

Moving from PURE DI to a DI CONTAINER, on the other hand, might make you lose this overview. That's because DI CONTAINERS use reflection to build object graphs at runtime, compared to specifying them at compile time using a programming language.[14] When an application is well designed, however, we found that this loss becomes less of a problem.[15] We experienced that the amount of navigation we needed to do from a class to its DEPENDENCIES and back decreased when an application's maintainability increased.

Still, this difference between PURE DI and a DI CONTAINER is something to take into consideration, because it might influence your choice of one over another. Section 12.3 goes into detail about when to use a DI CONTAINER and when to stick with PURE DI.

This chapter concludes the first part of the book. The purpose of part 1 was to *put DI on the map* and to introduce DI in general. In this chapter, you've seen examples of CONSTRUCTOR INJECTION. We also introduced METHOD INJECTION and COMPOSITION ROOT as patterns related to DI. In the next chapter, we'll dive deeper into these and other design patterns.

Summary

- Refactoring existing applications towards a more maintainable, loosely coupled design is hard. Big rewrites, on the other hand, are often riskier and expensive.
- The use of view models can simplify the view, because the incoming data is shaped specifically for the view.
- Because views are harder to test, the dumber the view, the better. It also simplifies the work of a UI designer who might work on the view.
- When you limit the amount of VOLATILE DEPENDENCIES within the domain layer, you get a higher degree of decoupling, reuse, and TESTABILITY.
- When building applications, the outside-in approach facilitates more rapid prototyping, which can shorten the feedback cycle.

---

[14] Some DI CONTAINERS let you visualize object graphs, but this is something that's only done at runtime, not when you look at the code.

[15] "Well designed" is subjective, but following SOLID principles has proven to be an important instrument in making a well-designed application. We'll discuss the SOLID acronym in chapter 10.

- When you want a high degree of modularity in your application, you need to apply the CONSTRUCTOR INJECTION pattern and build object graphs in the COMPOSITION ROOT, which is located close to the application's entry point.
- Programming to interfaces is a cornerstone of DI. It allows you to replace, mock, and INTERCEPT a DEPENDENCY, without having to make changes to its consumers. When implementation and ABSTRACTION are placed in different assemblies, it enables whole libraries to be replaced.
- Programming to interfaces doesn't mean that all classes should implement an interface. Short-lived objects, such as ENTITIES, view models, and DTOs, typically contain no behavior that requires mocking, INTERCEPTION, decoration, or replacement.
- With respect to DI, it doesn't matter whether you use interfaces or purely abstract classes. From a general development perspective, as authors, we typically prefer interfaces over abstract classes.
- A *reusable library* is a library that has clients that aren't known at compile time. Reusable libraries are typically shipped via NuGet. Libraries that only have callers within the same (Visual Studio) solution aren't considered to be reusable libraries.
- DI is closely related to the DEPENDENCY INVERSION PRINCIPLE. This principle implies that you should program against interfaces, and that a layer must be in control over the interfaces it uses.
- The use of a DI CONTAINER can help in making the application's COMPOSITION ROOT more maintainable, but it won't magically make tightly coupled code loosely coupled. For an application to become maintainable, it must be designed with DI patterns and techniques in mind.

Part 2

Catalog

Part 1 provided an overview of DI, discussing the purpose and benefits of DI. Even though chapter 3 contained an extensive example, we're sure the first chapters still left you with some unresolved questions. In part 2, we'll dig a little deeper to answer some of those questions.

As the title implies, part 2 presents a complete catalog of patterns, anti-patterns, and code smells. Some people dislike design patterns, because they find them dry or too abstract. Personally, we love patterns, because they provide us with a high-level language that makes us more efficient and concise when we discuss software design. It's our intent to use this catalog to provide a pattern language for DI. Although a pattern description must contain some generalizations, we've made each pattern concrete, using examples. You can read all three chapters in sequence, but each item in the catalog is also written so that you can read it by itself.

Chapter 4 contains a mini catalog of DI design patterns. In a sense, these patterns constitute prescriptive guidance on how to implement DI, but you should be aware that we don't consider them to be of equal importance. CONSTRUCTOR INJECTION and COMPOSITION ROOT are by far the most important design patterns, whereas all the other patterns should be treated as fringe cases that can be applied in specialized circumstances.

Whereas chapter 4 gives you a set of generalized solutions, chapter 5 contains a catalog of situations to avoid. These anti-patterns describe common, but incorrect ways to address typical DI challenges. In each case, the anti-pattern describes how to identify occurrences and how to resolve the issue. It's important to know and understand these anti-patterns to avoid the traps that they represent, and, just as chapter 4 presents two dominatingly important patterns, the most important anti-pattern is SERVICE LOCATOR, the antithesis of DI.

As you apply DI to real-life programming tasks, you'll run into some challenges. We think we've all had moments of doubt where we feel that we understand a tool or technique, and yet we think, "In theory, this may work, but my case is special." When we find ourself thinking like this, it's clear to us that we have more to learn.

During our career, we've seen a particular set of problems appear again and again. Each of these problems has a general solution you can apply to move your code towards one of the DI patterns from chapter 4. Chapter 6 contains a catalog of these common problems, or code smells, and their corresponding solutions.

We expect this to be the most useful part of the book, because it's the most enduring. Hopefully, you'll return to these chapters months and even years after you first read them.

DI patterns

In this chapter

- Composing object graphs with COMPOSITION ROOT

- Statically declaring required DEPENDENCIES with CONSTRUCTOR INJECTION

- Passing DEPENDENCIES outside the COMPOSITION ROOT with METHOD INJECTION

- Declaring optional DEPENDENCIES with PROPERTY INJECTION

- Understanding which pattern to use

Like all professionals, cooks have their own jargon that enables them to communicate about complex food preparation in a language that often sounds esoteric to the rest of us. It doesn't help that most of the terms they use are based on the French language (unless you already speak French, that is). Sauces are a great example of the way cooks use their professional terminology. In chapter 1, we briefly discussed *sauce béarnaise*, but we didn't elaborate on the taxonomy that surrounds it.

A *sauce béarnaise* is really a *sauce hollandaise* where the lemon juice is replaced by a reduction of vinegar, shallots, chervil, and tarragon. Other sauces are based on sauce hollandaise, including Mark's favorite, *sauce mousseline*, which is made by folding whipped cream into the hollandaise.

Did you notice the jargon? Instead of saying, "carefully mix the whipped cream into the sauce, taking care not to collapse it," we used the term *folding*. Instead of saying, "thickening and intensifying the flavor of vinegar," we used the term *reduction*. Jargon allows you to communicate concisely and effectively.

In software development, we have a complex and impenetrable jargon of our own. You may not know what the cooking term *bain-marie* refers to, but we're pretty sure most chefs would be utterly lost if you told them that "strings are immutable classes, which represent sequences of Unicode characters." And when it comes to talking about how to structure code to solve particular types of problems, we have design patterns that give names to common solutions. In the same way that the terms *sauce hollandaise* and *fold* help us succinctly communicate how to make *sauce mousseline*, design patterns help us talk about how code is structured.

We've already named quite a few software design patterns in the previous chapters. For instance, in chapter 1 we talked about the patterns Abstract Factory, Null Object, Decorator, Composite, Adapter, Guard Clause, Stub, Mock, and Fake. Although, at this point, you might not be able to recall each of them, you probably won't feel that uncomfortable if we talk about design patterns. We human beings like to name reoccurring patterns, even if they're simple.

Don't worry if you have only a limited knowledge of design patterns in general. The main purpose of a design pattern is to provide a detailed and self-contained description of a particular way of attaining a goal—a recipe, if you will. And besides, you already saw examples of three out of the four basic DI design patterns that we'll describe in this chapter:

- *COMPOSITION ROOT*—Describes where and how you should compose an application's object graphs.
- *CONSTRUCTOR INJECTION*—Allows a class to statically declare its required DEPENDENCIES.
- *METHOD INJECTION*—Enables you to provide a DEPENDENCY to a consumer when either the DEPENDENCY or the consumer might change for each operation.
- *PROPERTY INJECTION*—Allows clients to optionally override some class's default behavior, where this default behavior is implemented in a LOCAL DEFAULT.

This chapter is structured to provide a catalog of patterns. For each pattern, we'll provide a short description, a code example, advantages and disadvantages, and so on. You can read about all four patterns introduced in this chapter in sequence or only read the ones that interest you. The most important patterns are COMPOSITION ROOT and CONSTRUCTOR INJECTION, which you should use in most situations—the other patterns become more specialized as the chapter progresses.

4.1   COMPOSITION ROOT

Where should we compose object graphs?
AS CLOSE AS POSSIBLE TO THE APPLICATION'S ENTRY POINT.

When you're creating an application from many loosely coupled classes, the composition should take place as close to the application's entry point as possible. The Main method is the entry point for most application types. The COMPOSITION ROOT composes the object graph, which subsequently performs the actual work of the application.

DEFINITION   A COMPOSITION ROOT is a single, logical location in an application where modules are composed together.

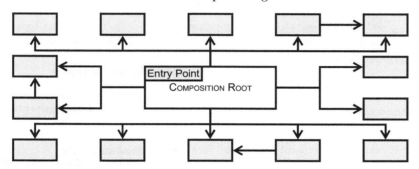

Figure 4.1   Close to the application's entry point, the COMPOSITION ROOT takes care of composing object graphs of loosely coupled classes. The COMPOSITION ROOT takes a direct dependency on all modules in the system.

In the previous chapter, you saw that most classes used CONSTRUCTOR INJECTION. By doing so, they pushed the responsibility for the creation of their DEPENDENCIES up to their consumers. Such consumers, however, also pushed the responsibility for creating their DEPENDENCIES up to their consumers.

You can't delay the creation of your objects indefinitely. There must be a location where you create your object graphs. You should concentrate this creation into a single area of your application. This place is called the COMPOSITION ROOT.

WARNING   If you use a DI CONTAINER, the COMPOSITION ROOT should be the only place where you use the DI CONTAINER. Using a DI CONTAINER outside the COMPOSITION ROOT leads to the SERVICE LOCATOR anti-pattern, which we discuss in the next chapter.

In the previous chapter, this resulted in the object graph that you saw in listing 3.13 (figure 4.1). This listing also shows that all components from all application layers are constructed in the COMPOSITION ROOT.

Listing 4.1　The application's object graph from chapter 3

| UI component

```
new HomeController(
    new ProductService(          ◄──────── Domain component
        new SqlProductRepository(
            new CommerceContext(connectionString)),   ┤ Data access components
        new AspNetUserContextAdapter()));◄────┐
                                              └ UI component
```

If you were to have a console application that was written to operate on this particular object graph, it might look as shown in the following listing.

Listing 4.2　The application's object graph as part of a console application

```
public static class Program
{
    public static void Main(string[] args)   ◄─── The application's entry point
    {
        string connectionString = args[0];   ◄─── Extracts a connection string from the
                                                   supplied command-line arguments

        HomeController controller =
            CreateController(connectionString);   ◄─── Requests that the
                                                        application's COMPOSITION ROOT
        var result = controller.Index();            build a new controller instance

        var vm = (FeaturedProductsViewModel)result.Model;

        Console.WriteLine("Featured products:");

        foreach (var product in vm.Products)
        {
            Console.WriteLine(product.SummaryText);
        }
    }
                                                     Acts as the application's
    private static HomeController CreateController(   ◄─── COMPOSITION ROOT
        string connectionString)
    {
        var userContext = new ConsoleUserContext();   ◄─── IUserContext implementation
                                                            that allows the ProductService
        return                                              to function and calculate the
            new HomeController(                             discounts
                new ProductService(
                    new SqlProductRepository(   ─┐ Builds the application's object graph
                        new CommerceContext(
                            connectionString)),
                    userContext));
    }
}
```

In this example, the COMPOSITION ROOT is separated from the Main method. This isn't required, however—the COMPOSITION ROOT isn't a method or a class, it's a concept. It can be part of the Main method, or it can span multiple classes, as long as they all reside in a single module. Separating it into its own method helps to ensure that the composition is consolidated and not otherwise interspersed with subsequent application logic.

4.1.1 How COMPOSITION ROOT works

When you write loosely coupled code, you create many classes to create an application. It can be tempting to compose these classes at many different locations in order to create small subsystems, but that limits your ability to INTERCEPT those systems to modify their behavior. Instead, you should compose classes in one single area of your application.

When you look at CONSTRUCTOR INJECTION in isolation, you may wonder, doesn't it defer the decision about selecting a DEPENDENCY to another place? Yes, it does, and that's a good thing. This means that you get a central place where you can connect collaborating classes.

The COMPOSITION ROOT acts as a third party that connects consumers with their services. The longer you defer the decision on how to connect classes, the more you keep your options open. Thus, the COMPOSITION ROOT should be placed as close to the application's entry point as possible.

Even a modular application that uses loose coupling and late binding to compose itself has a root that contains the entry point into the application. Examples follow:

- A .NET Core console application is a library (.dll) containing a Program class with a Main method.
- An ASP.NET Core web application also is a library containing a Program class with a Main method.
- UWP and WPF applications are executables (.exe) with an App.xaml.cs file.

Many other technologies exist, but they have one thing in common: one module contains the entry point of the application—this is the root of the application. Don't be misled into thinking that the COMPOSITION ROOT is part of your UI layer. Even if you place the COMPOSITION ROOT in the same assembly as your UI layer, as we'll do in the next example, the COMPOSITION ROOT isn't part of that layer.

Assemblies are a *deployment artifact*: you split code into multiple assemblies to allow code to be deployed separately. An architectural layer, on the other hand, is a *logical artifact*: you can group multiple logical artifacts in a single deployment artifact. Even though the assembly that holds both the COMPOSITION ROOT and the UI layer depends on all other modules in the system, the UI layer itself doesn't.

IMPORTANT The COMPOSITION ROOT isn't part of the UI layer, even though it might be placed in the same assembly.

It's not a requirement for the COMPOSITION ROOT to be placed in the same project as your UI layer. You can move the UI layer out of the application's root project. The advantage of this is that you can prevent the project that holds the UI layer from taking on a dependency (for instance, the data access layer project in chapter 3). This makes it impossible for UI classes to accidentally depend on data access classes. The downside of this approach, however, is that it isn't always easy to do. With ASP.NET Core MVC, for instance, it's trivial to move controllers and view models to a separate project, but it can be quite challenging to do the same with your views and client resources.

Separating the presentation technology from the COMPOSITION ROOT might not be that beneficial, either, because a COMPOSITION ROOT is specific to the application. COMPOSITION ROOTS aren't reused.

You shouldn't attempt to compose classes in any of the other modules, because that approach limits your options. All classes in application modules should use CONSTRUCTOR INJECTION (or, in rare cases, one of the other two patterns from this chapter), and then leave it up to the COMPOSITION ROOT to compose the application's object graph. Any DI CONTAINER in use should be limited to the COMPOSITION ROOT.

> **NOTE** Moving the composition of classes out of the COMPOSITION ROOT leads to either the CONTROL FREAK or SERVICE LOCATOR anti-patterns, which we'll discuss in the next chapter.

In an application, the COMPOSITION ROOT should be the sole place that knows about the structure of the constructed object graphs. Application code not only relinquishes control over its DEPENDENCIES, it also relinquishes knowledge about its DEPENDENCIES. Centralizing this knowledge simplifies development. This also means that application code can't pass on DEPENDENCIES to other threads that run parallel to the current operation, because a consumer has no way of knowing whether it's safe to do so. Instead, when spinning off concurrent operations, it's the job of the COMPOSITION ROOT to create a new object graph for each concurrent operation.

The COMPOSITION ROOT in listing 4.2 showed an example of PURE DI. The COMPOSITION ROOT pattern, however, is both applicable to PURE DI and DI CONTAINERS. In the next section, we'll describe how a DI CONTAINER can be used in a COMPOSITION ROOT.

4.1.2 Using a DI CONTAINER in a COMPOSITION ROOT

As described in chapter 3, a DI CONTAINER is a software library that can automate many of the tasks involved in composing objects and managing their lifetimes. But it can be misused as a SERVICE LOCATOR and should only be used as an engine that composes object graphs. When you consider a DI CONTAINER from that perspective, it makes sense to constrain it to the COMPOSITION ROOT. This also significantly benefits the removal of any coupling between the DI CONTAINER and the rest of the application's code base.

> **NOTE** Only the COMPOSITION ROOT should have a reference to the DI CONTAINER, and it should only be referenced from the COMPOSITION ROOT. (The rest of the application has no reference to the container and instead relies on

the patterns described in this chapter.) Nor should the container be referenced by all other modules. DI CONTAINERS understand those patterns and use them to compose the application's object graph.

A COMPOSITION ROOT can be implemented with a DI CONTAINER. This means that you use the container to compose the entire application's object graph in a single call to its Resolve method. When we talk to developers about doing it like this, we can always tell that it makes them uncomfortable because they're afraid that it's terribly inefficient and bad for performance. You don't have to worry about that. That's almost never the case and, in the few situations where it is, there are ways to address the issue, as we'll discuss in section 8.4.2.

Don't worry about the performance overhead of using a DI CONTAINER to compose large object graphs. It's usually not an issue. In part 4, we'll do a deep dive into DI CONTAINERS and show how to use a DI CONTAINER inside the COMPOSITION ROOT.

When it comes to request-based applications, such as websites and services, you configure the container once, but resolve an object graph for each incoming request. The e-commerce web application in chapter 3 is an example of that.

4.1.3 Example: Implementing a COMPOSITION ROOT using PURE DI

The sample e-commerce web application must have a COMPOSITION ROOT to compose object graphs for incoming HTTP requests. As with all other ASP.NET Core web applications, the entry point is in the Main method. By default, however, the Main method of an ASP.NET Core application delegates most of the work to the Startup class. This Startup class is close enough to the application's entry point for us, and we'll use that as our COMPOSITION ROOT.

As in the previous example with the console application, we use PURE DI. This means you compose your object graphs using plain old C# code instead of a DI CONTAINER, as shown in the following listing.

Listing 4.3   The e-commerce application's `Startup` class

```
public class Startup
{
    public Startup(IConfiguration configuration)          ◄─── ASP.NET Core calls this constructor
    {                                                          on application startup.
        this.Configuration = configuration;
    }

    public IConfiguration Configuration { get; }

    public void ConfigureServices(            ◄─── By convention, ASP.NET calls this
        IServiceCollection services)               method. The supplied IServiceCollection
    {                                              instance lets you influence the default
        services.AddMvc();                         services that ASP.NET knows about.
```

```
services.AddHttpContextAccessor();          ◄──── Adds a service to the framework, which
                                                  retrieves the current HttpContext

var connectionString =
    this.Configuration.GetConnectionString(       Loads the application's
        "CommerceConnection");                     database connection string
                                                   from the configuration file
services.AddSingleton<IControllerActivator>(
    new CommerceControllerActivator(               Replaces the default
        connectionString));                        IControllerActivator with one
}                                                  that builds the object graphs

    ...
}
```

If you're not familiar with ASP.NET Core, here's a simple explanation: the `Startup` class is a necessity; it's where you apply the required plumbing. The interesting part is the `CommerceControllerActivator`. The entire setup for the application is encapsulated in the `CommerceControllerActivator` class, which we'll show shortly.

To enable wiring MVC controllers to the application, you must employ the appropriate SEAM in ASP.NET Core MVC, called an `IControllerActivator` (discussed in detail in section 7.3). For now, it's enough to understand that to integrate with ASP.NET Core MVC, you must create an Adapter for your COMPOSITION ROOT and tell the framework about it.

> **NOTE** Any well-designed framework provides the appropriate SEAMS to intercept the creation of framework types. These SEAMS are usually shaped as factory abstractions, as is MVC's `IControllerActivator`.

The `Startup.ConfigureServices` method only runs once. As a result, your `Commerce-ControllerActivator` class is a single instance that's only initialized once. Because you set up ASP.NET Core MVC with the custom `IControllerActivator`, MVC invokes its `Create` method to create a new controller instance for each incoming HTTP request (you can read about the details in section 7.3). The following listing shows the `CommerceControllerActivator`.

Listing 4.4   The application's `IControllerActivator` implementation

```
public class CommerceControllerActivator : IControllerActivator
{
    private readonly string connectionString;

    public CommerceControllerActivator(string connectionString)
    {
        this.connectionString = connectionString;
    }
```

```
public object Create(ControllerContext ctx)
{
    Type type = ctx.ActionDescriptor
        .ControllerTypeInfo.AsType();

    if (type == typeof(HomeController))
    {
        return
            new HomeController(
                new ProductService(
                    new SqlProductRepository(
                        new CommerceContext(
                            this.connectionString)),
                    new AspNetUserContextAdapter()));
    }
    else
    {
        throw new Exception("Unknown controller.");
    }
}
}
```

ASP.NET Core MVC calls this method for every request.

Builds the appropriate object graph if MVC asks for a HomeController

The e-commerce application currently only has one controller. Each new controller that you add will have its own if block.

Notice how the creation of HomeController in this example is almost identical to the application's object graph from chapter 3 that we showed in listing 4.1. When MVC calls Create, you determine the controller type and create the correct object graph based on this type.

In section 2.3.3, we discussed how only the COMPOSITION ROOT should rely on configuration files, because it's more flexible for reusable libraries to be imperatively configurable by their callers. You should also separate the loading of configuration values from the methods that do OBJECT COMPOSITION (as shown in listings 4.3 and 4.4). The Startup class of listing 4.3 loads the configuration, whereas the CommerceController-Activator of listing 4.4 only depends on the configuration value, not the configuration system. An important advantage of this separation is that it decouples OBJECT COMPOSITION from the configuration system in use, making it possible to test without the existence of a (valid) configuration file.

The COMPOSITION ROOT in this example is spread out across two classes, as shown in figure 4.2. This is expected. The important thing is that all classes are contained in the same module, which, in this case, is the application root.

The most important thing to notice in this figure is that these two classes are the only classes in the entire sample application that compose object graphs. The remaining application code only uses the CONSTRUCTOR INJECTION pattern.

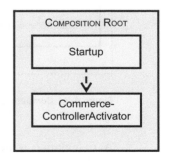

Figure 4.2 The COMPOSITION ROOT is spread across two classes, but they're defined within the same module.

4.1.4   *The apparent dependency explosion*

An often-heard complaint from developers is that the COMPOSITION ROOT causes the application's entry point to take a dependency on all other assemblies in the application. In their old, tightly coupled code bases, their entry point only needed to depend on the layer directly below. This seems backward because DI is meant to lower the required number of dependencies. They see the use of DI as causing an explosion of dependencies in their application's entry point—or so it seems.

This complaint comes from the fact that developers misunderstand how project dependencies work. To get a good view of what they're worried about, let's take a look at the dependency graph of Mary's application from chapter 2 and compare that with the dependency graph of the loosely coupled application of chapter 3 (figure 4.3).

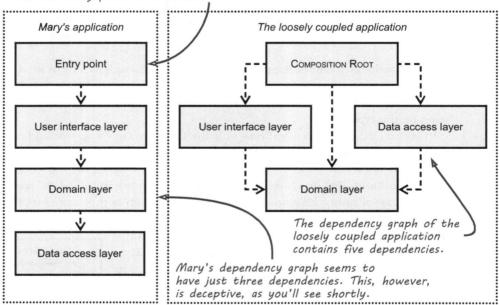

Figure 4.3   Comparing the dependency graph of Mary's application to that of the loosely coupled application

At first glance, it indeed looks as if there are two more dependencies in the loosely coupled application, compared to Mary's application with "only" three dependencies. The diagram, however, is misleading.

Changes to the data access layer also ripple through the UI layer and, as we discussed in the previous chapter, the UI layer can't be deployed without the data access layer.

Even though the diagram doesn't show it, there's a dependency between the UI and the data access layer. Assembly dependencies are in fact transitive.

NOTE *Transitivity* is a mathematical concept that states that when an element *a* is related to an element *b*, and *b* is related to an element *c*, then *a* is also related to *c*.

This transitive relationship means that because Mary's UI depends on the domain, and the domain depends on data access, the UI depends on data access too, which is exactly the behavior you'll experience when deploying the application. If you take a look at the dependencies between the projects in Mary's application, you'll see something different (figure 4.4).

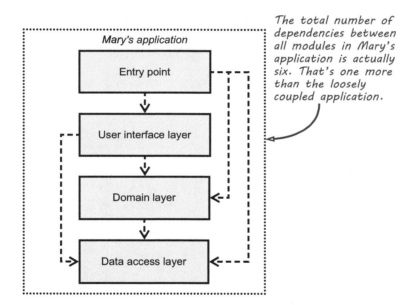

Figure 4.4 The dependencies between the libraries in Mary's application

As you can see, even in Mary's application, the entry point depends on all libraries. Both Mary's entry point and the COMPOSITION ROOT of the loosely coupled application have the same number of dependencies. Remember, though, that dependencies aren't defined by the number of modules, but the number of times each module depends on another module. As a result, the total number of dependencies between all modules in Mary's application is, in fact, six. That's one more than the loosely coupled application.

Now imagine an application with dozens of projects. It's not hard to imagine how the number of dependencies in a tightly coupled code base explodes compared with a loosely coupled code base. But, by writing loosely coupled code that applies the COMPOSITION ROOT pattern, you can lower the number of dependencies. As you've seen in the previous chapter, this lets you replace complete modules with different ones, which is harder in a tightly coupled code base.

The COMPOSITION ROOT pattern applies to all applications developed using DI, but only startup projects will have a COMPOSITION ROOT. A COMPOSITION ROOT is the result of removing the responsibility for the creation of DEPENDENCIES from consumers. To achieve this, you can apply two patterns: CONSTRUCTOR INJECTION and PROPERTY INJECTION. CONSTRUCTOR INJECTION is the most common and should be used almost exclusively. Because CONSTRUCTOR INJECTION is the most commonly used pattern, we'll discuss that next.

4.2 CONSTRUCTOR INJECTION

How do we guarantee that a necessary VOLATILE DEPENDENCY *is always available to the class we're currently developing?*

BY REQUIRING ALL CALLERS TO SUPPLY THE *VOLATILE DEPENDENCY* AS A PARAMETER TO THE CLASS'S CONSTRUCTOR.

When a class requires an instance of a DEPENDENCY, you can supply that DEPENDENCY through the class's constructor, enabling it to store the reference for future use.

DEFINITION CONSTRUCTOR INJECTION is the act of statically defining the list of required DEPENDENCIES by specifying them as parameters to the class's constructor.

The constructor signature is compiled with the type and is available for all to see. It clearly documents that the class requires the DEPENDENCIES it requests through its constructor. Figure 4.5 demonstrates this.

This figure shows that the consuming class HomeController needs an instance of the IProductService DEPENDENCY to work, so it requires the COMPOSITION ROOT (the client) to supply an instance via its constructor. This guarantees that the instance is available to HomeController when it's needed.

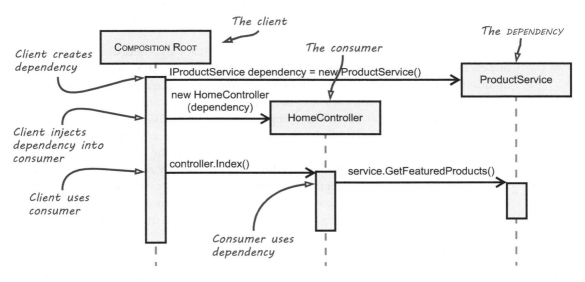

Figure 4.5 Constructing a HomeController instance with a required IProductService DEPENDENCY using CONSTRUCTOR INJECTION

4.2.1 HOW CONSTRUCTOR INJECTION works

The class that needs the DEPENDENCY must expose a public constructor that takes an instance of the required DEPENDENCY as a constructor argument. This should be the only publicly available constructor. If more than one DEPENDENCY is needed, additional constructor arguments can be added to the same constructor. Listing 4.5 shows the definition of the HomeController class of figure 4.5.

IMPORTANT   Constrain the design to a single (public) constructor. Because the constructor is the definition of a class's DEPENDENCIES, it makes little sense to have multiple definitions. Overloaded constructors lead to ambiguity: which constructor should the caller (or a DI CONTAINER) use?

Listing 4.5   Injecting a DEPENDENCY using CONSTRUCTOR INJECTION

Private instance field to store supplied DEPENDENCY

```
public class HomeController
{
    private readonly IProductService service;

    public HomeController(
        IProductService service)
    {
        if (service == null)
            throw new ArgumentNullException("service");

        this.service = service;
    }
}
```

Constructor that statically defines its DEPENDENCIES

Argument for supplying the required DEPENDENCY

Guard Clause to prevent clients from passing in null

Storing the DEPENDENCY in the private field for later use. The constructor contains no other logic than verifying and storing its incoming DEPENDENCIES

The IProductService DEPENDENCY is a required constructor argument of HomeController; any client that doesn't supply an instance of IProductService can't compile. But, because an interface is a reference type, a caller can pass in null as an argument to make the calling code compile. You need to protect the class against such misuse with a Guard Clause.[1] Because the combined efforts of the compiler and the Guard Clause guarantee that the constructor argument is valid if no exception is thrown, the constructor can store the DEPENDENCY for future use without knowing anything about the real implementation.

It's good practice to mark the field holding the DEPENDENCY as readonly. This guarantees that once the initialization logic of the constructor has executed, the field can't be modified. This isn't strictly required from a DI point of view, but it protects you from accidentally modifying the field (such as setting it to null) somewhere else in the depending class's code.

IMPORTANT   Keep the constructor free of any other logic to prevent it from performing any work on DEPENDENCIES. The SINGLE RESPONSIBILITY PRINCIPLE implies that members should do only one thing. Now that you're using the constructor to inject DEPENDENCIES, you should keep it free of other concerns. This makes the construction of your classes fast and reliable.

When the constructor has returned, the new instance of the class is in a consistent state with a proper instance of its DEPENDENCY injected into it. Because the constructed class holds a reference to this DEPENDENCY, it can use the DEPENDENCY as often as necessary from any of its other members. Its members don't need to test for null, because the instance is guaranteed to be present.

---

[1]   Martin Fowler et al., *Refactoring: Improving the Design of Existing Code* (Addison-Wesley, 1999), 250.

4.2.2 When to use CONSTRUCTOR INJECTION

CONSTRUCTOR INJECTION should be your default choice for DI. It addresses the most common scenario where a class requires one or more DEPENDENCIES, and no reasonable LOCAL DEFAULTS are available.

> **DEFINITION** A LOCAL DEFAULT is a default implementation of a DEPENDENCY that originates in the same module or layer.

LOCAL DEFAULT

When you're developing a class that has a DEPENDENCY, you probably have a particular implementation of that DEPENDENCY in mind. If you're writing a domain service that accesses a Repository, you're most likely planning to develop an implementation of a Repository that uses a relational database.

It would be tempting to make that implementation the default used by the class under development. But when such a prospective default is implemented in a different assembly, using it as a default means creating a hard reference to that other assembly, effectively violating many of the benefits of loose coupling described in chapter 1. Such implementation is the opposite of a LOCAL DEFAULT—it's a FOREIGN DEFAULT. A class that has a hard reference to a FOREIGN DEFAULT is applying the CONTROL FREAK anti-pattern. We'll discuss CONTROL FREAK in chapter 5.

Conversely, if the intended default implementation is defined in the same library as the consuming class, you won't have that problem. This is unlikely to be the case with Repositories, but such LOCAL DEFAULTS often arise as implementations of the Strategy pattern.[2]

> **WARNING** A LOCAL DEFAULT with DEPENDENCIES becomes a FOREIGN DEFAULT when one of its DEPENDENCIES is a FOREIGN DEFAULT. Transitivity strikes again.

CONSTRUCTOR INJECTION addresses the common scenario of an object requiring a DEPENDENCY with no reasonable LOCAL DEFAULT available, because it guarantees that the DEPENDENCY must be provided. If the depending class absolutely can't function without the DEPENDENCY, such a guarantee is valuable. Table 4.1 provides a summary of the advantages and disadvantages of CONSTRUCTOR INJECTION.

Table 4.1 CONSTRUCTOR INJECTION advantages and disadvantages

Advantages	Disadvantages
Injection guaranteed Easy to implement Statically declares a class's DEPENDENCIES	Frameworks that apply the CONSTRAINED CONSTRUCTION anti-pattern can make using CONSTRUCTOR INJECTION difficult.

---

[2] Erich Gamma et al., *Design Patterns*, 315.

In cases where the local library can supply a good default implementation, PROPERTY INJECTION can also be a good fit, but this is usually not the case. In the earlier chapters, we showed many examples of Repositories as DEPENDENCIES. These are good examples of DEPENDENCIES, where the local library can supply no good default implementation because the proper implementations belong in specialized data access libraries. Apart from the guaranteed injection already discussed, this pattern is also easy to implement using the structure presented in listing 4.5.

The main disadvantage to CONSTRUCTOR INJECTION is that if the class you're building is called by your current application framework, you might need to customize that framework to support it. Some frameworks, especially older ones, assume that your classes will have a parameterless constructor.[3] (This is called the CONSTRAINED CONSTRUCTION anti-pattern, and we'll discuss this in more detail in the next chapter.) In this case, the framework will need special help creating instances when a parameterless constructor isn't available. In chapter 7, we'll explain how to enable CONSTRUCTOR INJECTION for common application frameworks.

As previously discussed in section 4.1, an apparent disadvantage of CONSTRUCTOR INJECTION is that it requires that the entire DEPENDENCY graph be initialized immediately. Although this sounds inefficient, it's rarely an issue. After all, even for a complex object graph, we're typically talking about creating a few dozen new object instances, and creating an object instance is something the .NET Framework does extremely fast. Any performance bottleneck your application may have will appear in other places, so don't worry about it.[4]

NOTE   As previously stated, component constructors should be free from all logic except guard checks and storing incoming DEPENDENCIES. This makes construction fast and prevents most performance issues.

Extremely big object graphs

I (Steven) once had a conversation with a developer who switched DI CONTAINERS after having some severe performance problems with his old container. After switching, he reported a 300 to 400 ms speedup per web request, which is quite impressive. After doing some analysis on his application, though, I found out that, in some cases, an object graph was created that consisted of more than 19,000 object instances. No wonder this performed so poorly with some of the DI CONTAINERS.

The size of this object graph was unimaginable to me. I'd never seen anything this outrageously big before. Many of the classes in the system were huge, with way too many

---

[3]   ASP.NET Web Forms forced forms and custom controls to have a parameterless constructor, but with the introduction of .NET 4.7.2, this changed. ASP.NET forms and controls can now be constructed using CONSTRUCTOR INJECTION.

[4]   In extremely rare cases, this can be a real issue, but in chapter 8, we'll describe how to delay the creation of a DEPENDENCY as one possible remedy to this issue. For now, we'll merely observe that there may be a potential issue with initial load.

DEPENDENCIES. Twenty or more DEPENDENCIES were quite common.[5] Even commonly used classes had that many DEPENDENCIES, which caused the number of object instances in the object graphs to spiral out of control, or, as that developer himself said, "Real world sometimes goes beyond fantasies."

Although this story might seem to prove that performance could be an issue, the moral of the story is that well-designed systems hardly ever have this problem. In a well-designed system, classes only have a few DEPENDENCIES (up to four or five), and this makes object graphs quite narrow. Object graphs tend to get deeper in well-designed systems because of the ease with which you can apply multiple layers of Decorators.[6] But, in the end, the number of objects in the graphs of well-designed systems will stay within a few hundred at most. This means that under normal conditions, with a well-designed system, even a slower DI CONTAINER should typically cause no performance problems.

Now that you know that CONSTRUCTOR INJECTION is the preferred way of applying DI, let's take a look at some known examples. For this, we'll discuss CONSTRUCTOR INJECTION in the .NET BCL next.

4.2.3 Known use of CONSTRUCTOR INJECTION

Although CONSTRUCTOR INJECTION tends to be ubiquitous in applications employing DI, it isn't very present in the BCL. This is mainly because the BCL is a set of reusable libraries and not a full-fledged application. Two related examples where you can see a sort of CONSTRUCTOR INJECTION in the BCL is with the `System.IO.StreamReader` and `System.IO.StreamWriter` classes. Both take a `System.IO.Stream` instance in their constructors. Here's all of `StreamWriter`'s `Stream`-related constructors; the `StreamReader` constructors are similar:

```
public StreamWriter(Stream stream);
public StreamWriter(Stream stream, Encoding encoding);
public StreamWriter(Stream stream, Encoding encoding, int bufferSize);
```

`Stream` is an abstract class that serves as an ABSTRACTION on which `StreamWriter` and `StreamReader` operate to perform their duties. You can supply any `Stream` implementation in their constructors, and they'll use it, but they'll throw `ArgumentNullExceptions` if you try to slip them a `null` stream.

> **NOTE** For classes in a reusable class library (like the BCL), having multiple constructors often makes sense. For your application components, however, it doesn't.

Although the BCL provides examples where you can see CONSTRUCTOR INJECTION in use, it's always more instructive to see a working example. The next section walks you through a full implementation example.

---

[5] This is a code smell called *Constructor Over-injection*, which we'll discuss in section 6.1.

[6] In chapter 10, we'll create an example containing multiple layers of Decorators.

4.2.4   *Example: Adding currency conversions to the featured products*

Mary's boss says her app is working fine, but now some customers who are using it want to pay for goods in different currencies. Can she write some new code that enables the app to display and calculate costs in different currencies? Mary sighs and realizes that it's not going to be enough to hard-code in a few different currency conversions. She'll need to write code flexible enough to accommodate any currency over time. DI is calling again.

What Mary needs is both an object for representing money and its currency and an ABSTRACTION that allows converting money from one currency into another. She'll name the ABSTRACTION ICurrencyConverter. For simplicity, the Currency will only have a currency Code, and Money is composed of both a Currency and an Amount, as shown in figure 4.6.

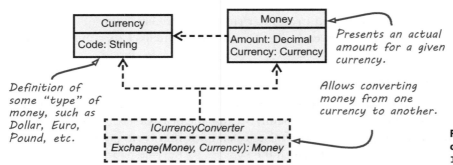

Figure 4.6   Exchanging currencies using ICurrencyConverter

The following listing shows the Currency and Money classes, and the ICurrency-Converter interface, as envisioned in figure 4.6.

Listing 4.6   Currency, Money, and the ICurrencyConverter interface

```
public interface ICurrencyConverter
{
    Money Exchange(Money money, Currency targetCurrency);
}

public class Currency
{
    public readonly string Code;

    public Currency(string code)
    {
        if (code == null) throw new ArgumentNullException("code");

        this.Code = code;
    }
}
```

```
public class Money
{
    public readonly decimal Amount;
    public readonly Currency Currency;

    public Money(decimal amount, Currency currency)
    {
        if (currency == null) throw new ArgumentNullException("currency");

        this.Amount = amount;
        this.Currency = currency;
    }
}
```

An ICurrencyConverter is likely to represent an out-of-process resource, such as a web service or a database that supplies conversion rates. This means that it'd be fitting to implement a concrete ICurrencyConverter in a separate project, such as a data access layer. Hence, there's no reasonable LOCAL DEFAULT.

At the same time, the ProductService class will need an ICurrencyConverter. CONSTRUCTOR INJECTION is a good fit. The following listing shows how the ICurrency-Converter DEPENDENCY is injected into ProductService.

Listing 4.7   Injecting an ICurrencyConverter into ProductService

```
public class ProductService : IProductService
{
    private readonly IProductRepository repository;
    private readonly IUserContext userContext;
    private readonly ICurrencyConverter converter;

    public ProductService(
        IProductRepository repository,
        IUserContext userContext,
        ICurrencyConverter converter)
    {
        if (repository == null)
            throw new ArgumentNullException("repository");
        if (userContext == null)
            throw new ArgumentNullException("userContext");
        if (converter == null)
            throw new ArgumentNullException("converter");

        this.repository = repository;
        this.userContext = userContext;
        this.converter = converter;
    }
}
```

Because the ProductService class already had a DEPENDENCY on IProductRepository and IUserContext, we add the new ICurrencyConverter DEPENDENCY as a third constructor argument and then follow the same sequence outlined in listing 4.5. Guard

Clauses guarantee that the DEPENDENCIES aren't null, which means it's safe to store them for later use in read-only fields. Because an ICurrencyConverter is guaranteed to be present in ProductService, it can be used from anywhere; for example, in the GetFeaturedProducts method as shown here.

Listing 4.8   ProductService using ICurrencyConverter

```
public IEnumerable<DiscountedProduct> GetFeaturedProducts()
{
    Currency userCurrency = this.userContext.Currency;    ◄─── Adds a Currency property to
                                                               IUserContext to get the user's
    var products =                                             preferred currency
        this.repository.GetFeaturedProducts();

    return
        from product in products
        let unitPrice = product.UnitPrice    ◄─── A product now has a
        let amount = this.converter.Exchange(     UnitPrice of type Money.
            money: unitPrice,
            targetCurrency: userCurrency)    Given some Money and a new Currency,
        select product                       invokes the ICurrencyConverter to
            .WithUnitPrice(amount)           provide an amount for the new currency
            .ApplyDiscountFor(this.userContext);
}
```

Notice that you can use the converter field without needing to check its availability in advance. That's because it's guaranteed to be present.

4.2.5   *Wrap-up*

CONSTRUCTOR INJECTION is the most generally applicable DI pattern available, and also the easiest to implement correctly. It applies when the DEPENDENCY is required. If you need to make the DEPENDENCY optional, you can change to PROPERTY INJECTION if it has a proper LOCAL DEFAULT.

> **WARNING**   DEPENDENCIES should hardly ever be optional. Optional DEPENDEN-CIES complicate the consuming component with null checks. Instead, make DEPENDENCIES required, and create and inject Null Object implementations in cases where there's no reasonable implementation available for the required DEPENDENCY.

Null Object pattern

The Null Object design pattern allows a consumer's DEPENDENCY to always be available, even in the absence of any real implementation.[7] By injecting an implementation that contains no behavior—the Null Object—the consumer can treat the DEPENDENCY transparently, without the need to be complicated with null checks.

---

[7]   Robert C. Martin et al., *Pattern Languages of Program Design 3* (Addison-Wesley, 1998), 5.

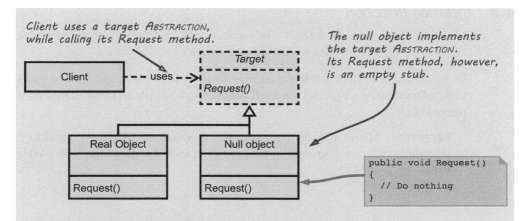

General structure of the Null Object pattern

Implementations of the Null Object pattern are typically empty, except in the case where the Null Object must return a value. In that case, the simplest correct value is typically returned.

From time to time, applications needs to produce output that allows developers or operation staff to analyze problems. Logging ABSTRACTIONS are an often-used method for doing so. Even though a class can be designed to support logging, the application it runs in might not require a particular class to log. Although you could let such a class check for the availability of a logger—for instance, using null checks—a more robust solution is to inject a Null Object implementation.

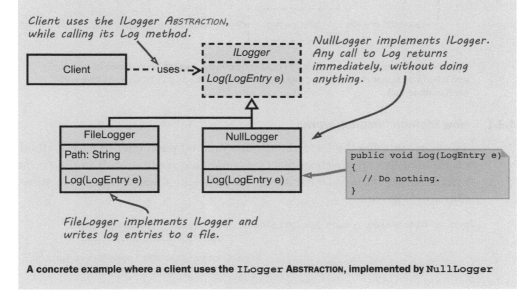

A concrete example where a client uses the ILogger ABSTRACTION, implemented by NullLogger

The next pattern in this chapter is METHOD INJECTION, which takes a slightly different approach. It tends to apply more to the situation where you already have a DEPENDENCY that you want to pass on to the collaborators you invoke.

4.3   METHOD INJECTION

How can we inject a DEPENDENCY into a class when it's different for each operation?
BY SUPPLYING IT AS A METHOD PARAMETER.

In cases where a DEPENDENCY can vary with each method call, or the consumer of such a DEPENDENCY can vary on each call, you can supply a DEPENDENCY via a method parameter.

DEFINITION   METHOD INJECTION supplies a consumer with a DEPENDENCY by passing it as method argument on a method called outside the COMPOSITION ROOT.

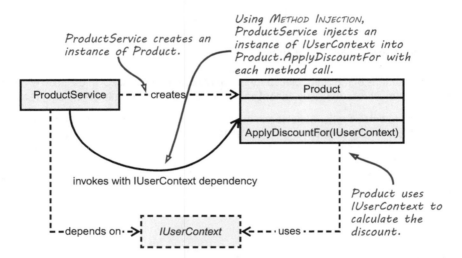

Figure 4.7   Using METHOD INJECTION, `ProductService` creates an instance of `Product` and injects an instance of `IUserContext` into `Product.ApplyDiscountFor` with each method call.

4.3.1   How METHOD INJECTION works

The caller supplies the DEPENDENCY as a method parameter in each method call. An example of this approach in Mary's e-commerce application is in the `Product` class, where the `ApplyDiscountFor` method accepts an `IUserContext` DEPENDENCY using METHOD INJECTION:

```
public DiscountedProduct ApplyDiscountFor(IUserContext userContext)
```

IUserContext is accepted using METHOD INJECTION

`IUserContext` presents contextual information for the operation to run, which is a common scenario for METHOD INJECTION. Often this context will be supplied to a method alongside a "proper" value, as shown in listing 4.9.

Listing 4.9 Passing a DEPENDENCY alongside a proper value

```
public decimal CalculateDiscountPrice(decimal price, IUserContext context)
{
    if (context == null) throw new ArgumentNullException("context");

    decimal discount = context.IsInRole(Role.PreferredCustomer) ? .95m : 1;

    return price * discount;
}
```

The price value parameter represents the value on which the method is supposed to operate, whereas context contains information about the current context of the operation; in this case, information about the current user. The caller supplies the DEPENDENCY to the method. As you've seen many times before, the Guard Clause guarantees that the context is available to the rest of the method body.

4.3.2 *When to use METHOD INJECTION*

METHOD INJECTION is different from other types of DI patterns in that the injection doesn't happen in a COMPOSITION ROOT but, rather, dynamically at invocation. This allows the caller to provide an operation-specific context, which is a common extensibility mechanism used in the .NET BCL. Table 4.2 provides a summary of the advantages and disadvantages of METHOD INJECTION.

Table 4.2 METHOD INJECTION advantages and disadvantages

Advantages	Disadvantages
Allows the caller to provide operation-specific context	Limited applicability
Allows injecting DEPENDENCIES into data-centric objects that aren't created inside the COMPOSITION ROOT	Causes the DEPENDENCY to become part of the public API of a class or its ABSTRACTION

There are two typical use cases for applying METHOD INJECTION:

- When the consumer of the injected DEPENDENCY varies on each call
- When the injected DEPENDENCY varies on each call to a consumer

The following sections show an example of each. Listing 4.9 is an example of how the consumer varies. This is the most common form, which is why we'll start with providing another example.

EXAMPLE: VARYING THE DEPENDENCY'S CONSUMER ON EACH METHOD CALL

When you practice Domain-Driven Design (DDD), it's common to create domain ENTITIES that contain domain logic, effectively mixing runtime data with behavior in the same class.[8] ENTITIES, however, are typically not created within the COMPOSITION ROOT. Take the following Customer ENTITY, for example.

---

[8] Eric Evans, *Domain-Driven Design: Tackling Complexity in the Heart of Software* (Addison-Wesley, 2004).

Listing 4.10   An ENTITY containing domain logic but no DEPENDENCIES (yet)

```
                              A domain ENTITY
public class Customer      ◄──────┘
{                                              The ENTITY's data members. This is
    public Guid Id { get; private set; }       the application's runtime data.
    public string Name { get; private set; }

    public Customer(Guid id, string name)      The constructor requires the ENTITY's
    {                                          data to be supplied. This way the
        ...                                    constructor can ensure the ENTITY is
    }                                          always created in a valid state.

    public void RedeemVoucher(Voucher voucher) ...    Lets the customer
                                                      redeem a voucher

    public void MakePreferred() ...     Promotes the customer
}                                       to Preferred status
```

The `RedeemVoucher` and `MakePreferred` methods in listing 4.10 are domain methods.
`RedeemVoucher` implements the domain logic that lets the customer redeem a voucher.
(You may have redeemed a voucher to get a discount when you purchased this book.)
`voucher` is a value object[9] used by the method. `MakePreferred`, on the other hand,
implements the domain logic that promotes the customer. A regular customer could
get upgraded to become a preferred customer, which might give certain advantages
and discounts, similar to being a frequent flyer airline customer.

ENTITIES that contain behavior besides their usual set of data members would easily
get a wide range of methods, each requiring their own DEPENDENCIES. Although you
might be tempted to use CONSTRUCTOR INJECTION to inject such DEPENDENCIES, that
leads to a situation where each such ENTITY needs to be created with all of its DEPEN-
DENCIES, even though only a few may be necessary for a given use case. This complicates testing the logic of an ENTITY, because all DEPENDENCIES need to be supplied to
the constructor, even though a test might only be interested in a few DEPENDENCIES.
METHOD INJECTION, as shown in the next listing, offers a better alternative.

Listing 4.11   An ENTITY using METHOD INJECTION

```
public class Customer
{
    public Guid Id { get; private set; }
    public string Name { get; private set; }

    public Customer(Guid id, string name)
    {
        ...
    }
```

---

[9]   As stated before in the footnote of section 4.4.1, Popsicle immutability allows a client to set a DEPEN-
DENCY during initialization.

```
public void RedeemVoucher(
    Voucher voucher,
    IVoucherRedemptionService service)
{
    if (voucher == null)
        throw new ArgumentNullException("voucher");
    if (service == null)
        throw new ArgumentNullException("service");

    service.ApplyRedemptionForCustomer(
        voucher,
        this.Id);
}
public void MakePreferred(IEventHandler handler)
{
    if (handler == null)
        throw new ArgumentNullException("handler");

    handler.Publish(new CustomerMadePreferred(this.Id));
}
}
```

Using METHOD INJECTION, both of the ENTITY's domain methods, RedeemVoucher and MakePreferred, accept the required DEPENDENCIES — IVoucherRedemptionService and IEventHandler. They validate the parameters and use the supplied DEPENDENCY.

Inside a `CustomerServices` component, the `Customer`'s `RedeemVoucher` method can be called while passing the `IVoucherRedemptionService` DEPENDENCY with the call, as shown next.

Listing 4.12 A component using METHOD INJECTION to pass a DEPENDENCY

```
public class CustomerServices : ICustomerServices
{
    private readonly ICustomerRepository repository;
    private readonly IVoucherRedemptionService service;

    public CustomerServices(
        ICustomerRepository repository,
        IVoucherRedemptionService service)
    {
        this.repository = repository;
        this.service = service;
    }

    public void RedeemVoucher(
        Guid customerId, Voucher voucher)
    {
        var customer =
            this.repository.GetById(customerId);

        customer.RedeemVoucher(voucher, this.service);

        this.repository.Save(customer);
    }
}
```

The CustomerServices class uses CONSTRUCTOR INJECTION to statically define its required DEPENDENCIES. IVoucherRedemptionService is one of those DEPENDENCIES.

The IVoucherRedemptionService DEPENDENCY is passed to an already constructed Customer ENTITY using METHOD INJECTION. Customer is created inside the ICustomerRepository implementation.

In listing 4.12, only a single `Customer` instance is requested from `ICustomerRepository`. But a single `CustomerServices` instance can be called over and over again using a multitude of customers and vouchers, causing the same `IVoucherRedemptionService` to be supplied to many different `Customer` instances. `Customer` is the consumer of the `IVoucherRedemptionService` DEPENDENCY and, while you're reusing the DEPENDENCY, you're varying the consumer.

This is similar to the first METHOD INJECTION example shown in listing 4.9 and the `ApplyDiscountFor` method discussed in listing 3.8. The opposite case is when you vary the DEPENDENCY while keeping its consumers around.

EXAMPLE: VARYING THE INJECTED DEPENDENCY ON EACH METHOD CALL

Imagine an add-in system for a graphical drawing application, where you want everyone to be able to plug in their own image effects. External image effects might require information about the runtime context, which can be passed on by the application to the image effect. This is a typical use case for applying METHOD INJECTION. You can define the following interface for applying those effects:

ABSTRACTION of add-ins that represent image effects. Image effects can be plugged into the application by implementing this ABSTRACTION.

```
public interface IImageEffectAddIn
{
    Bitmap Apply(
        Bitmap source,
        IApplicationContext context);
}
```

Allows the add-in to apply its effect to the source and then returns a new Bitmap with the effect applied

Provides contextual information to the image effect by the graphical application using METHOD INJECTION

The `IImageEffectAddIn`'s `IApplicationContext` DEPENDENCY can vary with each call to the `Apply` method, providing the effect with information about the context in which the operation is being invoked. Any class implementing this interface can be used as an add-in. Some implementations may not care about the `context` at all, whereas other implementations will.

A client can use a list of add-ins by calling each with a source `Bitmap` and a context to return an aggregated result, as shown in the next listing.

Listing 4.13   A sample add-in client

```
public Bitmap ApplyEffects(Bitmap source)
{
    if (source == null) throw new ArgumentNullException("source");

    Bitmap result = source;

    foreach (IImageEffectAddIn effect in this.effects)
    {
```

```
        result = effect.Apply(result, this.context);
    }

    return result;
}
```

The private `effects` field is a list of `IImageEffectAddIn` instances, which allows the client to loop through the list to invoke each add-in's `Apply` method. Each time the `Apply` method is invoked on an add-in, the operation's context, represented by the `context` field, is passed as a method parameter:

```
result = effect.Apply(result, this.context);
```

At times, the value and the operational context are encapsulated in a single ABSTRACTION that works as a combination of both. An important thing to note is this: as you've seen in both examples, the DEPENDENCY injected via METHOD INJECTION becomes part of the definition of the ABSTRACTION. This is typically desirable in case that DEPENDENCY contains runtime information that's supplied by its direct callers.

In cases where the DEPENDENCY is an implementation detail to the caller, you should try to prevent the ABSTRACTION from being "polluted"; therefore, CONSTRUCTOR INJECTION is a better pick. Otherwise, you could easily end up passing the DEPENDENCY from the top of our application's object graph all the way down, causing sweeping changes.

The previous examples all showed the use of METHOD INJECTION outside of the COMPOSITION ROOT. This is deliberate. METHOD INJECTION is unsuitable when used within the COMPOSITION ROOT. Within a COMPOSITION ROOT, METHOD INJECTION can initialize a previously constructed class with its DEPENDENCIES. Doing so, however, leads to TEMPORAL COUPLING and for that reason it's highly discouraged.

THE TEMPORAL COUPLING CODE SMELL

TEMPORAL COUPLING is a common problem in API design. It occurs when there's an implicit relationship between two or more members of a class, requiring clients to invoke one member before the other. This tightly couples the members in the temporal dimension. The archetypical example is the use of an `Initialize` method, although copious other examples can be found—even in the BCL. As an example, this usage of `System.ServiceModel.EndpointAddressBuilder` compiles but fails at runtime:

```
var builder = new EndpointAddressBuilder();
var address = builder.ToEndpointAddress();
```

It turns out that an URI is required before an `EndpointAddress` can be created. The following code compiles and succeeds at runtime:

```
var builder = new EndpointAddressBuilder();
builder.Uri = new UriBuilder().Uri;
var address = builder.ToEndpointAddress();
```

The API provides no hint that this is necessary, but there's a TEMPORAL COUPLING between the `Uri` property and the `ToEndpointAddress` method.

When applied inside the COMPOSITION ROOT, a *recurring pattern* is the use of some `Initialize` method, as shown in listing 4.14.

BAD
CODE

Listing 4.14   TEMPORAL COUPLING example

```
public class Component
{
    private ISomeInterface dependency;

    public void Initialize(
        ISomeInterface dependency)
    {
        this.dependency = dependency;
    }

    public void DoSomething()
    {
        if (this.dependency == null)
            throw new InvalidOperationException(
                "Call Initialize first.");

        this.dependency.DoStuff();
    }
}
```

The Initialize and DoSomething methods need to be invoked in a particular order, but this relationship is implicit. This causes TEMPORAL COUPLING.

The possibility to call DoSomething before Initialize forces the addition of this extra Guard Clause, which every public method of this class requires.

Semantically, the name of the `Initialize` method is a clue, but on a structural level, this API gives us no indication of TEMPORAL COUPLING. Thus, code like this compiles, but throws an exception at runtime:

```
var c = new Component();
c.DoSomething();
```

The solution to this problem should be obvious by now—you should apply CONSTRUCTOR INJECTION instead:

```
public class Component
{
    private readonly ISomeInterface dependency;

    public Component(ISomeInterface dependency)
    {
        if (dependency == null)
            throw new ArgumentNullException("dependency");

        this.dependency = dependency;
    }

    public void DoSomething()
    {
        this.dependency.DoStuff();
    }
}
```

WARNING   Don't store injected method DEPENDENCIES. This leads to TEMPORAL COUPLING, CAPTIVE DEPENDENCIES, or hidden side effects.[10] A method should use the DEPENDENCY or pass it on, and should refrain from storing such a DEPENDENCY. The use of METHOD INJECTION is quite common in the .NET BCL, so we'll look at an example next.

---

[10] We'll discuss CAPTIVE DEPENDENCIES in section 8.4.1.

4.3.3 Known use of METHOD INJECTION

The .NET BCL provides many examples of METHOD INJECTION, particularly in the System .ComponentModel namespace. You use System.ComponentModel.Design.IDesigner for implementing custom design-time functionality for components. It has an Initialize method that takes an IComponent instance so that it knows which component it's currently helping to design. (Note that this Initialize method causes TEMPORAL COUPLING.) Designers are created by IDesignerHost implementations that also take IComponent instances as parameters to create designers:

```
IDesigner GetDesigner(IComponent component);
```

This is a good example of a scenario where the parameter itself carries information. The component can carry information about which IDesigner to create, but at the same time, it's also the component on which the designer must subsequently operate.

Another example in the System.ComponentModel namespace is provided by the Type-Converter class. Several of its methods take an instance of ITypeDescriptorContext that, as the name says, conveys information about the context of the current operation, such as information about the type's properties. Because there are many such methods, we don't want to list them all, but here's a representative example:

```
public virtual object ConvertTo(ITypeDescriptorContext context,
    CultureInfo culture, object value, Type destinationType)
```

In this method, the context of the operation is communicated explicitly by the context parameter, whereas the value to be converted and the destination type are sent as separate parameters. Implementers can use or ignore the context parameter as they see fit.

ASP.NET Core MVC also contains several examples of METHOD INJECTION. You can use the IValidationAttributeAdapterProvider interface, for instance, to provide IAttributeAdapter instances. Its only method is this:

```
IAttributeAdapter GetAttributeAdapter(
    ValidationAttribute attribute, IStringLocalizer stringLocalizer)
```

ASP.NET Core allows properties of view models to be marked with ValidationAttribute. It's a convenient way to apply metadata that describes the validity of properties encapsulated in the view model.

Based on a ValidationAttribute, the GetAttributeAdapter method allows an IAttributeAdapter to be returned, which allows relevant error messages to be displayed in a web page. In the GetAttributeAdapter method, the attribute parameter is the object an IAttributeAdapter should be created for, whereas the stringLocalizer is the DEPENDENCY that's passed through METHOD INJECTION.

> **NOTE** When we recommend that CONSTRUCTOR INJECTION should be your preferred DI pattern, we're assuming that you generally build applications. On the other hand, if you're building a framework, METHOD INJECTION can be useful because it lets the framework pass information about the context to add-ins. This is one reason why you see METHOD INJECTION used so prolifically in the BCL. But even in application code, METHOD INJECTION can be useful.

Next, we'll see how Mary uses METHOD INJECTION in order to prevent code repetition. When we last saw Mary (in section 4.2), she was working on ICurrencyConverter: she injected it using CONSTRUCTOR INJECTION into the ProductService class.

4.3.4   *Example: Adding currency conversions to the Product ENTITY*

Listing 4.8 showed how the GetFeaturedProducts method called the ICurrency-Converter.Exchange method using the product's UnitPrice and the user's preferred currency in Mary's application. Here's that GetFeaturedProducts method again:

```
public IEnumerable<DiscountedProduct> GetFeaturedProducts()
{
    Currency currency = this.userContext.Currency;

    return
        from product in this.repository.GetFeaturedProducts()
        let amount = this.converter.Exchange(product.UnitPrice, currency)
        select product
            .WithUnitPrice(amount)
            .ApplyDiscountFor(this.userContext);
}
```

Conversions of Product ENTITIES from one Currency to another will be a recurring task in many parts of her application. For this reason, Mary likes to move the logic concerning the conversion of the Product out of ProductService and centralize it as part of the Product ENTITY. This prevents other parts of the system from repeating this code. METHOD INJECTION turns out to be a great candidate for this. Mary creates a new ConvertTo method in Product, as shown in the next listing.

Listing 4.15   Product ENTITY with ConvertTo method

```
public class Product
{
    public string Name { get; set; }
    public Money UnitPrice { get; set; }
    public bool IsFeatured { get; set; }          The ConvertTo method
                                                  accepts the Currency value.
    public Product ConvertTo(
        Currency currency,          ◄─────────   The ICurrencyConverter DEPENDENCY is
        ICurrencyConverter converter)  ◄──────   now injected using METHOD INJECTION.
    {
        if (currency == null)
            throw new ArgumentNullException("currency");
        if (converter == null)
            throw new ArgumentNullException("converter");

        var newUnitPrice =
            converter.Exchange(      ◄──────   The new unit price is
                this.UnitPrice,                determined by calling Exchange.
                currency);

        return this.WithUnitPrice(newUnitPrice);   ◄──────   A new Product instance is created
    }                                                         based on the original Product,
                                                              where the UnitPrice is replaced by
                                                              the newly constructed unit price.
```

```
    public Product WithUnitPrice(Money unitPrice)
    {
        return new Product
        {
            Name = this.Name,
            UnitPrice = unitPrice,
            IsFeatured = this.IsFeatured
        };
    }
    ...
}
```

With the new `ConvertTo` method, Mary refactors the `GetFeaturedProducts` method.

Listing 4.16 `GetFeaturedProducts` using `ConvertTo` method

```
public IEnumerable<DiscountedProduct> GetFeaturedProducts()
{
    Currency currency = this.userContext.Currency;

    return
        from product in this.repository.GetFeaturedProducts()
        select product
            .ConvertTo(currency, this.converter)     ◄
            .ApplyDiscountFor(this.userContext);
}
```

The **ICurrencyConverter** is now
supplied through METHOD INJECTION.

Instead of calling the `ICurrencyConverter.Exchange` method, as you've seen previously, `GetFeaturedProducts` now passes `ICurrencyConverter` on to the `ConvertTo` method using METHOD INJECTION. This simplifies the `GetFeaturedProducts` method and prevents any code duplication when Mary needs to convert products elsewhere in her code base. By using METHOD INJECTION instead of CONSTRUCTOR INJECTION, she avoided having to build up the `Product` ENTITY with all of its DEPENDENCIES. This simplifies construction and testing.

> **NOTE** Although we defined the `ICurrencyConverter` in section 4.2, we haven't yet talked about how the `ICurrencyConverter` class is implemented, because it's not that important from the point of view of either METHOD INJECTION or CONSTRUCTOR INJECTION. If you're interested to see how it's implemented, it's available in the book's accompanying source code.

Unlike the other DI patterns in this chapter, you mainly use METHOD INJECTION when you want to supply DEPENDENCIES to an already existing consumer. With CONSTRUCTOR INJECTION and PROPERTY INJECTION, on the other hand, you supply DEPENDENCIES to a consumer while it's being created.

The last pattern in this chapter is PROPERTY INJECTION, which allows you to override a class's LOCAL DEFAULT. Where METHOD INJECTION was solely applied outside the COMPOSITION ROOT, PROPERTY INJECTION, just as CONSTRUCTOR INJECTION, is applied from within the COMPOSITION ROOT.

4.4   PROPERTY INJECTION

How do we enable DI as an option in a class when we have a good LOCAL DEFAULT?

BY EXPOSING A WRITABLE PROPERTY THAT LETS CALLERS SUPPLY A DEPENDENCY
IF THEY WANT TO OVERRIDE THE DEFAULT BEHAVIOR.

When a class has a good LOCAL DEFAULT, but you still want to leave it open for extensibility, you can expose a writable property that allows a client to supply a different implementation of the class's DEPENDENCY than the default. As figure 4.8 shows, clients wanting to use the Consumer class as is can create an instance of the class and use it without giving it a second thought, whereas clients wanting to modify the behavior of the class can do so by setting the DEPENDENCY property to a different implementation of IDependency.

DEFINITION   PROPERTY INJECTION allows a LOCAL DEFAULT to be replaced via a public settable property. PROPERTY INJECTION is also known as SETTER INJECTION.

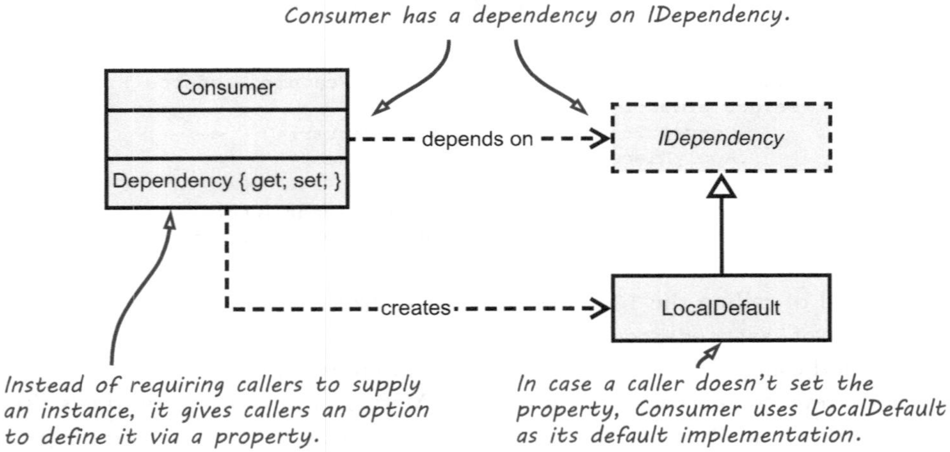

Figure 4.8   PROPERTY INJECTION

4.4.1   How PROPERTY INJECTION works

The class that uses the DEPENDENCY must expose a public writable property of the DEPENDENCY's type. In a bare-bones implementation, this can be as simple as the following listing.

Listing 4.17   PROPERTY INJECTION

```
public class Consumer
{
    public IDependency Dependency { get; set; }
}
```

Consumer depends on IDependency. Clients can supply implementations of IDependency by setting the Dependency property.

NOTE In contrast to CONSTRUCTOR INJECTION, you can't mark the Dependency property's backing field as readonly, because you allow callers to modify the property at any given time during a consumer's lifetime.

Other members of the depending class can use the injected DEPENDENCY to perform their duties, like this:

```
public void DoSomething()
{
    this.Dependency.DoStuff();
}
```

Unfortunately, such an implementation is fragile. That's because the Dependency property isn't guaranteed to return an instance of IDependency. Code like this would throw a NullReferenceException if the value of the Dependency property is null:

```
var instance = new Consumer();

instance.DoSomething();
```
← **This call causes an exception, because we forgot to set instance.Dependency.**

This issue can be solved by letting the constructor set a default instance on the property, combined with a proper Guard Clause in the property's setter. Another complication arises if clients switch the DEPENDENCY in the middle of the class's lifetime:

```
var instance = new Consumer();

instance.Dependency = new SomeImplementation();
```
← **Sets the Dependency property with a valid implementation**
```
instance.DoSomething();

instance.Dependency = new SomeOtherImplementation();
```
←
```
instance.DoSomething();
```
Changes the Dependency property in the middle of the class's lifetime. This might cause a problem for Consumer.

This can be addressed by introducing an internal flag that only allows a client to set the DEPENDENCY during initialization.[11]

The example in section 4.4.4 shows how you can deal with these complications. But before we get to that, we'd like to explain when it's appropriate to use PROPERTY INJECTION.

4.4.2 *When to use PROPERTY INJECTION*

PROPERTY INJECTION should only be used when the class you're developing has a good LOCAL DEFAULT, and you still want to enable callers to provide different implementations of the class's DEPENDENCY. It's important to note that PROPERTY INJECTION is best used when the DEPENDENCY is *optional*. If the DEPENDENCY is required, CONSTRUCTOR INJECTION is always a better pick.

---

[11] Eric Lippert calls this *Popsicle immutability*. Eric Lippert, "Immutability in C# Part One: Kinds of Immutability," 2007, https://mng.bz/y2Eq/.

In chapter 1, we discussed good reasons for writing code with loose coupling, thus isolating modules from each other. But loose coupling can also be applied to classes within a single module with great success. This is often done by introducing ABSTRACTIONS within a module and letting classes within that module communicate via ABSTRACTIONS, instead of being tightly coupled to each other. The main reasons for applying loose coupling within a module boundary is to open classes for extensibility and for ease of testing.

NOTE   The concept of opening a class for extensibility is captured by the OPEN/ CLOSED PRINCIPLE that, briefly put, states that a class should be open for extensibility, but closed for modification. When you implement classes following the OPEN/CLOSED PRINCIPLE, you may have a LOCAL DEFAULT in mind, but you still provide clients with a way to extend the class by replacing the DEPENDENCY with something else.

OPEN/CLOSED PRINCIPLE

Software entities (classes, modules, functions, and so on) that conform to the OPEN/ CLOSED PRINCIPLE have two primary attributes:

- *They're open for extension.* This means you can change or extend the behavior of such entity. This statement by itself is a bit dull, assuming your team owns the entire application, because you can always change the behavior of some part of the system. You go to its source code and you change it. This attribute, however, becomes interesting within the context of the next one.
- *They're closed for modification.* This means that when you extend the system, you must be able to do so without touching any of the existing source code. This can seem rather weird; how can you change a system if you can't alter its source code?

DI provides an important piece of the answer to this apparent conflict. It lets you replace or INTERCEPT classes to add or change behavior without either the consuming class nor its DEPENDENCY being aware of this. The OPEN/CLOSED PRINCIPLE pushes you to a design where every new feature request can be addressed by creating one or more new classes or modules without touching any of the existing ones.

When you're able to add new functional and non-functional requirements to your system without touching existing parts, it means that the problem at hand is isolated from other parts of the system. This leads to code that's easier to understand and test, and therefore maintain. That said, although being able to extend a system without having to change any existing code is a worthy ideal to strive for, it's an unreachable one. There'll always be cases where you'll have to change existing parts of the system.

As a developer, it's your job to find out what kind of changes are the most likely to occur in your application. Based on the understanding of how you expect a particular application or system to evolve, you should model it in such a way that you maximize maintainability. An important aspect of approaching this ideal is to prevent sweeping changes to the system from happening regularly.

Working with ABSTRACTIONS is one of the main topics in this book, and there's more to it. We'll explore some techniques that can help you make your applications open for extension but closed for modification in chapters 9 and 10.

NOTE The OPEN/CLOSED PRINCIPLE is closely related to the DRY principle.[12]

TIP Sometimes you only want to provide an extensibility point, leaving the LOCAL DEFAULT as a no-op.[13] In such cases, you can use the Null Object pattern to implement the LOCAL DEFAULT.

We haven't shown you any real examples of PROPERTY INJECTION so far because the applicability of this pattern is more limited, especially in the context of application development. Table 4.3 summarizes its advantages and disadvantages.

Table 4.3 PROPERTY INJECTION advantages and disadvantages

Advantages	Disadvantages
Easy to understand	Not entirely simple to implement robustly
	Limited applicability
	Only applicable to reusable libraries
	Causes TEMPORAL COUPLING

The main advantage of PROPERTY INJECTION is that it's so easy to understand. We've often seen this pattern used as a first attempt when people decide to adopt DI.

Appearances can be deceptive, though, and PROPERTY INJECTION is fraught with difficulties. It's challenging to implement it in a robust manner. Clients can forget to supply the DEPENDENCY because of the previously discussed problem of TEMPORAL COUPLING. Additionally, what would happen if a client tries to change the DEPENDENCY in the middle of the class's lifetime? This could lead to inconsistent or unexpected behavior, so you may want to protect yourself against that event.

Despite the downsides, it makes sense to use PROPERTY INJECTION when building a reusable library. It allows components to define sensible defaults, and this simplifies working with a library's API.

NOTE When building applications, on the other hand, we never use PROPERTY INJECTION, and you should do so sparingly. Even though you might have a LOCAL DEFAULT for a DEPENDENCY, CONSTRUCTOR INJECTION still provides you with a better alternative. CONSTRUCTOR INJECTION is simpler and more robust. You might think you need PROPERTY INJECTION to work around a cyclic DEPENDENCY, but that's a code smell, as we'll explain in chapter 6.

When developing applications, you wire up your classes in your COMPOSITION ROOT. CONSTRUCTOR INJECTION prevents you from forgetting to supply the DEPENDENCY. Even in the case that there's a LOCAL DEFAULT, such instances can be supplied to the

---

[12] The DRY principle—Don't Repeat Yourself—states that "Every piece of knowledge must have a single, unambiguous, authoritative representation within a system."

[13] NOP, no-op, and NOOP are short for *no operation*. It is an assembly language instruction that does nothing. The term *no op* has become a general term in computer science for an operation that does nothing.

constructor by the COMPOSITION ROOT. This simplifies the class and allows the COMPO-SITION ROOT to be in control over the value that all consumers get. This might even be a Null Object implementation.

> **TIP** Prevent the use of PROPERTY INJECTION as a solution to Constructor Over-injection. Classes with many DEPENDENCIES are a code smell and PROP-ERTY INJECTION won't lower the class's complexity. We'll discuss Constructor Over-injection in section 6.1.

The existence of a good LOCAL DEFAULT depends in part on the granularity of modules. The BCL ships as a rather large package; as long as the default stays within the BCL, it could be argued that it's also local. In the next section, we'll briefly touch on that subject.

4.4.3   *Known uses of PROPERTY INJECTION*

In the .NET BCL, PROPERTY INJECTION is a bit more common than CONSTRUCTOR INJECTION, probably because good LOCAL DEFAULTS are defined in many places, and also because this simplifies the default instantiation of most classes. For example, `System.ComponentModel.IComponent` has a writable `Site` property that allows you to define an `ISite` instance. This is mostly used in design time scenarios (for example, by Visual Studio) to alter or enhance a component when it's hosted in a designer. With that BCL example as an appetizer, let's move on to a more substantial example of using and implementing PROPERTY INJECTION.

4.4.4   *Example: PROPERTY INJECTION as an extensibility model of a reusable library*

Earlier examples in this chapter extended the sample application of the previous chapter. Although we could show you an example of PROPERTY INJECTION using the sample application, this would be misleading because PROPERTY INJECTION is hardly ever a good fit when building applications; CONSTRUCTOR INJECTION is almost always a better choice. Instead, we'd like to show you an example of a reusable library. In this case, we're looking at some code from Simple Injector.

Simple Injector is one of the DI CONTAINERS that's discussed in part 4. It helps you construct your application's object graphs. Chapter 14 will have an extensive discussion on Simple Injector, so we won't go into much detail about it here. From the perspective of PROPERTY INJECTION, how Simple Injector works isn't important.

As a reusable library, Simple Injector makes extensive use of PROPERTY INJECTION. Lots of its behavior can be extended, and the way this is done is by providing default implementations of its behavior. Simple Injector exposes properties that allow the user to change the default implementation. One of the behaviors that Simple Injector allows to be replaced is how the library selects the correct constructor for doing CONSTRUCTOR INJECTION.[14]

As we discussed in section 4.2, your classes should only have one constructor. Because of this, Simple Injector, by default, only allows classes that have just one public constructor to be created. In any other case, Simple Injector throws an exception. Simple Injector, however,

---

[14] To explain PROPERTY INJECTION, this example uses the CONSTRUCTOR INJECTION feature of a DI CON-TAINER. But don't worry, the example shows a property with a LOCAL DEFAULT and two Guard Clauses.

lets you override this behavior. This might be useful for certain narrow integration scenarios. For this, Simple Injector defines an `IConstructorResolutionBehavior` interface.[15] A custom implementation can be defined by the user, and the library-provided default can be replaced by setting the `ConstructorResolutionBehavior` property, as shown here:

```
var container = new Container();

container.Options.ConstructorResolutionBehavior =
    new CustomConstructorResolutionBehavior();
```

The `Container` is the central Facade[16] pattern in Simple Injector's API. It's used to specify the relationships between ABSTRACTIONS and implementations, and to build object graphs of these implementations. The class includes an `Options` property of type `ContainerOptions`. It includes a number of properties and methods that allow the default behavior of the library to be changed. One of those properties is `Constructor-ResolutionBehavior`. Here's a simplified version of the `ContainerOptions` class with its `ConstructorResolutionBehavior` property:

```
public class ContainerOptions          Assignment of the private resolutionBehavior field with the
{                                      DefaultConstructorResolutionBehavior LOCAL DEFAULT

    IConstructorResolutionBehavior resolutionBehavior =
        new DefaultConstructorResolutionBehavior();   ◄

    public IConstructorResolutionBehavior ConstructorResolutionBehavior
    {
        get
        {
            return this.resolutionBehavior;
        }
        set
        {                                       Guard Clause with null check
            if (value == null)    ◄
                throw new ArgumentNullException("value");

            if (this.Container.HasRegistrations)   ◄      Guard Clause with a
            {                                              variation of the discussed
                throw new InvalidOperationException(       internal flag that ensures
                    "The ConstructorResolutionBehav" +     Popsicle immutability[17]
                    "ior property cannot be changed" +
                    " after the first registration " +
                    "has been made to the container.";
            }

            this.resolutionBehavior = value;   ◄
        }
    }                          Stores the incoming DEPENDENCY in the
}                              private field, overriding the LOCAL DEFAULT
```

---

[15] This is an implementation of the Strategy pattern.

[16] Erich Gamma et al., *Design Patterns*, 208.

[17] As stated before in the footnote of section 4.4.1, Popsicle immutability allows a client to set a DEPENDENCY during initialization.

The ConstructorResolutionBehavior property can be changed multiple times as long as there are no registrations made in the container. This is important, because when registrations are made, Simple Injector uses the specified ConstructorResolutionBehavior to verify whether it'll be able to construct such a type by analyzing a class's constructor. If a user was able to change the constructor resolution behavior after registrations were made, it could impact the correctness of earlier registrations. This is because Simple Injector could, otherwise, end up using a different constructor for a component from that which it approved to be correct during the time of registration. This means that either all previous registrations should be reevaluated or the user should be prevented from being able to change the behavior after registrations are made. Because reevaluating can have hidden performance costs and is harder to implement, Simple Injector implements the latter approach.

Compared to CONSTRUCTOR INJECTION, PROPERTY INJECTION is more involved. It may look simple in its raw form (as shown in listing 4.19), but, properly implemented, it tends to be more complex.

You use PROPERTY INJECTION in a reusable library where the DEPENDENCY is optional and you have a good LOCAL DEFAULT. In cases where there's a short-lived object that requires the DEPENDENCY, you should use METHOD INJECTION. In other cases, you should use CONSTRUCTOR INJECTION.

This completes the last pattern in this chapter. The following section provides a short recap and explains how to select the right pattern for your job.

4.5 *Choosing which pattern to use*

The patterns presented in this chapter are a central part of DI. Armed with a COMPOSITION ROOT and an appropriate mix of injection patterns, you can implement PURE DI or use a DI CONTAINER. When applying DI, there are many nuances and finer details to learn, but these patterns cover the core mechanics that answer the question, "How do I inject my DEPENDENCIES?"

These patterns aren't interchangeable. In most cases, your default choice should be CONSTRUCTOR INJECTION, but there are situations where one of the other patterns affords a better alternative. Figure 4.9 shows a decision process that can help you decide on a proper pattern, but, if in doubt, choose CONSTRUCTOR INJECTION. You can't go terribly wrong with that choice.

The first thing to examine is whether the DEPENDENCY is something you need or something you already have but want to communicate to another collaborator. In most cases, you'll probably need the DEPENDENCY. But in add-in scenarios, you may want to convey the current context to an add-in. Every time the DEPENDENCY varies from operation to operation, METHOD INJECTION is a good candidate for an implementation.

Secondly, you'll need to know what kind of class needs the DEPENDENCY. In case you're mixing runtime data with behavior in the same class, as you might do in your domain ENTITIES, METHOD INJECTION is a good fit. In other cases, when you're writing

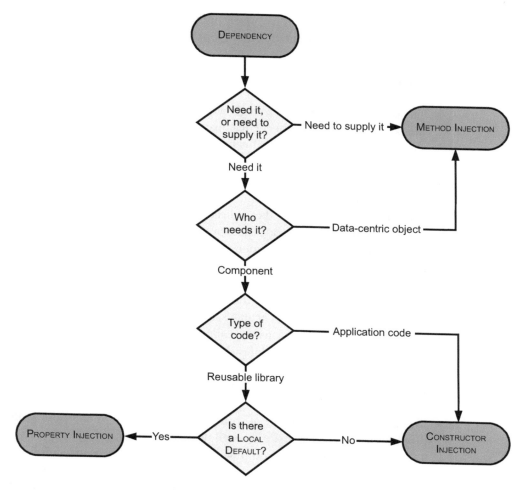

Figure 4.9 Pattern decision process. In most cases, you should choose CONSTRUCTOR INJECTION, but there are situations where one of the other DI patterns is a better fit.

application code, opposed to writing a reusable library, CONSTRUCTOR INJECTION automatically applies.

When it comes to writing application code, even the use of LOCAL DEFAULTS should be prevented in favor of having these defaults set in one central place in the application—the COMPOSITION ROOT. On the other hand, when writing a reusable library, a LOCAL DEFAULT is the deciding factor, as it can make explicitly assigning the DEPENDENCY optional—the default takes over if no overriding implementation is specified. This scenario can be effectively implemented with PROPERTY INJECTION.

CONSTRUCTOR INJECTION should be your default choice for DI. It's easy to understand and simpler to implement robustly than any of the other DI patterns. You can build entire applications with CONSTRUCTOR INJECTION alone, but knowing about the other patterns can help you choose wisely in the few cases where it doesn't fit perfectly. The next chapter approaches DI from the opposite direction and takes a look at ill-advised ways of using DI.

Summary

- The COMPOSITION ROOT is a single, logical location in an application where modules are composed together. The construction of your application's components should be concentrated into this single area of your application.
- Only startup projects will have a COMPOSITION ROOT.
- Although a COMPOSITION ROOT can be spread out across multiple classes, they should be in a single module.
- The COMPOSITION ROOT takes a direct dependency on all other modules in the system. Loosely coupled code that applies the COMPOSITION ROOT pattern lowers the overall number of dependencies between modules, subsystems, and layers, compared to tightly coupled code.
- Even though you might place the COMPOSITION ROOT in the same assembly as your UI or presentation layer, the COMPOSITION ROOT isn't part of those layers. Assemblies are deployment artifacts, whereas layers are logical artifacts.
- Where a DI CONTAINER is used, it should only be referenced from the COMPOSITION ROOT. All other modules should be oblivious to the existence of the DI CONTAINER.
- Use of a DI CONTAINER outside the COMPOSITION ROOT leads to the SERVICE LOCATOR anti-pattern.
- The performance overhead of using a DI CONTAINER to compose large object graphs is usually not an issue in a well-designed system.
- The COMPOSITION ROOT should be the sole place in the entire application that knows about the structure of the constructed object graphs. This means that application code can't pass on DEPENDENCIES to other threads that run parallel to the current operation, because a consumer has no way of knowing whether it's safe to do so. Instead, when spinning off concurrent operations, it's the COMPOSITION ROOT's job to create a new object graph for each concurrent operation.
- CONSTRUCTOR INJECTION is the act of statically defining the list of required DEPENDENCIES by specifying them as parameters to the class's constructor.
- A constructor that's used for CONSTRUCTOR INJECTION should do no more than apply Guard Clauses and store the receiving DEPENDENCIES. Other logic should be kept out of the constructor. This makes building object graphs fast and reliable.
- CONSTRUCTOR INJECTION should be your default choice for DI, because it's the most reliable and the easiest to apply correctly.
- CONSTRUCTOR INJECTION is well suited when a DEPENDENCY is required. It's important to note, however, that DEPENDENCIES should hardly ever be optional.

Optional DEPENDENCIES complicate the component with null checks. Inside the COMPOSITION ROOT, a Null Object implementation should instead be injected when there's no reasonable implementation available.

- Application components should only have a single constructor. Overloaded constructors lead to ambiguity. For reusable class libraries, like the BCL, having multiple constructors often makes sense; for application components, it doesn't.

- METHOD INJECTION is the act of passing DEPENDENCIES on method invocations.

- Where either a DEPENDENCY or a DEPENDENCY's consumer can differ for each operation, you can apply METHOD INJECTION. This can be useful for add-in scenarios where some runtime context needs to be passed along to the add-in's public API, or when a data-centric object requires a DEPENDENCY for a certain operation, as will often be the case with domain ENTITIES.

- METHOD INJECTION is unsuited for use inside the COMPOSITION ROOT because it leads to TEMPORAL COUPLING.

- A method that accepts a DEPENDENCY through METHOD INJECTION shouldn't store that DEPENDENCY. This leads to TEMPORAL COUPLING, CAPTIVE DEPENDENCIES, or hidden side effects. DEPENDENCIES should only be stored with CONSTRUCTOR INJECTION and PROPERTY INJECTION.

- A LOCAL DEFAULT is a default implementation of a DEPENDENCY that originates in the same module or layer.

- PROPERTY INJECTION allows class libraries to be open for extension, because it lets callers change the library's default behavior.

- PROPERTY INJECTION may look simple, but when properly implemented, it tends to be more complex compared to CONSTRUCTOR INJECTION.

- Beyond optional DEPENDENCIES within reusable libraries, the applicability of PROPERTY INJECTION is limited, and CONSTRUCTOR INJECTION is usually a better fit. CONSTRUCTOR INJECTION simplifies the class, allows the COMPOSITION ROOT to be in control over the value that all consumers get, and prevents TEMPORAL COUPLING.

DI anti-patterns

In this chapter

- Creating tightly coupled code with CONTROL FREAK

- Requesting a class's DEPENDENCIES with a
  SERVICE LOCATOR

- Making a VOLATILE DEPENDENCY globally available
  with AMBIENT CONTEXT

- Forcing a particular constructor signature with
  CONSTRAINED CONSTRUCTION

Many dishes require food to be cooked in a pan with oil. If you're not experienced with the recipe at hand, you might start heating the oil, and then turn your back to read the recipe. But once you're done cutting the vegetables, the oil is smoking. You might think that the smoking oil means the pan is hot and ready for cooking. This is a common misconception with inexperienced cooks. When oils start to smoke, they also start to break down. This is called their *smoke point.* Not only do most oils taste awful once heated past their smoke point, they form harmful compounds and lose beneficial antioxidants.

In the previous chapter, we briefly compared design patterns to recipes. A pattern provides a common language we can use to succinctly discuss a complex concept.

When the concept (or rather, the implementation) becomes warped, we have an anti-pattern on our hands.

> **DEFINITION** An *anti-pattern* is a commonly occurring solution to a problem, which generates decidedly negative consequences, although other documented solutions that prove to be more effective are available.[1]

Heating oil past its smoke point is a typical example of what can be considered to be a cooking anti-pattern. It's a commonly occurring mistake. Many inexperienced cooks do this because it seems a reasonable thing to do, but loss of taste and unhealthful foods are negative consequences.

Anti-patterns are, more or less, a formalized way of describing common mistakes that people make again and again. In this chapter, we'll describe some common anti-patterns related to DI. During our career, we've seen all of them in use in one form or other, and we've been guilty of applying all of them ourselves.

In many cases, anti-patterns represent sincere attempts at implementing DI in an application. But because of not fully complying with DI fundamentals, the implementations can morph into solutions that do more harm than good. Learning about these anti-patterns can give you an idea about what traps to be aware of as you venture into your first DI projects. But even if you've been applying DI for years, it's still easy to make mistakes.

> **WARNING** This chapter is different from the other chapters because most of the code we'll show you gives examples of how *not* to implement DI. Don't try this at home!

Anti-patterns can be fixed by refactoring the code toward one of the DI patterns introduced in chapter 4. Exactly how difficult it is to fix each occurrence depends on the details of the implementation. For each anti-pattern, we'll supply some generalized guidance on how to refactor it toward a better pattern.

> **NOTE** Because it isn't the main topic of this book, our coverage of refactoring from a DI anti-pattern to a DI pattern is constrained by the space of this chapter. If you're interested in learning more about how you can move an existing application in the direction of DI, an entire book discusses refactoring such applications: *Working Effectively with Legacy Code* (Michael C. Feathers, Prentice Hall, 2004). Although it doesn't deal exclusively with DI, it covers many of the same concepts we do here.

Legacy code sometimes requires drastic measures to make your code TESTABLE. This often means taking small steps to prevent accidentally breaking a previously working application. In some cases, an anti-pattern might be the most appropriate temporary solution. Even though the application of an anti-pattern might be an improvement

---

[1] William J. Brown et al., *AntiPatterns: Refactoring Software, Architectures, and Projects in Crisis* (Wiley Computer Publishing, 1998), 7.

over the original code, it's important to note that this doesn't make it any less an anti-pattern; other documented and repeatable solutions exist that are proven to be more effective. The anti-patterns covered in this chapter are listed in table 5.1.

Table 5.1   DI anti-patterns

Anti-pattern	Description
CONTROL FREAK	As opposed to INVERSION OF CONTROL, DEPENDENCIES are controlled directly.
SERVICE LOCATOR	An implicit service can serve DEPENDENCIES to consumers, but it isn't guaranteed to do so.
AMBIENT CONTEXT	Makes a single DEPENDENCY available through a static accessor.
CONSTRAINED CONSTRUCTION	Constructors are assumed to have a particular signature.

The rest of this chapter describes each anti-pattern in greater detail, presenting them in order of importance. You can read from start to finish or only read the ones you're interested in—each has a self-contained section. If you decide to read only part of this chapter, we recommend that you read CONTROL FREAK and SERVICE LOCATOR.

Just as CONSTRUCTOR INJECTION is the most important DI pattern, CONTROL FREAK is the most frequently occurring of the anti-patterns. It effectively prevents you from applying any kind of proper DI, so we'll need to focus on this anti-pattern before we address the others—and so should you. But because SERVICE LOCATOR looks like it's solving a problem, it's the most dangerous. We'll address that in section 5.2.

5.1 CONTROL FREAK

What's the opposite of INVERSION OF CONTROL? Originally the term INVERSION OF CONTROL was coined to identify the opposite of the normal state of affairs, but we can't talk about the "Business as Usual" anti-pattern. Instead, CONTROL FREAK describes a class that won't relinquish control of its VOLATILE DEPENDENCIES.

> **DEFINITION** The CONTROL FREAK anti-pattern occurs every time you depend on a VOLATILE DEPENDENCY in any place other than a COMPOSITION ROOT. It's a violation of the DEPENDENCY INVERSION PRINCIPLE that we discussed in section 3.1.2.

As an example, the CONTROL FREAK anti-pattern happens when you create a new instance of a VOLATILE DEPENDENCY by using the new keyword. The following listing demonstrates an implementation of the CONTROL FREAK anti-pattern.

BAD CODE

Listing 5.1 A CONTROL FREAK anti-pattern example

```
public class HomeController : Controller
{
    public ViewResult Index()
    {
        var service = new ProductService();

        var products = service.GetFeaturedProducts();
        return this.View(products);
    }
}
```

HomeController creates a new instance of the VOLATILE DEPENDENCY, ProductService, causing tightly coupled code.

Every time you create a VOLATILE DEPENDENCY, you explicitly state that you're going to control the lifetime of the instance and that no one else will get a chance to INTERCEPT that particular object. Although the new keyword is a code smell when it comes to VOLATILE DEPENDENCIES, you don't need to worry about using it for STABLE DEPENDENCIES.[2]

> **NOTE** In general, the new keyword isn't suddenly "illegal," but you should refrain from using it to get instances of VOLATILE DEPENDENCIES outside the COMPOSITION ROOT. Also, be aware of static classes. Static classes can also be VOLATILE DEPENDENCIES. Although you'll never use the new keyword on a static class, depending on them causes the same problems.

The most blatant example of CONTROL FREAK is when you make no effort to introduce ABSTRACTIONS in your code. You saw several examples of that in chapter 2 when Mary implemented her e-commerce application (section 2.1). Such an approach makes no attempt to introduce DI. But even where developers have heard about DI and composability, the CONTROL FREAK anti-pattern can often be found in some variation.

---

[2] *Code smells* are certain structures in code that indicate design problems with the code and impact its quality.

In the next sections, we'll show you some examples that resemble code we've seen used in production. In every case, the developers had the best intentions of programming to interfaces, but never understood the underlying forces and motivations.

5.1.1 Example: CONTROL FREAK through newing up DEPENDENCIES

Many developers have heard about the principle of programming to interfaces but don't understand the deeper rationale behind it. In an attempt to do the right thing or to follow best practices, they write code that doesn't make much sense. For example, in listing 3.9, you saw an example of a `ProductService` that uses an instance of the `IProduct-Repository` interface to retrieve a list of featured products. As a reminder, the following repeats the relevant code:

```
public IEnumerable<DiscountedProduct> GetFeaturedProducts()
{
    return
        from product in this.repository.GetFeaturedProducts()
        select product.ApplyDiscountFor(this.userContext);
}
```

The salient point is that the `repository` member variable represents an ABSTRACTION. In chapter 3, you saw how the `repository` field can be populated via CONSTRUCTOR INJECTION, but we've seen other, more naïve attempts. The following listing shows one such attempt.

BAD
CODE

> Listing 5.2   Newing up a `ProductRepository`

```
private readonly IProductRepository repository;

public ProductService()
{
    this.repository = new SqlProductRepository();
}
```

An example of the CONTROL FREAK anti-pattern, this directly creates a new instance in the constructor, causing tightly coupled code.

The `repository` field is declared as the `IProductRepository` interface, so any member in the `ProductService` class (such as `GetFeaturedProducts`) programs to an interface. Although this sounds like the right thing to do, not much is gained from doing so because, at runtime, the type will always be a `SqlProductRepository`. There's no way you can INTERCEPT or change the `repository` variable unless you change the code and recompile. Additionally, you don't gain much by defining a variable as an ABSTRACTION if you hard-code it to always have a specific concrete type. Directly newing up DEPENDENCIES is one example of the CONTROL FREAK anti-pattern.

Before we get to the analysis and possible ways to address the resulting issues generated by a CONTROL FREAK, let's look at some more examples to give you a better idea of the context and common failed attempts. In the next example, it's apparent that the solution isn't optimal. Most developers will attempt to refine their approach.

5.1.2 Example: CONTROL FREAK *through factories*

The most common and erroneous attempt to fix the evident problems from newing up DEPENDENCIES involves a factory of some sort. When it comes to factories, there are several options. We'll quickly cover each of the following:

- Concrete Factory
- Abstract Factory
- Static Factory

If told that she could only deal with the IProductRepository ABSTRACTION, Mary Rowan (from chapter 2) would introduce a ProductRepositoryFactory that would produce the instances she needs to get. Let's listen in as she discusses this approach with her colleague Jens. We predict that their discussion will, conveniently, cover the factory options we've listed.

> MARY: *We need an instance of* IProductRepository *in this* ProductService *class. But* IProductRepository *is an interface, so we can't just create new instances of it, and our consultant says that we shouldn't create new instances of* SqlProductRepository *either.*
>
> JENS: *What about some sort of factory?*
>
> MARY: *Yes, I was thinking the same thing, but I'm not sure how to proceed. I don't understand how it solves our problem. Look here—*

Mary starts to write some code to demonstrate her problem. This is the code that Mary writes:

```
public class ProductRepositoryFactory
{
    public IProductRepository Create()
    {
        return new SqlProductRepository();
    }
}
```

CONCRETE FACTORY

> MARY: *This* ProductRepositoryFactory *encapsulates knowledge about how to create* ProductRepository *instances, but it doesn't solve the problem, because we'd have to use it in the* ProductService *like this:*
>
> ```
> var factory = new ProductRepositoryFactory();
> this.repository = factory.Create();
> ```
>
> *See? Now we need to create a new instance of the* ProductRepositoryFactory *class in the* ProductService, *but that still hard-codes the use of* SqlProductRepository. *The only thing we've achieved is moving the problem into another class.*
>
> JENS: *Yes, I see—couldn't we solve the problem with an Abstract Factory instead?*

Let's pause Mary and Jens' discussion to evaluate what happened. Mary is entirely correct that a Concrete Factory class doesn't solve the CONTROL FREAK issue but only moves it around. It makes the code more complex without adding any value. `Product-Service` now directly controls the lifetime of the factory, and the factory directly controls the lifetime of `ProductRepository`, so you still can't INTERCEPT or replace the Repository instance at runtime.

> **NOTE** Don't conclude from this section that we generally oppose the use of Concrete Factory classes. A Concrete Factory can solve other problems, such as code repetition, by encapsulating complex creation logic. It, however, doesn't provide any value with regards to DI. Use it when it makes sense.

It's fairly evident that a Concrete Factory won't solve any DI problems, and we've never seen it used successfully in this fashion. Jens' comment about Abstract Factory sounds more promising.

ABSTRACT FACTORY

Let's resume Mary and Jens' discussion and hear what Jens has to say about Abstract Factory.

JENS: *What if we made the factory abstract, like this?*

```
public interface IProductRepositoryFactory
{
    IProductRepository Create();
}
```

This means we haven't hard-coded any references to `SqlProductRepository`*, and we can use the factory in the* `ProductService` *to get instances of* `IProductRepository`*.*

MARY: *But now that the factory is abstract, how do we get a new instance of it?*

JENS: *We can create an implementation of it that returns* `SqlProductService` *instances.*

MARY: *Yes, but how do we create an instance of that?*

JENS: *We just new it up in the* `ProductService` *… Oh. Wait—*

MARY: *That would put us back where we started.*

Mary and Jens quickly realize that an Abstract Factory doesn't change their situation. Their original conundrum was that they needed an instance of the abstract `IProductRepository`, and now they need an instance of the abstract `IProductRepositoryFactory` instead.

Abstract Factories are commonly overused

Abstract Factory is one of the patterns from the original design patterns book.[3] The Abstract Factory pattern is more common than you may realize. The names of the classes involved often hide this fact (for instance, by not ending in *Factory*).

When it comes to DI, however, Abstract Factories are often overused. In chapter 6, we'll return to the Abstract Factory pattern and see why it's more often than not a code smell.

---

[3] Erich Gamma et al., *Design Patterns: Elements of Reusable Object-Oriented Software* (Addison-Wesley, 1994), 87.

Now that Mary and Jens have rejected the Abstract Factory as a viable option, one damaging option is still open. Mary and Jens are about to reach a conclusion.

STATIC FACTORY

Let's listen as Mary and Jens decide on an approach that they think will work.

MARY: *Let's make a Static Factory. Let me show you:*

```
public static class ProductRepositoryFactory
{
    public static IProductRepository Create()
    {
        return new SqlProductRepository();
    }
}
```

Now that the class is static, we don't need to deal with how to create it.

JENS: *But we've still hard-coded that we return SqlProductRepository instances, so does it help us in any way?*

MARY: *We could deal with this via a configuration setting that determines which type of ProductRepository to create. Like this:*

```
public static IProductRepository Create()
{
    IConfigurationRoot configuration = new ConfigurationBuilder()
        .SetBasePath(Directory.GetCurrentDirectory())
        .AddJsonFile("appsettings.json")
        .Build();

    string repositoryType = configuration["productRepository"];

    switch (repositoryType)
    {
        case "sql": return new SqlProductRepository();
        case "azure": return AzureProductRepository();
        default: throw new InvalidOperationException("...");
    }
}
```

See? This way we can determine whether we should use the SQL Server–based implementation or the Microsoft Azure–based implementation, and we don't even need to recompile the application to change from one to the other.

JENS: *Cool! That's what we'll do. That consultant must be happy now!*

NOTE Mary and Jens' static ProductRepositoryFactory reads from the configuration file at runtime, but recall from section 2.3.3 that this is problematic: Only the finished application should rely on configuration files. Other parts of the application, such as the ProductRepositoryFactory, shouldn't request values from a configuration file but, instead, should be configurable by their callers.

There are several reasons why such a Static Factory doesn't provide a satisfactory solution to the original goal of programming to interfaces. Take a look at the DEPENDENCY graph in figure 5.1.

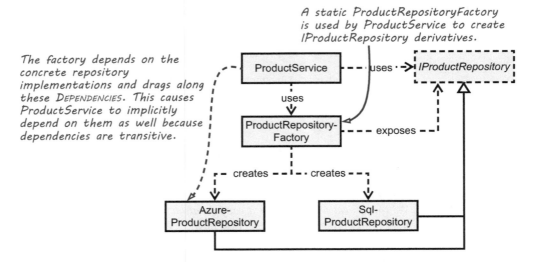

A static ProductRepositoryFactory is used by ProductService to create IProductRepository derivatives.

The factory depends on the concrete repository implementations and drags along these DEPENDENCIES. This causes ProductService to implicitly depend on them as well because dependencies are transitive.

Figure 5.1   DEPENDENCY graph for the proposed `ProductRepositoryFactory` solution

All classes need to reference the abstract `IProductRepository` as follows:

- `ProductService` because it consumes `IProductRepository` instances
- `ProductRepositoryFactory` because it creates `IProductRepository` instances
- `AzureProductRepository` and `SqlProductRepository` because they implement `IProductRepository`

`ProductRepositoryFactory` depends on both the `AzureProductRepository` and `SqlProductRepository` classes. Because `ProductService` directly depends on `ProductRepositoryFactory`, it also depends on both concrete `IProductRepository` implementations—recall from section 4.1.4 that dependencies are transitive.

> ### We're not making this up
>
> If we were the consultants in this example, we wouldn't be at all happy. In fact, such a solution was suggested on a project Mark was involved with, and Steven has experienced similar designs multiple times in the past. The project Mark was involved with was a pretty big project that targeted a central business area of a Fortune 500 company. Due to the complexity of the application, proper modularization was important. Unfortunately, Mark became involved with the project too late, and his suggestions were dismissed because they involved dramatic changes to the already-developed code base.
>
> Mark moved on to other projects, but later learned that although the team managed to deliver enough to fulfill the contract, the project was considered a failure and heads rolled. It'd be unreasonable to claim that the project failed only because DI wasn't employed, but the approach taken was symptomatic of a lack of proper design.

As long as `ProductService` has a dependency on the static `ProductRepositoryFactory`, you have unsolvable design issues. If you define the static `ProductRepositoryFactory` in the domain layer, it means that the domain layer needs to depend on the data access layer, because `ProductRepositoryFactory` creates a `SqlProductRepository` that's located in that layer. The data access layer, however, already depends on the domain layer because `SqlProductRepository` uses types and ABSTRACTIONS like `Product` and `IProductRepository` from that layer. This causes a circular reference between the two projects. Additionally, if you move `ProductRepositoryFactory` into the data access layer, you still need a dependency from the domain layer to the data access layer because `ProductService` depends on `ProductRepositoryFactory`. This still causes a circular dependency. Figure 5.2 shows this design issue.

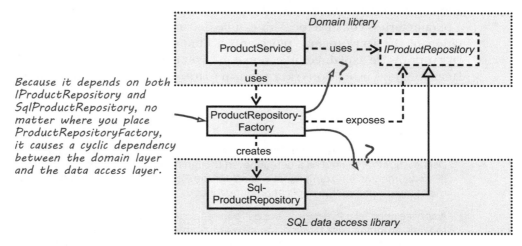

Figure 5.2 Cyclic dependency between the domain and the data access layers that's caused by the static `ProductRepositoryFactory`

No matter how you move your types around, the only way to prevent these circular dependencies between projects is by creating a single project for all types. This isn't a viable option, however, because it tightly couples the domain layer to the data access layer and disallows your data access layer from being replaced.

Instead of loosely coupled `IProductRepository` implementations, Mary and Jens end up with tightly coupled modules. Even worse, the factory always drags along all implementations—even those that aren't needed! If they host on Azure, they still need to distribute Commerce.SqlDataAccess.dll (for example) with their application.

If Mary and Jens ever need a third type of `IProductRepository`, they'll have to change the factory and recompile their solution. Although their solution may be configurable, it isn't extensible; if a separate team, or even company, needs to create a new Repository, they'll have no options without access to the source code. It's also impossible to replace the concrete `IProductRepository` implementations with test-specific implementations, because that requires defining the `IProductRepository` instance at runtime, instead of statically in a configuration file at design time.

In short, a Static Factory may seem to solve the problem but, in reality, only compounds it. Even in the best cases, it forces you to reference VOLATILE DEPENDENCIES. Another variation of this anti-pattern can be seen when overloaded constructors are used in combination with FOREIGN DEFAULTS, as you'll see in the next example.

5.1.3 Example: CONTROL FREAK through overloaded constructors

Constructor overloads are fairly common in many .NET code bases (including the BCL). Often, the many overloads provide reasonable defaults to one or two full-blown constructors that take all relevant parameters as input. (This practice is called *Constructor Chaining*.) At times, we see other uses when it comes to DI.

An all-too-common anti-pattern defines a test-specific constructor overload that allows you to explicitly define a DEPENDENCY, although the production code uses a parameterless constructor. This can be detrimental when the default implementation of the DEPENDENCY represents a FOREIGN DEFAULT rather than a LOCAL DEFAULT. As we explained in section 4.4.2, you typically want to supply all VOLATILE DEPENDENCIES using CONSTRUCTOR INJECTION — even those that could be a LOCAL DEFAULT.

FOREIGN DEFAULT

A FOREIGN DEFAULT is the opposite of a LOCAL DEFAULT. It's an implementation of a VOLATILE DEPENDENCY that's used as a default, even though it's defined in a different module than its consumer. As an example, let's consider the Repository implementations you saw in the sample e-commerce application throughout the previous chapters.

A service such as a `ProductService` requires an instance of an `IProductRepository` to work. In many cases, when you develop such applications, you have a reasonable implementation in mind: one that implements the desired functionality by reading and writing data to and from a relational database. It would be tempting to use such an implementation as the default. The problem is that the default implementation you have in mind (`SqlProductRepository`) is defined in a different module. This forces you to take an undesirable dependency on the data access layer.

Dragging along unwanted modules robs you of many of the benefits of loose coupling, which were discussed in chapter 1. It becomes harder to reuse the domain layer module because it drags along the data access module, although you may want to use that in a different context. It also makes parallel development more difficult because the `ProductService` class now depends directly on the `SqlProduct-Repository` class.

The following listing shows the `ProductService` class with a default and an overloaded constructor. It's an example of what *not* to do.

BAD CODE

> **Listing 5.3   ProductService with multiple constructors**

```
private readonly IProductRepository repository;

public ProductService()
    : this(new SqlProductRepository())
{
}

public ProductService(IProductRepository repository)
{
    if (repository == null)
        throw new ArgumentNullException("repository");

    this.repository = repository;
}
```

Parameterless constructor forwards the SqlProductRepository FOREIGN DEFAULT to the overloaded constructor. This causes the domain layer to be coupled to the SQL data access layer.

Injection constructor accepts a required IProductRepository and stores it in the repository field

At first sight, this coding style might seem like the best of both worlds. It allows fake DEPENDENCIES to be supplied for the sake of unit testing; whereas, the class can still be conveniently created without having to supply its DEPENDENCIES. The following example shows this style:

```
var productService = new ProductService();
```

By letting ProductService create the SqlProductRepository VOLATILE DEPENDENCY, you again force strong coupling between modules. Although ProductService can be reused with different IProductRepository implementations, by supplying them via the most flexible constructor overload while testing, it disables the ability to INTERCEPT the IProductRepository instance in the application.

Now that you've seen a few of examples of CONTROL FREAK, we hope you have a better idea what to look for—occurrences of the new keyword next to VOLATILE DEPENDENCIES. This may enable you to avoid the most obvious traps. But if you need to untangle yourself from an existing occurrence of this anti-pattern, the next section will help you deal with such a task.

5.1.4   Analysis of CONTROL FREAK

CONTROL FREAK is the antithesis of INVERSION OF CONTROL. When you directly control the creation of VOLATILE DEPENDENCIES, you end up with tightly coupled code, missing many (if not all) of the benefits of loose coupling outlined in chapter 1.

CONTROL FREAK is the most common DI anti-pattern. It represents the default way of creating instances in most programming languages, so it can be observed even in applications where developers have never considered DI. It's such a natural and deeply rooted way to create new objects that many developers find it difficult to discard. Even when they begin to think about DI, they have a hard time shaking the mindset that they must somehow control when and where instances are created. Letting go of that control can be a difficult mental leap to make; but, even if you make it, there are other, although lesser, pitfalls to avoid.

THE NEGATIVE EFFECTS OF THE CONTROL FREAK ANTI-PATTERN

With the tightly coupled code that's the result of CONTROL FREAK, many benefits of modular design are potentially lost. These were covered in each of the previous sections, but to summarize:

- *Although you can configure an application to use one of multiple preconfigured DEPENDENCIES, you can't replace them at will.* It isn't possible to provide an implementation that was created after the application was compiled, and it certainly isn't possible to provide specific instances as an implementation.
- *It becomes harder to reuse the consuming module because it drags with it DEPENDENCIES that may be undesirable in the new context.* As an example of this, consider a module that, through the use of a FOREIGN DEFAULT, depends on ASP.NET Core libraries. This makes it harder to reuse that module as part of an application that should't or can't depend on ASP.NET Core (for example, a Windows Service or mobile phone application).
- *It makes parallel development more difficult.* This is because the consuming application is tightly coupled to all implementations of its DEPENDENCIES.
- *TESTABILITY suffers.* Test Doubles can't be used as substitutes for the DEPENDENCY.

With careful design, you can still implement tightly coupled applications with clearly defined responsibilities so that maintainability doesn't suffer. But even so, the cost is too high, and you'll retain many limitations. Given the amount of effort required to accomplish that, there's no reason to continue investing in CONTROL FREAK. You need to move away from CONTROL FREAK and toward proper DI.

REFACTORING FROM CONTROL FREAK TOWARD DI

To get rid of CONTROL FREAK, you need to refactor your code toward one of the proper DI design patterns presented in chapter 4. As an initial step, you should use the guidance given in figure 4.9 to determine which pattern to aim for. In most cases, this will be CONSTRUCTOR INJECTION. The refactoring steps are as follows:

1. Ensure that you're programming to an ABSTRACTION. In the examples, this was already the case; but in other situations, you may need to first extract an interface and change variable declarations.
2. If you create a particular implementation of a DEPENDENCY in multiple places, move them all to a single creation method. Make sure this method's return value is expressed as the ABSTRACTION and not the concrete type.

3 Now that you have only a single place where you create the instance, move this creation out of the consuming class by implementing one of the DI patterns, such as CONSTRUCTOR INJECTION.

In the case of the `ProductService` examples in the previous sections, CONSTRUCTOR INJECTION is an excellent solution.

GOOD
CODE

> Listing 5.4 Refactoring away from CONTROL FREAK using CONSTRUCTOR INJECTION

```
public class ProductService : IProductService
{
    private readonly IProductRepository repository;

    public ProductService(IProductRepository repository)
    {
        if (repository == null)
            throw new ArgumentNullException("repository");

        this.repository = repository;
    }
}
```

CONTROL FREAK is by far the most damaging anti-pattern, but even when you have it under control, more subtle issues can arise. The next sections look at more anti-patterns. Although they're less problematic than CONTROL FREAK, they also tend to be easier to resolve, so be on the lookout, and fix them as they're discovered.

5.2   SERVICE LOCATOR

It can be difficult to give up on the idea of directly controlling DEPENDENCIES, so many developers take Static Factories (such as the one described in section 5.1.2) to new levels. This leads to the SERVICE LOCATOR anti-pattern.

> **DEFINITION** A SERVICE LOCATOR supplies application components outside the COMPOSITION ROOT with access to an unbounded set of VOLATILE DEPENDENCIES.

As it's most commonly implemented, the SERVICE LOCATOR is a Static Factory that can be configured with concrete services before the first consumer begins to use it. (But you'll equally also find abstract SERVICE LOCATORS.) This could conceivably happen in the COMPOSITION ROOT. Depending on the particular implementation, the SERVICE LOCATOR can be configured with code by reading a configuration file or by using a combination thereof. The following listing shows the SERVICE LOCATOR anti-pattern in action.

BAD
CODE

Listing 5.5   Using the SERVICE LOCATOR anti-pattern

```
public class HomeController : Controller
{
    public HomeController() { }          HomeController has a
                                         parameterless constructor.

    public ViewResult Index()
    {                                    HomeController requests an
        IProductService service =        IProductService instance from
            Locator.GetService<IProductService>();   the static Locator class.

        var products = service.GetFeaturedProducts();   Uses the requested
                                                        IProductService, as
        return this.View(products);                     usual
    }
}
```

Instead of statically defining the list of required DEPENDENCIES, HomeController has a parameterless constructor, requesting its DEPENDENCIES later. This hides these DEPENDENCIES from HomeController's consumers and makes HomeController harder to use and test. Figure 5.3 shows the interaction in listing 5.5, where you can see the relationship between the SERVICE LOCATOR and the ProductService implementation.

Years ago, it was quite controversial to call SERVICE LOCATOR an anti-pattern. The controversy is over: SERVICE LOCATOR is an anti-pattern. But don't be surprised to find code bases that have this anti-pattern sprinkled all over the place.

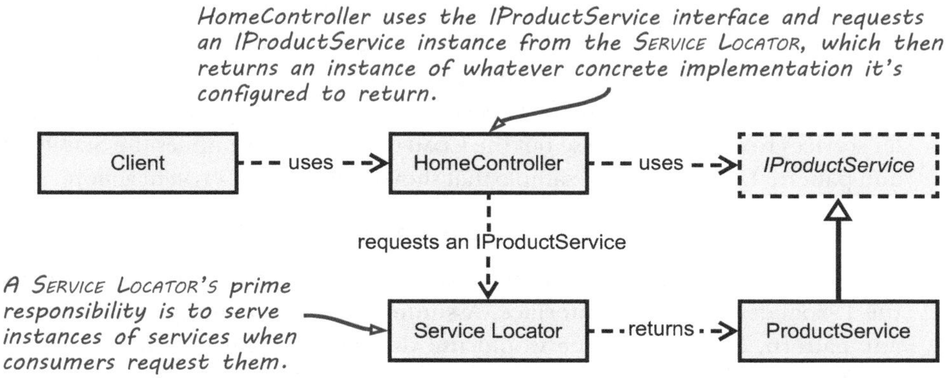

HomeController uses the IProductService interface and requests
an IProductService instance from the SERVICE LOCATOR, which then
returns an instance of whatever concrete implementation it's
configured to return.

A SERVICE LOCATOR'S prime
responsibility is to serve
instances of services when
consumers request them.

Figure 5.3 Interaction between `HomeController` and SERVICE LOCATOR

Our personal history with SERVICE LOCATOR

SERVICE LOCATOR and I (Mark) had an intense relationship for a couple of years before we parted ways. Although I can't remember exactly when I first came across a well-known article that described SERVICE LOCATOR as a pattern,[4] it provided me with a potential solution to a problem that I'd been pondering for some time: how to inject DEPENDENCIES. As described, the SERVICE LOCATOR pattern seemed like the answer to all my issues, and I quickly set forth to develop a reusable library based on the pattern, which I conveniently named "Service Locator."

In 2007, I released a complete rewrite of the library, targeting Enterprise Library 2.[5] Not long after that, I abandoned the library because I realized that it was an anti-pattern. Steven's story is quite similar to mine.

In 2009, the Common Service Locator (CSL) open source project was released.[6] CSL is a reusable library that implements the SERVICE LOCATOR pattern, similar to Mark's Service Locator library. It's an ABSTRACTION over the resolve API of DI CONTAINERS, which allows other reusable libraries to resolve DEPENDENCIES without having to take a hard dependency on a particular DI CONTAINER. Application developers are then able to plug in their own DI CONTAINER.

Inspired by the CSL, I (Steven) started to develop my own DI CONTAINER, a simple CSL implementation. Because of being a CSL implementation, I conveniently called my library "Simple Service Locator." Like Mark, it didn't take long for me to realize that SERVICE LOCATOR is an anti-pattern that neither application developers nor reusable libraries should use. I therefore removed the dependency on CSL and renamed the DI CONTAINER "Simple Injector" (https://simpleinjector.org).

---

[4] Martin Fowler, "Inversion of Control Containers and the Dependency Injection pattern," 2004, https://martinfowler.com/articles/injection.html.

[5] https://blogs.msdn.microsoft.com/ploeh/2007/03/15/service-locator-2-released/.

[6] https://github.com/unitycontainer/commonservicelocator.

It's important to note that if you look at only the static structure of classes, a DI CONTAINER looks like a SERVICE LOCATOR. The difference is subtle and lies not in the mechanics of implementation, but in how you use it. In essence, asking a container or locator to resolve a complete object graph from the COMPOSITION ROOT is proper usage. Asking it for granular services from anywhere else but the COMPOSITION ROOT implies the SERVICE LOCATOR anti-pattern. Let's review an example that shows SERVICE LOCATOR in action.

5.2.1   Example: `ProductService` using a SERVICE LOCATOR

Let's return to our tried-and-tested `ProductService`, which requires an instance of the `IProductRepository` interface. Assuming we were to apply the SERVICE LOCATOR anti-pattern, `ProductService` would use the static `GetService` method, as shown in the following listing.

BAD
CODE

Listing 5.6   Using a SERVICE LOCATOR inside a constructor

```
public class ProductService : IProductService
{
    private readonly IProductRepository repository;

    public ProductService()
    {
        this.repository = Locator.GetService<IProductRepository>();
    }

    public IEnumerable<DiscountedProduct> GetFeaturedProducts() { ... }
}
```

In this example, we implement the `GetService` method using generic type parameters to indicate the type of service being requested. You could also use a `Type` argument to indicate the type, if that's more to your liking.

As the following listing shows, this implementation of the `Locator` class is as short as possible. We could have added Guard Clauses and error handling, but we wanted to highlight the core behavior. The code could also include a feature that enables it to load its configuration from a file, but we'll leave that as an exercise for you.

Listing 5.7   A simple SERVICE LOCATOR implementation

```
public static class Locator
{
    private static Dictionary<Type, object> services =      ◀──  The static Locator class
        new Dictionary<Type, object>();                           holds all the configured
                                                                  services in an internal
    public static void Register<T>(T service)                     dictionary that maps
    {                                                             the abstract types to
        services[typeof(T)] = service;                            each concrete instance.
    }
```

```
public static T GetService<T>()
{
    return (T)services[typeof(T)];
}

public static void Reset()
{
    services.Clear();
}
}
```

> The **GetService** method allows resolving an arbitrary ABSTRACTION.

Clients such as `ProductService` can use the `GetService` method to request an instance of the abstract type `T`. Because this example code contains no Guard Clauses or error handling, the method throws a rather cryptic `KeyNotFoundException` if the requested type has no entry in the dictionary. You can imagine how to add code to throw a more descriptive exception.

The `GetService` method can only return an instance of the requested type if it has previously been inserted in the internal dictionary. This can be done with the `Register` method. Again, this example code contains no Guard Clause, so it would be possible to `Register` a `null` value, but a more robust implementation shouldn't allow that. This implementation also caches registered instances forever, but it isn't that hard to come up with an implementation that allows creating new instances on every call to `Get-Service`. In certain cases, particularly when unit testing, it's important to be able to reset the SERVICE LOCATOR. That functionality is provided by the `Reset` method, which clears the internal dictionary.

Classes like `ProductService` rely on the service to be available in the SERVICE LOCATOR, so it's important that it's previously configured. In a unit test, this could be done with a Test Double implemented by a Stub, as can be seen in the following listing.[7]

BAD CODE

> ### Listing 5.8   A unit test depending on a SERVICE LOCATOR

```
[Fact]
public void GetFeaturedProductsWillReturnInstance()
{
    // Arrange
    var stub = ProductRepositoryStub();

    Locator.Reset();

    Locator.Register<IProductRepository>(stub);

    var sut = new ProductService();
```

> Creates a Stub for the **IProductRepository** interface

> Resets the Locator to its default settings to prevent previous tests from influencing this test

> Uses the static **Register** method to configure the SERVICE LOCATOR with the Stub instance

---

[7]   For more on Test Doubles, see Gerard Meszaros' *xUnit Test Patterns: Refactoring Test Code* (Addison-Wesley, 2007), 522.

```
    // Act
    var result = sut.GetFeaturedProducts();
    
    // Assert
    Assert.NotNull(result);
}
```

Executes the required task for the test at hand; GetFeaturedProducts will now use ProductRepositoryStub. The internal use of Locator.GetService causes TEMPORAL COUPLING between Locator.Register and GetFeaturedProducts.

The example shows how the static `Register` method is used to configure the SERVICE LOCATOR with the Stub instance. If this is done before `ProductService` is constructed, as shown in the example, `ProductService` uses the configured Stub to work against `ProductRepository`. In the full production application, the SERVICE LOCATOR will be configured with the correct `ProductRepository` implementation in the COMPOSITION ROOT.

This way of locating DEPENDENCIES from the `ProductService` class definitely works if our only success criterion is that the DEPENDENCY can be used and replaced at will. But it has some serious shortcomings.

5.2.2 *Analysis of SERVICE LOCATOR*

SERVICE LOCATOR is a dangerous pattern because it almost works. You can locate DEPENDENCIES from consuming classes, and you can replace those DEPENDENCIES with different implementations—even with Test Doubles from unit tests. When you apply the analysis model outlined in chapter 1 to evaluate whether SERVICE LOCATOR can match the benefits of modular application design, you'll find that it fits in most regards:

- You can support late binding by changing the registration.
- You can develop code in parallel, because you're programming against interfaces, replacing modules at will.
- You can achieve good separation of concerns, so nothing stops you from writing maintainable code, but doing so becomes more difficult.
- You can replace DEPENDENCIES with Test Doubles, so TESTABILITY is ensured.

There's only one area where SERVICE LOCATOR falls short, and that shouldn't be taken lightly.

NEGATIVE EFFECTS OF THE SERVICE LOCATOR ANTI-PATTERN

The main problem with SERVICE LOCATOR is that it impacts the reusability of the classes consuming it. This manifests itself in two ways:

- The class drags along the SERVICE LOCATOR as a redundant DEPENDENCY.
- The class makes it non-obvious what its DEPENDENCIES are.

Let's first look at the DEPENDENCY graph for the `ProductService` from the example in section 5.2.1, shown in figure 5.4.

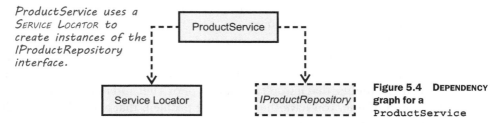

ProductService uses a SERVICE LOCATOR to create instances of the IProductRepository interface.

Figure 5.4 DEPENDENCY graph for a `ProductService`

In addition to the expected reference to `IProductRepository`, `ProductService` also depends on the `Locator` class. This means that to reuse the `ProductService` class, you must redistribute not only it and its relevant DEPENDENCY `IProductRepository`, but also the `Locator` DEPENDENCY, which only exists for mechanical reasons. If the `Locator` class is defined in a different module than `ProductService` and `IProductRepository`, new applications wanting to reuse `ProductService` must accept that module too.

Perhaps we could even tolerate that extra DEPENDENCY on `Locator` if it was truly necessary for DI to work. We'd accept it as a tax to be paid to gain other benefits. But there are better options (such as CONSTRUCTOR INJECTION) available, so this DEPENDENCY is redundant. Moreover, neither this redundant DEPENDENCY nor `IProductRepository`, its relevant counterpart, is explicitly visible to developers wanting to consume the `ProductService` class. Figure 5.5 shows that Visual Studio offers no guidance on the use of this class.

```
var ps = new ProductService (
    ProductService.ProductService ()
```

Figure 5.5 The only thing Visual Studio's IntelliSense can tell us about the `ProductService` class is that it has a parameterless constructor. Its DEPENDENCIES are invisible.

If you want to create a new instance of the `ProductService` class, Visual Studio can only tell you that the class has a parameterless constructor. But if you subsequently attempt to run the code, you get a runtime error if you forgot to register an `IProductRepository` instance with the `Locator` class. This is likely to happen if you don't intimately know the `ProductService` class.

NOTE Imagine that the code you write ships in an undocumented, obfuscated .dll. How easy would it be for someone else to use? It's possible to develop APIs that are close to self documenting, and although doing so takes practice, it's a worthy goal. The problem with SERVICE LOCATOR is that any component using it is being dishonest about its level of complexity. It looks simple as seen through the public API, but it turns out to be complex—and you won't find out until you try to run it.

The `ProductService` class is far from self documenting: you can't tell which DEPENDENCIES must be present before it'll work. In fact, the developers of `ProductService` may even decide to add more DEPENDENCIES in future versions. That would mean that code that works for the current version can fail in a future version, and you aren't going to get a compiler error that warns you. SERVICE LOCATOR makes it easy to inadvertently introduce breaking changes.

The use of generics may trick you into thinking that a SERVICE LOCATOR is strongly typed. But even an API like the one shown in listing 5.7 is weakly typed, because you can request any type. Being able to compile code invoking the `GetService<T>` method gives you no guarantee that it won't throw exceptions left and right at runtime.

When unit testing, you have the additional problem that a Test Double registered in one test case will lead to the Interdependent Tests code smell, because it remains in memory when the next test case is executed. It's therefore necessary to perform Fixture Teardown after every test by invoking `Locator.Reset()`.[8] This is something that you must manually remember to do, and it's easy to forget.

It's not about the mechanics

Although SERVICE LOCATORS come in different forms and shapes, a common signature looks something like this:

```
public T Resolve<T>()
```

It's easy to think that every API with this signature is a SERVICE LOCATOR, but that's not the case. In fact, this is the exact signature that most DI CONTAINERS expose. It's not the static structure of an API that determines it as a SERVICE LOCATOR, but rather the role the API plays in the application.

An important aspect of the SERVICE LOCATOR anti-pattern is that application components query for DEPENDENCIES instead of statically declaring them through their constructor. As explained previously, there are quite a few downsides to doing this. When code that's part of the COMPOSITION ROOT queries for DEPENDENCIES, however, these downsides don't exist.

Because the COMPOSITION ROOT already depends on everything else in the system (as we discussed in section 4.1), it's impossible for it to drag along an extra DEPENDENCY. By definition, it knows about every DEPENDENCY already. And it's impossible for the COMPOSITION ROOT to hide its DEPENDENCIES—from whom does it hide them? Its role is to build object graphs; it doesn't need to expose those DEPENDENCIES.

Querying for DEPENDENCIES, even if through a DI CONTAINER, becomes a SERVICE LOCATOR if used incorrectly. When application code (as opposed to infrastructure code) actively queries a service in order to be provided with required DEPENDENCIES, then it has become a SERVICE LOCATOR.

IMPORTANT A DI CONTAINER encapsulated in a COMPOSITION ROOT isn't a SERVICE LOCATOR—it's an infrastructure component.

---

[8] For more on Fixture Teardown, see Gerard Meszaros' *xUnit Test Patterns*, 100.

A SERVICE LOCATOR may seem innocuous, but it can lead to all sorts of nasty runtime errors. How do you avoid those problems? When you decide to get rid of a SERVICE LOCATOR, you need to find a way to do it. As always, the default approach should be CONSTRUCTOR INJECTION, unless one of the other DI patterns from chapter 4 provides a better fit.

REFACTORING FROM SERVICE LOCATOR TOWARD DI

Because CONSTRUCTOR INJECTION statically declares a class's DEPENDENCIES, it enables the code to fail at compile time, assuming you practice PURE DI. When you use a DI CONTAINER, on the other hand, you lose the ability to verify correctness at compile time. Statically declaring a class's DEPENDENCIES, however, still ensures that you can verify the correctness of your application's object graphs by asking the container to create all object graphs for you. You can do this at application startup or as part of a unit/ integration test.

Some DI CONTAINERS even take this a step further and allow doing more-complex analysis on the DI configuration. This allows detecting all kinds of common pitfalls. A SERVICE LOCATOR, on the other hand, will be completely invisible to a DI CONTAINER, making it impossible for it to do these kinds of verification on your behalf.

In many cases, a class that consumes a SERVICE LOCATOR may have calls to it spread throughout its code base. In such cases, it acts as a replacement for the new statement. When this is so, the first refactoring step is to consolidate the creation of each DEPENDENCY in a single method.

If you don't have a member field to hold an instance of the DEPENDENCY, you can introduce such a field and make sure the rest of the code uses this field when it consumes the DEPENDENCY. Mark the field `readonly` to ensure that it can't be modified outside the constructor. Doing so forces you to assign the field from the constructor using the SERVICE LOCATOR. You can now introduce a constructor parameter that assigns the field instead of the SERVICE LOCATOR, which can then be removed.

> **NOTE** Introducing a DEPENDENCY parameter to a constructor is likely to break existing consumers, so it's best to start with the top-most classes and work your way down the DEPENDENCY graph.

Refactoring a class that uses SERVICE LOCATOR is similar to refactoring a class that uses CONTROL FREAK. Section 5.1.4 contains further notes on refactoring CONTROL FREAK implementations to use DI.

At first glance, SERVICE LOCATOR may look like a proper DI pattern, but don't be fooled: it may explicitly address loose coupling, but it sacrifices other concerns along the way. The DI patterns presented in chapter 4 offer better alternatives with fewer drawbacks. This is true for the SERVICE LOCATOR anti-pattern, as well as the other anti-patterns presented in this chapter. Even though they're different, they all share the common trait that they can be resolved by one of the DI patterns from chapter 4.

5.3   AMBIENT CONTEXT

Related to SERVICE LOCATOR is the AMBIENT CONTEXT anti-pattern. Where a SERVICE LOCATOR allows global access to an unrestricted set of DEPENDENCIES, an AMBIENT CONTEXT makes a single strongly typed DEPENDENCY available through a static accessor.

> **DEFINITION**   An AMBIENT CONTEXT supplies application code outside the COMPOSITION ROOT with global access to a VOLATILE DEPENDENCY or its behavior by the use of static class members.

The following listing shows the AMBIENT CONTEXT anti-pattern in action.

BAD
CODE

Listing 5.9   Using the AMBIENT CONTEXT anti-pattern

```
public string GetWelcomeMessage()
{
    ITimeProvider provider = TimeProvider.Current;
    DateTime now = provider.Now;

    string partOfDay = now.Hour < 6 ? "night" : "day";

    return string.Format("Good {0}.", partOfDay);
}
```

The Current static property represents the AMBIENT CONTEXT, which allows access to an ITimeProvider instance. This hides the ITimeProvider DEPENDENCY and complicates testing.

In this example, `ITimeProvider` presents an ABSTRACTION that allows retrieving the system's current time. Because you might want to influence how time is perceived by the application (for instance, for testing), you don't want to call `DateTime.Now` directly. Instead of letting consumers call `DateTime.Now` directly, a good solution is to hide access to `DateTime.Now` behind an ABSTRACTION. It's all too tempting, however, to allow consumers to access the default implementation through a static property or method. In listing 5.9, the `Current` property allows access to the default `ITimeProvider` implementation.

AMBIENT CONTEXT is similar in structure to the Singleton pattern.[9] Both allow access to a DEPENDENCY by the use of static class members. The difference is that AMBIENT CONTEXT allows its DEPENDENCY to be changed, whereas the Singleton pattern ensures that its singular instance never changes.

> **NOTE**   The Singleton pattern should only be used either from within the COMPOSITION ROOT or when the DEPENDENCY is STABLE. On the other hand, when the Singleton pattern is abused to provide the application with global access to a VOLATILE DEPENDENCY, its effects are identical to those of the AMBIENT CONTEXT, as discussed in section 5.3.3.

The access to the system's current time is a common need. Let's dive a little bit deeper into the `ITimeProvider` example.

---

[9]   Erich Gamma et al., *Design Patterns*, 132.

5.3.1 Example: Accessing time through AMBIENT CONTEXT

There are many reasons one would need to exercise some control over time. Many applications have business logic that depends on time or the progression of it. In the previous example, you saw a simple case where we displayed a welcome message based on the current time. Two other examples include these:

- *Cost calculations based on day of the week.* In some businesses, it's normal for customers to pay more for services during the weekend.
- *Sending notifications to users using different communication channels based on the time of day.* For instance, the business might want email notifications to be sent during working hours, and by text message or pager, otherwise.

Because the need to work with time is such a widespread requirement, developers often feel the urge to simplify access to such a VOLATILE DEPENDENCY by using an AMBIENT CONTEXT. The following listing shows an example `ITimeProvider` ABSTRACTION.

> **Listing 5.10 An `ITimeProvider` ABSTRACTION**

```
public interface ITimeProvider
{
    DateTime Now { get; }          ◄─── Allows consumers to acquire
}                                        the system's current time
```

The following listing shows a simplistic implementation of the `TimeProvider` class for this `ITimeProvider` ABSTRACTION.

BAD CODE

> **Listing 5.11 A `TimeProvider` AMBIENT CONTEXT implementation**

```
                                         A static class that allows global
                                         access to a configured
public static class TimeProvider   ◄──── ITimeProvider implementation
{
    private static ITimeProvider current =
        new DefaultTimeProvider();  ◄──── Initialization of a LOCAL DEFAULT
                                          that uses the real system clock

    public static ITimeProvider Current  ◄──┐ Static property that allows global
    {                                        │ read/write access to the ITimeProvider
        get { return current; }              │ VOLATILE DEPENDENCY
        set { current = value; }
    }

    private class DefaultTimeProvider : ITimeProvider   ◄──┐ Default
    {                                                       │ implementation
        public DateTime Now { get { return DateTime.Now; } }│ that uses the
    }                                                       │ real system
}                                                           │ clock
```

Using the `TimeProvider` implementation, you can unit test the previously defined `GetWelcomeMessage` method. The following listing shows such test.

BAD CODE

Listing 5.12   A unit test depending on an AMBIENT CONTEXT

```
[Fact]
public void SaysGoodDayDuringDayTime()
{
    // Arrange
    DateTime dayTime = DateTime.Parse("2019-01-01 6:00");

    var stub = new TimeProviderStub { Now = dayTime };

    TimeProvider.Current = stub;

    var sut = new WelcomeMessageGenerator();

    // Act
    string actualMessage = sut.GetWelcomeMessage();

    // Assert
    Assert.Equal(expected: "Good day.", actual: actualMessage);
}
```

> Replaces the default implementation with a Stub that always returns the specified dayTime

> WelcomeMessageGenerator's API is dishonest because its constructor hides the fact that ITimeProvider is a required DEPENDENCY.

> There's TEMPORAL COUPLING between TimeProvider.Current and GetWelcomeMessage.

This is one variation of the AMBIENT CONTEXT anti-pattern. Other common variations you might encounter are these:

- *An AMBIENT CONTEXT that allows consumers to make use of the behavior of a globally configured DEPENDENCY.* With the previous example in mind, the `TimeProvider` could supply consumers with a static `GetCurrentTime` method that hides the used DEPENDENCY by calling it internally.
- *An AMBIENT CONTEXT that merges the static accessor with the interface into a single ABSTRACTION.* In respect to the previous example, that would mean that you have a single `TimeProvider` base class that contains both the `Now` instance property and the static `Current` property.
- *An AMBIENT CONTEXT where delegates are used instead of a custom-defined ABSTRACTION.* Instead of having a fairly descriptive `ITimeProvider` interface, you could achieve the same using a `Func<DateTime>` delegate.

AMBIENT CONTEXT can come in many shapes and implementations. Again, the caution regarding AMBIENT CONTEXT is that it provides either direct or indirect access to a VOLATILE DEPENDENCY by means of some static class member. Before doing the analysis and evaluating possible ways to fix the problems caused by AMBIENT CONTEXT, let's look at another common example of AMBIENT CONTEXT.

5.3.2 *Example: Logging through* AMBIENT CONTEXT

Another common case where developers tend to take a shortcut and step into the AMBIENT CONTEXT trap is when it comes to applying logging to their applications. Any real application requires the ability to write information about errors and other uncommon conditions to a file or other source for later analysis. Many developers feel that logging is such a special activity that it deserves "bending the rules." You might find code similar to that shown in the next listing even in the code bases of developers who are quite familiar with DI.

BAD CODE

> **Listing 5.13 AMBIENT CONTEXT when logging**

```
public class MessageGenerator
{
    private static readonly ILog Logger =
        LogManager.GetLogger(typeof(MessageGenerator));

    public string GetWelcomeMessage()
    {
        Logger.Info("GetWelcomeMessage called.");

        return string.Format(
            "Hello. Current time is: {0}.", DateTime.Now);
    }
}
```

Acquires an ILog VOLATILE DEPENDENCY through the static LogManager AMBIENT CONTEXT and stores it in a private static field. This hides the DEPENDENCY and makes it difficult to test MessageGenerator.

Uses the Logger field to log every time the method is called

There are several reasons why AMBIENT CONTEXT is so ubiquitous in many applications when it comes to logging. First, code like listing 5.13 is typically the first example that logging libraries show in their documentation. Developers copy those examples out of ignorance. We can't blame them; developers typically assume that the library designers know and communicate best practices. Unfortunately, this isn't always the case. Documentation examples are typically written for simplicity, not best practice, even if their designers understand those best practices.

Apart from that, developers tend to apply AMBIENT CONTEXT for loggers because they need logging in almost every class in their application. Injecting it in the constructor could easily lead to constructors with too many DEPENDENCIES. This is indeed a code smell called *Constructor Over-injection*, and we'll discuss it in chapter 6.

Jeff Atwood wrote a great blog post back in 2008 about the danger of logging.[10] A few of his arguments follow:

- Logging means more code, which obscures your application code.
- Logging isn't free, and logging a lot means constantly writing to disk.
- The more you log, the less you can find.
- If it's worth saving to a log file, it's worth showing in the user interface.

---

[10] https://blog.codinghorror.com/the-problem-with-logging/.

When working on Stack Overflow, Jeff removed most of the logging, relying exclusively on logging of unhandled exceptions. If it's an error, an exception should be thrown.

We wholeheartedly agree with Jeff's analysis, but would also like to approach this from a design perspective. We've found that with good application design, you'll be able to apply logging across common components, without having it pollute your entire code base. Chapter 10 describes in detail how to design such an application.

> **NOTE** By no means are we stating that you shouldn't log. Logging is a crucial part of any application, as it is in the applications we build. What we're saying, however, is that you should design your application in such way that there's only a handful of classes in your system affected by logging. If most of your application components are responsible for logging, your code becomes harder to maintain.

There are many other examples of AMBIENT CONTEXT, but these two examples are so common and widespread that we've seen them countless times in companies we've consulted with. (We've even been guilty of introducing AMBIENT CONTEXT implementations ourselves in the past.) Now that you've seen the two most common examples of AMBIENT CONTEXT, the next section discusses why it's a problem and how to deal with it.

5.3.3   *Analysis of AMBIENT CONTEXT*

AMBIENT CONTEXT is usually encountered when developers have a CROSS-CUTTING CONCERN as a VOLATILE DEPENDENCY, which is used ubiquitously. This ubiquitous nature makes developers think it justifies moving away from CONSTRUCTOR INJECTION. It allows them to hide DEPENDENCIES and avoids the necessity of adding the DEPENDENCY to many constructors in their application.

NEGATIVE EFFECTS OF THE AMBIENT CONTEXT ANTI-PATTERN

The problems with AMBIENT CONTEXT are related to the problems with SERVICE LOCATOR. Here are the main issues:

- The DEPENDENCY is hidden.
- Testing becomes more difficult.
- It becomes hard to change the DEPENDENCY based on its context.
- There's TEMPORAL COUPLING between the initialization of the DEPENDENCY and its usage.

When you hide a DEPENDENCY by allowing global access to it through AMBIENT CONTEXT, it becomes easier to hide the fact that a class has too many DEPENDENCIES. This is related to the Constructor Over-injection code smell and is typically an indication that you're violating the SINGLE RESPONSIBILITY PRINCIPLE.

When a class has many DEPENDENCIES, it's an indication that it's doing more than it should. It's theoretically possible to have a class with many DEPENDENCIES, while still having just "one reason to change."[11] The larger the class, however, the less likely it is to abide by this guidance. The use of AMBIENT CONTEXT hides the fact that classes might have become too complex, and need to be refactored.

---

[11] Robert C. Martin, *Agile Software Development, Principles, Patterns, and Practices* (Prentice Hall, 2003), 95.

AMBIENT CONTEXT also makes testing more difficult because it presents a global state. When a test changes the global state, as you saw in listing 5.12, it might influence other tests. This is the case when tests run in parallel, but even sequentially executed tests can be affected when a test forgets to revert its changes as part of its teardown. Although these test-related issues can be mitigated, it means building a specially crafted AMBIENT CONTEXT and either global or test-specific teardown logic. This adds complexity, whereas the alternative doesn't.

The use of an AMBIENT CONTEXT makes it hard to provide different consumers with different implementations of the DEPENDENCY. For instance, say you need part of your system to work with a moment in time that's fixed at the start of the current request, whereas other, possibly long-running operations, should get a DEPENDENCY that's live-updated.[12] Providing consumers with different implementations of the DEPENDENCY is exactly what happened in listing 5.13, as repeated here:

```
private static readonly ILog Logger =
    LogManager.GetLogger(typeof(MessageGenerator));
```

To be able to provide consumers with different implementations, the `GetLogger` API requires the consumer to pass along its appropriate type information. This needlessly complicates the consumer.

The use of an AMBIENT CONTEXT causes the usage of its DEPENDENCY coupled on a temporal level. Unless you initialize the AMBIENT CONTEXT in the COMPOSITION ROOT, the application fails when the class starts using the DEPENDENCY for the first time. We rather want our applications to fail fast instead.

I'm using an ABSTRACTION; what can go wrong?

I (Steven) once worked for a client that had an enormous code base that used logging in a fashion similar to listing 5.13. Logging was ever present. Because the developers wanted to prevent a direct dependency on the logging library in question, log4net,[13] they used another third-party library to provide them with an ABSTRACTION over logging libraries. This library was called Common.Logging.[14] What didn't help, though, was that the Common.Logging library mimicked the API of log4net, which hid the fact that their projects often accidentally contained a dependency on both libraries. This caused many classes to still depend on log4net. More importantly, even though the application designers hid the use of log4net behind an ABSTRACTION, there was still a dependency on a third-party library so that now every class depended on the AMBIENT CONTEXT provided by Common.Logging (similar to listing 5.13).

The problem started to surface when we discovered a bug in Common.Logging, which caused a call to the static `GetLogger` method to fail on certain developer machines when run inside of IIS. On those developer machines, it became impossible to start the application, because the first call to `LogManager.GetLogger` would fail. Unfortunately, for me, I was one of the two developers who had this problem.

---

[13] https://logging.apache.org/log4net/.

[14] https://github.com/net-commons/common-logging.

[12] This might seem far-fetched, but we've seen quite a few bugs in systems we've worked on over the years that were caused by requests passing midnight or daylight saving.

Although AMBIENT CONTEXT isn't as destructive as SERVICE LOCATOR, because it only hides a single VOLATILE DEPENDENCY opposed to an arbitrary number of DEPENDENCIES, it has no place in a well-designed code base. There are always better alternatives, which is what we describe in the next section.

REFACTORING FROM AMBIENT CONTEXT TOWARD DI

Don't be surprised to see AMBIENT CONTEXT even in code bases where the developers have a fairly good understanding of DI and the harm that SERVICE LOCATOR brings. It can be hard to convince developers to move away from AMBIENT CONTEXT, because they're so accustomed to using it. On top of that, although refactoring a single class toward DI isn't hard, the underlying problems like ineffective and harmful logging strategies are harder to change. Typically, there's lots of code that logs for reasons that aren't always clear. Finding out whether these logging statements could be removed or should be turned into exceptions instead can often be a slow process when the original developers are long gone. Still, assuming a code base already applies DI, refactoring away from AMBIENT CONTEXT toward DI is straightforward.

A class that consumes an AMBIENT CONTEXT typically contains one or a few calls to it, possibly spread over multiple methods. Because the first refactoring step is to centralize the call to the AMBIENT CONTEXT, the constructor is a good place to do this.

Create a `private readonly` field that can hold a reference to the DEPENDENCY and assign it with the AMBIENT CONTEXT's DEPENDENCY. The rest of the class's code can now use this new private field. The call to the AMBIENT CONTEXT can now be replaced with a constructor parameter that assigns the field and a Guard Clause that ensures the constructor parameter isn't null. This new constructor parameter will likely cause consumers to break. But if DI was applied already, this should only cause changes to the COMPOSITION ROOT and the class's tests. The following listing shows the (unsurprising) result of the refactoring, when applied to the `WelcomeMessageGenerator`.

GOOD
CODE

Listing 5.14 Refactoring away from AMBIENT CONTEXT to CONSTRUCTOR INJECTION

```
public class WelcomeMessageGenerator
{
    private readonly ITimeProvider timeProvider;

    public WelcomeMessageGenerator(ITimeProvider timeProvider)
    {
        if (timeProvider == null)
            throw new ArgumentNullException("timeProvider");

        this.timeProvider = timeProvider;
    }

    public string GetWelcomeMessage()
    {
        DateTime now = this.timeProvider.Now;
        ...
    }
}
```

Refactoring AMBIENT CONTEXT is relatively simple because, for the most part, you'll be doing it in an application that has already applied DI. For applications that don't, it's better to fix CONTROL FREAK and SERVICE LOCATOR problems first before tackling AMBIENT CONTEXT refactorings.

AMBIENT CONTEXT sounds like a great way to access commonly used CROSS-CUTTING CONCERNS, but looks are deceiving. Although less problematic than CONTROL FREAK and SERVICE LOCATOR, AMBIENT CONTEXT is typically a cover-up for larger design problems in the application. The patterns described in chapter 4 provide a better solution, and in chapter 10, we'll show how to design your applications in such way that logging and other CROSS-CUTTING CONCERNS can be applied more easily and transparently across the application.

The last anti-pattern considered in this chapter is CONSTRAINED CONSTRUCTION. This often originates from the desire to attain late binding.

5.4   *CONSTRAINED CONSTRUCTION*

The biggest challenge of properly implementing DI is getting all classes with DEPEN-
DENCIES moved to a COMPOSITION ROOT. When you accomplish this, you've already
come a long way. Even so, there are still some traps to look out for.

   A common mistake is to require DEPENDENCIES to have a constructor with a particular signature. This normally originates from the desire to attain late binding so that
DEPENDENCIES can be defined in an external configuration file and thereby changed
without recompiling the application.

> **DEFINITION**   CONSTRAINED CONSTRUCTION forces all implementations of a cer-
> tain ABSTRACTION to require their constructors to have an identical signature
> with the goal of enabling late binding.

Be aware that this section applies only to scenarios where late binding is desired. In scenarios where you directly reference all DEPENDENCIES from the application's root, you
won't have this problem. But then again, you won't have the ability to replace DEPEN-
DENCIES without recompiling the startup project, either. The following listing shows
the CONSTRAINED CONSTRUCTION anti-pattern in action.

BAD
CODE

> **Listing 5.15   CONSTRAINED CONSTRUCTION anti-pattern example**

```
public class SqlProductRepository : IProductRepository
{
    public SqlProductRepository(string connectionStr)          Forces exact
    {                                                           signatures for
    }                                                           constructors in the
}                                                               implementations of
                                                                IProductRepository
public class AzureProductRepository : IProductRepository
{
    public AzureProductRepository(string connectionStr)
    {
    }
}
```

All implementations of the IProductRepository ABSTRACTION are forced to have a constructor with the same signature. In this example, the constructor should have exactly
one argument of type string. Although it's perfectly fine for a class to have a DEPEN-
DENCY of type string, it's a problem for those implementations to be forced to have an
identical constructor signature. In section 1.2.2, we briefly touched on this issue. This
section examines it more carefully.

5.4.1   *Example: Late binding a ProductRepository*

In the sample e-commerce application, some classes depend on the IProductRepository
interface. This means that to create those classes, you first need to create an IProduct-
Repository implementation. At this point, you've learned that a COMPOSITION ROOT

is the correct place to do this. In an ASP.NET Core application, this typically means `Startup`. The following listing shows the relevant part that creates an instance of an `IProductRepository`.

BAD
CODE

Listing 5.16 Implicitly constraining the `ProductRepository` constructor

```
string connectionString = this.Configuration
    .GetConnectionString("CommerceConnectionString");
```
Reads the connection string from the application's configuration file

```
var settings =
    this.Configuration.GetSection("AppSettings");

string productRepositoryTypeName =
    settings.GetValue<string>("ProductRepositoryType");
```
Reads the name of the repository type to create from the AppSettings section of the configuration file

```
var productRepositoryType =
    Type.GetType(
        typeName: productRepositoryTypeName,
        throwOnError: true);
```
Loads the Type object of the repository type

```
var constructorArguments =
    new object[] { connectionString };

IProductRepository repository =
    (IProductRepository)Activator.CreateInstance(
        productRepositoryType, constructorArguments);
```
Creates an instance of the repository type, while expecting a particular signature. This call will fail for components that require a different constructor signature.

The following code shows the corresponding configuration file:

```
{
  "ConnectionStrings": {
    "CommerceConnectionString":
      "Server=.;Database=MaryCommerce;Trusted_Connection=True;"
  },
  "AppSettings": {
    "ProductRepositoryType": "SqlProductRepository, Commerce.SqlDataAccess"
  },
}
```

The first thing that should trigger suspicion is that a connection string is read from the configuration file. Why do you need a connection string if you plan to treat a Product-Repository as an ABSTRACTION?

Although it's perhaps a bit unlikely, you could choose to implement a Product-Repository with an in-memory database or an XML file. A REST-based storage service, such as the Windows Azure Table Storage Service, offers a more realistic alternative, although, once again this year, the most popular choice seems to be a relational database. The ubiquity of databases makes it all too easy to forget that a connection string implicitly represents an implementation choice.

To late bind an `IProductRepository`, you also need to determine which type has been chosen as the implementation. This can be done by reading an assembly-qualified type name from the configuration and creating a `Type` instance from that name. This in itself isn't problematic. The difficulty arises when you need to create an instance of that type. Given a `Type`, you can create an instance using the `Activator` class. The `CreateInstance` method invokes the type's constructor, so you must supply the correct constructor parameters to prevent an exception from being thrown. In this case, you supply a connection string.

If you didn't know anything else about the application other than the code in listing 5.16, you should by now be wondering why a connection string is passed as a constructor argument to an unknown type. It wouldn't make sense if the implementation was based on a REST-based web service or an XML file.

Indeed, it doesn't make sense because this represents an accidental constraint on the DEPENDENCY's constructor. In this case, you have an implicit requirement that any implementation of `IProductRepository` should have a constructor that takes a single string as input. This is in addition to the explicit constraint that the class must derive from `IProductRepository`.

NOTE The implicit constraint that the constructor should take a single string still leaves you a great degree of flexibility, because you can encode different information in strings to be decoded later. Suppose instead that the constraint is a constructor that takes a `TimeSpan` and a number, and you can begin to imagine how limiting that would be.

You could argue that an `IProductRepository` based on an XML file would also require a string as constructor parameter, although that string would be a filename and not a connection string. But, conceptually, it'd still be weird because you'd have to define that filename in the `connectionStrings` element of the configuration. (In any case, we think such a hypothetical `XmlProductRepository` should take an `XmlReader` as a constructor argument instead of a filename.)

TIP Modeling DEPENDENCY construction exclusively on explicit constraints (interface or base class) is a better and more flexible option.

5.4.2 *Analysis of CONSTRAINED CONSTRUCTION*

In the previous example, the implicit constraint required implementers to have a constructor with a single string parameter. A more common constraint is that all implementations should have a parameterless constructor, so that the simplest form of `Activator.CreateInstance` will work:

```
IProductRepository repository =
    (IProductRepository)Activator.CreateInstance(productRepositoryType);
```

Although this can be said to be the lowest common denominator, the cost in flexibility is significant. No matter how you constrain object construction, you lose flexibility.

NEGATIVE EFFECTS OF THE CONSTRAINED CONSTRUCTION ANTI-PATTERN

It might be tempting to declare that all DEPENDENCY implementations should have a parameterless constructor. After all, they could perform their initialization internally; for example, reading configuration data like connection strings directly from the configuration file. But this would limit you in other ways because you might want to compose an application as layers of instances that encapsulate other instances. In

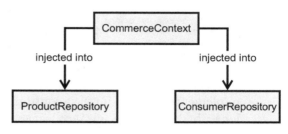

Figure 5.6   You want to create a single instance of the CommerceContext **class and inject that instance into both Repositories.**

some cases, for example, you might want to share an instance between different consumers, as illustrated in figure 5.6.

When you have more than one class requiring the same DEPENDENCY, you may want to share a single instance among all those classes. This is possible only when you can inject that instance from the outside. Although you could write code inside each of those classes to read type information from a configuration file and use `Activator.CreateInstance` to create the correct type of instance, it'd be really involved to share a single instance this way. Instead, you'd have multiple instances of the same class taking up more memory.

> **NOTE**   The fact that DI allows you to share a single instance among many consumers doesn't mean you should always do so. Sharing an instance saves memory but can introduce interaction-related problems, such as threading issues. Whether you want to share an instance is closely related to the concept of OBJECT LIFETIME, which is discussed in chapter 8.

Instead of imposing implicit constraints on how objects should be constructed, you should implement your COMPOSITION ROOT so that it can deal with any kind of constructor or factory method you may throw at it. Now let's take a look at how you can refactor toward DI.

REFACTORING FROM CONSTRAINED CONSTRUCTION TOWARD DI

How can you deal with having no constraints on components' constructors when you need late binding? It may be tempting to introduce an Abstract Factory that can create instances of the required ABSTRACTION and then require the implementations of those Abstract Factories to have a particular constructor signature. But doing so, however, is likely to cause complications of its own. Let's examine such an approach.

Imagine using an Abstract Factory for the IProductRepository ABSTRACTION. The Abstract Factory scheme dictates that you also need an IProductRepositoryFactory interface. Figure 5.7 illustrates this structure.

Figure 5.7   An attempt to use the Abstract Factory structure to solve the late-binding challenge

In this figure, IProductRepository represents the real DEPENDENCY. But to keep its implementers free of implicit constraints, you attempt to solve the late-binding challenge by introducing an IProductRepositoryFactory. This will be used to create instances of IProductRepository. A further requirement is that any factories have a particular constructor signature.

Now let's assume that you want to use an implementation of IProductRepository that requires an instance of IUserContext to work, as shown in the next listing.

Listing 5.17   SqlProductRepository that requires an IUserContext

```
public class SqlProductRepository : IProductRepository
{
    private readonly IUserContext userContext;
    private readonly CommerceContext dbContext;

    public SqlProductRepository(
        IUserContext userContext, CommerceContext dbContext)
    {
        if (userContext == null)
            throw new ArgumentNullException("userContext");
        if (dbContext == null)
            throw new ArgumentNullException("dbContext");

        this.userContext = userContext;
        this.dbContext = dbContext;
    }
}
```

The SqlProductRepository class implements the IProductRepository interface, but requires an instance of IUserContext. Because the only constructor isn't a parameterless constructor, IProductRepositoryFactory will come in handy.

Currently, you want to use an implementation of IUserContext that's based on ASP.NET Core. You call this implementation AspNetUserContextAdapter (as we discussed in listing 3.12). Because the implementation depends on ASP.NET Core, it isn't defined in the same assembly as SqlProductRepository. And, because you don't want to drag a reference to the library that contains AspNetUserContextAdapter along with SqlProductRepository, the only solution is to implement SqlProductRepositoryFactory in a different assembly than SqlProductRepository, as shown in figure 5.8.

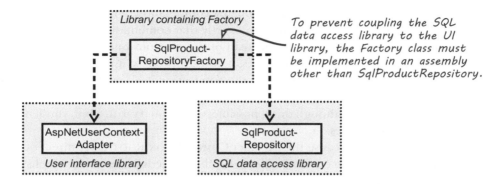

Figure 5.8 Dependency graph with `SqlProductRepositoryFactory` implemented in a separate assembly

The following listing shows a possible implementation for the `SqlProductRepository-Factory`.

BAD CODE

Listing 5.18 Factory that creates `SqlProductRepository` instances

```
public class SqlProductRepositoryFactory
    : IProductRepositoryFactory
{
    private readonly string connectionString;

    public SqlProductRepositoryFactory(
        IConfigurationRoot configuration)
    {
        this.connectionString =
            configuration.GetConnectionString(
                "CommerceConnectionString");
    }

    public IProductRepository Create()
    {
        return new SqlProductRepository(
            new AspNetUserContextAdapter(),
            new CommerceContext(this.connectionString));
    }
}
```

> **Constructor with a particular signature that all IProductRepositoryFactory implementations must have. By accepting Microsoft's IConfigurationRoot, the factory loads its required configuration values. It also throws an error during construction in case such a value is missing.**

> **Loads the connection string from the configuration file and stores it for later use**

> **Creates a new SqlProductRepository using DEPENDENCIES that are located in different assemblies**

Even though `IProductRepository` and `IProductRepositoryFactory` look like a cohesive pair, it's important to implement them in two different assemblies. This is because the factory must have references to all DEPENDENCIES to be able to wire them together correctly. By convention, the `IProductRepositoryFactory` implementation must again use CONSTRAINED CONSTRUCTION so that you can write the assembly-qualified type name in a configuration file and use `Activator.CreateInstance` to create an instance.

Every time you need to wire together a new combination of DEPENDENCIES, you must implement a new factory that wires up exactly that combination, and then configure the application to use that factory instead of the previous one. This means you can't define arbitrary combinations of DEPENDENCIES without writing and compiling code, but you can do it without recompiling the application itself. Such an Abstract Factory becomes an Abstract COMPOSITION ROOT that's defined in an assembly separate from the core application. Although this is possible, when you try to apply it, you'll notice the inflexibility that it causes.

Flexibility suffers because the Abstract COMPOSITION ROOT takes direct dependencies on concrete types in other libraries to fulfill the needs of the object graphs it builds. In the `SqlProductRepositoryFactory` example, the factory needs to create an instance of `AspNetUserContextAdapter` to pass to `SqlProductRepository`. But what if the core application wants to replace or INTERCEPT the `IUserContext` implementation? This forces changes to both the core application and the `SqlProductRepositoryFactory` project. Another problem is that it becomes quite hard for these Abstract Factories to manage OBJECT LIFETIME. This is the same problem as illustrated in figure 5.5.

To combat this inflexibility, the only feasible solution is to use a general-purpose DI CONTAINER. Because DI CONTAINERS analyze constructor signatures using reflection, the Abstract COMPOSITION ROOT doesn't need to know the DEPENDENCIES used to construct its components. The only thing the Abstract COMPOSITION ROOT needs to do is specify the mapping between the ABSTRACTION and the implementation. In other words, the SQL data access COMPOSITION ROOT needs to specify that in case the application requires an `IProductRepository`, an instance of `SqlProductRepository` should be created.

> **TIP**   Using a DI CONTAINER can be an effective solution to prevent CONSTRAINED CONSTRUCTION. In part 4, we'll go into detail about how DI CONTAINERS work and how to use them.

Abstract COMPOSITION ROOTs are only required when you truly need to be able to plug in a new assembly without having to recompile any part of the existing application. Most applications don't need this amount of flexibility. Although you might want to be able to replace the SQL data access layer with an Azure data access layer without having to recompile the domain layer, it's typically OK if this means you still have to make changes to the startup project.

> **NOTE**   The CONSTRAINED CONSTRUCTION anti-pattern only applies when you employ late binding. When you use early binding, the compiler ensures that you never introduce implicit constraints on how components are constructed. If you can get away with recompiling the startup project, you should keep your COMPOSITION ROOT centralized in the startup project. Late binding introduces extra complexity, and complexity increases maintenance costs.

Because DI is a set of patterns and techniques, no single tool can mechanically verify whether you've applied it correctly. In chapter 4, we looked at patterns that describe how DI can be used properly, but that's only one side of the coin. It's also important to study how it's possible to fail, even with the best of intentions. You can learn important lessons from failure, but you don't have to always learn from your own mistakes—sometimes you can learn from other people's mistakes.

In this chapter, we've described the most common DI mistakes in the form of anti-patterns. We've seen all these mistakes in real life on more than one occasion, and we confess to being guilty of all of them. By now, you should know what to avoid and what you should ideally be doing instead. There can still be issues that look as though they're hard to solve, however. The next chapter discusses such challenges and how to resolve them.

Summary

- An *anti-pattern* is a description of a commonly occurring solution to a problem that generates decidedly negative consequences.
- CONTROL FREAK is the most dominating of the anti-patterns presented in this chapter. It effectively prevents you from applying any kind of proper DI. It occurs every time you depend on a VOLATILE DEPENDENCY in any place other than a COMPOSITION ROOT.
- Although the new keyword is a code smell when it comes to VOLATILE DEPENDENCIES, you don't need to worry about using it for STABLE DEPENDENCIES. In general, the new keyword isn't suddenly illegal, but you should refrain from using it to get instances of VOLATILE DEPENDENCIES.
- CONTROL FREAK is a violation of the DEPENDENCY INVERSION PRINCIPLE.
- CONTROL FREAK represents the default way of creating instances in most programming languages, so it can be observed even in applications where developers have never considered DI. It's such a natural and deeply rooted way to create new objects that many developers find it difficult to discard.
- A FOREIGN DEFAULT is the opposite of a LOCAL DEFAULT. It's an implementation of a DEPENDENCY that's used as a default even though it's defined in a different module than its consumer. Dragging along unwanted modules robs you of many of the benefits of loose coupling.
- SERVICE LOCATOR is the most dangerous anti-pattern presented in this chapter because it looks like it's solving a problem. It supplies application components outside the COMPOSITION ROOT with access to an unbounded set of VOLATILE DEPENDENCIES.
- SERVICE LOCATOR impacts the reusability of the components consuming it. It makes it non-obvious to a component's consumers what its DEPENDENCIES are, makes such a component dishonest about its level of complexity, and causes its consuming components to drag along the SERVICE LOCATOR as a redundant DEPENDENCY.

- SERVICE LOCATOR prevents verification of the configuration of relationships between classes. CONSTRUCTOR INJECTION in combination with PURE DI allows verification at compile time; CONSTRUCTOR INJECTION in combination with a DI CONTAINER allows verification at application startup or as part of a simple automated test.

- A static SERVICE LOCATOR causes Interdependent Tests, because it remains in memory when the next test case is executed.

- It's not the mechanical structure of an API that determines it as a SERVICE LOCATOR, but rather the role the API plays in the application. Therefore, a DI CONTAINER encapsulated in a COMPOSITION ROOT isn't a SERVICE LOCATOR—it's an infrastructure component.

- AMBIENT CONTEXT supplies application code outside the COMPOSITION ROOT with global access to a VOLATILE DEPENDENCY or its behavior by using static class members.

- AMBIENT CONTEXT is similar in structure to the Singleton pattern with the exception that AMBIENT CONTEXT allows its DEPENDENCY to be changed. The Singleton pattern ensures that the single created instance will never change.

- AMBIENT CONTEXT is usually encountered when developers have a CROSS-CUTTING CONCERN as a DEPENDENCY that's used ubiquitously, making them think it justifies moving away from CONSTRUCTOR INJECTION.

- AMBIENT CONTEXT causes the VOLATILE DEPENDENCY to become hidden, complicates testing, and makes it difficult to change the DEPENDENCY based on its context.

- CONSTRAINED CONSTRUCTION forces all implementations of a certain ABSTRACTION to have a particular constructor signature with the goal of enabling late binding. It limits flexibility and might force implementations to do their initialization internally.

- CONSTRAINED CONSTRUCTION can be prevented by utilizing a general-purpose DI CONTAINER because DI CONTAINERS analyze constructor signatures using reflection.

- If you can get away with recompiling the startup project, you should keep your COMPOSITION ROOT centralized in the startup project and refrain from using late binding. Late binding introduces extra complexity, and complexity increases maintenance costs.

Code smells

In this chapter

- Handling Constructor Over-injection code smells
- Detecting and preventing overuse of Abstract Factories
- Fixing cyclic DEPENDENCY code smells

You may have noticed that I (Mark) have a fascination with sauce béarnaise—or sauce hollandaise. One reason is that it tastes so good; another is that it's a bit tricky to make. In addition to the challenges of production, it presents an entirely different problem: it must be served immediately (or so I thought).

This used to be less than ideal when guests arrived. Instead of being able to casually greet my guests and make them feel welcome and relaxed, I was frantically whipping the sauce in the kitchen, leaving them to entertain themselves. After a couple of repeat performances, my sociable wife decided to take matters into her own hands. We live across the street from a restaurant, so one day she chatted with the cooks to find out whether there's a trick that would enable me to prepare a genuine hollandaise well in advance. It turns out there is. Now I can serve a delicious sauce for my guests without first subjecting them to an atmosphere of stress and frenzy.

Each craft has its own tricks of the trade. This is also true for software development, in general, and for DI, in particular. Challenges keep popping up. In many cases, there are well-known ways to deal with them. Over the years, we've seen people struggle when learning DI, and many of the issues were similar in nature. In this chapter, we'll look at the most common code smells that appear when you apply DI to a code base and how you can resolve them. When we're finished, you should be able to better recognize and handle these situations when they occur.

Similar to the two previous chapters in this part of the book, this chapter is organized as a catalog—this time, a catalog of problems and solutions (or, if you will, refactorings). You can read each section independently or in sequence, as you prefer. The purpose of each section is to familiarize you with a solution to a commonly occurring problem so that you'll be better equipped to deal with it if it occurs. But first, let's define code smells.

> **DEFINITION**   "A *code smell* is a hint that something might be wrong, not a certainty. A perfectly good idiom may be considered a code smell because it's often misused, or because there's a simpler alternative that works better in most cases. Calling something a code smell is not an attack; it's a sign that a closer look is warranted." (http://wiki.c2.com/?CodeSmell)

Where an *anti-pattern* is a description of a commonly occurring solution to a problem that generates decidedly negative consequences, a code smell, on the other hand, is a code construct that might cause problems. Code smells simply warrant further investigation.

6.1   *Dealing with the Constructor Over-injection code smell*

Unless you have special requirements, CONSTRUCTOR INJECTION (we covered this in chapter 4) should be your preferred injection pattern. Although CONSTRUCTOR INJECTION is easy to implement and use, it makes developers uncomfortable when their constructors start looking something like that shown next.

CODE
SMELL

Listing 6.1   Constructor with many DEPENDENCIES

```
public OrderService(
    IOrderRepository orderRepository,
    IMessageService messageService,                   ┐  OrderService
    IBillingSystem billingSystem,                     ├─ DEPENDENCIES
    ILocationService locationService,                 │
    IInventoryManagement inventoryManagement)         ┘
{
    if (orderRepository == null)
        throw new ArgumentNullException("orderRepository");
    if (messageService == null)
        throw new ArgumentNullException("messageService");
    if (billingSystem == null)
        throw new ArgumentNullException("billingSystem");
    if (locationService == null)
        throw new ArgumentNullException("locationService");
    if (inventoryManagement == null)
        throw new ArgumentNullException("inventoryManagement");
```

```
    this.orderRepository = orderRepository;
    this.messageService = messageService;
    this.billingSystem = billingSystem;
    this.locationService = locationService;
    this.inventoryManagement = inventoryManagement;
}
```

Having many Dependencies is an indication of a Single Responsibility Principle (SRP) violation. SRP violations lead to code that's hard to maintain.

In this section, we'll look at the apparent problem of a growing number of constructor parameters and why Constructor Injection is a good thing rather than a bad thing. As you'll see, it doesn't mean you should accept long parameter lists in constructors, so we'll also review what you can do about those. You can refactor away from Constructor Over-injection in many ways, so we'll also discuss two common approaches you can take to refactor those occurrences, namely, Facade Services and domain events:

- Facade Services are abstract Facades[1] that are related to Parameter Objects.[2] Instead of combining components and exposing them as parameters, however, a Facade Service exposes only the encapsulated behavior, while hiding the constituents.
- With domain events, you capture actions that can trigger a change to the state of the application you're developing.

6.1.1 *Recognizing Constructor Over-injection*

When a constructor's parameter list grows too large, we call the phenomenon *Constructor Over-injection* and consider it a code smell.[3] It's a general issue unrelated to, but magnified by, DI. Although your initial reaction might be to dismiss Constructor Injection because of Constructor Over-injection, we should be thankful that a general design issue is revealed to us.

We can't say we blame anyone for disliking a constructor as shown in listing 6.1, but don't blame Constructor Injection. We can agree that a constructor with five parameters is a code smell, but it indicates a violation of the SRP rather than a problem related to DI.

> **NOTE** Constructor Injection makes it easy to spot SRP violations. Instead of feeling uneasy about Constructor Over-injection, you should embrace it as a fortunate side effect of Constructor Injection. It's a signal that alerts you when a class takes on too much responsibility.

Our personal threshold lies at four constructor arguments. When we add a third argument, we already begin considering whether we could design things differently, but we can live with four arguments for a few classes. Your limit may be different, but when you cross it, it's time to investigate.

---

[1] See Erich Gamma et al., *Design Patterns: Elements of Reusable Object-Oriented Software* (Addison-Wesley, 1994), 185.

[2] See Martin Fowler et al., *Refactoring: Improving the Design of Existing Code* (Addison-Wesley, 1999), 295.

[3] Jeffrey Palermo, "Constructor over-injection smell—follow up," 2010, https://mng.bz/jrzr.

How you refactor a particular class that has grown too big depends on the particular circumstances: the object model already in place, the domain, business logic, and so on. Splitting up a budding God Class into smaller, more focused classes according to well-known design patterns is always a good move.[4] Still, there are cases where business requirements oblige you to do many different things at the same time. This is often the case at the boundary of an application. Think about a coarse-grained web service operation that triggers many business events.

> **NOTE** A tempting, but erroneous, attempt to resolve Constructor Over-injection is through the introduction of PROPERTY INJECTION, perhaps even by moving those properties into a base class. Although the number of constructor DEPENDENCIES can be reduced by replacing them with properties, such a change doesn't lower the class's complexity, which should be your primary focus.

You can design and implement collaborators so that they don't violate the SRP. In chapter 9, we'll discuss how the Decorator[5] design pattern can help you stack CROSS-CUTTING CONCERNS instead of injecting them into consumers as services. This can eliminate many constructor arguments. In some scenarios, a single entry point needs to orchestrate many DEPENDENCIES. One example is a web service operation that triggers a complex interaction of many different services. The entry point of a scheduled batch job can face the same issue.

The sample e-commerce application that we look at from time to time needs to be able to receive orders. This is often best done by a separate application or subsystem because, at that point, the semantics of the transaction change. As long as you're looking at a shopping basket, you can dynamically calculate unit prices, exchange rates, and discounts. But when a customer places an order, all of those values must be captured and frozen as they were presented when the customer approved the order. Table 6.1 provides an overview of the order process.

Table 6.1   **When the order subsystem approves an order, it must perform a number of different actions.**

Action	Required DEPENDENCIES
Update the order	IOrderRepository
Send a receipt email to the customer	IMessageService
Notify the accounting system about the invoice amount	IBillingSystem
Select the best warehouses to pick and ship the order based on the items purchased and proximity to the shipping address	ILocationService, IInventoryManagement
Ask the selected warehouses to pick and ship the entire order or parts of it	IInventoryManagement

---

[4] A *God Class* is an object that controls too many other objects in the system and has grown beyond all logic to become *The Class That Does Everything*. See William J. Brown et al., *AntiPatterns: Refactoring Software, Architectures, and Projects in Crisis* (Wiley Computer Publishing, 1998), 73.

[5] See Erich Gamma et al., *Design Patterns*, 175.

Five different Dependencies are required just to approve an order. Imagine the other Dependencies you'd need to handle other order-related operations!

> **NOTE** Most examples you saw up to this page had Guard Clauses. By now, we think we've stressed the importance of Guard Clauses enough. For the sake of brevity, from this point on, we'll omit most of the Guard Clauses, starting with listing 6.2.

Let's review how this would look if the consuming `OrderService` class directly imported all of these Dependencies. The following listing gives a quick overview of the internals of this class.

CODE SMELL

Listing 6.2   Original `OrderService` class with many Dependencies

```
public class OrderService : IOrderService
{
    private readonly IOrderRepository orderRepository;
    private readonly IMessageService messageService;
    private readonly IBillingSystem billingSystem;
    private readonly ILocationService locationService;
    private readonly IInventoryManagement inventoryManagement;

    public OrderService(
        IOrderRepository orderRepository,
        IMessageService messageService,
        IBillingSystem billingSystem,
        ILocationService locationService,
        IInventoryManagement inventoryManagement)
    {
        this.orderRepository = orderRepository;
        this.messageService = messageService;
        this.billingSystem = billingSystem;
        this.locationService = locationService;
        this.inventoryManagement = inventoryManagement;
    }

    public void ApproveOrder(Order order)
    {
        this.UpdateOrder(order);        ◄────  Updates the database with
        this.Notify(order);      ◄───          the order's new status
    }
                                      Notifies other systems
    private void UpdateOrder(Order order)     about the order
    {
        order.Approve();
        this.orderRepository.Save(order);
    }

    private void Notify(Order order)
    {
        this.messageService.SendReceipt(new OrderReceipt { ... });
        this.billingSystem.NotifyAccounting(...);
        this.Fulfill(order);
    }
```

```
private void Fulfill(Order order)
{
    this.locationService.FindWarehouses(...);
    this.inventoryManagement.NotifyWarehouses(...);
}
```

| **Finds closest warehouse(s)**

| **Notifies warehouse(s) about order**

}

To keep the example manageable, we omitted most of the details of the class. But it's not hard to imagine such a class to be rather large and complex. If you let Order-Service directly consume all five DEPENDENCIES, you get many fine-grained DEPENDENCIES. The structure is shown in figure 6.1.

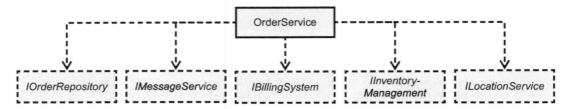

Figure 6.1   OrderService **has five direct** DEPENDENCIES**, which suggests an SRP violation.**

If you use CONSTRUCTOR INJECTION for the OrderService class (which you should), you have a constructor with five parameters. This is too many and indicates that Order-Service has too many responsibilities. On the other hand, all of these DEPENDENCIES are required because the OrderService class must implement all of the desired functionality when it receives a new order. You can address this issue by redesigning Order-Service using Facade Services refactoring. We'll show you how to do that in the next section.

6.1.2   *Refactoring from Constructor Over-injection to Facade Services*

When redesigning OrderService, the first thing you need to do is to look for natural clusters of interaction. The interaction between ILocationService and IInventoryManagement should immediately draw your attention, because you use them to find the closest warehouses that can fulfill the order. This could potentially be a complex algorithm.

After you've selected the warehouses, you need to notify them about the order. If you think about this a little further, ILocationService is an implementation detail of notifying the appropriate warehouses about the order. The entire interaction can be hidden behind an IOrderFulfillment interface, like this:

```
public interface IOrderFulfillment
{
    void Fulfill(Order order);
}
```

The next listing shows the implementation of the new `IOrderFulfillment` interface.

GOOD
CODE

Listing 6.3 `OrderFulfillment` **class**

```
public class OrderFulfillment : IOrderFulfillment
{
    private readonly ILocationService locationService;
    private readonly IInventoryManagement inventoryManagement;

    public OrderFulfillment(
        ILocationService locationService,
        IInventoryManagement inventoryManagement)
    {
        this.locationService = locationService;
        this.inventoryManagement = inventoryManagement;
    }

    public void Fulfill(Order order)
    {
        this.locationService.FindWarehouses(...);
        this.inventoryManagement.NotifyWarehouses(...);
    }
}
```

Interestingly, order fulfillment sounds a lot like a domain concept in its own right. Chances are that you discovered an implicit domain concept and made it explicit.

The default implementation of `IOrderFulfillment` consumes the two original DEPENDENCIES, so it has a constructor with two parameters, which is fine. As a further benefit, you've encapsulated the algorithm for finding the best warehouse for a given order into a reusable component. The new `IOrderFulfillment` ABSTRACTION is a Facade Service because it hides the two interacting DEPENDENCIES with their behavior.

> **DEFINITION** A *Facade Service* hides a natural cluster of interacting DEPENDENCIES, along with their behavior, behind a single ABSTRACTION.

This refactoring merges two DEPENDENCIES into one but leaves you with four DEPENDENCIES on the `OrderService` class, as shown in figure 6.2. You also need to look for other opportunities to aggregate DEPENDENCIES into a Facade.

The `OrderService` class only has four DEPENDENCIES, and the `OrderFulfillment` class contains two. That's not a bad start, but you can simplify `OrderService` even more. The next thing you may notice is that all the requirements involve notifying other systems about the order. This suggests that you can define a common ABSTRACTION that models notifications, perhaps something like this:

```
public interface INotificationService
{
    void OrderApproved(Order order);
}
```

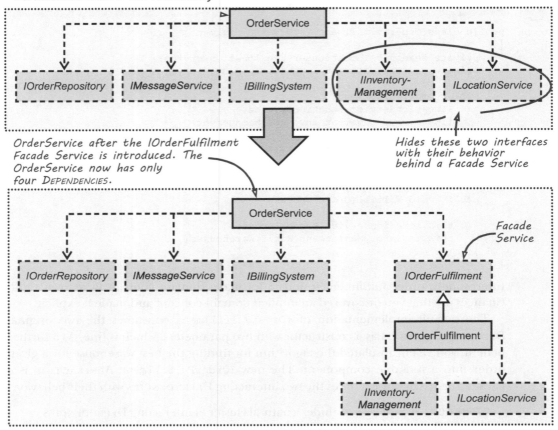

OrderService with its original five
DEPENDENCIES before the refactoring

OrderService after the IOrderFulfilment
Facade Service is introduced. The
OrderService now has only
four DEPENDENCIES.

Hides these two interfaces
with their behavior
behind a Facade Service

Facade
Service

Figure 6.2   Two DEPENDENCIES of `OrderService` **aggregated behind a Facade Service**

Each notification to an external system can be implemented using this interface. But you may wonder how this helps, because you've wrapped each DEPENDENCY in a new interface. The number of DEPENDENCIES didn't decrease, so did you gain anything?

Yes, you did. Because all three notifications implement the same interface, you can wrap them in a Composite[6] pattern as can be seen in listing 6.4. This shows another implementation of `INotificationService` that wraps a collection of `INotification-Service` instances and invokes the `OrderAccepted` method on all of those.

---

[6]   See Erich Gamma et al., *Design Patterns*, 163.

GOOD CODE

Listing 6.4   Composite wrapping `INotificationService` instances

```
public class CompositeNotificationService
    : INotificationService                        ◄─────────────  Implements
{                                                                 INotificationService

    IEnumerable<INotificationService> services;

    public CompositeNotificationService(                          Wraps a sequence of
        IEnumerable<INotificationService> services)   ◄───────── INotificationService instances
    {
        this.services = services;
    }

    public void OrderApproved(Order order)
    {
        foreach (var service in this.services)
        {                                                         Forwards an incoming call
            service.OrderApproved(order);            ◄────────── to all wrapped instances
        }
    }
}
```

CompositeNotificationService implements INotificationService and forwards an incoming call to its wrapped implementations. This prevents the consumer from having to deal with multiple implementations, which is an implementation detail. This means that you can let OrderService depend on a single INotificationService, which leaves just two DEPENDENCIES, as shown next.

GOOD CODE

Listing 6.5   Refactored `OrderService` with two DEPENDENCIES

```
public class OrderService : IOrderService
{
    private readonly IOrderRepository orderRepository;
    private readonly INotificationService notificationService;

    public OrderService(
        IOrderRepository orderRepository,
        INotificationService notificationService)
    {
        this.orderRepository = orderRepository;
        this.notificationService = notificationService;
    }

    public void ApproveOrder(Order order)
    {
        this.UpdateOrder(order);

        this.notificationService.OrderApproved(order);
    }

    private void UpdateOrder(Order order)
    {
        order.Approve();
        this.orderRepository.Save(order);
    }
}
```

From a conceptual perspective, this also makes sense. At a high level, you don't need to care about the details of how OrderService notifies other systems, but you do care that it does. This reduces OrderService to only two DEPENDENCIES, which is a more reasonable number.

From the consumer's perspective, OrderService is functionally unchanged, making this a true refactoring. On the other hand, on the conceptual level, Order-Service is changed. Its responsibility is now to receive an order, save it, and notify other systems. The details of which systems are notified and how this is implemented have been pushed down to a more detailed level. Figure 6.3 shows the final DEPENDENCIES of OrderService.

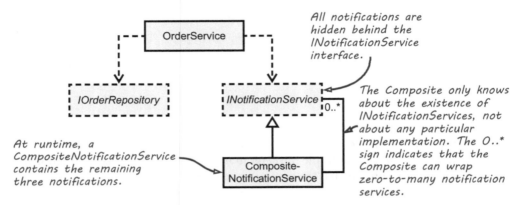

Figure 6.3   The final OrderService with refactored DEPENDENCIES

Using the CompositeNotificationService, you can now create the OrderService with its DEPENDENCIES.

Listing 6.6   COMPOSITION ROOT refactored using Facade Services

```
var repository = new SqlOrderRepository(connectionString);

var notificationService = new CompositeNotificationService(
    new INotificationService[]
    {
        new OrderApprovedReceiptSender(messageService),
        new AccountingNotifier(billingSystem),
        new OrderFulfillment(locationService, inventoryManagement)
    });

var orderServive = new OrderService(repository, notificationService);
```

Even though you consistently use CONSTRUCTOR INJECTION throughout, no single class's constructor ends up requiring more than two parameters. CompositeNotificationService takes an IEnumerable<INotificationService> as a single argument.

TIP Refactoring to Facade Services is more than just a party trick to get rid of too many DEPENDENCIES. The key is to identify natural clusters of interaction.

A beneficial side effect is that discovering these natural clusters draws previously undiscovered relationships and domain concepts out into the open. In the process, you turn implicit concepts into explicit concepts.[7] Each aggregate becomes a service that captures this interaction at a higher level, and the consumer's single responsibility becomes to orchestrate these higher-level services. You can repeat this refactoring if you have a complex application where the consumer ends up with too many DEPENDENCIES on Facade Services. Creating a Facade Service of Facade Services is a perfectly sensible thing to do.

The Facade Services refactoring is a great way to handle complexity in a system. But with regard to the `OrderService` example, we might even take this one step further, bringing us to domain events.

6.1.3 *Refactoring from Constructor Over-injection to domain events*

Listing 6.5 shows that all notifications are actions triggered when an order is approved. The following code shows this relevant part again:

```
this.notificationService.OrderApproved(order);
```

We can say that the act of an order being approved is of importance to the business. These kinds of events are called *domain events*, and it might be valuable to model them more explicitly in your applications.

DEFINITION The essence of a *domain event* is that you use it to capture actions that can trigger a change to the state of the application you're developing (https://martinfowler.com/eaaDev/DomainEvent.html).

Although the introduction of `INotificationService` is a great improvement to `OrderService`, it only solves the problem at the level of `OrderService` and its direct DEPENDENCIES. When applying the same refactoring technique to other classes in the system, one could easily imagine how `INotificationService` evolves toward something similar to the following listing.

BAD CODE

Listing 6.7 `INotificationService` with a growing number of methods

```
public interface INotificationService
{
    void OrderApproved(Order order);
    void OrderCancelled(Order order);
    void OrderShipped(Order order);
    void OrderDelivered(Order order);
    void CustomerCreated(Customer customer);
    void CustomerMadePreferred(Customer customer);
}
```

> Each method represents a domain event. ABSTRACTIONS with many members, however, typically violate the INTERFACE SEGREGATION PRINCIPLE, which we'll discuss in section 6.2.1.

---

[7] See Eric J. Evans' *Domain-Driven Design* (Addison-Wesley, 2003), 206–223.

Within any system of reasonable size and complexity, you'd easily get dozens of these domain events, which would lead to an ever-changing `INotificationService` interface. With each change to this interface, all implementations of that interface must be updated too. Additionally, ever-growing interfaces also causes ever-growing implementations. If, however, you promote the domain events to actual types and make them part of the domain, as shown in figure 6.4, an interesting opportunity to generalize even further arises.

Each class describes a specific change to system state. Both classes are simple data objects.

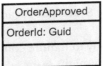

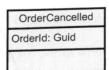

Even though these classes seem identical, giving each event its own class allows events to be mapped to components that can handle them in a strongly typed manner.

Figure 6.4 Domain events promoted to actual types. These types contain only data and no behavior.

The following listing shows the domain event code illustrated in figure 6.4.

Listing 6.8 `OrderApproved` and `OrderCancelled` domain event classes

```
public class OrderApproved
{
    public readonly Guid OrderId;

    public OrderApproved(Guid orderId)
    {
        this.OrderId = orderId;
    }
}

public class OrderCancelled
{
    public readonly Guid OrderId;

    public OrderCancelled(Guid orderId)
    {
        this.OrderId = orderId;
    }
}
```

Although both the `OrderApproved` and `OrderCancelled` classes have the same structure and are related to the same ENTITY, modelling them around their own class makes it easier to create code that responds to such a specific event. When each domain event in your system gets its own type, it lets you change `INotificationService` to a generic interface with a single method, as the following listing shows.

GOOD CODE

```
public interface IEventHandler<TEvent>
{
    void Handle(TEvent e);
}
```

◀— **We changed the name from INotificationService to IEventHandler to make it more apparent that this interface has a wider scope than just notifying other systems.**

Generics

Generics introduces the concept of *type parameters*, which allows the design of interfaces, classes, and methods that defer the specification of their types until they're declared and instantiated by client code. Using generics, such an interface, class, or method becomes a template.

The .NET Framework includes many types and methods that are generic, and you've most likely used many of them. In fact, we've already shown several examples throughout the course of this book:

- The `IEnumerable<T>` interface in several listings (for example, listing 2.3) in chapters 2 and 3
- The `DbSet<T>` class in listings 2.2 and 3.11
- The `AddSingleton<T>()` method in listing 4.3
- The `Dictionary<TKey, TValue>` class in listing 5.7

The `IEventHandler<TEvent>` interface of listing 6.9 isn't any different from those generic framework types and methods. If you're new to the concept of generics, we advise you to take a look at the topic in the C# programming guide.[8]

> **NOTE** Generic types and methods will pop up from time to time throughout the remainder of this book.

In the case of `IEventHandler<TEvent>`, a class deriving from the interface must specify a `TEvent` type—for the instance `OrderCancelled`—in the class declaration. This type will then be used as the parameter type for that class's `Handle` method. This allows one interface to unify several classes, despite differences in their types. In addition, it allows each of those implementations to be strongly typed, working exclusively off whatever type was specified as `TEvent`.

Based on this interface, you can now build the classes that respond to a domain event, like the `OrderFulfillment` class you saw previously. Based on the new `IEventHandler<TEvent>` interface, the original `OrderFulfillment` class, as shown in listing 6.3, changes to that displayed in the following listing.

---

[8] https://docs.microsoft.com/en-us/dotnet/csharp/programming-guide/generics/.

Listing 6.10 `OrderFulfillment` **class implementing** `IEventHandler<TEvent>`

```
public class OrderFulfillment                  Implements
    : IEventHandler<OrderApproved>    ◄──────  IEventHandler<OrderApproved>
{
    private readonly ILocationService locationService;
    private readonly IInventoryManagement inventoryManagement;

    public OrderFulfillment(
        ILocationService locationService,
        IInventoryManagement inventoryManagement)
    {
        this.locationService = locationService;
        this.inventoryManagement = inventoryManagement;     The logic inside the
    }                                                       Handle method is
                                                            identical to that in
    public void Handle(OrderApproved e)    ◄─────────────── listing 6.3.
    {
        this.locationService.FindWarehouses(...);
        this.inventoryManagement.NotifyWarehouses(...);
    }
}
```

The `OrderFulfillment` class implements `IEventHandler<OrderApproved>`, meaning that it acts on `OrderApproved` events. `OrderService` then uses the new `IEventHandler<TEvent>` interface, as figure 6.5 shows.

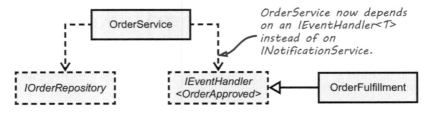

Figure 6.5 The `OrderService` **class depends on an** `IEventHandler<OrderApproved>` **interface, instead of** `INotificationService`.

Listing 6.11 shows an `OrderService` depending on `IEventHandler<OrderApproved>`. Compared to listing 6.5, the `OrderService` logic will stay almost unchanged.

Listing 6.11 `OrderService` **depending on** `IEventHandler<OrderApproved>`

```
public class OrderService : IOrderService
{
    private readonly IOrderRepository orderRepository;
    private readonly IEventHandler<OrderApproved> handler;
```

```
public OrderService(
    IOrderRepository orderRepository,
    IEventHandler<OrderApproved> handler)
{
    this.orderRepository = orderRepository;
    this.handler = handler;
}

public void ApproveOrder(Order order)
{
    this.UpdateOrder(order);

    this.handler.Handle(
        new OrderApproved(order.Id));
}
...
}
```

◄── **OrderService now depends on IEventHandler<OrderApproved> instead of INotificationService.**

◄── **Approving an order means you create an OrderApproved domain event and send it to the appropriate handlers for processing.**

Just as with the non-generic `INotificationService`, you still need a Composite that takes care of dispatching the information to the list of available handlers. This enables you to add new handlers to the application, without the need to change `OrderService`. Listing 6.12 shows this Composite. As you can see, it's similar to the `CompositeNotificationService` from listing 6.4.

Listing 6.12 Composite wrapping `IEventHandler<TEvent>` instances

```
public class CompositeEventHandler<TEvent> : IEventHandler<TEvent>
{
    private readonly IEnumerable<IEventHandler<TEvent>> handlers;

    public CompositeEventHandler(
        IEnumerable<IEventHandler<TEvent>> handlers)
    {
        this.handlers = handlers;
    }

    public void Handle(TEvent e)
    {
        foreach (var handler in this.handlers)
        {
            handler.Handle(e);
        }
    }
}
```

◄── **Wraps a collection of IEventHandler<TEvent> instances**

Wrapping a collection of `IEventHandler<TEvent>` instances, as does `CompositeEvent-Handler<TEvent>`, lets you add arbitrary event handler implementations to the system without having to make any changes to consumers of `IEventHandler<TEvent>`. Using the new `CompositeEventHandler<TEvent>`, you can create the `OrderService` with its DEPENDENCIES.

Listing 6.13   COMPOSITION ROOT for the `OrderService` refactored using events

```
var orderRepository = new SqlOrderRepository(connectionString);

var orderApprovedHandler = new CompositeEventHandler<OrderApproved>(
    new IEventHandler<OrderApproved>[]
    {
        new OrderApprovedReceiptSender(messageService),
        new AccountingNotifier(billingSystem),
        new OrderFulfillment(locationService, inventoryManagement)
    });

var orderService = new OrderService(orderRepository, orderApprovedHandler);
```

Likewise, the COMPOSITION ROOT will contain the configuration for the handlers of other domain events. The following code shows a few more event handlers for `Order-Cancelled` and `CustomerCreated`. We leave it up to the reader to extrapolate from this.

```
var orderCancelledHandler = new CompositeEventHandler<OrderCancelled>(
    new IEventHandler<OrderCancelled>[]
    {
        new AccountingNotifier(billingSystem),
        new RefundSender(orderRepository),
    });

var customerCreatedHandler = new CompositeEventHandler<CustomerCreated>(
    new IEventHandler<CustomerCreated>[]
    {
        new CrmNotifier(crmSystem),
        new TermsAndConditionsSender(messageService, termsRepository),
    });

var orderService = new OrderService(
    orderRepository, orderApprovedHandler, orderCancelledHandler);

var customerService = new CustomerService(
    customerRepository, customerCreatedHandler);
```

The beauty of a generic interface like `IEventHandler<TEvent>` is that the addition of new features won't cause any changes to either the interface nor any of the already existing implementations. In case you need to generate an invoice for your approved order, you only have to add a new implementation that implements `IEventHandler<OrderApproved>`. When a new domain event is created, no changes to `CompositeEventHandler<TEvent>` are required.

In a sense, `IEventHandler<TEvent>` becomes a template for common building blocks that the application relies on. Each building block responds to a particular event. As you saw, you can have multiple building blocks that respond to the same event. New building blocks can be plugged in without the need to change any existing business logic.

TIP A DI Container's Auto-Registration abilities is a great way to simplify your Composition Root. Chapters 13, 14, and 15 show how to register IEvent-Handler<TEvent> implementations using a DI Container.

Although the introduction of IEventHandler<TEvent> prevented the problem of an ever-growing INotificationService, it doesn't prevent the problem of an ever-growing OrderService class. This is something we'll address in great detail in chapter 10.

Reliable messaging

Promoting domain events to types in your system has more benefits than just improving the maintainability of the application. Consider the following scenario.

At peak hours, the web services of the warehouses may time out. But at that point in time, both the receipt has been sent and the billing system has been notified. Although it's possible to roll back the database update, it's impossible to roll back the notification—the customer has already been mailed.

Unfortunately, the problems with the billing system aren't the only ones. Recently, one of the web servers that runs the order-approval process crashed. The customer's confirmation mail got sent just before the crash, but neither the billing system nor the warehouses were notified. The customer never got the order. What should you do to mitigate these kinds of problems?

Although there are multiple ways to handle this scenario, domain events can help: they can be serialized and put on a durable message queue like MSMQ, Azure Queue, or a database table. Doing so allows you to let your OrderService only execute the following operations:

- Begin a transaction
- Update the order in the database as part of the transaction
- Publish the OrderAccepted event to a durable queue as part of the transaction[9]
- Commit the transaction

Only after the OrderAccepted event has been committed to the queue does it become available for further processing. At that point, you can pass it on to each of the available handlers for that particular event. Each handler can run in its own isolated transaction.[10] If one of the handlers fails, you could retry that specific handler without influencing the other handlers. You might even execute multiple handlers in parallel.

Processing messages using a durable queue is a form of *reliable messaging*. Reliable messaging gives certain guarantees about the successful transmission of messages. It's an effective solution for the scenario described, where servers can crash and external systems can become unavailable. As you can imagine, though, how to implement these reliable messaging patterns is outside the scope of this book.[11]

---

[9] The Outbox pattern is an excellent way to prevent distributed transactions. See http://gistlabs.com/2014/05/the-outbox/.

[10] This leads to eventual consistency. See https://en.wikipedia.org/wiki/Eventual_consistency for details.

[11] A great book that explains the basics of message theory, eventual consistency, and Publish/Subscribe is David Boike's *Learning NServiceBus*, 2nd Ed. (Packt Publishing, 2015).

We've found the use of domain events to be an effective model. It allows code to be defined on a more conceptual level, while letting you build more-robust software, especially where you have to communicate with external systems that aren't part of your database transaction. But no matter which refactoring approach you choose, be it Decorators, Facade Services, domain events, or perhaps another, the important takeaway here is that Constructor Over-injection is a clear sign that code smells. Don't ignore such a sign, but act accordingly.

Because Constructor Over-injection is a commonly recurring code smell, the next section discusses a more subtle problem that, at first sight, might look like a good solution to a set of recurring problems. But is it?

6.2 *Abuse of Abstract Factories*

When you start applying DI, one of the first difficulties you're likely to encounter is when ABSTRACTIONS depend on runtime values. For example, an online mapping site may offer to calculate a route between two locations, giving you a choice of how you want the route computed. Do you want the shortest route? The fastest route based on known traffic patterns? The most scenic route?

The first response from many developers in such cases would be to use an Abstract Factory. Although Abstract Factories do have their place in software, when it comes to DI—when factories are used as DEPENDENCIES in application components—they're often overused. In many cases, better alternatives exist.

In this section, we'll discuss two cases where better alternatives to Abstract Factories exist. In the first case, we'll discuss why Abstract Factories shouldn't be used to create stateful DEPENDENCIES with a short lifetime. After that, we'll discuss why it's generally better not to use Abstract Factories to select DEPENDENCIES based on runtime data.

6.2.1 *Abusing Abstract Factories to overcome lifetime problems*

When it comes to the abuse of Abstract Factories, a common code smell is to see parameterless factory methods that have a DEPENDENCY as the return type, as the next listing shows.

CODE
SMELL

> **Listing 6.14 Abstract Factory with parameterless `Create` method**

```
public interface IProductRepositoryFactory
{
    IProductRepository Create();      ◀─── A parameterless factory method
}                                          returning a new instance of a
                                           VOLATILE DEPENDENCY
```

Abstract Factories with parameterless `Create` methods are often used to allow consumers to control the lifetime of their DEPENDENCIES. In the following listing, `HomeController` controls the lifetime of `IProductRepository` by requesting it from the factory, and disposing of it when it finishes using it.

CODE SMELL

Listing 6.15 A `HomeController` explicitly managing its DEPENDENCY's lifetime

```
public class HomeController : Controller
{
    private readonly IProductRepositoryFactory factory;

    public HomeController(                          ◄─── Injects Abstract Factory
        IProductRepositoryFactory factory)               into the consumer
    {
        this.factory = factory;
    }
                                                    Abstract Factory creates
    public ViewResult Index()                       Repository instance, whose
    {                                               lifetime must be managed
        using (IProductRepository repository =      explicitly.
            this.factory.Create())      ◄──────────────
        {
                                                    Because IProductRepository
            var products =                          implements IDisposable, the created
                repository.GetFeaturedProducts();   instance should be disposed of when
                                                    the consumer is done. This makes
            return this.View(products);   ◄──────── IProductRepository a LEAKY
        }                                           ABSTRACTION, as we'll discuss shortly.
    }
}
```

The Repository is used. (points to `var products` / `repository.GetFeaturedProducts()`)

Figure 6.6 shows the sequence of communication between `HomeController` and its DEPENDENCIES.

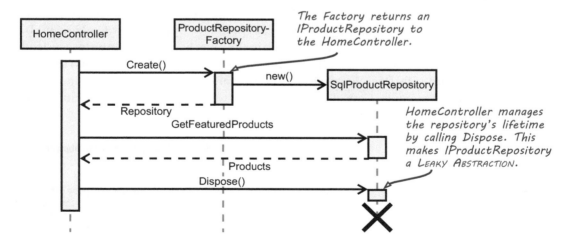

Figure 6.6 The consuming class `HomeController` controls the lifetime of its `IProductRepository` DEPENDENCY. It does so by requesting a Repository instance from the `IProductRepositoryFactory` DEPENDENCY and calling `Dispose` on the `IProductRepository` instance when it's done with it.

Disposing the Repository is required when the used implementation holds on to resources, such as database connections, that should be closed in a deterministic fashion. Although an implementation might require deterministic cleanup, that doesn't imply that it should be the responsibility of the consumer to ensure proper cleanup. This brings us to the concept of LEAKY ABSTRACTIONS.

THE LEAKY ABSTRACTION CODE SMELL

Just as Test-Driven Development (TDD) ensures TESTABILITY, it's safest to define interfaces first and then subsequently program against them. Even so, there are cases where you already have a concrete type and now want to extract an interface. When you do this, you must take care that the underlying implementation doesn't leak through. One way this can happen is if you only extract an interface from a given concrete type, but some of the parameter or return types are still concrete types defined in the library you want to abstract from. The following interface definition offers an example:

CODE SMELL

```
public interface IRequestContext
{
    HttpContext Context { get; }
}
```

◄——— **Application interface tries to abstract away from the ASP.NET runtime environment**

◄——— **The interface is still exposing HttpContext, which is part of ASP.NET. This is a LEAKY ABSTRACTION.**

If you need to extract an interface, you need to do it in a recursive manner, ensuring that all types exposed by the root interface are themselves interfaces. We call this *Deep Extraction*, and the result is *Deep Interfaces*.

This doesn't mean that interfaces can't expose any concrete classes. It's typically fine to expose behaviorless data objects, such as Parameter Objects, view models, and Data Transfer Objects (DTOs). They're defined in the same library as the interface instead of the library you want to abstract from. Those data objects are part of the ABSTRACTION.

Be careful with Deep Extraction: it doesn't always lead to the best solution. Take the previous example. Consider the following suspicious-looking implementation of a Deep Extracted IHttpContext interface:

CODE SMELL

```
public interface IHttpContext
{
    IHttpRequest Request { get; }
    IHttpResponse Response { get; }
    IHttpSession Session { get; }
    IPrincipal User { get; }
}
```

◄——— **Application-defined interface to abstract from ASP.NET's HttpContext**

The interface's members expose other application-defined interfaces that abstract from the members that HttpContext exposes. This can go many levels deep.

Although you might be using interfaces all the way down, it's still glaringly obvious that the HTTP model is leaking through. In other words, `IHttpContext` is still a LEAKY ABSTRACTION—and so are its sub-interfaces.

How should you model `IRequestContext` instead? To figure this out, you have to look at what its consumers want to achieve. For instance, if a consumer needs to find out the role of the user who sent the current web request, you might end up instead with the `IUserContext` we discussed in chapter 3:

GOOD CODE

```
public interface IUserContext
{
    bool IsInRole(Role role);
}
```

This `IUserContext` interface doesn't reveal to the consumer that it's running as part of an ASP.NET web application. As a matter of fact, this ABSTRACTION lets you run the same consumer as part of a Windows service or desktop application. It'll likely require the creation of a different `IUserContext` implementation, but its consumers are oblivious to this.

Always consider whether a given ABSTRACTION makes sense for implementations other than the one you have in mind. If it doesn't, you should reconsider your design. That brings us back to our parameterless factory methods.

PARAMETERLESS FACTORY METHODS ARE LEAKY ABSTRACTIONS

As useful as the Abstract Factory pattern can be, you must take care to apply it with discrimination. The DEPENDENCIES created by an Abstract Factory should conceptually require a runtime value, and the translation from a runtime value into an ABSTRACTION should make sense. If you feel the urge to introduce an Abstract Factory because you have a specific implementation in mind, you may have a LEAKY ABSTRACTION at hand.

Consumers that depend on `IProductRepository`, such as the `HomeController` from listing 6.15, shouldn't care about which instance they get. At runtime, you might need to create multiple instances, but as far as the consumer is concerned, there's only one.

> **IMPORTANT** Conceptually, there's only one instance of a service ABSTRACTION. During the lifetime of a consumer, it shouldn't be concerned with the possibility that multiple instances of a DEPENDENCY can exist. Anything otherwise would cause needless complication for consumers, which means the ABSTRACTION isn't designed for their benefit.

By specifying an `IProductRepositoryFactory` ABSTRACTION with a parameterless `Create` method, you let the consumer know that there are more instances of the given service, and that it has to deal with this. Because another implementation of `IProduct-Repository` might not require multiple instances or deterministic disposal at all, you're therefore leaking implementation details through the Abstract Factory with its parameterless `Create` method. In other words, you've created a LEAKY ABSTRACTION.

ABSTRACTIONS that implement IDisposable are LEAKY ABSTRACTIONS

Application code shouldn't be responsible for the management of the lifetime of objects. Putting this responsibility inside the application code means you increase complexity of that particular class and make it more complicated to test and maintain. We often see LIFETIME MANAGEMENT logic duplicated across the application, instead of being centralized in the COMPOSITION ROOT, which is what you're aiming for.

DI is no excuse for writing applications with memory leaks, so you must be able to explicitly close connections and other resources as soon as possible. On the other hand, any DEPENDENCY may or may not represent an out-of-process resource, so it would be a LEAKY ABSTRACTION if you were to model an ABSTRACTION to include a `Dispose` or `Close` method.

An ABSTRACTION generally shouldn't be disposable, as there's no way to foresee all of its possible implementations. Practically, any ABSTRACTION could end up requiring a disposable implementation at some point, whereas other implementations of the same ABSTRACTION continue relying exclusively on managed code.

This doesn't mean that classes shouldn't implement `IDisposable`. What this does mean, however, is that ABSTRACTIONS shouldn't implement `IDisposable`. Because the client only knows about the ABSTRACTION, it can't be responsible for managing the lifetime of that instance. We move this responsibility back to the COMPOSITION ROOT. We'll discuss LIFETIME MANAGEMENT in chapter 8.

Next, we'll discuss how to prevent this LEAKY ABSTRACTION code smell.

REFACTORING TOWARD A BETTER SOLUTION

Consuming code shouldn't be concerned with the possibility of there being more than one `IProductRepository` instance. You should therefore get rid of the `IProduct-RepositoryFactory` completely and instead let consumers depend solely on `IProduct-Repository`, which they should have injected using CONSTRUCTOR INJECTION. This advice is reflected in the following listing.

GOOD
CODE

> **Listing 6.16   `HomeController` without managing its DEPENDENCY's lifetime**

```
public class HomeController : Controller
{
    private readonly IProductRepository repository;

    public HomeController(
        IProductRepository repository)          ◀── Instead of injecting an Abstract
    {                                               Factory, IProductRepository itself is
        this.repository = repository;               injected directly into the consuming
    }                                               HomeController.

    public ViewResult Index()
```

```
    {
        var products =
            this.repository.GetFeaturedProducts();

        return this.View(products);
    }
}
```

> Instead of managing IProductRepository's lifetime by requesting it from an Abstract Factory and disposing of it, HomeController merely uses it. IProductRepository no longer implements IDisposable.

This code results in a simplified sequence of interactions between `HomeController` and its sole `IProductRepository` DEPENDENCY, as shown in figure 6.7.

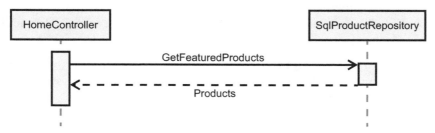

Figure 6.7 Compared to figure 6.6, removing the responsibility of managing IProduct-Repository's lifetime together with removing the IProductRepositoryFactory DEPENDENCY considerably simplifies interaction with HomeController's DEPENDENCIES.

Although removing LIFETIME MANAGEMENT simplifies the `HomeController`, you'll have to manage the Repository's lifetime somewhere in the application. A common pattern to address this problem is the Proxy pattern, an example of which is given in the next listing.

GOOD CODE

Listing 6.17 Delaying creation of SqlProductRepository using a Proxy

```
public class SqlProductRepositoryProxy : IProductRepository
{
    private readonly string connectionString;

    public SqlProductRepositoryProxy(string connectionString)
    {
        this.connectionString = connectionString;
    }

    public IEnumerable<Product> GetFeaturedProducts()
    {
        using (var repository = this.Create())
        {
            return repository.GetFeaturedProducts();
        }
    }

    private SqlProductRepository Create()
    {
        return new SqlProductRepository(
            this.connectionString);
    }
}
```

The Proxy forwards the call to the real IProductRepository implementation.

The Proxy creates and calls the SqlProductRepository internally only when its GetFeaturedProducts method is called. Such a Proxy should typically be part of the COMPOSITION ROOT to prevent the CONTROL FREAK anti-pattern.

The SqlProductRepository implementation still implements IDisposable. This way, the Proxy can manage its lifetime.

> ### Proxy design pattern
>
> The Proxy design pattern provides a surrogate or placeholder for another object to control access to it.[12] It allows deferring the full cost of its creation and initialization until you need to use it. A Proxy implements the same interface as the object it's surrogate for. It makes consumers believe they're talking to the real implementation.

Notice how `SqlProductRepositoryProxy` internally contains factory-like behavior with its private `Create` method. This behavior, however, is encapsulated within the Proxy and doesn't leak out, compared to the `IProductRepositoryFactory` Abstract Factory that exposes `IProductRepository` from its definition.

> **NOTE** Having factory-like behavior (like the `Create` method of listing 6.17) is typically unavoidable. Application-wide Factory ABSTRACTIONS, however, should be viewed with suspicion.

`SqlProductRepositoryProxy` is tightly coupled to `SqlProductRepository`. This would be an implementation of the CONTROL FREAK anti-pattern (section 5.1) if the `SqlProductRepositoryProxy` was defined in your domain layer. Instead, you should either define this Proxy in your data access layer that contains `SqlProductRepository` or, more likely, the COMPOSITION ROOT.

Because the `Create` method composes part of the object graph, the COMPOSITION ROOT is a well-suited location to place this Proxy class. The next listing shows the structure of the COMPOSITION ROOT using the `SqlProductRepositoryProxy`.

Listing 6.18   Object graph with the new `SqlProductRepositoryProxy`

```
new HomeController(
    new SqlProductRepositoryProxy(
        connectionString));
```

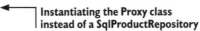 **Instantiating the Proxy class instead of a SqlProductRepository**

In the case that an ABSTRACTION has many members, it becomes quite cumbersome to create Proxy implementations. ABSTRACTIONS with many members, however, typically violate the INTERFACE SEGREGATION PRINCIPLE. Making ABSTRACTIONS more focused solves many problems, such as the complexity of creating Proxies, Decorators, and Test Doubles. We'll discuss this in more detail in section 6.3 and again come back to this subject in chapter 10.

---

[12] Erich Gamma et al., *Design Patterns*, 245.

INTERFACE SEGREGATION PRINCIPLE

The INTERFACE SEGREGATION PRINCIPLE (ISP) states that "No client should be forced to depend on methods it doesn't use."

This means that a consumer of an interface should use all the methods of a consumed DEPENDENCY. If there are methods on that ABSTRACTION that aren't used by a consumer, the interface is too large and, according to the ISP, the interface should be split up. This keeps a system decoupled and easier to refactor, change, and redeploy. Interfaces should therefore be designed to be specific. You don't want to lump too many responsibilities together into one interface, because it becomes too cumbersome to implement.

The ISP can be considered to be the conceptual underpinning of the SINGLE RESPONSIBILITY PRINCIPLE (SRP). The ISP states that interfaces should model only a single concept, whereas the SRP states that implementations should have only one responsibility.

The ISP may at first seem to be distantly related to DI. It's important because an interface that models too much pulls you in the direction of a particular implementation. It's often a smell of a LEAKY ABSTRACTION and makes it harder to replace DEPENDENCIES. This is because some of the interface members may make no sense in a context that's different to the one that drove the initial design.[13] In chapter 10, however, you'll learn that the ISP is crucial when it comes to effectively applying DI and ASPECT-ORIENTED PROGRAMMING.

That doesn't mean that there should always be a one-to-one relationship between an implementation and an ABSTRACTION, though. Sometimes you want to make interfaces smaller than their implementations, meaning that an implementation might implement more interfaces.[14]

The next section deals with the abuse of Abstract Factories to select the DEPENDENCY to return, based on the supplied runtime data.

6.2.2 *Abusing Abstract Factories to select DEPENDENCIES based on runtime data*

In the previous section, you learned that Abstract Factories should typically accept runtime values as input. Without them, you're leaking implementation details about the implementation to the consumer. This doesn't mean that an Abstract Factory that accepts runtime data is the correct solution to every situation. More often than not, it isn't.

In this section, we'll look at Abstract Factories that accept runtime data specifically to decide which DEPENDENCY to return. The example we'll look at is the online mapping site that offers to calculate a route between two locations, which we introduced at the start of section 6.2.

---

[13] Mark Seemann, "Interfaces are not abstractions," 2010, https://mng.bz/8yvz.

[14] For a detailed discussion, see Robert C. Martin, *Agile Software Development, Principles, Patterns, and Practices* (Prentice Hall, 2003), chapter 12.

To calculate a route, the application needs a routing algorithm, but it doesn't care which one. Each option represents a different algorithm, and the application can handle each routing algorithm as an ABSTRACTION to treat them all equally. You must tell the application which algorithm to use, but you won't know this until runtime because it's based on the user's choice.

In a web application, you can only transfer primitive types from the browser to the server. When the user selects a routing algorithm from a drop-down box, you must represent this by a number or a string.[15] An enum is a number, so on the server you can represent the selection using this RouteType:

```
public enum RouteType { Shortest, Fastest, Scenic }
```

What you need is an instance of IRouteAlgorithm that can calculate the route for you:

```
public interface IRouteAlgorithm
{
    RouteResult CalculateRoute(RouteSpecification specification);
}
```

Now you're presented with a problem. The RouteType is runtime data based on the user's choice. It's sent to the server with the request.

Listing 6.19   RouteController with its GetRoute method

```
public class RouteController : Controller
{
    public ViewResult GetRoute(
        RouteSpecification spec, RouteType routeType)
    {
        IRouteAlgorithm algorithm = ...         ◄─── Gets the IRouteAlgorithm for
                                                      the appropriate RouteType.
                                                      But how?

        var route = algorithm.CalculateRoute(spec);   ◄─── Calls the selected
                                                            IRouteAlgorithm

        var vm = new RouteViewModel      ─┐  Maps the returned
        {                                 │  route data to a
            ...                           │  RouteViewModel
        };                                │  that can be
                                          │  consumed by
        return this.View(vm);             ┘  the view
    }                    ◄─── Wraps the view model in an
}                             MVC ViewResult object using
                              MVC's View helper method
```

The question now becomes, how do you get the appropriate algorithm? If you hadn't been reading this chapter, your knee-jerk reaction to this challenge would probably be to introduce an Abstract Factory, like this:

```
public interface IRouteAlgorithmFactory
{
    IRouteAlgorithm CreateAlgorithm(RouteType routeType);
}
```

---

[15] To be pedantic, we can only transfer strings, but most web frameworks support type conversion for primitive types.

This enables you to implement a `GetRoute` method for `RouteController` by inject-ing `IRouteAlgorithmFactory` and using it to translate the runtime value to the `IRouteAlgorithm` DEPENDENCY you need. The following listing demonstrates the interaction.

CODE
SMELL

Listing 6.20   Using an `IRouteAlgorithmFactory` in `RouteController`

```
public class RouteController : Controller
{
    private readonly IRouteAlgorithmFactory factory;

    public RouteController(IRouteAlgorithmFactory factory)
    {
        this.factory = factory;
    }

    public ViewResult GetRoute(
        RouteSpecification spec, RouteType routeType)
    {
        IRouteAlgorithm algorithm =
            this.factory.CreateAlgorithm(routeType);

        var route = algorithm.CalculateRoute(spec);

        var vm = new RouteViewModel
        {
            ...
        };

        return this.View(vm);
    }
}
```

Uses the factory to map the runtime value of the routeType parameter to an IRouteAlgorithm

When you have that algorithm, you can use it to calculate the route and return the result.

The `RouteController` class's responsibility is to handle web requests. The `GetRoute` method receives the user's specification of origin and destination, as well as a selected `RouteType`. With an Abstract Factory, you map the runtime `RouteType` value to an `IRouteAlgorithm` instance, so you request an instance of `IRouteAlgorithmFactory` using CONSTRUCTOR INJECTION. This sequence of interactions between `RouteController` and its DEPENDENCIES is shown in figure 6.8.

The most simple implementation of `IRouteAlgorithmFactory` would involve a switch statement and return three different implementations of `IRouteAlgorithm` based on the input. But we'll leave this as an exercise for the reader.

Up until this point you might be wondering, "What's the catch? Why is this a code smell?" To be able to see the problem, we need to go back to the DEPENDENCY INVER-SION PRINCIPLE.

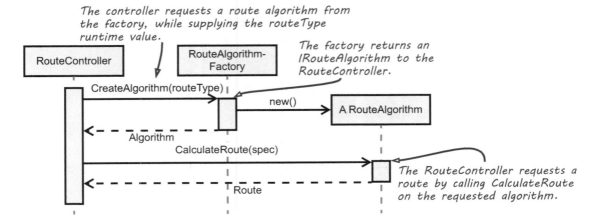

The controller requests a route algorithm from the factory, while supplying the routeType runtime value.

The factory returns an IRouteAlgorithm to the RouteController.

The RouteController requests a route by calling CalculateRoute on the requested algorithm.

Figure 6.8 `RouteController` **supplies the** `routeType` **runtime value to** `IRouteAlgorithmFactory`. **The factory returns an** `IRouteAlgorithm` **implementation, and** `RouteController` **requests a route by calling** `CalculateRoute`. **The interaction is similar to that of figure 6.6.**

ANALYSIS OF THE CODE SMELL

In chapter 3 (section 3.1.2), we talked about the DEPENDENCY INVERSION PRINCIPLE. We discussed how it states that ABSTRACTIONS should be owned by the layer using the ABSTRACTION. We explained that it's the consumer of the ABSTRACTION that should dictate its shape and define the ABSTRACTION in a way that suits its needs the most. When we go back to our RouteController and ask ourselves whether this is the design that suits RouteController the best, we'd argue that this design doesn't suit RouteController.

One way of looking at this is by evaluating the number of DEPENDENCIES Route-Controller has, which tells you something about the complexity of the class. As you saw in section 6.1, having a large number of DEPENDENCIES is a code smell, and a typical solution is to apply Facade Services refactoring.

When you introduce an Abstract Factory, you always increase the number of DEPENDENCIES a consumer has. If you only look at the constructor of RouteController, you may be led to believe that the controller only has one DEPENDENCY. But IRoute-Algorithm is also a DEPENDENCY of RouteController, even if it isn't injected into its constructor.

This increased complexity might not be obvious at first, but it can be felt instantly when you start unit testing RouteController. Not only does this force you to test the interaction RouteController has with IRouteAlgorithm, you also have to test the interaction with IRouteAlgorithmFactory.

REFACTORING TOWARD A BETTER SOLUTION

You can reduce the number of DEPENDENCIES by merging both IRouteAlgorithm-Factory and IRouteAlgorithm together, much like you saw with the Facade Services refactoring of section 6.1. Ideally, you'd want to use the Proxy pattern the same way you applied it in section 6.2.1. A Proxy, however, is only applicable in case the ABSTRACTION is supplied with all the data required to select the appropriate DEPENDENCY. Unfortunately, this prerequisite doesn't hold for IRouteAlgorithm because it's only supplied with a RouteSpecification, but not a RouteType.

Before you discard the Proxy pattern, it's important to verify whether it makes sense from a conceptual level to pass RouteType on to IRouteAlgorithm. If it does, it means that a CalculateRoute implementation contains all the information required to select both the proper algorithm and the runtime values the algorithm will need to calculate the route. In this case, however, passing RouteType on to IRouteAlgorithm is conceptually weird. An algorithm implementation will never need to use RouteType. Instead, to reduce the controller's complexity, you define an Adapter that internally dispatches to the appropriate route algorithm:

```
public interface IRouteCalculator
{
    RouteResult Calculate(RouteSpecification spec, RouteType routeType);
}
```

The following listing shows how RouteController gets simplified when it depends on IRouteCalculator instead of IRouteAlgorithmFactory.

GOOD CODE

Listing 6.21   Using an `IRouteCalculator` in `RouteController`

```
public class RouteController : Controller
{
    private readonly IRouteCalculator calculator;

    public RouteController(IRouteCalculator calculator)
    {
        this.calculator = calculator;
    }

    public ViewResult GetRoute(RouteSpecification spec, RouteType routeType)
    {
        var route = this.calculator.Calculate(spec, routeType);

        var vm = new RouteViewModel { ... };

        return this.View(vm);
    }
}
```

The use of IRouteCalculator reduces the number of DEPENDENCIES. There's now just one DEPENDENCY left.

Figure 6.9 shows the simplified interaction between `RouteController` and its sole DEPENDENCY. As you saw in figure 6.7, the interaction is reduced to a single method call.

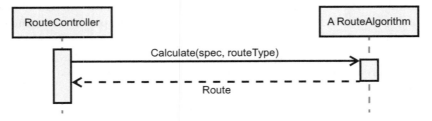

Figure 6.9   Compared to figure 6.8, by hiding `IRouteAlgorithmFactory` and `IRouteAlgorithm` behind a single `IRouteCalculator` ABSTRACTION, the interaction between `RouteController` and its (now single) DEPENDENCY is simplified.

You can implement an `IRouteCalculator` in many ways. One way is to inject `IRoute-AlgorithmFactory` into this `RouteCalculator`. This isn't our preference, though, because `IRouteAlgorithmFactory` would be a useless extra layer of indirection you could easily do without. Instead, you'll inject `IRouteAlgorithm` implementations into the `RouteCalculator` constructor.

Listing 6.22   `IRouteCalculator` wrapping a dictionary of `IRouteAlgorithms`

```
public class RouteCalculator : IRouteCalculator
{
    private readonly IDictionary<RouteType, IRouteAlgorithm> algorithms;

    public RouteCalculator(
        IDictionary<RouteType, IRouteAlgorithm> algorithms)
    {
        this.algorithms = algorithms;
    }

    public RouteResult Calculate(RouteSpecification spec, RouteType type)
    {
        return this.algorithms[type].CalculateRoute(spec);
    }
}
```

Using the newly defined `RouteCalculator`, `RouteController` can now be constructed like this:

```
var algorithms = new Dictionary<RouteType, IRouteAlgorithm>
{
    { RouteType.Shortest, new ShortestRouteAlgorithm() },
    { RouteType.Fastest, new FastestRouteAlgorithm() },
    { RouteType.Scenic, new ScenicRouteAlgorithm() }
};

new RouteController(
    new RouteCalculator(algorithms));
```

By refactoring from Abstract Factory to an Adapter, you effectively reduce the number of DEPENDENCIES between your components. Figure 6.10 shows the DEPENDENCY graph of the initial solution using the Factory, while figure 6.11 shows the object graph after refactoring.

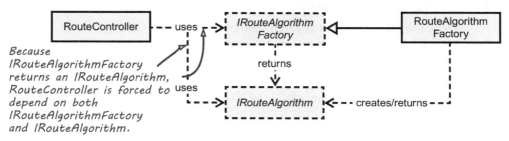

Because IRouteAlgorithmFactory returns an IRouteAlgorithm, RouteController is forced to depend on both IRouteAlgorithmFactory and IRouteAlgorithm.

Figure 6.10 The initial DEPENDENCY graph for `RouteController` with `IRouteAlgorithmFactory`

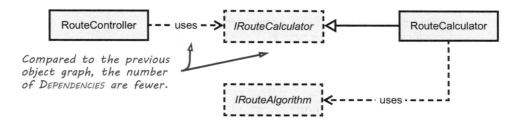

Compared to the previous object graph, the number of DEPENDENCIES are fewer.

Figure 6.11 The DEPENDENCY graph for `RouteController` when depending on `IRoute-Calculator` instead

When you use Abstract Factories to select DEPENDENCIES based on supplied runtime data, more often than not, you can reduce complexity by refactoring toward Adapters that don't expose the underlying DEPENDENCY like the Abstract Factory does. This, however, doesn't hold only when dealing with Abstract Factories. We'd like to generalize this point.

Typically, service ABSTRACTIONS shouldn't expose other service ABSTRACTIONS in their definition.[16] This means that a service ABSTRACTION shouldn't accept another service ABSTRACTION as input, nor should it have service ABSTRACTIONS as output parameters or as a return type. Application services that depend on other application services force their clients to know about both DEPENDENCIES.

> **NOTE** The previous is more of a guideline than a strict rule. There certainly are exceptions where returning ABSTRACTIONS makes the most sense, but beware that, when it comes to using them to resolve DEPENDENCIES, these situations aren't that common. For that reason, we see this as a code smell and not an anti-pattern.

---

[16] This is related to the principle of least knowledge.

The next code smell is a more exotic one, so you might not encounter it that often. Although the previously discussed code smells can go unnoticed, the next smell is hard to miss—your code either stops compiling or breaks at runtime.

6.3   *Fixing cyclic DEPENDENCIES*

Occasionally, DEPENDENCY implementations turn out to be cyclic. An implementation requires another DEPENDENCY whose implementation requires the first ABSTRACTION. Such a DEPENDENCY graph can't be satisfied. Figure 6.12 shows this problem.

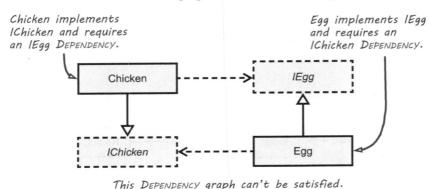

Chicken implements IChicken and requires an IEgg DEPENDENCY.

Egg implements IEgg and requires an IChicken DEPENDENCY.

This DEPENDENCY graph can't be satisfied.

Figure 6.12 DEPENDENCY cycle between Chicken and Egg

The following shows a simplistic example containing the cyclic DEPENDENCY of figure 6.12:

```
public class Chicken : IChicken
{
    public Chicken(IEgg egg) { ... }          Chicken depends
                                               on IEgg.
    public void HatchEgg() { ... }
}
                                Egg implements
public class Egg : IEgg          IEgg.                Egg depends on IChicken,
{                                                     which is implemented by
    public Egg(IChicken chicken) { ... }             Chicken.
}
```

With the previous example in mind, how can you construct an object graph consisting of these classes?

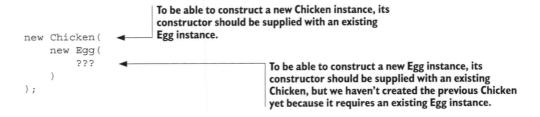

To be able to construct a new Chicken instance, its constructor should be supplied with an existing Egg instance.

```
new Chicken(
    new Egg(
        ???
    )
);
```

To be able to construct a new Egg instance, its constructor should be supplied with an existing Chicken, but we haven't created the previous Chicken yet because it requires an existing Egg instance.

What we've got here is your typical *the chicken or the egg* causality dilemma. The short answer is that you can't construct an object graph like this because both classes require the other object to exist before they're constructed. As long as the cycle remains, you can't possibly satisfy all DEPENDENCIES, and your applications won't be able to run. Clearly, something must be done, but what?

In this section, we'll look into the issue concerning cyclic DEPENDENCIES, including an example. When we're finished, your first reaction should be to try to redesign your DEPENDENCIES, because the problem is typically caused by your application's design. The main takeaway from this section, therefore, is this: DEPENDENCY *cycles are typically caused by an SRP violation.*

If redesigning your DEPENDENCIES isn't possible, you can break the cycle by refactoring from CONSTRUCTOR INJECTION to PROPERTY INJECTION. This represents a loosening of a class's invariants, so it isn't something you should do lightly.

6.3.1   *Example: DEPENDENCY cycle caused by an SRP violation*

Mary Rowan (our developer from chapter 2) has been developing her e-commerce application for some time now, and it's been quite successful in production. One day, however, Mary's boss pops around the door to request a new feature. The complaint is that when problems arise in production, it's hard to pinpoint who's been working on a certain piece of data in the system. One solution would be to store changes in an auditing table that records every change that every user in the system makes.

After thinking about this for some time, Mary comes up with the definition for an `IAuditTrailAppender` ABSTRACTION, as shown in listing 6.23. (Note that to demonstrate this code smell in a realistic setting, we need a somewhat complex example. The following example consists of three classes, and we'll spend a few pages explaining the code, before we get to its analysis.)

Listing 6.23   An `IAuditTrailAppender` ABSTRACTION

```
public interface IAuditTrailAppender          ◀──  Allows appending entries to the auditing table by
{                                                  passing in a domain ENTITY that's being altered
    void Append(Entity changedEntity);     ◀──  The base class from which
}                                              all ENTITIES derive
```

Mary uses SQL Server Management Studio to create an AuditEntries table that she can use to store the audit entries. The table definition is shown in table 6.2.

Table 6.2   Mary's AuditEntries table

Column Name	Data Type	Allow Nulls	Primary Key
Id	uniqueidentifier	No	Yes
UserId	uniqueidentifier	No	No

Table 6.2   Mary's AuditEntries table *(continued)*

Column Name	Data Type	Allow Nulls	Primary Key
TimeOfChange	DateTime	No	No
EntityId	uniqueidentifier	No	No
EntityType	varchar(100)	No	No

After creating her database table, Mary continues with the IAuditTrailAppender implementation, shown in the next listing.

Listing 6.24   SqlAuditTrailAppender appends entries to a SQL database table

```
public class SqlAuditTrailAppender : IAuditTrailAppender
{
    private readonly IUserContext userContext;
    private readonly CommerceContext context;
    private readonly ITimeProvider timeProvider;

    public SqlAuditTrailAppender(
        IUserContext userContext,
        CommerceContext context,
        ITimeProvider timeProvider)
    {
        this.userContext = userContext;
        this.context = context;
        this.timeProvider = timeProvider;
    }

    public void Append(Entity entity)
    {
        AuditEntry entry = new AuditEntry
        {
            UserId = this.userContext.CurrentUser.Id,
            TimeOfChange = this.timeProvider.Now,
            EntityId = entity.Id,
            EntityType = entity.GetType().Name
        };

        this.context.AuditEntries.Add(entry);
    }
}
```

> Recall that this is the ITimeProvider interface from listing 5.10.

> Constructs a new AuditEntry object that will be inserted into the AuditEntries table. This entry is constructed using the current system time, information specific to the supplied Entity, and the identity of the User executing the request.

An important part of an audit trail is relating a change to a user. To accomplish this, SqlAuditTrailAppender requires an IUserContext DEPENDENCY. This allows SqlAuditTrailAppender to construct the entry using the CurrentUser property on IUserContext. This is a property that Mary added some time ago for another feature.

Listing 6.25 shows Mary's current version of the `AspNetUserContextAdapter` (see listing 3.12 for the initial version).

Listing 6.25 `AspNetUserContextAdapter` with added `CurrentUser` property

```
public class AspNetUserContextAdapter : IUserContext
{
    private static HttpContextAccessor Accessor = new HttpContextAccessor();

    private readonly IUserRepository repository;

    public AspNetUserContextAdapter(
        IUserRepository repository)
    {
        this.repository = repository;
    }

    public User CurrentUser
    {
        get
        {
            var user = Accessor.HttpContext.User;
            string userName = user.Identity.Name;
            return this.repository.GetByName(userName);
        }
    }
    ...
}
```

The **new property** ─▶

◀── The IUserRepository DEPENDENCY was added by Mary to allow retrieving user information from the database.

Gets the name of the logged-in user from the HttpContext and uses it to request a User instance from the IUserRepository

While you were busy reading about DI patterns and anti-patterns, Mary's been busy too. `IUserRepository` is one of the ABSTRACTIONS she added in the meantime. We'll discuss her `IUserRepository` implementation shortly.

Mary's next step is to update the classes that need to be appended to the audit trail. One of the classes that needs to be updated is `SqlUserRepository`. It implements `IUser-Repository`, so this is a good moment to take a peek at it. The following listing shows the relevant parts of this class.

Listing 6.26 `SqlUserRepository` that needs to append to the audit trail

```
public class SqlUserRepository : IUserRepository
{
    public SqlUserRepository(
        CommerceContext context,
        IAuditTrailAppender appender)
    {
        this.appender = appender;
        this.context = context;
    }
```

◀── For the new audit trail feature, Mary adds a DEPENDENCY to IAuditTrailAppender into the constructor of SqlUserRepository.

```
public void Update(User user)
{
    this.appender.Append(user);
    ...
}

public User GetById(Guid id) { ... }

public User GetByName(string name) { ... }
}
```

The Update method is modified with a call to IAuditTrailAppender.Append. This allows an entry to be appended to the audit trail.

Original, unchanged code

This method is used by the CurrentUser property of the previously discussed AspNetUserContextAdapter.

Mary is almost finished with her feature. Because she added a constructor argument to the SqlUserRepository method, she's left with updating the COMPOSITION ROOT. Currently, the part of the COMPOSITION ROOT that creates AspNetUserContextAdapter looks like this:

```
var userRepository = new SqlUserRepository(context);

IUserContext userContext = new AspNetUserContextAdapter(userRepository);
```

Because IAuditTrailAppender was added as DEPENDENCY to the SqlUserRepository constructor, Mary tries to add it to the COMPOSITION ROOT:

```
var appender = new SqlAuditTrailAppender(
    userContext,
    context,
    timeProvider);

var userRepository = new SqlUserRepository(context, appender);

IUserContext userContext = new AspNetUserContextAdapter(userRepository);
```

Ouch! Mary gets a compile error on this line.

Unfortunately, Mary's changes don't compile. The C# compiler complains: "Cannot use local variable 'userContext' before it's declared."

Because SqlAuditTrailAppender depends on IUserContext, Mary tries to supply the SqlAuditTrailAppender with the userContext variable that she defined. The C# compiler doesn't accept this because such a variable must be defined before it's used. Mary tries to fix the problem by moving the definition and assignment of the userContext variable up, but this immediately causes the C# compiler to complain about the userRepository variable. But when she moves the userRepository variable up, the compiler complaints about the appender variable, which is used before it's declared.

Mary starts to realize she's in serious trouble—there's a cycle in her DEPENDENCY graph. Let's analyze what went wrong.

6.3.2   *Analysis of Mary's* DEPENDENCY *cycle*

The cycle in Mary's object graph appeared once she added the `IAuditTrailAppender` DEPENDENCY to the `SqlUserRepository` class. Figure 6.13 shows this DEPENDENCY cycle.

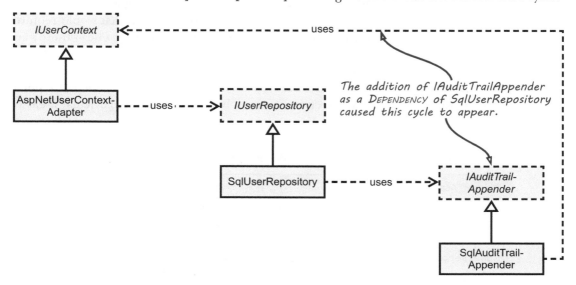

Figure 6.13   The DEPENDENCY **cycle involving** `AspNetUserContextAdapter`, `SqlUserRepository`, **and** `SqlAuditTrailAppender`

The figure shows the cycle in the object graph. The object graph, however, is part of the story. Another view we can use to analyze the problem is the method call graph as shown here:

```
UserService.UpdateMailAddress(Guid userId, string newMailAddress)
  ➥ SqlUserRepository.Update(User user)
      ➥ SqlAuditTrailAppender.Append(Entity changedEntity)
          ➥ AspNetUserContextAdapter.CurrentUser
              ➥ SqlUserRepository.GetByName(string name)
```

This call graph shows how the call would start with the `UpdateMailAddress` method of `UserService`, which would call into the `Update` method of the `SqlUserRepository` class. From there it goes into `SqlAuditTrailAppender`, then into `AspNetUserContext-Adapter` and, finally, it ends up in the `SqlUserRepository`'s `GetByName` method.

NOTE   We haven't discussed the `UserService` class because it isn't that interesting for this discussion.

What this method call graph shows is that although the object graph is cyclic, the method call graph isn't recursive. It would become recursive if GetByName again called SqlAuditTrailAppender.Append, for instance. That would cause the endless calling of other methods until the process ran out of stack space, causing a StackOverflow-Exception. Fortunately for Mary, the call graph isn't recursive, as that would require her to rewrite the methods. The cause of the problem lies somewhere else — there's an SRP violation.

When we take a look at the previously declared classes AspNetUserContextAdapter, SqlUserRepository, and SqlAuditTrailAppender, you might find it difficult to spot a possible SRP violation. All three classes seem to be focused on one particular area, as table 6.3 lists.

Table 6.3   The ABSTRACTIONS with their roles in the application

ABSTRACTION	Role	Methods
IAuditTrailAppender	Enables recording of important changes made by users	1 method
IUserContext	Provides consumers with information about the user on whose behalf the current request is executed	2 methods
IUserRepository	Provides operations around the retrieval, querying, and storage of users for a given persistence technology	3 methods

If you look more closely at IUserRepository, you can see that the functionality in the class is primarily grouped around the concept of a user. This is a quite broad concept. If you stick with this approach of grouping user-related methods in a single class, you'll see both IUserRepository and SqlUserRepository being changed quite frequently.

NOTE   Ever-changing ABSTRACTIONS are a strong indication of SRP violations. This also relates to the OPEN/CLOSED PRINCIPLE (OCP) as discussed in chapter 4, which states that you should be able to add features without having to change existing classes.

When we look at the SRP from the perspective of cohesion, we can ask ourselves whether the methods in IUserRepository are really that highly cohesive. How easy would it be to split the class up into multiple narrower interfaces and classes?

6.3.3   *Refactoring from SRP violations to resolve the DEPENDENCY cycle*

It might not always be easy to fix SRP violations, because that might cause rippling changes through the consumers of the ABSTRACTION. In the case of our little commerce application, however, it's quite easy to make the change, as the following listing shows.

GOOD
CODE

Listing 6.27   `GetByName` **moved into** `IUserByNameRetriever`

```
public interface IUserByNameRetriever
{
    User GetByName(string name);
}

public class SqlUserByNameRetriever : IUserByNameRetriever
{
    public SqlUserByNameRetriever(CommerceContext context)
    {
        this.context = context;
    }

    public User GetByName(string name) { ... }
}
```

> **GetByName method moved from IUserRepository to this new IUserByNameRetriever interface**

In the listing, the `GetByName` method is extracted from `IUserRepository` and `SqlUserRepository` into a new ABSTRACTION implementation pair named `IUserByNameRetriever` and `SqlUserByNameRetriever`. The new `SqlUserByNameRetriever` implementation doesn't depend on `IAuditTrailAppender`. The remaining part of `SqlUserRepository` is shown next.

GOOD
CODE

Listing 6.28   **The remaining part of** `IUserRepository` **and its implementation**

```
public interface IUserRepository
{
    void Update(User user);
    User GetById(Guid id);
}

public class SqlUserRepository : IUserRepository
{
    public SqlUserRepository(
        CommerceContext context,
        IAuditTrailAppender appender
    )
    {
        this.context = context;
        this.appender = appender;
    }

    public void Update(User user) { ... }
    public User GetById(Guid id) { ... }
}
```

> **Removes the GetByName method**

> **Removes the IUserContext DEPENDENCY**

NOTE The more methods a class has, the higher the chance it violates the SINGLE RESPONSIBILITY PRINCIPLE. This is also related to the INTERFACE SEGREGATION PRINCIPLE, which prefers narrow interfaces.

Mary gained a couple of things from this division. First of all, the new classes are smaller and easier to comprehend. Next, it lowers the chance of getting into the situation where Mary will be constantly updating existing code. And last, but not least, splitting the `SqlUserRepository` class breaks the DEPENDENCY cycle, because the new `SqlUserByNameRetriever` doesn't depend on `IAuditTrailAppender`. Figure 6.14 shows how the DEPENDENCY cycle was broken.

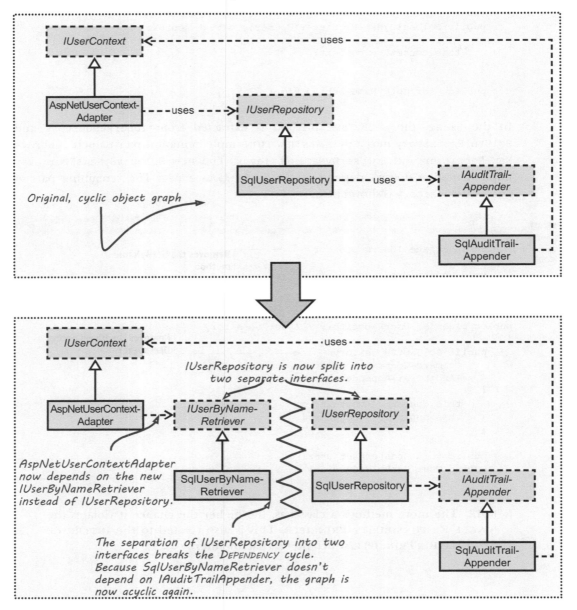

Figure 6.14   The separation of `IUserRepository` into two interfaces breaks the DEPENDENCY cycle.

The following code shows the new COMPOSITION ROOT that ties everything together:

```
var userContext = new AspNetUserContextAdapter(
    new SqlUserByNameRetriever(context));

var appender = new
    SqlAuditTrailAppender(
        userContext,
        context,
        timeProvider);

var repository = new SqlUserRepository(context, appender);
```

AspNetUserContextAdapter now depends on IUserByNameRetriever, because it requires the retrieval of users by their name.

Implementing an audit trail

The specific audit trail implementation in this section is chosen for the purpose of explaining DEPENDENCY cycles. However, this isn't typically how we'd implement such a feature ourselves. An audit trail is a CROSS-CUTTING CONCERN. The way Mary implemented it causes sweeping changes throughout many classes in the system. This is cumbersome and error prone, and it's a violation of both the OCP and the SRP.

A simpler solution would be to override the `DbContext.SaveChanges` method inside `CommerceContext`. A `DbContext` allows querying for changes using its `ChangeTracker` property. That prevents having to make sweeping changes and saves you from implementing this on any individual class and writing appropriate tests for this. Our preferred approach, however, would be to apply domain events as discussed in section 6.1. Where the previous method stores every changed ENTITY as an entry in an audit trail, domain events provide you with a trail at a higher, more functional level.

Let's take a previous example, where you try to update the user's mail address. When you publish a `UserMailAddressChanged` event, you can append that event to the trail. With it, you can store the ID of the user whose mail address was changed, the time this happened, and the user who made the change. This results in an audit trail that gives you an excellent view of what happened at every point in time. When you visualize the domain events for a given `Order` in the e-commerce web application, you might end up with the view shown in the following table.

Timeline for a given Order

Date	User	Description
2018-11-21 15:21	Mary Rowan	Order created
2018-11-21 15:26	Mary Rowan	Order approved
2018-11-21 15:27	Mary Rowan	Order paid
2018-11-22 08:10	[system]	Order shipped
2018-11-23 15:48	[system]	Order delivered

In chapter 10, we'll demonstrate yet another solution for implementing audit trails.

The most common cause of DEPENDENCY cycles is an SRP violation. Fixing the violation by breaking classes into smaller, more focused classes is typically a good solution, but there are also other strategies for breaking DEPENDENCY cycles.

6.3.4   *Common strategies for breaking DEPENDENCY cycles*

When we encounter a DEPENDENCY cycle, our first question is, "Where did I fail?" A DEPENDENCY cycle should immediately trigger a thorough evaluation of the root cause. Any cycle is a design smell, so your first reaction should be to redesign the involved part to prevent the cycle from happening in the first place. Table 6.4 shows some general directions you can take.

Table 6.4   Some redesign strategies for breaking DEPENDENCY cycles, ordered from most to least preferable strategy

Strategy	Description
Split classes	As you saw with the audit trail example, in most cases, you can split classes with too many methods into smaller classes to break the cycle.
.NET events	You can often break a cycle by changing one of the ABSTRACTIONS to raise events instead of having to explicitly invoke a DEPENDENCY to inform the DEPENDENCY that something happened. Events are particularly appropriate if one side only invokes void methods on its DEPENDENCY.
PROPERTY INJECTION	If all else fails, you can break the cycle by refactoring one class from CONSTRUCTOR INJECTION to PROPERTY INJECTION. This should be a last-ditch effort, because it only treats the symptoms.

Make no mistake: a DEPENDENCY cycle is a design smell. Your first priority should be to analyze the code to understand why the cycle appears. Still, sometimes you can't change the design, even if you understand the root cause of the cycle.

6.3.5   *Last resort: Breaking the cycle with PROPERTY INJECTION*

In some cases, the design error is out of your control, but you still need to break the cycle. In such cases, you can do this by using PROPERTY INJECTION, even if it's a temporary solution.

> **WARNING**   Only resort to solving cycles by using PROPERTY INJECTION as a last-ditch effort. It only treats the symptoms instead of curing the illness.

To break the cycle, you must analyze it to figure out where you can make a cut. Because using PROPERTY INJECTION suggests an optional rather than a required DEPENDENCY, it's important that you closely inspect all DEPENDENCIES to determine where cutting hurts the least.

In our audit trail example, you can resolve the cycle by changing the DEPENDENCY of SqlAuditTrailAppender from CONSTRUCTOR INJECTION to PROPERTY INJECTION. This means that you can create SqlAuditTrailAppender first, inject it into SqlUserRepository, and then subsequently assign AspNetUserContextAdapter to SqlAuditTrailAppender, as this listing shows.

CODE
SMELL

Listing 6.29 Breaking a DEPENDENCY cycle with PROPERTY INJECTION

```
var appender =
    new SqlAuditTrailAppender(context, timeProvider);    ◄──  Creates the appender
                                                               without an IUserContext
                                                               instance. This results in a
                                                               partially initialized instance.
var repository =
    new SqlUserRepository(context, appender);    ◄──  Injects the partially initialized
                                                       appender into the Repository.
var userContext = new
AspNetUserContextAdapter(
    new SqlUserByNameRetriever(context));

appender.UserContext = userContext;    ◄──  Uses PROPERTY INJECTION to finalize
                                             the initialization of the appender
                                             by injecting IUserContext.
```

Using PROPERTY INJECTION this way adds extra complexity to SqlAuditTrailAppender, because it must now be able to deal with a DEPENDENCY that isn't yet available. This leads to TEMPORAL COUPLING, as discussed in section 4.3.2.

NOTE As we stated previously in section 4.2.1, classes should never perform work involving DEPENDENCIES in their constructors. Besides making object construction slow and unreliable, using an injected DEPENDENCY might fail, because it may not yet be fully initialized.

If you don't want to relax any of the original classes in this way, a closely related approach is to introduce a Virtual Proxy, which leaves SqlAuditTrailAppender intact:[17]

CODE
SMELL

Listing 6.30 Breaking a DEPENDENCY cycle with a Virtual Proxy

```
var lazyAppender = new LazyAuditTrailAppender();    ◄──  Creates a
                                                          Virtual Proxy
var repository =
    new SqlUserRepository(context, lazyAppender);

var userContext = new
AspNetUserContextAdapter(
    new SqlUserByNameRetriever(context));    ──  Injects the real appender
                                                  into the property of the
lazyAppender.Appender =    ◄──────────────────────  Virtual Proxy
    new SqlAuditTrailAppender(
        userContext, context, timeProvider);
```

---

[17] Erich Gamma et al., *Design Patterns*, 208.

LazyAuditTrailAppender implements IAuditTrailAppender like SqlAuditTrail-Appender does. But it takes its IAuditTrailAppender DEPENDENCY through PROPERTY INJECTION instead of CONSTRUCTOR INJECTION, allowing you to break the cycle without violating the invariants of the original classes. The next listing shows the LazyAudit-TrailAppender Virtual Proxy.

Listing 6.31　A LazyAuditTrailAppender Virtual Proxy implementation

```
public class LazyAuditTrailAppender : IAuditTrailAppender
{
    public IAuditTrailAppender Appender { get; set; }        ◄─┐ Property that allows breaking
                                                                the DEPENDENCY cycle

    public void Append(Entity changedEntity)
    {
        if (this.Appender == null)     ◄──── Guard Clause
        {
            throw new InvalidOperationException("Appender was not set.");
        }

        this.Appender.Append(changedEntity);     ◄──── Forwards the call
    }
}
```

Always keep in mind that the best way to address a cycle is to redesign the API so that the cycle disappears. But in the rare cases where this is impossible or highly undesirable, you must break the cycle by using PROPERTY INJECTION in at least one place. This enables you to compose the rest of the object graph apart from the DEPENDENCY associated with the property. When the rest of the object graph is fully populated, you can inject the appropriate instance via the property. PROPERTY INJECTION signals that a DEPENDENCY is optional, so you shouldn't make the change lightly.

DI isn't particularly difficult when you understand a few basic principles. As you learn, however, you're guaranteed to run into issues that may leave you stumped for a while. This chapter addressed some of the most common issues people encounter. Together with the two preceding chapters, it forms a catalog of patterns, anti-patterns, and code smells. This catalog constitutes part 2 of the book. In part 3, we'll turn toward the three dimensions of DI: OBJECT COMPOSITION, LIFETIME MANAGEMENT, and INTERCEPTION.

Summary

- Ever-changing ABSTRACTIONS are a clear sign of SINGLE RESPONSIBILITY PRINCIPLE (SRP) violations. This also relates to the OPEN/CLOSED PRINCIPLE that states that you should be able to add features without having to change existing classes.
- The more methods a class has, the higher the chance it violates the SRP. This is also related to the INTERFACE SEGREGATION PRINCIPLE, which states that no client should be forced to depend on methods it doesn't use.
- Making ABSTRACTIONS thinner solves many problems, such as the complexity of creating Proxies, Decorators, and Test Doubles.

- A benefit of CONSTRUCTOR INJECTION is that it becomes more obvious when you violate the SRP. When a single class has too many DEPENDENCIES, it's a signal that you should redesign it.

- When a constructor's parameter list grows too large, we call the phenomenon Constructor Over-injection and consider it a code smell. It's a general code smell unrelated to, but magnified by, DI.

- You can redesign from Constructor Over-injection in many ways, but splitting up a large class into smaller, more focused classes according to well-known design patterns is always a good move.

- You can refactor away from Constructor Over-injection by applying Facade Services refactoring. A Facade Service hides a natural cluster of interacting DEPENDENCIES with their behavior behind a single ABSTRACTION.

- Facade Service refactoring allows discovering these natural clusters and draws previously undiscovered relationships and domain concepts out in the open. Facade Service is related to Parameter Objects but, instead of combining and exposing components, it exposes only the encapsulated behavior while hiding the constituents.

- You can refactor away from Constructor Over-injection by introducing domain events into your application. With domain events, you capture actions that can trigger a change to the state of the application you're developing.

- A LEAKY ABSTRACTION is an ABSTRACTION, such as an interface, that leaks implementation details, such as layer-specific types or implementation-specific behavior.

- ABSTRACTIONS that implement `IDisposable` are LEAKY ABSTRACTIONS. `IDisposable` should be put into effect within the implementation instead.

- Conceptually, there's only one instance of a service ABSTRACTION. ABSTRACTIONS that leak this knowledge to their consumers aren't designed with those consumers in mind.

- Service ABSTRACTIONS should typically not expose other service ABSTRACTIONS in their definition. ABSTRACTIONS that depend on other ABSTRACTIONS force their clients to know about both ABSTRACTIONS.

- When it comes to applying DI, Abstract Factories are often overused. In many cases, better alternatives exist.

- The DEPENDENCIES created by an Abstract Factory should conceptually require a runtime value. The translation from a runtime value into an ABSTRACTION should make sense on the conceptual level. If you feel the urge to introduce an Abstract Factory to be able to create instances of a concrete implementation, you may have a LEAKY ABSTRACTION on hand. Instead, the Proxy pattern provides you with a better solution.

- Having factory-like behavior inside some classes is typically unavoidable. Application-wide Factory ABSTRACTIONS, however, should be reviewed with suspicion.

- An Abstract Factory always increases the number of DEPENDENCIES a consumer has, along with its complexity.
- When you use Abstract Factories to select DEPENDENCIES based on supplied runtime data, more often than not, you can reduce complexity by refactoring towards Facades that don't expose the underlying DEPENDENCY.
- DEPENDENCY cycles are typically caused by SRP violations.
- Improving the design of the part of the application that contains the DEPENDENCY cycle should be your preferred option. In the majority of cases, this means splitting up classes into smaller, more focused classes.
- DEPENDENCY cycles can be broken using PROPERTY INJECTION. You should only resort to solving cycles by using PROPERTY INJECTION as a last-ditch effort. It only treats the symptoms instead of curing the illness.
- Classes should never perform work involving DEPENDENCIES in their constructors because the injected DEPENDENCY may not yet be fully initialized.

Part 3

Pure DI

In chapter 1, we gave a short outline of the three dimensions of DI: OBJECT COMPOSITION, LIFETIME MANAGEMENT, and INTERCEPTION. In this part of the book, we'll explore these dimensions in depth, providing each with their own chapter. Many DI CONTAINERS have features that directly relate to these dimensions. Some provide features in all three dimensions, whereas others only support some of them.

Because a DI CONTAINER is an optional tool, we feel it's more important to explain the underlying principles and techniques that containers typically use to implement these features. Given this, part 3 examines how to apply DI without using a DI CONTAINER at all. A practical do-it-yourself guide, this is what we call PURE DI.

Chapter 7 explains how to compose objects in various frameworks like ASP.NET Core MVC, Console Applications, and so on. Not all frameworks support DI equally well, and even among those that do, the details differ a lot. For each framework, it can be difficult to identify the SEAM that enables DI. Once that SEAM is found, however, you have a solution for all applications that use that particular framework. In chapter 7, we've done this work for the most common .NET application frameworks. Think of it as a catalog of framework SEAMS.

Although composing objects isn't particularly hard with PURE DI, you should begin to see the benefits of a real DI CONTAINER after reading about LIFETIME MANAGEMENT in chapter 8. It's possible to properly manage the lifetime of various objects in an object graph, but it requires more custom code than OBJECT COMPOSITION. And none of that code adds any particular business value to an application. In addition to explaining the basics of LIFETIME MANAGEMENT, chapter 8 also contains a catalog of common lifestyles. This catalog serves as a vocabulary for discussing lifestyles throughout part 4. Although you don't have to implement any of these by hand, it's good to know how they work.

The remaining chapters of part 3 explain the last dimension of DI: INTERCEPTION. In chapter 9, we'll look at the frequently occurring problem of implementing

CROSS-CUTTING CONCERNS in a component-based way. We'll do this by using the Decorator design pattern. Chapter 9 also functions as an introduction to the two chapters following it.

We'll look at the ASPECT-ORIENTED PROGRAMMING (AOP) paradigm in chapter 10 and see how a careful application design, based on the SOLID principles, enables you to create highly maintainable code, without the use of any special tooling. We consider this chapter the climax of the book—this is where many readers using the early access program said they began to see the contours of a tremendously powerful way to model software.

Besides applying SOLID design principles, there are other ways to practice ASPECT-ORIENTED PROGRAMMING. Instead of using patterns and principles, you can use specialized tooling such as compile-time weaving and dynamic INTERCEPTION tools. These are described in chapter 11.

Application composition

In this chapter

- Composing console applications
- Composing Universal Windows Programming (UWP) applications
- Composing ASP.NET Core MVC applications

Cooking a gourmet meal with several courses is a challenging undertaking, particularly if you want to partake in the consumption. You can't eat and cook at the same time, yet many dishes require last-minute cooking to turn out well. Professional cooks know how to resolve many of these challenges. Amidst many tricks of the trade, they use the general principle of *mise en place*, which can be loosely translated to *everything in place*.[1] Everything that can be prepared well in advance is, well, prepared in advance. Vegetables are cleaned and chopped, meats cut, stocks cooked, ovens preheated, tools laid out, and so on.

If ice cream is part of the dessert, it can be made the day before. If the first course contains mussels, they can be cleaned hours before. Even such a fragile component as sauce béarnaise can be prepared up to an hour before. When the guests are ready

---

[1] French pronunciation: mi zã 'plas.

211

to eat, only the final preparations are necessary: reheat the sauce while frying the meat, and so on. In many cases, this final composition of the meal need not take more than 5 to 10 minutes. Figure 7.1 illustrates the process.

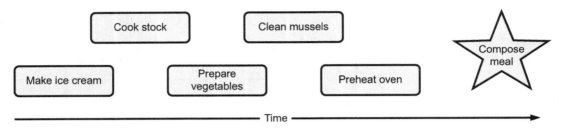

Figure 7.1 *Mise en place* **involves preparing all components of the meal well in advance so that the final composition of the meal can be done as quickly and effortlessly as possible.**

The principle of *mise en place* is similar to developing a loosely coupled application with DI. You can write all the required components well in advance and only compose them when you absolutely must.

As with all analogies, we can only take this one so far. In cooking, preparation and composition are separated by time, whereas in application development, separation occurs across modules and layers. Figure 7.2 shows how to compose the components in the COMPOSITION ROOT.

At runtime, the first thing that happens is OBJECT COMPOSITION. As soon as the object graph is wired up, OBJECT COMPOSITION is finished, and the constituent components take over. In this chapter, we'll focus on the COMPOSITION ROOTS of several application frameworks. In contrast to *mise en place*, OBJECT COMPOSITION doesn't happen as late as possible, but in a place where integration of the different modules is required.

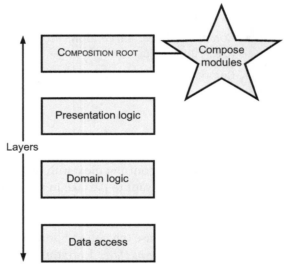

Figure 7.2 The COMPOSITION ROOT composes all the independent modules of the application.

DEFINITION   OBJECT COMPOSITION is the act of building up hierarchies of related components. This composition takes place inside the COMPOSITION ROOT.

OBJECT COMPOSITION is the foundation of DI, and it's one of the easiest parts to understand. You already know how to do it because you compose objects all the time when you create objects that contain other objects.

In section 4.1, we covered the basics of when and how to compose applications. This chapter doesn't repeat that information. Instead, we want to help you address some of the challenges that can arise as you compose objects. Those challenges stem not from OBJECT COMPOSITION itself, but from the application frameworks in which you work. These issues tend to be specific to each framework, and so are the resolutions. In our experience, these challenges pose some of the greatest obstacles to successfully applying DI, so we'll focus on them. Doing so will make the chapter less theoretical and more practical than the previous chapters.

> **NOTE** If you only want to read about applying DI in your framework of choice, you can skip ahead to that section in this chapter. Each section is intended to stand alone.

It's easy to compose an application's entire DEPENDENCY hierarchy when you have full control over the application's lifetime (as you do with command-line applications). But some frameworks in .NET (for example, ASP.NET Core) involve INVERSION OF CONTROL, which can sometimes make it more difficult to apply DI. Understanding each framework's SEAMS is key to applying DI for that particular framework. In this chapter, we'll examine how to implement COMPOSITION ROOTS in the most common .NET Core frameworks.

We'll begin each section with a general introduction to applying DI in a particular framework, followed by an extensive example built on the e-commerce example that runs throughout most of this book. We'll start with the easiest framework in which to apply DI, and then gradually work through the more complex frameworks. The easiest type to apply DI to is, by far, a console application, so we'll discuss this next.

> **NOTE** Some of the old .NET frameworks (such as PowerShell and older versions of ASP.NET Web Forms) are downright hostile environments in which to apply DI. The more recent .NET Core frameworks, on the other hand, are more DI-friendly. In this book, we mainly focus on those newer .NET Core frameworks. If you're interested in finding out how to apply DI to ASP.NET MVC, Web Forms, WCF, WPF, or PowerShell, grab the digital copy of the first edition of this book; it comes with your purchase of this edition. Chapter 7 discusses each in great detail.

7.1 Composing console applications

A console application is, hands down, the easiest type of application to compose. Contrary to most other .NET BCL application frameworks, a console application involves virtually no INVERSION OF CONTROL. When execution hits the application's entry point (usually the Main method in the Program class), you're on your own. There are no special events to subscribe to, no interfaces to implement, and precious few services you can use.

The `Program` class is a suitable COMPOSITION ROOT. In its `Main` method, you compose the application's modules and let them take over. There's nothing to it, but let's look at an example.

7.1.1 *Example: Updating currencies using the UpdateCurrency program*

In chapter 4, we looked at how to provide a currency conversion feature for the sample e-commerce application. Section 4.2.4 introduced the `ICurrencyConverter` ABSTRACTION that applies exchange rates from one currency to other currencies. Because `ICurrencyConverter` is an interface, we could have created many different implementations, but in the example, we used a database. The purpose of the example code in chapter 4 was to demonstrate how to retrieve and implement currency conversion, so we never looked at how to update exchange rates in the database.

> **NOTE** The complete source code of this example is available in the source code that accompanies the book.

To continue the example, let's examine how to write a simple .NET Core console application that enables an administrator or super-user to update the exchange rates without having to interact directly with the database. The console application talks to the database and processes the incoming command-line arguments. Because the purpose of this program is to update the exchange rates in the database, we'll call it UpdateCurrency. It takes two command-line arguments:

- The currency code
- The exchange rate from the primary currency (USD) to this currency

USD is the primary currency in our system, and we store all the exchange rates of other currencies relative it. For example, the exchange rate for USD to EUR is expressed as 1 USD costing 0.88 EUR (December 2018). When we want to update the exchange rate at the command line, it looks like this:

```
d:\> dotnet commerce\UpdateCurrency.dll EUR "0.88"
Updated: 0.88 EUR = 1 USD.
```

> **NOTE** In .NET Core, a console application is a .dll (not an .exe) that can be started by running the `dotnet` command with the name of the DLL as the first argument.

Executing the program updates the database and writes the new values back to the console. Let's look at how we build such a console application.

7.1.2 Building the COMPOSITION ROOT of the UpdateCurrency program

UpdateCurrency uses the default entry point for a console program: the Main method in the Program class. This acts as the COMPOSITION ROOT for the application.

Listing 7.1 The console application's COMPOSITION ROOT

```
class Program
{
    static void Main(string[] args)
    {
        string connectionString =                    Loads configuration
            LoadConnectionString();                   values

        CurrencyParser parser =                                    Builds the object graph
            CreateCurrencyParser(connectionString);

        ICommand command = parser.Parse(args);        Invokes the desired
        command.Execute();                            functionality
    }

    static string LoadConnectionString()
    {
        var configuration = new ConfigurationBuilder()
            .SetBasePath(AppContext.BaseDirectory)
            .AddJsonFile("appsettings.json", optional: false)
            .Build();

        return configuration.GetConnectionString(
            "CommerceConnectionString");
    }

    static CurrencyParser CreateCurrencyParser(string connectionString) ...
}
```

The Program class's only responsibilities are to load the configuration values, compose all relevant modules, and let the composed object graph take care of the functionality. In this example, the composition of the application's modules is extracted to the CreateCurrencyParser method, whereas the Main method is responsible for calling methods on the composed object graph. CreateCurrencyParser composes its object graph using hardwired DEPENDENCIES. We'll return to it shortly to examine how it's implemented.

Any COMPOSITION ROOT should only do four things: load configuration values, build the object graph, invoke the desired functionality, and, as we'll discuss in the next chapter, release the object graph. As soon as it has done that, it should get out of the way and leave the rest to the invoked instance.

> **NOTE** As we stated previously in section 4.1.3, you should separate the loading of configuration values from the methods that do OBJECT COMPOSITION, as shown in listing 7.1. This decouples OBJECT COMPOSITION from the configuration system in use, making it possible to test without the existence of a (valid) configuration file.

With this infrastructure in place, you can now ask `CreateCurrencyParser` to create a `CurrencyParser` that parses the incoming arguments and eventually executes the corresponding command. This example uses PURE DI, but it's straightforward to replace it with a DI CONTAINER like those covered in part 4.

7.1.3 Composing object graphs in `CreateCurrencyParser`

The `CreateCurrencyParser` method exists for the express purpose of wiring up all DEPENDENCIES for the UpdateCurrency program. The following listing shows the implementation.

Listing 7.2 `CreateCurrencyParser` method that composes the object graph

```
static CurrencyParser CreateCurrencyParser(string connectionString)
{
    IExchangeRateProvider provider =
        new SqlExchangeRateProvider(                      Composes the
            new CommerceContext(connectionString));       object graph

    return new CurrencyParser(provider);
}
```

In this listing, the object graph is rather shallow. The `CurrencyParser` class requires an instance of the `IExchangeRateProvider` interface, and you construct `SqlExchangeRateProvider` for communicating with the database in the `CreateCurrencyParser` method.

The `CurrencyParser` class uses CONSTRUCTOR INJECTION, so you pass it the `SqlExchangeRateProvider` instance that was just created. You then return the newly created `CurrencyParser` from the method. In case you're wondering, here's the constructor signature of `CurrencyParser`:

```
public CurrencyParser(IExchangeRateProvider exchangeRateProvider)
```

Recall that `IExchangeRateProvider` is an interface that's implemented by `SqlExchangeRateProvider`. As part of the COMPOSITION ROOT, `CreateCurrencyParser` contains a hard-coded mapping from `IExchangeRateProvider` to `SqlExchangeRateProvider`. The rest of the code, however, remains loosely coupled, because it consumes only the ABSTRACTION.

This example may seem simple, but it composes types from three different application layers. Let's briefly examine how these layers interact in this example.

7.1.4 A closer look at UpdateCurrency's layering

The COMPOSITION ROOT is where components from all layers are wired together. The entry point and the COMPOSITION ROOT constitute the only code of the executable. All implementation is delegated to lower layers, as figure 7.3 illustrates.

The diagram in figure 7.3 may look complicated, but it represents almost the entire code base of the console application. Most of the application logic consists of parsing the input arguments and choosing the correct command based on the input. All this takes place in the application services layer, which only talks directly with the domain layer via the IExchangeRateProvider interface and the Currency class.

IExchangeRateProvider is injected into CurrencyParser by the COMPOSITION ROOT and CurrencyParser is subsequently used as a factory to create ICommand instances used by the Program class. The data access layer supplies the SQL Server–based implementations of the domain ABSTRACTIONS. Although none of the other application classes talk directly to those implementations, CreateCurrencyParser maps the ABSTRACTIONS to the concrete classes.

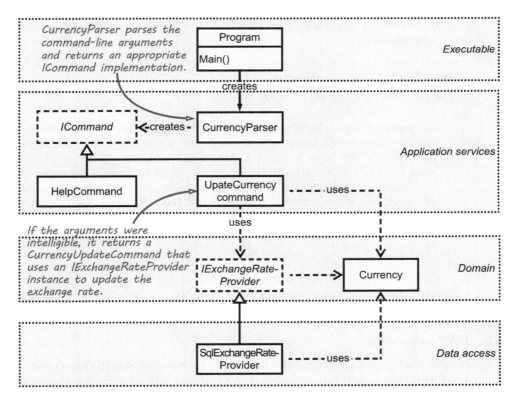

Figure 7.3 Component composition of the UpdateCurrency application

NOTE You might recall from section 6.2 that the use of Abstract Factories should be viewed with suspicion. In this case, however, using a factories is fine because only the COMPOSITION ROOT makes use of it.

Using DI with a console application is easy because there's virtually no external INVERSION OF CONTROL involved. The .NET Framework spins up the process and hands control to the Main method. This is similar to working with Universal Windows Programming (UWP), which allows OBJECT COMPOSITION without any SEAMS.

7.2 *Composing UWP applications*

Composing a UWP application is almost as easy as composing a console application. In this section, we'll implement a small UWP application for managing products of the e-commerce application using the Model-View-ViewModel (MVVM) pattern. We'll take a look at where to place the COMPOSITION ROOT, how to construct and initialize view models, how to bind views to their corresponding view models, and how to ensure we can navigate from one page to the next.

A UWP application's entry point is fairly uncomplicated, and although it doesn't provide SEAMS explicitly targeted at enabling DI, you can easily compose an application in any way you prefer.

What's a UWP application?

Microsoft has defined UWP this way:

The Universal Windows Platform (UWP) is the application platform for Windows 10. You can develop apps for UWP with just one API set, one application package, and one store to reach all Windows 10 devices (PC, tablet, phone, Xbox, HoloLens, Surface Hub, and more). It's easier to support a number of screen sizes and a variety of interaction models, whether it be touch, mouse and keyboard, a game controller, or a pen. At the core of UWP applications is the idea that users want their experiences to be common across all their devices, and they want to use whatever device is most convenient or productive for the task at hand.[2]

In this section, we won't be teaching UWP itself. Basic knowledge about building UWP applications is assumed.[3]

7.2.1 *UWP composition*

A UWP application's entry point is defined in its App class. As with most other classes in UWP, this class is split into two files: App.xaml and App.xaml.cs. You define what happens at application startup in the App.xaml.cs.

---

[2] Source: https://mng.bz/DVVg.

[3] To learn about UWP, see Ayan Chatterjee, *Building Apps for the Universal Windows Platform*, (Apress, 2017).

NOTE The code for this example is available in the source code that accompanies the book.

When you create a new UWP project in Visual Studio, the App.xaml.cs file defines an `OnLaunched` method that defines which page is shown when the application starts; in this case, `MainPage`.

Listing 7.3   `OnLaunched` method of the App.xaml.cs file

```
protected override void OnLaunched(LaunchActivatedEventArgs e)
{
    ...

    rootFrame.Navigate(typeof(MainPage), e.Arguments);

    ...
}
```

> Among other things, a default UWP project in Visual Studio navigates the user to the MainPage on launch by calling Frame.Navigate.

The `OnLaunched` method is similar to a console application's `Main` method—it's the entry point for your application. The `App` class becomes the application's COMPOSITION ROOT. You can use a DI CONTAINER or PURE DI to compose the page; the next example uses PURE DI.

7.2.2   Example: Wiring up a product-management rich client

The example in the previous section created our commerce console application for setting exchange rates. In this example, you'll create a UWP application that enables you to manage products. Figures 7.4 and 7.5 show screen captures of this application.

Figure 7.4   Product Management's main page is a list of products. You can edit or delete products by tapping on a row, or you can add a new product by tapping Add Product.

Figure 7.5   Product Management's product-edit page lets you change the product name and unit price in dollars. The application makes use of UWP's default command bar.

The entire application is implemented using the MVVM approach and contains the four layers shown in figure 7.6. We keep the part with the most logic isolated from the other modules; in this case, that's the presentation logic. The UWP client layer is a thin layer that does little apart from defining the UI and delegating implementation to the other modules.

The diagram in figure 7.6 is similar to what you've seen in previous chapters, with the addition of a presentation logic layer. The data access layer can directly connect to a database, as we did in the e-commerce web application, or it can connect to a product-management web service. How the information is stored isn't that relevant where the presentation logic layer is concerned, so we won't go into details about that in this chapter.

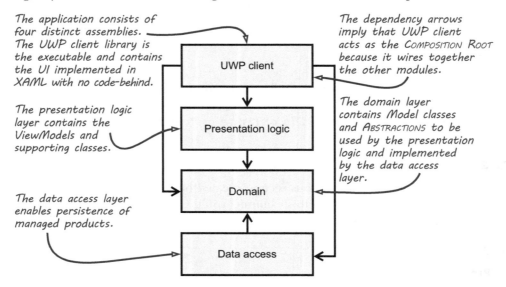

Figure 7.6   The four distinct assemblies of the product-management rich client application

MVVM

Model-View-ViewModel (MVVM) is a design pattern for which UWP is particularly well suited.[4] It divides UI code into three distinct responsibilities:

- *The Model is the underlying model for the application.* This is often, but not always, the domain model. It frequently consists of Plain Old CLR Objects (POCOs). Notice that the Model is usually expressed in a UI-neutral way; it doesn't assume that it'll be exposed directly by a UI, so it doesn't expose any UWP-specific functionality.
- *The View is the UI we look at.* In UWP, you can declaratively express the View in XAML and use data binding and data templating to present the data. It's possible

---

[4] Read more about MVVM in Josh Smith's "Patterns: WPF Apps With The Model-View-ViewModel Design Pattern," 2009, https://msdn.microsoft.com/en-us/magazine/dd419663.aspx.

> to express the views without the use of code-behind, and, in fact, it's often preferred, as it helps keep the views focused exclusively on UI.
> - *The ViewModel is the bridge between the View and the Model.* Each ViewModel is a class that translates and exposes the Model in a technology-specific way. In UWP, this means it may expose lists as `System.Collections.ObjectModel.ObservableCollection`, user actions as `System.Windows.Input.ICommand`, and so on.
>
> The role of the ViewModel in MVVM is different from the View Model in an MVC application. With MVC, the View Model is a behaviorless data object and is newed up in your application code. MVVM ViewModels, on the other hand, are components with DEPENDENCIES. In your UWP application, ViewModels will be composed using DI.

With MVVM, you assign a ViewModel to a page's `DataContext` property, and the data-binding and data-templating engines take care of presenting the data correctly as you spin up new ViewModels or change the data in the existing ViewModels. Before you can create the first `ViewModel`, however, you need to define some constructs that enable ViewModels to navigate to other ViewModels. Likewise, for a ViewModel to be initialized with the runtime data required when a page is shown to the user, you must let the ViewModels implement a custom interface. The following section addresses these concerns before getting to the meat of the application: the `MainViewModel`.

INJECTING DEPENDENCIES INTO THE `MainViewModel`

`MainPage` contains only XAML markup and no custom code-behind. Instead, it uses data binding to display data and handle user commands. To enable this, you must assign a `MainViewModel` to its `DataContext` property. This, however, is a form of PROPERTY INJECTION. We'd like to use CONSTRUCTOR INJECTION instead. To allow this, we remove the `MainPage`'s default constructor with an overloaded constructor that accepts the `MainViewModel` as an argument, where the constructor internally assigns that `DataContext` property:

```
public sealed partial class MainPage : Page
{
    public MainPage(MainViewModel vm)
    {
        this.InitializeComponent();

        this.DataContext = vm;
    }
}
```

`MainViewModel` exposes data, such as the list of products, as well as commands to create, update, or delete a product. Enabling this functionality depends on a service that provides access to the product catalog: the `IProductRepository` ABSTRACTION. Apart from `IProductRepository`, `MainViewModel` also needs a service that it can use to control its windowing environment, such as navigating to other pages. This other DEPENDENCY is called INavigationService:

```
public interface INavigationService
{
    void NavigateTo<TViewModel>(Action whenDone = null, object model = null)
        where TViewModel : IViewModel;
}
```

> **NOTE**   C# 4 introduced *optional method arguments*, which enable you to omit arguments for some parameters. In this case, the C# compiler supplies the call with the declared default. In the previous listing, both method parameters are optional. Listing 7.4 calls NavigateTo, sometimes omitting arguments.

The NavigateTo method is generic, so the type of ViewModel that it needs to navigate to must be supplied as its generic type argument. The method arguments are passed by the navigation service to the created ViewModel. For this to work, a ViewModel must implement IViewModel. For this reason, the NavigateTo method specifies the generic type constraint where TViewModel : IViewModel.[5] The following code snippet shows IViewModel:

```
public interface IViewModel
{
    void Initialize(Action whenDone, object model);   ◄─── Initializes a
}                                                           ViewModel
```

The Initialize method contains the same arguments as the INavigationService .NavigateTo method. The navigation service will invoke Initialize on a constructed ViewModel. The model represents the data that the ViewModel needs to initialize, such as a Product. The whenDone action allows the originating ViewModel to get notified when the user exits this ViewModel, as we'll discuss shortly.

Using the previous interface definitions, you can now construct a ViewModel for MainPage. The following listing shows MainViewModel in its full glory.

Listing 7.4   The `MainViewModel` class

```
public class MainViewModel : IViewModel,        ◄─── To be able to inform the view that it
    INotifyPropertyChanged                           should be updated, the ViewModel must
{                                                    implement INotifyPropertyChanged.
    private readonly INavigationService navigator;
    private readonly IProductRepository repository;
```

---

[5] Using generic type constraints, you can narrow the possible types that you can use as the generic type argument. This is verified for you by the C# compiler.

The ViewModel contains several properties that the XAML of MainPage binds to. Model is the list of products shown in the grid view; the ICommand properties represent the actions that are executed when their corresponding buttons are pressed.

```
public MainViewModel(
    INavigationService navigator,
    IProductRepository repository)
{
    this.navigator = navigator;
    this.repository = repository;

    this.AddProductCommand =
        new RelayCommand(this.AddProduct);
    this.EditProductCommand =
        new RelayCommand(this.EditProduct);
}

public IEnumerable<Product> Model { get; set; }
public ICommand AddProductCommand { get; }
public ICommand EditProductCommand { get; }

public event PropertyChangedEventHandler
    PropertyChanged = (s, e) => { };

public void Initialize(
    Action whenDone, object model)
{
    this.Model = this.repository.GetAll();
    this.PropertyChanged.Invoke(this,
        new PropertyChangedEventArgs("Model"));
}

private void AddProduct()
{
    this.navigator.NavigateTo<NewProductViewModel>(
        whenDone: this.GoBack);
}

private void EditProduct(object product)
{
    this.navigator.NavigateTo<EditProductViewModel>(
        whenDone: this.GoBack,
        model: product;
}

private void GoBack()
{
    this.navigator.NavigateTo<MainViewModel>();
}
}
```

The Initialize method is specified by the IViewModel interface, which every ViewModel is required to implement. In the case of MainViewModel, you don't use the arguments, but do load all products using the injected IProductRepository.

When the Add Product button (see figure 7.4) is pressed, this method will be invoked.

By calling the PropertyChanged event of the implemented INotifyPropertyChanged interface and supplying it with the name of the property being changed, UWP can figure out how the screen should be repainted.

On initialization, EditProductViewModel loads the product you want to edit. This requires you to pass the product ID with the call to NavigateTo.

When the user taps a row in the products table, the EditProduct method is invoked. With the call, UWP passes on the bound item from the list, which will be a Product from the Model collection.

The command methods, AddProduct and EditProduct, both instruct INavigation-Service to navigate to the page for the corresponding ViewModel. In the case of AddProduct, this corresponds to NewProductViewModel. The NavigateTo method is supplied with a delegate that'll be invoked by NewProductViewModel when the user finishes working on that page. This results in invoking the MainViewModel's GoBack method, which will navigate the application back to MainViewModel. To paint a complete picture, listing 7.5 shows a simplified version of the MainPage XAML definition and how the XAML is bound to the Model, EditProductCommand, and AddProduct-Command properties of MainViewModel.

Listing 7.5   XAML of MainPage

```
<Page x:Class="Ploeh.Samples.ProductManagement.UWPClient.MainPage"
    xmlns:commands="using:ProductManagement.PresentationLogic.UICommands"
    ...>
    <Grid>
        <Grid.RowDefinitions>
            ...
        </Grid.RowDefinitions>

        <GridView ItemsSource="{Binding Model}"
            commands:ItemClickCommand.Command="{Binding EditProductCommand}"
            IsItemClickEnabled="True">
            <GridView.ItemTemplate>
                <DataTemplate>
                    <Grid>
                        <Grid.ColumnDefinitions>
                            <ColumnDefinition Width="2*"/>
                            <ColumnDefinition Width="*"/>
                        </Grid.ColumnDefinitions>
                        <StackPanel Grid.Column="0">
                            <TextBlock Text="{Binding Name}" />
                        </StackPanel>
                        <StackPanel Grid.Column="1">
                            <TextBlock Text="{Binding UnitPrice}" />
                        </StackPanel>
                    </Grid>
                </DataTemplate>
            </GridView.ItemTemplate>
        </GridView>

        <CommandBar Grid.Row="5" Grid.ColumnSpan="3" Grid.Column="0">
            <AppBarToggleButton Icon="Add" Label="Add product"
                Command="{Binding AddProductCommand}" />
        </CommandBar>
    </Grid>
</Page>
```

NOTE The XAML's `GridView` uses a custom UI command named `ItemClick-Command` to allow taps and clicks on GridView rows to be bound to the View-Model's `EditProductCommand`. A discussion of this UI command is outside the scope of the book, but the custom command is available in the book's accompanying source code, where you can see the full version of the XAML.

Although the previous XAML makes use of the older `Binding` markup extension, as a UWP developer, you might be used to using the newer `x:Bind` markup extension. `x:Bind` gives compile-time support, but requires types to be fixed at compile time, typically defined in the view's code-behind class. Because you bind to a ViewModel that's stored in the untyped `DataContext` property, you lose compile-time support and, therefore, need to fall back to the `Binding` markup extension.[6]

The two main elements in the `MainPage` XAML are a `GridView` and a `CommandBar`. The `GridView` is used to display the available products and bind to both the `Model` and `EditProductCommand` properties; its `DataTemplate` binds to the `Name` and `UnitPrice` properties of the `Model`'s `Product` elements. The `CommandBar` displays a generic ribbon with operations that the user is allowed to invoke. The `CommandBar` binds to the `Add-ProductCommand` property. With the definitions of `MainViewModel` and `MainPage`, you can now start wiring up the application.

WIRING UP `MainViewModel`

Before wiring up `MainViewModel`, let's take a look at all the classes involved in this DEPENDENCY graph. Figure 7.7 shows the graph for the application, starting with `MainPage`.

Now that you've identified all the building blocks of the application, you can compose it. To do this, you must create both a `MainViewModel` and a `MainPage`, and then inject the ViewModel to the `MainPage`'s constructor. To wire up `MainViewModel`, you have to compose it with its DEPENDENCIES:

```
IViewModel vm = new MainViewModel(navigationService, productRepository);
Page view = new MainPage(vm);
```

As you saw in listing 7.3, the default Visual Studio template calls `Frame .Navigate(Type)`. The `Navigate` method creates a new `Page` instance on your behalf and shows that page to the user. There's no way to supply a `Page` instance to `Navigate`, but you can work around this by manually assigning the page created to the `Content` property of the application's main `Frame`:

```
var frame = (Frame)Window.Current.Content;
frame.Content = view;
```

Because these are the important pieces to glue the application together, this is exactly what you'll do in the COMPOSITION ROOT.

---

[6] See the MSDN article, "Data Binding in Depth", https://mng.bz/mz9P.

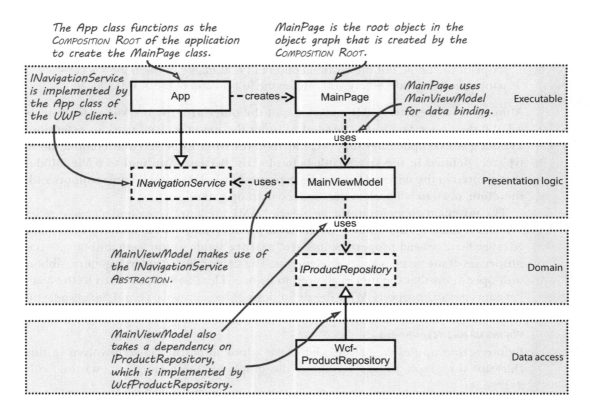

Figure 7.7   DEPENDENCY graph of the product-management rich client

7.2.3   *Implementing the COMPOSITION ROOT in the UWP application*

There are many ways to create the COMPOSITION ROOT. For this example, we chose to place both the navigation logic and the construction of View/ViewModel pairs inside the App.xaml.cs file to keep the example relatively succinct. The application's COMPOSITION ROOT is displayed in figure 7.8 .

> **NOTE** An important part of the COMPOSITION ROOT is the COMPOSER. It's a unifying term to refer to any object or method that composes DEPENDENCIES and is discussed in more detail in the next chapter.

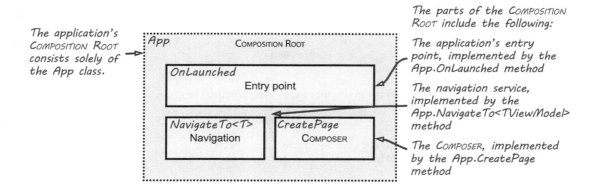

The parts of the COMPOSITION ROOT include the following:

The application's entry point, implemented by the App.OnLaunched method

The navigation service, implemented by the App.NavigateTo<TViewModel> method

The COMPOSER, implemented by the App.CreatePage method

The application's COMPOSITION ROOT consists solely of the App class.

Figure 7.8   The product-management rich client's COMPOSITION ROOT

The next listing shows our COMPOSITION ROOT in action.

Listing 7.6   The product-management App class containing the COMPOSITION ROOT

```
public sealed partial class App : Application, INavigationService
{
    protected override void OnLaunched(          The application's
        LaunchActivatedEventArgs e)              entry point
    {
        if (Window.Current.Content == null)
        {                                              On launch, creates a new
            Window.Current.Content = new Frame();      Frame and activates it
            Window.Current.Activate();
            this.NavigateTo<MainViewModel>(null, null);    Creates a new
        }                                                  MainPage and
    }                                                      MainViewModel
                                                           pair, and shows
    public void NavigateTo<TViewModel>(                    the MainPage to
        Action whenDone, object model)                     the user
        where TViewModel : IViewModel
    {
        var page = this.CreatePage(typeof(TViewModel));    NavigateTo
        var viewModel = (IViewModel)page.DataContext;      triggers the
                                                           composition and
        viewModel.Initialize(whenDone, model);             initialization,
                                                           ensuring the
        var frame = (Frame)Window.Current.Content;         created page is
        frame.Content = page;                              displayed.
    }
}
```

```
private Page CreatePage(Type vmType)
{
    var repository = new WcfProductRepository();

    if (vmType == typeof(MainViewModel))
    {
        return new MainPage(
            new MainViewModel(this, repository));
    }
    else if (vmType == typeof(EditProductViewModel))
    {
        return new EditProductPage(
            new EditProductViewModel(repository));
    }
    else if (vmType == typeof(NewProductViewModel))
    {
        return new NewProductPage(
            new NewProductViewModel(repository));
    {
    else
    {
        throw new Exception("Unknown view model.");
    }
    ...
}
```

> **CreatePage constructs the requested View/ViewModel pair by composing the ViewModel and injects it into the view's constructor. Note that MainViewModel depends on an INavigationService, but because the App class implements INavigationService, it can be injected into the MainViewModel directly using the keyword this.**

The CreatePage factory method is similar to the COMPOSITION ROOT examples we discussed in section 4.1. It consists of a big list of else if statements to construct the correct pair accordingly.

NOTE   For simplicity, CreatePage of listing 7.6 creates new Page instances on every call. This isn't strictly required, but is easier to implement.

UWP offers a simple place for a COMPOSITION ROOT. All you need to do is remove the call to Frame.Navigate(Type) from OnLaunched and set Frame.Content with a manually created Page class, which is composed using a ViewModel and its DEPENDENCIES.

In most other frameworks, there's a higher degree of INVERSION OF CONTROL, which means we need to be able to identify the correct extensibility points to wire up the desired object graph. One such framework is ASP.NET Core MVC.

7.3   *Composing ASP.NET Core MVC applications*

ASP.NET Core MVC was built and designed to support DI. It comes with its own internal composition engine that you can use to build up its own components; although, as you'll see, it doesn't enforce the use of a DI CONTAINER for your application components. You can use PURE DI or whichever DI CONTAINER you like.[7]

---

[7] The ASP.NET Core designers, however, defined an ABSTRACTION over DI CONTAINERS with the intention of allowing third-party DI CONTAINERS to completely replace the built-in implementation. In our opinion, this was a grave mistake, causing pain and frustration for those who maintain DI CONTAINERS. Due to time and page constraints, a discussion of this is outside the scope of the book. Our advice, however, is to keep the built-in DI CONTAINER, even if you use a third-party DI CONTAINER to construct your application components. For more information about this, see https://simpleinjector.org/blog/2016/06/.

In this section, you'll learn how to use the main extensibility point of ASP.NET Core MVC, which allows you to plug in your logic for composing controller classes with their DEPENDENCIES. This section looks at ASP.NET Core MVC from the perspective of DI OBJECT COMPOSITION. There's a lot more to building ASP.NET Core applications than we can address in a single chapter, however. If you want to learn more about how to build applications with ASP.NET Core, take a look at Andrew Lock's *ASP.NET Core in Action* (Manning, 2018). After that, we'll take a look at how to plug in custom middleware that requires DEPENDENCIES.

> **NOTE** In ASP.NET "classic," Microsoft developed separate frameworks for MVC and Web API. With ASP.NET Core, Microsoft created one unifying framework to handle both MVC and Web API under the umbrella of ASP.NET Core MVC. From the perspective of DI, wiring a Web API is identical to an MVC application in ASP.NET Core. This means that this section applies to building Web APIs in .NET Core too.

As is always the case with practicing DI in an application framework, the key to applying it is finding the correct extensibility point. In ASP.NET Core MVC, this is an interface called `IControllerActivator`. Figure 7.9 illustrates how it fits into the framework.

Controllers are central to ASP.NET Core MVC. They handle requests and determine how to respond. If you need to query a database, validate and save incoming data, invoke domain logic, and so on, you initiate such actions from a controller. A controller shouldn't do such things itself, but rather delegate the work to the appropriate DEPENDENCIES. This is where DI comes in.

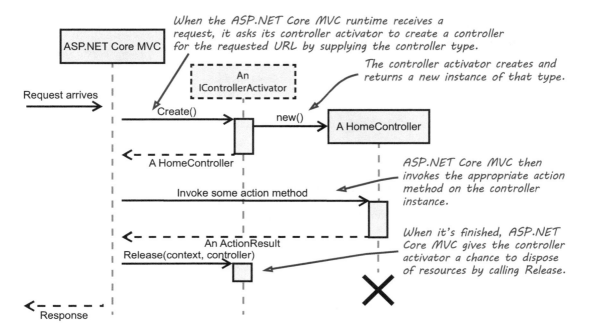

Figure 7.9   The ASP.NET Core MVC request pipeline

You want to be able to supply DEPENDENCIES to a given controller class, ideally by CONSTRUCTOR INJECTION. This is possible with a custom IControllerActivator.

7.3.1   *Creating a custom controller activator*

Creating a custom controller activator isn't particularly difficult. It requires you to implement the IControllerActivator interface:

```
public interface IControllerActivator
{
    object Create(ControllerContext context);
    void Release(ControllerContext context, object controller);
}
```

The Create method provides a ControllerContext that contains information such as the HttpContext and the controller type. This is the method where you get the chance to wire up all required DEPENDENCIES and supply them to the controller before returning the instance. You'll see an example in a moment.

If you created any resources that need to be explicitly disposed of, you can do that when the Release method is called. We'll go into further details about releasing components in the next chapter. A more practical way to ensure that DEPENDENCIES are disposed of is to add them to the list of disposable request objects using the HttpContext.Response.RegisterForDispose method. Although implementing a custom controller activator is the hard part, it won't be used unless we tell ASP.NET Core MVC about it.

USING A CUSTOM CONTROLLER ACTIVATOR IN ASP.NET CORE

A custom controller activator can be added as part of the application startup sequence—usually in the Startup class. They're used by calling AddSingleton<IControllerActivator> on the IServiceCollection instance. The next listing shows the Startup class from the sample e-commerce application.

> Listing 7.7   **Commerce application's Startup class**

```
public class Startup
{
    public Startup(IConfiguration configuration)
    {
        this.Configuration = configuration;
    }

    public IConfiguration Configuration { get; }

    public void ConfigureServices(IServiceCollection services)
    {
        services.AddMvc();

        var controllerActivator = new CommerceControllerActivator(
            Configuration.GetConnectionString("CommerceConnectionString"));

        services.AddSingleton<IControllerActivator>(controllerActivator);
    }
```

```
        public void Configure(ApplicationBuilder app, IHostingEnvironment env)
        {
            ...
        }
    }
}
```

This listing creates a new instance of the custom `CommerceControllerActivator`. By adding it to the list of known services using `AddSingleton`, you ensure the creation of controllers is INTERCEPTED by your custom controller activator. If this code looks vaguely familiar, it's because you saw something similar in section 4.1.3. Back then, we promised to show you how to implement a custom controller activator in chapter 7, and what do you know? This is chapter 7.

EXAMPLE: IMPLEMENTING THE `CommerceControllerActivator`

As you might recall from chapters 2 and 3, the e-commerce sample application presents the visitor of the website with a list of products and their prices. In section 6.2, we added a feature that allowed users to calculate a route between two locations. Although we've shown several snippets of the COMPOSITION ROOT, we didn't show a complete example. Together with listing 7.7's `Startup` class, listing 7.8's `CommerceControllerActivator` class shows a complete COMPOSITION ROOT.

The e-commerce sample application needs a custom controller activator to wire up controllers with their required DEPENDENCIES. Although the entire object graph is considerably deeper, from the perspective of the controllers themselves, the union of all immediate DEPENDENCIES is as small as two items (figure 7.10).

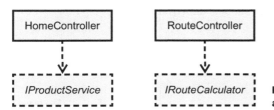

Figure 7.10 Two controllers in the sample application with their DEPENDENCIES

The following listing shows a `CommerceControllerActivator` that composes both `HomeController` and `RouteController` with their DEPENDENCIES.

> **Listing 7.8 Creating controllers using a custom controller activator**

```
public class CommerceControllerActivator : IControllerActivator
{
    private readonly string connectionString;

    public CommerceControllerActivator(string connectionString)
    {
        this.connectionString = connectionString;
    }
```

```
public object Create(ControllerContext context)
{
    Type type = context.ActionDescriptor
        .ControllerTypeInfo.AsType();

    if (type == typeof(HomeController))
    {
        return this.CreateHomeController();
    }
    else if (type == typeof(RouteController))
    {
        return this.CreateRouteController();
    }
    else
    {
        throw new Exception("Unknown controller " + type.Name);
    }
}

private HomeController CreateHomeController()
{
    return new HomeController(
        new ProductService(
            new SqlProductRepository(
                new CommerceContext(
                    this.connectionString)),
            new AspNetUserContextAdapter())));
}

private RouteController CreateRouteController()
{
    var routeAlgorithms = ...;
    return new RouteController(
        new RouteCalculator(routeAlgorithms));
}

public void Release(
    ControllerContext context, object controller)
{
}
}
```

Gets the controller Type to create from ControllerContext

Returns the appropriate controller based on the given type, assuming the requested type is either HomeController or RouteController

Explicitly wires up the controllers with the required DEPENDENCIES and returns them. Both types use CONSTRUCTOR INJECTION, so you supply the DEPENDENCIES through their constructors.

We leave the Release method empty for now, as we'll get back to this in section 8.2.

NOTE As we stated before, ASP.NET Core contains its own built-in DI CONTAINER (which we'll discuss in chapter 15). Alternatively, you could use this built-in DI CONTAINER to register your DEPENDENCIES. In chapter 12, we'll discuss how to decide whether to use PURE DI or a DI CONTAINER. In this part of the book, we'll stick to using PURE DI.

When a CommerceControllerActivator instance is registered in Startup, it correctly creates all requested controllers with the required DEPENDENCIES. Besides controllers, other common components that often require the use of DI are what ASP.NET Core calls middleware.

7.3.2 Constructing custom middleware components using PURE DI

ASP.NET Core makes it relatively easy to plug in extra behavior in the request pipeline. Such behavior can influence the request and response. In ASP.NET Core, these extensions to the request pipeline are called *middleware*. A typical use of hooking up middleware to the request pipeline is through the Use extension method:

Runs some code before continuing with the rest of the pipeline

Runs some code after the rest of the pipeline has run

```
var logger =
    loggerFactory.CreateLogger("Middleware");

app.Use(async (context, next) =>
{
    logger.LogInformation("Request started");

    await next();

    logger.LogInformation("Request ended");
});
```

Creates an ILogger instance for use by the middleware

Lets you register a lambda expression to run with each request. The context argument is an HttpContext, and the next argument is a Func<Task>.

A call to next() causes the rest of the pipeline to run. Because next() returns a Task, you must await the results of that Task.

> **NOTE** This is the first time in the book that we show a code sample that uses the C# 5.0 async and await keywords. If you're a C# developer, you've probably come across examples of asynchronous programming already because ASP.NET Core is built around an asynchronous programming model. A discussion about asynchronous programming, however, is out of the scope of this book.[8] Fortunately, when it comes to applying DI, asynchronous programming isn't an issue, because construction of object graphs should always be fast, should never depend on any I/O, and, therefore, should always be synchronous.

More often, however, more work needs to be done prior to or after the request's main logic runs. You might therefore want to extract such middleware logic into its own class. This prevents your Startup class from being cluttered and gives you the opportunity to unit test this logic, should you want to do so. You can extract the body of our previous Use lambda to an Invoke method on a newly created LoggingMiddleware class:

```
public class LoggingMiddleware
{
    private readonly ILogger logger;

    public LoggingMiddleware(ILogger logger)
    {
        this.logger = logger;
    }

    public async Task Invoke(
        HttpContext context, Func<Task> next)
    {
```

A constructor accepts the required DEPENDENCY.

The Invoke method contains the logic that was previously supplied in-line.

---

[8] For guidance on asynchronous programming, when to use it, and how to use the async and await keywords, see https://docs.microsoft.com/en-us/dotnet/csharp/async.

```
        this.logger.LogInformation("Request started");
        await next();
        this.logger.LogInformation("Request ended");
    }
}
```

With the middleware logic now moved into the LoggingMiddleware class, the Startup configuration can be minimized to the following code:

```
var logger = loggerFactory.CreateLogger("Middleware");

app.Use(async (context, next) =>
{
    var middleware = new LoggingMiddleware(logger);

    await middleware.Invoke(context, next);
});
```

Constructs a new middleware component with its DEPENDENCIES

Invokes the middleware by passing the context and next arguments

> **NOTE** When the object graph of the created middleware component becomes more complex, it may become necessary to move the creation of the component into the location where your other components are composed. In our previous example, that would be the CommerceControllerActivator. But we'll leave this as an exercise for the reader.

The great thing about ASP.NET Core MVC is that it was designed with DI in mind, so, for the most part, you only need to know and use a single extensibility point to enable DI for an application. OBJECT COMPOSITION is one of three important dimensions of DI (the others being LIFETIME MANAGEMENT and INTERCEPTION).

In this chapter, we've shown you how to compose applications from loosely coupled modules in a variety of different environments. Some frameworks actually make it easy. When you're writing console applications and Windows clients (such as UWP), you're more or less in direct control of what's happening at the application's entry point. This provides you with a distinct and easily implemented COMPOSITION ROOT. Other frameworks, such as ASP.NET Core, make you work a little harder, but they still provide SEAMS you can use to define how the application should be composed. ASP.NET Core was designed with DI in mind, so composing an application is as easy as implementing a custom IControllerActivator and adding it to the framework.

Without OBJECT COMPOSITION, there's no DI, but you may not yet have fully realized the implications for OBJECT LIFETIME when we move the creation of objects out of the consuming classes. You may find it self evident that the external caller (often a DI CONTAINER) creates new instances of DEPENDENCIES —but when are injected instances deallocated? And what if the external caller doesn't create new instances each time, but instead hands you an existing instance? These are topics for the next chapter.

Summary

- OBJECT COMPOSITION is the act of building up hierarchies of related components, which takes place inside the COMPOSITION ROOT.

- A COMPOSITION ROOT should only do four things: load configuration values, build object graphs, invoke the desired functionality, and release the object graphs.

- Only the COMPOSITION ROOT should rely on configuration files because it's more flexible for libraries to be imperatively configurable by their callers.

- Separate the loading of configuration values from the methods that do OBJECT COMPOSITION. This makes it possible to test OBJECT COMPOSITION without the existence of a configuration file.

- Model View ViewModel (MVVM) is a design in which the ViewModel is the bridge between the view and the model. Each ViewModel is a class that translates and exposes the model in a technology-specific way. In MVVM, ViewModels are the application components that will be composed using DI.

- In a console application, the `Program` class is a suitable COMPOSITION ROOT.

- In a UWP application, the `App` class is a suitable COMPOSITION ROOT, and its `OnLaunched` method is the main entry point.

- In an ASP.NET Core MVC application, the `IControllerActivator` is the correct extensibility point to plug in OBJECT COMPOSITION.

- A practical way to ensure that DEPENDENCIES are disposed of in ASP.NET Core is to use the `HttpContext.Response.RegisterForDispose` method to add them to the list of disposable request objects.

- Middleware can be added to ASP.NET Core by registering a function to the pipeline that implements a small part of the COMPOSITION ROOT. This composes the middleware component and invokes it.

Object lifetime

8

In this chapter

- Managing DEPENDENCY LIFETIME
- Working with disposable DEPENDENCIES
- Using SINGLETON, TRANSIENT, and SCOPED LIFESTYLES
- Preventing or fixing bad LIFESTYLE choices

The passing of time has a profound effect on most food and drink, but the consequences vary. Personally, we find 12-month-old Gruyère more interesting than 6-month-old Gruyère, but Mark prefers his asparagus fresher than either of those.[1] In many cases, it's easy to assess the proper age of an item; but in certain cases, doing so becomes complex. This is most notable when it comes to wine (see figure 8.1).

Wines tend to get better with age—until they suddenly become too old and lose most of their flavor. This depends on many factors, including the origin and vintage of the wine. Although wines interest us, we don't ever expect we'll be able to predict when a wine will peak. For that, we rely on experts: books at home and sommeliers at restaurants. They understand wines better than we do, so we happily let them take control.

---

[1] Steven, however, doesn't like asparagus at any age, but does prefer his whiskey of older age.

Figure 8.1 Wine, cheese, and asparagus. Although the combination may be a bit off, their age greatly affects their overall qualities.

Unless you dove straight into this chapter without reading any of the previous ones, you know that letting go of control is a key concept in DI. This stems from the Inversion of Control principle, where you delegate control of your Dependencies to a third party, but it also implies more than just letting someone else pick an implementation of a required Abstraction. When you allow a Composer to supply a Dependency, you must also accept that you can't control its lifetime.

> **DEFINITION** Composer is a unifying term to refer to any object or method that composes Dependencies. It's an important part of the Composition Root. The Composer is often a DI Container, but it can also be any method that constructs object graphs manually (using Pure DI).

Just as the sommelier intimately knows the contents of the restaurant's wine cellar and can make a far more informed decision than we can, we should trust the Composer to be able to control the lifetime of Dependencies more efficiently than the consumer. Composing and managing components is its single responsibility.

In this chapter, we'll explore DEPENDENCY LIFETIME MANAGEMENT. Understanding this topic is important because, just as you can have a subpar experience if you drink a wine at the wrong age (both your own age and the wine's), you can experience degraded performance from configuring DEPENDENCY LIFETIME incorrectly. Even worse, you may get the LIFETIME MANAGEMENT equivalent of spoiled food: resource leaks. Understanding the principles of correctly managing the lifecycles of components should enable you to make informed decisions to configure your applications correctly.

We'll start with a general introduction to DEPENDENCY LIFETIME MANAGEMENT, followed by a discussion about disposable DEPENDENCIES. This first part of the chapter is meant to provide all the background information and guiding principles you need in order to make knowledgeable decisions about your own applications' lifecycles, scope, and configurations.

After that, we'll look at different lifetime strategies. This part of the chapter takes the form of a catalog of available LIFESTYLES. In most cases, one of these stock LIFESTYLE patterns will provide a good match for a given challenge, so understanding them in advance equips you to deal with many difficult situations.

DEFINITION   A LIFESTYLE is a formalized way of describing the intended lifetime of a DEPENDENCY.

We'll finish the chapter with some bad habits, or anti-patterns, concerning LIFETIME MANAGEMENT. When we're finished, you should have a good grasp of LIFETIME MANAGEMENT and common LIFESTYLE do's and don'ts. First, let's look at OBJECT LIFETIME and how it relates to DI in general.

8.1   *Managing DEPENDENCY LIFETIME*

Up to this point, we've mostly discussed how DI enables you to compose DEPENDENCIES. The previous chapter explored this subject in great detail, but, as we alluded to in section 1.4, OBJECT COMPOSITION is just one aspect of DI. Managing OBJECT LIFETIME is another.

The first time we were introduced to the idea that the scope of DI includes LIFETIME MANAGEMENT, we failed to understand the deep connection between OBJECT COMPOSITION and OBJECT LIFETIME. We finally got it, and it's simple, so let's take a look!

In this section, we'll introduce LIFETIME MANAGEMENT and how it applies to DEPENDENCIES. We'll look at the general case of composing objects and how it has implications for the lifetimes of DEPENDENCIES. First, we'll investigate why OBJECT COMPOSITION implies LIFETIME MANAGEMENT.

8.1.1   *Introducing LIFETIME MANAGEMENT*

When we accept that we should let go of our psychological need for control over DEPENDENCIES and instead request them through CONSTRUCTOR INJECTION or one of the other DI patterns, we must let go completely. To understand why, we'll examine the issue progressively. Let's begin by reviewing what the standard .NET object lifecycle means for DEPENDENCIES. You likely already know this, but bear with us for the next half page while we establish the context.

SIMPLE DEPENDENCY LIFECYCLE

You know that DI means you let a third party (typically our COMPOSITION ROOT) serve the DEPENDENCIES you need. This also means you must let it manage the DEPENDENCIES' lifetimes. This is easiest to understand when it comes to object creation. Here's a (slightly restructured) code fragment from the sample e-commerce application's COMPOSITION ROOT. (You can see the complete example in listing 7.8.)

```
var productRepository =
    new SqlProductRepository(
        new CommerceContext(connectionString));

var productService =
    new ProductService(
        productRepository,
        userContext);
```

We hope that it's evident that the `ProductService` class doesn't control when `productRepository` is created. In this case, `SqlProductRepository` is likely to be created within the same millisecond; but as a thought experiment, we could insert a call to `Thread.Sleep` between these two lines of code to demonstrate that you can arbitrarily separate them over time. That would be a pretty weird thing to do, but the point is that not all objects of a DEPENDENCY graph have to be created at the same time.

Consumers don't control creation of their DEPENDENCIES, but what about destruction? As a general rule, you don't control when objects are destroyed in .NET. The garbage collector cleans up unused objects, but unless you're dealing with disposable objects, you can't explicitly destroy an object.

> **NOTE** We use the term *disposable object* as shorthand for referring to object instances of types that implement the `IDisposable` interface.

Objects are eligible for garbage collection when they go out of scope. Conversely, they last as long as someone else holds a reference to them. Although a consumer can't explicitly destroy an object—that's up to the garbage collector—it can keep the object alive by holding on to the reference. This is what you do when you use CONSTRUCTOR INJECTION, because you save the DEPENDENCY in a private field:

```
public class HomeController
{
    private readonly IProductService service;

    public HomeController(IProductService service)    ◀── Injects a DEPENDENCY into
    {                                                       the class's constructor
        this.service = service;    ◀── Saves the reference to the DEPENDENCY in
    }                                  a private field, keeping the DEPENDENCY
}                                      alive at least as long as the consuming
                                       HomeController instance is alive
```

This means that when the consumer goes out of scope, so can the DEPENDENCY. Even when a consumer goes out of scope, however, the DEPENDENCY can live on if other objects hold a reference to it. Otherwise, it'll be garbage collected. Because you're an experienced .NET developer, this is probably old news to you, but now the discussion should begin to get more interesting.

ADDING COMPLEXITY TO THE DEPENDENCY LIFECYCLE

Until now our analysis of the DEPENDENCY lifecycle has been mundane, but now we can add some complexity. What happens when more than one consumer requires the same DEPENDENCY? One option is to supply each consumer their own instance, as shown in figure 8.2.

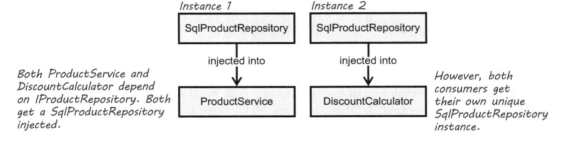

Both ProductService and DiscountCalculator depend on IProductRepository. Both get a SqlProductRepository injected.

However, both consumers get their own unique SqlProductRepository instance.

Figure 8.2   Composing multiple, unique instances of a DEPENDENCY

The following listing composes multiple consumers with multiple instances of the same DEPENDENCY, shown in figure 8.2.

Listing 8.1   Composing with multiple instances of the same DEPENDENCY

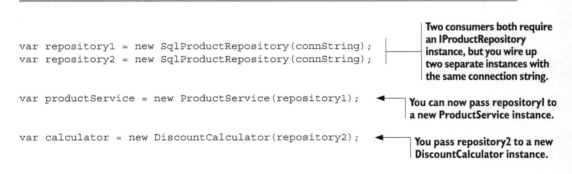

```
var repository1 = new SqlProductRepository(connString);
var repository2 = new SqlProductRepository(connString);

var productService = new ProductService(repository1);

var calculator = new DiscountCalculator(repository2);
```

Two consumers both require an IProductRepository instance, but you wire up two separate instances with the same connection string.

You can now pass repository1 to a new ProductService instance.

You pass repository2 to a new DiscountCalculator instance.

When it comes to the lifecycles of each Repository in listing 8.1, nothing has changed compared to the previously discussed sample e-commerce application's COMPOSITION ROOT. Each DEPENDENCY goes out of scope and is garbage-collected when its consumers go out of scope. This can happen at different times, but the situation is only marginally different than before. It would be a somewhat different situation if both consumers were to share the same DEPENDENCY, as shown in figure 8.3.

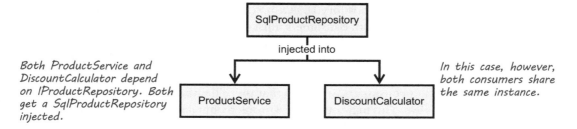

Both ProductService and DiscountCalculator depend on IProductRepository. Both get a SqlProductRepository injected.

In this case, however, both consumers share the same instance.

Figure 8.3 Reusing the same instance of a DEPENDENCY by injecting it into multiple consumers

When you apply this to listing 8.1, you get the code in listing 8.2.

Listing 8.2 Composing with a single instance of the same DEPENDENCY

```
var repository = new SqlProductRepository(connString);

var productService = new ProductService(repository);

var calculator = new DiscountCalculator(repository);
```

Instead of creating two different SqlProductRepository instances, you create a single instance that you inject into both consumers. Both save the reference for later use.

When comparing listings 8.1 and 8.2, you don't find that one is inherently better than the other. As we'll discuss in section 8.3, there are several factors to consider when it comes to when and how you want to reuse a DEPENDENCY.

NOTE The consumers are blissfully unaware that the DEPENDENCY is shared. Because they both accept whichever version of the DEPENDENCY they're given, no modification of the source code is necessary to accommodate this change in DEPENDENCY configuration. This is a result of the LISKOV SUBSTITUTION PRINCIPLE.

LISKOV SUBSTITUTION PRINCIPLE

As it was originally stated, the LISKOV SUBSTITUTION PRINCIPLE is an academic and abstract concept defined by Barbara Liskov in 1987. But in object-oriented design, we can paraphrase it as follows: "Methods that consume ABSTRACTIONS must be able to use any class derived from that ABSTRACTION without noticing the difference."

We must be able to substitute the ABSTRACTION for an arbitrary implementation without changing the correctness of the system. Failing to adhere to the LISKOV SUBSTITUTION PRINCIPLE makes applications fragile, because it disallows replacing DEPENDENCIES, and doing so might cause a consumer to break.

The lifecycle for the Repository DEPENDENCY has changed distinctly, compared with the previous example. Both consumers must go out of scope before the variable repository can be eligible for garbage collection, and they can do so at different times. The situation becomes less predictable when the DEPENDENCY reaches the end of its lifetime. This trait is only reinforced when the number of consumers increases.

Given enough consumers, it's likely that there'll always be one around to keep the DEPENDENCY alive. This may sound like a problem, but it rarely is: instead of a multitude of similar instances, you have only one, which saves memory. This is such a desirable quality that we formalize it in a LIFESTYLE pattern called the SINGLETON LIFESTYLE. Don't confuse this with the Singleton design pattern, although there are similarities.[2] We'll go into greater detail about this subject in section 8.3.1.

The key point to appreciate is that the COMPOSER has a greater degree of influence over the lifetime of DEPENDENCIES than any single consumer. The COMPOSER decides when instances are created, and by its choice of whether to share instances, it determines whether a DEPENDENCY goes out of scope with a single consumer, or whether all consumers must go out of scope before the DEPENDENCY can be released.

> **DEFINITION**   *Releasing* is the process of determining which DEPENDENCIES can be dereferenced and possibly disposed of. The COMPOSITION ROOT requests an object graph from the COMPOSER. After the COMPOSITION ROOT has finished working with that resolved graph, it informs the COMPOSER that it has finished with the graph. The COMPOSER can then decide which of the DEPENDENCIES of that particular graph can be released.

This is comparable to visiting a restaurant with a good sommelier. The sommelier spends a large proportion of the day managing and evolving the wine cellar: buying new wines, sampling the available bottles to track how they develop, and working with the chefs to identify optimal matches to the food being served. When we're presented with the wine list, it includes only what the sommelier deems fit to offer for today's menu. We're free to select a wine according to our personal taste, but we don't presume to know more about the restaurant's selection of wines and how they go with the food than the sommelier does. The sommelier will often decide to keep lots of bottles in stock for years; and as you'll see in the next section, a COMPOSER may decide to keep instances alive by holding on to their references.

8.1.2   *Managing lifetime with PURE DI*

The previous section explained how you can vary the composition of DEPENDENCIES to influence their lifetimes. In this section, we'll look at how to implement this using PURE DI, while applying the two most commonly used LIFESTYLES: TRANSIENT and SINGLETON.

---

[2]   Erich Gamma et al., *Design Patterns: Elements of Reusable Object-Oriented Software* (Addison-Wesley, 1994), 127.

In chapter 7, you created specialized classes to compose applications. One of these was a `CommerceControllerActivator` for an ASP.NET Core MVC application—our Composer. Listing 7.8 shows the implementation of its `Create` method.

As you may recall, the `Create` method creates the entire object graph on the fly each time it's invoked. Each Dependency is private to the issued controller, and there's no sharing. When the controller instance goes out of scope (which it does every time the server has replied to a request), all the Dependencies go out of scope too. This is often called a Transient Lifestyle, which we'll talk more about in section 8.3.2.

Let's analyze the object graphs created by the `CommerceControllerActivator` and shown in figure 8.4 to see if there's room for improvement. Both the `AspNetUserContextAdapter` and `RouteCalculator` classes are completely stateless services, so there's no reason to create a new instance every time you need to service a request. The connection string is also unlikely to change, so you can reuse it across requests. The `SqlProductRepository` class, on the other hand, relies on an Entity Framework `DbContext` (implemented by our `CommerceContext`), which mustn't be shared across requests.[3]

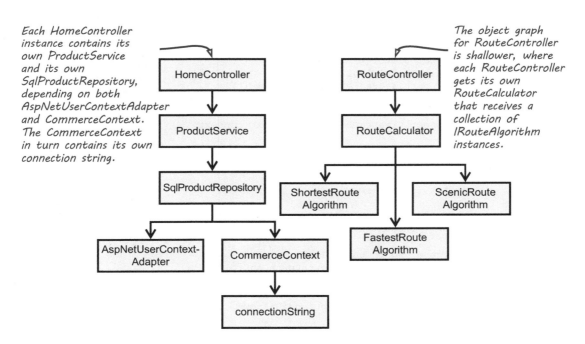

Figure 8.4 Object graphs as created by `CommerceControllerActivator`, **which creates** `HomeController` **and** `RouteController` **instances with their Dependencies**

---

[3] Entity Framework `DbContext` instances aren't thread-safe and can't be used by multiple requests in parallel.

Given this particular configuration, a better implementation of CommerceController-Activator would reuse the same instances of both AspNetUserContextAdapter and RouteCalculator, while creating new instances of ProductService and SqlProduct-Repository. In short, you should configure AspNetUserContextAdapter and RouteCalculator to use the SINGLETON LIFESTYLE, and ProductService and Sql-ProductRepository as TRANSIENT. The following listing shows how to implement this change.

Listing 8.3   Managing lifetime within the CommerceControllerActivator

```
public class CommerceControllerActivator : IControllerActivator
{
    private readonly string connectionString;
    private readonly IUserContext userContext;          Read-only fields to store
    private readonly RouteCalculator calculator;        SINGLETON DEPENDENCIES

    public CommerceControllerActivator(string connectionString)
    {
        this.connectionString = connectionString;

        this.userContext =                              Creates SINGLETON
            new AspNetUserContextAdapter();             DEPENDENCIES and stores
                                                        them in private fields.
        this.calculator =                               This way they can be
            new RouteCalculator(                        reused throughout the
                this.CreateRouteAlgorithms());          application's lifetime by
    }                                                   all requests.

    public object Create(ControllerContext context)
    {
        Type type = context.ActionDescriptor
            .ControllerTypeInfo.AsType();

        switch (type.Name)
        {
            case "HomeController":
                return this.CreateHomeController();

            case "RouteController":
                return this.CreateRouteController();

            default:
                throw new Exception("Unknown controller " + type.Name);
        }
    }
}
```

```
    private HomeController CreateHomeController()
    {
        return new HomeController(
            new ProductService(
                new SqlProductRepository(
                    new CommerceContext(
                        this.connectionString)),
                this.userContext));
    }

    private RouteController CreateRouteController()
    {
        return new RouteController(this.calculator);
    }

    public void Release(ControllerContext context,
        object controller) { ... }
}
```

> **Creates TRANSIENT instances each time the CommerceControllerActivator is asked to create a new instance. The earlier created SINGLETONS are injected into these TRANSIENTS.**

> **We'll leave the Release method empty for now and get back to it in section 8.2.**

NOTE The readonly keyword of listing 8.3 provides an extra guarantee that once assigned, these SINGLETON instances are permanent and can't be replaced. Apart from that guarantee, however, readonly is in no way required when implementing the SINGLETON LIFESTYLE.

In an MVC application, it's practical to load configuration values in the Startup class. That's why in listing 8.3, the connection string is supplied to the constructor of the CommerceControllerActivator.

The code in listing 8.3 is functionally equivalent to the code in listing 7.8—it's just slightly more efficient because some of the DEPENDENCIES are shared. By holding on to the DEPENDENCIES you create, you can keep them alive for as long as you want. In this example, CommerceControllerActivator created both SINGLETON DEPENDENCIES as soon as it was initialized, but it could also have used lazy initialization.

The ability to fine-tune each DEPENDENCY's LIFESTYLE can be important for performance reasons, but can also be important for correct behavior. For instance, the Mediator design pattern relies on a shared director through which several components communicate.[4] This only works when the Mediator is shared among the involved collaborators.

So far, we've discussed how INVERSION OF CONTROL implies that consumers can't manage the lifetimes of their DEPENDENCIES, because they don't control creation of objects; and because .NET uses garbage collection, consumers can't explicitly destroy objects, either. This leaves a question unanswered: what about disposable DEPENDENCIES? We'll now turn our attention to that delicate question.

8.2 Working with disposable DEPENDENCIES

Although .NET is a managed platform with a garbage collector, it can still interact with unmanaged code. When this happens, .NET code interacts with unmanaged memory that isn't garbage-collected. To prevent memory leaks, you must have a mechanism with which to deterministically release unmanaged memory. This is the key purpose of the IDisposable interface.

---

[4] Erich Gamma et al., *Design Patterns*, 273.

It's likely that some DEPENDENCY implementations will contain unmanaged resources. As an example, ADO.NET connections are disposable because they tend to use unmanaged memory. As a result, database-related implementations like Repositories backed by databases are likely to be disposable themselves. How should we model disposable DEPENDENCIES? Should we also let ABSTRACTIONS be disposable? That might look like this:

```
public interface IMyDependency : IDisposable
```

IMPORTANT This is technically possible but not a particularly good idea. It's a design smell that, as we explained in section 6.2.1, indicates a LEAKY ABSTRACTION.

If you feel the urge to add IDisposable to your interface, it's probably because you have a particular implementation in mind. But you must not let that knowledge leak through to the interface design. Doing so would make it more difficult for other classes to implement the interface and would introduce vagueness into the ABSTRACTION.

Who's responsible for disposing of a disposable DEPENDENCY? Could it be the consumer?

8.2.1 *Consuming disposable DEPENDENCIES*

For the sake of argument, imagine that you have a disposable ABSTRACTION like the following IOrderRepository interface.

Listing 8.4 `IOrderRepository` implementing `IDisposable`

```
public interface IOrderRepository : IDisposable
```

How should an OrderService class deal with such a DEPENDENCY? Most design guidelines (including Visual Studio's built-in Code Analysis) would insist that if a class holds a disposable resource as a member, it should itself implement IDisposable and dispose of the resource. The next listing shows how.

Listing 8.5 `OrderService` depending on disposable DEPENDENCY

```
public sealed class OrderService : IDisposable        ◄──┐ OrderService also implements
{                                                         │ IDisposable.
    private readonly IOrderRepository repository;

    public OrderService(IOrderRepository repository)
    {
        this.repository = repository;
    }

    public void Dispose()                                   Implements Dispose and disposes
    {                                                        the IOrderRepository DEPENDENCY
        this.repository.Dispose();        ◄──
    }
}
```

But this turns out to be a bad idea because the `repository` member was originally injected, and it can be shared by other consumers:

```
var repository =
    new SqlOrderRepository(connectionString);

var validator = new OrderValidator(repository);
var orderService = new OrderService(repository);

orderService.AcceptOrder(order);
orderService.Dispose();

validator.Validate(order);
```

A single instance of SqlOrderRepository is injected into both OrderValidator and OrderService. These two instances share the same instance of the IOrderRepository DEPENDENCY.

If OrderService disposes of its injected IOrderRepository at a later point in time, it destroys OrderValidator's DEPENDENCY too.

This causes exceptions to be thrown when OrderValidator tries to use it in its Validate method.

It would be less dangerous not to dispose of the injected Repository, but this means you're ignoring the fact that the ABSTRACTION is disposable. Besides, in this case, the ABSTRACTION exposes more members than used by the client, which is an INTERFACE SEGREGATION PRINCIPLE violation (see section 6.2.1). Declaring an ABSTRACTION as deriving from `IDisposable` provides no benefit.

Then again, there can be scenarios where you need to signal the beginning and end of a short-lived scope; `IDisposable` is sometimes used for that purpose. Before we examine how a COMPOSER can manage the lifetime of a disposable DEPENDENCY, we should consider how to deal with such ephemeral disposables.

> **DEFINITION** An *ephemeral disposable* is an object with a clear and short lifetime that typically doesn't exceed a single method call.

CREATING EPHEMERAL DISPOSABLES

Many APIs in the .NET BCL use `IDisposable` to signal that a particular scope has ended. One of the more prominent examples is WCF proxies.

WCF proxies and IDisposable

All autogenerated Windows Communication Foundation (WCF) proxies implement `IDispos-able`, and it's important to remember to invoke the `Dispose` method on a proxy as soon as possible.[5] Many bindings automatically create a session on the service when they submit the first request, and this session lingers in the service until it times out or is explicitly disposed of.

If you forget to dispose of the WCF proxies after use, the number of sessions increases until you hit the limit for concurrent connections from the same source. When you reach the limit, exceptions are thrown. Too many sessions also place an undue burden on the service, so disposing of WCF proxies as soon as possible is important.

---

[5] Although it's impossible to create services with .NET Core, you can still consume them from a .NET Core application.

It's important to remember that the use of IDisposable for such purposes need not indicate a LEAKY ABSTRACTION, because these types aren't always ABSTRACTIONS in the first place. On the other hand, some of them are; and when that's the case, how do you deal with them?

Fortunately, after an object is disposed of, you can't reuse it. If you want to invoke the same API again, you must create a new instance. As an example that fits well with how you use WCF proxies or ADO.NET commands, you create the proxy, invoke its operations, and dispose of it as soon as you're finished. How can you reconcile this with DI if you consider disposable ABSTRACTIONS to be LEAKY ABSTRACTIONS?

As always, hiding the messy details behind an interface can be helpful. Returning to the UWP application from section 7.2, we used an IProductRepository ABSTRACTION to hide the details of communicating with a data store from the presentation logic layer. During this discussion, we ignored the details of such an implementation because it wasn't that relevant at that moment. But let's assume that the UWP application must communicate with a WCF web service. From the EditProductViewModel's perspective, this is how you delete a product:

> You ask the injected Repository to delete the product by supplying the product ID. EditProductViewModel can safely hold a reference to the Repository because the IProductRepository interface doesn't derive from IDisposable.

```
private void DeleteProduct()
{
    this.productRepository.Delete(this.Model.Id);   ◄─────
    this.whenDone();
}
```

Another picture forms when we look at the WCF implementation of that interface. Here's the implementation of WcfProductRepository with its Delete method.

Listing 8.6   Using a WCF channel as an ephemeral disposable

```
public class WcfProductRepository : IProductRepository
{
    private readonly ChannelFactory<IProductManagementService> factory;

    public WcfProductRepository(
        ChannelFactory<IProductManagementService> factory)
    {
        this.factory = factory;
    }

    public void Delete(Guid productId)
    {
        using (var channel =
            this.factory.CreateChannel())
        {
            channel.DeleteProduct(productId);
        }
    }
    ...
}
```

> The Delete method creates a WCF channel, which is an ephemeral disposable. The channel is both created and disposed of within the same method call.

The `WcfProductRepository` class has no mutable state, so you inject a `Channel-Factory<TChannel>` that you can use to create a channel. *Channel* is just another word for a WCF proxy, and it's the autogenerated client interface you get for free when you create a service reference with Visual Studio or svcutil.exe.

Because this interface derives from `IDisposable`, you can wrap it in a `using` statement. You then use the channel to delete the product. When you exit the `using` scope, the channel is disposed of.

> **WARNING** Although the `using` statement is a best practice when it comes to working with short-lived disposables, this doesn't hold true when it comes to WCF. Against all guidelines, WCF proxy classes can throw exceptions when calling `Dispose`. This causes you to lose the original exception information, in case an exception was thrown within the `using` block. Instead of relying on a `using` statement, you must write a `finally` block and ignore any exceptions thrown by `Dispose`. We only referenced `using` here to demonstrate the general concept of implementing an ephemeral disposable.[6]

Every time you invoke a method on the `WcfProductRepository` class, it quickly opens a new channel and disposes of it after use. Its lifetime is extremely short, which is why we call such a disposable ABSTRACTION an ephemeral disposable.

But wait! Didn't we claim that a disposable ABSTRACTION is a LEAKY ABSTRACTION? Yes, we did, but we have to balance pragmatic concerns against principles. In this case, at least, `WcfProductRepository` and `IProductManagementService` are defined in the same WCF-specific library. This ensures that the LEAKY ABSTRACTION can be confined to code that has a reasonable expectation of knowing about and managing that complexity.

Notice that the ephemeral disposable is never injected into the consumer. Instead, a factory is used, and you use that factory to control the lifetime of the ephemeral disposable.

`ChannelFactory<TChannel>` is thread-safe and can be injected as a SINGLETON. In this case, you might wonder why we choose to inject `ChannelFactory<TChannel>` into the `WcfProductRepository`'s constructor; you can create it internally and store it in a `static` field. This, however, causes `WcfProductRepository` to be implicitly dependent on a configuration file, which needs to exist to create a new `WcfProduct-Repository`. As we discussed in 2.3.3, only the finished application should rely on configuration files.

In summary, disposable ABSTRACTIONS are LEAKY ABSTRACTIONS. Sometimes we must accept such a leak to avoid bugs (such as refused WCF connections); but when we do that, we should do our best to contain that leak so it doesn't propagate throughout an entire application. We've now examined how to consume disposable DEPENDENCIES. Let's turn our attention to how we can serve and manage them for consumers.

---

6   For more information, see https://mng.bz/5Y6z.

8.2.2   *Managing disposable DEPENDENCIES*

Because we so adamantly insist that disposable ABSTRACTIONS are LEAKY ABSTRACTIONS, the consequence is that ABSTRACTIONS shouldn't be disposable. On the other hand, sometimes implementations are disposable; if you don't properly dispose of them, you'll have resource leaks in your applications. Someone or something must dispose of them.

> **TIP**   Strive to implement services so they don't hold references to disposables, but rather create and dispose of them on demand as illustrated in listing 8.6. This makes memory management simpler because the service can be garbage collected like other objects.

As always, this responsibility falls on the COMPOSER. It, better than anything else, knows when it creates a disposable instance, so it also knows when the instance needs to be disposed of. It's easy for the COMPOSER to keep a reference to the disposable instance and invoke its `Dispose` method at an appropriate time. The challenge lies in identifying when it's the appropriate time. How do you know when all consumers have gone out of scope?

Unless you're informed when that happens, you don't know. Often, however, your code lives inside some sort of context with a well-defined lifetime, as well as events that tell you when a specific scope completes. In ASP.NET Core, for instance, you can scope instances around a single web request. At the end of a web request, the framework tells `IControllerActivator`, which is typically our COMPOSER, that it should release all DEPENDENCIES for a given object. It's then up to the COMPOSER to keep track of those DEPENDENCIES and to decide whether anything must be disposed of based on their LIFESTYLES.

RELEASING DEPENDENCIES

Releasing an object graph isn't the same as disposing of it. As we stated in the introduction, *releasing* is the process of determining which DEPENDENCIES can be dereferenced and possibly disposed of, and which DEPENDENCIES should be kept alive to be reused. It's the COMPOSER that decides whether a released object should be disposed of or reused.

The release of an object graph is a signal to the COMPOSER that the root of the graph is going out of scope, so if the root itself implements `IDisposable`, then it should be disposed of. But the root's DEPENDENCIES can be shared with other roots, so the COMPOSER may decide to keep some of them around, because it knows other objects still rely on them. Figure 8.5 illustrates the sequence of events.

To release DEPENDENCIES, a COMPOSER must track all the disposable DEPENDENCIES it has ever served, and to which consumers it has served them, so that it can dispose of them when the last consumer is released. And a COMPOSER must take care to dispose of objects in the correct order.

> **WARNING**   An object might require its DEPENDENCIES to be called during disposal, which causes problems when these DEPENDENCIES are already disposed of. Disposal should therefore happen in the opposite order of creation—this means from the outside in.

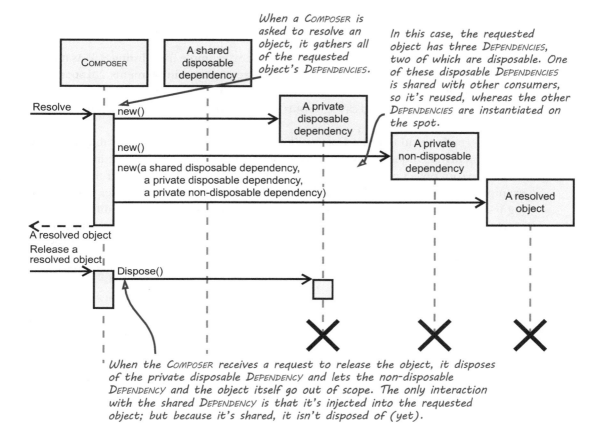

When a COMPOSER is asked to resolve an object, it gathers all of the requested object's DEPENDENCIES.

In this case, the requested object has three DEPENDENCIES, two of which are disposable. One of these disposable DEPENDENCIES is shared with other consumers, so it's reused, whereas the other DEPENDENCIES are instantiated on the spot.

When the COMPOSER receives a request to release the object, it disposes of the private disposable DEPENDENCY and lets the non-disposable DEPENDENCY and the object itself go out of scope. The only interaction with the shared DEPENDENCY is that it's injected into the requested object; but because it's shared, it isn't disposed of (yet).

Figure 8.5   The sequence of events for releasing DEPENDENCIES

Should I dispose of a DbContext?

CommerceContext is our project-specific version of Entity Framework Core's DbContext, which implements IDisposable. In the past, we've witnessed many discussions with colleagues and developers on online forums about the need to dispose of DbContext instances. These discussions typically came from the observation that a DbContext uses database connections as ephemeral disposables; connections are opened and closed in the same method call. Calling SaveChanges on DbContext, for instance, creates and opens a database connection, and then disposes of that connection once all changes are saved.

Well, things have changed in Entity Framework Core 2.0. With the introduction of version 2, it now supports DbContext pooling, a feature similar to ADO.NET's connection pooling. It allows the same DbContext instance to be reused, which can improve application performance under certain conditions. DbContext instances, however, are returned back to their pool when Dispose is called, so not calling Dispose on a DbContext instance might starve the pool.

The moral of this story is that you should always make sure disposable objects are correctly disposed of. Even if you determined that you could omit a call to Dispose in your specific case, an external component, such as Entity Framework Core, is free to change that behavior any time in the future.

NOTE To learn about Entity Framework Core in detail, the book *Entity Framework Core in Action* by Jon Smith (Manning, 2018) is a good place to start.

Let's go back to the CommerceControllerActivator example from listing 8.3. As it turns out, there's a bug in that listing, because CommerceContext implements IDisposable. The code in listing 8.3 creates new instances of CommerceContext, but it never disposes of those instances. This could cause resource leaks, so let's fix that bug with a new version of the COMPOSER.

First, keep in mind that the COMPOSER for a web application must be able to service many concurrent requests, so it has to associate each CommerceContext instance with either the root object it creates or with the request it's associated with. In the following example, we'll use the request to track disposable objects, because this saves us from having to define a static dictionary instance. A static mutable state is more difficult to use correctly, because it must be implemented in a thread-safe manner. The next listing shows how CommerceControllerActivator resolves requests for HomeController instances.

> **Listing 8.7 Associating disposable DEPENDENCIES with a web request**

```
private HomeController CreateHomeController(ControllerContext context)
{
    var dbContext =                                          ← Creates the instance that
        new CommerceContext(this.connectionString);            requires disposal

    TrackDisposable(context, dbContext);     ← Tracks that instance by associating
                                               it with the current request
    return new HomeController(
        new ProductService(
            new SqlProductRepository(dbContext),
            this.userContext));
}

private static void TrackDisposable(
    ControllerContext context, IDisposable disposable)
{
    IDictionary<object, object> items =
        context.HttpContext.Items;

    object list;

    if (!items.TryGetValue("Disposables", out list))
    {
        list = new List<IDisposable>();
        items["Disposables"] = list;
    }

    ((List<IDisposable>)list).Add(disposable);
}
```

The TrackDisposable method stores disposable instances in a list that's associated with the request by storing it in the HttpContext .Items dictionary. If the list doesn't exist, it'll be created. The disposable instance is appended to the list.

The CreateHomeController method starts by resolving all the DEPENDENCIES. This is similar to the implementation in listing 8.3, but before returning the resolved service, it must store the DEPENDENCY with the request in such a way that it can be disposed of when the controller gets released. The application flow of listing 8.7 is shown in figure 8.6.

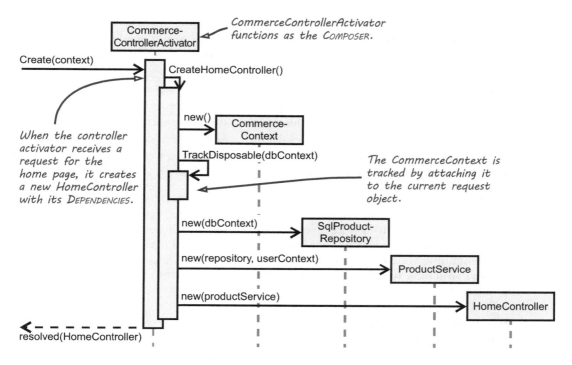

Figure 8.6 Tracking disposable DEPENDENCIES

When we implemented the CommerceControllerActivator in listing 7.8, we left the Release method empty. So far, we haven't implemented this method, relying on the garbage collector to do the job; but with disposable DEPENDENCIES, it's essential that you take this opportunity to clean up. Here's the implementation.

Listing 8.8 Releasing disposable DEPENDENCIES

```
public void Release(ControllerContext context, object controller)
{
    var disposables =
        (List<IDisposable>)context.HttpContext
            .Items["Disposables"];

    if (disposables != null)
    {
        disposables.Reverse();

        foreach (IDisposable disposable in disposables)
        {
            disposable.Dispose();
        }
    }
}
```

Gets the list of tracked disposables from the items dictionary

Loops through the collection and disposes of all instances one by one

Reverses the order of the list of disposables so instances can be disposed of in the opposite order of their creation

This `Release` method takes a shortcut that prevents some disposables from being disposed of if an exception is thrown. If you're meticulous, you'll need to ensure that disposal of instances continues, even if one throws an exception, preferably by using `try` and `finally` statements. We'll leave this as an exercise for the reader.

In the context of ASP.NET Core MVC, the given solution using `TrackDisposable` and `Release` can be reduced to a simple call to `HttpContext.Response.RegisterForDispose`, because that would effectively do the same thing. It both implements opposite-order disposal and continues disposing of objects in case of a failure. Because this chapter isn't about ASP.NET Core MVC in particular, we wanted to provide you with a more generic solution that illustrates the basic idea.

> **TIP** DI CONTAINERS are particularly good at LIFETIME MANAGEMENT. DI CONTAINERS can deal with complex combinations of LIFESTYLES, and they offer opportunities, such as a `Release` method, to explicitly release components when you're finished with them. When you find yourself in the situation where maintaining your COMPOSITION ROOT using PURE DI becomes difficult, consider switching to a DI CONTAINER instead. (We'll go into more detail when discussing DI CONTAINERS in chapter 12.)

WHERE SHOULD DEPENDENCIES BE RELEASED?

After reading all this, two questions remain: where should object graphs be released, and who is responsible for doing this? It's important to note that the code that has requested an object graph is also responsible for requesting its release. Because the request for an object graph is typically part of the COMPOSITION ROOT, so is the initiation of its release.

> **NOTE** Releasing will be demanded after the COMPOSITION ROOT has finished using the resolved root object.

The following listing shows the `Main` method of the console application of section 7.1 again, but now with an additional `Release` method.

Listing 8.9   The COMPOSITION ROOT that releases the resolved object graph

```
static void Main(string[] args)
{
    string connStr = LoadConnectionString();

    CurrencyParser parser =                        Requests a CurrencyParser
        CreateCurrencyParser(connStr);             root object

    ICommand command = parser.Parse(args);         Uses that root object
    command.Execute();

    Release(parser);          Demands its release after
}                             the operation is completed
```

When building a console application, you're in full control of the application. As we discussed in section 7.1, there's no INVERSION OF CONTROL. If you're using a framework, you'll often see the framework take control over both requesting the object graph and demanding its release. ASP.NET Core MVC is a good example of this. In the case of MVC, it's the framework that calls CommerceControllerActivator's Create and Release methods. In between those calls, it uses a resolved controller instance.

We've now discussed LIFETIME MANAGEMENT in some detail. As a consumer, you can't manage the lifetime of injected DEPENDENCIES; that responsibility falls on the COMPOSER who can decide to share a single instance among many consumers or give each consumer its own private instance. These SINGLETON and TRANSIENT LIFESTYLES are only the most common members of a larger set of LIFESTYLES, and we'll use the next section to work our way through a catalog of the most common lifecycle strategies.

8.3 *LIFESTYLE catalog*

Now that we've covered the principles behind LIFETIME MANAGEMENT, we'll spend some time looking at common LIFESTYLE patterns. As we described in the introduction, a LIFESTYLE is a formalized way of describing the intended lifetime of a DEPENDENCY. This gives us a common vocabulary, just as design patterns do. It makes it easier to reason about when and how a DEPENDENCY is expected to go out of scope—and if it'll be reused.

This section discusses the three most common LIFESTYLES described in table 8.1. Because you've already encountered both SINGLETON and TRANSIENT, we'll begin with those.

Table 8.1   Lifestyle patterns covered in this section

Name	Description
SINGLETON	A single instance is perpetually reused.
TRANSIENT	New instances are always served.
SCOPED	At most, one instance of each type is served per an implicitly or explicitly defined scope.

> **NOTE** We use comparable examples throughout this section. But to allow us to focus on the essentials, we'll compose shallow hierarchies, and we'll sometimes ignore the issue with disposable DEPENDENCIES to avoid that added complexity.

The use of a SCOPED LIFESTYLE is widespread; most exotic LIFESTYLES are variations of it. Compared to advanced LIFESTYLES, a SINGLETON LIFESTYLE may seem mundane, but it's nevertheless a common and appropriate lifecycle strategy.

8.3.1 *The SINGLETON LIFESTYLE*

In this book, we've implicitly used the SINGLETON LIFESTYLE from time to time. The name is both clear and somewhat confusing at the same time. It makes sense, however, because the resulting behavior is similar to the Singleton design pattern, but the structure is different.

> **NOTE** Within the scope of a single COMPOSER, there'll only be one instance of a component with the SINGLETON LIFESTYLE. Each and every time a consumer requests the component, the same instance is served.

With both the SINGLETON LIFESTYLE and the Singleton design pattern, there's only one instance of a DEPENDENCY, but the similarity ends there. The Singleton design pattern provides a global point of access to its instance, which is similar to the AMBIENT CONTEXT anti-pattern we discussed in section 5.3. A consumer, however, can't access a SINGLETON-scoped DEPENDENCY through a static member. If you ask two different COMPOSERS to serve an instance, you'll get two different instances. It's important, therefore, that you don't confuse the SINGLETON LIFESTYLE with the Singleton design pattern.

Because only a single instance is in use, the SINGLETON LIFESTYLE generally consumes a minimal amount of memory and is efficient. The only time this isn't the case is when the instance is used rarely but consumes large amounts of memory. In such cases, the instance can be wrapped in a Virtual Proxy, as we'll discuss in section 8.4.2.

WHEN TO USE THE SINGLETON LIFESTYLE

Use the SINGLETON LIFESTYLE whenever possible. Two main issues that might prevent you from using a SINGLETON follow:

- *When a component isn't thread-safe.* Because the SINGLETON instance is potentially shared among many consumers, it must be able to handle concurrent access.
- *When one of the component's DEPENDENCIES has a lifetime that's expected to be shorter, possibly because it isn't thread-safe.* Giving the component a SINGLETON LIFESTYLE would keep its DEPENDENCIES alive for too long. In that case, such a DEPENDENCY becomes a CAPTIVE DEPENDENCY. We'll go into more detail about CAPTIVE DEPENDENCIES in section 8.4.1.

All stateless services are, by definition, thread-safe, as are immutable types and, obviously, classes specifically designed to be thread-safe. In these cases, there's no reason not to configure them as SINGLETONS.

In addition to the argument for efficiency, some DEPENDENCIES may work as intended only if they're shared. For example, this is the case for implementations of the Circuit Breaker[7] design pattern that we'll discuss in chapter 9, as well as in-memory caches. In these cases, it's essential that the implementations are thread-safe.

Let's take a closer look at an in-memory Repository. We'll explore an example of this next.

---

[7] Michael T. Nygard, *Release It! Design and Deploy Production-Ready Software* (Pragmatic Bookshelf, 2007), 104.

EXAMPLE: USING A THREAD-SAFE IN-MEMORY REPOSITORY

Let's once more turn our attention to implementing a CommerceControllerActivator like those from sections 7.3.1 and 8.1.2. Instead of using a SQL Server–based IProduct-Repository, could use a thread-safe, in-memory implementation. For an in-memory data store to make sense, it must be shared among all requests, so it has to be thread-safe. This is illustrated in figure 8.7.

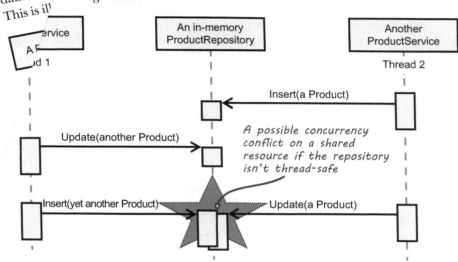

Figure 8.7 When multiple `ProductService` instances running on separate threads access a shared resource, such as an in-memory `IProductRepository`, you must ensure that the shared resource is thread-safe.

Instead of explicitly implementing such a Repository using the Singleton design pattern, you should use a concrete class and scope it appropriately using the SINGLETON LIFESTYLE. The next listing shows how a COMPOSER can return new instances every time it's asked to resolve a HomeController, whereas IProductRepository is shared among all instances.

Listing 8.10 Managing a SINGLETON LIFESTYLE

```
public class CommerceControllerActivator : IControllerActivator
{
    private readonly IUserContext userContext;
    private readonly IProductRepository repository;

    public CommerceControllerActivator()
    {
        this.userContext = new FakeUserContext();
        this.repository = new InMemoryProductRepository();
    }
    ...
```

Creates SINGLETONS in the COMPOSER's constructor

Storage locations for SINGLETON instances keep the SINGLETON DEPENDENCIES referenced for the lifetime of the COMPOSER.

```
private HomeController CreateHomeController()
{
    return new HomeController(
        new ProductService(
            this.repository,
            this.userContext));
}
}
```

Every time the ~~POSER is asked~~ to resolve a Ho~~ntroller~~ instance, it creat~~es a~~ ProductService wi~~th two~~ TRANSIENT SINGLETONS injected two

Note that in this example, both `repository` and `userContext` enco~~de~~ LIFESTYLES. You can, however, mix LIFESTYLES if you want. Figure 8.8 ~~SINGLETON~~ pens with `CommerceControllerActivator` at runtime. ~~what hap-~~

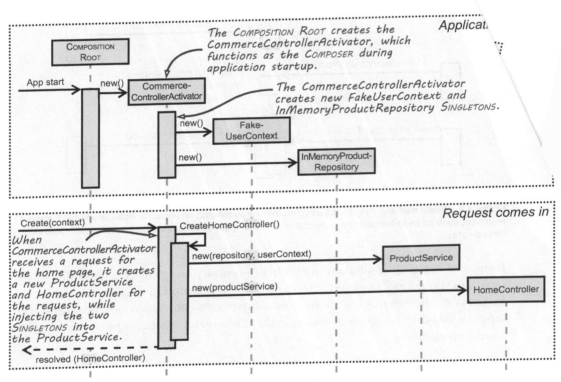

Figure 8.8   Composing SINGLETONS using `CommerceControllerActivator`

The SINGLETON LIFESTYLE is one of the easiest LIFESTYLES to implement. All it requires is that you keep a reference to the object and serve the same object every time it's requested. The instance doesn't go out of scope until the COMPOSER goes out of scope. When that happens, the COMPOSER should dispose of the object if it's a disposable type.

Another LIFESTYLE that's trivial to implement is the TRANSIENT LIFESTYLE. Let's look at that next.

8.3.2 *The TRANSIENT LIFESTYLE*

The TRANSIENT LIFESTYLE involves returning a new instance every time it's requested. Unless the instance returned implements `IDisposable`, there's nothing to keep track of. Conversely, when the instance implements `IDisposable`, the COMPOSER must keep it in mind and explicitly dispose of it when asked to release the applicable object graph. Most of the examples in this book of constructed object graphs implicitly used the TRANSIENT LIFESTYLE.

> **WARNING** When it comes to the TRANSIENT LIFESTYLE, be aware that DI CONTAINERS can behave differently. Although some DI CONTAINERS track TRANSIENT components and tend to dispose of them when their consumer goes out of scope, others don't and, therefore, the TRANSIENTS aren't disposed.

It's worth noting that in desktop and similar applications, we tend to resolve the entire object hierarchy only once: at application startup. This means that even for TRANSIENT components, only a few instances could be created, and they can be around for a long time. In the degenerate case where there's only one consumer per DEPENDENCY, the end result of resolving a graph of pure TRANSIENT components is equivalent to resolving a graph of pure SINGLETONS, or any mix thereof. This is because the graph is resolved only once, so the difference in behavior is never realized.

WHEN TO USE THE TRANSIENT LIFESTYLE

The TRANSIENT LIFESTYLE is the safest choice of LIFESTYLES, but also one of the least efficient. It can cause a myriad of instances to be created and garbage collected, even when a single instance would have sufficed.

If you have doubts about the thread-safety of a component, however, the TRANSIENT LIFESTYLE is safe, because each consumer has its own instance of the DEPENDENCY. In many cases, you can safely exchange the TRANSIENT LIFESTYLE for a SCOPED LIFESTYLE, where access to the DEPENDENCY is also guaranteed to be sequential.

EXAMPLE: RESOLVING MULTIPLE REPOSITORIES

You saw several examples of using the TRANSIENT LIFESTYLE earlier in this chapter. In listing 8.3, the Repository is created and injected on the spot in the resolving method, and the COMPOSER keeps no reference to it. In listings 8.8 and 8.9, you subsequently saw how to deal with a TRANSIENT disposable component.

In these examples, you may have noticed that the `userContext` stays a SINGLETON throughout. This is a purely *stateless service*, so there's no reason to create a new instance for every `ProductService` created. The noteworthy point is that you can mix DEPENDENCIES with different LIFESTYLES.

> **WARNING** Although you can mix DEPENDENCIES with different LIFESTYLES, you should make sure that a consumer only has DEPENDENCIES with a lifetime that's equal to or exceeds its own, because a consumer will keep its DEPENDENCIES alive by storing them in its `private` fields. Failing to do so leads to CAPTIVE DEPENDENCIES, which we'll address in section 8.4.1.

When multiple components require the same DEPENDENCY, each is given a separate instance. The following listing shows a method resolving an ASP.NET Core MVC controller.

Listing 8.11   Resolving TRANSIENT AspNetUserContextAdapter instances

```
private HomeController CreateHomeController()
{
    return new HomeController(
        new ProductService(
            new SqlProductRepository(this.connStr),
            new AspNetUserContextAdapter(),
            new SqlUserRepository(
                this.connStr,
                new AspNetUserContextAdapter())));
}
```

> **Both the ProductService and SqlUserRepository classes require an IUserContext DEPENDENCY. When the AspNetUserContextAdapter is transient, each consumer gets its own private instance, so ProductService gets one instance, and SqlUserRepository gets another.**

The TRANSIENT LIFESTYLE implies that every consumer receives a private instance of the DEPENDENCY, even when multiple consumers in the same object graph have the same DEPENDENCY (as is the case in the previous listing). If many consumers share the same DEPENDENCY, this approach can be inefficient; but if the implementation isn't thread-safe, the more efficient SINGLETON LIFESTYLE is inappropriate. In such cases, the SCOPED LIFESTYLE may be a better fit.

8.3.3   *The SCOPED LIFESTYLE*

As users of a web application, we'd like a response from the application as quickly as possible, even when other users are accessing the system at the same time. We don't want our request to be put on a queue together with all the other users' requests. We might have to wait an inordinate amount of time for a response if there are many requests ahead of ours. To address this issue, web applications handle requests concurrently. The ASP.NET Core infrastructure shields us from this by letting each request execute in its own context and with its own instance of controllers (if you use ASP.NET Core MVC).

Because of concurrency, DEPENDENCIES that aren't thread-safe can't be used as SINGLETONS. On the other hand, using them as TRANSIENTS can be inefficient or even downright problematic if you need to share a DEPENDENCY between different consumers within the same request.

Although the ASP.NET Core engine executes a single request asynchronously, and the execution of a single request typically involves multiple threads, it does guarantee that code is executed in a sequential manner—at least when you properly await asynchronous operations.[8] This means that if you can share a DEPENDENCY within a single request, thread-safety isn't an issue. Section 8.4.3 provides more details on how the asynchronous, multi-threaded approach works in ASP.NET Core.

---

[8]   Threads are still used sequentially, one after the other, not in parallel.

Although the concept of a web request is limited to web applications and web services, the concept of a *request* is broader. Most long-running applications use requests to execute single operations. For example, when building a service application that processes items one by one from a queue, you can imagine each processed item as an individual request, consisting of its own set of DEPENDENCIES.

The same could hold for desktop or phone applications. Although the top root types (views or ViewModels) could potentially live for a long time, you could see a button press as a request, and you could scope this operation and give it its own isolated bubble with its own set of DEPENDENCIES. This leads to the concept of a SCOPED LIFESTYLE, where you decide to reuse instances within a given scope. Figure 8.9 demonstrates how the SCOPED LIFESTYLE works.

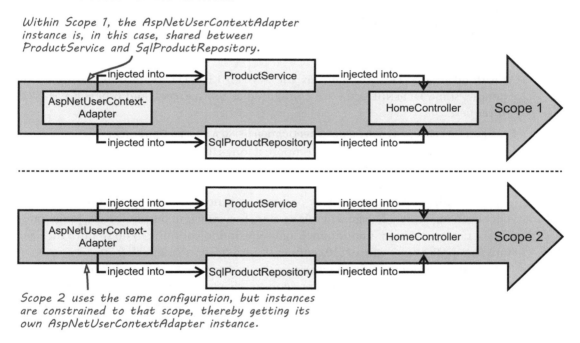

Within Scope 1, the AspNetUserContextAdapter instance is, in this case, shared between ProductService and SqlProductRepository.

Scope 2 uses the same configuration, but instances are constrained to that scope, thereby getting its own AspNetUserContextAdapter instance.

Figure 8.9 The SCOPED LIFESTYLE indicates that you create, at most, one instance per specified scope.

DEFINITION SCOPED DEPENDENCIES behave like SINGLETON DEPENDENCIES within a single, well-defined scope or request but aren't shared across scopes. Each scope has its own cache of associated DEPENDENCIES.

Note that DI CONTAINERS might have specialized versions of the SCOPED LIFESTYLE that target a specific technology. Also, any disposable components should be disposed of when the scope ends.

WHEN TO USE THE SCOPED LIFESTYLE

The SCOPED LIFESTYLE makes sense for long-running applications that are tasked with processing operations that need to run with some degree of isolation. Isolation is required when these operations are processed in parallel, or when each operation contains its own state. Web applications are a great example of where the SCOPED LIFESTYLE works well, because web applications typically process requests in parallel, and those requests typically contain some mutable state that's specific to the request. But even if a web application starts some background operation that isn't related to a web request, the SCOPED LIFESTYLE is valuable. Even these background operations can typically be mapped to the concept of a request.

> **TIP**   If you ever need to compose an Entity Framework Core DbContext in a web request, a SCOPED LIFESTYLE is an excellent choice. DbContext instances aren't thread-safe, but you typically only want to have one DbContext instance per web request.

As with all LIFESTYLES, you can mix the SCOPED LIFESTYLE with others so that, for example, some DEPENDENCIES are configured as SINGLETONS, and others are shared per request.

EXAMPLE: COMPOSING A LONG-RUNNING APPLICATION USING A SCOPED DBCONTEXT

In this example, you'll see how to compose a long-running console application with a scoped DbContext DEPENDENCY. This console application is a variation of the Update-Currency program we discussed in section 7.1.

Just as with the UpdateCurrency program, this new console application reads currency exchange rates. The goal of this version, however, is to output the exchange rates of a particular currency amount once a minute and to continue to do so until the user stops the application. Figure 8.10 outlines the application's main classes.

The CurrencyMonitoring program reuses the SqlExchangeRateProvider and CommerceContext from the UpdateCurrency program of chapter 7 and the ICurrencyConverter ABSTRACTION from chapter 4. The ICurrencyRepository ABSTRACTION and its accompanying SqlCurrencyRepository implementation are new. The CurrencyRateDisplayer is also new and is specific to this program; it's shown in the following listing.

Listing 8.12   The `CurrencyRateDisplayer` class

```
public class CurrencyRateDisplayer
{
    private readonly ICurrencyRepository repository;
    private readonly ICurrencyConverter converter;

    public CurrencyRateDisplayer(
        ICurrencyRepository repository,
        ICurrencyConverter converter)
    {
        this.repository = repository;
        this.converter = converter;
    }
```

```
        public void DisplayRatesFor(Money amount)
        {
            Console.WriteLine(
                "Exchange rates for {0} at {1}:",
                amount,
                DateTime.Now);

            IEnumerable<Currency> currencies =
                this.repository.GetAllCurrencies();      // Loads all known currencies

            foreach (Currency target in currencies)
            {
                Money rate = this.converter.Exchange(    // Calculates the exchange rates for the given
                    amount,                              // amount in the target currency
                    target);

                Console.WriteLine(rate);                 // Prints the requested exchange rates to the console
            }
        }
    }
```

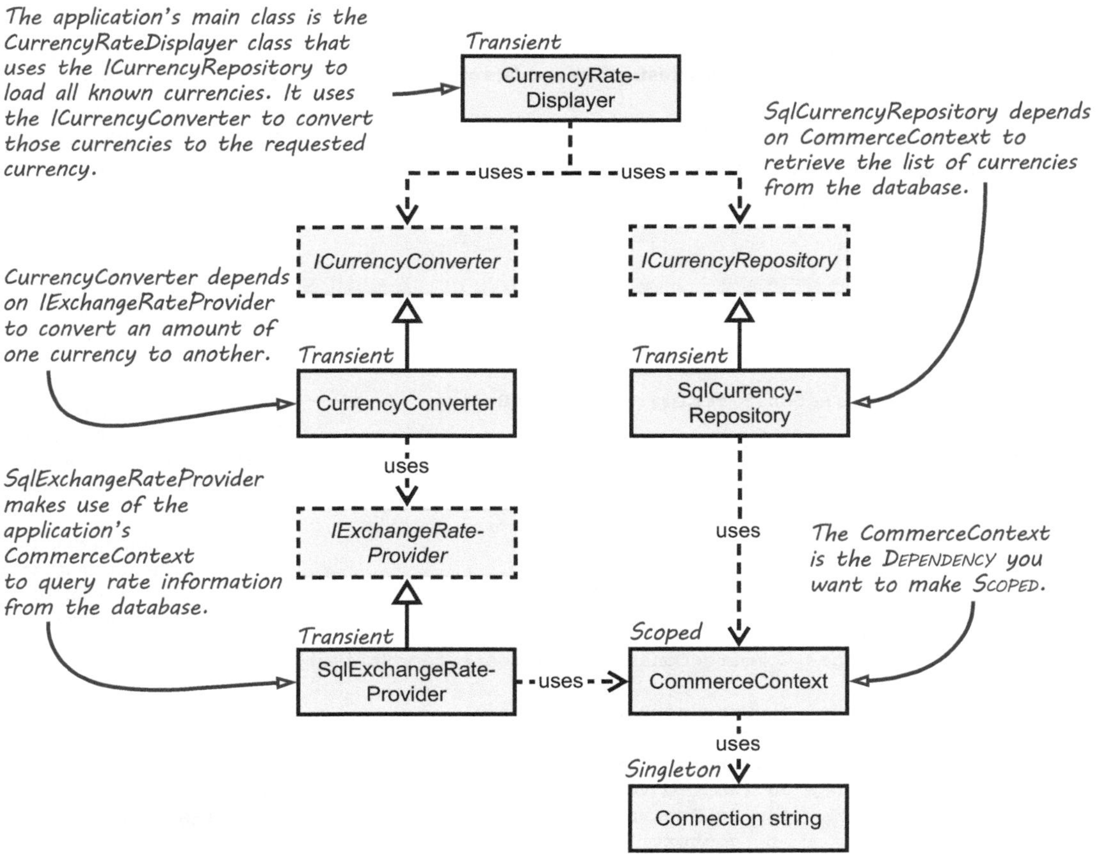

The application's main class is the CurrencyRateDisplayer class that uses the ICurrencyRepository to load all known currencies. It uses the ICurrencyConverter to convert those currencies to the requested currency.
Transient
CurrencyRate-Displayer
uses
uses
SqlCurrencyRepository depends on CommerceContext to retrieve the list of currencies from the database.
ICurrencyConverter
ICurrencyRepository
CurrencyConverter depends on IExchangeRateProvider to convert an amount of one currency to another.
Transient
CurrencyConverter
Transient
SqlCurrency-Repository
uses
SqlExchangeRateProvider makes use of the application's CommerceContext to query rate information from the database.
IExchangeRate-Provider
uses
The CommerceContext is the DEPENDENCY you want to make SCOPED.
Transient
SqlExchangeRate-Provider
uses
Scoped
CommerceContext
uses
Singleton
Connection string

Figure 8.10 The class diagram of the CurrencyMonitoring program

You can run the application from the command line using `"EUR 1.00"` as argument. Doing so outputs the following text:

```
Exchange rates for EUR 1.00000 at 12/10/2018 22:55:00.
CAD 1.48864
USD 1.13636
DKK 7.46591
EUR 1.00000
GBP 0.89773
```

To piece the application together, you need to create the application's COMPOSITION ROOT. The COMPOSITION ROOT, in this case, consists of two classes, as shown in figure 8.11.

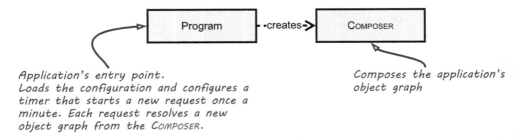

Figure 8.11   **The application's infrastructure consists of two classes, `Program` and `Composer`.**

The `Program` class uses the `Composer` class to resolve the application's object graph. Listing 8.13 shows the `Composer` class with its `CreateRateDisplayer` method. It ensures that for each resolve, only one instance of the scoped `CommerceContext` DEPENDENCY is created.

Listing 8.13   The `Composer` class, responsible for composing object graphs

```
public class Composer
{
    private readonly string connectionString;        ◄──  Storage fields for SINGLETONS. In
                                                           this case, there's only a connection
    public Composer(string connectionString)               string, but a typical application
    {                                                      will have more singleton instances.
        this.connectionString = connectionString;
    }
                                                           Public method that allows
    public CurrencyRateDisplayer CreateRateDisplayer()  ◄──  the transient root type
    {                                                      CurrencyRateDisplayer to
        var context =                                      be composed
            new CommerceContext(this.connectionString);

        return new CurrencyRateDisplayer(
            new SqlCurrencyRepository(
                context),          ◄──  Injects the SCOPED
            new CurrencyConverter(      DEPENDENCIES into a
                new SqlExchangeRateProvider(   transient object graph
                    context)));    ◄──
    }
}
```

Creates the SCOPED DEPENDENCIES

The remaining part of the CompOSITION ROOT is the application's entry point: the Program class. It's responsible for reading the input arguments and configuration file, and setting up the Timer that runs once a minute to display exchange rates. The following listing shows it in full glory.

Listing 8.14 The application's entry point that manages scopes

```
public static class Program
{
    private static Composer composer;

    public static void Main(string[] args)
    {
        var money = new Money(
            currency: new Currency(code: args[0]),
            amount: decimal.Parse(args[1]));

        composer = new Composer(LoadConnectionString());

        var timer = new Timer(interval: 60000);

        timer.Elapsed += (s, e) => DisplayRates(money);
        timer.Start();

        Console.WriteLine("Press any key to exit.");
        Console.ReadLine();
    }

    private static void DisplayRates(Money money)
    {
        CurrencyRateDisplayer displayer =
            composer.CreateRateDisplayer();

        displayer.DisplayRatesFor(money);
    }

    private static string LoadConnectionString() { ... }
}
```

Creates new Money based on the incoming command-line arguments. This is the amount for which the exchange rates will be displayed.

Creates a System .Timers.Timer.[9] Triggers the Timer once a minute. When an interval elapses, calls the DisplayRates method.

After the timer is started, the program waits for user input and quits when that happens.

The COMPOSER is requested to resolve a CurrencyRateDisplayer for the current request.

The Program class configures a Timer that calls the DisplayRates method when it elapses. Even though you only call DisplayRates once per minute, in this example, you could easily call DisplayRates in parallel over multiple threads or even make DisplayRates asynchronous. This would still work because each call creates and manages its set of scoped instances, allowing each operation to run in isolation from the others.

> **NOTE** As a simplification, the previous example omitted the release of the created object graph. Listings 8.7 and 8.8 demonstrate this concept in the context of an ASP.NET Core MVC application. A solution that works with a console application would look similar, so we'll leave that as an exercise for you.

---

[9] The System.Timers.Timer class is part of .NET Standard 2.0 and .NET Core 2.0.

Whereas a Transient Lifestyle implies that every consumer receives a private instance of a Dependency, a Scoped Lifestyle ensures that all consumers of all resolved graphs for that scope get the same instance. Besides common Lifestyle patterns, such as Singleton, Transient, and Scoped, there are also patterns that you can define as code smells or even anti-patterns. A few of those bad Lifestyle choices are discussed in the following section.

8.4   *Bad Lifestyle choices*

As we all know, some lifestyle choices are bad for our health, smoking being one of them. The same holds true when it comes to applying Lifestyles in DI. You can make many mistakes. In this section, we discuss the choices shown in table 8.2.

Table 8.2   Bad Lifestyle choices covered in this section

Subject	Type	Description
Captive Dependencies	Bug	Keeps Dependencies referenced beyond their expected lifetime
Leaky Abstractions	Design issue	Uses Leaky Abstractions, leaking Lifestyle choices to consumers
Per-thread Lifestyle	Bug	Causes concurrency bugs by tying instances to the lifetime of a thread

As table 8.2 states, Captive Dependencies and the per-thread Lifestyle can cause bugs in your application. More often than not, these bugs only appear after deploying the application to production, because they are concurrency related. When we start the application, as developers, we typically run it for a short period of time, one request at a time. The same holds true for testers that typically go through the application in an orderly fashion. This might hide such problems, which only pop up when multiple users access the application concurrently.

When we leak details of our Lifestyle choices to our consumers, this typically won't lead to bugs—or at least, not immediately. It does, however, complicate the Dependency's consumers and their tests, and might cause sweeping changes throughout the code base. In the end, this increases the chance of bugs.

8.4.1   *Captive Dependencies*

When it comes to lifetime management, a common pitfall is that of Captive Dependencies. This happens when a Dependency is kept alive by a consumer for longer than you intended it to be. This might even cause it to be reused by multiple threads or requests concurrently, even though the Dependency isn't thread-safe.

> **DEFINITION** A Captive Dependency is a Dependency that's inadvertently kept alive for too long because its consumer was given a lifetime that exceeds the Dependency's expected lifetime.

An all-too-common example of a CAPTIVE DEPENDENCY is when a short-lived DEPENDENCY is injected into a SINGLETON consumer. A SINGLETON is kept alive for the lifetime of the COMPOSER, and so will its DEPENDENCY. The following listing illustrates this problem.

BAD CODE

Listing 8.15 CAPTIVE DEPENDENCY example

```
public class Composer
{
    private readonly IProductRepository repository;

    public Composer(string connectionString)
    {
        this.repository = new SqlProductRepository(
            new CommerceContext(connectionString));
    }
    ...
}
```

Creates SqlProductRepository as SINGLETON and stores it for reuse

Injects CommerceContext into the SINGLETON. CommerceContext has now become a CAPTIVE DEPENDENCY; it isn't thread-safe and isn't intended to be reused by multiple threads.

Because there's only one instance of `SqlProductRepository` for the entire application, and `CommerceContext` is referenced by `SqlProductRepository` in its private field, there will be effectively just one instance of `CommerceContext` too. This is a problem, because `CommerceContext` isn't thread-safe and isn't intended to outlive a single request. Because `CommerceContext` is kept captive by `SqlProductRepository` past its expected release time, we call `CommerceContext` a CAPTIVE DEPENDENCY.

IMPORTANT A component should only reference DEPENDENCIES that have an expected lifetime that's equal to or longer than that of the component itself.

CAPTIVE DEPENDENCIES are a common problem when you're working with a DI CONTAINER. This is caused by the dynamic nature of DI CONTAINERS that make it easy to lose track of the shape of the object graphs you're building. As the previous example showed, however, the problem can also arise when working with PURE DI. By carefully structuring code in the PURE DI COMPOSITION ROOT, you can reduce the chance of running into this problem. The following listing shows an example of this approach.

Listing 8.16 Mitigating CAPTIVE DEPENDENCIES with PURE DI

```
public class CommerceControllerActivator : IControllerActivator
{
    private readonly string connStr;
    private readonly IUserContext userContext;

    public CommerceControllerActivator(string connectionString)
    {
        this.connStr = connectionString;
        this.userContext =
            new AspNetUserContextAdapter();
    }
```

Storage fields for SINGLETONS

Creates SINGLETONS

```
public object Create(ControllerContext ctx)
{
    var context = new CommerceContext(this.connStr);          ⎱ Creates SCOPED
    var provider = new SqlExchangeRateProvider(context);      ⎰ DEPENDENCIES


    Type type = ctx.ActionDescriptor
        .ControllerTypeInfo.AsType();

    if (type == typeof(HomeController))
    {
        return this.CreateHomeController(context);   ◄──────  Supplies factory
    }                                                         methods with the
    else if (type == typeof(ExchangeController))              created SCOPED
    {                                                         DEPENDENCIES
        return this.CreateExchangeController(
            context, provider);          ◄──────────────────
    }
    else
    {
        throw new Exception("Unknown controller " + type.Name);
    }
}

private HomeController CreateHomeController(
    CommerceContext context)
{                                                     Composes object graph
    return new HomeController(                         containing TRANSIENT,
        new ProductService(                            SCOPED, and SINGLETON
            new SqlProductRepository(                  instances
                context),
            this.userContext));
}

private RouteController CreateExchangeController(
    CommerceContext context,
    IExchangeRateProvider provider) { ... }
}
```

NOTE   When working with a DI CONTAINER, the problem of CAPTIVE DEPEN-
DENCIES is so widespread that some DI CONTAINERS will do analysis on constructed object graphs to detect them.[10]

Listing 8.16 separates the creation of all DEPENDENCIES into three distinct phases.
When you separate these phases, it becomes much easier to detect and prevent CAP-
TIVE DEPENDENCIES. These phases are

- SINGLETONS created during application start-up
- Scoped instances created at the start of a request
- Based on the request, a particular object graph that consists of TRANSIENT,
  SCOPED, and SINGLETON instances

---

[10] All DI CONTAINERS covered in this book contain features for the detection of CAPTIVE DEPENDENCIES.

With this model, all the application's SCOPED DEPENDENCIES are created for each request, even when they aren't used. This might seem inefficient, but remember that, as we discussed in section 4.2.2, component constructors should be free from all logic except guard checks and when storing incoming DEPENDENCIES. This makes construction fast and prevents most performance issues; the creation of a few unused DEPENDENCIES is a non-issue.

From a misconfiguration perspective, CAPTIVE DEPENDENCIES are one of the most common, hardest-to-spot configurations or programming errors related to bad LIFESTYLE choices. More often than we'd like to admit, we've wasted many hours trying to find bugs caused by CAPTIVE DEPENDENCIES. That's why we consider tool support for spotting CAPTIVE DEPENDENCIES invaluable when you're using a DI CONTAINER. Although CAPTIVE DEPENDENCIES are typically caused by configuration or programming errors, other inconvenient LIFESTYLE choices are design flaws, such as when you're forcing LIFESTYLE choices on consumers.

8.4.2　*Using LEAKY ABSTRACTIONS to leak LIFESTYLE choices to consumers*

Another case where you might end up with a bad LIFESTYLE choice is when you need to postpone the creation of a DEPENDENCY. When you have a DEPENDENCY that's rarely needed and is costly to create, you might prefer to create such an instance on the fly, after the object graph is composed. This is a valid concern. What isn't, however, is pushing such a concern on to the DEPENDENCY's consumers. If you do this, you're leaking details about the implementation and implementation choices of the COMPOSITION ROOT to the consumer. The DEPENDENCY becomes a LEAKY ABSTRACTION, and you're violating the DEPENDENCY INVERSION PRINCIPLE.

In this section, we'll show two common examples of how you can cause your LIFESTYLE choice to be leaked to a DEPENDENCY's consumer. Both examples have the same solution: create a wrapper class that hides the LIFESTYLE choice and functions as an implementation of the original ABSTRACTION rather than the LEAKY ABSTRACTION.

Lazy<T> AS A LEAKY ABSTRACTION

Let's again return to our regularly reused `ProductService` example that was first introduced in listing 3.9. Let's imagine that one of its DEPENDENCIES is costly to create, and not all code paths in the application require its existence.

This is something you might be tempted to solve by using .NET's `System.Lazy<T>` class. A `Lazy<T>` allows access to an underlying value through its `Value` property. That value, however, will only be created when it's requested for the first time. After that, the `Lazy<T>` caches the value for as long as the `Lazy<T>` instance exists.

This is useful, because it allows you to delay the creation of DEPENDENCIES. It's an error, however, to inject `Lazy<T>` directly into a consumer's constructor, as we'll discuss later. The next listing shows an example of such an erroneous use of `Lazy<T>`.

BAD
CODE

Listing 8.17   `Lazy<T>` as LEAKY ABSTRACTION

```
public class ProductService : IProductService
{
    private readonly IProductRepository repository;
    private readonly Lazy<IUserContext> userContext;

    public ProductService(
        IProductRepository repository,
        Lazy<IUserContext> userContext)
    {
        this.repository = repository;
        this.userContext = userContext;
    }

    public IEnumerable<DiscountedProduct> GetFeaturedProducts()
    {
        return
            from product in this.repository
                .GetFeaturedProducts()
            select product.ApplyDiscountFor(
                this.userContext.Value);
    }
}
```

> Instead of depending on IUserContext, ProductService now depends on Lazy<IUserContext>. This way, the IUserContext instance is created only when it's needed. This is bad because Lazy<IUserContext> is a LEAKY ABSTRACTION.

> The Value property on Lazy<IUserContext> ensures that the IUserContext DEPENDENCY is created once. When the GetFeaturedProducts method on IProductRepository returns an empty list, the select clause is never executed, and the Value property will never get called, preventing IUserContext from being created.

Listing 8.18 shows the structure of the COMPOSITION ROOT for the `ProductService` of listing 8.17.

BAD
CODE

Listing 8.18   Composing a `ProductService` that depends on `Lazy<IUserContext>`

```
Lazy<IUserContext> lazyUserContext =
    new Lazy<IUserContext>(
        () => new AspNetUserContextAdapter());

new HomeController(
    new ProductService(
        new SqlProductRepository(
            new CommerceContext(connectionString)),
        lazyUserContext));
```

> Delays the creation of the real AspNetUserContextAdapter DEPENDENCY by wrapping its creation inside the Lazy<IUserContext>

> Because ProductService now depends on Lazy<IUserContext> rather than IUserContext, you inject Lazy<IUserContext> directly into its constructor.

After seeing this code, you might wonder what's so bad about it. The following discussion lists several problems with such a design, but it's important that you know there's nothing wrong with the use of `Lazy<T>` inside your COMPOSITION ROOT—injecting `Lazy<T>` into an application component, however, leads to LEAKY ABSTRACTIONS. Now, back to the problems.

First, letting a consumer depend on `Lazy<IUserContext>` complicates the consumer and its unit tests. You might think that having to call `userContext.Value` is a small price to pay for being able to lazy load an expensive DEPENDENCY, but it isn't. When creating unit tests, not only do you have to create `Lazy<T>` instances that wrap the original DEPENDENCY, but you also have to write extra tests to verify whether that `Value` isn't being called at the wrong time.

Because making the DEPENDENCY lazy seems important enough as a performance optimization, it would be weird not to verify whether you implemented it correctly. This is, at least, one extra test you need to write for every consumer of that DEPENDENCY. There might be dozens of consumers for such a DEPENDENCY, and they all need the extra tests to verify their correctness.

Second, changing an existing DEPENDENCY to a lazy DEPENDENCY later in the development process causes sweeping changes throughout the application. This can present a serious amount of effort when there are dozens of consumers for that DEPENDENCY, because, as discussed in the previous point, not only do the consumers themselves need to be altered, but all of their tests need to be changed too. Making these kinds of rippling changes is time consuming and risky.

To prevent this, you could make all DEPENDENCIES lazy by default, because, in theory, every DEPENDENCY could potentially become expensive in the future. This would prevent you from having to make any future cascading changes. But this would be madness, and we hope you agree that this isn't a good path to pursue. This is especially true if you consider that every DEPENDENCY could potentially become a list of implementations, as we'll discuss shortly. This would lead to making all DEPENDENCIES `IEnumerable<Lazy<T>>` by default, which would be, even more so, insane.

Last, because the amount of changes you have to make and the number of tests you need to add, it becomes quite easy to make programming mistakes that would completely nullify these changes. For instance, if you create a new component that accidentally depends on `IUserContext` instead of `Lazy<IUserContext>`, it means that every graph that contains that component will always get an eagerly loaded `IUserContext` implementation.

This doesn't mean that you aren't allowed to construct your DEPENDENCIES lazily, though. We'd like, however, to repeat our statement from section 4.2.1: you should keep the constructors of your components free of any logic other than Guard Clauses and the storing of incoming DEPENDENCIES. This makes the construction of your classes fast and reliable, and will prevent such components from ever becoming expensive to instantiate.

In some cases, however, you'll have no choice; for instance, when dealing with third-party components you have little control over. In that case, `Lazy<T>` is a great tool. But rather than letting all consumers depend on `Lazy<T>`, you should hide `Lazy<T>` behind a Virtual Proxy and place that Virtual Proxy within the COMPOSITION ROOT.[11] The following listing provides an example of this.

---

[11] For more on Virtual Proxies, see Erich Gamma et. al., *Design Patterns*, 208.

GOOD
CODE

Listing 8.19   Virtual Proxy wrapping `Lazy<T>`

```
public class LazyUserContextProxy : IUserContext        ◀────|  Implements IUserContext
{
    private readonly Lazy<IUserContext> userContext;        ◀──  Depends on Lazy<IUserContext>
                                                                 to allow the IUserContext to be
    public LazyUserContextProxy(                                 constructed lazily
        Lazy<IUserContext> userContext)
    {
        this.userContext = userContext;
    }                                                            Only when the Proxy's
                                                                 IsInRole method is invoked
    public bool IsInRole(Role role)                             will the real IUserContext
    {                                                            implementation be
        IUserContext real = this.userContext.Value;             constructed and invoked.
        return real.IsInRole(role);
    }
}
```

This new `LazyUserContextProxy` allows `ProductService` to dependent on `IUser-Context` instead of `Lazy<IUserContext>`. Here's `ProductService`'s new constructor:

```
public ProductService(
    IProductRepository repository,
    IUserContext userContext)
```

The next listing shows how you can compose the object graph for `HomeController` while injecting `LazyUserContextProxy` into `ProductService`.

GOOD
CODE

Listing 8.20   Composing a `ProductService` by injecting a Virtual Proxy

```
IUserContext lazyProxy =
    new LazyUserContextProxy(                               Creates the Virtual Proxy
        new Lazy<IUserContext>(                             that wraps a Lazy<T>,
            () => new AspNetUserContextAdapter()));         allowing the creation of
                                                            the real DEPENDENCY in a
new HomeController(                                          lazy fashion
    new ProductService(
        new SqlProductRepository(
            new CommerceContext(connectionString)),
        lazyProxy));        ◀────     Because LazyUserContextProxy implements
                                      IUserContext, you're now able to let ProductService
                                      depend on IUserContext while injecting
                                      LazyUserContextProxy into its constructor.
```

As listing 8.19 shows, it's not a bad thing per se to have a class depending on `Lazy<T>`, but you want to centralize this inside the COMPOSITION ROOT and only have a single class that takes this dependency on `Lazy<IUserContext>`. Depending on `Func<T>` has practically the same effect as depending on `Lazy<T>`, and the solution is similar. Doing so prevents your code from being complicated, unit tests from being added, sweeping changes from being made, and unfortunate bugs from being introduced. As you'll see next, the same arguments hold for injecting IEnumerable<T> too.

IEnumerable<T> AS A LEAKY ABSTRACTION

Just as with using Lazy<T> to delay the creation of DEPENDENCIES, there are many cases where you need to work with a collection of DEPENDENCIES of a certain ABSTRACTION. For this purpose, you can make use of one of the BCL collection ABSTRACTIONS, such as IEnumerable<T>. Although, in itself, there's nothing wrong with using IEnumerable<T> as an ABSTRACTION to present a collection of DEPENDENCIES, using it in the wrong place can, once again, lead to a LEAKY ABSTRACTION. The following listing shows how IEnumerable<T> can be used incorrectly.

BAD CODE

Listing 8.21 IEnumerable<T> as a LEAKY ABSTRACTION

```
public class Component
{
    private readonly IEnumerable<ILogger> loggers;

    public Component(IEnumerable<ILogger> loggers)        ◄─── Injects a collection of
    {                                                          ILogger DEPENDENCIES
        this.loggers = loggers;
    }

    public void DoSomething()
    {
        foreach (var logger in this.loggers)              ◄─── Loops through the collection
        {                                                      and operates on them
            logger.Log("DoSomething called");
        }

        ...
    }
}
```

> **NOTE** We'll ignore for a moment the advice of section 5.3.2, where we stated that you shouldn't pollute your application's code base with logging. Chapter 10 describes in detail how to design your application to account for CROSS-CUTTING CONCERNS.

We'd like to prevent consumers from having to deal with the fact that there might be multiple instances of a certain DEPENDENCY. This is an implementation detail that's leaking out through the IEnumerable<ILogger> DEPENDENCY. As we explained previously, every DEPENDENCY could potentially have multiple implementations, but your consumers shouldn't need to be aware of this. Just as with the previous Lazy<T> example, this leakage increases the system's complexity and maintenance costs when you have multiple consumers of such a DEPENDENCY, because every consumer has to deal with looping over the collection. So do consumer's tests.

Although experienced developers spit out `foreach` constructs like this in a matter of seconds, things get more complicated when the collection of DEPENDENCIES needs to be processed differently. For example, let's say that logging should continue even if one of the loggers fails:

```
foreach (var logger in this.loggers)
{
    try
    {
        logger.Log("DoSomething called");
    }
    catch                                    Empty catch clause allows
    {                                        continuing logging in case
    }                                        of a failure
}
```

Or, perhaps you not only want to continue processing, but also log that error to the next logger. This way, the next logger functions as a fallback for the failed logger:

```
for (int index = 0; index < this.loggers.Count; index++)
{
    try                                              Forwards the call to
    {                                                the underlying logger
        this.loggers[index].Log("DoSomething called");    implementation
    }
    catch (Exception ex)
    {
        if (loggers.Count > index + 1)          Forwards the exception to the
        {                                       fallback logger, which is the
            loggers[index + 1].Log(ex);         next logger, if any, in the list
        }
    }
}
```

Or perhaps—well, we think you get the idea. It'd be rather painful to have these kinds of code constructs all over the place. If you want to change your logging strategy, it causes you to make cascading changes throughout the application. Ideally, we'd like to centralize this knowledge to one single location.

You can fix this design problem using the Composite design pattern. You should be familiar with the Composite design pattern by now, as we've discussed it in chapters 1 and 6 (see figure 1.8, and listings 6.4 and 6.12). The next listing shows a Composite for `ILogger`.

Listing 8.22   Composite wrapping `IEnumerable<T>`

GOOD
CODE

```
public class CompositeLogger : ILogger          CompositeLogger implements ILogger.
{
    private readonly IList<ILogger> loggers;

    public CompositeLogger(IList<ILogger> loggers)
    {
```

CompositeLogger depends on IList<ILogger>
to allow forwarding the log requests to all
available ILogger components.

```
        this.loggers = loggers;
    }
    public void Log(LogEntry entry)
    {
        for (int index = 0; index < this.loggers.Count; index++)
        {
            try
            {
                this.loggers[index].Log(entry);
            }
            catch (Exception ex)
            {
                if (loggers.Count > index + 1)
                {
                    var logger = loggers[index + 1];
                    logger.Log(new LogEntry(ex));
                }
            }
        }
    }
}
```

Implements ILogger's Log method. In this case, we assume ILogger contains one single method accepting a LogEntry method.[12]

Wraps the exception thrown by the failed logger in a LogEntry object so it can be passed on to the fallback logger

The following snippet shows how you can compose the object graph for `Component` using this new `CompositeLogger`, keeping `Component` dependent on a single `ILogger` instead of an `IEnumerable<ILogger>`:

GOOD
CODE

```
ILogger composite =
    new CompositeLogger(new ILogger[]
    {
        new SqlLogger(connectionString),
        new WindowsEventLogLogger(source: "MyApp"),
        new FileLogger(directory: "c:\\logs")
    });

new Component(composite);
```

Constructs a Composite with multiple ILogger implementations

Constructs the new Component using the Composite

As you've seen many times before, good application design follows the DEPENDENCY INVERSION PRINCIPLE and prevents LEAKY ABSTRACTIONS. This results in cleaner code that's more maintainable and more resilient to programming errors. Let's now look at a different smell, which doesn't affect the application's design per se, but potentially causes hard-to-fix concurrency problems.

8.4.3   *Causing concurrency bugs by tying instances to the lifetime of a thread*

Sometimes you're dealing with DEPENDENCIES that aren't thread-safe but don't necessarily need to be tied to the lifetime of a request. A tempting solution is to synchronizing the lifetime of such a DEPENDENCY to the lifetime of a thread. Although seductive, such practice is error prone.

---

[12] To get an idea of why we defined ILogger using a single Log method, take a look at the following Stack Overflow question: https://mng.bz/QgdG.

> **WARNING**   Some DI CONTAINERS refer to this method as the *per-thread* LIFE-STYLE and have built-in support for it—avoid this!

Listing 8.23 shows how the `CreateCurrencyParser` method, previously discussed in listing 7.2, makes use of a `SqlExchangeRateProvider` DEPENDENCY. This is created once for each thread in the application.

BAD CODE

Listing 8.23   A DEPENDENCY's lifetime tied to the lifetime of a thread

```
[ThreadStatic]
private static CommerceContext context;

static CurrencyParser CreateCurrencyParser(
    string connectionString)
{
    if (context == null)
    {
        context = new CommerceContext(
            connectionString);
    }

    return new CurrencyParser(
        new SqlExchangeRateProvider(context),
        context);
}
```

A static field is marked with the **[ThreadStatic]** attribute. The CLR ensures that such a field isn't shared between threads, instead providing each executing thread a separate instance of the field. If the field is accessed on a different thread, it'll contain a different value.

In case the thread on which the current code is executing doesn't have an initialized CommerceContext yet, a new instance is created and stored in the corresponding thread-static field.

Injects the per-thread DEPENDENCY into a transient object graph

Although this might look innocent, that couldn't be further from the truth. We'll discuss two problems with this listing next.

THE LIFETIME OF A THREAD IS OFTEN UNCLEAR

It can be hard to predict what the lifespan of a thread is. When you create and start a thread using `new Thread().Start()`, you'll get a fresh block of thread-static memory. This means that if you call `CreateCurrencyParser` in such a thread, the thread-static fields will all be unset, resulting in new instances being created.

When starting threads from the thread pool using `ThreadPool.QueueUserWorkItem`, however, you'll possibly get an existing thread from the pool or a newly created thread, depending on what's in the thread pool. Even if you aren't creating threads yourself, the framework might be (as we've discussed regarding, for example, ASP.NET Core). This means that while some threads have a lifetime that's rather short, others live for the duration of the entire application. Further complications arise when operations aren't guaranteed to run on a single thread.

ASYNCHRONOUS APPLICATION MODELS CAUSE MULTI-THREADING ISSUES

Modern application frameworks are inherently asynchronous in nature. Even though your code might not implement the new asynchronous programming patterns using the `async` and `await` keywords, the framework you're using might still decide to finish a request on a different thread than it was started on. ASP.NET Core is, for instance, completely built around this asynchronous programming model. But even older frameworks, such as ASP.NET Web API and ASP.NET Web Forms, allow requests to run asynchronously.

This is a problem for DEPENDENCIES that are tied to a particular thread. When a request continues on a different thread, it still references the same DEPENDENCIES, even though some of them are tied to the original thread. Figure 8.12 illustrates this.

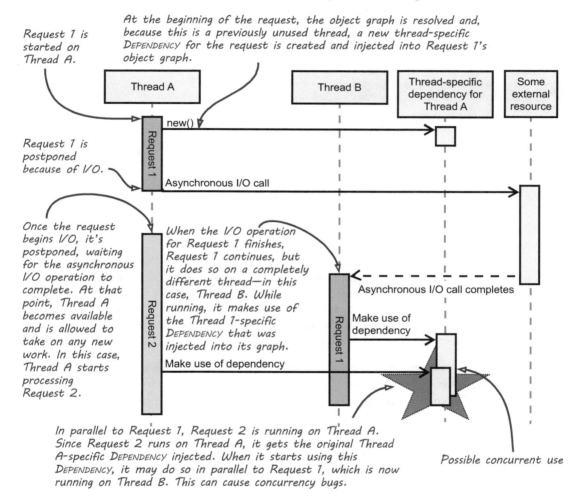

Figure 8.12 Thread-specific DEPENDENCIES can cause concurrency bugs in asynchronous environments.

NOTE The object graph of Request 1 in figure 8.12 moves from one thread to another, although the DEPENDENCY is thread specific. The DEPENDENCY effectively becomes a CAPTIVE DEPENDENCY once the object graph is moved to another thread.

Using thread-specific DEPENDENCIES while running in an asynchronous context is a particularly bad idea, because it could lead to concurrency problems, which are typically hard to find and reproduce. Such a problem would only occur if the thread-specific DEPENDENCY isn't thread-safe—they typically aren't. Otherwise, the SINGLETON LIFESTYLE would have worked just fine.

The solution to this problem is to scope things around a request or operation, and there are several ways to achieve this. Instead of linking the lifetime of the DEPENDENCY to that of a thread, make its lifetime scoped to the request, as discussed in section 8.3.3. The following listing demonstrates this once more.

GOOD
CODE

Listing 8.24   Storing SCOPED DEPENDENCIES in local variables

```
static CurrencyParser CreateCurrencyParser(
    string connectionString)
{
    var context = new CommerceContext(           Creates the SCOPED
        connectionString);                       DEPENDENCY

    return new CurrencyParser(                    Injects the SCOPED DEPENDENCY
        new SqlExchangeRateProvider(context),     into a transient object graph
        context);
}
```

> **NOTE** The given solution could reduce the lifetime of the DEPENDENCY considerably. This typically won't be a problem, but if it is, consider pooling the DEPENDENCY, or wrap access to a thread-static DEPENDENCY behind a proxy, which only accesses the DEPENDENCY from within its method. This prevents the DEPENDENCY from being accidentally moved from thread to thread. We'll leave this as an exercise for the reader.

The LIFESTYLES examined in this chapter represent the most common types, but you may have more exotic needs that aren't satisfactorily addressed. When we find ourselves in such a situation, our immediate response should be to realize that our approach must be wrong, and if we change our design a bit, everything will fit nicely into standard patterns.

This realization is often a disappointment, but it leads to better and more maintainable code. The point is that if you feel the need to implement a custom LIFESTYLE or create a LEAKY ABSTRACTION, you should first seriously reconsider your design. For this reason, we decided to leave specialized LIFESTYLES out of this book. We can often handle such situations better with a redesign or INTERCEPTION, as you'll see in the next chapter.

Summary

- COMPOSER is a unifying term, referring to any object or method that composes DEPENDENCIES. It's an important part of the COMPOSITION ROOT.

- The COMPOSER can be a DI CONTAINER, but it can also be any method that constructs object graphs manually using PURE DI.

- The COMPOSER has a greater degree of influence over the lifetime of DEPENDENCIES than any single consumer can have. The COMPOSER decides when instances are created, and, by its choice of whether to share instances, it determines whether a DEPENDENCY goes out of scope with a single consumer or whether all consumers must go out of scope before the DEPENDENCY can be released.

- A LIFESTYLE is a formalized way of describing the intended lifetime of a DEPENDENCY.

- The ability to fine tune each DEPENDENCY's LIFESTYLE is important for performance reasons but can also be important for correct behavior. Some DEPENDENCIES must be shared between several consumers for the system to work correctly.

- The LISKOV SUBSTITUTION PRINCIPLE states that you must be able to substitute the ABSTRACTION for an arbitrary implementation without changing the correctness of the system.

- Failing to adhere to the LISKOV SUBSTITUTION PRINCIPLE makes applications fragile, because it disallows replacing DEPENDENCIES that might cause a consumer to break.

- An *ephemeral disposable* is an object with a clear and short lifetime that typically doesn't exceed a single method call.

- Diligently work to implement services so they don't hold references to disposables, but rather create and dispose of them on demand. This makes memory management simpler, because the service can be garbage collected like other objects.

- The responsibility of disposing of DEPENDENCIES falls to the COMPOSER. It, better than anything else, knows when it creates a disposable instance, so it also knows that the instance needs to be disposed of.

- *Releasing* is the process of determining which DEPENDENCIES can be dereferenced and (possibly) disposed of. The COMPOSITION ROOT signals the COMPOSER to release a resolved DEPENDENCY.

- A COMPOSER must take care of the correct order of disposal for objects. An object might require its DEPENDENCIES to be called during disposal, which causes problems if these DEPENDENCIES are already disposed of. Disposal should, therefore, happen in the opposite order of object creation.

- The TRANSIENT LIFESTYLE involves returning a new instance every time it's requested. Each consumer gets its own instance of the DEPENDENCY.

- Within the scope of a single COMPOSER, there'll only be one instance of a component with the SINGLETON LIFESTYLE. Each time a consumer requests the component, the same instance is served.

- SCOPED DEPENDENCIES behave like singletons within a single, well-defined scope or request, but aren't shared across scopes. Each scope has its own set of associated DEPENDENCIES.

- The SCOPED LIFESTYLE makes sense for long-running applications that are tasked with processing operations that need to run in some degree of isolation. Isolation is required when these operations are processed in parallel, or when each operation contains its own state.

- If you ever need to compose an Entity Framework Core DbContext in a web request, a SCOPED LIFESTYLE is an excellent choice. DbContext instances aren't thread-safe, but you typically only want one DbContext instance per web request.

- Object graphs can consist of DEPENDENCIES of different LIFESTYLES, but you should make sure that a consumer only has DEPENDENCIES with a lifetime that's equal to or exceeds its own, because a consumer will keep its DEPENDENCIES alive. Failing to do so leads to CAPTIVE DEPENDENCIES.

- A CAPTIVE DEPENDENCY is a DEPENDENCY that's inadvertently kept alive for too long, because its consumer was given a lifetime that exceeds the DEPENDENCY's expected lifetime.

- CAPTIVE DEPENDENCIES are a common source of bugs when working with a DI CONTAINER, although the problem can also arise when working with PURE DI.

- When applying PURE DI, a careful structure of the COMPOSITION ROOT can reduce the chance of running into problems.

- When working with a DI CONTAINER, CAPTIVE DEPENDENCIES are such a widespread problem that some DI CONTAINERS perform analysis on constructed object graphs to detect them.

- Sometimes you need to postpone the creation of a DEPENDENCY. Injecting the DEPENDENCY as a Lazy<T>, Func<T>, or IEnumerable<T>, however, is a bad idea because it causes the DEPENDENCY to become a LEAKY ABSTRACTION. Instead, you should hide this knowledge behind a Proxy or Composite.

- Don't bind the lifetime of a DEPENDENCY to the lifetime of a thread. The lifetime of a thread is often unclear, and using it in an asynchronous framework can cause multi-threading issues. Instead, use a proper SCOPED LIFESTYLE or hide access to the thread-static value behind a Proxy.

Interception

In this chapter

- Intercepting calls between two collaborating objects
- Understanding the Decorator design pattern
- Applying CROSS-CUTTING CONCERNS using Decorators

One of the most interesting things about cooking is the way you can combine many ingredients, some of them not particularly savory in themselves, into a whole that's greater than the sum of its parts. Often, you start with a simple ingredient that provides the basis for the meal, and then modify and embellish it until the end result is a delicious dish.

Consider a veal cutlet. If you were desperate, you could eat it raw, but in most cases you'd prefer to fry it. But if you slap it on a hot pan, the result will be less than stellar. Apart from the burned flavor, it won't taste like much. Fortunately, there are lots of steps you can take to enhance the experience:

- Frying the cutlet in butter prevents burning the meat, but the taste is likely to remain bland.
- Adding salt enhances the taste of the meat.
- Adding other spices, such as pepper, makes the taste more complex.

- Breading it with a mixture that includes salt and spices not only adds to the taste, but also envelops the original ingredient in a new texture. At this point, you're getting close to having a *cotoletta*.[1]
- Slitting open a pocket in the cutlet and adding ham, cheese, and garlic into the pocket before breading it takes us over the top. Now you have *veal cordon bleu*, a most excellent dish.

The difference between a burned veal cutlet and veal cordon bleu is significant, but the basic ingredient is the same. The variation is caused by the things you add to it. Given a veal cutlet, you can embellish it without changing the main ingredient to create a different dish.

With loose coupling, you can perform a similar feat when developing software. When you program to an interface, you can transform or enhance a core implementation by wrapping it in other implementations of that interface. You already saw a bit of this technique in action in listing 8.19, where we used this technique to modify an expensive DEPENDENCY's lifetime by wrapping it in a Virtual Proxy.[2]

This approach can be generalized, providing you with the ability to INTERCEPT a call from a consumer to a service. This is what we'll cover in this chapter.

Like the veal cutlet, we start out with a basic ingredient and add more ingredients to make the first ingredient better, but without changing the core of what it was originally. INTERCEPTION is one of the most powerful abilities that you gain from loose coupling. It enables you to apply the SINGLE RESPONSIBILITY PRINCIPLE and Separation of Concerns with ease.

In the previous chapters, we expended a lot of energy maneuvering code into a position where it's truly loosely coupled. In this chapter, we'll start harvesting the benefits of that investment. The overall structure of this chapter is pretty linear. We'll start with an introduction to INTERCEPTION, including an example. From there, we'll move on to talk about CROSS-CUTTING CONCERNS. This chapter is light on theory and heavy on examples, so if you're already familiar with this subject, you can consider moving directly to chapter 10, which discusses ASPECT-ORIENTED PROGRAMMING.

> **DEFINITION**   CROSS-CUTTING CONCERNS are aspects of a program that affect a larger part of the application. They're often non-functional requirements. They don't directly relate to any particular feature, but, rather, are applied to existing functionality.

When you're done with this chapter, you should be able to use INTERCEPTION to develop loosely coupled code using the Decorator design pattern. You should gain the ability to successfully observe Separation of Concerns and apply CROSS-CUTTING CONCERNS, all while keeping your code in good condition.

---

[1]   Cotoletta is the Italian word for breaded veal cutlet.

[2]   Erich Gamma et al., *Design Patterns: Elements of Reusable Object-Oriented Software* (Addison-Wesley, 1994), 207.

This chapter starts with a basic, introductory example, building toward increasingly complex notions and examples. The final, and most advanced, concept can be quickly explained in the abstract. But, because it'll probably only make sense with a solid example, the chapter culminates with a comprehensive, multipage demonstration of how it works. Before we get to that point, however, we must start at the beginning, which is to introduce INTERCEPTION.

9.1   *Introducing* INTERCEPTION

The concept of INTERCEPTION is simple: we want to be able to intercept the call between a consumer and a service, and to execute some code before or after the service is invoked. And we want to do so in such a way that neither the consumer nor the service has to change.

> **DEFINITION**   INTERCEPTION is the ability to intercept calls between two collaborating components in such a way that you can enrich or change the behavior of the DEPENDENCY without the need to change the two collaborators themselves.

For example, imagine you want to add security checks to a `SqlProductRepository` class. Although you could do this by changing `SqlProductRepository` itself or by changing a consumer's code, with INTERCEPTION, you apply security checks by intercepting calls to `SqlProductRepository` using some intermediary piece of code. In figure 9.1, a normal call from a consumer to a service is intercepted by an intermediary that can execute its own code before or after passing the call to the real service.

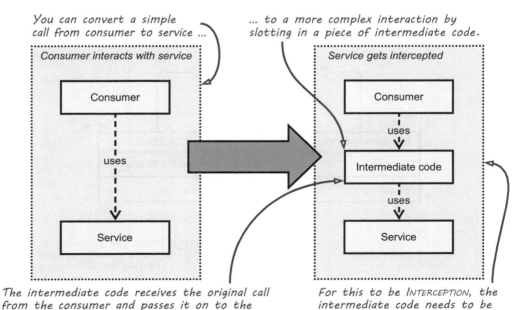

Figure 9.1   INTERCEPTION in a nutshell

IMPORTANT The set of software design principles and patterns around DI (such as, but not limited to, loose coupling and the LISKOV SUBSTITUTION PRINCIPLE) are the enablers of INTERCEPTION. Without these principles and patterns, it's impossible to apply INTERCEPTION.

In this section, you're going to get acquainted with INTERCEPTION and learn how, at its core, it's an application of the Decorator design pattern. Don't worry if your knowledge of the Decorator pattern is a bit rusty; we'll start with a description of this pattern as part of the discussion. When we're done, you should have a good understanding of how Decorators work. We'll begin by looking at a simple example that showcases the pattern, and follow up with a discussion of how INTERCEPTION relates to the Decorator pattern.

9.1.1   *Decorator design pattern*

As is the case with many other patterns, the Decorator pattern is an old and well-described design pattern that predates DI by a decade. It's such a fundamental part of INTERCEPTION that it warrants a refresher.

The Decorator pattern was first described in the book *Design Patterns: Elements of Reusable Object-Oriented Software* by Erich Gamma et al. (Addison-Wesley, 1994). The pattern's intent is to "attach additional responsibilities to an object dynamically. Decorators provide a flexible alternative to subclassing for extending functionality."[3]

As figure 9.2 shows, a Decorator works by wrapping one implementation of an ABSTRACTION in another implementation of the same ABSTRACTION. This wrapper delegates operations to the contained implementation, while adding behavior before and/or after invoking the wrapped object.

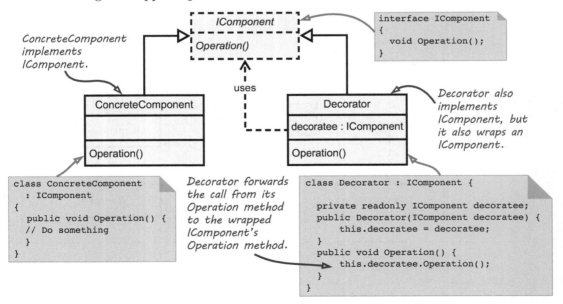

Figure 9.2   General structure of the Decorator pattern

---

3   Erich Gamma et al., *Design Patterns*, 175.

The ability to attach responsibilities dynamically means that you can make the decision to apply a Decorator at runtime rather than having this relationship baked into the program at compile time, which is what you'd do with subclassing.

A Decorator can wrap another Decorator, which wraps another Decorator, and so on, providing a "pipeline" of interception. Figure 9.3 shows how this works. At the core, there must be a self-contained implementation that performs the desired work.

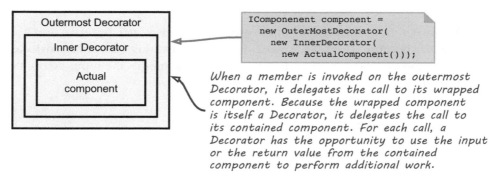

Figure 9.3   Like a set of Russian nesting dolls, a Decorator wraps another Decorator that wraps a self-contained component.[4]

Let's say, for instance, that you have an ABSTRACTION called `IGreeter` that contains a `Greet` method:

```
public interface IGreeter
{
    string Greet(string name);
}
```

For this ABSTRACTION, you can create a simple implementation that creates a formal greeting:

```
public class FormalGreeter : IGreeter
{
    public string Greet(string name)
    {
        return "Hello, " + name + ".";
    }
}
```

The simplest Decorator implementation is one that delegates the call to the decorated object without doing anything at all:

```
public class SimpleDecorator : IGreeter
{
    private readonly IGreeter decoratee;

    public SimpleDecorator(IGreeter decoratee)
```

A Decorator wraps a component of the same ABSTRACTION as it implements.

---

4   Russian nesting dolls are also known as Matryoshka dolls: a set of wooden dolls of decreasing size nested one inside another.

```
{
    this.decoratee = decoratee;
}

public string Greet(string name)
{
    return this.decoratee.Greet(name);
}
}
```

The call to Greet is passed without any changes to the decorated component; its return value is directly returned as well.

Figure 9.4 shows the relationship between IGreeter, FormalGreeter, and SimpleDecorator. Because SimpleDecorator doesn't do anything except forward the call, it's pretty useless. Instead, a Decorator can choose to modify the input before delegating the call.

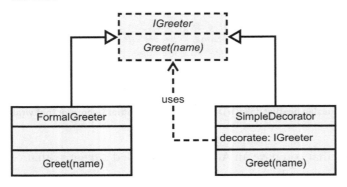

Figure 9.4   **Both SimpleDecorator and FormalGreeter implement IGreeter, while SimpleDecorator wraps an IGreeter and forwards any calls from its Greet method to the Greet method of the decoratee.**

NOTE   In the following code examples, we focus on the Greet method, because the rest of the Decorator's code will stay the same.

Let's take a look at the Greet method of a TitledGreeterDecorator class:

```
public string Greet(string name)
{
    string titledName = "Mr. " + name;
    return this.decoratee.Greet(titledName);
}
```

In a similar move, the Decorator may decide to modify the return value before returning it when you create a NiceToMeetYouGreeterDecorator:

```
public string Greet(string name)
{
    string greet = this.decoratee.Greet(name);
    return greet + " Nice to meet you.";
}
```

Given the two previous examples, you can wrap the latter around the former to compose a combination that modifies both input and output:

```
IGreeter greeter =
    new NiceToMeetYouGreeterDecorator(
        new TitledGreeterDecorator(
            new FormalGreeter()));
```

```
string greet = greeter.Greet("Samuel L. Jackson");
Console.WriteLine(greet);
```

This produces the following output:

```
FormalGreater              input    FormalGreater
  ┌─────┴─────┐       ┌───────┴───────┐┌
  Hello, Mr. Samuel L. Jackson! Nice to meet you.
          └─┬─┘              └───────┬───────┘

     TitledGreeterDecorator        NiceToMeetYouGreeterDecorator
```

A Decorator may also decide not to invoke the underlying implementation:

```
public string Greet(string name)
{
    if (name == null)          ◄───────   A Guard Clause provides a
    {                                      default behavior for null input,
        return "Hello world!";             in which case, the wrapped
    }                                      component isn't invoked at all.

    return this.decoratee.Greet(name);
}
```

Not invoking the underlying implementation is more consequential than delegating the call. Although there's nothing inherently wrong with skipping the decoratee, the Decorator now replaces, rather than enriches, the original behavior.[5] A more common scenario is to stop execution by throwing an exception, as we'll discuss in section 9.2.3.

What differentiates a Decorator from any class containing DEPENDENCIES is that the wrapped object implements the same ABSTRACTION as the Decorator. This enables a COMPOSER to replace the original component with a Decorator without changing the consumer. The wrapped object is often injected into the Decorator declared as the abstract type—it wraps the interface, not a specific, concrete implementation. In that case, the Decorator must adhere to the LISKOV SUBSTITUTION PRINCIPLE and treat all decorated objects equally.

That's it. There isn't much more to the Decorator pattern than this. You've already seen Decorators in action several places in this book. The `SecureMessageWriter` example in section 1.2.2, for instance, is a Decorator. Now let's look at a concrete example of how we can use a Decorator to implement a CROSS-CUTTING CONCERN.

9.1.2 *Example: Implementing auditing using a Decorator*

In this example, we'll implement auditing for the `IUserRepository` again. As you might recall, we discussed auditing in section 6.3, where we used it as an example when explaining how to fix DEPENDENCY cycles. With *auditing*, you record all of the important actions users make in a system for later analysis.

---

[5]   You could argue that it's no longer an application of the Decorator pattern, but rather of the Chain of Responsibility pattern (Erich Gamma et al., *Design Patterns*, 251). These two patterns, however, are closely related. We call it Decorator, to keep it simple.

Auditing is a common example of a CROSS-CUTTING CONCERN: it may be required, but the core functionality of reading and editing users shouldn't be affected by auditing. This is exactly what we did in section 6.3. Because we injected the IAuditTrail-Appender interface into the SqlUserRepository itself, we forced it to know about and to implement auditing. This is a SINGLE RESPONSIBILITY PRINCIPLE violation. The SINGLE RESPONSIBILITY PRINCIPLE suggests that we shouldn't let SqlUserRepository implement auditing; given this, using a Decorator is a better alternative.

IMPLEMENTING AN AUDITING DECORATOR FOR THE USER REPOSITORY

You can implement auditing with a Decorator by introducing a new AuditingUser-RepositoryDecorator class that wraps another IUserRepository and implements auditing. Figure 9.5 illustrates how the types relate to each other.

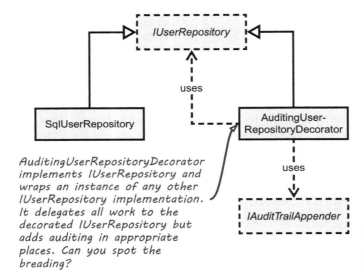

AuditingUserRepositoryDecorator implements IUserRepository and wraps an instance of any other IUserRepository implementation. It delegates all work to the decorated IUserRepository but adds auditing in appropriate places. Can you spot the breading?

Figure 9.5 AuditingUser-RepositoryDecorator adds auditing to any IUser-Repository implementation.

In addition to a decorated IUserRepository, AuditingUserRepositoryDecorator also needs a service that implements auditing. For this, you can use IAuditTrail-Appender from section 6.3. The following listing shows this implementation.

Listing 9.1 Declaring an AuditingUserRepositoryDecorator

```
public class AuditingUserRepositoryDecorator
    : IUserRepository                              ◄──── Implements and
{                                                        decorates IUserRepository
    private readonly IAuditTrailAppender appender;
    private readonly IUserRepository decoratee;

    public AuditingUserRepositoryDecorator(
        IAuditTrailAppender appender,
        IUserRepository decoratee)                 ◄────
    {
```

```
        this.appender = appender;
        this.decoratee = decoratee;
    }

    ...

}
```

`AuditingUserRepositoryDecorator` implements the same ABSTRACTION that it decorates. It uses standard CONSTRUCTOR INJECTION to request an `IUserRepository` that it can wrap and to which it can delegate its core implementation. In addition to the decorated Repository, it also requests an `IAuditTrailAppender` it can use to audit the operations implemented by the decorated Repository. The following listing shows sample implementations of two methods on `AuditingUserRepositoryDecorator`.

Listing 9.2   Implementing `AuditingUserRepositoryDecorator`

```
public User GetById(Guid id)
{                                              Omits auditing on
    return this.decoratee.GetById(id);         read operations
}


public void Update(User user)
{                                              Write operation
    this.decoratee.Update(user);               decorated with auditing
    this.appender.Append(user);
}
```

Not all operations need auditing. A common requirement is to audit all create, update, and delete operations, while ignoring read operations. Because the `GetById` method is a pure read operation, you delegate the call to the decorated Repository and immediately return the result. The `Update` method, on the other hand, must be audited. You still delegate the implementation to the decorated Repository, but after the delegated method returns successfully, you use the injected `IAuditTrailAppender` to audit the operation.

A Decorator, like `AuditingUserRepositoryDecorator`, is similar to the breading around the veal cutlet: it embellishes the basic ingredient without modifying it. The breading itself isn't an empty shell, but comes with its own list of ingredients. Real breading is made from breadcrumbs and spices; similarly, `AuditingUserRepository-Decorator` contains an `IAuditTrailAppender`.

Note that the injected `IAuditTrailAppender` is itself an ABSTRACTION, which means that you can vary the implementation independently of `AuditingUserRepository-Decorator`. All the `AuditingUserRepositoryDecorator` class does is coordinate the actions of the decorated `IUserRepository` and `IAuditTrailAppender`. You can write any implementation of `IAuditTrailAppender` you like, but in listing 6.24, we chose to build one based on the Entity Framework. Let's see how you can wire up all relevant DEPENDENCIES to make this work.

COMPOSING `AuditingUserRepositoryDecorator`

In chapter 8, you saw several examples of how to compose a `HomeController` instance. Listing 8.11 provided a simple implementation concerning instances with a TRANSIENT LIFESTYLE. The following listing shows how you can compose this `HomeController` using a decorated `SqlUserRepository`.

Listing 9.3   Composing a Decorator

```
private HomeController CreateHomeController()
{
    var context = new CommerceContext();

    IAuditTrailAppender appender =
        new SqlAuditTrailAppender(
            this.userContext,
            context);

    IUserRepository userRepository =
        new AuditingUserRepositoryDecorator(
            appender,
            new SqlUserRepository(context));

    IProductService productService =
        new ProductService(
            new SqlProductRepository(context),
            this.userContext,
            userRepository);

    return new HomeController(productService);
}
```

Creates a new instance of SqlUserRepository. Injects both the SqlUserRepository and a SQL Server–based IAuditTrailAppender implementation into a Decorator instance. SqlUserRepository and AuditingUserRepositoryDecorator are both IUserRepository instances.

Instead of injecting SqlUserRepository directly into a ProductService instance, injects the Decorator that wraps SqlUserRepository. ProductService sees only the IUserRepository interface and knows nothing about either the SqlUserRepository or the Decorator.

WARNING Listing 9.3 is a simplified example that ignores lifetime issues. Because `CommerceContext` is a disposable type, the code could cause resource leaks. A more correct implementation would be an interpolation of listing 9.3 with the model discussed in section 8.3.3, but we're sure you'll appreciate that it starts to get rather complex at that point.

Notice that you were able to add behavior to `IUserRepository` without changing the source code of existing classes. You didn't have to change `SqlUserRepository` to add auditing. Recall from section 4.4.2 that this is a desirable trait known as the OPEN/CLOSED PRINCIPLE.

Now that you've seen an example of intercepting the concrete `SqlUserRepository` with a decorating `AuditingUserRepositoryDecorator`, let's turn our attention to writing clean and maintainable code in the face of inconsistent or changing requirements, and to addressing CROSS-CUTTING CONCERNS.

9.2   *Implementing CROSS-CUTTING CONCERNS*

Most applications must address aspects that don't directly relate to any particular feature, but, rather, address a wider matter. These concerns tend to touch many otherwise unrelated areas of code, even in different modules or layers. Because they cut across a wide area of the code base, we call them CROSS-CUTTING CONCERNS. Table 9.1 lists some examples. This table isn't a comprehensive listing; rather, it's an illustrative sampling.

Table 9.1   Common examples of CROSS-CUTTING CONCERNS

Aspect	Description
Auditing	Any data-altering operation should leave an audit trail including time-stamp, the identity of the user who performed the change, and information about what changed. You saw an example of this in section 9.1.2.
Logging	Slightly different than auditing, logging tends to focus on recording events that reflect the state of the application. This could be events of interest to IT operations staff, but might also be business events.
Performance monitoring	Slightly different than logging because this deals more with recording performance than specific events. If you have Service Level Agreements (SLAs) that can't be monitored via standard infrastructure, you must implement your own performance monitoring. Custom Windows performance counters are a good choice for this, but you must still add some code that captures the data.
Validation	Operations typically need to be called with valid data. This can be either simple user input validation or more complex business rule validation. Although validation itself is always dependent on its context, the invocation of that validation and the processing of the validation results often isn't and can be considered to be cross-cutting.
Security	Some operations should only be allowed for certain users, often based on membership in roles or groups, and you must enforce this.
Caching	You can often increase performance by implementing caches, but there's no reason why a specific data access component should deal with this aspect. You may want the ability to enable or disable caching for different data access implementations.
Error handling	An application may need to handle certain exceptions and log them, transform them, or show a message to the user. You can use an error-handling Decorator to deal with errors in a proper way.
Fault tolerance	Out-of-process resources are guaranteed to be unavailable from time to time. Relational databases need to process transactional operations to prevent data corruption, which can lead to deadlocks. Using a Decorator, you can implement fault tolerance patterns, such as a Circuit Breaker, to address this.

When you draw diagrams of layered application architecture, CROSS-CUTTING CONCERNS are often represented as vertical blocks placed beside the layers. This is shown in figure 9.6.

In this section, we'll look at some examples that illustrate how to use INTERCEPTION in the form of Decorators to address CROSS-CUTTING CONCERNS. From table 9.1, we'll pick the fault tolerance, error handling, and security aspects to get a feel for implementing aspects. As is the case with many other concepts, INTERCEPTION can be easy to understand in the abstract, but the devil is in the details. It takes exposure to properly absorb the technique, and that's why this section shows three examples. When we're done with these, you should have a clearer picture of what INTERCEPTION is and how you can apply

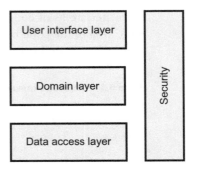

Figure 9.6   In application architecture diagrams, CROSS-CUTTING CONCERNS are typically represented by vertical blocks that span all layers. In this case, security is a CROSS-CUTTING CONCERN.

it. Because you already saw an introductory example in section 9.1.2, we'll take a look at a more complex example to illustrate how INTERCEPTION can be used with arbitrarily complex logic.

9.2.1   *Intercepting with a Circuit Breaker*

Any application that communicates with an out-of-process resource will occasionally find that the resource is unavailable. Network connections go down, databases go offline, and web services get swamped by Distributed Denial of Service (DDOS) attacks. In such cases, the calling application must be able to recover and appropriately deal with the issue.

Most .NET APIs have default timeouts that ensure that an out-of-process call doesn't block the consuming thread forever. Still, in a situation where you receive a timeout exception, how do you treat the next call to the faulting resource? Do you attempt to call the resource again? Because a timeout often indicates that the other end is either offline or swamped by requests, making a new blocking call may not be a good idea. It would be better to assume the worst and throw an exception immediately. This is the rationale behind the Circuit Breaker pattern.

Circuit Breaker is a stability pattern that adds robustness to an application by failing fast instead of hanging and consuming resources as it hangs. This is a good example of a non-functional requirement and a true CROSS-CUTTING CONCERN, because it has little to do with the feature implemented in the out-of-process call.

The Circuit Breaker pattern itself is a bit complex and can be intricate to implement, but you only need to make that investment once. You could even implement it in a reusable library if you liked, where you could easily apply it to multiple components by employing the Decorator pattern.

THE CIRCUIT BREAKER PATTERN

The Circuit Breaker design pattern takes its name from the electric switch of the same name.[6] It's designed to cut the connection when a fault occurs, preventing the fault from propagating.

In software applications, once a timeout or similar communications error occurs, it can make a bad situation worse if you keep hammering a downed system. If the remote system is swamped, multiple retries can take it over the edge — a pause might give it a chance to recover. On the calling tier, threads blocked waiting for timeouts can make the consuming application unresponsive, forcing a user to wait for an error message. It's better to detect that communications are down and fail fast for a period of time.

The Circuit Breaker design addresses this by tripping the switch when an error occurs. It usually includes a timeout that makes it retry the connection later; this way, it can automatically recover when the remote system comes back up. Figure 9.7 illustrates a simplified view of the state transitions in a Circuit Breaker.

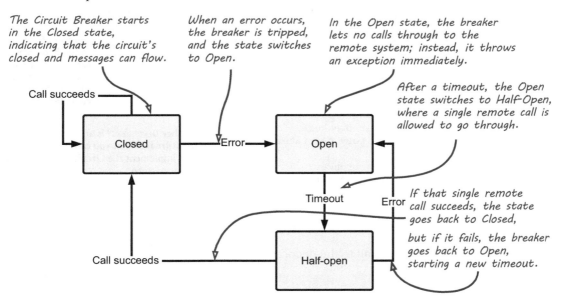

Figure 9.7 Simplified state transition diagram of the Circuit Breaker pattern

You may want to make a Circuit Breaker more complex than described in figure 9.7. First, you may not want to trip the breaker every time a sporadic error occurs but, rather, use a threshold. Second, you should only trip the breaker on certain types of errors. Timeouts and communication exceptions are fine, but a `NullReferenceException` is likely to indicate a bug instead of an intermittent error.

---

[6] Michael T. Nygard, *Release It! Design and Deploy Production-Ready Software* (Pragmatic Bookshelf, 2007), 104.

Let's look at an example that shows how the Decorator pattern can be used to add Circuit Breaker behavior to an existing out-of-process component. In this example, we'll focus on applying the reusable Circuit Breaker, but not on how it's implemented.

EXAMPLE: CREATING A CIRCUIT BREAKER FOR `IProductRepository`

In section 7.2, we created a UWP application that communicates with a backend data source, such as a WCF or Web API service, using the `IProductRepository` interface. In listing 8.6, we used a `WcfProductRepository` that implements `IProductRepository` by invoking the WCF service operations. Because this implementation has no explicit error handling, any communication error will bubble up to the caller.

This is an excellent scenario in which to use a Circuit Breaker. You'd like to fail fast once exceptions start occurring; this way, you won't block the calling thread and swamp the service. As the next listing shows, you start by declaring a Decorator for `IProduct-Repository` and requesting the necessary DEPENDENCIES via CONSTRUCTOR INJECTION.

Listing 9.4   Decorating with a Circuit Breaker

```
public class CircuitBreakerProductRepositoryDecorator
    : IProductRepository
{
    private readonly ICircuitBreaker breaker;
    private readonly IProductRepository decoratee;

    public CircuitBreakerProductRepositoryDecorator(
        ICircuitBreaker breaker,
        IProductRepository decoratee)
    {
        this.breaker = breaker;
        this.decoratee = decoratee;
    }

    ...
}
```

Decorator of IProductRepository, meaning that it both implements and wraps an implementation of IProductRepository

The other DEPENDENCY is an ICircuitBreaker that you can use to implement the Circuit Breaker pattern.

You can now wrap any call to the decorated `IProductRepository`.

Listing 9.5   Applying a Circuit Breaker to the `Insert` method

```
public void Insert(Product product)
{
    this.breaker.Guard();

    try
    {
        this.decoratee.Insert(product);
        this.breaker.Succeed();
    }
    catch (Exception ex)
    {
        this.breaker.Trip(ex);
        throw;
    }
}
```

Checks the state of the Circuit Breaker

Invokes the decorated Repository and calls Succeed when the call succeeds

When the call to Insert fails, trips the Circuit Breaker

The first thing you need to do before you invoke the decorated Repository is check the state of the Circuit Breaker. The `Guard` method lets you through when the state is either Closed or Half-Open, whereas it throws an exception when the state is Open. This ensures that you fail fast when you have reason to believe that the call isn't going to succeed. If you make it past the `Guard` method, you can attempt to invoke the decorated Repository. If the call fails, you trip the breaker. In this example, we're keeping things simple, but in a proper implementation, you should only catch and trip the breaker from a selection of exception types.

From both the Closed and Half-Open states, tripping the breaker puts you back in the Open state. From the Open state, a timeout determines when you move back to the Half-Open state.

Conversely, you signal the Circuit Breaker if the call succeeds. If you're already in the Closed state, you stay in the Closed state. If you're in the Half-Open state, you transition back to Closed. It's impossible to signal success when the Circuit Breaker is in the Open state, because the `Guard` method ensures that you never get that far.

All other methods of `IProductRepository` look similar, with the only difference being the method they invoke on the `decoratee` and an extra line of code for methods that return a value. You can see this variation inside the `try` block for the `GetAll` method:

```
var products = this.decoratee.GetAll();
this.breaker.Succeed();
return products;
```

Because you must indicate success to the Circuit Breaker, you have to hold the return value of the decorated repository before returning it. That's the only difference between methods that return a value and methods that don't.

At this point, you've left the implementation of `ICircuitBreaker` open, but the real implementation is a completely reusable complex of classes that employ the State design pattern.[7] Although we aren't going to dive deeper into the implementation of `CircuitBreaker` here, the important message is that you can INTERCEPT with arbitrarily complex code.

> **NOTE** If you're curious about the implementation of the `CircuitBreaker` class, it's available in the code that accompanies this book.

COMPOSING THE APPLICATION USING THE CIRCUIT BREAKER IMPLEMENTATION

To compose an `IProductRepository` with Circuit Breaker functionality added, you can wrap the Decorator around the real implementation:

```
var channelFactory = new ChannelFactory<IProductManagementService>("*");

var timeout = TimeSpan.FromMinutes(1);

ICircuitBreaker breaker = new CircuitBreaker(timeout);
```

---

[7]   Erich Gamma et al., *Design Patterns, 305.*

```
IProductRepository repository =
   new CircuitBreakerProductRepositoryDecorator(
       breaker,
       new WcfProductRepository(channelFactory));
```

Decorates the WcfProductRepository

In listing 7.6, we composed a UWP application from several DEPENDENCIES, including a WcfProductRepository instance in listing 8.6. You can decorate this WcfProduct-Repository by injecting it into a CircuitBreakerProductRepositoryDecorator instance, because it implements the same interface. In this example, you create a new instance of the CircuitBreaker class every time you resolve DEPENDENCIES. That corresponds to the TRANSIENT LIFESTYLE.

In a UWP application, where you only resolve the DEPENDENCIES once, using a TRANSIENT Circuit Breaker isn't an issue but, in general, this isn't the optimal lifestyle for such functionality. There'll only be a single web service at the other end. If this service becomes unavailable, the Circuit Breaker should disconnect all attempts to connect to it. If several instances of CircuitBreakerProductRepositoryDecorator are in use, this should happen for all of them.

A more compact ICircuitBreaker

As presented here, the ICircuitBreaker interface contains three members: Guard, Succeed, and Trip. An alternative interface definition could accept a delegate to reduce the footprint to a single method:

```
public interface ICircuitBreaker
{
    T Execute<T>(Func<T> action);
}
```

This would allow you to more succinctly use ICircuitBreaker in each method, like this:

```
public IEnumerable<Product> GetAll()
{
    return this.breaker.Execute(() => this.decoratee.GetAll());
}
```

We chose to use the more explicit and old-fashioned version of ICircuitBreaker, because we want you to be able to focus on the current topic of INTERCEPTION. Although we personally like continuation passing, we think it might be more distracting than helpful in this context. Whether we ultimately choose one interface definition over the other doesn't change the conclusion of the current chapter.

There's an obvious case for setting up CircuitBreaker with the SINGLETON lifetime, but that also means that it must be thread-safe. Due to its nature, CircuitBreaker maintains state; thread-safety must be explicitly implemented. This makes the implementation even more complex.

Despite its complexity, you can easily INTERCEPT an IProductRepository instance with a Circuit Breaker. Although the first INTERCEPTION example in section 9.1.2 was fairly simple, the Circuit Breaker example demonstrates that you can intercept a class with a CROSS-CUTTING CONCERN. The CROSS-CUTTING CONCERN can easily be more complex than the original implementation.

The Circuit Breaker pattern ensures that an application fails fast instead of tying up precious resources. Ideally, the application wouldn't crash at all. To address this issue, you can implement some kinds of error handling with INTERCEPTION.

9.2.2 *Reporting exceptions using the Decorator pattern*

DEPENDENCIES are likely to throw exceptions from time to time. Even the best-written code will (and should) throw exceptions if it encounters situations it can't deal with. Clients that consume out-of-process resources fall into that category. A class like `Wcf-ProductRepository` from the sample UWP application is one example. When the web service is unavailable, the Repository will start throwing exceptions. A Circuit Breaker doesn't change this fundamental trait. Although it INTERCEPTS the WCF client, it still throws exceptions—it does so quicker.

You can use INTERCEPTION to add error handling. You don't want to burden a DEPENDENCY with error handling. Because a DEPENDENCY should be viewed as a reusable component that can be consumed in many different scenarios, it wouldn't be possible to add an exception-handling strategy to the DEPENDENCY that would fit all scenarios. It would also be a violation of the SINGLE RESPONSIBILITY PRINCIPLE if you did.

By using INTERCEPTION to deal with exceptions, you follow the OPEN/CLOSED PRINCIPLE. It allows you to implement the best error-handling strategy for any given situation. Let's look at an example.

In the previous example, we wrapped `WcfProductRepository` in a Circuit Breaker for use with the product-management client application, which was originally introduced in section 7.2.2. A Circuit Breaker only deals with errors by making certain that the client fails fast, but it still throws exceptions. If left unhandled, they'll cause the application to crash, so you should implement a Decorator that knows how to handle some of those errors.

Instead of a crashing application, you might prefer a message box that tells the user that the operation didn't succeed and that they should try again later. In this example, when an exception is thrown, it should pop up a message as shown in figure 9.8.

Figure 9.8 The product-management application handles communication exceptions by showing a message to the user. Notice that in this case, the error message originates from the Circuit Breaker instead of the underlying communication failure.

Implementing this behavior is easy. The same way you did in section 9.2.1, you add a new `ErrorHandlingProductRepositoryDecorator` class that decorates the `IProduct-Repository` interface. Listing 9.6 shows a sample of one of the methods of that interface, but they're all similar.

> **Listing 9.6 Handling exceptions with `ErrorHandlingProductRepositoryDecorator`**

```
public void Insert(Product product)
{
    try
    {
        this.decoratee.Insert(product);          ◄───── Delegates to
    }                                                    the decoratee
    catch (CommunicationException ex)
    {
        this.AlertUser(ex.Message);              ◄───── Alerts the user
    }
    catch (InvalidOperationException ex)
    {
        this.AlertUser(ex.Message);              ◄─────┘
    }
}
```

The `Insert` method is representative of the entire implementation of the `ErrorHandling-ProductRepositoryDecorator` class. You attempt to invoke the `decoratee` and alert the user with the error message if an exception is thrown. Notice that you only handle a particular set of known exceptions, because it can be dangerous to suppress all exceptions. Alerting the user involves formatting a string and showing it to the user using the `MessageBox.Show` method. This is done inside the `AlertUser` method.

Once again, you added functionality to the original implementation (`WcfProduct-Repository`) by implementing the Decorator pattern. You're following both the SINGLE RESPONSIBILITY PRINCIPLE and the OPEN/CLOSED PRINCIPLE by continually adding new types instead of modifying existing code. By now, you should be seeing a pattern that suggests a more general arrangement than a Decorator. Let's briefly glance at a final example, implementing security.

9.2.3 *Preventing unauthorized access to sensitive functionality using a Decorator*

Security is another common CROSS-CUTTING CONCERN. We want to secure our applications as much as possible to prevent unauthorized access to sensitive data and functionality.

> **NOTE** Security is a big topic that encompasses many areas, including the disclosure of sensitive information and breaking into networks.[8] In this section, we'll touch briefly on the subject of authorization: making sure that only authorized people (or systems) can perform certain actions.

---

[8] For a thorough treatment of security, you may want to read Michael Howard and David LeBlanc, *Writing Secure Code*, 2nd Ed. (Microsoft Press, 2003).

Similar to how we used Circuit Breaker, we'd like to INTERCEPT a method call and check whether the call should be allowed. If not, instead of allowing the call to be made, an exception should be thrown. The principle is the same; the difference lies in the criterion we use to determine the validity of the call.

A common approach to implementing authorization logic is to employ role-based security by checking the user's role(s) against a hard-coded value for the operation at hand. If we stick with our IProductRepository, we might start out with a SecureProduct-RepositoryDecorator. Because, as you've seen in the previous sections, all methods look similar, the following listing only shows two method implementations.

Listing 9.7 Explicitly checking authorization with a Decorator

```
public class SecureProductRepositoryDecorator
    : IProductRepository
{
    private readonly IUserContext userContext;
    private readonly IProductRepository decoratee;

    public SecureProductRepositoryDecorator(
        IUserContext userContext,
        IProductRepository decoratee)
    {
        this.userContext = userContext;
        this.decoratee = decoratee;
    }

    public void Delete(Guid id)
    {
        this.CheckAuthorization();
        this.decoratee.Delete(id);
    }

    public IEnumerable<Product> GetAll()
    {
        return this.decoratee.GetAll();
    }
    ...
    private void CheckAuthorization()
    {
        if (!this.userContext.IsInRole(
            Role.Administrator))
        {
            throw new SecurityException(
                "Access denied.");
        }
    }
}
```

The Decorator depends on IUserContext, which enables it to check the current user's role.

The Delete method starts with a Guard Clause that explicitly checks if the current user is allowed to execute this operation. If not, it immediately throws an exception. Only if the current user has the required role do you allow it past the Guard Clause to invoke the decorated Repository.

Not all methods require permission checks. In this application, only create, update, and delete (CUD) operations do. Every user in this system is allowed to query all products.

The required role for the CUD operations is hard-coded to the Administrator role. If the user isn't in that role, an exception is thrown.

NOTE   The Decorator examples in listings 9.2, 9.5, 9.6, and 9.7 only showed part of the Decorator's code because all methods of the Decorator looked similar.

In our current design, for a given CROSS-CUTTING CONCERN, the implementation based on a Decorator tends to be repetitive. Implementing a Circuit Breaker involves applying the same code template to all methods of the `IProductRepository` interface. Had you wanted to add a Circuit Breaker to another ABSTRACTION, you would've had to apply the same code to more methods.

With the security Decorator, it got even worse because we required some of the methods to be extended, whereas others are mere pass-through operations. But the overall problem is identical.

If you need to apply this CROSS-CUTTING CONCERN to a different ABSTRACTION, this too will cause code duplication, which can cause major maintainability issues as the system gets bigger. As you might imagine, there are ways to prevent code duplication, bringing us to the important topic of ASPECT-ORIENTED PROGRAMMING, which we'll discuss in the next chapter.

Summary

- INTERCEPTION is the ability to intercept calls between two collaborating components in such a way that you can enrich or change the behavior of the DEPENDENCY without the need to change the two collaborators themselves.
- Loose coupling is the enabler of INTERCEPTION. When you program to an interface, you can transform or enhance a core implementation by wrapping it in other implementations of that interface.
- At its core, INTERCEPTION is an application of the Decorator design pattern.
- The Decorator design pattern provides a flexible alternative to subclassing by attaching additional responsibilities to an object dynamically. It works by wrapping one implementation of an ABSTRACTION in another implementation of the same ABSTRACTION. This allows Decorators to be nested like Russian nesting dolls.
- CROSS-CUTTING CONCERNS are non-functional aspects of code that typically cut across a wide area of the code base. Common examples of CROSS-CUTTING CONCERNS are auditing, logging, validation, security, and caching.
- Circuit Breaker is a stability design pattern that adds robustness to a system by cutting connections when a fault occurs in order to prevent the fault from propagating.

Aspect-Oriented Programming by design

In this chapter

- Recapping the SOLID principles
- Using ASPECT-ORIENTED PROGRAMMING to prevent code duplication
- Using SOLID to achieve ASPECT-ORIENTED PROGRAMMING

There's a big difference between cooking at home and working in a professional kitchen. At home, you can take all the time you want to prepare your dish, but in a commercial kitchen, efficiency is key. *Mise en place* is an important aspect of this. This is more than in-advance preparation of ingredients; it's about having all the required equipment set up, including your pots, pans, chopping boards, tasting spoons, and anything that's an essential part of your workspace.

The ergonomics and layout of the kitchen is also a major factor in the efficiency of a kitchen. A badly laid out kitchen can cause pinch points, high levels of disruption, and context switching for staff. Features like dedicated stations with associated specialized equipment help to minimize the movement of staff, avoid (unnecessary) multitasking, and encourage concentration on the task at hand. When this is done well, it helps to improve the efficiency of the kitchen as a whole.

In software development, the code base is our kitchen. Teams work together for years in the same kitchen, and the right architecture is essential to be efficient and consistent, keeping code repetition to a minimum. Your "guests" depend on your successful kitchen strategy.

One of the key architectural strategies you can use to improve your software ergonomics is ASPECT-ORIENTED PROGRAMMING (AOP). This can come in the form of equipment (tools) or a solid layout (software design). AOP is strongly related to INTERCEPTION. To fully appreciate the potential of INTERCEPTION, you must study the concept of AOP and software design principles like SOLID.

This chapter starts with an introduction to AOP. Because one of the most effective ways to apply AOP is through well-known design patterns and object-oriented principles, this chapter continues with a recap of the five SOLID principles, which were discussed in previous chapters throughout the book.

A common misconception is that AOP requires tooling. In this chapter, we'll demonstrate that this isn't the case: We'll show how you can use SOLID software design as a driver of AOP and an enabler of an efficient, consistent, and maintainable code base. In the next chapter, we'll discuss two well-known forms of AOP that require special tooling. Both forms, however, exhibit considerable disadvantages over the purely design-driven form of AOP discussed in this chapter.

If you're already familiar with SOLID and the basics of AOP, you can jump directly into section 10.3, which contains the meat of this chapter. Otherwise, you can continue with our introduction to ASPECT-ORIENTED PROGRAMMING.

10.1   *Introducing AOP*

AOP was invented at the Xerox Palo Alto Research Center (PARC) in 1997, where Xerox engineers designed AspectJ, an AOP extension to the Java language. AOP is a paradigm that focuses around the notion of applying CROSS-CUTTING CONCERNS effectively and maintainably. It's a fairly abstract concept that comes with its own set of jargon, most of which isn't pertinent to this discussion.

> **DEFINITION**   ASPECT-ORIENTED PROGRAMMING aims to reduce boilerplate code required for implementing CROSS-CUTTING CONCERNS and other coding patterns. It does this by implementing such patterns in a single place and applying them to a code base either declaratively or based on convention, without modifying the code itself.

The auditing and Circuit Breaker examples in sections 9.1.2 and 9.2.1 showed only a few representative methods, because all methods were implemented in the same way. We didn't want to add several pages of nearly identical code to our discussion because it would've detracted from the point we were making.

The following listing shows the `CircuitBreakerProductRepositoryDecorator`'s `Delete` method again.

Listing 10.1 `Delete` method of `CircuitBreakerProductRepositoryDecorator`

```
public void Delete(Product product)
{
    this.breaker.Guard();

    try
    {
        this.decoratee.Delete(product);
        this.breaker.Succeed();
    }
    catch (Exception ex)
    {
        this.breaker.Trip(ex);
        throw;
    }
}
```

Listing 10.2 shows how similar the methods of `CircuitBreakerProductRepository-Decorator` are. This listing only shows the `Insert` method, but we're confident that you can extrapolate how the rest of the implementation would look.

CODE SMELL

Listing 10.2 Violating the DRY principle by duplicating Circuit Breaker logic

```
public void Insert(Product product)
{
    this.breaker.Guard();

    try
    {
        this.decoratee.Insert(product);          ◄──  This line is the only difference between
        this.breaker.Succeed();                        this listing and listing 10.1. Instead of
    }                                                  calling Delete, this line calls Insert.
    catch (Exception ex)
    {
        this.breaker.Trip(ex);
        throw;
    }
}
```

The purpose of this listing is to illustrate the repetitive nature of Decorators used as aspects in our current design. The only difference between the `Delete` and `Insert` methods is that they each invoke their own corresponding method on the decorated Repository.

Even though we've successfully delegated the Circuit Breaker implementation to a separate class via the `ICircuitBreaker` interface, this plumbing code violates the DRY principle. It tends to be reasonably unchanging, but it's still a liability. Every time you want to add a new member to a type you decorate, or when you want to apply a Circuit Breaker to a new ABSTRACTION, you must apply the same plumbing code. This repetitiveness can become a problem if you want to maintain such an application.

NOTE   AOP as a paradigm focuses on working around the problem of *repetition*.

Sticking with our auditing example from chapter 9, we've already established that you don't want to put the auditing code inside the `SqlProductRepository` implementation, because that would violate the SINGLE RESPONSIBILITY PRINCIPLE (SRP). But neither do you want to have dozens of auditing Decorators for each Repository ABSTRACTION in the system. This would also cause severe code duplication and, likely, sweeping changes, which is an OPEN/CLOSED PRINCIPLE (OCP) violation. Instead, you want to declaratively state that you want to apply the auditing aspect to a certain set of methods of all Repository ABSTRACTIONS in the system and implement this auditing aspect once.

You'll find tools, frameworks, and architectural styles that enable AOP. In this chapter, we'll discuss the most ideal form of AOP. The next chapter will discuss dynamic INTERCEPTION and compile-time weaving as tool-based forms of AOP. These are the three major methods of AOP.[1] Table 10.1 lists the methods we'll discuss, with a few of the major advantages and disadvantages of each.

Table 10.1   Common AOP methods

Method	Description	Advantages	Disadvantages
SOLID	Applies aspects using Decorators around reusable ABSTRACTIONS defined for groups of classes based on their behavior.	■ Doesn't require any tooling. ■ Aspects are easy to implement. ■ Focuses on design. ■ Makes the system more maintainable.	■ Not always easy to apply in legacy systems.
Dynamic INTERCEPTION	Causes the runtime generation of Decorators based on the application's ABSTRACTIONS. These Decorators are injected with tool-specific aspects, called *Interceptors*.	■ Easy to add to existing or legacy applications with relatively little changes, assuming the application already programs to interfaces. ■ Keeps the compiled application decoupled from the used dynamic INTERCEPTIONlibrary ■ Good tooling is freely available.	■ Causes aspects to be strongly coupled to the AOP tool. ■ Loses compile-time support. ■ Causes the convention to be fragile and error prone.

---

[1]   Other AOP methods exist, but those are either similar or out of fashion in the .NET world, so we ignore them in this book. Be aware, however, that each method discussed comes with its own subset of variations.

Table 10.1 Common AOP methods *(continued)*

Method	Description	Advantages	Disadvantages
Compile-time weaving	Aspects are added to an application in a post-compilation process. The most common form is IL weaving, where an external tool reads the compiled assembly, modifies it by applying the aspects, and replaces the original assembly with the modified one.	■ Easy to add to existing or legacy applications with relatively few changes, even if the application doesn't program to interfaces.	■ Injecting VOLATILE DEPENDENCIES into aspects causes TEMPORAL COUPLING or Interdependent Tests. ■ Aspects are woven in at compile time, making it impossible to call code without the aspect applied. This complicates testing and reduces flexibility. ■ Compile-time weaving is the antithesis of DI.

As stated previously, we'll get back to dynamic INTERCEPTION and compile-time weaving in the next chapter. But before we dive into using SOLID as a driver for AOP, let's start with a short recap of the SOLID principles.

10.2 *The SOLID principles*

You may have noticed a denser-than-usual usage of terms such as SINGLE RESPONSIBILITY PRINCIPLE, OPEN/CLOSED PRINCIPLE, and LISKOV SUBSTITUTION PRINCIPLE in chapter 9 and in the previous section. Together with the INTERFACE SEGREGATION PRINCIPLE (ISP) and DEPENDENCY INVERSION PRINCIPLE (DIP), they make up the SOLID acronym. We've discussed all five of them independently throughout the course of this book, but this section provides a short summary to refresh your mind, because understanding those principles is important for the remainder of this chapter.

> **NOTE** Who doesn't want to write solid software? Software that can withstand the test of time and provide value to its users sounds like a worthy goal, so we introduce SOLID as an acronym because building quality software just makes sense.

All these patterns and principles are recognized as valuable guidance for writing clean code. The general purpose of this section is to relate this established guidance to DI, emphasizing that DI is only a means to an end. We, therefore, use DI as an enabler of maintainable code.

None of the principles encapsulated by SOLID represent absolutes. They're guidelines that can help you write clean code. To us, they represent goals that help us decide which direction we should take our applications. We're always happy when we succeed; but sometimes we don't.

The following sections go through the SOLID principles and summarize what we've already explained about them throughout the course of this book. Each section is a brief overview—we omit examples in those sections. We'll return to this in section 10.3, where we walk through a realistic example that shows why a violation of the SOLID principles can become problematic from a maintainability perspective. For now, we'll recap the five SOLID principles.

10.2.1 SINGLE RESPONSIBILITY PRINCIPLE (SRP)

In section 2.1.3, we described how the SRP states that every class should have a single reason to change. Violating this principle causes classes to become more complex and harder to test and maintain.

More often than not, however, it can be challenging to see whether a class has multiple reasons to change. What can help in this respect is looking at the SRP from the perspective of cohesion. *Cohesion* is defined as the functional relatedness of the elements of a class or module. The lower the amount of relatedness, the lower the cohesion; and the lower the cohesion, the greater the possibility a class violates the SRP. In section 10.3, we'll discuss cohesion with a concrete example.

It can be difficult to stick to, but if you practice DI, one of the many benefits of CONSTRUCTOR INJECTION is that it becomes more obvious when you violate the SRP. In the auditing example in section 9.1.2, you were able to adhere to the SRP by separating responsibilities into separate types: `SqlUserRepository` deals only with storing and retrieving product data, whereas `AuditingUserRepositoryDecorator` concentrates on persisting the audit trail in the database. The `AuditingUserRepositoryDecorator` class's single responsibility is to coordinate the actions of `IUserRepository` and `IAuditTrailAppender`.

10.2.2 OPEN/CLOSED PRINCIPLE (OCP)

As we discussed in section 4.4.2, the OCP prescribes an application design that prevents you from having to make sweeping changes throughout the code base; or, in the vocabulary of the OCP, a class should be open for extension, but closed for modification. A developer should be able to extend the functionality of a system without needing to modify the source code of any existing classes.

Because they both try to prevent sweeping changes, there's a strong relationship between the OCP principle and the Don't Repeat Yourself (DRY) principle. OCP, however, focuses on code, whereas DRY focuses on knowledge.

> ## Don't Repeat Yourself (DRY)
>
> In their book, *The Pragmatic Programmer*, Andy Hunt and Dave Thomas coined the acronym DRY, short for *Don't Repeat Yourself*, which they formulate this way:
>
> *Every piece of knowledge must have a single, unambiguous, authoritative representation within a system.*[2]
>
> We developers work in systems where knowledge isn't stable. Having such knowledge duplicated makes it difficult to keep everything in sync. Our understanding of both the system and the requirements change—often rapidly. DRY states that we should strive to centralize every piece of knowledge in a single place. DRY goes beyond mere code: it also holds for documentation.

You can make a class extensible in many ways, including virtual methods, injection of Strategies, and the application of Decorators.[3] But no matter the details, DI makes this possible by enabling you to compose objects.

10.2.3   LISKOV SUBSTITUTION PRINCIPLE (LSP)

In section 8.1.1, we described that all consumers of DEPENDENCIES should observe the LSP when they invoke their DEPENDENCIES, because every DEPENDENCY should behave as defined by its ABSTRACTION. This allows you to replace the originally intended implementation with another implementation of the same ABSTRACTION, without worrying about breaking a consumer. Because a Decorator implements the same ABSTRACTION as the class it wraps, you can replace the original with a Decorator, but only if that Decorator adheres to the contract given by its ABSTRACTION.

This was exactly what we did in listing 9.3 when we substituted the original `SqlUserRepository` with `AuditingUserRepositoryDecorator`. You could do this without changing the code of the consuming `ProductService`, because any implementation should adhere to the LSP. `ProductService` requires an instance of `IUserRepository` and, as long as it talks exclusively to that interface, any implementation will do.

The LSP is a foundation of DI. When consumers don't observe it, there's little advantage in injecting DEPENDENCIES, because you can't replace them at will, and you'll lose many (if not all) benefits of DI.

10.2.4   INTERFACE SEGREGATION PRINCIPLE (ISP)

In section 6.2.1, you learned that the ISP promotes the use of fine-grained ABSTRACTIONS, rather than wide ABSTRACTIONS. Any time a consumer depends on an ABSTRACTION where some of its members are unused, the ISP is violated.

---

[2] Andy Hunt and Dave Thomas, *The Pragmatic Programmer* (Addison-Wesley, 2000), 27.

[3] For more on Strategies, see Erich Gamma et al., *Design Patterns: Elements of Reusable Object-Oriented Software* (Addison-Wesley, 1994), 315.

The ISP can, at first, seem to be distantly related to DI, but that's probably because we ignored this principle for most of this book. That'll change in section 10.3, where you'll learn that the ISP is crucial when it comes to effectively applying ASPECT-ORIENTED PROGRAMMING.

10.2.5 DEPENDENCY INVERSION PRINCIPLE (DIP)

When we discussed the DIP in section 3.1.2, you learned that much of what we're trying to accomplish with DI is related to the DIP. The principle states that you should program against ABSTRACTIONS, and that the consuming layer should be in control of the shape of a consumed ABSTRACTION. The consumer should be able to define the ABSTRACTION in a way that benefits itself the most. If you find yourself adding members to an interface to satisfy the needs of other, specific implementations—including potential future implementations—then you're almost certainly violating the DIP.

10.2.6 SOLID principles and INTERCEPTION

Design patterns (such as Decorator) and guidelines (such as SOLID principles) have been around for many years and are generally regarded as beneficial. In these sections, we provide an indication of how they relate to DI.

The SOLID principles have been relevant throughout the book's chapters. But it's when we start talking about INTERCEPTION and how it relates to Decorators that the benefits of adhering to the SOLID principles stands out. Some are subtler than others, but adding behavior (such as auditing) by using a Decorator is a clear application of both the OCP and the SRP, the latter allowing us to create implementations with specifically defined scopes.

In the previous sections, we took a short detour through common patterns and principles to understand the relationship DI has with other established guidelines. Armed with this knowledge, let's now turn our attention back to the goal of the chapter, which is to write clean and maintainable code in the face of inconsistent or changing requirements, as well as the need to address CROSS-CUTTING CONCERNS.

10.3 SOLID as a driver for AOP

In section 10.1, you learned that the primary aim of AOP is to keep your CROSS-CUTTING CONCERNS DRY. As we discussed in section 10.2, there's a strong relationship between the OCP and the DRY principle. They both strive for the same objective, which is to minimize repetition and prevent sweeping changes.

From that perspective, the code repetition that you witnessed with `AuditingUser-RepositoryDecorator`, `CircuitBreakerProductRepositoryDecorator`, and `Secure-ProductRepositoryDecorator` in chapter 9 (listings 9.2, 9.4, and 9.7) are a strong indication that we were violating the OCP. AOP seeks to address this by separating out extensible behavior (aspects) into separate components that can easily be applied to a variety of implementations.

A common misconception, however, is that AOP requires tooling. AOP tool vendors are all to eager to keep this fallacy alive. Our preferred approach is to practice *AOP by design*, which means you apply patterns and principles first, before reverting to specialized AOP tooling like dynamic INTERCEPTION libraries.

In this section, we'll do just that. We'll look at AOP from a design perspective by taking a close look at the IProductService ABSTRACTION we introduced in chapter 3. We'll analyze which SOLID principles we're violating and why such violations are problematic. After that, we'll address these violations step by step with the goal of making the application more maintainable, preventing the need to make sweeping changes in the future. Be prepared for some mental discomfort—and even cognitive dissonance—as we defy your beliefs on how to design software. Buckle up, and get ready for the ride.

10.3.1 *Example: Implementing product-related features using IProductService*

Let's dive right in by looking at the IProductService ABSTRACTION that you built in chapter 3 as part of the sample e-commerce application's domain layer. The following listing shows this interface as originally defined in listing 3.5.

```
public interface IProductService
{
    IEnumerable<DiscountedProduct> GetFeaturedProducts();
}
```

When looking at an application's design from the perspective of SOLID principles in general, and the OCP in particular, it's important to take into consideration how the application has changed over time, and from there predict future changes. With this in mind, you can determine whether the application is closed for modification to the changes that are most likely to happen in the future.

NOTE   The more experience you have in the application's domain and with software development, in general, the more likely you are to make good predictions about future changes. That's why it's typically difficult to get the design right immediately when starting a project.

It's important to note that even with a SOLID design, there can come a time where a change becomes sweeping. Being 100% closed for modification is neither possible nor desirable. Besides, conforming to the OCP is expensive. It takes considerable effort to find and design the appropriate ABSTRACTIONS, although too many ABSTRACTIONS can have a negative impact on the complexity of the application. Your job is to balance the risks and the costs and come up with a global optimum.

Because you should be looking at how the application evolves, evaluating IProduct-Service at a single point in time isn't that helpful. Fortunately, Mary Rowan (our developer from chapter 2), has been working on her e-commerce application for some time now, and a number of features have been implemented since we last looked over her shoulder. The next listing shows how Mary has progressed.

Listing 10.4 The evolved IProductService interface

```
public interface IProductService
{
    IEnumerable<DiscountedProduct> GetFeaturedProducts();
    void DeleteProduct(Guid productId);
    Product GetProductById(Guid productId);
    void InsertProduct(Product product);
    void UpdateProduct(Product product);
    Paged<Product> SearchProducts(
        int pageIndex, int pageSize,
        Guid? manufacturerId, string searchText);
    void UpdateProductReviewTotals(
        Guid productId, ProductReview[] reviews);
    void AdjustInventory(
        Guid productId, bool decrease, int quantity);
    void UpdateHasTierPricesProperty(Product product);
    void UpdateHasDiscountsApplied(
        Guid productId, string discountDescription);
}
```

New features added by Mary during the course of the last few chapters. As we'll discuss shortly, this small code snippet exhibits three SOLID violations.

As you can see, quite a few new features have been added to the application. Some are typical CRUD operations, such as UpdateProduct, whereas others address more-complex use cases, such as UpdateHasTierPricesProperty. Still others are for retrieving data, such as SearchProducts and GetProductById.

NOTE Don't worry if the functionality of these new methods isn't clear to you; the details of this interface and what each method does aren't that relevant to this discussion.

Although Mary started off with good intentions when she defined the first version of IProductService in listing 10.3, the fact that this interface needs to be updated every time a new product-related feature is implemented is a clear indication that something's wrong.

If you extrapolate this to make a prediction, can you expect this interface to be updated again soon? The answer to that question is a clear "Yes!" As a matter of fact, Mary already has several features in her backlog, concerning cross-sellings, product pictures, and product reviews that would all cause changes to IProductService.[4]

What this teaches us is that, in this particular application, new features concerning products are added on a regular basis. Because this is an e-commerce application, this isn't a world-shattering observation. But because this is both a central part of the code base and under frequent change, the need to improve the design arises. Let's analyze the current design with SOLID principles in mind.

---

[4] Have you ever seen lists like Other Customers Bought or Related Items in web shops? Those are cross-sellings. *Cross-selling* is the action or practice of selling an additional product or service to a customer.

10.3.2 *Analysis of IProductService from the perspective of SOLID*

Concerning the five SOLID principles discussed in section 10.2, Mary's design violates three out of five SOLID principles, namely, the ISP, SRP, and OCP. We'll start with the first one: IProductService violates the ISP.

IProductService VIOLATES THE ISP

There's one obvious violation—IProductService violates the ISP. As explained in section 10.2.4, the ISP prescribes the use of fine-grained ABSTRACTIONS over wide ABSTRACTIONS. From the perspective of the ISP, IProductService is rather wide. With listing 10.4 in mind, it's easy to believe that there'll be no single consumer of IProduct-Service that'll use all its methods. Most consumers would typically use one method or a few at most. But how is this violation a problem?

A part of the code base where wide interfaces directly cause trouble is during testing. HomeController's unit tests, for instance, will define an IProductService Test Double implementation, but such a Test Double is required to implement all its members, even though HomeController itself only uses one method.[5] Even if you could create a reusable Test Double, you typically still want to assert that unrelated methods of IProductService aren't called by HomeController. The following listing shows a Mock IProductService implementation that asserts unexpected methods aren't called.

BAD CODE

> **Listing 10.5 A reusable Mock IProductService base class**

```
public abstract class MockProductService : IProductService
{
    public virtual void DeleteProduct(Guid productId)
    {
        Assert.True(false, "Should not be called.");      ◀─── All method
    }                                                          implementations fail.

    public virtual Product GetProductById(Guid id)
    {
        Assert.True(false, "Should not be called.");      ◀───┘
        return null;
    }

    public virtual void InsertProduct(Product product)
    {
        Assert.True(false, "Should not be called.");      ◀───
    }
                    ┌── List of methods goes on. You'll need
    . . .       ◀──┘    to implement all 10 methods.
}
```

---

[5] Listing 3.4 shows how HomeController's Index method solely calls GetFeaturedProducts() on IProductService.

All methods are implemented to fail by calling `Assert.True` using a value of `false`. The `Assert.True` method is part of the xUnit testing framework.[6] By passing `false`, the assertion fails, and the currently running test also fails.

To preserve precious trees, listing 10.5 only shows a few of `MockProductService`'s methods, but we think you get the picture. You wouldn't have to implement this big list of failing methods if the interface was specific to `HomeController`'s needs; in that case, `HomeController` is expected to call all its DEPENDENCY's methods, and you wouldn't have to do this check.

`IProductService` VIOLATES THE **SRP**

Because the ISP is the conceptual underpinning of the SRP, an ISP violation typically indicates an SRP violation in its implementations, as is the case here. SRP violations can sometimes be hard to detect, and you might argue that a `ProductService` implementation has one responsibility, namely, handling product-related use cases.

The concept of product-related use cases, however, is extremely vague and broad. Rather, you want classes that have only one reason to change. `ProductService` definitely has multiple reasons to change. For instance, any of the following reasons causes `ProductService` to change:

- Changes to how discounts are applied
- Changes to how inventory adjustments are processed
- Adding search criteria for products
- Adding a new product-related feature

Not only does `ProductService` have many reasons to change, its methods are most likely not cohesive. A simple way to spot low cohesion is to check how easy it is to move some of the class's functionality to a new class. The easier this is, the lower the relatedness of the two parts, and the more likely SRP is violated.

Perhaps `UpdateHasTierPricesProperty` and `UpdateHasDiscountsApplied` share the same DEPENDENCIES, but that'd be about it; they aren't cohesive. As a result, the class will likely be complex, which can cause maintainability problems. `ProductService` should, therefore, be split into multiple classes. But that raises this question: how many classes and which methods should be grouped together, if any? Before we get into that, let's first inspect how the design around `IProductService` violates the OCP.

`IProductService` VIOLATES THE **OCP**

To test whether the code violates the OCP, you first have to determine what kind of changes to this part of the application you can expect. After that, you can ask the question, "Does this design cause sweeping changes when expected changes are made?"

---

[6]   Calling `Assert.True` with a `false` argument is a bit confusing, but xUnit lacks a convenient `Assert.Fail` method.

You can expect two quite likely changes to happen during the course of the lifetime of the e-commerce application. First, new features will need to be added (Mary already has them on her backlog). Second, Mary likely also needs to apply CROSS-CUTTING CONCERNS. With these expected changes, the obvious answer to the question is, "Yes, the current design does cause sweeping changes." Sweeping changes happen both when adding new features and when adding new aspects.

When a new product-related feature is added, the change ripples through all IProduct-Service implementations, which will be the main ProductService implementation, and also all Decorators and Test Doubles. When a new CROSS-CUTTING CONCERN is added, there'll likely be rippling changes to the system too, because, besides adding a new Decorator for IProductService, you'll also be adding Decorators for ICustomerService, IOrderService, and all other I...Service ABSTRACTIONS. Because each ABSTRACTION potentially contains dozens of methods, the aspect's code would be repeated many times, as we discussed in section 10.1.

> **NOTE** The amount of changes you need to make to the existing Decorators grows proportionally with the amount of features in the system. This makes adding new aspects and features more expensive over time, up to the point that adding features becomes too costly.

In table 9.1, we summed up a wide range of possible aspects you might need to implement. At the start of a project, you might not know which ones you'll need. But even though you might not know exactly which CROSS-CUTTING CONCERNS you may need to add, it'd be a fairly well-educated guess to assume that you do need to add some during the course of the project, as Mary does.

CONCLUDING OUR ANALYSIS OF IProductService

From the previous analysis, you can conclude that, together with its implementations, listing 10.4 violates three out of five SOLID principles. Although from the perspective of AOP, you might be tempted to use either dynamic INTERCEPTION (section 11.1) or compile-time weaving tools (section 11.2) to apply aspects, we argue that this only solves part of the problem; namely, how to effectively apply CROSS-CUTTING CONCERNS in a maintainable fashion. The use of tools doesn't fix the underlying design issues that still cause maintainability problems in the long run.

> **TIP** Although you shouldn't reject tool-based methods of AOP immediately, your first instinct should be to improve the application's design. Only when that doesn't solve the maintainability issues should you resort to the use of tooling.

As we'll discuss in sections 11.1.2 and 11.2.2, both methods of AOP have their own particular sets of disadvantages. But let's take a look at whether we can get to a more SOLID and maintainable design with Mary's app.

10.3.3 *Improving design by applying SOLID principles*

In this section, we'll improve the application's design step by step by doing the following:

- Separate the reads from the writes
- Fix the ISP and SRP violations by splitting interfaces and implementations
- Fix the OCP violation by introducing Parameter Objects and a common interface for implementations
- Fix the accidentally introduced LSP violation by defining a generic ABSTRACTION

STEP 1: SEPARATING READS FROM WRITES

One of the problems with Mary's current design is that the majority of aspects applied to IProductService are only required by a subset of its methods. Although an aspect such as security typically applies to all features, aspects such as auditing, validation, and fault tolerance will usually only be required around the parts of the application that change state. An aspect such as caching, on the other hand, may only make sense for methods that read data without changing state. You can simplify the creation of Decorators by splitting IProductService into a read-only and write-only interface, as shown in figure 10.1.

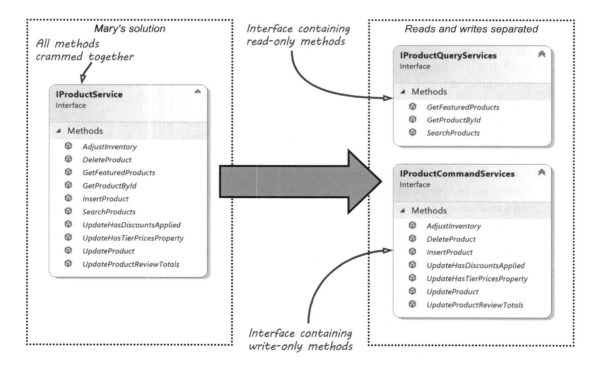

Figure 10.1   **Separating** IProductService **into a read-only** IProductQueryServices **ABSTRACTION and a write-only** IProductCommandServices **ABSTRACTION**

NOTE We use the term *query* for operations that only read state but don't change the state of the system, and *command* for operations that change the state of the system but don't produce any results. This terminology stems from the COMMAND-QUERY SEPARATION (CQS) principle. Mary already applied CQS with `IProductService` on the method level, but by splitting the interface, she now propagates CQS to the interface level.

COMMAND-QUERY SEPARATION

COMMAND-QUERY SEPARATION (CQS) was coined by Bertrand Meyer in *Object-Oriented Software Construction* (ISE Inc., 1988). CQS has become an influential object-oriented principle that promotes the idea that each method should either

- Return a result, but not change the observable state of the system
- Change the state, but not produce any value

Meyer called the value-producing methods *queries* and the state-changing methods *commands*. The idea behind this separation is that methods become easier to reason about when they're either a query or a command, but not both.

The advantage of this split is that the new interfaces are finer-grained than before. This reduces the risk of you having to depend on methods that you don't need. When you create a Decorator that applies a transaction to the executed code, for instance, only `IProductCommandServices` will need to be decorated, which eliminates the need to implement the `IProductQueryServices`'s methods. It also makes the implementations smaller and simpler to reason about.

Although this split is an improvement over the original `IProductService` interface, this new design still causes sweeping changes. As before, implementing a new product-related feature causes a change to many classes in the application. Although you reduced the likelihood of a class being changed by half, a change still causes about the same amount of classes to be touched. This brings us to the second step.

STEP 2: FIXING ISP AND SRP BY SPLITTING INTERFACES AND IMPLEMENTATIONS

Because splitting the wide interface pushes us in the right direction, let's take this a step further. We'll focus our attention on `IProductCommandServices` and ignore `IProductQueryServices`.

Let's try something radical here. Let's break up `IProductCommandServices` into multiple one-membered interfaces. Figure 10.2 shows how the `ProductCommandServices` implementation is segregated into seven classes, each with their own one-membered interface.

In figure 10.2 , you moved each method of the `IProductCommandServices` interface into a separate interface and gave each interface its own class. Listing 10.6 shows a few of those interface definitions.

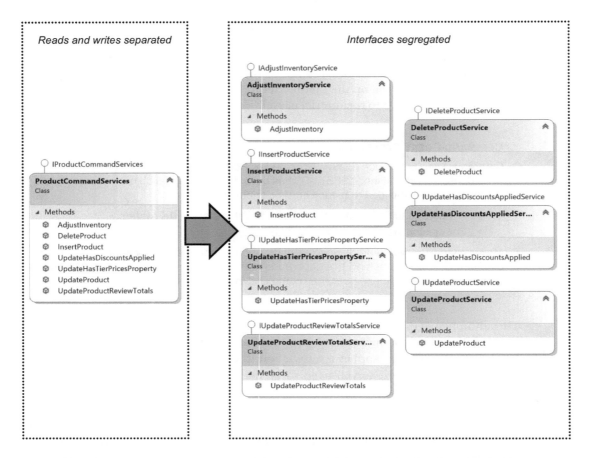

Figure 10.2   The `IProductCommandServices` interface containing seven members is replaced with seven, one-membered interfaces. Each interface gets its own corresponding implementation.

Listing 10.6   The big interface segregated into one-membered interfaces

```
public interface IAdjustInventoryService
{
    void AdjustInventory(Guid productId, bool decrease, int quantity);
}

public interface IUpdateProductReviewTotalsService
{
    void UpdateProductReviewTotals(Guid productId, ProductReview[] reviews);
}

public interface IUpdateHasDiscountsAppliedService
{
    void UpdateHasDiscountsApplied(Guid productId, string description);
}
...
```
The other four interfaces are omitted for brevity.

This might scare the living daylights out of you, but it might not be as bad as it seems. Here are some compelling advantages to this change:

- Every interface is segregated. No client will be forced to depend on methods it doesn't use.
- When you create a one-to-one mapping from interface to implementation, each use case in the application gets its own class. This makes classes small and focused — they have a single responsibility.
- Adding a new feature means the addition of a new interface-implementation pair. No changes have to be made to existing classes that implement other use cases.

Even though this new design conforms to the ISP and the SRP, it still causes sweeping changes when it comes to creating Decorators. Here's how:

- With the `IProductCommandServices` interface split into seven, one-membered interfaces, there'll be seven Decorator implementations per aspect. With 10 aspects, for instance, this means 70 Decorators.
- Making changes to an existing aspect causes sweeping changes throughout a large set of classes, because each aspect is spread out over many Decorators.

This new design causes each class in the application to be focused around one particular use case, which is great from the perspective of the SRP and the ISP. But, because these classes have no commonality to which you can apply aspects, you're forced to create many Decorators with almost identical implementations. It'd be nice if you were able to define a single interface for all command operations in the code base. That would greatly reduce the code duplication around aspects and the number of Decorator classes to one Decorator per aspect.

When you look at listing 10.6, it might be hard to see how these interfaces have any similarity. They all return `void`, but all have a differently named method, and each method has a different set of parameters. There's no commonality to extract from that — or is there?

STEP 3: FIXING OCP USING PARAMETER OBJECTS

What if you extract the method parameters of each command method into a Parameter Object? Most refactoring tools allow such refactoring with a few simple keystrokes.

> **DEFINITION** A *Parameter Object* is a group of parameters that naturally go together.[7]

---

[7] Martin Fowler et al., *Refactoring: Improving the Design of Existing Code* (Addison-Wesley, 1999), 285.

The next listing shows the result of this refactoring.

Listing 10.7   Wrapping method parameters in a Parameter Object

```
public interface IAdjustInventoryService
{
    void Execute(AdjustInventory command);
}
```

> Instead of accepting a list of parameters, IAdjustInventoryService now accepts one single parameter of the new AdjustInventory Parameter Object. That class groups all the method's parameters. Its method is renamed to a more generic name, Execute.

```
public class AdjustInventory
{
    public Guid ProductId { get; set; }
    public bool Decrease { get; set; }
    public int Quantity { get; set; }
}
```

> AdjustInventory contains IAdjustInventoryService's grouped method parameters. It's a Parameter Object; it contains no behavior.

```
public interface IUpdateProductReviewTotalsService
{
    void Execute(UpdateProductReviewTotals command);
}
```

```
public class UpdateProductReviewTotals
{
    public Guid ProductId { get; set; }
    public ProductReview[] Reviews { get; set; }
}
```

> The two method parameters of IUpdateProductReviewTotalsService are now grouped together in the new UpdateProductReviewTotals Parameter Object.

> Same refactoring applied to this interface. It now accepts UpdateProductReviewTotals as its sole parameter.

It's important to note that even though both `AdjustInventory` and `UpdateProduct-ReviewTotals` Parameter Objects are concrete objects, they're still part of their ABSTRACTION. As we mentioned in section 3.1.1, because they're mere data objects without behavior, hiding their values behind an ABSTRACTION would be rather useless. If you moved the implementations into a different assembly, the Parameter Objects would stay in the same assembly as their ABSTRACTION. Also, these extracted Parameter Objects become the definition of a command operation. We therefore typically refer to these objects themselves as *commands*.

> **TIP**   It's perfectly fine for command Parameter Objects to have a single parameter—or even no parameters at all.

Both the `InsertProduct` and `UpdateHasTierPricesProperty` commands will have a single parameter of type `Product`. Inserting a product, however, is something completely different than updating a product's `HasTierPrices` property. Again, the command type itself becomes the definition of a command operation.

With these refactorings, you effectively changed the code from 1 interface and implementation with 7 methods, to 7 interfaces and 14 classes. At this point, you might think we're certifiably nuts and perhaps you're ready to toss this book out the window. This might be the mental discomfort we warned about at the beginning of this section. Bear with us, because increasing the number of classes in your system might not be as bad as it might seem at first, and this refactoring will get us somewhere. Promise.

> **IMPORTANT** Although this refactoring increases the number of files in the project, assuming that each class and interface gets its own file in the project, you didn't change the executable code. Every method still contains the same amount of code as before. You gave each use case its own data object, and each class now handles a single use case.

With the previous refactoring, a pattern emerges:

- Every ABSTRACTION contains a single method.
- Every method is named `Execute`.
- Every method returns `void`.
- Every method has one single input parameter.

You can now extract a common interface from this pattern. Here's how:

```
public interface ICommandService          ◄────┐ One interface to rule them all!
{
    void Execute(object command);
}
```

If you implement the command services using this new `ICommandService` interface, it results in the code in listing 10.8. Note that this new interface definition can likely be used to replace other `I...Service` ABSTRACTIONS too.

Listing 10.8 AdjustInventoryService implementing ICommandService

```
public class AdjustInventoryService : ICommandService      ◄─── Implements ICommandService
{                                                               instead of IAdjustInventoryService
    readonly IInventoryRepository repository;

    public AdjustInventoryService(              ◄───────── Uses CONSTRUCTOR INJECTION to inject
        IInventoryRepository repository)                   the class's DEPENDENCIES
    {
        this.repository = repository;
    }
                                                    Execute accepts a value of type
    public void Execute(object cmd)                 object, but because you know
    {                                               AdjustInventoryService gets supplied
        var command = (AdjustInventory)cmd;    ◄─── with an AdjustInventory command
                                                    message, you perform a cast.
        Guid id = command.ProductId;           ┐ Accesses the command's parameters
        bool decrease = command.Decrease;      │ and executes the appropriate code.
        int quantity = command.Quantity;       ┤ This is the code that was originally
        ...                                    │ placed in the AdjustInventory method
    }                                          ┘ of the ProductService class.
}
```

Figure 10.3 shows how the number of interfaces are reduced from seven back to one. Now, however, you extract the method parameters into a Parameter Object per service.

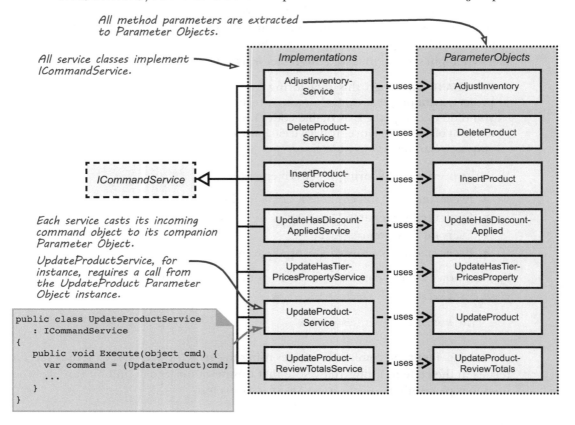

Figure 10.3   The number of interfaces is reduced from seven to one `ICommandService` by extracting method parameters into Parameter Objects.

As we stated previously, the Parameter Objects are part of the ABSTRACTION. Collapsing all interfaces into one single interface makes this even more apparent. The Parameter Object has become the definition of a use case—it has become the contract. Consumers can get this `ICommandService` injected into their constructor and call its `Execute` method by supplying the appropriate Parameter Object.

Listing 10.9   `InventoryController` depending on `ICommandService`

```
public class InventoryController : Controller
{
    private readonly ICommandService service;

    public InventoryController(ICommandService service)
    {
```
◀ **Injects ICommandService into the MVC controller class**

```
        this.service = service;
    }

    [HttpPost]
    public ActionResult AdjustInventory(
        AdjustInventoryViewModel viewModel)
    {
        if (!this.ModelState.IsValid)
        {
            return this.View(viewModel);
        }

        AdjustInventory command = viewModel.Command;

        this.service.Execute(command);

        return this.RedirectToAction("Index");
    }
}
```

In case the posted data is valid, passes on the command to the ICommandService for execution

AdjustInventoryViewModel wraps the AdjustInventory command as a property.

The `AdjustInventoryViewModel` wraps the `AdjustInventory` command as a property. This is convenient, because `AdjustInventory` is part of the ABSTRACTION and only contains data specific to the use case. `AdjustInventory` will be model-bound by the MVC framework, together with its surrounding `AdjustInventoryViewModel`, when the user posts back the request.

> **NOTE** If you noticed that listing 10.9 violates the LSP, we applaud you. We'll get to that violation in a moment.

USING `ICommandService` TO IMPLEMENT CROSS-CUTTING CONCERNS
Having a single interface for all your command service calls in the code base provides a huge advantage. Because all the application's state-changing use cases now implement this single interface, you can now create a single Decorator per aspect and wrap it around each and every implementation. To prove this point, the following listing shows the implementation of a transaction aspect as a Decorator for the `ICommandService`.

Listing 10.10 Implementing a transaction aspect based on `ICommandService`

```
public class TransactionCommandServiceDecorator
    : ICommandService
{
    private readonly ICommandService decoratee;

    public TransactionCommandServiceDecorator(
        ICommandService decoratee)
    {
        this.decoratee = decoratee;
    }

    public void Execute(object command)
    {
        using (var scope = new TransactionScope())
```

```
        {
            this.decoratee.Execute(command);

            scope.Complete();
        }
    }
}
```

Because this Decorator is like what you saw many times in chapter 9, we think it needs little explaining, except perhaps the `TransactionScope` class.

TransactionScope

The `System.Transactions.TransactionScope` class of the System.Transactions.dll lets you wrap any arbitrary piece of code in a transaction. Any `DbTransaction` created during the lifetime of that scope is automatically enlisted in the same transaction. This is a powerful concept that makes it possible to apply transactions to multiple pieces of code that belong to the same business operation, without having to pass along transactions through the call stack.

Compared to the full .NET framework, .NET Core doesn't support distributed transactions, because this requires the Microsoft Distributed Transaction Coordinator (MSDTC) service, which has no equivalent on platforms other than Windows. This is an advantage, because we feel that, in general, distributed transactions should be prevented anyway. With .NET Core, however, you can still use `TransactionScope` to enlist operations in a transaction to a single data source.

Using this new Decorator, you can now compose an `InventoryController` by injecting a new `AdjustInventoryService` that gets INTERCEPTED by a `Transaction-CommandServiceDecorator`:

```
ICommandService service =
    new TransactionCommandServiceDecorator(
        new AdjustInventoryService(repository));

new InventoryController(service);
```

This design effectively prevents sweeping changes both when new features are added and when new CROSS-CUTTING CONCERNS need to be applied. This design is now truly closed for modification because

- Adding a new (command) feature means creating a new command Parameter Object and a supporting `ICommandService` implementation. No existing classes need to be changed.
- Adding a new feature doesn't force the creation of new Decorators nor the change of existing Decorators.
- Adding a new CROSS-CUTTING CONCERN to the application can be done by adding a single Decorator.
- Changing a CROSS-CUTTING CONCERN results in changing a single class.

> **IMPORTANT** Even though you moved from the situation of listing 10.4, where you had 2 types (the IProductService interface and its implementation), into the situation shown in figure 10.3, where you have 15 types (1 interface, 7 Parameter Objects, and 7 service implementations), the maintainability of the application improved dramatically because sweeping changes will be rare. This leads to the important realization that the number of classes in itself is a bad metric for measuring maintainability.

Some developers argue against having this many classes in their system, because they feel it complicates navigating through the project. This, however, only happens when you don't structure your project properly. In this example, all product-related operations can be placed in a namespace called MyApp.Services.Products, effectively grouping those operations together, similar to what Mary's IProductService did. Instead of having the grouping at the class level, you now have it at the project level, which is a great benefit, because the project structure immediately shows you the application's behavior.

Now that you've fixed the previously analyzed SOLID violations, you might think that we're done with our refactoring. But, unfortunately, these changes accidentally introduced a new SOLID violation. Let's look at that next.

ANALYZING THE NEW ACCIDENTAL LSP VIOLATION

As mentioned, the definition of ICommandService accidentally introduced a new SOLID violation, namely, the LSP. The InventoryController of listing 10.9 exhibits this violation.

As we discussed in section 10.2.3, the LSP says that you must be able to substitute an ABSTRACTION for an arbitrary implementation of that same ABSTRACTION without changing the correctness of the client. According to the LSP, because the Adjust-InventoryService implements the ICommandService, you should be able to substitute it for a different implementation without breaking the InventoryController. The following listing shows an altered object composition for InventoryController.

BAD CODE

> **Listing 10.11 Substituting** AdjustInventoryService

```
ICommandService service =
    new TransactionCommandServiceDecorator(
        new UpdateProductReviewTotalsService(
            repository));

new InventoryController(service);
```

Instead of injecting an AdjustInventoryService, you inject an UpdateProductReviewTotalsService. This compiles, but completely breaks InventoryController—an LSP violation.

The following shows the Execute method for UpdateProductReviewTotalsService:

```
public void Execute(object cmd)
{
    var command = (UpdateProductReviewTotals)cmd;
    ...
}
```

This cast fails when Execute is supplied with a command of type AdjustInventory.

InventoryController gets an ICommandService injected into its constructor. It passes on the AdjustInventory command to that injected ICommandService. Because the injected ICommandService is an UpdateProductReviewTotalsService, it'll try to cast the incoming command to UpdateProductReviewTotals. Because it'll be unable to cast AdjustInventory to UpdateProductReviewTotals, however, the cast fails. This breaks InventoryController and therefore violates the LSP.

> **NOTE** DI CONTAINERS compose object graphs based on the type information retrieved from the type's constructor arguments. Because their primary method for OBJECT COMPOSITION is based on this, DI CONTAINERS are bad for handling ambiguous ABSTRACTIONS. LSP violations, therefore, tend to complicate your COMPOSITION ROOT when using a DI CONTAINER. Or, put differently, the use of a DI CONTAINER makes LSP violations more obvious, just as CONSTRUCTOR INJECTION makes SRP violations more obvious.

Although one could argue that it's up to the COMPOSITION ROOT to supply the correct implementation, the ICommandService interface still causes ambiguity, and it prevents the compiler from verifying whether the composition of our object graph makes sense. LSP violations tend to make a system fragile. Furthermore, the untyped command method argument that Execute methods consume requires every ICommandService implementation to contain a cast, which can be considered a code smell in its own right. Let's fix this violation.

STEP 4: FIXING LSP USING A GENERIC ABSTRACTION

Here's a rather elegant solution to this seemingly intractable design deadlock. All you have to do to fix this issue is redefine ICommandService.

GOOD CODE

Listing 10.12   A generic ICommandService implementation

```
public interface ICommandService<TCommand>        ◀──┐  TCommand is the generic type argument.
{                                                     │  It specifies the type of command that an
    void Execute(TCommand command);                   │  implementation will execute.
}
```

You might be confused as to how making the interface generic helps. To help clarify this, the next listing shows how you would implement ICommandService<TCommand>.

GOOD CODE

Listing 10.13   AdjustInventoryService implementing ICommandService<TCommand>

```
                                                  ┌ Implements an
                                                  │ ICommandService<TCommand>,
                                                  │ indicating that this class handles
public class AdjustInventoryService               │ AdjustInventory messages
    : ICommandService<AdjustInventory>    ◀───────┘
{
    private readonly IInventoryRepository repository;

    public AdjustInventoryService(
        IInventoryRepository repository)
```

```
    {
        this.repository = repository;
    }

    public void Execute(AdjustInventory command)
    {
        var productId = command.ProductId;

        ...
    }
}
```

> **Because the class implements ICommandService<AdjustInventory>, its Execute method now accepts an AdjustInventory instead of an object.**

> **Because Execute now directly accepts an AdjustInventory, the parameter command can be used directly without any casts.**

IMPORTANT Do you remember how we defined an IEventHandler<TEvent> ABSTRACTION in listing 6.9? The signature of this new ICommandService<TCommand> is identical to IEventHandler<TEvent>'s, and that's no coincidence. This is the kind of structure that'll frequently emerge when you apply SOLID principles to your code base—that is, one-membered generic interfaces that accept and/or return messages based on their generic types.

Many frameworks and online reference architecture samples have different names for an interface similar to the previous examples. They might be named IHandler<T>, ICommandHandler<T>, IMessageHandler<T>, or IHandleMessages<T>. Some ABSTRACTIONS are asynchronous and return a Task, whereas others add a CancellationToken as a method argument. Sometimes the method is called Handle or HandleAsync. Although named differently, the idea and the effect it has on the maintainability of your application, however, is the same.

Although the additional compile-time support in the implementation is certainly a nice plus, the main reason for the generic ICommandService<TCommand> is to prevent violating the LSP in its clients. The following listing shows how injecting ICommand-Service<TCommand> into the InventoryController fixes the LSP.

GOOD
CODE

Listing 10.14 InventoryController depending on ICommandService<TCommand>

```
public class InventoryController : Controller
{
    private readonly ICommandService<AdjustInventory> service;

    public InventoryController(
        ICommandService<AdjustInventory> service)
    {
        this.service = service;
    }

    public ActionResult AdjustInventory(
```

> **Injects a specific ICommandService<AdjustInventory>, indicating that you want to execute AdjustInventory commands. This prevents the accidental injection of services that handle UpdateProductReviewTotals or any other command type.**

```
        AdjustInventoryViewModel viewModel)
    {
        ...

        AdjustInventory command = viewModel.Command;

        this.service.Execute(command);

        return this.RedirectToAction("Index");
    }
}
```

> The service parameter only accepts AdjustInventory as a command type. It becomes impossible to supply it with a different type of message — that wouldn't compile.

TIP If your programming language doesn't support generics, you might find the use of the non-generic ICommandService interface mixed with the Mediator design pattern an acceptable workaround.[8] In that case, you introduce an additional ABSTRACTION, the Mediator, which accepts arbitrary commands and gets injected into consumers. The Mediator's job is to dispatch a supplied command to the correct ICommandService implementation.

Changing the non-generic ICommandService into the generic ICommandService<TCommand> fixes our last SOLID violation. This would be a good time to reap the benefits of our new design.

APPLYING TRANSACTION HANDLING USING THE GENERIC ABSTRACTION

Although there's more to a generic one-membered ABSTRACTION than just CROSS-CUTTING CONCERNS, the ability to apply aspects in a way that doesn't cause sweeping changes is one of the greatest benefits of such a design. As with the non-generic ICommandService interface, ICommandService<TCommand> still allows the creation of a single Decorator per aspect. Listing 10.15 shows a rewrite of the transaction Decorator of listing 10.10 using the new generic ICommandService<TCommand> ABSTRACTION.

GOOD
CODE

> **Listing 10.15   Implementing a generic transaction aspect**

```
public class TransactionCommandServiceDecorator<TCommand>
    : ICommandService<TCommand>
{
    private readonly ICommandService<TCommand> decoratee;

    public TransactionCommandServiceDecorator(
        ICommandService<TCommand> decoratee)
    {
        this.decoratee = decoratee;
    }
```

---

8 Erich Gamma et al., *Design Patterns*, 273.

```
    public void Execute(TCommand command)
    {
        using (var scope = new TransactionScope())
        {
            this.decoratee.Execute(command);

            scope.Complete();
        }
    }
}
```

Using the ICommandService<TCommand> interface and the TransactionCommand-ServiceDecorator<TCommand> Decorator, your COMPOSITION ROOT becomes the following:

```
new InventoryController(
    new TransactionCommandServiceDecorator<AdjustInventory>(
        new AdjustInventoryService(repository)));
```

This brings us to the point where this one-membered generic ABSTRACTION starts to steal the show. This is when you start adding more CROSS-CUTTING CONCERNS.

10.3.4 *Adding more CROSS-CUTTING CONCERNS*

The examples of CROSS-CUTTING CONCERNS we discussed in section 9.2 all focused on applying aspects at the boundary of Repositories (such as in listings 9.4 and 9.7). In this section, however, we shift the focus one level up in the layered architecture, from the data access library's repository to the domain library's IProductService.

This shift is deliberate, because you'll find that Repositories aren't the right granular level for applying many CROSS-CUTTING CONCERNS effectively. A single business action defined in the domain layer would potentially call multiple Repositories, or call the same Repository multiple times. If you were to apply, for instance, a transaction at the level of the repository, it'd still mean that the business operation could potentially run in dozens of transactions, which would endanger the correctness of the system.

A single business operation should typically run in a single transaction. This level of granularity holds not only for transactions, but other types of operations as well.

The domain library implements business operations, and it's at this boundary that you typically want to apply many CROSS-CUTTING CONCERNS. The following lists some examples. It isn't a comprehensive listing, but it'll give you a sense of what you could apply on that level:

- *Auditing*—Although you could implement auditing around Repositories, as you did in the AuditingUserRepositoryDecorator of listing 9.1, this presents a list of changes to individual ENTITIES, and you lose the overall picture—that is, why the change happened. Reporting changes to individual ENTITIES might be suited for CRUD-based applications, but if the application implements more-complex use cases that influence more than a single ENTITY, it becomes beneficial to pull auditing a level up and store information about the executed command. We'll show an auditing example next.

- *Logging*—As we alluded to in section 5.3.2, a good application design can prevent unnecessary logging statements spread across the entire code base. Logging any executed business operation with its data provides you with detailed information about the call, which typically removes the need to log at the start of each method.

- *Performance monitoring*—Since 99% of the time executing a request is typically spent running the business operation itself, ICommandService<TCommand> becomes an ideal boundary for plugging in performance monitoring.

- *Security*—Although you might try to restrict access on the level of the repository, this is typically too fine-grained, because you more likely want to restrict access at the level of the business operation. You can mark your commands with either a permitted role or a permission, which makes it trivial to apply security concerns around all business operations using a single Decorator. We'll show an example shortly.

- *Fault tolerance*—Because you want to apply transactions around your business operations, as we've shown in listing 10.15, other fault-tolerant aspects should typically be applied on the same level. Implementing a database deadlock retry aspect, for instance, is a good example. Such a mechanism should always be applied around a transaction aspect.

- *Validation*—As we demonstrated in listings 10.9 and 10.14, the command can become part of the web request's submitted data. By enriching commands with Data Annotations' attributes, the command's data will also be validated by MVC.[9] As an extra safety measure, you can create a Decorator that validates an incoming command using Data Annotations' static Validator class.[10]

The following sections take a look at how you can implement two of these aspects on top of ICommandService<TCommand>.

EXAMPLE: IMPLEMENTING AN AUDITING ASPECT

Listings 9.1 and 9.2 defined an auditing Decorator for IUserRepository, while reusing the IAuditTrailAppender from listing 6.23. If you apply auditing on ICommandService<TCommand> instead, you're at the ideal level of granularity, because the command contains all interesting use case–specific data you might want to record. If you enrich this data and metadata with some contextual information, such as username and the current system time, you're pretty much done. The next listing shows an auditing Decorator on top of ICommandService<TCommand>.

---

[9] System.ComponentModel.DataAnnotations is a framework-agnostic data validation library by Microsoft.

[10] For an example of such a Decorator, see https://simpleinjector.org/aop#decoration.

GOOD CODE

> **Listing 10.16 Implementing a generic auditing aspect for business operations**

```
public class AuditingCommandServiceDecorator<TCommand>
    : ICommandService<TCommand>
{
    private readonly IUserContext userContext;
    private readonly ITimeProvider timeProvider;
    private readonly CommerceContext context;
    private readonly ICommandService<TCommand> decoratee;

    public AuditingCommandServiceDecorator(
        IUserContext userContext,
        ITimeProvider timeProvider,
        CommerceContext context,
        ICommandService<TCommand> decoratee)
    {
        this.userContext = userContext;
        this.timeProvider = timeProvider;
        this.context = context;
        this.decoratee = decoratee;
    }

    public void Execute(TCommand command)
    {
        this.decoratee.Execute(command);
        this.AppendToAuditTrail(command);
    }

    private void AppendToAuditTrail(TCommand command)
    {
        var entry = new AuditEntry
        {
            UserId = this.userContext.CurrentUser.Id,
            TimeOfExecution = this.timeProvider.Now,
            Operation = command.GetType().Name,
            Data = Newtonsoft.Json.JsonConvert
                .SerializeObject(command)
        };

        this.context.AuditEntries.Add(entry);
        this.context.SaveChanges();
    }
}
```

Recall that this is the ITimeProvider interface from listing 5.10.

Besides appending the user and the time of execution to the audit trail, the Decorator stores the name of the command and a serialized representation of its data too. This information is gathered using reflection and, in this case, you use the well-known JSON.NET serialization library (https://www.newtonsoft.com/json) that converts the command data to a readable JSON format.

NOTE This Decorator combines the auditing logic and the decorating logic. Whether this is good practice depends on the amount of logic inside the Decorator, whether you need this auditing logic to be reused by other classes, and in which module you locate the Decorator. Because you can now apply this Decorator around all business operations, we argue there's little reason to share this logic with other classes. For that reason, we merged the two classes together. Because of the dependency on CommerceContext, however, this Decorator should be placed in either the data access layer or the COMPOSITION ROOT.

When Mary runs the application using the `AuditingCommandService-Decorator<TCommand>`, the Decorator produces the information in the auditing table, shown in table 10.2.

Table 10.2 Example audit trail

User	Time	Operation	Data
Mary	2018-12-24 11:20	AdjustInventory	{ ProductId: "ae361...00bc", Decrease: false, Quantity: 2 }
Mary	2018-12-24 11:21	UpdateHasTierPricesProperty	{ Product: { Id: "ae361...00bc", Name: "Gruyère", UnitPrice: 48.50, IsFeatured: true } }
Mary	2018-12-24 11:25	UpdateHasDiscountsApplied	{ ProductId: "ae361...00bc", DiscountDescription: "Test" }
Mary	2018-12-24 15:11	AdjustInventory	{ ProductId: "5435...a845", Decrease: true, Quantity: 1 }
Mary	2018-12-24 15:12	UpdateProductReviewTotals	{ ProductId: "5435...a845", Reviews: [{ Rating: 5, Text: "nice!" }] }

As stated previously, `AuditingCommandServiceDecorator<TCommand>` uses reflection to get the name of the command and convert the command to a JSON format. Although JSON is human readable, you probably don't want to show this to your end users. Still, this is a good format to use for backend auditing purposes. Using this information, you'll be able to efficiently see what happened in your system, by whom, and at which point in time. It would even allow you to replay an operation if it failed for some reason or to use this information to perform a realistic stress test on the system. You could deserialize the information from this table back to commands and run them through the system.

As we described in section 6.3.2, domain events are another well-suited technique that can also be used for auditing. This auditing aspect, however, only records a user's successful action. Although an auditor might not be interested in failures, we as developers certainly are. It isn't hard to imagine how you'd use the same mechanism to record the same data and include a stack trace when the operation fails.

> **IMPORTANT** The application design went from an RPC-like method-calling model to a message-passing model. These messages can be serialized, queued, logged, and replayed—all abilities that are harder to achieve with a method-calling model, such as the initial `IProductService` implementation from listing 10.4.

> ## Well-designed applications have few code lines that log
>
> When you use an ABSTRACTION that wraps around a business transaction, like `ICommand-Service<TCommand>` does, the method parameters become an easily serializable package of data, as you saw in listing 10.16. A single Decorator, therefore, lets you apply logging across a wide range of methods in the application.
>
> This might not solve all your logging needs, but when an application gets more complex, we've experienced that the ABSTRACTIONS of a well-designed SOLID application allow the definition of a few Decorators that provide us with 98% of the logging needs of our applications. But there are other practices you need to apply to prevent having to log at too many places in the application:
>
> - Instead of logging unexpected situations while continuing execution, throw exceptions.[11]
> - Instead of catching unexpected exceptions, logging, and continuing in the middle of an operation, prefer leaving exceptions unhandled and let them bubble up the call stack. Letting an operation fail fast allows exceptions to be logged at a single location at the top of the call stack and prevents giving users the illusion that their request completed successfully.
> - Make methods small.[12] Not only does this improve the readability of code but, in the case of thrown exceptions, the stack trace gives you more information about which path the application went through at the time of the exception.

Likewise, you can use this information for performance monitoring in the same way, where you store an additional timespan next to the time and the operation details. This easily allows you to monitor which operations become slower over time. Before showing you an example of the new COMPOSITION ROOT with `AuditingCommand-ServiceDecorator<TCommand>` applied, we'll first take a look at how you can use passive attributes to implement a security aspect.

EXAMPLE: IMPLEMENTING A SECURITY ASPECT

During our discussion about CROSS-CUTTING CONCERNS in section 9.2, you implemented a `SecureProductRepositoryDecorator` in listing 9.7. Because that Decorator was specific to `IProductRepository`, it was clear what role the Decorator should grant access to. In the example, access to the write methods of `IProductRepository` was restricted to the `Administrator` role.

With this new generic model, a single Decorator is wrapped around all business operations, not just the product CRUD operations. Some operations also need to be executable by other roles, which makes the hard-coded `Administrator` role unsuited for this generic model. You can implement such a security check on top of a generic ABSTRACTION in many ways, but one compelling method is through the use of passive attributes.

---

[11] See, for example, Jeff Atwood, "The Problem With Logging" 2008, https://blog.codinghorror.com/the-problem-with-logging/.

[12] See, for example, Robert C. Martin, *Clean Code* (Prentice Hall, 2009).

DEFINITION   A *passive attribute* provides metadata rather than behavior. Passive attributes prevent the CONTROL FREAK anti-pattern, because aspect attributes that include behavior are often VOLATILE DEPENDENCIES.[13]

When you stick to role-based security as an example of authorization, you can specify a PermittedRoleAttribute.

Listing 10.17   A passive `PermittedRoleAttribute`

```
public class PermittedRoleAttribute : Attribute
{
    public readonly Role Role;

    public PermittedRoleAttribute(Role role)
    {
        this.Role = role;
    }
}

public enum Role
{
    PreferredCustomer,
    Administrator,
    InventoryManager
}
```

This passive attribute allows classes to be enriched with metadata about the permitted role.

Wraps the application's Role enumeration that defines the application's fixed set of roles

The Role enumeration containing the application's known roles. You first saw this enum in section 3.1.2.

You can use this attribute to enrich commands with metadata about which role is allowed to execute an operation.

GOOD
CODE

Listing 10.18   Enriching commands with security-related metadata

```
[PermittedRole(Role.InventoryManager)]
public class AdjustInventory
{
    public Guid ProductId { get; set; }
    public bool Decrease { get; set; }
    public int Quantity { get; set; }
}

[PermittedRole(Role.Administrator)]
public class UpdateProductReviewTotals
{
    public Guid ProductId { get; set; }
    public ProductReview[] Reviews { get; set; }
}
```

Marks commands with the PermittedRoleAttribute while specifying the allowed role. In this case, AdjustInventory can be executed by users with the role InventoryManager, although only administrators are authorized to execute UpdateProductReviewTotals.

IMPORTANT   Notice how the permitted role in listing 10.18 becomes part of the definition of a command.

---

[13] Mark Seemann, "Passive attributes" 2014, https://blog.ploeh.dk/2014/06/13/passive-attributes/.

There's a big difference between applying aspect attributes, as we'll discuss in section 11.2, and a passive attribute, such as the `PermittedRoleAttribute`. Compared to aspect attributes, passive attributes are decoupled from the aspect that use their values, which is one of the main problems with compile-time weaving, as you'll see in chapter 11. The passive attribute doesn't have a direct relationship with the aspect. This allows the metadata to be reused by multiple aspects, perhaps in different ways.

TIP Prefer creating a domain-specific attribute over reusing an attribute that's tied to a specific framework. For instance, if you use the ASP.NET Core's `[Authorize]` attribute, that would drag along a dependency to Microsoft .AspNetCore.Authorization.dll, which wouldn't be appropriate if you were to reuse the domain in, for example, a Windows service application.

Like you've seen previously, adding the security behavior is a matter of creating the Decorator and wrapping it around the real implementation. Listing 10.19 shows such a Decorator. It makes use of the `PermittedRoleAttribute` that's supplied to commands, as listing 10.18 showed.

GOOD CODE

Listing 10.19 `SecureCommandServiceDecorator<TCommand>`

```
public class SecureCommandServiceDecorator<TCommand>
    : ICommandService<TCommand>
{
    private static readonly Role PermittedRole = GetPermittedRole();      ◄─────── Gets the role permitted to
                                                                                   execute this command

    private readonly IUserContext userContext;
    private readonly ICommandService<TCommand> decoratee;

    public SecureCommandServiceDecorator(
        IUserContext userContext,         ◄───────  The Decorator depends on an
        ICommandService<TCommand> decoratee)       IUserContext that allows it to
    {                                               check the current user's role.
        this.decoratee = decoratee;
        this.userContext = userContext;
    }
                                                   Before delegating the call to the
    public void Execute(TCommand command)          decoratee, verifies whether the user
    {                                              is allowed to execute this operation
        this.CheckAuthorization();       ◄────────┘
        this.decoratee.Execute(command);
    }

    private void CheckAuthorization()
    {
        if (!this.userContext.IsInRole(PermittedRole))    ◄───  In case the user isn't part
        {                                                       of the specified role,
            throw new SecurityException();                      throws an exception. This
        }                                                       lets the operation fail fast.
    }                                                           Logging of the exception
}                                                               can be done higher up the
                                                                call stack.
```

```
private static Role GetPermittedRole()
{
    var attribute = typeof(TCommand)
        .GetCustomAttribute<PermittedRoleAttribute>();

    if (attribute == null)
    {
        throw new InvalidOperationException(
            "[PermittedRole] missing.");
    }

    return attribute.Role;
}
```

Uses reflection to get the **PermittedRoleAttribute** specified on the command type

In case no attribute is defined on the command type, you could assume that every user is allowed to execute the command, but that would be a security risk. Instead, it throws an exception, forcing every command to have the attribute applied.

Authorization flavors

You can specify authorization on commands and other message types in many ways. Here are some ideas:

- *If commands are always accessible by a single role, consider placing the command in a namespace that's named after its role instead of applying an attribute.* For instance, you can place administrative commands in the namespace MyApp .Domain.Commands.Administrator and let the Decorator analyze this namespace. This also gives you a nice intuitive project structure because commands are grouped by their permitted role.
- *Instead of working with roles, a common model is working with permissions.* Permissions allow access to be configured in a more fine-grained manner. A command can be marked with a specific permission. This hard-codes the list of application permissions rather than roles and allows an administrator to manage the link between users, roles, and permissions.
- *Next to role-based security, your application might require row-based security.* In the context of the e-commerce application, this could mean that certain groups of products can only be managed by users located in certain regions. In other words, even though multiple users might be in the same role, row-based security can still make a specific product accessible to some users in a role, but inaccessible to others from that same role.[14]

We could give you tons of examples of Decorators that can be wrapped around business transactions, but there's a limit to the number of pages a book can have. Besides, at this point, we think you're starting to get the picture about how to apply Decorators on top of ICommandService<TCommand>. Let's piece everything together inside the COMPOSITION ROOT.

---

[14] For inspiration on how to handle row-based security, see this online discussion: https://github.com/ dotnetjunkie/solidservices/issues/4.

Composing object graphs using generic Decorators

In the previous sections, you declared three Decorators implementing security, transaction management, and auditing. You need to apply these Decorators around a real implementation in your COMPOSITION ROOT. Figure 10.4 shows how the Decorators are wrapped around a command service like a set of Russian nesting dolls.

If you apply all three previously defined Decorators to your COMPOSITION ROOT, you end up with the code shown next.

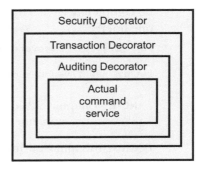

Figure 10.4   Enriching a real command service with auditing, transaction, and security aspects

---

Listing 10.20   Decorating `AdjustInventoryService`

```
ICommandService<AdjustInventory> service =
    new SecureCommandServiceDecorator<AdjustInventory>(
        this.userContext,
        new TransactionCommandServiceDecorator<AdjustInventory>(
            new AuditingCommandServiceDecorator<AdjustInventory>(
                this.userContext,
                this.timeProvider,
                context,
                new AdjustInventoryService(repository))));

return new InventoryController(service);
```

Because the application is expected to get many `ICommandService<TCommand>` implementations, most of the implementations would require the same decorators. Listing 10.20, therefore, would lead to lots of code repetition inside the COMPOSITION ROOT. This is something that's easily fixed by extracting the repeated Decorator creation into its own method.

Listing 10.21   Extracting the composition of Decorators to a reusable method

```
private ICommandService<TCommand> Decorate<TCommand>(
    ICommandService<TCommand> decoratee, CommerceContext context)
{
    return
        new SecureCommandServiceDecorator<TCommand>(
            this.userContext,
            new TransactionCommandServiceDecorator<TCommand>(
                AuditingCommandServiceDecorator<TCommand>(
                    this.userContext,
                    this.timeProvider,
                    context,              ◄─── Wraps the decoratee parameter
                    decoratee))));              in the list of Decorators
}
```

Extracting the Decorators into the `Decorate` method allows the Composition Root to be completely DRY. The creation of `AdjustInventoryService` is reduced to a simple one-liner:

```
var service = Decorate(new AdjustInventoryService(repository), context);

return new InventoryController(service);
```

> **NOTE** Chapter 12 demonstrates how to Auto-Register `ICommandService` `<TCommand>` implementations and apply Decorators using a DI Container.

Because this almost brings us to the end of this section about using SOLID principles as a driver for AOP, let's reflect for a moment on what we've achieved and how this relates to the bigger picture of application design.

10.3.5 *Conclusion*

In this chapter, you refactored the domain layer's big `IProductService`, which consisted of several command methods, into a single `ICommandService<TCommand>` Abstraction, where each command got its own message and associated implementation for handling that message. This refactoring didn't change any of the original application logic; you did, however, make the concept of commands explicit.

An important observation is that these domain commands are now exposed as a clear artifact in the system, and their handlers are marked with a single interface. This methodology is similar to what you implicitly practice when working with application frameworks such as ASP.NET Core MVC. MVC Controllers are typically defined by inheriting from the `Controller` Abstraction; this allows MVC to find them using reflection, and it presents a common API for interacting with them. This practice is valuable at a larger scale in the application's design, as you've seen with these commands where you gave their handlers a common API (a single `Execute` method). This allowed aspects to be applied effectively and without code repetition.

Besides commands, there are other artifacts in the system that you might want to design in a similar fashion in order to be able to apply Cross-Cutting Concerns. A common artifact that deserves to be exposed more clearly is that of a query. At the start of section 10.3.3, after you split up `IProductService` into a read and write interface, we focused your attention on `IProductCommandServices` and ignored `IProductQueryServices`. Queries deserve an Abstraction of their own. Due to space constraints, however, a discussion of this is outside the scope of this book.[15]

Our point, however, is that in many types of applications, it's possible to determine a commonality between groups of related components as you did in this chapter. This might help with applying Cross-Cutting Concerns more effectively and also supplies you with an explicit and compiler-verified coding convention.

---

[15] For a discussion of such an Abstraction, see Steven van Deursen, "Meanwhile... on the query side of my architecture" 2011, https://cuttingedge.it/blogs/steven/pivot/entry.php?id=92.

But the goal of this chapter wasn't to state that the ICommandService<TCommand> ABSTRACTION is the way to design your applications. The important takeaway from this chapter should be that designing applications according to SOLID is the way to keep applications maintainable. As we demonstrated, this can, for the most part, be achieved without the use of specialized AOP tooling. This is important, because those tools come with their own sets of limitations and problems, which is something we'll go into deeper in the next chapter. We have found, however, a certain set of design structures to be applicable to many line-of-business (LOB) applications — an ICommandService-like ABSTRACTION being one of them.

This doesn't mean that it's always easy to apply SOLID principles. On the contrary, it can be difficult. As stated previously, it takes time, and you'll never be 100% SOLID. Your job as software developer is to find the sweet spot; applying DI and SOLID at the right moments will absolutely boost your chances of getting closer to that.

DI shines when it comes to applying recognized object-oriented principles such as SOLID. In particular, the loosely coupled nature of DI lets you use the Decorator pattern to follow the OCP as well as the SRP. This is valuable in a wide range of situations, because it enables you to keep your code clean and well organized, especially when it comes to addressing CROSS-CUTTING CONCERNS.

But let's not beat around the bush. Writing maintainable software is hard, even when you try to apply the SOLID principles. Besides, you often work in projects that aren't designed to stand the test of time. It might be unfeasible or dangerous to make big architectural changes. At those times, using AOP tooling might be your only viable option, even if it presents you with a temporary solution. Before you decide to use these tools, it's important to understand how they work and what their weaknesses are, especially compared to the design philosophy described in this chapter. This will be the subject of the next chapter.

Summary

- The SINGLE RESPONSIBILITY PRINCIPLE (SRP) states that each class should have only one reason to change. This can be viewed from the perspective of cohesion. *Cohesion* is defined as the functional relatedness of the elements of a class or module. The lower the amount of relatedness, the lower the cohesion; and the lower the cohesion, the greater the chance a class violates the SRP.

- The OPEN/CLOSED PRINCIPLE (OCP) prescribes an application design that prevents you from having to make sweeping changes throughout the code base. A strong relationship between the OCP and the DRY principle is that they both strive for the same objective.

- The Don't Repeat Yourself (DRY) principle states that every piece of knowledge must have a single, unambiguous, authoritative representation within a system.

- The LISKOV SUBSTITUTION PRINCIPLE (LSP) states that every implementation should behave as defined by its ABSTRACTION. This lets you replace the originally intended implementation with another implementation of the same ABSTRACTION without worrying about breaking a consumer. It's a foundation of DI. When consumers don't observe it, there's little advantage in injecting DEPENDENCIES, because you can't replace DEPENDENCIES at will, and you lose many (if not all) benefits of DI.

- The INTERFACE SEGREGATION PRINCIPLE (ISP) promotes the use of fine-grained ABSTRACTIONS rather than wide ABSTRACTIONS. Any time a consumer depends on an ABSTRACTION where some of the members stay unused, this principle is violated. This principle is crucial when it comes to effectively applying ASPECT-ORIENTED PROGRAMMING.

- The DEPENDENCY INVERSION PRINCIPLE (DIP) states that you should program against ABSTRACTIONS and that the consuming layer should be in control of the shape of a consumed ABSTRACTION. The consumer should be able to define the ABSTRACTION in a way that benefits itself the most.

- These five principles together form the SOLID acronym. None of the SOLID principles represents absolutes. They're guidelines that can help you write clean code.

- ASPECT-ORIENTED PROGRAMMING (AOP) is a paradigm that focuses on the notion of applying CROSS-CUTTING CONCERNS effectively and maintainably.

- The most compelling AOP technique is SOLID. A SOLID application prevents code duplication during normal application code and implementation of CROSS-CUTTING CONCERNS. Using SOLID techniques can also help developers avoid the use of specific AOP tooling.

- Even with a SOLID design, there likely will come a time where a change becomes sweeping. Being 100% closed for modification is neither possible nor desirable. Conforming to the OCP takes considerable effort when finding and designing the appropriate ABSTRACTIONS, although too many ABSTRACTIONS can have a negative impact on the complexity of the application.

- COMMAND-QUERY SEPARATION (CQS) is an influential object-oriented principle that states that each method should either return a result but not change the observable state of the system, or change the state but not produce any value.

- Placing command methods and query methods in different ABSTRACTIONS simplifies applying CROSS-CUTTING CONCERNS, because the majority of aspects need to be applied to either commands or queries, but not both.

- A Parameter Object is a group of parameters that naturally go together. The extraction of Parameter Objects allows the definition of a reusable ABSTRACTION that can be implemented by a large group of components. This allows these components to be handled similarly and CROSS-CUTTING CONCERNS to be applied effectively.

- Rather than a component's ABSTRACTION, these extracted Parameter Objects become the definition of a distinct operation or use case in the system.
- Although splitting larger classes into many smaller classes with Parameter Objects can drastically increase the number of classes in a system, it can also dramatically improve the maintainability of a system. The number of classes in a system is a bad metric for measuring maintainability.
- CROSS-CUTTING CONCERNS should be applied at the right granular level in the application. For all but the simplest CRUD applications, Repositories aren't the right granular level for most CROSS-CUTTING CONCERNS. With the application of SOLID principles, reusable one-membered ABSTRACTIONS typically emerge as the levels where CROSS-CUTTING CONCERNS need to be applied.

Tool-based Aspect-Oriented Programming

In this chapter

- Using dynamic INTERCEPTION to apply Interceptors using generated Decorators

- Advantages and disadvantages of dynamic INTERCEPTION

- Using compile-time weaving to apply CROSS-CUTTING CONCERNS

- Why compile-time weaving is the antithesis of DI

This chapter is a continuation of the Aspect-Oriented Programming (AOP) discussion that we started in chapter 10. Where chapter 10 described AOP in its purest form—namely, applying AOP solely using SOLID design practices—this chapter approaches AOP from a tool-based perspective. We'll discuss two common methods for applying AOP: dynamic INTERCEPTION and compile-time weaving.

In case the design approach of chapter 10 is too radical, dynamic INTERCEPTION will be your next best pick, which is why we'll discuss it first. Dynamic INTERCEPTION might be a good temporary solution until the right time arrives to start making the kinds of improvements discussed in the last chapter.

Compile-time weaving is the opposite of DI, and we consider it to be an anti-pattern. We feel it's important, however, to include a discussion on compile-time weaving, because it's a well-known form of AOP, and we want to make it clear that it isn't a viable alternative to DI.

TIP   Our coverage of these tools is limited to the topic of DI. If you're interested in learning more about tool-based AOP, there's a book on this topic: *AOP in .NET*, by Matthew D. Groves (Manning, 2013).

11.1   *Dynamic INTERCEPTION*

The code listings of section 10.1, which implement the `Delete` and `Insert` methods of `CircuitBreakerProductRepositoryDecorator`, contained code duplication. The following listing shows this code again.

CODE
SMELL

Listing 11.1   Violating the DRY principle (repeated)

```
public void Delete(Product product)
{
    this.breaker.Guard();

    try
    {
        this.decoratee.Delete(product);
        this.breaker.Succeed();
    }
    catch (Exception ex)
    {
        this.breaker.Trip(ex);
        throw;
    }
}

public void Insert(Product product)
{
    this.breaker.Guard();

    try
    {
        this.decoratee.Insert(product);
        this.breaker.Succeed();
    }
    catch (Exception ex)
    {
        this.breaker.Trip(ex);
        throw;
    }
}
```

The code of these two methods looks a lot like a template. They're almost identical, with the only difference being the calls to the Delete and Insert methods.

The hardest part of implementing a Decorator as an aspect is to design the template. After that, it's a rather mechanical process:

1 Create a new Decorator class
2 Derive from the desired interface
3 Implement each interface member by applying the template

This process is so repetitive that you can use a tool to automate it. Among the many powerful features of the .NET Framework is the ability to dynamically emit types. This makes it possible to write code that generates a fully functional class at runtime. Such a class has no underlying source code file, but is compiled directly from some abstract model. This enables you to automate the generation of Decorators that are created at runtime. As figure 11.1 shows, this is what dynamic INTERCEPTION enables you to do.

After the object graph for the dynamically generated Decorator and its DEPENDENCIES is created, the Decorator can be used as a stand-in for the real class. Because it implements the real class's ABSTRACTION, it can be injected into clients that use that ABSTRACTION. Figure 11.2 describes the flow of method calls when the client calls into its INTERCEPTED ABSTRACTION.

To use dynamic INTERCEPTION, you must still write the code that implements the aspect. This could be the plumbing code required for the Circuit Breaker aspect as

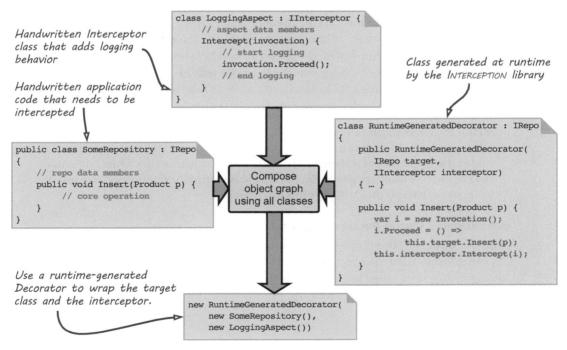

Figure 11.1 A dynamic INTERCEPTION library generates a Decorator class at runtime. This happens once per given ABSTRACTION (in this case, for `IRepo`). After the generation process completes, you can request that the INTERCEPTION library create new instances of that Decorator for you, while you supply both the `target` and the `interceptor`.

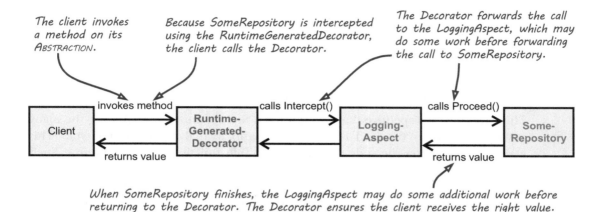

Figure 11.2 **The flow of method calls when the client calls into its INTERCEPTED ABSTRACTION**

shown in listing 11.1. Once you've done this, you must tell the dynamic INTERCEPTION library about the ABSTRACTIONS it should apply the aspect to. Enough with the theory, let's see an example.

11.1.1 *Example: INTERCEPTION with Castle Dynamic Proxy*

With its repetitive code, the Circuit Breaker aspect from listing is a good candidate for dynamic INTERCEPTION. While you can write the code that generates Decorators at runtime, this is a rather involved operation, and besides, there are already excellent tools available. Instead of taking you through the tedious process of generating code by hand, we'll start using a tool directly. As an example, let's see how you can reduce code duplication with Castle Dynamic Proxy's INTERCEPTION capabilities.

> **NOTE** Castle Dynamic Proxy is the *de facto* standard tool for dynamic INTER-CEPTION in .NET. It's free and open source. In fact, most DI CONTAINERS use it under the hood for their dynamic INTERCEPTION functionality. Other dynamic INTERCEPTION tools are available, but Castle is mature and has stood the test of time, so we'll focus on Castle for this discussion.

IMPLEMENTING A CIRCUIT BREAKER INTERCEPTOR

Implementing an Interceptor for Castle requires that you implement its `Castle .DynamicProxy.IInterceptor` interface, which consists of a single method. The following listing shows how to implement the Circuit Breaker from listing 11.1. Distinct from that listing, however, the following shows the entire class.

Listing 11.2   Implementing the Circuit Breaker Interceptor with Dynamic Proxy

```
public class CircuitBreakerInterceptor
    : Castle.DynamicProxy.IInterceptor                    ◄──── To implement an Interceptor, you
{                                                               must implement the IInterceptor
                                                                interface defined by Castle.
    private readonly ICircuitBreaker breaker;

    public CircuitBreakerInterceptor(          ◄──── An Interceptor can be composed inside
        ICircuitBreaker breaker)                     the COMPOSITION ROOT. This enables you
    {                                                to use CONSTRUCTOR INJECTION in your
        this.breaker = breaker;                      Interceptor aspects.
    }


    public void Intercept(IInvocation invocation)     ◄─────────────────┐
    {                                        There's only one method to implement, and
        this.breaker.Guard();                you implement it by applying the same code
                                                     that you used repeatedly when you
        try                                  implemented the CircuitBreakerProduct-
        {                                                   RepositoryDecorator.
            invocation.Proceed();     ◄────┐
                                           Instructs Castle to let the call proceed
            this.breaker.Succeed();        to the decorated instance
        }
        catch (Exception ex)
        {
            this.breaker.Trip(ex);
            throw;
        }
    }
}
```

The main difference from listing 11.1 is that instead of delegating the method call to a specific method, you must be more general, because you apply this code to potentially any method. The IInvocation interface passed to the Intercept method as a parameter represents the method call. It might, for example, represent the call to the Insert(Product) method. The Proceed method is one of the key members of this interface, because it enables you to let the call proceed to the next implementation on the stack.

The IInvocation interface enables you to assign a return value before letting the call proceed. It also provides access to detailed information about the method call. From the invocation parameter, you can get information about the name and parameter values of the method, as well as other information about the current method call. Implementing the Interceptor is the hard part. The next step is easy.

APPLYING THE INTERCEPTOR INSIDE THE COMPOSITION ROOT USING PURE DI

The following listing shows how you can incorporate the CircuitBreakerInterceptor into your COMPOSITION ROOT.

Listing 11.3   Incorporating the Interceptor into the COMPOSITION ROOT

```
var generator =
    new Castle.DynamicProxy.ProxyGenerator();

var timeout = TimeSpan.FromMinutes(1);

var breaker = new CircuitBreaker(timeout);

var interceptor =
    new CircuitBreakerInterceptor(breaker);

var wcfRepository = new WcfProductRepository();

IProductRepository repository = generator
    .CreateInterfaceProxyWithTarget<IProductRepository>(
        wcfRepository,
        interceptor);
```

Castle's **ProxyGenerator** can generate Proxy types at runtime.[1]

The Interceptor accepts an instance of **ICircuitBreaker** in its constructor using CONSTRUCTOR INJECTION.

Creates the real **IProductRepository** instance

Requests that Castle creates a Decorator (the Proxy) based on the **IProductRepository** interface and wraps it around both the original Repository instance and the newly created Interceptor

TIP   For good performance, `Castle.DynamicProxy.ProxyGenerator` should typically be created once and cached for the lifetime of the application.

This example shows that, although Castle is in control of the construction of the `IProductRepository` Decorator and the injection of its DEPENDENCIES, you can still bootstrap your application using PURE DI. In the next section, we'll analyze dynamic INTERCEPTION and discuss its advantages and disadvantages.

11.1.2 *Analysis of dynamic INTERCEPTION*

When we compare the tool-based AOP approach of dynamic INTERCEPTION to the *AOP by design* approach discussed in the previous chapter, we find a number of similarities between the two:

- Each enables you to address CROSS-CUTTING CONCERNS when you program against ABSTRACTIONS.
- As with plain old Decorators, Interceptors can use CONSTRUCTOR INJECTION, which makes them DI-friendly and decoupled from the code they're decorating. These characteristics allow both your business code and your aspects to be easily tested.
- Aspects can be centralized in the COMPOSITION ROOT, which prevents code duplication, and in case your Visual Studio solution contains multiple applications, it allows the aspects to be applied in one COMPOSITION ROOT, but not the other.

Despite these similarities, there are some differences that make dynamic INTERCEPTION less than ideal. Table 11.1 summarizes the downsides, which we'll discuss next.

---

[1] *Proxy* is Castle's terminology for a Decorator.

Table 11.1   Disadvantages of dynamic INTERCEPTION

Disadvantage	Summary
Loss of compile-time support.	INTERCEPTION code tends to be more complicated than a Decorator, which makes it harder to read and maintain.
Aspects are tighly coupled to the tooling.	This coupling makes it harder to test and forces the Interceptor to be part of the COMPOSITION ROOT in order to prevent other assemblies from requiring a DEPENDENCY on the dynamic INTERCEPTION library.
Not universally applicable.	Aspects can only be applied at the boundaries of methods that are virtual or abstract, such as methods that are part of an interface definition.
Doesn't fix underlying design problems.	You still end up with a system that's only marginally more maintainable than the existing design and considerably less maintainable than a more SOLID-based design.

LOSS OF COMPILE-TIME SUPPORT

Compared to plain old Decorators, dynamic INTERCEPTION involves a fair deal of runtime reflection calls any time an Interceptor is used. With Castle, for instance, the `IInvocation` interface contains an `Arguments` property that returns an array of `object` instances that contains the list of method arguments. Reading and changing those values involves casting and boxing in case of value types like integer and boolean. From a performance perspective, this constant burden of reflection will be, for the most part, negligible. Your typical I/O operations, such as database reads and writes, cost orders of magnitude more.

This use of reflection, however, does complicate the Interceptors you write. When handling the list of method arguments and return types, you'll have to write the proper casting and type checking, and possibly communicate casting errors more effectively. An Interceptor, therefore, tends to be more complicated than a Decorator, which makes it harder to read and maintain.

ASPECTS ARE STRONGLY COUPLED TO TOOLING

Compared to plain old Decorators, the Interceptors you write with dynamic INTER-CEPTION are strongly coupled to the INTERCEPTION library you use. The `Circuit-BreakerInterceptor` of listing 11.2 is a good example of this. This Interceptor implements `Castle.DynamicProxy.IInterceptor` and makes use of the `Castle .DynamicProxy.IInvocation` ABSTRACTION.

Although less pervasive than compile-time weaving, as you'll see in section 11.2, this leads to all aspects being coupled to a Castle Dynamic Proxy library. This coupling introduces an extra dependency on an external library that needs to be learned, which brings extra costs and risks to the project. We'll explain this in detail in section 12.3.1 .

NOT UNIVERSALLY APPLICABLE

Because dynamic INTERCEPTION works by wrapping existing ABSTRACTIONS with dynamically generated Decorators, the behavior of a class can only be extended at the ABSTRACTION's method boundaries. Private methods can't be INTERCEPTED because they're not part of the interface.

This limitation also holds true when practicing AOP by design. With AOP by design, however, this is typically less of a problem, because you design your ABSTRACTIONS in such a way that there's only a need to apply aspects at the boundaries of the ABSTRACTIONS.[2] When you apply dynamic INTERCEPTION, on the other hand, you typically accept the status quo because, if you didn't, you'd end up practicing AOP by design.

IT DOESN'T FIX UNDERLYING DESIGN PROBLEMS

In chapter 10, we extensively discussed the design problems that existed with the big IProductService interface and how they could be fixed by applying SOLID principles. As discussed, these problems have a bigger impact on the system beyond any issues regarding CROSS-CUTTING CONCERNS.

You can use dynamic INTERCEPTION, however, when you accept the status quo of the application's current design. You want to be able to apply CROSS-CUTTING CONCERNS without having to apply large refactorings. The disadvantage of this is that you only solve part of the problem. You'll still end up with a system that's only marginally more maintainable than the existing design and considerably less maintainable than a more SOLID-based design This is because dynamic INTERCEPTION only considers the application of CROSS-CUTTING CONCERNS — not other parts of your code.

Applying dynamic INTERCEPTION requires you to program to interfaces and to use the DI patterns from chapter 4. Another form of AOP that doesn't require programming to interfaces is compile-time weaving. This may sound attractive at first, but as we'll discuss next, it's a DI anti-pattern.

11.2 Compile-time weaving

When we as developers write C# code, the C# compiler transforms our code to Microsoft Intermediate Language (IL). IL is read by the Common Language Runtime (CLR) Just-In-Time (JIT) compiler and is translated on the spot to machine instructions for execution by the CPU.[3] You'll most likely be familiar with the basics of this process.

Compile-time weaving is a common AOP technique that alters this compilation process. It uses special tools to read a compiled assembly produced by our (C#) compiler, modifies it, and writes it back to disk, effectively replacing the original assembly. Figure 11.3 shows this process.

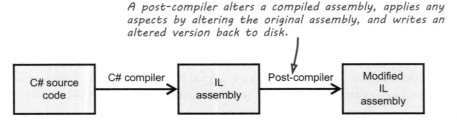

A post-compiler alters a compiled assembly, applies any aspects by altering the original assembly, and writes an altered version back to disk.

Figure 11.3 Compile-time weaving process

---

[2] In fact, we consider the need to INTERCEPT private methods a code smell.

[3] This is a simplification; in some environments, IL is interpreted rather than JIT compiled.

Altering an originally compiled assembly in a post-compilation process is done with the intention of weaving aspects into the original source code, as shown in figure 11.4.

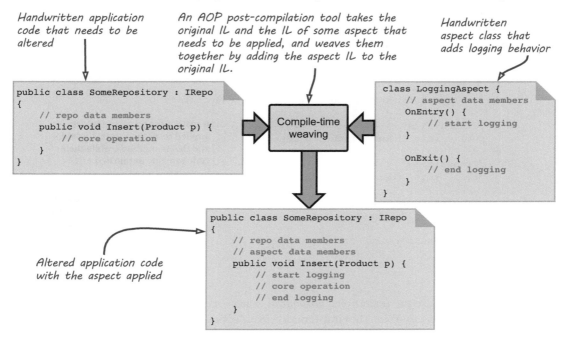

Figure 11.4 Compile-time weaving, visualized

But, as alluring as it may seem at first, when applied to VOLATILE DEPENDENCIES, the use of compile-time weaving comes with issues that make this technique problematic from a maintainability perspective. Because of these downsides, as explained throughout this section, we consider compile-time weaving to be the opposite of DI—it's a DI anti-pattern.

> **IMPORTANT** Compile-time weaving isn't a desirable method of applying AOP for VOLATILE DEPENDENCIES. Favor applying the SOLID principles, or fall back to dynamic INTERCEPTION if that isn't possible.

As we stated in the introduction, we found it important to discuss compile-time weaving even though it's a DI anti-pattern. Compile-time weaving is such a well-known form of AOP that we have to warn against its use. Before we discuss why it's problematic, we'll begin with an example.

11.2.1 *Example: Applying a transaction aspect using compile-time weaving*

Attributes share a trait with Decorators: although they may add or imply a modification of behavior of a member, they leave the signature and original source code unchanged. In section 9.2.3, you applied a security aspect using a Decorator. Compile-time weaving tools, however, let you declare aspects by placing attributes on classes, their members, and even assemblies.

It sounds attractive to use this concept to apply CROSS-CUTTING CONCERNS. Wouldn't it be nice if you could decorate a method or class with a [Transaction] attribute, or even a custom [CircuitBreaker] attribute and, in this way, apply the aspect with a single line of declarative code? The following listing shows how a custom TransactionAttribute aspect attribute gets applied directly to the methods of SqlProductRepository.

Listing 11.4   Applying a [Transaction] aspect attribute to SqlProductRepository

```
public class SqlProductRepository : IProductRepository
{
    [Transaction]
    public void Insert(Product product) ...

    [Transaction]
    public void Update(Product product) ...

    [Transaction]
    public void Delete(Guid id) ...

    public IEnumerable<Product> GetAll() ...

    ...
}
```

A custom aspect attribute gets applied to all the Insert, Update, and Delete methods, while their code remains untouched.

Not all methods require transaction logic, so this method isn't marked with the attribute.

NOTE We use the term *aspect attribute* to denote a custom attribute declared on a class or its members that implements or signifies an aspect.

Although there are many compile-time weaving tools you can choose from, in this section, we'll use PostSharp (https://www.postsharp.net/), which is a commercial tool. The next listing shows the definition of TransactionAttribute using PostSharp.

Listing 11.5   Implementing a TransactionAttribute aspect with PostSharp

```
[AttributeUsage(AttributeTargets.Method |
    AttributeTargets.Class |
    AttributeTargets.Assembly,
    AllowMultiple = false)]
[PostSharp.Serialization.PSerializable]
[PostSharp.Extensibility.MulticastAttributeUsage(
    MulticastTargets.Method,
    TargetMemberAttributes =
        MulticastAttributes.Instance |
        MulticastAttributes.Static)]
public class TransactionAttribute
    : PostSharp.Aspects.OnMethodBoundaryAspect
{

    public override void OnEntry(
        MethodExecutionArgs args)
    {
        args.MethodExecutionTag =
            new TransactionScope();
    }
```

Required attributes for PostSharp aspects

By inheriting from the PostSharp OnMethodBoundaryAspect attribute, you can apply the aspect to the boundary of a decorated method, just as you would do with a Decorator.

Implements the aspect by overriding the OnEntry, OnSuccess, and OnExit methods

```
public override void OnSuccess(
    MethodExecutionArgs args)
{
    var scope = (TransactionScope)
        args.MethodExecutionTag;
    scope.Complete();
}

public override void OnExit(
    MethodExecutionArgs args)
{
    var scope = (TransactionScope)
        args.MethodExecutionTag;
    scope.Dispose();
}
}
```

Implements the aspect by overriding the OnEntry, OnSuccess, and OnExit methods

Because you want to wrap a transaction around some arbitrary piece of code, you need to override three of the methods of OnMethodBoundaryAspect—namely, OnEntry, OnSuccess, and OnExit. During OnEntry, you create a new TransactionScope, and during OnExit, you dispose of the scope. OnExit is guaranteed to be called. PostSharp will wrap its call in a finally block. Only when the wrapped operation succeeds will you want to invoke the Complete method. That's why you implement this in the OnSuccess method. You make use of the MethodExecutionTag property to transfer the created TransactionScope from method to method.

NOTE For a discussion on TransactionScope, see section 10.3.3.

While looking at listing 11.4 in isolation, you might find these attributes attractive, but if you compare the code in listing 11.5 to the same aspect in a Decorator (listing 10.15), there's quite a lot of boilerplate. You need to override multiple methods, apply all kinds of attributes, and pass state from method to method.

NOTE When comparing the TransactionCommandServiceDecorator<TCommand> of listing 10.15 with the implementation of the PostSharp aspect in listing 11.5, we appreciate how much cleaner a Decorator is to write. Decorators can be written in a way that's more natural for developers. Especially when it comes to writing code that contains catch, finally, or using blocks, a SOLID Decorator—and even the dynamic INTERCEPTION approach—is superior in simplicity and maintainability to compile-time weaving as offered by tools such as PostSharp.

This would perhaps be a small price to pay if this would increase maintainability, but there are other, more limiting issues with compile-time weaving that make it unsuitable as a method to apply VOLATILE DEPENDENCIES as CROSS-CUTTING CONCERNS.

11.2.2 Analysis of compile-time weaving

In relationship to DI, compile-time weaving comes with two specific disadvantages. In this section, we'll discuss these limitations. While there are other downsides to compile-time weaving, the two described in table 11.2 capture the core issue that makes it an undesirable method for DI.

Table 11.2   Disadvantages of compile-time weaving from a DI perspective

Disadvantage	Summary
DI-unfriendly	There's no good way to inject VOLATILE DEPENDENCIES into compile-time weaving aspects. The alternatives cause TEMPORAL COUPLING, CAPTIVE DEPENDENCIES, and Interdependent Tests.
Compile-time coupling	Aspects are woven in at compile time, making it impossible to call code without the aspect applied. This complicates testing and reduces flexibility.

COMPILE-TIME WEAVING ASPECTS ARE DI-UNFRIENDLY

When it comes to applying CROSS-CUTTING CONCERNS, you'll find yourself regularly working with VOLATILE DEPENDENCIES. As you learned in chapter 1, VOLATILE DEPENDENCIES are the focal point of DI. With VOLATILE DEPENDENCIES, your default choice should be to use CONSTRUCTOR INJECTION, because it statically defines the list of required DEPENDENCIES.

Unfortunately, it isn't possible to use CONSTRUCTOR INJECTION with compile-time weaving aspects. Take a look at the next listing, where we try to use CONSTRUCTOR INJECTION with a Circuit Breaker aspect.

BAD CODE

> **Listing 11.6   Injecting a DEPENDENCY into an aspect using CONSTRUCTOR INJECTION**

```
[PostSharp.Serialization.PSerializable]          ◄────┐ Other attributes omitted for brevity
public class CircuitBreakerAttribute
    : OnMethodBoundaryAspect
{
    private readonly ICircuitBreaker breaker;

    public CircuitBreakerAttribute(          ◄───── Attempts to use CONSTRUCTOR INJECTION to
        ICircuitBreaker breaker)                    get the aspect's VOLATILE DEPENDENCY. This
    {                                               won't work, as we show next.
        this.breaker = breaker;
    }

    public override void OnEntry(          Uses the breaker VOLATILE DEPENDENCY
        MethodExecutionArgs args)          inside the OnEntry, OnSuccess, and
    {                                      OnException methods
        this.breaker.Guard();          ◄────
    }

    ...
}
```

This attempt to apply CONSTRUCTOR INJECTION to this aspect class fails miserably. Remember, you're defining an attribute that represents separate code, which will be woven into the methods you'll be working with at compile time. In .NET, attributes can only have primitive types, such as strings and integers, in their constructor.

Even if attributes could have more complex DEPENDENCIES, there'd be no way for you to supply an instance of this aspect with an `ICircuitBreaker` instance, because the aspect is constructed at a completely different time and location from where you'd construct `ICircuitBreaker` instances. Instances of attributes, like the `CircuitBreaker-Attribute`, are created by the .NET runtime, and there's no way for you to influence their creation. You have no means of injecting the DEPENDENCY into the attribute's constructor as part of, for instance, the COMPOSITION ROOT:

```
[CircuitBreakerAttribute(???)]
```
What to inject here? And how?

This issue, however, isn't limited to working with attributes. Even if the AOP framework uses a mechanism other than attributes, its post-compiler weaves the aspect code into your normal code at compile time and makes it part of the assembly's code. Your object graphs, on the other hand, are constructed at runtime as part of the COMPOSITION ROOT. These two models don't mix well. CONSTRUCTOR INJECTION isn't possible with compile-time weaving.

AMBIENT CONTEXT and SERVICE LOCATOR are two workarounds for this issue. Both workarounds are, however, hacks with considerable downsides of their own. For the sake of argument, let's take a look at how to work around the problem using an AMBIENT CONTEXT. The following listing shows the definition of a public static `Breaker` property in the Circuit Breaker aspect.

BAD CODE

> **Listing 11.7 Using a DEPENDENCY inside an aspect using an AMBIENT CONTEXT**

```
public class CircuitBreakerAttribute
    : OnMethodBoundaryAspect
{
    public static ICircuitBreaker Breaker { get; set; }

    public override void OnEntry(
        MethodExecutionArgs args)
    {
        Breaker.Guard();
    }

    ...
}
```

A public static property that lets you set the ICircuitBreaker interface inside the COMPOSITION ROOT when the application starts. This is the AMBIENT CONTEXT anti-pattern.

As you learned in section 5.3.2, among other things, the AMBIENT CONTEXT causes TEMPORAL COUPLING. This means that if you forget to set the `Breaker` property, the application fails with a `NullReferenceException`, because the DEPENDENCY isn't optional.

Further, because your only option is to set the property once during application startup, it needs to be defined as `static`. But this might lead to problems of its own: this could cause the `ICircuitBreaker` to become a CAPTIVE DEPENDENCY, as explained in section 8.4.1.

Such a `static` property causes Interdependent Tests because its value remains in memory when the next test case is executed. It's therefore necessary to perform Fixture Teardown after each and every test.[4] This is something that we must always remember to do—it's easy to forget. For this reason, compile-time weaving aspects that use an AMBIENT CONTEXT to access VOLATILE DEPENDENCIES aren't easy to test.

> **NOTE** You can mitigate CAPTIVE DEPENDENCIES with the use of Factory or Proxy implementations for `ICircuitBreaker`, but we think at this point, you've started to understand the complexity a static property causes.

The other workaround is SERVICE LOCATOR, but compared to AMBIENT CONTEXT, it'd only make things worse. SERVICE LOCATOR exhibits the same problems with Interdependent Tests and TEMPORAL COUPLING. On top of that, its access to an unbound set of VOLATILE DEPENDENCIES makes it non-obvious as to what its DEPENDENCIES are, and it drags along the SERVICE LOCATOR as a redundant DEPENDENCY. Because SERVICE LOCATOR is the worse choice, we spare you an example and jump directly into the second disadvantage of compile-time weaving—coupling at compile time.

COMPILE-TIME WEAVING CAUSES COUPLING AT COMPILE TIME

Although compile-time weaving decouples your *source* code from your aspects, it still causes your *compiled* code to be tightly coupled with the woven aspects. This is a problem, because CROSS-CUTTING CONCERNS often depend on an external system. This problem becomes obvious when you write unit tests, because a unit test must be able to run in isolation. You want to test a class's logic itself without interdependency with its VOLATILE DEPENDENCIES. You don't want your unit test crossing process and network boundaries, because communication with a database, filesystem, or other external system will influence the reliability and performance of your tests. In other words, compile-time woven aspects impact TESTABILITY.

But even with broadly defined integration tests, compile-time weaving will still cause problems. In an integration test, you test a part of the system in integration with other parts. This lowers the level of isolation, but enables you to find out how individual components work when integrated with others. If you were testing `SqlProductRepository`, for instance, it wouldn't make sense to unit test it, because all this Repository does is query the database. You therefore want to test this component's interaction with the database.

But even in that case, you typically wouldn't want to have all aspects applied during testing. The use of a `[CheckAuthorization]` aspect, for instance, might force such a test to go through some sort of login process to verify whether the component can successfully store and retrieve products. It's important to see whether such an authorization aspect works as expected. Having to run this as part of your test setup for every integration test, unfortunately, makes these tests harder to maintain and, possibly, a lot slower.

---

[4]   For more on Fixture Teardown, see Gerard Meszaros, *xUnit Test Patterns: Refactoring Test Code* (Addison-Wesley, 2007), 100.

A funnier problem manifests itself if you also have caching enabled. In such a case, you could write an automated test with the intent to query the database, but never do so because the test code hits the cache. For this reason, you want to have full control over which aspects are applied to which test and when, in case those aspects are related to VOLATILE DEPENDENCIES. Compile-time weaving complicates this tremendously.

COMPILE-TIME WEAVING IS UNSUITABLE FOR USE ON VOLATILE DEPENDENCIES

The aim of DI is to manage VOLATILE DEPENDENCIES by introducing SEAMS into your application. This enables you to centralize the composition of your object graphs inside the COMPOSITION ROOT.

This is the complete opposite of what you achieve when applying compile-time weaving: it causes VOLATILE DEPENDENCIES to be coupled to your code at compile time. This makes it impossible to use proper DI techniques and to safely compose complete object graphs in the application's COMPOSITION ROOT. It's for this reason that we say that compile-time weaving is the opposite of DI — using compile-time weaving on VOLATILE DEPENDENCIES is an anti-pattern.

> **IMPORTANT** We're explicitly talking about the use of compile-time weaving in combination with VOLATILE DEPENDENCIES. From a DI point of view, STABLE DEPENDENCIES aren't that interesting. While you might find value in applying STABLE DEPENDENCIES using compile-time weaving, there's no value in applying VOLATILE DEPENDENCIES using compile-time weaving.

Favor applying SOLID principles, falling back to dynamic INTERCEPTION if that isn't possible. On that note, we can now leave PURE DI behind in part 3 and move on to read about DI CONTAINERS in part 4. There, you'll learn how DI CONTAINERS can fix some of the challenges you might face.

Summary

- Dynamic INTERCEPTION is an ASPECT-ORIENTED PROGRAMMING (AOP) technique that automates the generation of Decorators to be emitted at runtime. Aspects are written as Interceptors, which are injected into a runtime-generated Decorator.
- Dynamic INTERCEPTION exhibits the following disadvantages:
  - Loss of compile-time support.
  - Aspects are strongly coupled to the tooling.
  - Not universally applicable.
  - Doesn't fix underlying design problems.

- To prevent or delay making design changes like the ones we suggested in chapter 10, dynamic INTERCEPTION might be a good temporary solution until its time to start making these kinds of improvements.
- Compile-time weaving is an AOP technique that alters the compilation process. It uses special tools to alter a compiled assembly using IL manipulation. It isn't a desirable method of applying AOP to VOLATILE DEPENDENCIES.

- In relation to DI, compile-time weaving exhibits the following problems:
  - Compile-time weaving aspects are DI-unfriendly.
  - Compile-time weaving causes tight coupling at compile time.

- Favor applying SOLID principles, falling back to dynamic INTERCEPTION if that isn't possible.

Part 4

DI Containers

The previous parts of the book have been about the various principles and patterns that together define DI. As chapter 3 explained, a DI CONTAINER is an optional tool that you can use to implement a lot of the general-purpose infrastructure that you would otherwise have to implement if you were using PURE DI.

Throughout the book, we've kept the discussion container agnostic, which means we've only taught you PURE DI. Don't interpret this as a recommendation of PURE DI per se; rather, we want you to see DI in its purest form, untainted by any particular container's API.

Many excellent DI CONTAINERS are available for the .NET platform. In chapter 12, we'll discuss when you should use one of these containers and when you should stick with PURE DI. The remaining chapters in part 4 cover a selection of three free and open source DI CONTAINERS. In each chapter, we provide detailed coverage of that particular container's API as it relates to the dimensions covered in part 3, as well as various other issues that traditionally cause beginners grief. The containers covered are Autofac (chapter 13), Simple Injector (chapter 14), and Microsoft.Extensions .DependencyInjection (chapter 15).

Given unlimited space and time, we wanted to include all containers, but alas, that wasn't possible. We excluded all but one of the containers covered in the first edition. Those excluded include Castle Windsor, StructureMap, String.NET, Unity, and MEF. For more information on those, grab your copy of the first edition (you get it free with this edition). Also, we considered, but didn't include, Ninject, which is one of the more popular DI CONTAINERS. At the time of writing, there is no .NET Core–compatible version available, which was a criterion for inclusion.

All the containers described are open source projects with fast release cycles. Before we discuss the containers in this part, chapter 12 goes into more detail about what a container is, what it helps you with, and how to decide when to use a DI CONTAINER or stick with using PURE DI.

Because of its market share, we simply couldn't exclude Autofac, even though we covered it in the first edition. Autofac is the most popular DI CONTAINER for .NET. Chapter 13 is dedicated to it. And although we included Microsoft.Extensions .DependencyInjection (MS.DI), we're skeptical of it, because it's limited in functionality. However, we felt obliged to cover it, because many developers are inclined to use the built-in tooling first before switching to third-party tooling. Chapter 15 will explain what MS.DI can and can't do.

Each chapter follows a common template. This may give you a certain sense of déjà vu as you read the same sentence for the third time. We consider it an advantage, because it should make it easy for you to quickly find similar sections across different chapters if you want to compare how a specific feature is addressed across containers.

These chapters are meant as inspiration. If you have yet to pick a favorite DI CONTAINER, you can read through all three chapters to compare them, but you can also just read the one that particularly interests you. The information presented in part 4 was accurate at the time of writing, but always be sure to consult more up-to-date sources as well.

DI Container introduction

In this chapter

- Using configuration files to enable late binding

- Explicitly registering components in a
  DI CONTAINER with CONFIGURATION AS CODE

- Applying Convention over Configuration in a
  DI CONTAINER with AUTO-REGISTRATION

- Choosing between applying PURE DI or using
  a DI CONTAINER

When I (Mark) was a kid, my mother and I would occasionally make ice cream. This didn't happen too often because it required work, and it was hard to get right. Real ice cream is based on a *crème anglaise*, which is a light custard made from sugar, egg yolks, and milk or cream. If heated too much, this mixture curdles. Even if you manage to avoid this, the next phase presents more problems. Left alone in the freezer, the cream mixture crystallizes, so you have to stir it at regular intervals until it becomes so stiff that this is no longer possible. Only then will you have a good, homemade ice cream. Although this is a slow and labor-intensive process, if you want to — and you have the necessary ingredients and equipment—you can use this technique to make ice cream.

Today, some 35 years later, my mother-in-law makes ice cream with a frequency unmatched by myself and my mother at much younger ages—not because she loves making ice cream, but because she uses technology to help her. The technique is still the same, but instead of regularly taking out the ice cream from the freezer and stirring it, she uses an electric ice cream maker to do the work for her (see figure 12.1).

DI is first and foremost a technique, but you can use technology to make things easier. In part 3, we described DI as a technique. Here, in part 4, we take a look at the technology that can be used to support the DI technique. We call this technology DI CONTAINERS.

DEFINITION   A DI CONTAINER is a software library that provides DI functionality and automates many of the tasks involved in OBJECT COMPOSITION, INTERCEPTION, and LIFETIME MANAGEMENT. It's an engine that resolves and manages object graphs.

Figure 12.1   An Italian ice cream maker. As with making ice cream, with better technology, you can accomplish programming tasks more easily and quickly.

In this chapter, we'll look at DI Containers as a concept—how they fit into the overall topic of DI—as well as some patterns and practices concerning their usage. We'll also look at some examples along the way.

This chapter begins with a general introduction to DI Containers, including a description of a concept called Auto-Wiring, followed by a section on various configuration options. You can read about each of these configuration options in isolation, but we think it'd be beneficial to at least read about Configuration as Code before you read about Auto-Registration.

The last section is different. It focuses on the advantages and disadvantages of using DI Containers and helps you decide whether the use of a DI Container is beneficial to you and your applications. We think this an important part that everyone should read, regardless of their experience with DI and DI Containers. This section can be read in isolation, although it would be beneficial to read the sections on Configuration as Code and Auto-Registration first.

The purpose of this chapter is to give you a good understanding of what a DI Container is and how it fits in with the rest of the patterns and principles in this book. In a sense, you can view this chapter as an introduction to part 4 of the book. Here, we'll talk about DI Containers in general, whereas in the following chapters, we'll talk about specific containers and their APIs.

12.1 Introducing DI Containers

A DI Container is a software library that can automate many of the tasks involved in Object Composition, Lifetime Management, and Interception. Although it's possible to write all the required infrastructure code with Pure DI, it doesn't add much value to an application. On the other hand, the task of composing objects is of a general nature and can be resolved once and for all; this is what's known as a *Generic Subdomain.*[1] Given this, using a general-purpose library can make sense. It's not much different than implementing logging or data access; logging application data is the kind of problem that can be addressed by a general-purpose logging library. The same is true for composing object graphs.

In this section, we'll discuss how DI Containers compose object graphs. We'll also show you some examples to give you a general sense of what using a container and an implementation might look like.

12.1.1 Exploring containers' Resolve API

A DI Container is a software library like any other software library. It exposes an API that you can use to compose objects, and composing an object graph is a single method call. DI Containers also require you to configure them prior to composing objects. We'll revisit that in section 12.2.

Here, we'll show you some examples of how DI Containers can resolve object graphs. As examples in this section, we'll use both Autofac and Simple Injector applied

---

[1] Eric J. Evans, *Domain-Driven Design: Tackling Complexity in the Heart of Software* (Addison-Wesley, 2004), 406.

to an ASP.NET Core MVC application. Refer to section 7.3 for more detailed information about how to compose ASP.NET Core MVC applications.

You can use a DI CONTAINER to resolve controller instances. This functionality can be implemented with all three DI CONTAINERS covered in the following chapters, but we'll show only a couple of examples here.

RESOLVING CONTROLLERS WITH VARIOUS DI CONTAINERS

Autofac is a DI CONTAINER with a fairly pattern-conforming API. Assuming you already have an Autofac container instance, you can resolve a controller by supplying the requested type:

```
var controller = (HomeController)container.Resolve(typeof(HomeController));
```

You'll pass `typeof(HomeController)` to the `Resolve` method and get back an instance of the requested type, fully populated with all the appropriate DEPENDENCIES. The `Resolve` method is weakly typed and returns an instance of `System.Object`; this means you'll need to cast it to something more specific, as the example shows.

Many of the DI CONTAINERS have APIs that are similar to Autofac's. The corresponding code for Simple Injector looks nearly identical to Autofac's, even though instances are resolved using the `SimpleInjector.Container` class. With Simple Injector, the previous code would look like this:

```
controller = (HomeController)container.GetInstance(typeof(HomeController));
```

The only real difference is that the `Resolve` method is called `GetInstance`. You can extract a general shape of a DI CONTAINER from these examples.

RESOLVING OBJECT GRAPHS WITH DI CONTAINERS

A DI CONTAINER is an engine that resolves and manages object graphs. Although there's more to a DI CONTAINER than resolving objects, this is a central part of any container's API. The previous examples show that containers have a weakly typed method for that purpose. With variations in names and signatures, that method looks like this:

```
object Resolve(Type serviceType);
```

As the previous examples demonstrate, because the returned instance is typed as `System.Object`, you often need to cast the return value to the expected type before using it. Many DI CONTAINERS also offer a generic version for those cases where you know which type to request at compile time. They often look like this:

```
T Resolve<T>();
```

Instead of supplying a `Type` method argument, such an overload takes a type parameter (`T`) that indicates the requested type. The method returns an instance of `T`. Most containers throw an exception if they can't resolve the requested type.

> **WARNING** The signature of the `Resolve` method is extremely powerful and versatile. You can request an instance of any type and your code still compiles. In fact, the `Resolve` method fits the signature of a SERVICE LOCATOR. As discussed in 5.2, you'll need to exercise care not to use your DI CONTAINER as a SERVICE LOCATOR by calling `Resolve` outside the COMPOSITION ROOT.

If we view the `Resolve` method in isolation, it almost looks like magic. From the compiler's perspective, it's possible to ask it to resolve instances of arbitrary types. How does the container know how to compose the requested type, including all DEPENDENCIES? It doesn't; you'll have to tell it first. You do so using a configuration that maps ABSTRACTIONS to concrete types. We'll return to this topic in section 12.2.

If a container has insufficient configuration to fully compose a requested type, it'll normally throw a descriptive exception. As an example, consider the following `HomeController` we first discussed in listing 3.4. As you might remember, it contains a DEPENDENCY of type `IProductService`:

```
public class HomeController : Controller
{
    private readonly IProductService productService;

    public HomeController(IProductService productService)
    {
        this.productService = productService;
    }

    ...
}
```

With an incomplete configuration, Simple Injector has exemplary exception messages like this one:

> *The constructor of type HomeController contains the parameter with name 'productService'*
> *and type IProductService, which isn't registered. Please ensure IProductService is registered*
> *or change the constructor of HomeController.*

In the previous example, you can see that Simple Injector can't resolve `HomeController`, because it contains a constructor argument of type `IProductService`, but Simple Injector wasn't told which implementation to return when `IProductService` was requested. If the container is correctly configured, it can resolve even complex object graphs from the requested type. If something is missing from the configuration, the container can provide detailed information about what's missing. In the next section, we'll take a closer look at how this is done.

12.1.2 *AUTO-WIRING*

DI CONTAINERS thrive on the static information compiled into all classes. Using reflection, they can analyze the requested class and figure out which DEPENDENCIES are needed.

As explained in section 4.2, CONSTRUCTOR INJECTION is the preferred way of applying DI and, because of this, all DI CONTAINERS inherently understand CONSTRUCTOR INJECTION. Specifically, they compose object graphs by combining their own configuration with the information extracted from the classes' type information. This is called AUTO-WIRING.

> **DEFINITION** AUTO-WIRING is the ability to automatically compose an object graph from maps between ABSTRACTIONS and concrete types by making use of type information supplied by the compiler and the Common Language Runtime (CLR).

Most DI CONTAINERS also understand PROPERTY INJECTION, although some require you to explicitly enable it. Considering the downsides of PROPERTY INJECTION (as explained in section 4.4), this is a good thing. Figure 12.2 describes the general algorithm most DI CONTAINERS follow to AUTO-WIRE an object graph.

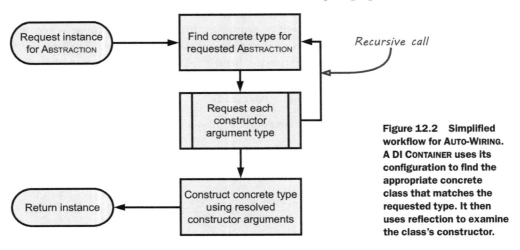

Figure 12.2 Simplified workflow for AUTO-WIRING. A DI CONTAINER uses its configuration to find the appropriate concrete class that matches the requested type. It then uses reflection to examine the class's constructor.

As shown, a DI CONTAINER finds the concrete type for a requested ABSTRACTION. If the constructor of the concrete type requires arguments, a recursive process starts where the DI CONTAINER repeats the process for each argument type until all constructor arguments are satisfied. When this is complete, the container constructs the concrete type while injecting the recursively resolved DEPENDENCIES.

> **NOTE** Most DI CONTAINERS implement optimizations that allow consecutive requests to execute faster. How these optimizations are performed differs from container to container. As we alluded in section 4.2.2, a DI CONTAINER typically doesn't pose significant performance overhead to your application. I/O is the most important bottleneck for an average application, and optimizing I/O generally produces more gains than optimizing OBJECT COMPOSITION.

In section 12.2, we'll take a closer look at how containers can be configured. For now, the most important thing to understand is that at the core of the configuration is a list of mappings between ABSTRACTIONS and their represented concrete classes. That sounds a bit theoretical, so we think an example will be helpful.

12.1.3 *Example: Implementing a simplistic DI CONTAINER that supports AUTO-WIRING*

To demonstrate how AUTO-WIRING works, and to show that there's nothing *magical* about DI CONTAINERS, let's look at a simplistic DI CONTAINER implementation that's able to build complex object graphs using AUTO-WIRING.

WARNING Listing 12.1 is marked as bad code, which, in this context, means that although you can use this code to play around with the concept, you should never use it in a real application. As we'll explain in more detail in section 12.3, you should either use PURE DI or one of the existing commonly used and well-tested DI CONTAINERS. This listing is purely for educational purposes — do not use this at work!

Listing 12.1 shows this simplistic DI CONTAINER implementation. It doesn't support LIFETIME MANAGEMENT, INTERCEPTION, or many other important features. The only supported feature is AUTO-WIRING.

BAD
CODE

Listing 12.1   A simplistic DI CONTAINER that supports AUTO-WIRING

```
public class AutoWireContainer
{                                                          Contains a set of mappings
    Dictionary<Type, Func<object>> registrations =
        new Dictionary<Type, Func<object>>();

    public void Register(
        Type serviceType, Type componentType)
    {                                                      Creates a new registration and adds
        this.registrations[serviceType] =                 the mapping for the service type to
            () => this.CreateNew(componentType);           the registrations dictionary
    }

    public void Register(
        Type serviceType, Func<object> factory)            You can supply the container
    {                                                      with a Func<T> delegate
        this.registrations[serviceType] = factory;         yourself, optionally
    }                                                      bypassing AUTO-WIRING.

    public object Resolve(Type type)
    {
        if(this.registrations.ContainsKey(type))
        {
            return this.registrations[type]();
        }                                                  Resolves a complete object graph

        throw new InvalidOperationException(
            "No registration for " + type);
    }

    private object CreateNew(Type componentType)
    {                                                      Creates a new instance
        var ctor =                                         of a component
            componentType.GetConstructors()[0];

        var dependencies =
            from p in ctor.GetParameters()
            select this.Resolve(p.ParameterType);

        return Activator.CreateInstance(
            componentType, dependencies.ToArray());
    }
}
```

The `AutoWireContainer` contains a set of registrations. A *registration* is a mapping between an ABSTRACTION (the service type) and a component type. The ABSTRACTION is presented as the dictionary's key, whereas its value is a `Func<object>` delegate that allows constructing a new instance of a component that implements the ABSTRACTION. The `Register` method registers a new registration by telling the container which component should be created for a given service type. You only specify which component to create, not how.

The `Register` method adds the mapping for the service type to the `registrations` dictionary. Optionally, the `Register` method can supply the container with a `Func<T>` delegate directly. This bypasses its AUTO-WIRING abilities. It will call the supplied delegate instead.

The `Resolve` methods allows resolving a complete object graph. It gets the `Func<T>` from the `registrations` dictionary for the requested `serviceType`, invokes it, and returns its value. In case there's no registration for the requested type, `Resolve` throws an exception. And finally, `CreateNew` creates a new instance of a component by iterating over the component's constructor parameters and calling back into the container recursively. It does so by calling `Resolve` for each parameter, while supplying the parameter's Type. When all the type's DEPENDENCIES are resolved in this way, it constructs the type itself by using reflection (using the `System.Activator` class).

NOTE   The `AutoWireContainer`'s `CreateNew` method contains the meat of the example in listing 12.1. It uses reflection to analyze the type information to recursively call back into the container to get the type's DEPENDENCIES and once more to create the type itself. `CreateNew` implements AUTO-WIRING.

An `AutoWireContainer` instance can be configured to compose arbitrary object graphs. Back in chapter 3 in listing 3.13, you created a `HomeController` using PURE DI. The next listing repeats that listing from chapter 3. We'll use that as an example to demonstrate the AUTO-WIRING capabilities previously defined in `AutoWireContainer`.

Listing 12.2   Composing an object graph for `HomeController` using PURE DI

```
new HomeController(
    new ProductService(
        new SqlProductRepository(
            new CommerceContext(connectionString)),
        new AspNetUserContextAdapter()));
```

Instead of composing this object graph by hand, as done in the previous listing, you can use the `AutoWireContainer` to register the five required components. To do this, you must map these five components to their appropriate ABSTRACTION. Table 12.1 lists these mappings.

Table 12.1 Mapping types to support AUTO-WIRING of HomeController

ABSTRACTION	Concrete type
HomeController	HomeController
IProductService	ProductService
IProductRepository	SqlProductRepository
CommerceContext	CommerceContext
IUserContext	AspNetUserContextAdapter

Listing 12.3 shows how you can use the AutoWireContainer's Register methods to add the required mappings specified in table 12.1. Note that this listing uses CONFIGURATION AS CODE. We'll discuss CONFIGURATION AS CODE in section 12.2.2.

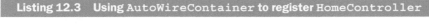

Listing 12.3 Using AutoWireContainer to register HomeController

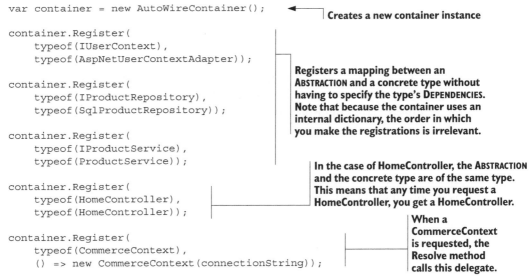

```
var container = new AutoWireContainer();          ◀── Creates a new container instance

container.Register(
    typeof(IUserContext),
    typeof(AspNetUserContextAdapter));

container.Register(                               Registers a mapping between an
    typeof(IProductRepository),                   ABSTRACTION and a concrete type without
    typeof(SqlProductRepository));                having to specify the type's DEPENDENCIES.
                                                  Note that because the container uses an
container.Register(                               internal dictionary, the order in which
    typeof(IProductService),                      you make the registrations is irrelevant.
    typeof(ProductService));
                                                  In the case of HomeController, the ABSTRACTION
container.Register(                               and the concrete type are of the same type.
    typeof(HomeController),                        This means that any time you request a
    typeof(HomeController));                       HomeController, you get a HomeController.

container.Register(                               When a
    typeof(CommerceContext),                      CommerceContext
    () => new CommerceContext(connectionString)); is requested, the
                                                  Resolve method
                                                  calls this delegate.
```

NOTE When a CommerceContext is requested, you create the context by hand, instead of making use of AUTO-WIRING. Hand wiring is required because CommerceContext contains the connectionString parameter, which is a primitive type string.

You might find the mapping for HomeController in table 12.1 and listing 12.3 confusing, because it maps to itself instead of mapping to an ABSTRACTION. This is a common practice, however, especially when dealing with types that are at the top of the object graph, such as MVC controllers.

You saw something similar in listings 4.4, 7.8, and 8.3, where you created a new Home-Controller instance when a HomeController type was requested. The main difference between those listings and listing 12.3 is that the latter uses a DI CONTAINER instead of PURE DI.

> **NOTE** Instead of hand wiring CommerceContext, you could have tried AUTO-WIRING the CommerceContext while adding an extra registration for the connectionString. Because connectionString is of type String, however, this would cause ambiguity. Remember that DI CONTAINERS resolve DEPENDENCIES based on their type, but there could be many configuration values of type String required by application components. When that's the case, the container would be unable to determine which value to use because they'd all have the same type. Hand wiring CommerceContext solves this problem.

Listing 12.3 effectively registered all components required for the composition of an object graph of HomeController. You can now use the configured AutoWireContainer to create a new HomeController.

Listing 12.4   Using AutoWireContainer to resolve a HomeController

```
object controller = container.Resolve(typeof(HomeController));
```

When the AutoWireContainer's Resolve method is called to request a new Home-Controller type, the container will call itself recursively until it has resolved all of its required DEPENDENCIES. After this, a new HomeController instance is created, while supplying the resolved DEPENDENCIES to its constructor. Figure 12.3 shows the recursive process, using a somewhat unconventional representation to visualize recursive calls. The container instance is spread out over four separate vertical time lines. Because there are multiple levels of recursive calls, folding them into one single line, as is the norm with UML sequence diagrams, would be quite confusing.

When the DI CONTAINER receives a request for a HomeController, the first thing it'll do is look up the type in its configuration. HomeController is a concrete class, which you mapped to itself. The container then uses reflection to inspect HomeController's one and only constructor with the following signature:

```
public HomeController(IProductService productService)
```

Because this constructor isn't a parameterless constructor, it needs to repeat the process for the IProductService constructor argument when following the general flow-chart from figure 12.2. The container looks up IProductService in its configuration and finds that it maps to the concrete ProductService class. The single public constructor for ProductService has this signature:

```
public ProductService(
    IProductRepository repository,
    IUserContext userContext)
```

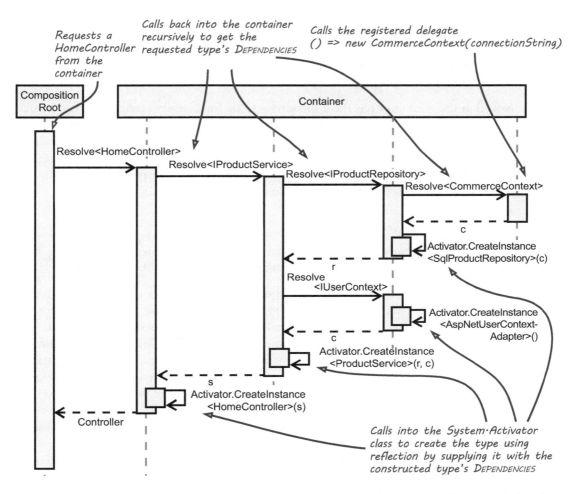

Figure 12.3 The COMPOSITION ROOT requests a `HomeController` from the `container`, which recursively calls back into itself to request `HomeController`'s DEPENDENCIES.

That's still not a parameterless constructor, and now there are two constructor arguments to deal with. The container takes care of each in order, so it starts with the `IProductRepository` interface that, according to the configuration, maps to `SqlProductRepository`. That `SqlProductRepository` has a public constructor with this signature:

```
public SqlProductRepository(CommerceContext context)
```

That's again not a parameterless constructor, so the container needs to resolve `CommerceContext` to satisfy `SqlProductRepository`'s constructor. `CommerceContext`, however, is registered in listing 12.3 using the following delegate:

```
() => new CommerceContext(connectionString)
```

This syntax for defining anonymous functions is also known as a *lambda* expression.

The container calls that delegate, which results in a new CommerceContext instance. This time, no AUTO-WIRING is used.

> **IMPORTANT**   When you start using a DI CONTAINER, it's not required that you abandon hand wiring object graphs altogether.

Now that the container has the appropriate value for CommerceContext, it can invoke the SqlProductRepository constructor. It has now successfully handled the Repository parameter for the ProductService constructor, but it'll need to hold on to that value for a while longer; it also needs to take care of ProductService's userContext constructor parameter. According to the configuration, IUserContext maps to the concrete AspNetUserContextAdapter class, which has this public constructor:

```
public AspNetUserContextAdapter()
```

> **NOTE**   You might recall from listing 3.12 that AspNetUserContextAdapter didn't specify a constructor at all. If you don't specify any constructors on a class, the C# compiler compiles the class using a parameterless public constructor.

Because AspNetUserContextAdapter contains a parameterless constructor, it can be created without having to resolve any DEPENDENCIES. It can now pass the new AspNetUserContextAdapter instance to the ProductService constructor. Together with the SqlProductRepository from before, it now fulfills the ProductService constructor and invokes it via reflection. Finally, it passes the newly created ProductService instance to the HomeController constructor and returns the HomeController instance. Figure 12.4 shows how the general workflow presented in figure 12.2 maps to the AutoWireContainer from listing 12.1.

The advantage of using a DI CONTAINER's AUTO-WIRING capabilities as shown in listing 12.3 rather than using PURE DI as shown in listing 12.2 is that with PURE DI, any change to a component's constructor needs to be reflected in the COMPOSITION ROOT. AUTO-WIRING, on the other hand, makes the COMPOSITION ROOT more resilient to such changes.

For example, let's say you need to add a CommerceContext DEPENDENCY to AspNetUserContextAdapter in order for it to query the database. The following listing shows the change that needs to be made to the COMPOSITION ROOT when you apply PURE DI.

Listing 12.5   COMPOSITION ROOT for the changed AspNetUserContextAdapter

```
new HomeController(
    new ProductService(
        new SqlProductRepository(
            new CommerceContext(connectionString)),
        new AspNetUserContextAdapter(
            new CommerceContext(connectionString))));
```

CommerceContext is now injected into AspNetUserContextAdapter.

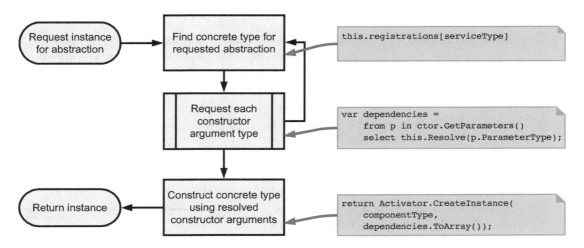

Figure 12.4   Simplified workflow for Auto-Wiring mapped to the code from listing 12.1. The `registrations` dictionary is queried for the concrete type, its constructor parameters get resolved, and the concrete type is created using its resolved Dependencies.

With Auto-Wiring, on the other hand, no changes to the Composition Root are required in this case. AspNetUserContextAdapter is Auto-Wired, and because its new Commerce-Context Dependency was already registered, the container will be able to satisfy the new constructor argument and will happily construct a new AspNetUserContextAdapter.

IMPORTANT   Although Auto-Wiring can decrease the required maintenance to the Composition Root, this still doesn't mean you should always prefer a DI Container over Pure DI. As stated previously, section 12.3 goes into more detail about when Pure DI is better.

This is how Auto-Wiring works, although DI Containers also need to take care of Lifetime Management and, perhaps, address Property Injection as well as other, more specialized, creational requirements.

WARNING   The AutoWireContainer from listing 12.1 will cause a StackOverflowException when there's a Dependency cycle in an object graph.[2] StackOverflowExceptions are problematic because they'll crash the application, making it hard to find out what exactly went wrong. This is one of the many reasons you should always prefer one of the available DI Containers over a home-grown implementation. Most of the modern popular DI Containers detect cycles without causing the process to be terminated.

The salient point is that Constructor Injection statically advertises the Dependency requirements of a class, and DI Containers use that information to Auto-Wire complex object graphs. A container must be configured before it can compose object graphs. Registration of components can be done in various ways.

---

[2]   We discussed Dependency cycles in section 6.3.

12.2 *Configuring DI* CONTAINERS

Although the `Resolve` method is where most of the action happens, you should expect to spend most of your time with a DI CONTAINER's configuration API. Resolving object graphs is, after all, a single method call.

DI CONTAINERS tend to support two or three of the common configuration options shown in figure 12.5. Some don't support configuration files, and others also lack support for AUTO-REGISTRATION, whereas CONFIGURATION AS CODE support is ubiquitous. Most allow you to mix several approaches in the same application. Section 12.2.4 discusses why you'd want to use a mixed approach.

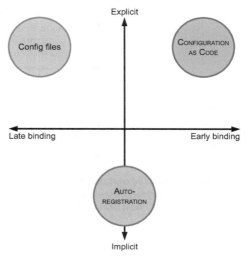

These three configuration options have different characteristics that make them useful in different situations. Both configuration files and CONFIGURATION AS CODE tend to be explicit, because they require you to register each component individually. AUTO-REGISTRATION, on the other hand, is more implicit because it uses conventions to register a set of components by a single rule.

Figure 12.5   The most common ways to configure a DI CONTAINER **shown against dimensions of explicitness and the degree of binding**

When you use CONFIGURATION AS CODE, you compile the container configuration into an assembly, whereas file-based configuration enables you to support late binding, where you can change the configuration without recompiling the application. In that dimension, AUTO-REGISTRATION falls somewhere in the middle, because you can ask it to scan a single assembly known at compile time or, alternatively, to scan all assemblies in a predefined folder that might be unknown at compile time. Table 12.2 lists the advantages and disadvantages of each option.

Table 12.2   Configuration options

Style	Description	Advantages	Disadvantages
Configuration files	Mappings are specified in configuration files (typically in XML or JSON format)	■ Supports replacement without recompilation	■ No compile-time checks ■ Verbose and brittle
CONFIGURATION AS CODE	Code explicitly determines mappings	■ Compile-time checks ■ High degree of control	■ No support for replacement without recompilation

Style	Description	Advantages	Disadvantages
Auto-Registration	Rules are used to locate suitable components using reflection and to build the mappings.	■ Supports replacement without recompilation ■ Less effort required ■ Helps enforce conventions to make a code base more consistent	■ No compile-time checks ■ Less control ■ May seem more abstract at first

Historically, DI Containers started out with configuration files, which also explains why the older libraries still support this. But this feature has been downplayed in favor of more conventional approaches. That's why more recently developed DI Containers, such as Simple Injector and Microsoft.Extensions.DependencyInjection, don't have any built-in support for file-based configuration.

> **IMPORTANT** You shouldn't go back and reconfigure the container once you've started resolving object graphs—that will only give you grief. This is related to the Register Resolve Release pattern (https://mng.bz/D8Ew).

Although Auto-Registration is the most modern option, it isn't the most obvious place to start. Because of its implicitness, it may seem more abstract than the more explicit options, so instead, we'll cover each option in historical order, starting with configuration files.

12.2.1 Configuring containers with configuration files

When DI Containers first appeared back in the early 2000s, they all used XML as a configuration mechanism—most things did back then. Experience with XML as a configuration mechanism later revealed that this is rarely the best option.

XML tends to be verbose and brittle. When you configure a DI Container in XML, you identify various classes and interfaces, but you have no compiler support to warn you if you misspell something. Even if the class names are correct, there's no guarantee that the required assembly is going to be in the application's probing path.

> **NOTE** In recent years, JSON has also become a popular way of expressing configurations. The format is cleaner and easier to read than XML, but it still exhibits the same characteristics: it's as brittle and verbose as XML.

To add insult to injury, the expressiveness of XML is limited compared to that of plain code. This sometimes makes it hard or impossible to express certain configurations in a configuration file that are otherwise trivial to express in code. In listing 12.3, for instance, you registered the CommerceContext using a lambda expression. Such a lambda expression can be expressed in neither XML nor JSON.

The advantage of configuration files, on the other hand, is that you can change the behavior of the application without recompilation. This is valuable if you develop software that ships to thousands of customers, because it gives them a way to customize the application. But if you write an internal application or a website where you control the deployment environment, it's often easier to recompile and redeploy the application when you need to change the behavior.

> **IMPORTANT**   Configuration files are as much a part of your COMPOSITION ROOT as is CONFIGURATION AS CODE and AUTO-REGISTRATION. Using configuration files, therefore, doesn't make your COMPOSITION ROOT smaller, it just moves it. Use configuration files only for those parts of your DI configuration that require late binding. Prefer CONFIGURATION AS CODE or AUTO-REGISTRATION in all other parts of your configuration.

A DI CONTAINER is often configured with files by pointing it to a particular configuration file. The following example uses Autofac as an example.

> **NOTE**   Because Autofac is the only DI CONTAINER covered in this book that has built-in support for configuration files, it makes sense to use it for an example.

In this example, you'll configure the same classes as in section 12.1.3. A large part of the task is to apply the configuration outlined in table 12.1, but you must also supply a similar configuration to support composition of the `HomeController` class. The following listing shows the configuration necessary to get the application up and running.

Listing 12.6   Configuring Autofac with a JSON configuration file

```
{
  "defaultAssembly": "Commerce.Web",          defaultAssembly helps write
  "components": [                              types in a shorter fashion.
  {
    "services": [{
      "type":
        "Commerce.Domain.IUserContext, Commerce.Domain"
    }],                                                       Simple mapping
    "type":
      "Commerce.Web.AspNetUserContextAdapter"
  },
  {
    "services": [{
      "type": "Commerce.Domain.IProductRepository, Commerce.Domain"
    }],
    "type": "Commerce.SqlDataAccess.SqlProductRepository, Commerce.
      SqlDataAccess"
  },
  {
    "services": [{
      "type": "Commerce.Domain.IProductService, Commerce.Domain"
    }],
    "type":
      "Commerce.Domain.ProductService, Commerce.Domain"    If a type maps to
  },                                                       itself, the services
  {                                                        array can be
    "type": "Commerce.Web.Controllers.HomeController"      omitted.
  },
```

```
{
  "type": "Commerce.SqlDataAccess.CommerceContext,
    ➥Commerce.SqlDataAccess",
  "parameters": {
    "connectionString":
      "Server=.;Database=MaryCommerce;Trusted_
    ➥Connection=True;"
  }
}]
}
```

Specifies a connection string as the value to a constructor parameter named connectionString

In this example, if you don't specify an assembly-qualified type name in a type or interface reference, `defaultAssembly` will be assumed to be the default assembly. For a simple mapping, full type names must be used, including namespace and assembly name. Because `AspNetUserContextAdapter` excluded the name of the assembly, Autofac looks for it in the `Commerce.Web` assembly, which you defined as the `defaultAssembly`.

As you can see from even this simple code listing, JSON configuration tends to be quite verbose. Simple mappings like the one from the `IUserContext` interface to the `AspNetUserContextAdapter` class require quite a lot of text in the form of brackets and fully qualified type names.

As you may recall, `CommerceContext` takes a connection string as input, so you need to specify how the value of this string is found. By adding `parameters` to a mapping, you can specify values by their parameter name—in this case, `connectionString`. Loading the configuration into the container is done with the following code.

Listing 12.7 Reading configuration files using Autofac

```
var builder = new Autofac.ContainerBuilder();

IConfigurationRoot configuration =
    new ConfigurationBuilder()
    .AddJsonFile("autofac.json")
    .Build();

builder.RegisterModule(
    new Autofac.Configuration.ConfigurationModule(
        configuration));
```

Allows adding mapping between ABSTRACTIONS and concrete types

Loads the autofac.json configuration file from listing 12.6 using .NET Core's configuration system

Wraps the created configuration in an Autofac module that processes the configuration file and maps the components to registrations in Autofac

Autofac is the only DI CONTAINER included in this book that supports configuration files, but there are other DI CONTAINERS not covered here that continue to support configuration files. The exact schema is different for each container, but the overall structure tends to be similar, because you need to map an ABSTRACTION to an implementation.

WARNING   As your application grows in size and complexity, so will your configuration file. It can grow to become a real stumbling block. This is because it models coding concepts such as classes, parameters, and such, but without the benefits of the compiler, debugging options, and so forth. Configuration files tend to become brittle and opaque to errors, so only use this approach when you need late binding.

Configuration files don't scale

I (Steven) once worked for a big client that maintained a product that contained over a hundred man-years of code. DI was applied ubiquitously, which was an absolute plus. To support OBJECT COMPOSITION, however, they used Spring.NET as their DI CONTAINER, which solely supported XML configuration files at the time. To make matters worse, the version of Spring.NET they used didn't support AUTO-WIRING. This not only required every mapping to be explicitly defined in big XML files, but every constructor DEPENDENCY needed to be specified too. With over a dozen teams working on that code base, these Spring.NET XML configuration files were not only verbose, brittle, and maintenance heavy, they also caused merge conflicts on a regular basis.

Because of the verbosity, fragility, lack of compiler support, and bad performance of those XML configuration files, many development hours were wasted on a daily basis, which was something the developers all realized. They'd have been better off if they had decided to practice PURE DI instead from the beginning.[3] In their case, PURE DI wouldn't by itself have solved their merge conflicts, but at least the compiler would help catch most of the errors earlier.

TIP   Although configuration files can work in a small application, or when used for small portions of your application, they don't scale. Avoid using configuration files as your default method of DI configuration. As we'll discuss in section 12.3, use either PURE DI or AUTO-REGISTRATION.

Don't let the absence of support for handling configuration files influence your choice of a DI CONTAINER too much. As described previously, only true late-bound components should be defined in configuration files, which will unlikely be more than a handful. Even with absence of support from your container, types can be loaded from configuration files in a few simple statements, as shown in listing 1.2.

Because of the disadvantages of verbosity and brittleness, you should prefer the other alternatives for configuring containers. CONFIGURATION AS CODE is similar to configuration files in granularity and concept, but obviously uses code instead of configuration files.

---

[3]   Their choice of XML-based OBJECT COMPOSITION wasn't weird, considering that at the time development for the product started, everybody was using XML.

12.2.2 Configuring containers using CONFIGURATION AS CODE

Perhaps the easiest way to compose an application is to hard code the construction of object graphs. This may seem to go against the whole spirit of DI, because it determines the concrete implementations that should be used for all ABSTRACTIONS at compile time. But if done in a COMPOSITION ROOT, it only violates one of the benefits listed in table 1.1, namely, late binding.

The benefit of late binding is lost if DEPENDENCIES are hard-coded, but, as we mentioned in chapter 1, this may not be relevant for all types of applications. If your application is deployed in a limited number of instances in a controlled environment, it can be easier to recompile and redeploy the application if you need to replace modules:

> *I often think that people are over-eager to define configuration files. Often a programming language makes a straightforward and powerful configuration mechanism.*[4]
>
> MARTIN FOWLER

When you use CONFIGURATION AS CODE, you explicitly state the same discrete mappings as when you use configuration files—only you use code instead of XML or JSON.

DEFINITION In the context of DI CONTAINERS, CONFIGURATION AS CODE allows the container's configuration to be stored as source code. Each mapping between an ABSTRACTION and a particular implementation is expressed explicitly and directly in code.

All modern DI CONTAINERS fully support CONFIGURATION AS CODE as the successor to configuration files; in fact, most of them present this as the default mechanism, with configuration files as an optional feature. As stated previously, some don't even offer support for configuration files at all. The API exposed to support CONFIGURATION AS CODE differs from DI CONTAINER to DI CONTAINER, but the overall goal is still to define discrete mappings between ABSTRACTIONS and concrete types.

TIP Prefer CONFIGURATION AS CODE over configuration files unless you need late binding. The compiler can be helpful, and the Visual Studio build system automatically copies all required assemblies to the output folder. And if you do need late binding, only use a configuration file for the parts of the configuration that need to be late bound, which is typically just a tiny subset of the types in the entire application.

Let's take a look how to configure the e-commerce application using CONFIGURATION AS CODE with Microsoft.Extensions.DependencyInjection. For this, we'll use an example that configures the sample e-commerce application with code.

---

[4] Martin Fowler, "Inversion of Control Containers and the Dependency Injection pattern," 2004, https://martinfowler.com/articles/injection.html.

In section 12.2.1, you saw how to configure the sample e-commerce application with configuration files using Autofac. We could also demonstrate CONFIGURATION AS CODE with Autofac, but, to make this chapter a bit more interesting, we'll instead use Microsoft.Extensions.DependencyInjection in this example. Using Microsoft's configuration API, you can express the configuration from listing 12.6 more compactly, as shown here.

Listing 12.8   Configuring Microsoft.Extensions.DependencyInjection with code

```
var services = new ServiceCollection();

services.AddSingleton<
    IUserContext,
    AspNetUserContextAdapter>();

services.AddTransient<
    IProductRepository,
    SqlProductRepository>();

services.AddTransient<
    IProductService,
    ProductService>();

services.AddTransient<HomeController>();

services.AddScoped<CommerceContext>(
    p => new CommerceContext(connectionString));
```

Defines mappings between ABSTRACTIONS and implementations

Adds AUTO-WIRED mappings between ABSTRACTIONS and concrete types

Overload that takes the concrete type as a generic type argument

Overload that allows mapping an ABSTRACTION to a Func<T> delegate

ServiceCollection is Microsoft's equivalent to Autofac's ContainerBuilder, which defines the mappings between ABSTRACTIONS and implementations. The Add-Transient, AddScoped, and AddSingleton methods are used to add AUTO-WIRED mappings between ABSTRACTIONS and concrete types for their specific LIFESTYLE. These methods are generic, which results in more condensed code with the additional benefit of getting some extra compile-time checking. In case a concrete type maps to itself, instead of having an ABSTRACTION mapping to a concrete type, there's a convenient overload that just takes in the concrete type as a generic type argument. And, just as with the AutoWireContainer example of listing 12.1, the API of this DI CONTAINER contains an overload that allows mapping an ABSTRACTION to a Func<T> delegate.

> **NOTE** If this looks familiar, that isn't a surprise: it's conceptually almost identical to our sample code in listing 12.3. There, we established a proof of concept for how AUTO-WIRING is accomplished.

In listing 12.8, we took the liberty of demonstrating the registration of components using the three common lifestyles: SINGLETON, TRANSIENT, and SCOPED. The following chapters show how to configure lifestyles for each container in more detail.

Compare this code with listing 12.6, and notice how much more compact it is—even though it does the exact same thing. A simple mapping like the one from IProductService to ProductService is expressed with a single method call.

Not only is CONFIGURATION AS CODE much more compact than configurations expressed in a configuration file, it also enjoys compiler support. The type arguments used in listing 12.8 represent real types that the compiler checks. Generics go even a step further, because the use of generic type constraints such as Microsoft's API applies allows the compiler to check whether the supplied concrete type matches the ABSTRACTION. If a conversion isn't possible, the code won't compile.

Although CONFIGURATION AS CODE is safe and easy to use, it still requires more maintenance than you might like. Every time you add a new type to an application, you must also remember to register it—and many registrations end up being similar. AUTO-REGISTRATION addresses this issue.

12.2.3 *Configuring containers by convention using AUTO-REGISTRATION*

Considering the registrations of listing 12.8, it might be completely fine to have these few lines of code in your project. When a project grows, however, so will the amount of registrations required to set up the DI CONTAINER. In time, you're likely to see many similar registrations appear. They'll typically follow a common pattern. The following listing shows how these registrations can start to look somewhat repetitive.

> **Listing 12.9   Repetition in registrations when using CONFIGURATION AS CODE**

```
services.AddTransient<IProductRepository, SqlProductRepository>();
services.AddTransient<ICustomerRepository, SqlCustomerRepository>();
services.AddTransient<IOrderRepository, SqlOrderRepository>();
services.AddTransient<IShipmentRepository, SqlShipmentRepository>();
services.AddTransient<IImageRepository, SqlImageRepository>();

services.AddTransient<IProductService, ProductService>();
services.AddTransient<ICustomerService, CustomerService>();
services.AddTransient<IOrderService, OrderService>();
services.AddTransient<IShipmentService, ShipmentService>();
services.AddTransient<IImageService, ImageService>();
```

Repeatedly writing registration code like that violates the DRY principle. It also seems like an unproductive piece of infrastructure code that doesn't add much value to the application. You can save time and make fewer errors if you can automate the registration of components, assuming those components follow some sort of convention. Many DI CONTAINERS provide AUTO-REGISTRATION capabilities that let you introduce your own conventions and apply *Convention over Configuration*.

> **DEFINITION** AUTO-REGISTRATION is the ability to automatically register components in a container by scanning one or more assemblies for implementations of desired ABSTRACTIONS, based on a certain convention. AUTO-REGISTRATION is sometimes referred to as *Batch Registration* or *Assembly Scanning*.

Convention over Configuration

An increasingly popular architectural model is the concept of *Convention over Configuration*. Instead of writing and maintaining a lot of configuration code, you can agree on conventions that affect the code base. The way ASP.NET Core MVC finds controllers based on controller names is a great example of a simple convention:[5]

- A request comes in for a controller named *Home*.
- The default controller factory searches through a list of well-known namespaces for a class named `HomeController`. If it finds such a class, it's a match.
- The default controller factory forwards the type of the class to the controller activator, which constructs an instance of the controller.

The convention here is that a controller must be named *[ControllerName]Controller*.

Conventions can be applied to more than ASP.NET Core MVC controllers. The more conventions you add, the more you can automate the various parts of the container configuration.

TIP   Convention over Configuration has more advantages than just supporting DI configuration. It makes your code more consistent, because it automatically works, as long as you follow your conventions.

In reality, you may need to combine AUTO-REGISTRATION with CONFIGURATION AS CODE or configuration files, because you may not be able to fit every single component into a meaningful convention. But the more you can move your code base towards conventions, the more maintainable it will be.

Autofac supports AUTO-REGISTRATION, but we thought it would be more interesting to use yet another DI CONTAINER to configure the sample e-commerce application using conventions. Because we like to restrain the examples to the DI CONTAINERS discussed in this book, and because Microsoft.Extensions.DependencyInjection doesn't have any AUTO-REGISTRATION facilities, we'll use Simple Injector to illustrate this concept.

Looking back at listing 12.9, you'll likely agree that the registrations of the various data access components are repetitive. Can we express some sort of convention around them? All five concrete Repository types of listing 12.9 share some characteristics:

- They're all defined in the same assembly.
- Each concrete class has a name that ends with *Repository*.
- Each implements a single interface.

It seems that an appropriate convention would express these similarities by scanning the assembly in question and registering all classes that match the convention. Even though Simple Injector does support AUTO-REGISTRATION, its AUTO-REGISTRATION

---

[5]   The description of this convention for finding MVC controllers is simplified. In reality, there's more to it (see https://mng.bz/lED8).

API focuses around the registration of groups of types that share the same interface. Its API, by itself, doesn't allow you to express this convention, because there's no single interface that describes this group of repositories.

At first, this omission might seem rather awkward, but defining a custom LINQ query on top of .NET's reflection API is typically easy to write, provides more flexibility, and prevents you from having to learn another API—assuming you're familiar with LINQ and .NET's reflection API. The following listing shows such a convention using a LINQ query.

Listing 12.10   Convention for scanning repositories using Simple Injector

```
var assembly =
    typeof(SqlProductRepository).Assembly;        │  Selects an assembly for the convention

var repositoryTypes =
    from type in assembly.GetTypes()                  Defines a LINQ query that locates
    where !type.Abstract                              all types in the assembly that fit
    where type.Name.EndsWith("Repository")            the criterion of being concrete
    select type;                                      and ending with Repository

foreach (Type type in repositoryTypes)
{                                                     Iterates over the LINQ query
    container.Register(                               to register each type
        type.GetInterfaces().Single(), type);
}
```

Each of the classes that make it through the `where` filters during iteration should be registered against their interface. For example, because `SqlProductRepository`'s interface is an `IProductRepository`, it'll end up as a mapping from `IProductRepository` to `SqlProductRepository`.

This particular convention scans the assembly that contains the data access components. You could get a reference to that assembly in many ways, but the easiest way is to pick a representative type, such as `SqlProductRepository`, and get the assembly from that, as shown in listing 12.10. You could also have chosen a different class or found the assembly by name.

> **NOTE**   With Microsoft.Extensions.DependencyInjection, the code of the convention of listing 12.10 would be almost identical. Only the body of the `foreach` loop would be different, because that's the only place the DI CONTAINER's API is called.

Comparing this convention against the four registrations in listing 12.9, you may think that the benefits of this convention look negligible. Indeed, because there are only four data access components in the current example, the amount of code statements has increased with the convention. But this convention scales much better. Once you write it, it handles hundreds of components without any additional effort.

You can also address the other mappings from listings 12.6 and 12.8 with conventions, but there wouldn't be much value in doing so. As an example, you can register all services with this convention:

```
var assembly = typeof(ProductService).Assembly;

var serviceTypes =
    from type in assembly.GetTypes()
    where !type.Abstract
    where type.Name.EndsWith("Service")
    select type;

foreach (Type type in serviceTypes)
{
    container.Register(type.GetInterfaces().Single(), type);
}
```

This convention scans the identified assembly for all concrete classes where the name ends with *Service* and registers each type against the interface it implements. This effectively registers `ProductService` against the `IProductService` interface, but because you currently don't have any other matches for this convention, nothing much is gained. It's only when more services are added, as indicated in listing 12.9, that it starts to make sense to formulate a convention.

Defining conventions by hand with the use of LINQ might make sense for types all deriving from their own interface, as you've seen previously with the repositories. But when you start to register types that are based on a generic interface, as we extensively discussed in section 10.3.3, this strategy starts to break down rather quickly—querying generic types through reflection is typically not a pleasant thing to do.[6]

That's why Simple Injector's AUTO-REGISTRATION API is built around the registration of types based on a generic ABSTRACTION, such as the `ICommandService<TCommand>` interface from listing 10.12. Simple Injector allows the registration of all `ICommandService<TCommand>` implementations to be done in a single line of code.

> **Listing 12.11** AUTO-REGISTERING implementations based on a generic ABSTRACTION

```
Assembly assembly = typeof(AdjustInventoryService).Assembly;

container.Register(typeof(ICommandService<>), assembly);
```

NOTE `ICommandService<>` is the C# syntax for specifying the open-generic version, accomplished by omitting the `TCommand` generic type argument.

By supplying a list of assemblies to one of its `Register` overloads, Simple Injector iterates through these assemblies to find any non-generic, concrete types that implement `ICommandService<TCommand>`, while registering each type by its specific

---

[6] You'll have to find implementations of the generic interface, consider types that implement multiple interfaces, register all Decorators for all implementations, and so forth.

`ICommandService<TCommand>` interface. This has the generic type argument `TCommand` filled in with an actual type.

> **DEFINITION** A generic type that has its generic type arguments filled in (for example, `ICommandService<AdjustInventory>`), is called a *closed generic*. Likewise, when you have just the generic type definition itself (for example, `ICommandService<TCommand>`), such a type is referred to as *open generic*.

In an application with four `ICommandService<TCommand>` implementations, the previous API call would be equivalent to the following CONFIGURATION AS CODE listing.

CODE SMELL

Listing 12.12   Registering implementations using CONFIGURATION AS CODE

```
container.Register(typeof(ICommandService<AdjustInventory>),
    typeof(AdjustInventoryService));
container.Register(typeof(ICommandService<UpdateProductReviewTotals>),
    typeof(UpdateProductReviewTotalsService));
container.Register(typeof(ICommandService<UpdateHasDiscountsApplied>),
    typeof(UpdateHasDiscountsAppliedService));
container.Register(typeof(ICommandService<UpdateHasTierPricesProperty>),
    typeof(UpdateHasTierPricesPropertyService));
```

Iterating a list of assemblies to find appropriate types, however, isn't the only thing you can achieve with Simple Injector's AUTO-REGISTRATION API. Another powerful feature is the registration of generic Decorators, like the ones you saw in listings 10.15, 10.16, and 10.19. Instead of manually composing the hierarchy of Decorators, as you did in listing 10.21, Simple Injector allows Decorators to be applied using its `RegisterDecorator` method overloads.

Listing 12.13   Registering generic Decorators using AUTO-REGISTRATION

```
container.RegisterDecorator(
    typeof(ICommandService<>),
    typeof(AuditingCommandServiceDecorator<>));

container.RegisterDecorator(
    typeof(ICommandService<>),
    typeof(TransactionCommandServiceDecorator<>));

container.RegisterDecorator(
    typeof(ICommandService<>),
    typeof(SecureCommandServiceDecorator<>));
```

> **RegisterDecorator is supplied with the open-generic ICommandService<TCommand> service type and the open-generic implementation for the Decorator. Using this information, Simple Injector wraps every ICommandService<TCommand> that it resolves with the appropriate Decorators.**

Simple Injector applies Decorators in order of registration, which means that, in respect to listing 12.13, the auditing Decorator is wrapped using the transaction Decorator, and the transaction Decorator is wrapped with the security Decorator, resulting in an object graph identical to the one shown in listing 10.21.

Registration of open-generic types can be seen as a form of AUTO-REGISTRATION because a single method call to `RegisterDecorator` can result in a Decorator being applied to many registrations.[7] Without this form of AUTO-REGISTRATION for generic Decorator classes, you'd be forced to register each closed version of each Decorator for each closed `ICommandService<TCommand>` implementation individually, as the following listing shows.

BAD CODE

Listing 12.14   **Registering generic Decorators using CONFIGURATION AS CODE**

```
container.RegisterDecorator(
    typeof(ICommandService<AdjustInventory>),
    typeof(AuditingCommandServiceDecorator<AdjustInventory>));
container.RegisterDecorator(
    typeof(ICommandService<AdjustInventory>),
    typeof(TransactionCommandServiceDecorator<AdjustInventory>));
container.RegisterDecorator(
    typeof(ICommandService<AdjustInventory>),
    typeof(SecureCommandServiceDecorator<AdjustInventory>));

container.RegisterDecorator(
    typeof(ICommandService<UpdateProductReviewTotals>),
    typeof(AuditingCommandServiceDecorator<UpdateProductReviewTotals>));
container.RegisterDecorator(
    typeof(ICommandService<UpdateProductReviewTotals>),
    typeof(TransactionCommandServiceDecorator<UpdateProductReviewTotals>));
container.RegisterDecorator(
    typeof(ICommandService<UpdateProductReviewTotals>),
    typeof(SecureCommandServiceDecorator<UpdateProductReviewTotals>));

container.RegisterDecorator(
    typeof(ICommandService<UpdateHasDiscountsApplied>),
    typeof(AuditingCommandServiceDecorator<UpdateHasDiscountsApplied>));
container.RegisterDecorator(
    typeof(ICommandService<UpdateHasDiscountsApplied>),
    typeof(TransactionCommandServiceDecorator<UpdateHasDiscountsApplied>));
container.RegisterDecorator(
    typeof(ICommandService<UpdateHasDiscountsApplied>),
    typeof(SecureCommandServiceDecorator<UpdateHasDiscountsApplied>));
```

. . .   ◀────┐ **Other registrations are omitted for brevity.**

The code in this listing is cumbersome and error prone. Additionally, it would cause an exponential growth of the COMPOSITION ROOT.

> **TIP** The most prominent downside of AUTO-REGISTRATION is that you lose some control. It must be possible to AUTO-WIRE every component that's picked up by the AUTO-REGISTRATION facility. When there's a particular component that requires hand wiring, it should be excluded from AUTO-REGISTRATION to prevent errors.

---

[7] On top of that, there's a lot going on in the background. For instance, if the Decorator contains generic-type constraints, Simple Injector automatically finds out whether the Decorator is applicable to a given registration based on these type constraints. Doing this by hand would be cumbersome and error prone.

In a system that adheres to the SOLID principles, you create many small and focused classes, but existing classes are less likely to change, increasing maintainability. AUTO-REGISTRATION prevents the COMPOSITION ROOT from constantly being updated. It's a powerful technique that has the potential to make the DI CONTAINER invisible. Once appropriate conventions are in place, you may have to modify the container configuration only on rare occasions.

12.2.4 *Mixing and matching configuration approaches*

So far, you've seen three different approaches to configuring a DI CONTAINER:

- Configuration files
- CONFIGURATION AS CODE
- AUTO-REGISTRATION

None of these are mutually exclusive. You can choose to mix AUTO-REGISTRATION with specific mappings of abstract-to-concrete types, and even mix all three approaches to have some AUTO-REGISTRATION, some CONFIGURATION AS CODE, and some of the configuration in configuration files for late binding purposes.

As a rule of thumb, you should prefer AUTO-REGISTRATION as a starting point, complemented by CONFIGURATION AS CODE to handle more special cases. You should reserve configuration files for cases where you need to be able to vary an implementation without recompiling the application—which is rarer than you may think.

Now that we've covered how to configure a DI CONTAINER and how to resolve object graphs with one, you should have a good idea about how to use them. Using a DI CONTAINER is one thing, but understanding *when* to use one is another.

12.3 *When to use a DI* CONTAINER

In the previous parts of this book, we solely used PURE DI as our method of OBJECT COMPOSITION. This wasn't just for educational purposes. Complete applications can be built using PURE DI alone.

In section 12.2, we talked about the different configuration methods of DI CONTAINERS and how the use of AUTO-REGISTRATION can increase maintainability of your COMPOSITION ROOT. But the use of DI CONTAINERS comes with additional costs and disadvantages over PURE DI. Most, if not all, DI CONTAINERS are open source, so they're free in a monetary sense. But because developer hours are typically the most expensive part of software development, anything that increases the time it takes to develop and maintain software is a cost, which is what we'll talk about here.

In this section, we'll compare the advantages and disadvantages, so you can make an educated decision about when to use a DI CONTAINER and when to stick to PURE DI. Let's start with an often overlooked aspect of using libraries such as DI CONTAINERS, which is that they introduce costs and risks.

12.3.1 *Using third-party libraries involves costs and risks*

When a library is free in a monetary sense, we developers often tend to ignore the other costs involved in using it. A DI CONTAINER might be considered a STABLE DEPENDENCY (section 1.3.1), so from a DI perspective, using one isn't an issue. But there are other concerns to consider. As with any third-party library, using a DI CONTAINER comes with costs and risks.

The most obvious cost of any library is its learning curve—it takes time to learn to use a new library. You have to learn its API, its behavior, its quirks, and its limitations. When you're with a team of developers, most of them will have to understand how to work with that library in one way or another. Having just one developer that knows how to work with the tool might save costs in the short run, but such a practice is in itself a liability to the continuity of your project.[8]

A library's behavior, quirks, and limitations might not exactly suit your needs. A library might be opinionated towards a different model than the one your software is built around.[9] This is typically something you only find out while you're learning to use it. As you apply it to your code base, you may find that you need to implement various workarounds. This can result in much yak shaving.

It is, therefore, hard to estimate how much money the use of a new library will save the project because of the learning costs that are often hard to realistically estimate. The accumulated time spent on learning the API of a third-party library is time not spent building the application itself, and therefore represents a real cost.

Besides the direct cost of learning to work with a library, there are risks involved in taking a dependency on such a library. One risk is that the developers stop maintaining and supporting a library you're using.[10] When such an event occurs, it introduces extra costs to the project because it can force you to switch libraries. In that case, you're paying the previously discussed learning costs all over again with the additional costs of migrating and testing the application again.

> **TIP** Because of these costs and risks, care should be taken in selecting the right libraries for your project. When starting a new project, to mitigate the risks, it's therefore advisable to limit the amount of external libraries your team needs to become familiar with.

---

[8] This is often referred to as the *bus factor*. The bus factor is the minimum number of team members that have to suddenly disappear from a project (get hit by a bus) before the project stalls due to lack of knowledgeable or competent personnel.

[9] The library maker's opinions might be an opportunity for you and your team to learn something, but it might simply be a different opinion, incompatible with yours.

[10] This isn't a risk with third-party libraries only. Even Microsoft, one of the organizations most committed to long-term support of their technologies, has been known to break compatibility or abandon technologies. Examples include Workflow Foundation, Silverlight, Visual Studio LightSwitch, Windows Phone, and Windows RT. These days, Microsoft seems to be back to a more stable commitment to long-term support. The point is that one can never be certain.

This all sounds like an argument against using external libraries, but that isn't the case. You wouldn't be productive without external libraries, because you'd have to reinvent the wheel. If not using an external library means building such a library yourself, you'll often be worse off. (And we developers tend to underestimate the time it takes to write, test, and maintain such a piece of software.)

With DI CONTAINERS, however, you're in a somewhat different situation. That's because the alternative to using an external DI CONTAINER library isn't to build your own, but to apply PURE DI.

Don't build your own DI CONTAINER

At first sight, listing 12.1 might seem to imply that a DI CONTAINER can be written in a few lines of code. Although listing 12.1 sketches the first steps in writing a DI CONTAINER, there's a clear reason it's flagged as bad code.

The code in listing 12.1 is a naive implementation that, as we stated earlier, lacks many crucial capabilities. A fully functional DI CONTAINER should support LIFETIME MANAGEMENT, INTERCEPTION, AUTO-REGISTRATION, and DEPENDENCY cycle detection; communicate configuration mistakes effectively; have properly designed extensibility points; rest on great documentation; and much, much more. This isn't something you'll be able to do in a couple of weeks.

From experience, I (Steven) can tell you that it takes years for such a library to become stable and mature. And although it might be a great learning experience for you as a developer, it doesn't help your project or your company, because your focus should be on producing business value.[11]

This doesn't mean you should never create a new open source library such as a DI CONTAINER. Innovation is an important aspect of our industry, and the creation of new libraries helps with this. Sometimes we need radical new ideas, and this sometimes means we need to build new libraries and frameworks based on those ideas. You should, however, be cautious about spending your employer's money on this, because it'll cost your employer way more than you initially envision.

As you learned in section 4.1, interaction with the DI CONTAINER should be limited to the COMPOSITION ROOT. This already reduces the risk when it must be replaced. But even in that case, it can be a time-consuming endeavor to replace the DI CONTAINER and become familiar with a new API and design philosophy.

The major advantage of PURE DI is that it's easy to learn. You don't have to learn the API of any DI CONTAINER and, although individual classes still use DI, once you find the COMPOSITION ROOT, it'll be evident what's going on and how object graphs are constructed. Although newer IDEs make this less of a problem, it can be difficult for a new developer on a team to get a sense of the constructed object graph and to find the implementation for a class's DEPENDENCY when a DI CONTAINER is used.

---

[11] Writing and maintaining Simple Injector and supporting its community gave me a lot of knowledge, which eventually led to me becoming the coauthor of this book.

With PURE DI, this is less of a problem, because object graph construction is hard coded in the COMPOSITION ROOT. Besides being easier to learn, PURE DI gives you a shorter feedback cycle in case there's an error in your composition of objects. Let's look at that next.

12.3.2 *PURE DI gives a shorter feedback cycle*

DI CONTAINER techniques, such as AUTO-WIRING and AUTO-REGISTRATION, depend on the use of reflection. This means that, at runtime, the DI CONTAINER will analyze constructor arguments using reflection or even query through complete assemblies to find types based on conventions in order to compose complete object graphs. Consequently, configuration errors are only detected at runtime when an object graph is resolved. Compared to PURE DI, the DI CONTAINER assumes the compiler's role of code verification.

> **IMPORTANT**   PURE DI has a big advantage that's often overlooked: it's strongly typed. This allows the compiler to provide feedback about correctness, which is the fastest feedback that you can get.

When a COMPOSITION ROOT is well structured so that the creation of SINGLETONS and SCOPED instances are separated (see listings 8.10 and 8.13, for instance), it allows the compiler to detect CAPTIVE DEPENDENCIES, as discussed in section 8.4.1.

As we discussed in section 3.2.2, because of strong typing, PURE DI also has the advantage of giving you a clearer picture of the structure of the application's object graphs. This is something that you'll lose immediately when you start using a DI CONTAINER.

But strong typing cuts both ways because, as we discussed in section 12.1.3, it also means that every time you refactor a constructor, you'll break the COMPOSITION ROOT. If you're sharing a library (domain model, utility, data access component, and so on) between applications, you may have more than one COMPOSITION ROOT to maintain. How much of a burden this is depends on how often you refactor constructors, but we've seen projects where this happens several times each day. With multiple developers working on a single project, this can easily lead to merge conflicts, which cost time to fix.

Although the compiler will give rapid feedback when using PURE DI, the amount of validations it can do is limited. It'll be able to report missing DEPENDENCIES due to changes to constructors and to some extent CAPTIVE DEPENDENCIES, but, among other things, it will fail to detect the following:

- Failing constructor invocations due to exceptions thrown from within the constructor's body (for example, failing Guard Clauses)
- Whether disposable components are disposed of when they go out of scope
- When classes that are supposed to be SINGLETON or SCOPED are again (accidentally) created in a different part of the COMPOSITION ROOT, possibly with a different lifestyle[12]

---

[12] These defects are sometimes referred to as Torn LIFESTYLES (https://simpleinjector.org/diatl) and Ambiguous LIFESTYLES (https://simpleinjector.org/diaal).

When using PURE DI, the size of the COMPOSITION ROOT grows linearly with the size of the application. When an application is small, its COMPOSITION ROOT will also be small. This makes its COMPOSITION ROOT clean and manageable, and previously listed defects will be easy to spot. But when the COMPOSITION ROOT grows, it becomes easier to miss such defects.

This is something that the use of a DI CONTAINER can mitigate. Most DI CONTAINERS automatically detect a disposable component on your behalf and might detect common pitfalls, such as CAPTIVE DEPENDENCIES.[13]

12.3.3 *The verdict: When to use a DI CONTAINER*

If you use a DI CONTAINER's CONFIGURATION AS CODE abilities (as discussed in section 12.2.2), explicitly registering each and every component using the container's API, you lose the rapid feedback from strong typing. On the other hand, the maintenance burden is also likely to drop because of AUTO-WIRING. Still, you'll need to register each new class when you introduce it, which is a linear growth, and you and your team have to learn the specific API of that container. But even if you're already familiar with its API, there's still the risk of having to replace it someday. You might lose more than you gain.

Ultimately, if you can wield a DI CONTAINER in a sufficiently sophisticated way, you can use it to define a set of conventions using AUTO-REGISTRATION (as discussed in section 12.2.3). These conventions define a rule set that your code should adhere to, and as long as you stick to those rules, things just work. The container drops to the background, and you rarely need to touch it.

> **IMPORTANT** The use of Convention over Configuration using AUTO-REGISTRA-TION can minimize the amount of maintenance on the COMPOSITION ROOT to almost zero.

AUTO-REGISTRATION takes time to learn, and is weakly typed, but, if done right, it enables you to focus on code that adds value instead of infrastructure. An additional advantage is that it creates a positive feedback mechanism, forcing a team to produce code that's consistent with the conventions. Figure 12.6 visualizes the trade-off between PURE DI and using a DI CONTAINER.

As we stated in section 12.2.4, none of the available approaches are mutually exclusive. Although you might find a single COMPOSITION ROOT to contain a mix of all configuration styles, a COMPOSITION ROOT should either be focused around PURE DI with, perhaps, a few late-bound types, or around AUTO-REGISTRATION with, optionally, a limited amount of CONFIGURATION AS CODE, PURE DI, and configuration files. A COMPOSITION ROOT that focuses around CONFIGURATION AS CODE is pointless and should therefore be avoided.

---

[13] The three DI CONTAINERS discussed in this book all detect CAPTIVE DEPENDENCIES to some extent.

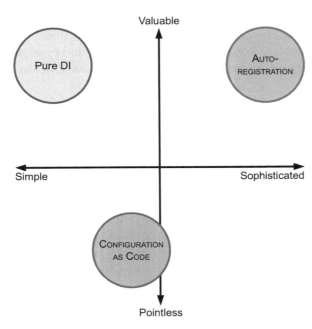

Figure 12.6 **PURE DI can be valuable because it's simple, although a DI CONTAINER can be either valuable or pointless, depending on how it's used. When it's used in a sufficiently sophisticated way (using AUTO-REGISTRATION), we consider a DI CONTAINER to offer the best value/cost ratio.**

The question then becomes this: when should you choose PURE DI, and when should you use AUTO-REGISTRATION? We, unfortunately, can't give any hard numbers on this. It depends on the size of the project, the amount of experience you and your team have with a DI CONTAINER, and the calculation of risk.

In general, though, you should use PURE DI for COMPOSITION ROOTS that are small and switch to AUTO-REGISTRATION when maintaining such a COMPOSITION ROOT becomes a problem. Bigger applications with many classes that can be captured by several conventions can benefit from using AUTO-REGISTRATION.[14]

Automagical

I (Mark) once worked for a client where I applied convention-based AUTO-REGISTRATION in a code base. The other developers weren't too happy with it because they found it too *automagical*. They fully embraced DI and used TDD, but weren't keen on using a DI CONTAINER, because they weren't familiar with its API.

In many cases, the conventions worked as advertised. When developers introduced new classes or interfaces, the DI CONTAINER discovered the new types and correctly configured them. Once in a while, however, developers (including myself) would implement a feature in a way not anticipated by the conventions. When that happened, it was necessary to adjust the conventions.

The other developers didn't understand—and weren't interested in learning—how to work with the DI CONTAINER's API, so whenever a change was required, I had to implement

---

[14] We also promote the idea of keeping applications relatively small. This inevitably leads to the concept of *Bounded Contexts*. See Eric J. Evans, *Domain-Driven Design, 335*.

> it. I became a critical resource, and occasionally a bottleneck. When I left the project, I expected the remaining team to rip out the DI CONTAINER and replace it with PURE DI. When I returned a year later, I wasn't surprised to learn that this was exactly what they had done. I can't say that I blamed them.

The other thing we won't tell you is which DI CONTAINER to choose. Selecting a DI CONTAINER involves more than technical evaluation. You must also evaluate whether the licensing model is acceptable, whether you trust the people or organization that develops and maintains the DI CONTAINER, how it fits into your organization's IT strategy, and so on. Your search for the right DI CONTAINER also shouldn't be limited to the containers listed in this book. For example, many excellent DI CONTAINERS for the .NET platform are available to choose from.

A DI CONTAINER can be a helpful tool if you use it correctly. The most important thing to understand is that the use of DI in no way depends on the use of a DI CONTAINER. An application can be made from many loosely coupled classes and modules, and none of these modules knows anything about a container. The most effective way to make sure that application code is unaware of any DI CONTAINER is by limiting its use to the COMPOSITION ROOT. This prevents you from inadvertently applying the SERVICE LOCATOR anti-pattern, because it constrains the container to a small, isolated area of the code.

Used in this way, a DI CONTAINER becomes an engine that takes care of part of the application's infrastructure. It composes object graphs based on its configuration. This can be particularly beneficial if you employ Convention over Configuration. If suitably implemented, it can take care of composing object graphs, and you can concentrate your efforts on implementing new features. The container will automatically discover new classes that follow the established conventions and make them available to consumers. The final three chapters of this book cover Autofac (chapter 13), Simple Injector (chapter 14), and Microsoft.Extensions.DependencyInjection (chapter 15).

Summary

- A DI CONTAINER is a library that provides DI functionality. It's an engine that resolves and manages object graphs.
- DI in no way hinges on the use of a DI CONTAINER. A DI CONTAINER is a useful, but optional, tool.
- AUTO-WIRING is the ability to automatically compose an object graph from maps between ABSTRACTIONS and concrete types by making use of the type information as supplied by the compiler and the Common Language Runtime (CLR).
- CONSTRUCTOR INJECTION statically advertises the DEPENDENCY requirements of a class, and DI CONTAINERS use that information to AUTO-WIRE complex object graphs.

- AUTO-WIRING makes a COMPOSITION ROOT more resilient to change.
- When you start using a DI CONTAINER, you're not required to abandon hand wiring object graphs altogether. You can use hand wiring in parts of your configuration when this is more convenient.
- When using a DI CONTAINER, the three configuration styles are configuration files, CONFIGURATION AS CODE, and AUTO-REGISTRATION.
- Configuration files are as much a part of your COMPOSITION ROOT as CONFIGURATION AS CODE and AUTO-REGISTRATION. Using configuration files, therefore, doesn't make your COMPOSITION ROOT smaller, it just moves it.
- As your application grows in size and complexity, so will your configuration file. Configuration files tend to become brittle and opaque to errors, so only use this approach when you need late binding.
- Don't let the absence of support for handling configuration files influence your choice for picking a DI CONTAINER. Types can be loaded from configuration files in a few simple statements.
- CONFIGURATION AS CODE allows the container's configuration to be stored as source code. Each mapping between an ABSTRACTION and a particular implementation is expressed explicitly and directly in code. This method is preferred over configuration files unless you need late binding.
- Convention over Configuration is the application of conventions to your code to facilitate easier registration.
- AUTO-REGISTRATION is the ability to automatically register components in a container by scanning one or more assemblies for implementations of desired ABSTRACTIONS, which is a form of Convention over Configuration.
- AUTO-REGISTRATION helps avoid constantly updating the COMPOSITION ROOT and is, therefore, preferred over CONFIGURATION AS CODE.
- Using external libraries such as DI CONTAINERS incurs costs and risks; for example, the cost of learning a new API and the risk of the library being abandoned.
- Avoid building your own DI CONTAINER. Either use one of the existing, well-tested, and freely available DI CONTAINERS, or practice PURE DI. Creating and maintaining such a library takes a lot of effort, which is effort not spent producing business value.
- The big advantage of PURE DI is that it's strongly typed. This allows the compiler to provide feedback about correctness, which is the fastest feedback that you can get.
- You should use PURE DI for COMPOSITION ROOTS that are small and switch to AUTO-REGISTRATION whenever maintaining such COMPOSITION ROOTS becomes a problem. Bigger applications with many classes that can be captured by several conventions can greatly benefit from using AUTO-REGISTRATION.

The Autofac DI Container

In this chapter

- Working with Autofac's basic registration API
- Managing component lifetime
- Configuring difficult APIs
- Configuring sequences, Decorators, and Composites

In the previous chapters, we discussed patterns and principles that apply to DI in general, but, apart from a few examples, we've yet to take a detailed look at how to apply them using any particular DI CONTAINER. In this chapter, you'll see how these overall patterns map to Autofac. You'll need to be familiar with the material from the previous chapters to fully benefit from this.

Autofac is a fairly comprehensive DI CONTAINER that offers a carefully designed and consistent API. It's been around since late 2007 and is, at the time of writing, one of the most popular containers.[1]

---

[1] No official statistics exist on DI CONTAINER usage, so our assessment is based on the average NuGet downloads per day.

In this chapter, we'll examine how Autofac can be used to apply the principles and patterns presented in parts 1–3. This chapter is divided into four sections. You can read each section independently, though the first section is a prerequisite for the other sections, and the fourth section relies on some methods and classes introduced in the third section.

This chapter should enable you to get started, as well as deal with the most common issues that can come up as you use Autofac on a daily basis. It's not a complete treatment of Autofac; that would take several more chapters or perhaps a whole book in itself. If you want to know more about Autofac, the best place to start is at the Autofac home page at https://autofac.org.

13.1   *Introducing Autofac*

In this section, you'll learn where to get Autofac, what you get, and how you start using it. We'll also look at common configuration options. Table 13.1 provides fundamental information that you're likely to need to get started.

Table 13.1   Autofac at a glance

Question	Answer
Where do I get it?	From Visual Studio, you can get it via NuGet. The package name is *Autofac*. Alternatively, the NuGet package can be downloaded from the GitHub repository (https://github.com/autofac/Autofac/releases).
Which platforms are supported?	.NET 4.5 (without a .NET Core SDK) and .NET Standard 1.1 (.NET Core 1.0, Mono 4.6, Xamarin.iOS 10.0, Xamarin.Mac 3.0, Xamarin.Android 7.0, UWP 10.0, Windows 8.0, Windows Phone 8.1). Older builds that support .NET 2.0 and Silverlight are available via NuGet history.
How much does it cost?	Nothing. It's open source.
How is it licensed?	MIT License.
Where can I get help?	You can get commercial support from companies associated with the Autofac developers. Read more about the options at https://autofac.readthedocs.io/en/latest/support.html. Other than commercial support, Autofac is still open source software with a thriving ecosystem, so you're also likely (but not guaranteed) to get help by posting on Stack Overflow at https://stackoverflow.com or by using the official forum at https://groups.google.com/group/autofac.
On which version is this chapter based?	4.9.0-beta1

Using Autofac isn't that different from using the other DI CONTAINERS that we'll discuss in the following chapters. As with Simple Injector and Microsoft.Extensions .DependencyInjection, usage is a two-step process, as figure 13.1 illustrates. First, you configure a `ContainerBuilder`, and when you're done with that, you use it to build a container to resolve components.

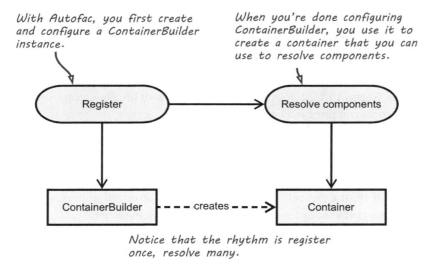

With Autofac, you first create and configure a ContainerBuilder instance.

When you're done configuring ContainerBuilder, you use it to create a container that you can use to resolve components.

Notice that the rhythm is register once, resolve many.

Figure 13.1   The pattern for using Autofac is to first configure it, and then resolve components.

When you're done with this section, you should have a good feeling for the overall usage pattern of Autofac, and you should be able to start using it in well-behaved scenarios—where all components follow proper DI patterns like CONSTRUCTOR INJECTION. Let's start with the simplest scenario and see how you can resolve objects using an Autofac container.

13.1.1 Resolving objects

The core service of any DI CONTAINER is to compose object graphs. In this section, we'll look at the API that lets you compose object graphs with Autofac.

By default, Autofac requires you to register all relevant components before you can resolve them. This behavior, however, is configurable. The following listing shows one of the simplest possible uses of Autofac.

Listing 13.1   Simplest possible use of Autofac

```
var builder = new ContainerBuilder();

builder.RegisterType<SauceBéarnaise>();

IContainer container = builder.Build();

ILifetimeScope scope = container.BeginLifetimeScope();

SauceBéarnaise sauce = scope.Resolve<SauceBéarnaise>();
```

As figure 13.1 shows, you need a `ContainerBuilder` instance to configure components. Here, you register the concrete `SauceBéarnaise` class with `builder` so that when you ask it to build a container, the resulting container is configured with the `SauceBéarnaise` class. This again enables you to resolve the `SauceBéarnaise` class from the container.

With Autofac, however, you never resolve from the root container itself, but from a lifetime scope. Section 13.2.1 goes into more detail about lifetime scope and why resolving from the root container is a bad thing.

> **WARNING**   With Autofac, resolving from the root container directly is a bad practice. This can easily lead to memory leaks or concurrency bugs. Instead, you should always resolve from a lifetime scope.

If you don't register the `SauceBéarnaise` component, attempting to resolve it throws a `ComponentNotRegisteredException` with the following message:

> *The requested service "Ploeh.Samples.MenuModel.SauceBéarnaise" has not been registered. To avoid this exception, either register a component to provide the service, check for service registration using IsRegistered(), or use the ResolveOptional() method to resolve an optional dependency.*

Not only can Autofac resolve concrete types with parameterless constructors, it can also AUTO-WIRE a type with other DEPENDENCIES. All these DEPENDENCIES need to be registered. For the most part, you'll want to program to interfaces, because this introduces loose coupling. To support this, Autofac lets you map ABSTRACTIONS to concrete types.

MAPPING ABSTRACTIONS TO CONCRETE TYPES

Whereas your application's root types will typically be resolved by their concrete types, loose coupling requires you to map ABSTRACTIONS to concrete types. Creating instances based on such maps is the core service offered by any DI CONTAINER, but you must still define the map. In this example, you map the `IIngredient` interface to the concrete `SauceBéarnaise` class, which allows you to successfully resolve `IIngredient`:

```
var builder = new ContainerBuilder();

builder.RegisterType<SauceBéarnaise>()
    .As<IIngredient>();          ◄──────────────── Maps a concrete type to an ABSTRACTION

IContainer container = builder.Build();

ILifetimeScope scope = container.BeginLifetimeScope();

IIngredient sauce = scope.Resolve<IIngredient>();   ◄────── Resolves the SauceBéarnaise class
```

The `As<T>` method allows a concrete type to be mapped to a particular ABSTRACTION. Because of the previous `As<IIngredient>()` call, `SauceBéarnaise` can now be resolved as `IIngredient`.

You use the `ContainerBuilder` instance to register types and define maps. The `RegisterType` method lets you register a concrete type.

As you saw in listing 13.1, you can stop right there if you only want to register the SauceBéarnaise class. You can also continue with the As method to define how the concrete type should be registered.[2]

> **WARNING** Contrary to Simple Injector and Microsoft.Extensions.DependencyInjection, there are no generic type constraints in effect between the types defined by the RegisterType and As methods. This means that it's possible to map incompatible types. The code will compile, but you'll get an exception at runtime when the ContainerBuilder builds the container.

In many cases, the generic API is all you need. Although it doesn't offer the same degree of type safety as some other DI CONTAINERS, it's still a readable way to configure the container. Still, there are situations where you need a more weakly typed way to resolve services. With Autofac, this is also possible.

RESOLVING WEAKLY TYPED SERVICES

Sometimes you can't use a generic API, because you don't know the appropriate type at design time. All you have is a Type instance, but you'd still like to get an instance of that type. You saw an example of that in section 7.3, where we discussed ASP.NET Core MVC's IControllerActivator class. The relevant method is this:

```
object Create(ControllerContext context);
```

As shown previously in listing 7.8, the ControllerContext captures the controller's Type, which you can extract using the ControllerTypeInfo property of the ActionDescriptor property:

```
Type controllerType = context.ActionDescriptor.ControllerTypeInfo.AsType();
```

Because you only have a Type instance, you can't use the generic Resolve<T> method, but must resort to a weakly typed API. Autofac offers a weakly typed overload of the Resolve method that lets you implement the Create method like this:

```
Type controllerType = context.ActionDescriptor.ControllerTypeInfo.AsType();
return scope.Resolve(controllerType);
```

The weakly typed overload of Resolve lets you pass the controllerType variable directly to Autofac. Typically, this means you have to cast the returned value to some ABSTRACTION, because the weakly typed Resolve method returns object. In the case of IControllerActivator, however, this isn't required, because ASP.NET Core MVC doesn't require controllers to implement any interface or base class.

No matter which overload of Resolve you use, Autofac guarantees that it'll return an instance of the requested type or throw an exception if there are DEPENDENCIES that can't be satisfied. When all required DEPENDENCIES have been properly configured, Autofac can AUTO-WIRE the requested type.

---

[2] With Autofac, you start with the concrete type and map it to an ABSTRACTION. This is the reverse of most other DI CONTAINERS, which start with the ABSTRACTION and map it to a concrete type.

In the previous example, `scope` is an instance of `Autofac.ILifetimeScope`. To be able to resolve the requested type, all loosely coupled DEPENDENCIES must have been previously configured. There are many ways to configure Autofac, and the next section reviews the most common ones.

13.1.2 Configuring the `ContainerBuilder`

As we discussed in section 12.2, you can configure a DI CONTAINER in several conceptually different ways. Figure 12.5 reviewed the options: configuration files, CONFIGURATION AS CODE, and AUTO-REGISTRATION. Figure 13.2 shows these options again.

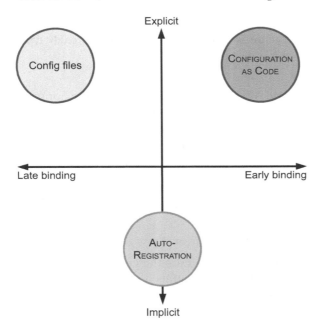

Figure 13.2   The most common ways to configure a DI CONTAINER shown against dimensions of explicitness and the degree of binding

The core configuration API is centered on code and supports both CONFIGURATION AS CODE and convention-based AUTO-REGISTRATION. Support for configuration files can be plugged in using the Autofac.Configuration NuGet package. Autofac supports all three approaches and lets you mix them all within the same container. In this section, you'll see how to use each of these three types of configuration sources.

CONFIGURING THE `ContainerBuilder` USING CONFIGURATION AS CODE

In section 13.1, you saw a brief glimpse of Autofac's strongly typed configuration API. Here, we'll examine it in greater detail.

All configurations in Autofac use the API exposed by the `ContainerBuilder` class, although most of the methods you use are extension methods. One of the most commonly used methods is the `RegisterType` method that you've already seen:

```
builder.RegisterType<SauceBéarnaise>().As<IIngredient>();
```

Registering SauceBéarnaise as IIngredient hides the concrete class so that you can no longer resolve SauceBéarnaise with this registration. But you can easily fix this by using an overload of the As method that lets you specify that the concrete type maps to more than one registered type:

```
builder.RegisterType<SauceBéarnaise>().As<SauceBéarnaise, IIngredient>();
```

Instead of registering the class only as IIngredient, you can register it as both itself and the interface it implements. This enables the container to resolve requests for both SauceBéarnaise and IIngredient. As an alternative, you can also chain calls to the As method:

```
builder.RegisterType<SauceBéarnaise>()
    .As<SauceBéarnaise>()
    .As<IIngredient>();
```

This produces the same result as in the previous example. The difference between the two registrations is simply a matter of style.

Three generic overloads of the As method let you specify one, two, or three types. If you need to specify more, there's also a non-generic overload that you can use to specify as many types as you like.

Torn LIFESTYLES

In this section, we've shown how you can call As multiple times to register a component as multiple service types. The following example shows this once more:

```
builder.RegisterType<SauceBéarnaise>()
    .As<SauceBéarnaise>()
    .As<IIngredient>();
```

You might be tempted to think this is equivalent to the following code:

```
builder.RegisterType<SauceBéarnaise>();
builder.RegisterType<SauceBéarnaise>().As<IIngredient>();
```

The former example, however, isn't equivalent to the latter. This becomes apparent when you change the LIFESTYLE from TRANSIENT to, for instance, SINGLETON.

BAD
CODE

```
builder.RegisterType<SauceBéarnaise>().SingleInstance();
builder.RegisterType<SauceBéarnaise>().As<IIngredient>()
    .SingleInstance();
```

Although you might expect there to only be one SauceBéarnaise instance for the lifetime of the container, splitting up the registration causes Autofac to create a separate instance per RegisterType call. The LIFESTYLE of SauceBéarnaise is therefore considered to be *torn*.

WARNING Supplying multiple service types to the As method isn't the same as making multiple RegisterType calls. Each call will get its own cache, which can cause the lifetime to be torn when the chosen LIFESTYLE is other than TRANSIENT.

In real applications, you always have more than one ABSTRACTION to map, so you must configure multiple mappings. This is done with multiple calls to RegisterType:

```
builder.RegisterType<SauceBéarnaise>().As<IIngredient>();
builder.RegisterType<Course>().As<ICourse>();
```

This example maps IIngredient to SauceBéarnaise, and ICourse to Course. There's no overlap of types, so it should be pretty evident what's going on. But you can also register the same ABSTRACTION several times:

```
builder.RegisterType<SauceBéarnaise>().As<IIngredient>();
builder.RegisterType<Steak>().As<IIngredient>();
```

Here, you register IIngredient twice. If you resolve IIngredient, you get an instance of Steak. The last registration wins, but previous registrations aren't forgotten. Autofac handles multiple configurations for the same ABSTRACTION well, but we'll get back to this topic in section 13.4.

There are more-advanced options available for configuring Autofac, but you can configure an entire application with the methods shown here. But to save yourself from too much explicit maintenance of container configuration, you could instead consider a more convention-based approach using AUTO-REGISTRATION.

CONFIGURING THE ContainerBuilder USING AUTO-REGISTRATION

In many cases, registrations will be similar. Such registrations are tedious to maintain, and explicitly registering each and every component might not be the most productive approach, as we discussed in section 12.3.3.

Consider a library that contains many IIngredient implementations. You can configure each class individually, but it'll result in numerous similar-looking calls to the RegisterType method. What's worse is that every time you add a new IIngredient implementation, you must also explicitly register it with the ContainerBuilder if you want it to be available. It'd be more productive to state that all implementations of IIngredient found in a given assembly should be registered.

This is possible using the RegisterAssemblyTypes method. This method lets you specify an assembly and configure all selected classes from this assembly into a single statement. To get the Assembly instance, you can use a representative class (in this case, Steak):

```
Assembly ingredientsAssembly = typeof(Steak).Assembly;

builder.RegisterAssemblyTypes(ingredientsAssembly).As<IIngredient>();
```

The RegisterAssemblyTypes method returns the same interface as the RegisterType method, so many of the same configuration options are available. This is a strong feature, because it means that you don't have to learn a new API to use AUTO-REGISTRATION.

In the previous example, we used the `As` method to register all types in the assembly as `IIngredient` services. The previous example also unconditionally configures all implementations of the `IIngredient` interface, but you can provide filters that let you select only a subset. Here's a convention-based scan where you add only classes whose name starts with *Sauce*:

```
Assembly ingredientsAssembly = typeof(Steak).Assembly;

builder.RegisterAssemblyTypes(ingredientsAssembly)
    .Where(type => type.Name.StartsWith("Sauce"))
    .As<IIngredient>();
```

When you register all types in an assembly, you can use a predicate to define a selection criterion. The only difference from the previous code example is the inclusion of the `Where` method, where you select only those types whose names start with *Sauce*.

There are many other methods that let you provide various selection criteria. The `Where` method gives you a filter that only lets those types through that match the predicate, but there's also an `Except` method that works the other way around.

Apart from selecting the correct types from an assembly, another part of AUTO-REGISTRATION is defining the correct mapping. In the previous examples, we used the `As` method with a specific interface to register all selected types against that interface. But sometimes you'll want to use different conventions.

Let's say that instead of interfaces, you use abstract base classes, and you want to register all types in an assembly where the name ends with *Policy*. For this purpose, there are several other overloads of the `As` method, including one that takes a `Func<Type, Type>` as input:

```
Assembly policiesAssembly = typeof(DiscountPolicy).Assembly;

builder.RegisterAssemblyTypes(policiesAssembly)
    .Where(type => type.Name.EndsWith("Policy"))
    .As(type => type.BaseType);
```

TIP Think of `RegisterAssemblyTypes` as the plural of `RegisterType`.

You can use the code block provided to the `As` method for every single type whose name ends with *Policy*. This ensures that all classes with the *Policy* suffix will be registered against their base class, so that when the base class is requested, the container will resolve it to the type mapped by this convention. Convention-based registration with Autofac is surprisingly easy and uses an API that closely mirrors the API exposed by the singular `RegisterType` method.

AUTO-REGISTRATION OF GENERIC ABSTRACTIONS USING `AsClosedTypesOf`

During the course of chapter 10, you refactored the big, obnoxious `IProductService` interface to the `ICommandService<TCommand>` interface of listing 10.12. Here's that ABSTRACTION again:

```
public interface ICommandService<TCommand>
{
    void Execute(TCommand command);
}
```

As discussed in chapter 10, every command Parameter Object represents a use case and, apart from any Decorators that implement CROSS-CUTTING CONCERNS, there'll be a single implementation per use case. The `AdjustInventoryService` of listing 10.8 was given as an example. It implemented the "adjust inventory" use case. The next listing shows this class again.

> **Listing 13.2   The `AdjustInventoryService` from chapter 10**

```
public class AdjustInventoryService : ICommandService<AdjustInventory>
{
    private readonly IInventoryRepository repository;

    public AdjustInventoryService(IInventoryRepository repository)
    {
        this.repository = repository;
    }

    public void Execute(AdjustInventory command)
    {
        var productId = command.ProductId;

        ...

    }
}
```

Any reasonably complex system will easily implement hundreds of use cases. This is an ideal candidate for using AUTO-REGISTRATION. With Autofac, this couldn't be easier, as the following listing shows.

> **Listing 13.3   AUTO-REGISTRATION of `ICommandService<TCommand>` implementations**

```
Assembly assembly = typeof(AdjustInventoryService).Assembly;

builder.RegisterAssemblyTypes(assembly)
    .AsClosedTypesOf(typeof(ICommandService<>));
```

As in the previous listings, you make use of the `RegisterAssemblyTypes` method to select classes from the supplied assembly. Instead of calling `As`, however, you call `AsClosedTypesOf` and supply the open-generic `ICommandService<TCommand>` interface.

Using the supplied open-generic interface, Autofac iterates through the list of assembly types and registers all types that implement a closed-generic version of `ICommand-Service<TCommand>`. What this means, for instance, is that `AdjustInventoryService` is registered, because it implements `ICommandService<AdjustInventory>`, which is a closed-generic version of `ICommandService<TCommand>`.

The `RegisterAssemblyTypes` method takes a `params` array of `Assembly` instances, so you can supply as many assemblies to a single convention as you'd like. It's not a far-fetched thought to scan a folder for assemblies and supply them all to implement add-in functionality. In that way, add-ins can be added without recompiling a core application. This is one way to implement late binding; another is to use configuration files.

CONFIGURING THE ContainerBuilder USING CONFIGURATION FILES

When you need to change a container's registrations without recompiling the application, configuration files are a viable option. As we stated in section 12.2.1, you should use configuration files only for those types of your DI configuration that require late binding: prefer CONFIGURATION AS CODE or AUTO-REGISTRATION in all other types and all other parts of your configuration.

The most natural way to use configuration files is to embed those into the standard .NET application configuration file. This is possible, but you can also use a standalone configuration file if you need to vary the Autofac configuration independently of the standard .config file. Whether you want to do one or the other, the API is almost the same.

> **NOTE** Autofac's configuration support is implemented in a separate assembly. To use this feature, you must add a reference to the `Autofac.Configuration` assembly (https://mng.bz/1Q4V).

Once you have a reference to `Autofac.Configuration`, you can ask the `Container-Builder` to read component registrations from the standard .config file like this:

```
var configuration = new ConfigurationBuilder()
    .AddJsonFile("autofac.json")
    .Build();

builder.RegisterModule(
    new ConfigurationModule(configuration));
```

> **Loads the autofac.json configuration file using .NET Core's configuration system. By default, the configuration file will be located in the application's root directory.**

> **Wraps the created configuration in an Autofac module that processes the configuration file and maps file-based registrations in Autofac. That module is added to the builder using RegisterModule.**

Here's a simple example that maps the `IIngredient` interface to the `Steak` class:

```
{
  "defaultAssembly": "Ploeh.Samples.MenuModel",
  "components": [
  {
    "services": [{
      "type": "Ploeh.Samples.MenuModel.IIngredient"
    }],
    "type": "Ploeh.Samples.MenuModel.Steak"
  }]
}
```

> **The defaultAssembly construct lets you write types in a shorter fashion. If you don't specify an assembly-qualified type name in a type or interface reference, it'll be assumed to be in the default assembly.**

> **Simple mapping from IIngredient to Steak. Specifying a type is done using a fully qualified type name, but you can omit the assembly name if the type is defined in the default assembly, as it is in this case.**

The type name must include the namespace so that Autofac can find that type. Because both types are located in the default assembly `Ploeh.Samples.MenuModel`, the assembly name can be omitted in this case. Although the `defaultAssembly` attribute is optional, it's a nice feature that can save you from a lot of typing if you have many types defined in the same assembly.

The `components` element is a JSON array of `component` elements. The previous example contained a single component, but you can add as many component elements as you like. In each element, you must specify a concrete type with the `type` attribute. This is the only required attribute. To map the `Steak` class to `IIngredient`, you can use the optional `services` attribute.

A configuration file is a good option when you need to change the configuration of one or more components without recompiling the application, but because it tends to be quite brittle, you should reserve it for only those occasions. Use either AUTO-REGISTRATION or CONFIGURATION AS CODE for the main part of the container's configuration.

> **TIP** Remember that the last configuration of a type wins! You can use this behavior to overwrite hard-coded configurations with XML configurations. To do this, you must remember to read in the XML configuration after any other components have been configured.

This section introduced the Autofac DI CONTAINER and demonstrated these fundamental mechanics: how to configure a `ContainerBuilder` and, subsequently, how to use the constructed container to resolve services. Resolving services is easily done with a single call to the `Resolve` method, so the complexity involves configuring the container. This can be done in several different ways, including imperative code and configuration files.

Until now, we've only looked at the most basic API, so there are more-advanced areas we have yet to cover. One of the most important topics is how to manage component lifetime.

13.2 *Managing lifetime*

In chapter 8, we discussed LIFETIME MANAGEMENT, including the most common conceptual LIFESTYLES such as SINGLETON, SCOPED, and TRANSIENT. Autofac supports several different LIFESTYLES, enabling you to configure the lifetime of all services. The LIFESTYLES shown in table 13.2 are available as part of the API.

> **NOTE** In Autofac, LIFESTYLES are called *instance scopes*.

Table 13.2 Autofac instance scopes (LIFESTYLES)

Autofac name	Pattern name	Comments
Per-dependency	TRANSIENT	This is the default instance scope. Instances are tracked by the container.
Single instance	SINGLETON	Instances are disposed of when the container is disposed of.
Per-lifetime scope	SCOPED	Ties the lifetime of components together with a lifetime scope (see section 13.2.1).

TIP The default Transient Lifestyle is the safest, but not always the most efficient. Singleton is a more effective choice for thread-safe services, but you must remember to explicitly register those services.

Autofac's implementations of Transient and Singleton are equivalent to the general Lifestyles described in chapter 8, so we won't spend much time on them in this chapter. Instead, in this section, you'll see how you can define Lifestyles for components both in code and with configuration files. We'll also look at Autofac's concept of lifetime scopes and how they can be used to implement the Scoped Lifestyle. By the end of this section, you should be able to use Autofac's Lifestyles in your own application. Let's start by reviewing how to configure instance scopes for components.

13.2.1 *Configuring instance scopes*

In this section, we'll review how to manage component instance scopes with Autofac. Instance scopes are configured as part of registering components, and you can define them both with code and via a configuration file. We'll look at each in turn.

CONFIGURING INSTANCE SCOPES WITH CODE

Instance scope is defined as part of the registrations you make on a `ContainerBuilder` instance. It's as easy as this:

```
builder.RegisterType<SauceBéarnaise>().SingleInstance();
```

This configures the concrete `SauceBéarnaise` class as a Singleton so that the same instance is returned each time `SauceBéarnaise` is requested. If you want to map an Abstraction to a concrete class with a specific lifetime, you can use the usual `As` method and place the `SingleInstance` method call wherever you like. These two registrations are functionally equivalent:

```
builder                               builder
    .RegisterType<SauceBéarnaise>()       .RegisterType<SauceBéarnaise>()
    .As<IIngredient>()                    .SingleInstance()
    .SingleInstance();                    .As<IIngredient>();
```

Notice that the only difference is that we've swapped the `As` and `SingleInstance` method calls. Personally, we prefer the sequence on the left, because the `Register-Type` and `As` method calls form a mapping between a concrete class and an Abstraction. Keeping them close together makes the registration more readable, and you can then state the instance scope as a modification to the mapping.

Although Transient is the default instance scope, you can explicitly state it. These two examples are equivalent:

```
builder                               builder
    .RegisterType<SauceBéarnaise>();      .RegisterType<SauceBéarnaise>()
                                          .InstancePerDependency();
```

Configuring instance scope for convention-based registrations is done using the same method as for singular registrations:

```
Assembly ingredientsAssembly = typeof(Steak).Assembly;

builder.RegisterAssemblyTypes(ingredientsAssembly).As<IIngredient>()
    .SingleInstance();
```

You can use `SingleInstance` and the other related methods to define the instance scope for all registrations in a convention. In the previous example, you defined all `IIngredient` registrations as SINGLETON. In the same way that you can register components both in code and in a configuration file, you can also configure instance scope in both places.

CONFIGURING INSTANCE SCOPES WITH CONFIGURATION FILES

When you need to define components in a configuration file, you might want to configure their instance scopes in the same place; otherwise, it would result in all components getting the same default LIFESTYLE. This is easily done as part of the configuration schema you saw in section 13.1.2. You can use the optional `instance-scope` attribute to declare the LIFESTYLE.

Listing 13.4   Using the optional `instance-scope` attribute

```
{
  "defaultAssembly": "Ploeh.Samples.MenuModel",
  "components": [
  {
    "services": [{
      "type": "Ploeh.Samples.MenuModel.IIngredient"
    }],
    "type": "Ploeh.Samples.MenuModel.Steak",          Adds instance scope to
    "instance-scope": "single-instance"       ◀──     configure a SINGLETON
  }]
}
```

Compared to the example in section 13.1.2, the only difference is the added `instance-scope` attribute that configures the instance as a SINGLETON. When you omit the `instance-scope` attribute, `per-dependency` is used, which is Autofac's equivalent to TRANSIENT.

Both in code and in a file, it's easy to configure instance scopes for components. In all cases, it's done in a rather declarative fashion. Although configuration is easy, you must not forget that some LIFESTYLES involve long-lived objects that use resources as long as they're around.

13.2.2 *Releasing components*

As discussed in section 8.2.2, it's important to release objects when you're done with them. Autofac has no explicit `Release` method but instead uses a concept called *lifetime scopes*. A lifetime scope can be regarded as a throw-away copy of the container. As figure 13.3 illustrates, it defines a boundary where components can be reused.

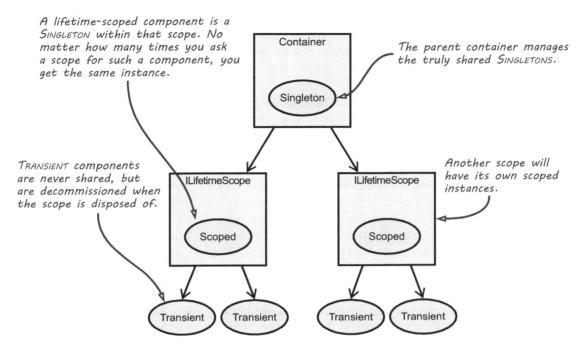

A lifetime-scoped component is a *Singleton* within that scope. No matter how many times you ask a scope for such a component, you get the same instance.

The parent container manages the truly shared *Singletons*.

Transient components are never shared, but are decommissioned when the scope is disposed of.

Another scope will have its own scoped instances.

Figure 13.3 **Autofac's lifetime scopes act as containers that can share components for a limited duration or purpose.**

A *lifetime scope* defines a derived container that you can use for a particular duration or purpose; the most obvious example is a web request. You spawn a scope from a container so that the scope inherits all the SINGLETONS tracked by the parent container, but the scope also acts as a container of local SINGLETONS. When a lifetime-scoped component is requested from a lifetime scope, you always receive the same instance. The difference from true SINGLETONS is that if you query a second scope, you'll get another instance.

NOTE TRANSIENT components still act as they should, whether you resolve them from the root container or a lifetime scope.

One of the important features of lifetime scopes is that they allow you to properly release components when the scope completes. You create a new scope with the `BeginLifetimeScope` method and release all appropriate components by invoking its `Dispose` method like so:

Creates a scope from the root container

```
using (var scope = container.BeginLifetimeScope())
{
    IMeal meal = scope.Resolve<IMeal>();      ← Resolves a meal from the
                                                 newly created scope
    meal.Consume();   ←┐ Consumes the meal
}  ←┐ Releases the meal by ending the using block
```

You create a new scope from the container by invoking the `BeginLifetimeScope` method. The return value implements `IDisposable` so you can wrap it in a `using` block. Because it also implements the same interface that the container itself implements, you can use the scope to resolve components in exactly the same way as with the container itself.

When you're done with a lifetime scope, you can dispose of it. This happens automatically with a `using` block when you exit the block, but you can also choose to explicitly dispose of it by invoking the `Dispose` method. When you dispose of a scope, you also release all the components that were created by the lifetime scope. In the example, it means that you release the meal object graph.

DEPENDENCIES of a component are always resolved at or below the component's lifetime scope. For example, if you need a TRANSIENT DEPENDENCY injected into a SINGLETON, that TRANSIENT DEPENDENCY comes from the root container even if you're resolving the SINGLETON from a nested lifetime scope. This will track the TRANSIENT within the root container and prevent it from being disposed of when the lifetime scope gets disposed of. The SINGLETON consumer would otherwise break, because it's kept alive in the root container while depending on a component that was disposed of.

> **NOTE** Remember that releasing a disposable component isn't the same as disposing of it. It's a signal to the container that the component is eligible for decommissioning. If the component is SCOPED, it'll be disposed of; otherwise, if it's a SINGLETON, it remains active until the root container is disposed of.

Earlier in this section, you saw how to configure components as SINGLETONS or TRANSIENTS. Configuring a component to have its instance scope tied to a lifetime scope is done in a similar way:

```
builder.RegisterType<SauceBéarnaise>()
    .As<IIngredient>()
    .InstancePerLifetimeScope();
```

Similar to the SingleInstance and InstancePerDependency methods, you use the InstancePerLifetimeScope method to state that the component's lifetime should follow the lifetime scope that created the instance.

> **IMPORTANT** Autofac tracks most components—even disposable TRANSIENTS—so it's important to resolve all components from a lifetime scope and dispose of the scope after use. Resolving scoped instances from the root container causes the same instance to always be returned. This'll cause concurrency bugs when such a scoped component isn't thread-safe. When the root container is used to resolve a disposable TRANSIENT, even though new instances are created on each call to `Resolve`, instances are kept alive as well, in order to allow them to be disposed of when the container is disposed of. Because the root container won't be disposed of until the application stops, this causes memory leaks.

Due to their nature, SINGLETONS are never released for the lifetime of the container itself. Still, you can release even those components if you don't need the container any longer. This is done by disposing of the container itself:

```
container.Dispose();
```

In practice, this isn't nearly as important as disposing of a scope because the lifetime of a container tends to correlate closely with the lifetime of the application it supports. You normally keep the container around as long as the application runs, so you'd only dispose of it when the application shuts down. In this case, memory would be reclaimed by the operating system.

This completes our tour of Lifetime Management with Autofac. Components can be configured with mixed instance scopes, and this is true even when you register multiple implementations of the same Abstraction. But until now, you've allowed the container to wire Dependencies by implicitly assuming that all components use Auto-Wiring. This isn't always the case. In the next section, we'll review how to deal with classes that must be instantiated in special ways.

13.3 Registering difficult APIs

Until now, we've considered how you can configure components that use Constructor Injection. One of the many benefits of Constructor Injection is that DI Containers like Autofac can easily understand how to compose and create all classes in a Dependency graph. This becomes less clear when APIs are less well behaved.

In this section, you'll see how to deal with primitive constructor arguments and static factories. These all require special attention. Let's start by looking at classes that take primitive types, such as strings or integers, as constructor arguments.

13.3.1 Configuring primitive Dependencies

As long as you inject Abstractions into consumers, all is well. But it becomes more difficult when a constructor depends on a primitive type, such as a string, a number, or an enum. This is particularly the case for data access implementations that take a connection string as constructor parameter, but it's a more general issue that applies to all strings and numbers.

Conceptually, it doesn't always make sense to register a string or number as a component in a container. But with Autofac, this is at least possible. Consider as an example this constructor:

```
public ChiliConCarne(Spiciness spiciness)
```

In this example, `Spiciness` is an enum:

```
public enum Spiciness { Mild, Medium, Hot }
```

> **TIP** As a rule of thumb, enums are code smells and should be refactored to polymorphic classes.[3] But they serve us well for this example.

If you want all consumers of `Spiciness` to use the same value, you can register `Spiciness` and `ChiliConCarne` independently of each other. This snippet shows how:

```
builder.Register<Spiciness>(c => Spiciness.Medium);
builder.RegisterType<ChiliConCarne>().As<ICourse>();
```

---

[3] See Martin Fowler et al., *Refactoring: Improving the Design of Existing Code* (Addison-Wesley, 1999), 82.

When you subsequently resolve `ChiliConCarne`, it'll have a `Spiciness` value of `Medium`, as will all other components with a DEPENDENCY on `Spiciness`. If you'd rather control the relationship between `ChiliConCarne` and `Spiciness` on a finer level, you can use the `WithParameter` method. Because you want to supply a concrete value for the `Spiciness` parameter, you can use the `WithParameter` overload that takes a parameter name and a value:

```
builder.RegisterType<ChiliConCarne>().As<ICourse>()
    .WithParameter(
        "spiciness",        ◄──────────────────────────┤ Name of the parameter
        Spiciness.Hot);   ◄───────┐ Value to inject
```

Both options described here use AUTO-WIRING to provide a concrete value to a component. As discussed in section 13.4, this has advantages and disadvantages. A more convenient solution, however, is to extract the primitive DEPENDENCIES into Parameter Objects.

In section 10.3.3, we discussed how the introduction of Parameter Objects allowed mitigating the OPEN/CLOSED PRINCIPLE violation that `IProductService` caused. Parameter Objects, however, are also a great tool to mitigate ambiguity.

The `Spiciness` of a course, for instance, could be described in the more general term *flavoring*. Flavoring might include other properties, such as saltiness. In other words, you can wrap the `Spiciness` and `ExtraSalty` in a `Flavoring` class:[4]

```
public class Flavoring
{
    public readonly Spiciness Spiciness;
    public readonly bool ExtraSalty;

    public Flavoring(Spiciness spiciness, bool extraSalty)
    {
        this.Spiciness = spiciness;
        this.ExtraSalty = extraSalty;
    }
}
```

TIP As we mentioned in section 10.3.3, it's perfectly fine for Parameter Objects to have one parameter. The goal is to remove ambiguity, but not just on the technical level. Such a Parameter Object's name might do a better job describing what your code does on a functional level, as the `Flavoring` class so elegantly does.

With the introduction of the `Flavoring` Parameter Object, it now becomes easy to AUTO-WIRE any `ICourse` implementation that requires some flavoring:

```
var flavoring = new Flavoring(Spiciness.Medium, extraSalty: true);
builder.RegisterInstance<Flavoring>(flavoring);

builder.RegisterType<ChiliConCarne>().As<ICourse>();
```

---

[4] From a culinary perspective, Mark shivers at the concept of extra saltiness. Savory food should have appropriate amounts of salt, but not extra.

Now you have a single instance of the `Flavoring` class. `Flavoring` becomes a configuration object for `ICourses`. Because there'll only be one `Flavoring` instance, you can register it in Autofac using `RegisterInstance`.

> **NOTE** Avoid injecting Parameter Objects that function as application-wide configuration objects. Instead, prefer narrow, focused, Parameter Objects that only contain the values a particular consumer requires. This communicates more clearly what configuration values a component uses, and simplifies testing. In general terms, injecting application-wide configuration objects is an INTERFACE SEGREGATION PRINCIPLE violation.

Extracting primitive DEPENDENCIES into Parameter Objects should be your preference over the previously discussed options because Parameter Objects remove ambiguity, both at the functional and the technical levels. It does, however, require a change to a component's constructor, which might not always be feasible. In this case, the use of `WithParameter` is your second-best pick.

13.3.2 *Registering objects with code blocks*

Another option for creating a component with a primitive value is to use the `Register` method. It lets you supply a delegate that creates the component:

```
builder.Register<ICourse>(c => new ChiliConCarne(Spiciness.Hot));
```

You already saw the `Register` method when we discussed the registration of `Spiciness` in section 13.3.1. Here, the `ChiliConCarne` constructor is invoked with a `Spiciness` value of `Hot` every time the `ICourse` service is resolved.

> **NOTE** The `Register` method is type-safe, but it disables AUTO-WIRING.

When it comes to the `ChiliConCarne` class, you have a choice between AUTO-WIRING or using a code block. Other classes can be more restrictive: they can't be instantiated through a public constructor. Instead, you must use some sort of factory to create instances of the type. This is always troublesome for DI CONTAINERS, because, by default, they look after public constructors. Consider this example constructor for the public `JunkFood` class:

```
internal JunkFood(string name)
```

Even though the `JunkFood` class might be public, the constructor is internal. In this example, instances of `JunkFood` should instead be created through the static `JunkFoodFactory` class:

```
public static class JunkFoodFactory
{
    public static JunkFood Create(string name)
    {
        return new JunkFood(name);
    }
}
```

From Autofac's perspective, this is a problematic API, because there are no unambiguous and well-established conventions around static factories. It needs help—and you can give that help by providing a code block it can execute to create the instance:

```
builder.Register<IMeal>(c => JunkFoodFactory.Create("chicken meal"));
```

This time, you use the `Register` method to create the component by invoking a static factory within the code block. With that in place, `JunkFoodFactory.Create` is invoked every time `IMeal` is resolved and the result returned.

When you end up writing the code to create the instance, how is this better than invoking the code directly? By using a code block inside a `Register` method call, you still gain something:

- *You map from `IMeal` to `JunkFood`.* This allows consuming classes to stay loosely coupled.
- *Instance scope can still be configured.* Although the code block will be invoked to create the instance, it may not be invoked every time the instance is requested. It is by default, but if you change it to a SINGLETON, the code block will only be invoked once, with the result cached and reused thereafter.

In this section, you've seen how you can use Autofac to deal with more-difficult creational APIs. You can use the `WithParameter` method to wire constructors with services to maintain a semblance of AUTO-WIRING, or you can use the `Register` method with a code block for a more type-safe approach. We have yet to look at how to work with multiple components, so let's now turn our attention in that direction.

13.4 *Working with multiple components*

As alluded to in section 12.1.2, DI CONTAINERS thrive on distinctness but have a hard time with ambiguity. When using CONSTRUCTOR INJECTION, a single constructor is preferred over overloaded constructors, because it's evident which constructor to use when there's no choice. This is also the case when mapping from ABSTRACTIONS to concrete types. If you attempt to map multiple concrete types to the same ABSTRACTION, you introduce ambiguity.

Despite the undesirable qualities of ambiguity, you often need to work with multiple implementations of a single ABSTRACTION.[5] This can be the case in situations like these:

- Different concrete types are used for different consumers.
- DEPENDENCIES are sequences.
- Decorators or Composites are in use.

---

[5] As a matter of fact, having many ABSTRACTIONS with only one implementation is a design smell described by the Reused Abstraction Principle. See Jason Gorman, "Reused Abstractions Principle (RAP)," 2010, http://www.codemanship.co.uk/parlezuml/blog/?postid=934.

In this section, we'll look at each of these cases and see how Autofac addresses each in turn. When we're done, you should be able to register and resolve components even when multiple implementations of the same ABSTRACTION are in play. Let's first see how you can provide more fine-grained control than AUTO-WIRING provides.

13.4.1 *Selecting among multiple candidates*

AUTO-WIRING is convenient and powerful but provides little control. As long as all ABSTRACTIONS are distinctly mapped to concrete types, you have no problems. But as soon as you introduce more implementations of the same interface, ambiguity rears its ugly head. Let's first recap how Autofac deals with multiple registrations of the same ABSTRACTION.

CONFIGURING MULTIPLE IMPLEMENTATIONS OF THE SAME SERVICE

As you saw in section 13.1.2, you can register multiple implementations of the same interface like this:

```
builder.RegisterType<Steak>().As<IIngredient>();
builder.RegisterType<SauceBéarnaise>().As<IIngredient>();
```

This example registers both the `Steak` and `SauceBéarnaise` classes as the `IIngredient` service. The last registration wins, so if you resolve `IIngredient` with `scope.Resolve<IIngredient>()`, you'll get a `SauceBéarnaise` instance.

> **TIP** The last registration of a given service defines the default instance for that type. You can register a type with `.PreserveExistingDefaults()` if you don't want your registration to take precedence over previous registrations.

You can also ask the container to resolve all `IIngredient` components. Autofac has no dedicated method to do that, but instead relies on relationship types (https://mng.bz/P429). A *relationship type* is a type that indicates a relationship that the container can interpret. As an example, you can use `IEnumerable<T>` to indicate that you want all services of a given type:

```
IEnumerable<IIngredient> ingredients =
    scope.Resolve<IEnumerable<IIngredient>>();
```

Notice that we use the normal `Resolve` method, but that we request `IEnumerable<IIngredient>`. Autofac interprets this as a convention and gives us all the `IIngredient` components it has.

> **TIP** As an alternative to `IEnumerable<T>`, you can also request an array. The results are equivalent; in both cases, you get all the components of the requested type.

When you register components, you can give each registration a name that you can later use to select among the different components. This code snippet shows that process:

```
builder.RegisterType<Steak>().Named<IIngredient>("meat");
builder.RegisterType<SauceBéarnaise>().Named<IIngredient>("sauce");
```

As always, you start with the `RegisterType` method, but instead of following up with the `As` method, you use the `Named` method to specify a service type as well as a name. This enables you to resolve named services by supplying the same name to the `Resolve-Named` method:

```
IIngredient meat = scope.ResolveNamed<IIngredient>("meat");
IIngredient sauce = scope.ResolveNamed<IIngredient>("sauce");
```

> **NOTE** A named component doesn't count as a default component. If you only register named components, you can't resolve a default instance of the service. But nothing prevents you from also registering a default (unnamed) component with the `As` method. You can even do it in the same statement by method chaining.

Naming components with strings is a fairly common feature of DI CONTAINERS. But Autofac also lets you identify components with arbitrary keys:

```
object meatKey = new object();
builder.RegisterType<Steak>().Keyed<IIngredient>(meatKey);
```

The key can be any object, and you can subsequently use it to resolve the component:

```
IIngredient meat = scope.ResolveKeyed<IIngredient>(meatKey);
```

Given that you should always resolve services in a single COMPOSITION ROOT, you should normally not expect to deal with such ambiguity on this level. If you do find yourself invoking the `Resolve` method with a specific name or key, consider if you can change your approach to be less ambiguous. You can also use named or keyed instances to select among multiple alternatives when configuring DEPENDENCIES for a given service.

REGISTERING NAMED DEPENDENCIES

As useful as AUTO-WIRING is, sometimes you need to override the normal behavior to provide fine-grained control over which DEPENDENCIES go where; it can also be that you need to address an ambiguous API. As an example, consider this constructor:

```
public ThreeCourseMeal(ICourse entrée, ICourse mainCourse, ICourse dessert)
```

In this case, you have three identically typed DEPENDENCIES, each of which represents a different concept. In most cases, you want to map each of the DEPENDENCIES to a separate type. The following listing shows how you could choose to register the ICourse mappings.

Listing 13.5   Registering named courses

```
builder.RegisterType<Rillettes>().Named<ICourse>("entrée");
builder.RegisterType<CordonBleu>().Named<ICourse>("mainCourse");
builder.RegisterType<MousseAuChocolat>().Named<ICourse>("dessert");
```

Here, you register three named components, mapping the Rillettes to an instance named *entrée*, CordonBleu to an instance named *mainCourse*, and the MousseAuChocolat to an instance named *dessert*. Given this configuration, you can now register the Three-CourseMeal class with the named registrations.

This turns out to be surprisingly complex. In the following listing, we'll first show you what it looks like, and then we'll subsequently pick apart the example to understand what's going on.

Listing 13.6   Overriding AUTO-WIRING

The WithParameter method provides parameter values for the ThreeCourseMeal constructor. One of its overloads takes two arguments.

```
builder.RegisterType<ThreeCourseMeal>().As<IMeal>()
    .WithParameter(
        (p, c) => p.Name == "entrée",
        (p, c) => c.ResolveNamed<ICourse>("entrée"))
    .WithParameter(
        (p, c) => p.Name == "mainCourse",
        (p, c) => c.ResolveNamed<ICourse>("mainCourse"))
    .WithParameter(
        (p, c) => p.Name == "dessert",
        (p, c) => c.ResolveNamed<ICourse>("dessert"));
```

A predicate matching the constructor parameter to a specific name; in this case, mainCourse

Resolves the value to be injected into the constructor parameter; in this case, dessert

Let's take a closer look at what's going on here. The WithParameter method overload wraps around the ResolvedParameter class, which has this constructor:

```
public ResolvedParameter(
    Func<ParameterInfo, IComponentContext, bool> predicate,
    Func<ParameterInfo, IComponentContext, object> valueAccessor);
```

The predicate parameter is a test that determines whether the valueAccessor delegate will be invoked. When predicate returns true, valueAccessor is invoked to provide the value for the parameter. Both delegates take the same input: information about the parameter in the form of a ParameterInfo object and an IComponentContext that can be used to resolve other components. When Autofac uses the ResolvedParameter instances, it provides both of these values when it invokes the delegates.

As listing 13.6 shows, the resulting registration is rather verbose. With the aid of two self-written helper methods, however, you can simplify the registration considerably:

```
builder.RegisterType<ThreeCourseMeal>().As<IMeal>()
    .WithParameter(Named("entrée"), InjectWith<ICourse>("entrée"))
    .WithParameter(Named("mainCourse"), InjectWith<ICourse>("mainCourse"))
    .WithParameter(Named("dessert"), InjectWith<ICourse>("dessert"));
```

By introducing the `Named` and `InjectWith<T>` helper methods, you simplified the registration, reduced its verbosity, and at the same time, made it easier to read what's going on. It almost starts to read like poetry (or a well-aged bottle of wine):

create thy `ThreeCourseMeal`, *with a parameter Named entrée,* `InjectedWith` *an* `ICourse` *named entrée.*

The following code shows the two new methods:

```
Func<ParameterInfo, IComponentContext, bool> Named(string name)
{
    return (p, c) => p.Name == name;
}

Func<ParameterInfo, IComponentContext, object> InjectWith<T>(string name)
{
    return (p, c) => c.ResolveNamed<T>(name);
}
```

When called, both methods create a new delegate that wraps the supplied `name` argument. Sometimes there's no other way than to use the `WithParameter` method for each and every constructor parameter, but in other cases, you can take advantage of conventions.

RESOLVING NAMED COMPONENTS BY CONVENTION

If you examine listing 13.6 closely, you'll notice a repetitive pattern. Each call to `With-Parameter` addresses only a single constructor parameter, but each `valueAccessor` does the same thing: it uses the `IComponentContext` to resolve an `ICourse` component with the same name as the parameter.

There's no requirement that says you must name the component after the constructor parameter, but when this is the case, you can take advantage of this convention and rewrite listing 13.6 in a simpler way. The following listing demonstrates how.

Listing 13.7   Overriding AUTO-WIRING with a convention

```
builder.RegisterType<ThreeCourseMeal>().As<IMeal>()
    .WithParameter(
        (p, c) => true,
        (p, c) => c.ResolveNamed(p.Name, p.ParameterType));
```

It might be a little surprising, but you can address all three constructor parameters of the `ThreeCourseMeal` class with the same `WithParameter` call. You do that by stating that this instance will handle any parameter Autofac might throw at it. Because you only use this method to configure the `ThreeCourseMeal` class, the convention only applies within this limited scope.

As the predicate always returns `true`, the second code block will be invoked for all three constructor parameters. In all three cases, it'll ask `IComponentContext` to resolve a component that has the same name and type as the parameter. This is functionally the same as what you did in listing 13.6.

> **WARNING** Identifying parameters by their names is convenient but not refactoring-safe. If you rename a parameter, you can break the configuration (depending on your refactoring tool).

As in listing 13.6, you can create a simplified version of listing 13.7. But we'll leave this as an exercise for the reader.

Overriding AUTO-WIRING by explicitly mapping parameters to named components is a universally applicable solution. You can do this even if you configure the named components in one part of the COMPOSITION ROOT and the consumer in a completely different part, because the only identification that ties a named component together with a parameter is the name. This is always possible but can be brittle if you have many names to manage. When the original reason prompting you to use named components is to deal with ambiguity, a better solution is to design your own API to get rid of that ambiguity. It often leads to a better overall design.

In the next section, you'll see how to use the less ambiguous and more flexible approach, where you allow any number of courses in a meal. To this end, you must learn how Autofac deals with lists and sequences.

13.4.2 *Wiring sequences*

In section 6.1.1, we discussed how CONSTRUCTOR INJECTION acts as a warning system for SINGLE RESPONSIBILITY PRINCIPLE violations. The lesson then was that instead of viewing Constructor Over-Injection as a weakness of the CONSTRUCTOR INJECTION pattern, you should rather rejoice that it makes problematic design so obvious.

When it comes to DI CONTAINERS and ambiguity, we see a similar relationship. DI CONTAINERS generally don't deal with ambiguity in a graceful manner. Although you can make a good DI CONTAINER like Autofac deal with it, it can seem awkward. This is often an indication that you could improve on the design of your code.

> **TIP** If configuring a certain part of your API is difficult with Autofac, take a step back and reevaluate your design against the patterns and principles presented in this book. More often than not, configuration difficulties are caused by an application design that doesn't follow these patterns or violates these principles. Making your overall design better not only improves the application's maintainability, but also makes it easier to configure Autofac.

Instead of feeling constrained by Autofac, you should embrace its conventions and let it guide you toward a better and more consistent design. In this section, we'll look at an example that demonstrates how you can refactor away from ambiguity, as well as show how Autofac deals with sequences, arrays, and lists.

REFACTORING TO A BETTER COURSE BY REMOVING AMBIGUITY

In section 13.4.1, you saw how the `ThreeCourseMeal` and its inherent ambiguity forced you to abandon AUTO-WIRING and instead use `WithParameter`. This should prompt you to reconsider the API design. For example, a simple generalization moves toward an implementation of IMeal that takes an arbitrary number of ICourse instances, instead of exactly three, as was the case with the ThreeCourseMeal class:

```
public Meal(IEnumerable<ICourse> courses)
```

Notice that instead of requiring three distinct ICourse instances in the constructor, the single dependency on an IEnumerable<ICourse> instance lets you provide any number of courses to the Meal class—from zero to ... a lot! This solves the issue with ambiguity, because there's now only a single DEPENDENCY. In addition, it also improves the API and implementation by providing a single, general-purpose class that can model different types of meals, from a simple meal with a single course to an elaborate 12-course dinner.

In this section, we'll look at how you can configure Autofac to wire up Meal instances with appropriate ICourse DEPENDENCIES. When you're done, you should have a good idea of the options available when you need to configure instances with sequences of DEPENDENCIES.

AUTO-WIRING SEQUENCES

Autofac has a good understanding of sequences, so if you want to use all registered components of a given service, AUTO-WIRING just works. As an example, you can configure the IMeal service like this:

```
builder.RegisterType<Rillettes>().As<IIngredient>();
builder.RegisterType<CordonBlue>().As<IIngredient>();
builder.RegisterType<MousseAuChocolat>().As<IIngredient>();

builder.RegisterType<Meal>().As<IMeal>();
```

Notice that this is a completely standard mapping from a concrete type to an ABSTRACTION. Autofac automatically understands the Meal constructor and determines that the correct course of action is to resolve all ICourse components. When you resolve IMeal, you get a Meal instance with the ICourse components: Rillettes, CordonBleu, and MousseAuChocolat.

Autofac automatically handles sequences, and, unless you specify otherwise, it does what you'd expect it to do: it resolves a sequence of DEPENDENCIES to all registered components of that type. Only when you need to explicitly pick some components from a larger set do you need to do more. Let's see how you can do that.

PICKING ONLY SOME COMPONENTS FROM A LARGER SET

Autofac's default strategy of injecting all components is often the correct policy, but as figure 13.4 shows, there may be cases where you want to pick only some registered components from the larger set of all registered components.

> **NOTE** The need to inject a subset of a complete collection isn't a common scenario, but it does demonstrate how to solve more-complex needs that you might encounter.

When you previously let Autofac AUTO-WIRE all configured instances, it corresponded to the situation depicted on the right side of the figure. If you want to register a

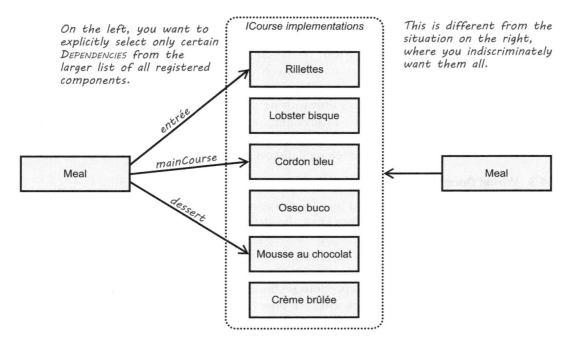

Figure 13.4   Picking components from a larger set of all registered components

component as shown on the left side, you must explicitly define which components should be used. In order to achieve this, you can use the WithParameter method the way you did in listings 13.6 and 13.7. This time, you're dealing with the Meal constructor that only takes a single parameter. The following listing demonstrates how you can implement the value-providing part of WithParameter to explicitly pick named components from the IComponentContext.

Listing 13.8   Injecting named components into a sequence

```
builder.RegisterType<Meal>().As<IMeal>()
    .WithParameter(
        (p, c) => true,
        (p, c) => new[]
        {
            c.ResolveNamed<ICourse>("entrée"),
            c.ResolveNamed<ICourse>("mainCourse"),
            c.ResolveNamed<ICourse>("dessert")
        });
```

As you saw in section 13.4.1, the WithParameter method takes two delegates as input parameters. The first is a predicate that's used to determine if the second delegate should be invoked. In this case, you decide to be a bit lazy and return true. You know that the Meal class has only a single constructor parameter, so this'll work. But if you later refactor the Meal class to take a second constructor parameter, this may not work correctly anymore. It might be safer to define an explicit check for the parameter type.

The second delegate provides the value for the parameter. You use `IComponentContext` to resolve three named components into an array. The result is an array of `ICourse` instances, which is compatible with `IEnumerable<ICourse>`.

Autofac natively understands sequences; unless you need to explicitly pick only some components from all services of a given type, Autofac automatically does the right thing. AUTO-WIRING works not only with single instances, but also for sequences, and the container maps a sequence to all configured instances of the corresponding type. A perhaps less intuitive use of having multiple instances of the same ABSTRACTION is the Decorators design pattern, which we'll discuss next.

13.4.3 *Wiring Decorators*

In section 9.1.1, we discussed how the Decorator design pattern is useful when implementing CROSS-CUTTING CONCERNS. By definition, Decorators introduce multiple types of the same ABSTRACTION. At the very least, you have two implementations of an ABSTRACTION: the Decorator itself and the decorated type. If you stack the Decorators, you can have even more. This is another example of having multiple registrations of the same service. Unlike the previous sections, these registrations aren't conceptually equal but rather DEPENDENCIES of each other.

There are multiple strategies for applying Decorators in Autofac, such as using the previously discussed `WithParameter` or using code blocks, as we discussed in section 13.3.2. In this section, however, we'll focus on the use of the `RegisterDecorator` and `RegisterGenericDecorator` methods because they make configuring Decorators a no-brainer.

DECORATING NON-GENERIC ABSTRACTIONS WITH `RegisterDecorator`

Autofac has built-in support for Decorators via the `RegisterDecorator` method. The following example shows how to use this method to apply `Breading` to a `VealCutlet`:

Registers the VealCutlet as a default IIngredient

Registers Breading as a Decorator of IIngredient. When resolving an IIngredient, Autofac returns a VealCutlet wrapped inside Breading.

```
builder.RegisterType<VealCutlet>()
    .As<IIngredient>();

builder.RegisterDecorator<Breading, IIngredient>();
```

As you learned in chapter 9, you get Cordon Bleu when you slit open a pocket in the veal cutlet and add ham, cheese, and garlic into the pocket before breading the cutlet. The following example shows how to add a `HamCheeseGarlic` Decorator in between `VealCutlet` and the `Breading` Decorator:

```
builder.RegisterType<VealCutlet>()
    .As<IIngredient>();

builder.RegisterDecorator<HamCheeseGarlic,
    IIngredient>();

builder.RegisterDecorator<Breading, IIngredient>();
```

Adds a new Decorator

By placing this new registration before the `Breading` registration, the `HamCheeseGarlic` Decorator is wrapped first. This results in an object graph equal to the following PURE DI version:

```
new Breading(
    new HamCheeseGarlic(
        new VealCutlet()));
```

VealCutlet is wrapped by HamCheeseGarlic, which is wrapped by Breading.

NOTE Autofac applies Decorators in the order of registration.

Chaining Decorators using the `RegisterDecorator` method is easy in Autofac. Likewise, you can apply generic Decorators, as you'll see next.

DECORATING GENERIC ABSTRACTIONS WITH `RegisterGenericDecorator`

During the course of chapter 10, we defined multiple generic Decorators that could be applied to any `ICommandService<TCommand>` implementation. In the remainder of this chapter, we'll set our ingredients and courses aside, and take a look at how to register these generic Decorators using Autofac. The following listing demonstrates how to register all `ICommandService<TCommand>` implementations with the three Decorators presented in section 10.3.

> **Listing 13.9 Decorating generic AUTO-REGISTERED ABSTRACTIONS**

```
builder.RegisterAssemblyTypes(assembly)
    .AsClosedTypesOf(typeof(ICommandService<>));

builder.RegisterGenericDecorator(
    typeof(AuditingCommandServiceDecorator<>),
    typeof(ICommandService<>));

builder.RegisterGenericDecorator(
    typeof(TransactionCommandServiceDecorator<>),
    typeof(ICommandService<>));

builder.RegisterGenericDecorator(
    typeof(SecureCommandServiceDecorator<>),
    typeof(ICommandService<>));
```

As you saw in listing 13.3, listing 13.9 uses `Register-AssemblyTypes` to register arbitrary `ICommand-Service<TCommand>` implementations. To register generic Decorators, however, Autofac provides a different method—`RegisterGenericDecorator`. The result of the configuration of listing 13.9 is figure 13.5, which we discussed previously in section 10.3.4.

You can configure Decorators in different ways, but in this section, we focused on Autofac's methods that were explicitly designed for this task. Autofac lets you work with multiple instances in several different ways: you can register components as alternatives to each other, as peers resolved as sequences,

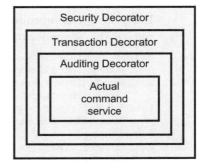

Figure 13.5 Enriching a real command service with transaction, auditing, and security aspects

or as hierarchical Decorators. In many cases, Autofac figures out what to do, but you can always explicitly define how services are composed if you need more-explicit control.

Although consumers that rely on sequences of DEPENDENCIES can be the most intuitive use of multiple instances of the same ABSTRACTION, Decorators are another good example. But there's a third and perhaps a bit surprising case where multiple instances come into play, which is the Composite design pattern.

13.4.4 *Wiring Composites*

During the course of this book, we discussed the Composite design pattern on several occasions. In section 6.1.2, for instance, you created a `CompositeNotification-Service` (listing 6.4) that both implemented `INotificationService` and wrapped a sequence of `INotificationService` implementations.

WIRING NON-GENERIC COMPOSITES

Let's take a look at how you can register Composites like the `CompositeNotification-Service` from chapter 6 in Autofac. The following listing shows this class again.

> **Listing 13.10 The `CompositeNotificationService` Composite from chapter 6**

```
public class CompositeNotificationService : INotificationService
{
    private readonly IEnumerable<INotificationService> services;

    public CompositeNotificationService(
        IEnumerable<INotificationService> services)
    {
        this.services = services;
    }

    public void OrderApproved(Order order)
    {
        foreach (INotificationService service in this.services)
        {
            service.OrderApproved(order);
        }
    }
}
```

Registering a Composite requires that it be added as a default registration while injecting it with a sequence of named instances:

```
builder.RegisterType<OrderApprovedReceiptSender>()
    .Named<INotificationService>("service");
builder.RegisterType<AccountingNotifier>()
    .Named<INotificationService>("service");
builder.RegisterType<OrderFulfillment>()
    .Named<INotificationService>("service");

builder.Register(c =>
    new CompositeNotificationService(
        c.ResolveNamed<IEnumerable<INotificationService>>("service")))
    .As<INotificationService>();
```

Here, three `INotificationService` implementations are registered by the same name, *service*, using the AUTO-WIRING API of Autofac. The `CompositeNotificationService`, on the other hand, is registered using a delegate. Inside the delegate, the Composite is newed up manually and injected with an `IEnumerable<INotificationService>`. By specifying the service name, the previous named registrations are resolved.

Because the number of notification services will likely grow over time, you can reduce the burden on your COMPOSITION ROOT by applying AUTO-REGISTRATION. Using the `RegisterAssemblyTypes` method, you can turn the previous list of registrations in a simple one-liner.

Listing 13.11 Registering `CompositeNotificationService`

```
builder.RegisterAssemblyTypes(assembly)
    .Named<INotificationService>("service");

builder.Register(c =>
    new CompositeNotificationService(
        c.ResolveNamed<IEnumerable<INotificationService>>("service")))
    .As<INotificationService>();
```

This looks reasonably simple, but looks are deceiving. `RegisterAssemblyTypes` will register any non-generic implementation that implements `INotificationService`. When you try to run the previous code, depending on which assembly your Composite is located in, Autofac might throw the following exception:

> *Circular component dependency detected: CompositeNotificationService -> INotificationService[] -> CompositeNotificationService -> INotificationService[] -> CompositeNotificationService.*

Autofac detected a cyclic DEPENDENCY. (We discussed DEPENDENCY cycles in detail in section 6.3.) Fortunately, its exception message is pretty clear. It describes that `CompositeNotificationService` depends on `INotificationService[]`. The `CompositeNotificationService` wraps a sequence of `INotificationService`, but that sequence itself again contains `CompositeNotificationService`. What this means is that `CompositeNotificationService` is an element of the sequence that's injected into `CompositeNotificationService`. This is an object graph that's impossible to construct.

`CompositeNotificationService` became a part of the sequence because Autofac's `RegisterAssemblyTypes` registers all non-generic `INotificationService` implementations it finds. In this case, `CompositeNotificationService` was placed in the same assembly as all other implementations.

There are multiple ways around this. The simplest solution is to move the Composite to a different assembly; for instance, the assembly containing the COMPOSITION ROOT. This prevents `RegisterAssemblyTypes` from selecting the type, because it's provided with a particular `Assembly` instance. Another option is to filter the

CompositeNotificationService out of the list. An elegant way of doing this is using the Except method:

```
builder.RegisterAssemblyTypes(assembly)
    .Except<CompositeNotificationService>()
    .Named<INotificationService>("service");
```

Composite classes, however, aren't the only classes that might require removal. You'll have to do the same for any Decorator. This isn't particularly difficult, but because there'll typically be more Decorator implementations, you might be better off querying the type information to find out whether the type represents a Decorator or not. The following example shows how you can filter out Decorators as well, using a custom IsDecoratorFor helper method:

```
builder.RegisterAssemblyTypes(assembly)
    .Except<CompositeNotificationService>()
    .Where(type => !IsDecoratorFor<INotificationService>(type))
    .Named<INotificationService>("service");
```

And the following example shows the IsDecoratorFor method:

```
private static bool IsDecoratorFor<T>(Type type)
{
    return typeof(T).IsAssignableFrom(type) &&
        type.GetConstructors()[0].GetParameters()
            .Any(p => p.ParameterType == typeof(T));
}
```

The IsDecoratorFor method expects a type to have a single constructor. A type is considered to be a Decorator when it both implements the given T ABSTRACTION and its constructor also requires a T.

WIRING GENERIC COMPOSITES

In section 13.4.3, you saw how using Autofac's RegisterGenericDecorator method made registering generic Decorators child's play. In this section, we'll take a look at how you can register Composites for generic ABSTRACTIONS.

In section 6.1.3, you specified the CompositeEventHandler<TEvent> class (listing 6.12) as a Composite implementation over a sequence of IEventHandler<TEvent> implementations. Let's see if you can register the Composite with its wrapped event handler implementations.

Let's start with AUTO-REGISTRATION of the event handlers. As you've seen previously, this is done using the RegisterAssemblyTypes method:

```
builder.RegisterAssemblyTypes(assembly)
    .As(type =>
        from interfaceType in type.GetInterfaces()
        where interfaceType.IsClosedTypeOf(typeof(IEventHandler<>))
        select new KeyedService("handler", interfaceType));
```

This example makes use of the As overload that allows supplying a sequence of Autofac .Core.KeyedService instances. A KeyedService class is a small data object that combines both a key and a service type.

Autofac runs any type it finds in the assembly through the As method. You can use a LINQ query to find the type's implemented interface that's a closed-generic version of IEventHandler<TEvent>. For most types in the assembly, this query won't yield any results, because most types don't implement IEventHandler<TEvent>. For those types, no registration is added to ContainerBuilder.

Even though this is quite complex, generic Composites and Decorators don't have to be filtered out. RegisterAssemblyTypes only selects non-generic implementations. Generic types, such as CompositeEventHandler<TEvent>, won't cause any problem, and don't have to be filtered out or moved to a different assembly. This is fortunate, because it wouldn't be fun at all to have to write a version of IsDecoratorFor that could handle generic ABSTRACTIONS.

What remains is the registration for CompositeEventHandler<TEvent>. Because this type is generic, you can't use the Register overload that takes in a predicate. Instead, you use RegisterGeneric. This method allows making a mapping between a generic implementation and its ABSTRACTION, similar to what you saw with RegisterGeneric-Decorator. To get the sequence of named registrations to be injected into the Composite's constructor argument, you can once more use the versatile WithParameter method:

```
builder.RegisterGeneric(typeof(CompositeEventHandler<>))
    .As(typeof(IEventHandler<>))
    .WithParameter(
        (p, c) => true,
        (p, c) => c.ResolveNamed("handler", p.ParameterType));
```

Because CompositeEventHandler<TEvent> contains a single constructor parameter, you simplify the registration to apply to all parameters by letting the predicate return true.

The WithParameter delegates are called when a closed IEventHandler<TEvent> is requested. Therefore, at the time of invocation, you can get the type of the constructor parameter by calling p.ParameterType. For example, if an IEventHandler<Order-Approved> is requested, the parameter type will be IEnumerable<IEvent-Handler<OrderApproved>>. By passing this type on to the ResolveNamed method with the sequence name *handler*, Autofac resolves the previously registered sequence of named instances that implement IEventHandler<OrderApproved>.

Although the registration of Decorators is simple, this unfortunately doesn't hold for Composites. Autofac hasn't been designed—yet—with the Composite design pattern in mind. It's likely this will change in a future version.

This completes our discussion of the Autofac DI CONTAINER. In the next chapter, we'll turn our attention to Simple Injector.

Summary

- The Autofac DI CONTAINER offers a fairly comprehensive API and addresses many of the trickier situations you typically encounter when you use DI CONTAINERS.

- An important overall theme for Autofac seems to be one of explicitness. It doesn't attempt to guess what you mean, but rather offers an easy-to-use API that provides you with options to explicitly enable features.

- Autofac enforces stricter separation of concerns between configuring and consuming a container. You configure components using a `ContainerBuilder` instance, but a `ContainerBuilder` can't resolve components. When you're done configuring a `ContainerBuilder`, you use it to build an `IContainer` that you can use to resolve components.

- With Autofac, resolving from the root container directly is a bad practice. This can easily lead to memory leaks or concurrency bugs. Instead, you should always resolve from a lifetime scope.

- Autofac supports the standard LIFESTYLES: TRANSIENT, SINGLETON, and SCOPED.

- Autofac allows working with ambiguous constructors and types by providing an API that allows supplying code blocks. This allows any code that creates a service to be executed.

The Simple Injector DI Container

In this chapter

- Working with Simple Injector's basic registration API
- Managing component lifetime
- Configuring difficult APIs
- Configuring sequences, Decorators, and Composites

In the previous chapter, we looked at the Autofac DI CONTAINER, created by Nicholas Blumhardt in 2007. Three years later, Steven created Simple Injector, which we'll examine in this chapter. We'll give Simple Injector the same treatment that we gave Autofac in the last chapter. You'll see how you can use Simple Injector to apply the principles and patterns presented in parts 1–3.

This chapter is divided into four sections. You can read each section independently, though the first section is a prerequisite for the other sections, and the fourth section relies on some methods and classes introduced in the third section. You can read this chapter apart from the rest of the chapters in part 4, specifically to learn about Simple Injector, or you can read it together with the other chapters to compare DI CONTAINERS.

Although this chapter isn't a complete treatment of the Simple Injector container, it gives enough information that you can start using it. This chapter includes information on how to deal with the most common questions that may come up as you use Simple Injector. For more information about this container, see the Simple Injector home page at https://simpleinjector.org.

14.1 Introducing Simple Injector

In this section, you'll learn where to get Simple Injector, what you get, and how to start using it. We'll also look at common configuration options. Table 14.1 provides fundamental information that you're likely to need to get started.

Table 14.1   Simple Injector at a glance

Question	Answer
Where do I get it?	From Visual Studio, you can get it via NuGet. The package name is *SimpleInjector*.
Which platforms are supported?	.NET 4.0 and .NET Standard 1.0 (.NET Core 1.0, Mono 4.6, Xamarin.iOS 10.0, Xamarin.Mac 3.0, Xamarin.Android 7.0, UWP 10.0, Windows 8.0, Windows Phone 8.1).
How much does it cost?	Nothing. It's open source.
How is it licensed?	MIT License
Where can I get help?	There's no guaranteed support, but you're likely to get help in the official forum at https://simpleinjector.org/forum or by asking your question on Stack Overflow at https://stackoverflow.com/.
On which version is this chapter based?	4.4.3

At a high level, using Simple Injector isn't that different from using the other DI CONTAINERS. As with the Autofac DI CONTAINER (covered in chapter 13) and the Microsoft.Extensions.DependencyInjection DI CONTAINER (covered in chapter 15), usage is a two-step process, as figure 14.1 illustrates.

As you might remember from chapter 13, to facilitate the two-step process, Autofac uses a `ContainerBuilder` class that produces an `IContainer`. Simple Injector, on the other hand, integrates both registration and resolution in the same `Container` instance. Still, it forces the registration to be a two-step process by disallowing any explicit registrations to be made after the first service is resolved.

Although resolution isn't that different, Simple Injector's registration API does differ quite a lot from how most DI CONTAINERS work. In its design and implementation, it eliminates many pitfalls that are a common cause of bugs. We've discussed most of these

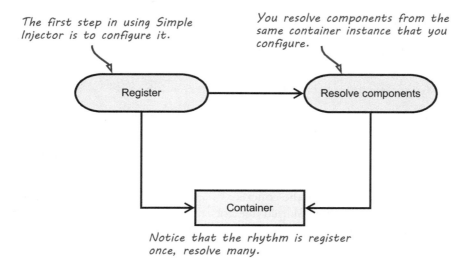

The first step in using Simple Injector is to configure it.

You resolve components from the same container instance that you configure.

Register → Resolve components

Container

Notice that the rhythm is register once, resolve many.

Figure 14.1   The pattern for using Simple Injector. First, you configure a `Container`, and then, using the same container instance, you resolve components from it.

pitfalls throughout the book, so in this chapter, we'll discuss the following differences between Simple Injector and other DI CONTAINERS:

- Scopes are ambient, allowing object graphs to always be resolved from the container itself to prevent memory and concurrency bugs.
- Sequences are registered through a different API to prevent accidental duplicate registrations from overriding each other.
- Primitive types can't be registered directly to prevent registrations from becoming ambiguous.
- Object graphs can be verified to spot common configuration errors, such as CAPTIVE DEPENDENCIES.

When you're done with this section, you should have a good feeling for the overall usage pattern of Simple Injector, and you should be able to start using it in well-behaved scenarios—where all components follow proper DI patterns, such as CONSTRUCTOR INJECTION. Let's start with the simplest scenario and see how you can resolve objects using a Simple Injector container.

14.1.1   *Resolving objects*

The core service of any DI CONTAINER is to compose object graphs. In this section, we'll look at the API that lets you compose object graphs with Simple Injector.

If you remember the discussion about resolving components with Autofac, you may recall that Autofac requires you to register all relevant components before you can resolve them. This isn't the case with Simple Injector; if you request a concrete type with a parameterless constructor, no configuration is necessary. The following listing shows one of the simplest possible uses of Simple Injector.

Listing 14.1   Simplest possible use of Simple Injector

```
var container = new Container();          ◄──────┘ Creates container

SauceBéarnaise sauce =
    container.GetInstance<SauceBéarnaise>();    ◄──────┘ Resolves concrete instance
```

Given an instance of `SimpleInjector.Container`, you can use the generic `GetInstance` method to get an instance of the concrete `SauceBéarnaise` class. Because this class has a parameterless constructor, Simple Injector automatically creates an instance of it. No explicit configuration of the container is necessary.

> **NOTE** The `GetInstance<T>` method is equivalent to Autofac's `Resolve<T>` method.

As you learned in section 12.1.2, AUTO-WIRING is the ability to automatically compose an object graph by making use of the type information. Because Simple Injector supports AUTO-WIRING, even in the absence of a parameterless constructor, it can create instances without configurations as long as the involved constructor parameters are all concrete types, and all parameters in the entire tree have leaf types with parameterless constructors. As an example, consider this `Mayonnaise` constructor:

```
public Mayonnaise(EggYolk eggYolk, SunflowerOil oil)
```

Although the mayonnaise recipe is a bit simplified, suppose both `EggYolk` and `Sunflower-Oil` are concrete classes with parameterless constructors. Although `Mayonnaise` itself has no parameterless constructor, Simple Injector creates it without any configuration:

```
var container = new Container();
Mayonnaise mayo = container.GetInstance<Mayonnaise>();
```

This works because Simple Injector is able to figure out how to create all required constructor parameters. But as soon as you introduce loose coupling, you must configure Simple Injector by mapping ABSTRACTIONS to concrete types.

MAPPING ABSTRACTIONS TO CONCRETE TYPES

Although Simple Injector's ability to AUTO-WIRE concrete types certainly can come in handy from time to time, loose coupling requires you to map ABSTRACTIONS to concrete types. Creating instances based on such maps is the core service offered by any DI CONTAINER, but you must still define the map. In this example, you map the `IIngredient` interface to the concrete `SauceBéarnaise` class, which allows you to successfully resolve `IIngredient`:

```
var container = new Container();

container.Register<IIngredient, SauceBéarnaise>();
```
◄——— **Maps an ABSTRACTION to a particular implementation**

```
IIngredient sauce =
    container.GetInstance<IIngredient>();
```
◄——— **Resolves SauceBéarnaise as an IIngredient**

You use the `Container` instance to register types and define maps. Here, the generic `Register` method allows an ABSTRACTION to be mapped to a particular implementation. This lets you register a concrete type. Because of the previous `Register` call, `SauceBéarnaise` can now be resolved as `IIngredient`.

> **NOTE** The `Register<TService, TImplementation>` method contains *generic type constraints*. This means that an incompatible type mapping will be caught by the compiler.

In many cases, the generic API is all you need. Still, there are situations where you need a more weakly typed way to resolve services. This is also possible.

RESOLVING WEAKLY TYPED SERVICES

Sometimes you can't use a generic API, because you don't know the appropriate type at design time. All you have is a `Type` instance, but you'd still like to get an instance of that type. You saw an example of that in section 7.3, where we discussed ASP.NET Core MVC's `IControllerActivator` class. The relevant method is this one:

```
object Create(ControllerContext context);
```

As shown previously in listing 7.8, the `ControllerContext` captures the controller's `Type`, which you can extract using the `ControllerTypeInfo` property of the `Action-Descriptor` property:

```
Type controllerType = context.ActionDescriptor.ControllerTypeInfo.AsType();
```

Because you only have a `Type` instance, you can't use the generic `GetInstance<T>` method, but must resort to a weakly typed API. Simple Injector offers a weakly typed overload of the `GetInstance` method that lets you implement the `Create` method like this:

```
Type controllerType = context.ActionDescriptor.ControllerTypeInfo.AsType();
return container.GetInstance(controllerType);
```

The weakly typed overload of `GetInstance` lets you pass the `controllerType` variable directly to Simple Injector. Typically, this means you have to cast the returned value to some ABSTRACTION because the weakly typed `GetInstance` method returns `object`. In the case of `IControllerActivator`, however, this isn't required, because ASP.NET Core MVC doesn't require controllers to implement any interface or base class.

No matter which overload of `GetInstance` you use, Simple Injector guarantees that it'll return an instance of the requested type or throw an exception if there are

DEPENDENCIES that can't be satisfied. When all required DEPENDENCIES have been properly configured, Simple Injector can AUTO-WIRE the requested type.

To be able to resolve the requested type, all loosely coupled DEPENDENCIES must have been previously configured. You can configure Simple Injector in many ways; the next section reviews the most common ones.

14.1.2 *Configuring the container*

As we discussed in section 12.2, you can configure a DI CONTAINER in several conceptually different ways. Figure 12.5 reviewed the options: configuration files, CONFIGURATION AS CODE, and AUTO-REGISTRATION. Figure 14.2 shows these options again.

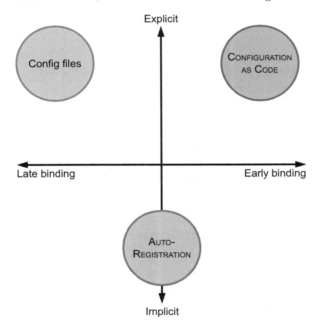

Figure 14.2   The most common ways to configure a DI CONTAINER shown against dimensions of explicitness and the degree of binding.

Simple Injector's core configuration API is centered on code and supports both CONFIGURATION AS CODE and convention-based AUTO-REGISTRATION. File-based configuration is left out completely. This shouldn't be an obstacle to using Simple Injector because, as we discussed in chapter 12, this configuration method should generally be avoided. Still, if your application requires late binding, it's quite easy to add a file-based configuration yourself, as we'll discuss later in this section.

Simple Injector lets you mix all three approaches. In this section, you'll see how to use each of these three types of configuration sources.

CONFIGURING THE CONTAINER USING CONFIGURATION AS CODE

In section 14.1, you saw a brief glimpse of Simple Injector's strongly typed configuration API. Here, we'll examine it in greater detail.

All configuration in Simple Injector uses the API exposed by the `Container` class. One of the most commonly used methods is the `Register` method that you've already seen:

```
container.Register<IIngredient, SauceBéarnaise>();
```

Because you want to program to interfaces, most of your components will depend on ABSTRACTIONS. This means that most components will be registered by their corresponding ABSTRACTION. When a component is the topmost type in the object graph, it's not uncommon to resolve it by its concrete type instead of its ABSTRACTION. MVC controllers, for instance, are resolved by their concrete type.

> **TIP** Even though Simple Injector allows resolving concrete unregistered types, make sure you register your topmost types explicitly. This allows Simple Injector to verify your complete object graph, including these root types. This often leads to the detection of otherwise hidden configuration errors. Section 14.2.4 goes into more detail about verification.

In general, you would register a type either by its ABSTRACTION or by its concrete type, but not both. There are exceptions to this rule, however. In Simple Injector, registering a component both by its concrete type and its ABSTRACTION is simply a matter of adding an extra registration:

```
container.Register<IIngredient, SauceBéarnaise>();
container.Register<SauceBéarnaise>();
```

Instead of registering the class only as `IIngredient`, you can register it as both itself and the interface it implements. This enables the container to resolve requests for both `SauceBéarnaise` and `IIngredient`.

> **NOTE** In section 13.1.2, we warned about Torn LIFESTYLES when calling `RegisterType` twice for the same component in Autofac. With Simple Injector, however, this isn't a problem. Under the hood, Simple Injector automatically deduplicates `SauceBéarnaise`'s registrations and prevents `SauceBéarnaise`'s LIFESTYLE from being torn.

In real applications, you always have more than one ABSTRACTION to map, so you must configure multiple mappings. This is done with multiple calls to `Register`:

```
container.Register<IIngredient, SauceBéarnaise>();
container.Register<ICourse, Course>();
```

This example maps `IIngredient` to `SauceBéarnaise`, and `ICourse` to `Course`. There's no overlap of types, so it should be pretty evident what's going on. But what would happen if you register the same ABSTRACTION several times?

```
container.Register<IIngredient, SauceBéarnaise>();
container.Register<IIngredient, Steak>();      ◀─────── Throws an exception
```

Here, you register `IIngredient` twice, which results in an exception being thrown on the second line with the following message:

> *Type IIngredient has already been registered. If your intention is to resolve a collection of IIngredient implementations, use the Collection.Register overloads. For more information, see https://simpleinjector.org/coll1.*

In contrast to most other DI CONTAINERS, Simple Injector doesn't allow stacking up registrations to build up a sequence of types, as the previous code snippet shows. Its API explicitly separates the registration of sequences from single ABSTRACTION mappings.[1] Instead of making multiple calls to `Register`, Simple Injector forces you to use the registration methods of the `Collection` property, such as `Collection.Register`:

```
container.Collection.Register<IIngredient>(
    typeof(SauceBéarnaise),
    typeof(Steak));
```

> **NOTE** Simple Injector uses the term *collection* where we use *sequence*. For the most part, you can use the terms interchangeably.

This example registers all ingredients in one single call. Alternatively, you can use `Collection.Append` to add implementations to a sequence of ingredients:

```
container.Collection.Append<IIngredient, SauceBéarnaise>();
container.Collection.Append<IIngredient, Steak>();
```

With the previous registrations, any component that depends on `IEnumerable-<IIngredient>` gets a sequence of ingredients injected. Simple Injector handles multiple configurations for the same ABSTRACTION well, but we'll get back to this topic in section 14.4.

Although there are more-advanced options available for configuring Simple Injector, you can configure an entire application with the methods shown here. But to save yourself from too much explicit maintenance of container configuration, you could instead consider a more convention-based approach using AUTO-REGISTRATION.

CONFIGURING THE CONTAINER USING AUTO-REGISTRATION

In many cases, registrations will be similar. Such registrations are tedious to maintain, and explicitly registering each and every component might not be the most productive approach, as we discussed in section 12.3.3.

Consider a library that contains many `IIngredient` implementations. You can configure each class individually, but it'll result in an ever-changing list of `Type` instances supplied to the `Collection.Register` method. What's worse is that, every time you add a new `IIngredient` implementation, you must also explicitly register it with the `Container` if you want it to be available. It'd be more productive to state that all implementations of `IIngredient` found in a given assembly should be registered.

---

[1] For a detailed discussion on why this is so, see https://simpleinjector.org/separate-collections.

This is possible using some of the `Register` and `Collection.Register` method over-loads. These particular overloads let you specify an assembly and configure all selected classes from this assembly in a single statement. To get the `Assembly` instance, you can use a representative class; in this case, `Steak`:

```
Assembly ingredientsAssembly = typeof(Steak).Assembly;

container.Collection.Register<IIngredient>(ingredientsAssembly);
```

The previous example unconditionally configures all implementations of the `IIngredient` interface, but you can provide filters that enable you to select only a subset. Here's a conven-tion-based scan where you add only classes whose name starts with *Sauce*:

```
Assembly assembly = typeof(Steak).Assembly;

var types = container.GetTypesToRegister<IIngredient>(assembly)
    .Where(type => type.Name.StartsWith("Sauce"));

container.Collection.Register<IIngredient>(types);
```

This scan makes use of the `GetTypesToRegister` method, which searches for types without registering them. This allows you to filter the selection using a predicate. Instead of supplying `Collection.Register` using a list of assemblies, you now supply it with a list of `Type` instances.

Apart from selecting the correct types from an assembly, another part of AUTO-REGISTRATION is defining the correct mapping. In the previous examples, you used the `Collection.Register` method with a specific interface to register all selected types against that interface. Sometimes, however, you may want to use different conventions. Let's say that instead of interfaces, you use abstract base classes, and you want to register all types in an assembly where the name ends with *Policy* by their base type:

```
Assembly policiesAssembly = typeof(DiscountPolicy).Assembly;

var policyTypes =                                    ← Gets all types in the assembly
    from type in policiesAssembly.GetTypes()
    where type.Name.EndsWith("Policy")               ← Filters by the Policy suffix
    select type;

foreach (Type type in policyTypes)
{                                                    Registers each policy
    container.Register(type.BaseType, type);         ← component by its base class
}
```

In this example, you hardly use any part of the Simple Injector API. Instead, you use the reflection and LINQ APIs provided by the .NET framework to filter and get the expected types.

Even though Simple Injector's convention-based API is limited, by making use of existing .NET framework APIs, convention-based registrations are still surprisingly easy. The Simple Injector's convention-based API mainly focuses around the registration of sequences and generic types. This becomes a different ball game when it comes to generics, which is why Simple Injector has explicit support for registering types based on generic ABSTRACTIONS, as we'll discuss next.

AUTO-REGISTRATION OF GENERIC ABSTRACTIONS

During the course of chapter 10, you refactored the big, obnoxious `IProductService` interface to the `ICommandService<TCommand>` interface of listing 10.12. Here's that ABSTRACTION again:

```
public interface ICommandService<TCommand>
{
    void Execute(TCommand command);
}
```

As discussed in chapter 10, every command Parameter Object represents a use case, and there'll be a single implementation per use case. The `AdjustInventoryService` of listing 10.8 was given as an example. It implemented the "adjust inventory" use case. The next listing shows this class again.

Listing 14.2   The `AdjustInventoryService` from chapter 10

```
public class AdjustInventoryService : ICommandService<AdjustInventory>
{
    private readonly IInventoryRepository repository;

    public AdjustInventoryService(IInventoryRepository repository)
    {
        this.repository = repository;
    }

    public void Execute(AdjustInventory command)
    {
        var productId = command.ProductId;

        ...
    }
}
```

Any reasonably complex system will easily implement hundreds of use cases, and these are ideal candidates for using AUTO-REGISTRATION. With Simple Injector, this couldn't be simpler.

Listing 14.3   AUTO-REGISTRATION of `ICommandService<TCommand>` implementations

```
Assembly assembly = typeof(AdjustInventoryService).Assembly;

container.Register(typeof(ICommandService<>), assembly);
```

In contrast to the previous listing that used `Collection.Register`, you again make use of `Register`. This is because there'll always be exactly one implementation of a requested command service; you don't want to inject a sequence of command services.

Using the supplied open-generic interface, Simple Injector iterates through the list of assembly types and registers types that implement a closed-generic version of `ICommandService<TCommand>`. What this means, for instance, is that `AdjustInventory-Service` is registered because it implements `ICommandService<AdjustInventory>`, which is a closed-generic version of `ICommandService<TCommand>`.

Not all `ICommandService<TCommand>` implementations will be registered, though. Simple Injector skips open-generic implementations, Decorators, and Composites, as they often require special registration. We'll discuss this in section 14.4.

The `Register` method takes a `params` array of `Assembly` instances, so you can supply as many assemblies as you like to a single convention. It's not a far-fetched idea to scan a folder for assemblies and supply them all to implement add-in functionality where add-ins can be added without recompiling a core application. (For an example, see https://simpleinjector.org/registering-plugins-dynamically.) This is one way to implement late binding; another is to use configuration files.

CONFIGURING THE CONTAINER USING CONFIGURATION FILES

When you need to be able to change a configuration without recompiling the application, configuration files are a good option. The most natural way to use configuration files is to embed them into a standard .NET application configuration file. This is possible, but you can also use a standalone configuration file if you need to be able to vary the Simple Injector configuration independently of the standard .config file.

> **TIP** As we stated in section 12.2.1, you should use configuration files only for those types in your DI configuration that require late binding. Prefer CONFIGURATION AS CODE or AUTO-REGISTRATION in all other types and all other parts of your configuration.

As stated in the beginning of this section, there's no explicit support in Simple Injector for file-based configuration. By making use of .NET Core's built-in configuration system, however, loading registrations from a configuration file is rather straightforward. For this purpose, you can define your own configuration structure that maps ABSTRACTIONS to implementations. Here's a simple example that maps the `IIngredient` interface to the `Steak` class.

> **Listing 14.4 Simple mapping from `IIngredient` to `Steak` using a configuration file**

```
{
  "registrations": [
    {
      "service":
        "Ploeh.Samples.MenuModel.IIngredient, Ploeh.Samples.MenuModel",
      "implementation":
        "Ploeh.Samples.MenuModel.Steak, Ploeh.Samples.MenuModel"
    }
  ]
}
```

> **NOTE**   The structure of this configuration sample closely follows that of Auto-fac, because it's a quite natural format.

The `registrations` element is a JSON array of `registration` elements. The previous example contained a single registration, but you can add as many `registration` elements as you like. In each element, you must specify a concrete type with the `implementation` attribute. To map the `Steak` class to `IIngredient`, you can use the `service` attribute.

Using .NET Core's built-in configuration system, you can load a configuration file and iterate through it. You then append the defined registrations to the container:

```
var config = new ConfigurationBuilder()
    .AddJsonFile("simpleinjector.json")
    .Build();

var registrations = config
    .GetSection("registrations").GetChildren();

foreach (var reg in registrations)
{
    container.Register(
        Type.GetType(reg["service"]),
        Type.GetType(reg["implementation"]));
}
```

Loads the simpleinjector.json configuration file using .NET Core's configuration system. By default, the config file will be located in the application's root directory.

Loads the list of registrations from the configuration file

Iterates through the list of registrations. Adds each registration to Simple Injector using its supplied service and implementation types as defined in the configuration file.

A configuration file is a good option when you need to change the configuration of one or more components without recompiling the application, but because it tends to be quite brittle, you should reserve it for only those occasions and use either AUTO-REGISTRATION or CONFIGURATION AS CODE for the main part of the container's configuration.

This section introduced the Simple Injector DI CONTAINER and demonstrated these fundamental mechanics: how to configure a `Container`, and, subsequently, how to use it to resolve services. Resolving services is easily done with a single call to the `GetInstance` method, so the complexity involves configuring the container. This can be done in several different ways, including imperative code and configuration files.

Until now, we've only looked at the most basic API; we have yet to cover more-advanced areas. One of the most important topics is how to manage component lifetime.

14.2   *Managing lifetime*

In chapter 8, we discussed LIFETIME MANAGEMENT, including the most common conceptual LIFESTYLES such as TRANSIENT, SINGLETON, and SCOPED. Simple Injector's LIFESTYLE supports mapping to these three LIFESTYLES. The LIFESTYLES shown in table 14.2 are available as part of the API.

Table 14.2 Simple Injector LIFESTYLES

Simple Injector name	Pattern name	Comments
Transient	TRANSIENT	This is the default LIFESTYLE. TRANSIENT instances aren't tracked by the container and, therefore, are never disposed of. Using its diagnostic services, Simple Injector warns if you register a disposable component as TRANSIENT.
Singleton	SINGLETON	Instances are disposed of when the container is disposed of.
Scoped	SCOPED	Template for LIFESTYLES that allows scoping instances. A SCOPED LIFESTYLE is defined by the `ScopedLifestyle` base class, and there are several `ScopedLifestyle` implementations. The most commonly used LIFESTYLE for a .NET Core application is `AsyncScopedLifestyle`. Instances are tracked for the lifetime of the scope and are disposed of when the scope is disposed of.

TIP The default TRANSIENT LIFESTYLE is the safest, but not always the most efficient. SINGLETON is a more efficient choice for thread-safe services, but you must remember to explicitly register those services.

Simple Injector's implementations of TRANSIENT and SINGLETON are equivalent to the general LIFESTYLES described in chapter 8, so we won't spend much time on them in this chapter. Instead, in this section, you'll see how you can define LIFESTYLES for components in code. We'll also look at Simple Injector's concept of ambient scoping and how it can simplify working with the container. We'll then cover how Simple Injector can verify and diagnose its configuration to prevent common configuration errors. By the end of this section, you should be able to use Simple Injector's LIFESTYLES in your own application. Let's start by reviewing how to configure LIFESTYLES for components.

14.2.1 Configuring LIFESTYLES

In this section, we'll review how to manage LIFESTYLES with Simple Injector. A LIFESTYLE is configured as part of registering components. It's as easy as this:

```
container.Register<SauceBéarnaise>(Lifestyle.Singleton);
```

This example configures the concrete SauceBéarnaise class as a SINGLETON so that the same instance is returned each time SauceBéarnaise is requested. If you want to map an ABSTRACTION to a concrete class with a specific lifetime, you can use the usual Register overload with two generic arguments, while supplying it with the Lifestyle.Singleton:

```
container.Register<IIngredient, SauceBéarnaise>(Lifestyle.Singleton);
```

Although TRANSIENT is the default LIFESTYLE, you can explicitly state it. These two examples are equivalent under the default configuration:[2]

```
container.Register<IIngredient, SauceBéarnaise>(
    Lifestyle.Transient);
```

Explicitly supplies TRANSIENT to a registration

```
container.Register<IIngredient, SauceBéarnaise>();
```

TRANSIENT is the default LIFESTYLE and can be omitted.

Configuring LIFESTYLES for convention-based registrations can be done in several ways. When registering a sequence, for instance, one of the options is to supply the `Collection.Register` method with a list of `Registration` instances:

```
Assembly assembly = typeof(Steak).Assembly;

var types = container.GetTypesToRegister<IIngredient>(assembly);

container.Collection.Register<IIngredient>(
    from type in types
    select Lifestyle.Singleton.CreateRegistration(type, container));
```

You can use `Lifestyle.Singleton` to define the LIFESTYLE for all registrations in a convention. In this example, you define all `IIngredient` registrations as SINGLETON by supplying them all as a `Registration` instance to the `Collection.Register` overload.[3]

> **NOTE** A `Registration` is the Simple Injector class that's responsible for the construction of the expression tree, which describes the creation of a type based on its LIFESTYLE. `Registration` objects are constructed by Simple Injector under the hood when you call most of the `Register` overloads, but you can also create them directly. This is useful in scenarios like this one.

When it comes to configuring LIFESTYLES for components, there are many options. In all cases, it's done in a rather declarative fashion. Although configuration is typically easy, you mustn't forget that some LIFESTYLES involve long-lived objects, which use resources as long as they're around.

14.2.2 Releasing components

As discussed in section 8.2.2, it's important to release objects when you're done with them. Similar to Autofac, Simple Injector has no explicit `Release` method, but instead uses a concept called *scopes*. A scope can be regarded as a request-specific cache. As figure 14.3 illustrates, it defines a boundary where components can be reused.

A `Scope` defines a cache that you can use for a particular duration or purpose; the most obvious example is a web request. When a scoped component is requested from a `Scope`, you always receive the same instance. The difference from true SINGLETONS is that if you query a second scope, you'll get another instance.

---

[2] The default LIFESTYLE can be changed by setting `Container.Options.DefaultLifestyle` to anything other than `Lifestyle.Transient`.

[3] Another interesting option is to override Simple Injector's default `ILifestyleSelection-Behavior`. See https://simpleinjector.org/xtpls.

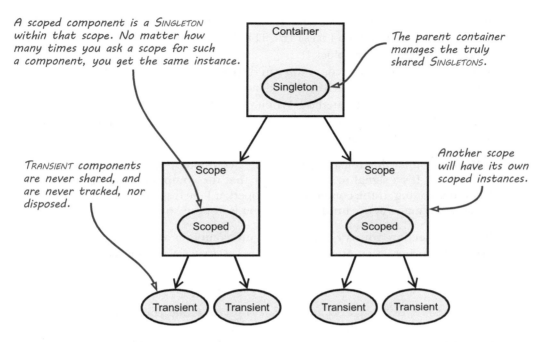

A scoped component is a SINGLETON within that scope. No matter how many times you ask a scope for such a component, you get the same instance.

The parent container manages the truly shared SINGLETONS.

TRANSIENT components are never shared, and are never tracked, nor disposed.

Another scope will have its own scoped instances.

Figure 14.3 Simple Injector's `Scope` acts as a request-specific cache that can share components for a limited duration or purpose.

One of the important features of scopes is that they let you properly release components when the scope completes. You create a new scope with the `BeginScope` method of a particular `ScopedLifestyle` implementation and release all appropriate components by invoking its `Dispose` method:

```
using (AsyncScopedLifestyle.BeginScope(container))
{
    IMeal meal = container.GetInstance<IMeal>();

    meal.Consume();
}
```

Creates a scope for the container

Resolves a meal from the container within the context of the created scope

Consumes the meal

Releases the meal by ending the using block

This example shows how `IMeal` is resolved from the `Container` instance, instead of being resolved from a `Scope` instance. This isn't a typo—the container automatically "knows" in which active scope it's operating. The next section discusses this in more detail.

TIP Simple Injector contains several NuGet packages that help to integrate it with common application frameworks. Some of these packages automatically ensure that a scope wraps around a web request. To find out what's the best way to integrate Simple Injector with your framework of choice, see the integration guide (https://simpleinjector.org/integration).

In the previous example, a new scope is created by invoking the `BeginScope` method on the corresponding SCOPED LIFESTYLE. The return value implements `IDisposable`, so you can wrap it in a `using` block.

When you're done with a scope, you can dispose of it with a `using` block. This happens automatically when you exit the block, but you can also choose to explicitly dispose of it by invoking the `Dispose` method. When you dispose of a scope, you also release all the components that were created during that scope. In the example, it means that you release the meal object graph.

> **NOTE**   Remember that releasing a disposable component isn't the same as disposing of it. It's a signal to the container that the component is eligible for decommissioning. If the component is scoped, it'll be disposed of; if it's a SINGLETON, it remains active until the container is disposed of.

Earlier in this section, you saw how to configure components as SINGLETONS or TRANSIENTS. Configuring a component to have its LIFESTYLE tied to a scope is done in a similar way:

```
container.Register<IIngredient, SauceBéarnaise>(Lifestyle.Scoped);
```

Similar to `Lifestyle.Singleton` and `Lifestyle.Transient`, you can use the `Lifestyle.Scoped` value to state that the component's lifetime should live for the duration of the scope that created the instance. This call by itself, however, would cause the container to throw the following exception:

> *To be able to use the Lifestyle.Scoped property, please ensure that the container is configured with a default scoped lifestyle by setting the Container.Options.DefaultScopedLifestyle property with the required scoped lifestyle for your type of application. For more information, see https://simpleinjector.org/scoped.*

Before you can use the `Lifestyle.Scoped` value, Simple Injector requires that you set the `Container.Options.DefaultScopedLifestyle` property. Simple Injector has multiple `ScopedLifestyle` implementations that are sometimes specific to a framework. This means you'll have to explicitly configure the `ScopedLifestyle` implementation that works best for your type of application. For ASP.NET Core applications, the proper SCOPED LIFESTYLE is the `AsyncScopedLifestyle`, which you can configure like this:

```
var container = new Container();

container.Options.DefaultScopedLifestyle =
    new AsyncScopedLifestyle();

container.Register<IIngredient, SauceBéarnaise>(
    Lifestyle.Scoped);
```

Before making any registrations to the container, you register the AsyncScopedLifestyle as the default SCOPED LIFESTYLE.

Now you can use the Lifestyle.Scoped value to make scoped registrations.

> **TIP**   Because of Simple Injector's ambient scopes, you can always resolve directly from the `Container` without being afraid of the accidental memory leaks that would occur were you to do this with a DI CONTAINER, such as Autofac. In case you resolve a SCOPED DEPENDENCY from the container while there's no active scope, Simple Injector throws a descriptive exception.

Due to their nature, SINGLETONS are never released for the lifetime of the container itself. Still, you can release even those components if you don't need the container any longer. This is done by disposing of the container itself:

```
container.Dispose();
```

In practice, this isn't nearly as important as disposing of a scope, because the lifetime of a container tends to correlate closely with the lifetime of the application it supports. You normally keep the container around as long as the application runs, so you only dispose of it when the application shuts down. In this case, memory would be reclaimed by the operating system.

As we mentioned earlier in this section, with Simple Injector, you always resolve objects from the container—not from a scope. This works because scopes are ambient in Simple injector. Let's look at ambient scopes next.

14.2.3 Ambient scopes

With Simple Injector, the previous example of the creation and disposal of the scope shows how you can always resolve instances from the `Container`, even if you resolve scoped instances. The following example shows this again:

```
using (AsyncScopedLifestyle.BeginScope(container))
{
    IMeal meal = container.GetInstance<IMeal>();     ◄────┐ With Simple Injector, you always
                                                           resolve from the container.
    meal.Consume();
}
```

This reveals an interesting feature of Simple Injector, which is that scope instances are ambient and are globally available in the context in which they're running. The following listing shows this behavior.

Listing 14.5 Ambient scopes in Simple Injector

```
var container = new Container();

container.Options.DefaultScopedLifestyle =
    new AsyncScopedLifestyle();                     Requests the currently active scope for the
                                                    configured SCOPED LIFESTYLE; in this case,
                                                    AsyncScopedLifestyle. Because there's no active
Scope scope1 = Lifestyle.Scoped                     scope yet, this method returns the value null.
    .GetCurrentScope(container);

using (Scope scope2 =                               When GetCurrentScope is called when
    AsyncScopedLifestyle.BeginScope(container))      there is an active scope, it returns that
{                                                    scope. In this case, the value of scope3
    Scope scope3 = Lifestyle.Scoped                  will be equal to scope2.
        .GetCurrentScope(container);
}                                                   After disposing of the scope, it becomes
                                                    unlisted. This results in the call to
Scope scope4 = Lifestyle.Scoped                     GetCurrentScope returning null again.
    .GetCurrentScope(container);
```

This behavior is similar to that of .NET's `TransactionScope` class.[4] When you wrap an operation with a `TransactionScope`, all database connections opened within that operation will automatically be part of the same transaction.

> **IMPORTANT**   Ambient scopes shouldn't be confused with AMBIENT CONTEXT. AMBIENT CONTEXT supplies application code outside the COMPOSITION ROOT with global access to a VOLATILE DEPENDENCY or its behavior. Because a DI CONTAINER's scopes will only be used inside the COMPOSITION ROOT, ambient scopes don't expose the same problems as AMBIENT CONTEXT does.

In general, you won't use the `GetCurrentScope` method a lot, if at all. The `Container` uses this under the hood on your behalf when you start resolving instances. Still, it demonstrates nicely that `Scope` instances can be retrieved and are accessible from the container.

A `ScopedLifestyle` implementation, such as the previous `AsyncScopedLifestyle`, stores its created `Scope` instance for later use, which allows it to be retrieved within the same context. It's the particular `ScopedLifestyle` implementation that defines when code runs in the same context. The `AsyncScopedLifestyle`, for instance, stores the `Scope` internally in an `System.Threading.AsyncLocal<T>`.[5] This allows scopes to flow from method to method, even if an asynchronous method continues on a different thread, as this example demonstrates:

```
using (AsyncScopedLifestyle.BeginScope(container))
{
    IMeal meal = container.GetInstance<IMeal>();

    await meal.Consume();          ◄─────  This asynchronous call might cause
                                           the remaining code of the method
                                           to continue on a different thread.
    meal = container.GetInstance<IMeal>();    ◄──┐ The object graph is guaranteed to
}                                                │ be resolved on the same scope.
```

Although ambient scopes might be confusing at first, their usage typically simplifies working with Simple Injector. For instance, you won't have to worry about getting memory leaks when resolving from the container, because Simple Injector manages this transparently on your behalf. `Scope` instances will never be cached in the root container, which is something you need to be cautious about with the other containers described in this book. Another area in which Simple Injector excels is the ability to detect common misconfigurations.

14.2.4 *Diagnosing the container for common lifetime problems*

Compared to PURE DI, registration and building object graphs in a DI CONTAINER is more implicit. This makes it easy to accidentally misconfigure the container. For that reason, many DI CONTAINERS have a function that allows all registrations to be iterated to enable verifying whether all can be resolved, and Simple Injector is no exception.

---

[4] See https://mng.bz/jrQP.

[5] See https://mng.bz/WeD1.

Being able to resolve an object graph, however, is no guarantee of the correctness of the configuration, as the CAPTIVE DEPENDENCY pitfall of section 8.4.1 illustrates. A CAPTIVE DEPENDENCY is a misconfiguration of the lifetime of a component. In fact, most errors concerning working with DI CONTAINERS are related to lifetime misconfigurations.

Because DI CONTAINER misconfigurations are so common and often difficult to trace, Simple Injector lets you verify its configuration, which goes beyond the simple instantiation of object graphs that most DI CONTAINERS support. On top of that, Simple Injector scans the object graphs for common misconfigurations—CAPTIVE DEPENDENCIES being one of them.

Therefore, the configure step of Simple Injector's two-step process, as outlined in figure 14.1, exists of two substeps. Figure 14.4 shows this process.

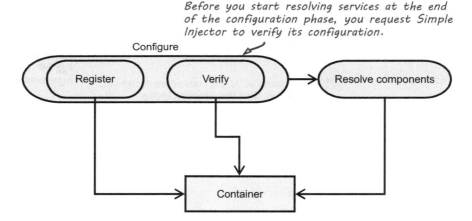

Figure 14.4 The pattern for using Simple Injector is to configure it, including verifying it, and then to resolve components.

The easiest way to let Simple Injector diagnose and detect configuration errors is by calling the Container's Verify method, as shown in the following listing.

Listing 14.6 Verifying the container

```
var container = new Container();

container.Register<IIngredient, Steak>();

container.Verify();
```

Registers all components for a fully functional application

After the last registration, calls Verify to ensure all registrations are verified

LETTING THE CONTAINER DETECT CAPTIVE DEPENDENCIES

The CAPTIVE DEPENDENCY misconfiguration is one that Simple Injector detects. Now let's see how you can cause `Verify` to trip on a CAPTIVE DEPENDENCY using the `Mayonnaise` ingredient of section 14.1.1. Its constructor contained two DEPENDENCIES:

```
public Mayonnaise(EggYolk eggYolk, SunflowerOil oil)
```

The following listing registers `Mayonnaise` with its two DEPENDENCIES. But it misconfigures `Mayonnaise` as SINGLETON, whereas its `EggYolk` DEPENDENCY is registered as TRANSIENT.

> **Listing 14.7   Causing the container to detect a CAPTIVE DEPENDENCY**

```
var container = new Container();

container.Register<EggYolk>(Lifestyle.Transient);
container.Register<Mayonnaise>(Lifestyle.Singleton);
container.Register<SunflowerOil>(Lifestyle.Singleton);

container.Verify();
```

Because of the short expiration of egg yolk, it's registered as TRANSIENT.

Mayonnaise depends on EggYolk, but is accidentally registered as SINGLETON.

Because of the previous misconfiguration, this method throws an exception.

When you call `Register`, Simple Injector only performs some rudimentary validations. This includes checking that the type isn't abstract, that it has a public constructor, and the like. It won't check for problems such as CAPTIVE DEPENDENCIES at that stage, because registrations can be made in any arbitrary order. In listing 14.7, for instance, `SunflowerOil` is registered after `Mayonnaise`, even though it's a DEPENDENCY of `Mayonnaise`. It's completely valid to do so. It's only after the configuration is completed that verification can be performed. When you run this code example, the call to `Verify` fails with the following exception message:

> *The configuration is invalid. The following diagnostic warnings were reported:*

> *-[Lifestyle Mismatch] Mayonnaise (Singleton) depends on EggYolk (Transient). See the Error property for detailed information about the warnings. Please see https:// simpleinjector.org/diagnostics how to fix problems and how to suppress individual warnings.*

> **NOTE**   Simple Injector calls CAPTIVE DEPENDENCIES *Lifestyle Mismatches.*

An interesting observation here is that Simple Injector doesn't allow TRANSIENT DEPENDENCIES to be injected into SINGLETON consumers. This is the opposite of Autofac. With Autofac, TRANSIENTS are implicitly expected to live as long as their consumer, which means that in Autofac, this situation is never considered to be a CAPTIVE DEPENDENCY. For that reason, Autofac calls a TRANSIENT `InstancePerDependency`, which pretty much describes its behavior: each consumer's DEPENDENCY that's configured as TRANSIENT is expected to get its own instance. Because of that, Autofac only detects the injection of scoped components into SINGLETONS as CAPTIVE DEPENDENCIES.

Although this might sometimes be exactly the behavior you need, in most cases, it's not. More often, Transient components are expected to live for a brief period of time, whereas injecting them into a Singleton consumer causes the component to live for as long as the application lives. Because of this, Simple Injector's motto is: "better safe than sorry," which is why it throws an exception. Sometimes you might need to suppress such warnings in cases where you know best.

Suppressing warnings on individual registrations

In case you want to ignore EggYolk's expiration date, Simple Injector lets you suppress the check on that particular registration.

Listing 14.8   Suppressing a diagnostic warning

```
var container = new Container();

Registration reg = Lifestyle.Transient        ◁ Creates a Transient
    .CreateRegistration<EggYolk>(container);     Registration for EggYolk

reg.SuppressDiagnosticWarning(
    DiagnosticType.LifestyleMismatch,          ◁ Suppresses the Captive Dependency
    justification: "I like to eat rotten eggs.");  diagnostic warning with a
                                                   description of why this is needed
container.AddRegistration(typeof(EggYolk), reg);  ◁ Adds the Registration
                                                     to the container
container.Register<Mayonnaise>(Lifestyle.Singleton);
container.Register<SunflowerOil>(Lifestyle.Singleton);

container.Verify();
```

SuppressDiagnosticWarning contains a required justification argument. It isn't used by SuppressDiagnosticWarning at all, but serves as a reminder so that you don't forget to document why the warning is suppressed.

> **NOTE**   For a description of all the available diagnostic checks, see https://simpleinjector.org/diagnostics.

This completes our tour of Lifetime Management with Simple Injector. Components can be configured with mixed Lifestyles, and this is even true when you register multiple implementations of the same Abstraction.

Until now, you've allowed the container to wire Dependencies by implicitly assuming that all components use Constructor Injection. But this isn't always the case. In the next section, we'll review how to deal with classes that must be instantiated in special ways.

14.3   *Registering difficult APIs*

Until now, we've considered how you can configure components that use Constructor Injection. One of the many benefits of Constructor Injection is that DI Containers like Simple Injector can easily understand how to compose and create all classes in a Dependency graph. This becomes less clear when APIs are less well behaved.

In this section, you'll see how to deal with primitive constructor arguments and static factories. These all require special attention. Let's start by looking at classes that take primitive types, such as strings or integers, as constructor arguments.

14.3.1 Configuring primitive DEPENDENCIES

As long as you inject ABSTRACTIONS into consumers, all is well. But it becomes more difficult when a constructor depends on a primitive type, such as a string, a number, or an enum. This is particularly the case for data access implementations that take a connection string as constructor parameter, but it's a more general issue that applies to all string and numeric types.

Conceptually, it doesn't make sense to register a string or number as a component in a container. In particular, when AUTO-WIRING is used, the registration of primitive types causes ambiguity. Take string, for instance. Where one component might require a database connection string, another might require a file path. The two are conceptually different, but because AUTO-WIRING works by selecting DEPENDENCIES based on their type, they become ambiguous. For that reason, Simple Injector blocks the registration of primitive DEPENDENCIES. Consider as an example this constructor:

```
public ChiliConCarne(Spiciness spiciness)
```

In this example, `Spiciness` is an enum:

```
public enum Spiciness { Mild, Medium, Hot }
```

> **TIP** As a rule of thumb, enums are code smells and should be refactored to polymorphic classes.[6] But they serve us well for this example.

You might be tempted to register `ChiliConCarne` as in the following example. That won't work!

```
container.Register<ICourse, ChiliConCarne>();
```

This line causes an exception with the following message:

> *The constructor of type ChiliConCarne contains parameter 'spiciness' of type Spiciness, which cannot be used for constructor injection because it's a value type.*

When you want to resolve `ChiliConCarne` with a medium `Spiciness`, you'll have to depart from AUTO-WIRING and instead use a delegate:[7]

```
container.Register<ICourse>(() => new ChiliConCarne(Spiciness.Medium));
```

> **NOTE** This `Register` method is type-safe but disables AUTO-WIRING.

---

[6] Martin Fowler et al, *Refactoring: Improving the Design of Existing Code* (Addison-Wesley, 1999), 82.

[7] Simple Injector allows overriding its default behavior of disallowing primitive types by replacing the default `IDependencyInjectionBehavior` implementation. A discussion about this, however, is outside the scope of this book. For more details, see https:/simpleinjector.org/xtppi.

The downside of using delegates is that the registration has to be changed when the ChiliConCarne constructor changes. When you add an IIngredient DEPENDENCY to the ChiliConCarne constructor, for instance, the registration must be updated:

```
container.Register<ICourse>(() =>
    new ChiliConCarne(
        Spiciness.Medium,
        container.GetInstance<IIngredient>()));
```

◄─── **Registers a delegate that creates ChiliConCarne when invoked**

◄─── **Calls back into the container to get an IIngredient and injects it manually into the constructor**

Besides the additional maintenance in the COMPOSITION ROOT, and because of the lack of AUTO-WIRING, the use of delegates disallows Simple Injector from verifying the validity of the relationship between ChiliConCarne and its IIngredient DEPENDENCY. The delegate hides the fact that this DEPENDENCY exists. This isn't always a problem, but it can complicate diagnosing problems that are caused due to misconfigurations. Because of these downsides, a more convenient solution is to extract the primitive DEPENDENCIES into Parameter Objects.

14.3.2 *Extracting primitive DEPENDENCIES to Parameter Objects*

In section 10.3.3, we discussed how the introduction of Parameter Objects allowed mitigating the OPEN/CLOSED PRINCIPLE violation that IProductService caused. Parameter Objects, however, are also a great tool to mitigate ambiguity. For example, the Spiciness of a course could be described in more general terms as a flavoring. Flavoring might include other properties, such as saltiness, so you can wrap Spiciness and the saltiness in a Flavoring class:

```
public class Flavoring
{
    public readonly Spiciness Spiciness;
    public readonly bool ExtraSalty;

    public Flavoring(Spiciness spiciness, bool extraSalty)
    {
        this.Spiciness = spiciness;
        this.ExtraSalty = extraSalty;
    }
}
```

As we mentioned in section 10.3.3, it's perfectly fine for Parameter Objects to have one parameter. The goal is to remove ambiguity, and not just on the technical level. Such a Parameter Object's name might do a better job describing what your code does on a functional level, as the Flavoring class so elegantly does. With the introduction of the Flavoring Parameter Object, it now becomes possible to AUTO-WIRE any ICourse implementation that requires some flavoring:

```
var flavoring = new Flavoring(Spiciness.Medium, extraSalty: true);
container.RegisterInstance<Flavoring>(flavoring);

container.Register<ICourse, ChiliConCarne>();
```

This code creates a single instance of the `Flavoring` class. `Flavoring` becomes a configuration object for courses. Because there'll only be one `Flavoring` instance, you can register it in Simple Injector using `RegisterInstance`.

> **TIP** Avoid injecting Parameter Objects that function as application-wide configuration objects. Instead, prefer narrow, focused, Parameter Objects that only contain the values a particular consumer requires. This communicates more clearly what configuration values a component uses and simplifies testing. In general terms, injecting application-wide configuration objects is an INTERFACE SEGREGATION PRINCIPLE violation.

Extracting primitive DEPENDENCIES into Parameter Objects should be your preference over the previously discussed option, because Parameter Objects remove ambiguity, at both the functional and technical levels. It does, however, require a change to a component's constructor, which might not always be feasible. In this case, registering a delegate is your second-best pick.

14.3.3 *Registering objects with code blocks*

As we discussed in the previous section, one of the options for creating a component with a primitive value is to use the `Register` method. This lets you supply a delegate that creates the component. Here's that registration again:

```
container.Register<ICourse>(() => new ChiliConCarne(Spiciness.Hot));
```

The `ChiliConCarne` constructor is invoked with `Hot` `Spiciness` every time the `ICourse` service is resolved. Instead of Simple Injector figuring out the constructor arguments, however, you write the constructor invocation yourself using a code block.

When it comes to application classes, you typically have a choice between AUTO-WIRING or using a code block. But other classes are more restrictive: they can't be instantiated through a public constructor. Instead, you must use some sort of factory to create instances of the type. This is always troublesome for DI CONTAINERS because, by default, they look after public constructors.

> **TIP** By default, Simple Injector is able to instantiate internal classes too, as long as their constructor is defined as `public`. This behavior, however, can be overridden by replacing the default `IConstructorResolutionBehavior` implementation (https://simpleinjector.org/xtpcr).

Consider this example constructor for the public `JunkFood` class:

```
internal JunkFood(string name)
```

Even though the `JunkFood` class might be public, the constructor is internal. In the next example, instances of `JunkFood` should instead be created through the static `JunkFoodFactory` class:

```
public static class JunkFoodFactory
{
    public static JunkFood Create(string name)
    {
        return new JunkFood(name);
    }
}
```

From Simple Injector's perspective, this is a problematic API, because there are no unambiguous and well-established conventions around static factories. It needs help—and you can give that help by providing a code block it can execute to create the instance:

```
container.Register<IMeal>(() => JunkFoodFactory.Create("chicken meal"));
```

This time, you use the Register method to create the component by invoking a static factory within the code block. JunkFoodFactory.Create is invoked every time IMeal is resolved, and the result is returned.

When you end up writing the code to create the instance, how is this in any way better than invoking the code directly? By using a code block inside a Register method call, you still gain something:

- *You map from IMeal to JunkFood.* This allows consuming classes to stay loosely coupled.
- *You can still configure LIFESTYLES.* Although the code block will be invoked to create the instance, it may not be invoked every time the instance is requested. It is by default, but if you change it to a SINGLETON, the code block will only be invoked once, and the result cached and reused thereafter.

In this section, you've seen how you can use Simple Injector to deal with more-difficult APIs. You can use the Register method with a code block for a more type-safe approach. We have yet to look at how to work with multiple components, so let's now turn our attention in that direction.

14.4　*Working with multiple components*

As alluded to in section 12.1.2, DI CONTAINERS thrive on distinctness but have a hard time with ambiguity. When using CONSTRUCTOR INJECTION, a single constructor is preferred over overloaded constructors, because it's evident which constructor to use when there's no choice. This is also the case when mapping from ABSTRACTIONS to concrete types. If you attempt to map multiple concrete types to the same ABSTRACTION, you introduce ambiguity.

> **NOTE** Where most containers contain some heuristic for picking the right constructor in cases where a class has multiple overloaded constructors, by default, Simple Injector throws an exception, which explains that the type's definition is ambiguous. Although this behavior can be overridden (see https://simpleinjector.org/xtpcr) as stated in section 4.2.3, our advice is to prevent creating components with multiple constructors.

Despite the undesirable qualities of ambiguity, you often need to work with multiple implementations of a single ABSTRACTION.[8] This can be the case in these situations:

- Different concrete types are used for different consumers.
- DEPENDENCIES are sequences.
- Decorators or Composites are in use.

In this section, we'll look at each of these cases and see how Simple Injector addresses each one in turn. When we're done, you should be able to register and resolve components even when multiple implementations of the same ABSTRACTION are in play. Let's first see how you can provide fine-grained control in the case of ambiguity.

14.4.1 *Selecting among multiple candidates*

AUTO-WIRING is convenient and powerful but provides little control. As long as all ABSTRACTIONS are distinctly mapped to concrete types, you have no problems. But as soon as you introduce more implementations of the same interface, ambiguity rears its ugly head. Let's first recap how Simple Injector deals with multiple registrations of the same ABSTRACTION.

CONFIGURING MULTIPLE IMPLEMENTATIONS OF THE SAME SERVICE

As you saw in section 14.1.2, you can register multiple implementations of the same interface like this:

```
container.Collection.Register<IIngredient>(
    typeof(SauceBéarnaise),
    typeof(Steak));
```

This example registers both the `Steak` and `SauceBéarnaise` classes as a sequence of `IIngredient` services. You can ask the container to resolve all `IIngredient` components. Simple Injector has a dedicated method to do that: `GetAllInstances` gets an `IEnumerable` with all registered ingredients. Here's an example:

```
IEnumerable<IIngredient> ingredients =
    container.GetAllInstances<IIngredient>();
```

You can also ask the container to resolve all `IIngredient` components using `GetInstance` instead:

```
IEnumerable<IIngredient> ingredients =
    container.GetInstance<IEnumerable<IIngredient>>();
```

Notice that you request `IEnumerable<IIngredient>`, but you use the normal `GetInstance` method. Simple Injector interprets this as a convention and gives you all the `IIngredient` components it has.

---

[8] As a matter of fact, having many ABSTRACTIONS with only one implementation is a design smell described by the Reused Abstraction Principle. See Jason Gorman, "Reused Abstractions Principle (RAP)," 2010, http://www.codemanship.co.uk/parlezuml/blog/?postid=934.

TIP As an alternative to IEnumerable<T>, you can also request ABSTRACTIONS like IList<T>, ICollection<T>, IReadOnlyList<T>, and IReadOnlyCollection<T>. The results are equivalent: in all cases, you get all the components of the requested type.

When there are multiple implementations of a certain ABSTRACTION, there'll often be a consumer that depends on a sequence. Sometimes, however, components need to work with a fixed set or a subset of DEPENDENCIES of the same ABSTRACTION, which is what we'll discuss next.

REMOVING AMBIGUITY USING CONDITIONAL REGISTRATIONS

As useful as AUTO-WIRING is, sometimes you need to override the normal behavior to provide fine-grained control over which DEPENDENCIES go where, but it may also be that you need to address an ambiguous API. As an example, consider this constructor:

```
public ThreeCourseMeal(ICourse entrée, ICourse mainCourse, ICourse dessert)
```

In this case, you have three identically typed DEPENDENCIES, each of which represents a different concept. In most cases, you want to map each of the DEPENDENCIES to a separate type. With most DI CONTAINERS, the typical solution for this type of problem is to use keyed or named registrations, as you saw with Autofac in the previous chapter. With Simple Injector, the solution is typically to change the registration of the DEPENDENCY instead of the consumer. The following listing shows how you could choose to register the ICourse mappings.

> **Listing 14.9　Registering courses based on the constructor's parameter names**

```
container.Register<IMeal, ThreeCourseMeal>();          ◄──  The ThreeCourseMeal is made using
                                                            the usual AUTO-WIRING registration.
container.RegisterConditional<ICourse, Rillettes>(
    c => c.Consumer.Target.Name == "entrée");

container.RegisterConditional<ICourse, CordonBleu>(
    c => c.Consumer.Target.Name == "mainCourse");

container
    .RegisterConditional<ICourse, MousseAuChocolat>(
    c => c.Consumer.Target.Name == "dessert");
```

The three courses are registered conditionally, based on the name of the target of the consuming type. A target can either be a property or a constructor parameter; and, in this case, the targets are ThreeCourseMeal's constructor parameters.

Let's take a closer look at what's going on here. The RegisterConditional method accepts a Predicate<PredicateContext> value, which allows it to determine whether a registration should be injected into the consumer or not. It has the following signature:

```
public void RegisterConditional<TService, TImplementation>(
    Predicate<PredicateContext> predicate)
    where TImplementation : class, TService
    where TService : class;
```

`System.Predicate<T>` is a .NET delegate type. The `predicate` value will be invoked by Simple Injector. If `predicate` returns `true`, it uses the registration for the given consumer. Otherwise, Simple Injector expects another conditional registration to have a delegate that returns `true`. It throws an exception when it can't find a registration, because, in that case, the object graph can't be constructed. Likewise, it throws an exception when there are multiple registrations that are applicable.

Simple Injector is strict and never assumes to *know* what you intended to select, as we discussed previously regarding components with multiple constructors. This does mean, though, that Simple Injector always calls all predicates of all applicable conditional registrations to find possible overlapping registrations. This might seem inefficient, but those predicates are only called when a component is resolved for the first time. Any following resolution has all the information available, which means additional resolutions are fast.

> **WARNING**   Identifying parameters by their names is convenient but not refactoring-safe. If you rename a parameter, you can break the configuration (depending on your refactoring tool).

By overriding AUTO-WIRING using conditional registered components, you allow Simple Injector to build the entire object graph without having to revert to registering a code block, as we discussed in section 14.3.3. This is useful when working with Simple Injector because of the previously discussed diagnostic capabilities. The use of code blocks blinds a container, which might cause configuration mistakes to stay undetected for too long.

In the next section, you'll see how to use the less ambiguous and more flexible approach where you allow any number of courses in a meal. To this end, you must learn how Simple Injector deals with lists and sequences.

14.4.2 *Wiring sequences*

In section 6.1.1, we discussed how CONSTRUCTOR INJECTION acts as a warning system for SINGLE RESPONSIBILITY PRINCIPLE violations. The lesson then was that instead of viewing Constructor Over-injection as a weakness of the CONSTRUCTOR INJECTION pattern, you should rather rejoice that it makes a problematic design so obvious.

When it comes to DI CONTAINERS and ambiguity, we see a similar relationship. DI CONTAINERS generally don't deal with ambiguity in a graceful manner. Although you can make a good DI CONTAINER like Simple Injector deal with it, it can seem awkward. This is often an indication that you could improve the design of your code.

> **TIP**   If configuring a certain part of your API is difficult with Simple Injector, take a step back and reevaluate your design against the patterns and principles presented in this book. More often than not, configuration difficulties are caused by an application design that doesn't follow these patterns or violates these principles. Making your overall design better not only improves the application's maintainability, but also makes it easier to configure Simple Injector.

Instead of feeling constrained by Simple Injector, you should embrace its conventions and let it guide you toward a better and more consistent design. In this section, we'll look at an example that demonstrates how you can refactor away from ambiguity, as well as show how Simple Injector deals with sequences.

REFACTORING TO A BETTER COURSE BY REMOVING AMBIGUITY

In section 14.4.1, you saw how the `ThreeCourseMeal` and its inherent ambiguity forced you to complicate your registration. This should prompt you to reconsider the API design. A simple generalization moves toward an implementation of `IMeal` that takes an arbitrary number of `ICourse` instances instead of exactly three, as was the case with the `ThreeCourseMeal` class:

```
public Meal(IEnumerable<ICourse> courses)
```

Notice that, instead of requiring three distinct `ICourse` instances in the constructor, the single DEPENDENCY on an `IEnumerable<ICourse>` instance lets you provide any number of courses to the `Meal` class—from zero to ... a lot! This solves the issue with ambiguity, because there's now only a single DEPENDENCY. In addition, it also improves the API and implementation by providing a single, general-purpose class that can model different types of meal: from a simple meal with a single course to an elaborate 12-course dinner.

In this section, we'll look at how you can configure Simple Injector to wire up `Meal` instances with appropriate `ICourse` DEPENDENCIES. When you're done, you should have a good idea of the options available when you need to configure instances with sequences of DEPENDENCIES.

AUTO-WIRING SEQUENCES

Simple Injector has a good understanding of sequences, so if you want to use all registered components of a given service, AUTO-WIRING just works. As an example, given a set of configured `ICourse` instances, you can configure the `IMeal` service like this:

```
container.Register<IMeal, Meal>();
```

Notice that this is a completely standard mapping from an ABSTRACTION to a concrete type. Simple Injector automatically understands the `Meal` constructor and determines that the correct course of action is to resolve all `ICourse` components. When you resolve `IMeal`, you get a `Meal` instance with the `ICourse` components. This still requires you to register the sequence of `ICourse` components, for instance, using AUTO-REGISTRATION:

```
container.Collection.Register<ICourse>(assembly);
```

Simple Injector automatically handles sequences, and unless you specify otherwise, it does what you'd expect it to do: it resolves a sequence of DEPENDENCIES for all registrations of that ABSTRACTION. Only when you need to explicitly pick only some components from a larger set do you need to do more. Let's see how you can do that.

PICKING ONLY SOME COMPONENTS FROM A LARGER SET

Simple Injector's default strategy of injecting all components is often the correct policy, but as figure 14.5 shows, there may be cases where you want to pick only some registered components from the larger set of all registered components.

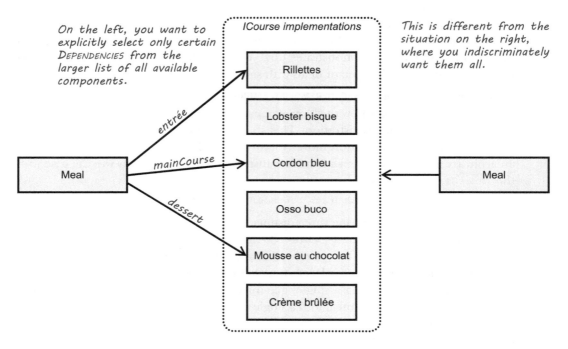

Figure 14.5   Picking components from a larger set of all registered components

> **NOTE**   The need to inject a subset of a complete collection isn't a common scenario, but it does demonstrate how to solve more-complex needs that you might encounter.

When you previously let Simple Injector Auto-Register and Auto-Wire all configured instances, it corresponded to the situation depicted on the right side of the figure. If you want to register a component as shown on the left side, you must explicitly define which components should be used. In order to achieve this, you can use the Collection.Create method, which allows creating a subset of a sequence. The following listing shows how to inject a subset of a sequence into a consumer.

Listing 14.10   Injecting a sequence subset into a consumer

```
IEnumerable<ICourse> coursesSubset1 =
    container.Collection.Create<ICourse>(
        typeof(Rillettes),                      ⟵ Creates a sequence of three courses
        typeof(CordonBleu),
        typeof(MousseAuChocolat));

IEnumerable<ICourse> coursesSubset2 =
    container.Collection.Create<ICourse>(
        typeof(CeasarSalad),                    ⟵ Creates another sequence with a
        typeof(ChiliConCarne),                     different subset of courses
        typeof(MousseAuChocolat));

                                                Creates a single instance of Meal by injecting
container.RegisterInstance<IMeal>(              the first sequence, and maps it to IMeal
    new Meal(sourcesSubset1));
```

The `Collection.Create` method lets you create a sequence of a given ABSTRACTION. The sequence itself won't be registered in the container—this can be done using `Collection.Register`. By calling `Collection.Create` multiple times for the same ABSTRACTION, you can create multiple sequences that are all different subsets, as shown in listing 14.10.

What might be surprising about listing 14.10 is that the call to `Collection.Create` doesn't create the courses at that point in time. Instead, the sequence is a stream. Only when you start iterating the sequence will it start to resolve instances. Because of this behavior, the sequence subset can be safely injected into the SINGLETON `Meal` without causing any harm. We'll go into more detail about streams in section 14.4.5.

Simple Injector natively understands sequences. Unless you need to explicitly pick only some components from all services of a given type, Simple Injector automatically does the right thing.

AUTO-WIRING works not only with single instances, but also for sequences; the container maps a sequence to all configured instances of the corresponding type. A perhaps less intuitive use of having multiple instances of the same ABSTRACTION is the Decorator design pattern, which we'll discuss next.

14.4.3 *Wiring Decorators*

In section 9.1.1, we discussed how the Decorator design pattern is useful when implementing CROSS-CUTTING CONCERNS. By definition, Decorators introduce multiple types of the same ABSTRACTION. At the very least, you have two implementations of an ABSTRACTION: the Decorator itself and the decorated type. If you stack the Decorators, you can have even more. This is another example of having multiple registrations of the same service. Unlike the previous sections, these registrations aren't conceptually equal, but rather DEPENDENCIES of each other.

Simple Injector has built-in support for registering Decorators using the `Register-Decorator` method. And, in this section, we'll discuss both registrations of non-generic and generic ABSTRACTIONS. Let's start with the former.

DECORATING NON-GENERIC ABSTRACTIONS

Using the `RegisterDecorator` method, you can elegantly register a Decorator. The following example shows how to use this method to apply `Breading` to a `VealCutlet`:

```
var c = new Container();

c.Register<IIngredient, VealCutlet>();          ◄——— Registers VealCutlet as IIngredient

c.RegisterDecorator<IIngredient, Breading>();   ◄——— Registers Breading as Decorator of
                                                     IIngredient. When resolving
                                                     IIngredient, Simple Injector returns
                                                     VealCutlet wrapped inside Breading.
```

As you learned in chapter 9, you get veal cordon bleu when you slit open a pocket in the veal cutlet and add ham, cheese, and garlic into the pocket before breading the cutlet. The following example shows how to add a `HamCheeseGarlic` Decorator in between `VealCutlet` and the `Breading` Decorator:

```
var c = new Container();

c.Register<IIngredient, VealCutlet>();

c.RegisterDecorator<IIngredient, HamCheeseGarlic>();          ◄───┘ Adds a new Decorator

c.RegisterDecorator<IIngredient, Breading>();
```

By placing this new registration before the `Breading` registration, the `HamCheese-Garlic` Decorator will be wrapped first. This results in an object graph equal to the following PURE DI version:

```
new Breading(
    new HamCheeseGarlic(
        new VealCutlet()));
```
│ **VealCutlet is wrapped by HamCheeseGarlic,**
│ **which is wrapped by Breading.**

NOTE   Decorators are applied in the order of registration.

Chaining Decorators using the `RegisterDecorator` method is easy in Simple Injector. Likewise, you can apply generic Decorators, as you'll see next.

DECORATING GENERIC ABSTRACTIONS

During the course of chapter 10, we defined multiple generic Decorators that could be applied to any `ICommandService<TCommand>` implementation. In the remainder of this chapter, we'll set our ingredients and courses aside, and take a look at how to register these generic Decorators using Simple Injector. The following listing demonstrates how to register all `ICommandService<TCommand>` implementations with the three Decorators presented in section 10.3.

> **Listing 14.11   Decorating generic AUTO-REGISTERED ABSTRACTIONS**

```
container.Register(
    typeof(ICommandService<>), assembly);          │   Registers arbitrary
                                                   │   ICommandService<TCommand>
container.RegisterDecorator(                       │   implementations
    typeof(ICommandService<>),
    typeof(AuditingCommandServiceDecorator<>));

container.RegisterDecorator(
    typeof(ICommandService<>),                     ──┘ Registers generic Decorators
    typeof(TransactionCommandServiceDecorator<>));

container.RegisterDecorator(
    typeof(ICommandService<>),
    typeof(SecureCommandServiceDecorator<>));
```

As in listing 14.3, you use a `Register` overload to register arbitrary `ICommand-Service<TCommand>` implementations by scanning assemblies. To register generic Decorators, you use the `RegisterDecorator` method that accepts two `Type` instances. The result of the configuration of listing 14.11 is figure 14.6, which we discussed previously in section 10.3.4.

When it comes to Simple Injector's support for Decorators, this is only the tip of the iceberg. Several `RegisterDecorator` overloads allow Decorators to be made conditionally, like the previously discussed `RegisterConditional` overload of listing 14.9. A discussion of this and other features, however, is out of the scope of this book.[9]

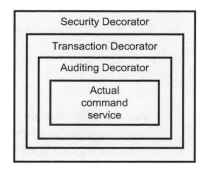

Figure 14.6   Enriching a real command service with transaction, auditing, and security aspects

Simple Injector lets you work with multiple Decorator instances in several different ways. You can register components as alternatives to each other, as peers resolved as sequences, or as hierarchical Decorators. In many cases, Simple Injector figures out what to do. You can always explicitly define how services are composed if you need more-explicit control.

In this section, we focused on Simple Injector's methods that were explicitly designed for configuring Decorators. Although consumers that rely on sequences of DEPENDENCIES can be the most intuitive use of multiple instances of the same ABSTRACTION, Decorators are another good example. But there's a third and perhaps a bit surprising case where multiple instances come into play, which is the Composite design pattern.

14.4.4   *Wiring Composites*

During the course of this book, we discussed the Composite design pattern on several occasions. In section 6.1.2, for instance, you created a `CompositeNotification-Service` (listing 6.4) that both implemented `INotificationService` and wrapped a sequence of `INotificationService` implementations.

WIRING NON-GENERIC COMPOSITES

Let's take a look at how you can register Composites, such as the `Composite-NotificationService` from chapter 6 in Simple Injector. The following listing shows this class again.

> **Listing 14.12   The `CompositeNotificationService` Composite from chapter 6**

```
public class CompositeNotificationService : INotificationService
{
    private readonly IEnumerable<INotificationService> services;
```

---

[9]   For a detailed discussion, see https://simpleinjector.org/aop.

```
public CompositeNotificationService(
    IEnumerable<INotificationService> services)
{
    this.services = services;
}

public void OrderApproved(Order order)
{
    foreach (INotificationService service in this.services)
    {
        service.OrderApproved(order);
    }
}
}
```

Because the Simple Injector API separates the registration of sequences from non-sequence registrations, the registration of Composites couldn't be any easier. You can register the Composite as a single registration, while registering its Dependencies as a sequence:

```
container.Collection.Register<INotificationService>(
    typeof(OrderApprovedReceiptSender),
    typeof(AccountingNotifier),
    typeof(OrderFulfillment),
);
```

container.Register<INotificationService, CompositeNotificationService>();

In the previous example, three INotificationService implementations are registered as a sequence using Collection.Register. The CompositeNotificationService, on the other hand, is registered as single, non-sequence registration. All types are Auto-Wired by Simple Injector. Using the previous registration, when an INotificationService is resolved, it results in an object graph similar to the following Pure DI representation:

```
return new CompositeNotificationService(new INotificationService[]
{
    new OrderApprovedReceiptSender(),
    new AccountingNotifier(),
    new OrderFulfillment()
});
```

Because the number of notification services will likely grow over time, you can reduce the burden on your Composition Root by applying Auto-Registration using the Collection.Register overload that accepts an Assembly. This lets you turn the previous list of types into a simple one-liner:

container.Collection.Register<INotificationService>(assembly);

```
container.Register<INotificationService, CompositeNotificationService>();
```

You may recall from chapter 13 that a similar construct in Autofac didn't work, because Autofac's Auto-Registration would register the Composite as well as part of the sequence. This, however, isn't the case with Simple Injector. It's Collection.Register method automatically filters out any Composite types and prevents them from being registered as part of the sequence.

Composite classes, however, aren't the only classes that will automatically be removed from the list by Simple Injector. Simple Injector also detects Decorators in the same way. This behavior makes working with Decorators and Composites in Simple Injector a breeze. The same holds true for working with generic Composites.

WIRING GENERIC COMPOSITES

In section 14.4.2, you saw how Simple Injector's `RegisterDecorator` method made registering generic Decorators look like child's play. In this section, we'll take a look at how you can register Composites for generic ABSTRACTIONS.

In section 6.1.3, you specified the `CompositeEventHandler<TEvent>` class (listing 6.12) as a Composite implementation over a sequence of `IEventHandler<TEvent>` implementations. Let's see if you can register the Composite with its wrapped event handler implementations. We'll start with the AUTO-REGISTRATION of the event handlers:

```
container.Collection.Register(typeof(IEventHandler<>), assembly);
```

In contrast to the registration of `ICommandService<T>` implementations in listing 14.3, you now use `Collection.Register` instead of `Register`. That's because there'll potentially be multiple handlers for a particular type of event. This means you have to explicitly state that you know there'll be more implementations for the single event type. Were you to have accidentally called `Register` instead of `Collection.Register`, Simple Injector would have thrown an exception similar to the following:

> *In the supplied list of types or assemblies, there are 3 types that represent the same closed-generic type IEventHandler<OrderApproved>. Did you mean to register the types as a collection using the Collection.Register method instead? Conflicting types: OrderApprovedReceiptSender, AccountingNotifier, and OrderFulfillment.*

A nice thing about this message is that it already indicates you most likely should be using `Collection.Register` instead of `Register`. But it's also possible that you accidentally added an invalid type that was picked up. As we explained before, when it comes to ambiguity, Simple Injector forces you to be explicit, which is helpful in detecting errors.

What remains is the registration for `CompositeEventHandler<TEvent>`. Because `CompositeEventHandler<TEvent>` is a generic type, you'll have to use the `Register` overload that accepts `Type` arguments:

```
container.Register(
    typeof(IEventHandler<>),
    typeof(CompositeEventHandler<>));
```

Because the Composite's goal is to hide the existence of the sequence, the Composite is registered as single, non-sequence mapping.

Using this registration, when a particular closed `IEventHandler<TEvent>` ABSTRACTION is requested (for example, `IEventHandler<OrderApproved>`), Simple Injector determines the exact `CompositeEventHandler<TEvent>` type to create. In this case, this is rather straightforward, because requesting an `IEventHandler<OrderApproved>` results in a `CompositeEventHandler<OrderApproved>` getting resolved. In other cases, determining the exact closed type can be a rather complex process, but Simple Injector handles this well.

Working with sequences is rather straightforward in Simple Injector. When it comes to resolving and injecting sequences, however, Simple Injector behaves differently compared to other DI CONTAINERS in a captivating way. As we alluded earlier, Simple Injector handles sequences as streams.

14.4.5 *Sequences are streams*

In section 14.1, you registered a sequence of ingredients as follows:

```
container.Collection.Register<IIngredient>(
    typeof(SauceBéarnaise),
    typeof(Steak));
```

As shown previously, you can ask the container to resolve all IIngredient components using either the GetAllInstances or GetInstance methods. Here's the example using GetInstance again:

```
IEnumerable<IIngredient> ingredients =
    container.GetInstance<IEnumerable<IIngredient>>();
```

You might expect the call to GetInstance<IEnumerable<IIngredient>>() to create an instance of both classes, but this couldn't be further from the truth. When resolving or injecting an IEnumerable<T>, Simple Injector doesn't prepopulate the sequence with all ingredients right away. Instead, IEnumerable<T> behaves like a stream.[10] What this means is that the returned IEnumerable<IIngredient> is an object that's able to produce new IIngredient instances when it's iterated. This is similar to streaming data from disk using a System.IO.FileStream or a database using a System.Data.SqlClient.SqlDataReader, where data arrives in small chunks rather than prefetching all the data in one go.

> **NOTE** Simple Injector is, to our knowledge, the only DI CONTAINER that streams sequences of ABSTRACTIONS.

The following example shows how iterating a stream multiple times can produce new instances:

Iterates the ingredients stream to resolve the first ingredient, which is SauceBéarnaise, using LINQ's Enumerable.First extension method

```
IEnumerable<IIngredient> stream =
    container.GetAllInstance<IIngredient>();

IIngredient ingredient1 = stream.First();
IIngredient ingredient2 = stream.First();         Iterates the ingredients stream again

object.ReferenceEquals(ingredient1, ingredient2);
```

Returns false because every time the stream is iterated, the container is requested to resolve an instance

---

[10] As a matter of fact, all sequence ABSTRACTIONS like IList<T> and ICollection<T> behave like streams in Simple Injector.

When a stream is iterated, it calls back into the container to resolve elements of the sequence based on their appropriate LIFESTYLE. This means that if the type is registered as TRANSIENT, new instances are always produced, as the previous example showed. When the type is SINGLETON, however, the same instance is returned every time:

```
var c = new Container();

c.Collection.Append<IIngredient, SauceBéarnaise>();
c.Collection.Append<IIngredient, Steak>(
    Lifestyle.Singleton);

var s = c.GetInstance<IEnumerable<IIngredient>>();

object.ReferenceEquals(s.First(), s.First());
object.ReferenceEquals(s.Last(), s.Last());
```

Appends both ingredients to the IIngredient sequence, while registering Steak as SINGLETON

Returns false

Returns true

NOTE The calls to `First` stop iterating the stream after the first instance is returned, which means that only `SauceBéarnaise` is created, whereas no `Steak` instance gets created. What might be surprising, though, is that the calls to `Last` don't cause the creation of both the first and the last element, but only the last, which isn't something you would expect when working with streams. This is caused by an optimization in `Enumerable.Last` in combination with the object that Simple Injector returns.

The returned sequence implements `IList<T>`. This might seem odd when you consider the sequence to be a stream, but this is possible because the number of items in the sequence is fixed after the configuration phase ends. `Enumerable.Last` has an optimization for `IList<T>`, allowing it to only request the last element using `List<T>`'s indexer without having to iterate the complete list.

Although streaming isn't a common trait under DI CONTAINERS, it has a few interesting advantages. First, when injecting a stream into a consumer, the injection of the stream itself is practically free, because no instance is created at that point in time.[11] This is useful when the list of elements is big, and not all elements are needed during the lifetime of the consumer. Take the following Composite `ILogger` implementation, for instance. It's a variation of the Composite of listing 8.22 but, in this case, the Composite stops logging directly after one of the wrapped loggers succeeds.

Listing 14.13 A Composite that processes part of the injected stream

```
public class CompositeLogger : ILogger
{
    private readonly IEnumerable<ILogger> loggers;

    public CompositeLogger(
        IEnumerable<ILogger> loggers)
    {
        this.loggers = loggers;
    }
```

Implements ILogger

Depends on IEnumerable<ILogger>

---

[11] The stream itself is a SINGLETON and will only get created once.

```
public void Log(LogEntry entry)                          ┌─ Iterates through the
{                                                        │  sequence of loggers
    foreach (ILogger logger in this.loggers)    ◄────────┘
    {
        try
        {
            logger.Log(entry);          ┌─ Breaks out of the loop when the
            break;           ◄──────────┘  logger doesn't throw an exception
        }
        catch { }    ◄──────────┐ Ignores any exception thrown by the logger and
    }                           └ continues to the next logger in the sequence
}
}
```

As you saw in section 14.4.4, you can register the `CompositeLogger` and the sequence of `ILogger` implementations as follows:

```
container.Collection.Register<ILogger>(assembly);
container.Register<ILogger, CompositeLogger>(Lifestyle.Singleton);
```

In this case, you registered the `CompositeLogger` as SINGLETON because it's stateless, and its only DEPENDENCY, the `IEnumerable<ILogger>`, is itself a SINGLETON. The effect of the `CompositeLogger` and `ILogger` sequences as SINGLETONS is that the injecting of `CompositeLogger` is practically free. Even when a consumer calls its DEPENDENCY's `Log` method, this typically only results in the creation of the first `ILogger` implementation of the sequence—not all of them.

A second advantage of sequences being streams is that, as long as you only store the reference to `IEnumerable<ILogger>`, as listing 14.13 showed, the sequence's elements can never accidentally become CAPTIVE DEPENDENCIES. The previous example already showed this. The SINGLETON `CompositeLogger` could safely depend on `IEnumerable<ILogger>`, because it also is a SINGLETON, even though its produced services might not be.

In this section, you've seen how to deal with multiple components such as sequences, Decorators, and Composites. This ends our discussion of Simple Injector. In the next chapter, we'll turn our attention to Microsoft.Extensions.DependencyInjection.

Summary

- Simple Injector is a modern DI CONTAINER that offers a fairly comprehensive feature set, but its API is quite different from most DI CONTAINERS. The following are a few of its characteristic attributes:

  - Scopes are ambient.
  - Sequences are registered using `Collection.Register` instead of appending new registrations of the same ABSTRACTION.
  - Sequences behave as streams.
  - The container can be diagnosed to find common configuration pitfalls.

- An important overall theme for Simple Injector is one of strictness. It doesn't attempt to guess what you mean and tries to prevent and detect configuration errors through its API and diagnostic facility.

- Simple Injector enforces a strict separation of registration and resolution. Although you use the same `Container` instance for both register and resolve, the `Container` is locked after first use.

- Because of Simple Injector's ambient scopes, resolving from the root container directly is good practice and encouraged: it doesn't lead to memory leaks or concurrency bugs.

- Simple Injector supports the standard LIFESTYLES: TRANSIENT, SINGLETON, and SCOPED.

- Simple Injector has excellent support for registration of sequences, Decorators, Composites, and generics.

The Microsoft.Extensions .DependencyInjection DI Container

In this chapter

- Working with Microsoft.Extensions .DependencyInjection's registration API
- Managing component lifetime
- Configuring difficult APIs
- Configuring sequences, Decorators, and Composites

With the introduction of ASP.NET Core, Microsoft introduced its own DI CONTAINER, Microsoft.Extensions.DependencyInjection, as part of the Core framework. In this chapter, we shorten that name to *MS.DI*.

Microsoft built MS.DI to simplify Dependency management for framework and third-party component developers working with ASP.NET Core. Microsoft's intention was to define a DI CONTAINER with a minimal, lowest common denominator feature set that all other DI CONTAINERS could conform to.

In this chapter, we'll give MS.DI the same treatment that we gave Autofac and Simple Injector. You'll see to which degree MS.DI can be used to apply the principles and patterns laid forth in parts 1–3. Even though MS.DI is integrated in ASP.NET Core, it can also be used separately, which is why, in this chapter, we treat it as such.

During the course of this chapter, however, you'll find that MS.DI is so limited in functionality that we deem it unsuited for development of any reasonably sized application that practices loose coupling and follows the principles and patterns described in this book. If MS.DI isn't suited, then why use an entire chapter covering it in this book? The most important reason is that MS.DI looks at a first glance so much like the other DI CONTAINERS that you need to spend some time with it to understand the differences between it and mature DI CONTAINERS. Because it's part of .NET Core, it may be tempting to use this built-in container if you don't understand its limitations. The purpose of this chapter is to reveal these limitations so you can make an informed decision.

NOTE You can skip this chapter if MS.DI doesn't interest you and you've already decided to use another DI CONTAINER.

This chapter is divided into four sections. You can read each section independently, though the first section is a prerequisite for the other sections, and the fourth section relies on some methods and classes introduced in the third section. You can read the chapter in isolation from the rest of part 4, specifically to learn about MS.DI, or you can read it together with the other chapters to compare DI CONTAINERS. The focus of this chapter is to show how MS.DI relates to and implements the patterns and principles described in parts 1–3.

15.1 *Introducing Microsoft.Extensions.DependencyInjection*

In this section, you'll learn where to get MS.DI, what you get, and how you start using it. We'll also look at common configuration options. Table 15.1 provides fundamental information that you're likely to need to get started.

Table 15.1 Microsoft.Extensions.DependencyInjection at a glance

Question	Answer
Where do I get it?	It's automatically included if you create a new ASP.NET Core application, but you can also manually add it to other application types. From Visual Studio, you can get it via NuGet. The package name is Microsoft.Extensions.DependencyInjection.
Which platforms are supported?	.NET Standard 2.0 (.NET Core 2.0, .NET Framework 4.6.1, Mono 5.4, Xamarin.iOS 10.14, Xamarin.Android 8.0, UWP 10.0.16299).
How much does it cost?	Nothing. It's open source.
How is it licensed?	Apache License, Version 2.0
Where can I get help?	Because this is an official Microsoft .NET product, there's guaranteed commercial support at https://www.microsoft.com/net/support/policy. For noncommercial—unguaranteed—support, you're likely to get help by asking on Stack Overflow at https://stackoverflow.com/.
On which version is this chapter based?	2.1.0

At a high level, using MS.DI isn't that different from Autofac (discussed in chapter 13). Its usage is a two-step process, as figure 15.1 illustrates. Compared to Simple Injector, however, with MS.DI this two-step process is explicit: first, you configure a `Service-Collection`, and when you're done with that, you use it to build a `ServiceProvider` that can be used to resolve components.

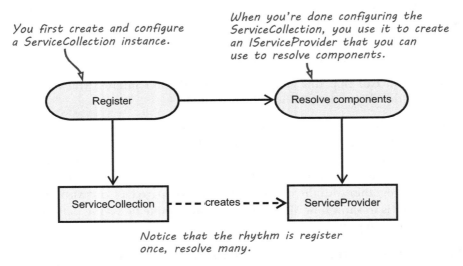

Figure 15.1   The pattern for using Microsoft.Extensions.DependencyInjection is to first configure it and then resolve components.

When you're done with this section, you should have a good feeling for the overall usage pattern of MS.DI, and you should be able to start using it in well-behaved scenarios—where all components follow proper DI patterns, such as CONSTRUCTOR INJECTION. Let's start with the simplest scenario and see how you can resolve objects using an MS.DI container.

15.1.1   *Resolving objects*

The core service of any DI CONTAINER is to compose object graphs. In this section, we'll look at the API that enables you to compose object graphs with MS.DI. MS.DI requires you to register all relevant components before you can resolve them. The following listing shows one of the simplest possible uses of MS.DI.

Listing 15.1   Simplest possible use of MS.DI

```
var services = new ServiceCollection();

services.AddTransient<SauceBéarnaise>();

ServiceProvider container =
    services.BuildServiceProvider(validateScopes: true);
```

```
IServiceScope scope = container.CreateScope();

SauceBéarnaise sauce =
    scope.ServiceProvider.GetRequiredService<SauceBéarnaise>();
```

As was already implied by figure 15.1, you need a `ServiceCollection` instance to configure components. MS.DI's `ServiceCollection` is the equivalent of Autofac's `ContainerBuilder`.

Here, you register the concrete `SauceBéarnaise` class with `services`, so that when you ask it to build a container, the resulting container is configured with the `Sauce-Béarnaise` class. This again enables you to resolve the `SauceBéarnaise` class from the container. If you don't register the `SauceBéarnaise` component, the attempt to resolve it throws a `InvalidOperationException` with the following message:

No service for type 'Ploeh.Samples.MenuModel.SauceBéarnaise' has been registered.

NOTE When creating an ASP.NET Core application, the hosting environment creates the `ServiceCollection` for you. In that case, you only have to consume it, as shown in listing 7.7. In this chapter, however, we'll treat MS.DI as the other DI CONTAINERS, which means we'll show how to use it in a less integrated environment.

As listing 15.1 shows, with MS.DI, you never resolve from the root container itself but from an `IServiceScope`. Section 15.2.1 goes into more detail about what an `IService-Scope` is.

WARNING With MS.DI, avoid resolving from the root container. This can easily lead to memory leaks or concurrency bugs. Instead, you should always resolve from a scope, as listing 15.1 shows.

As a safety measure, always build the `ServiceProvider` using the `BuildService-Provider` overload with the `validateScopes` argument set to `true`, as shown in listing 15.1. This prevents the accidental resolution of SCOPED instances from the root container. With the introduction of ASP.NET Core 2.0, `validateScopes` is automatically set to `true` by the framework when the application is running in the development environment, but it's best to enable validation even outside the development environment as well. This means you'll have to call `BuildServiceProvider(true)` manually.

Not only can MS.DI resolve concrete types with parameterless constructors, it can also AUTO-WIRE a type with other DEPENDENCIES. All these DEPENDENCIES need to be registered. For the most part, you want to program to interfaces, because this introduces loose coupling. To support this, MS.DI lets you map ABSTRACTIONS to concrete types.

MAPPING ABSTRACTIONS TO CONCRETE TYPES

Whereas our application's root types will typically be resolved by their concrete types as listing 15.1 showed, loose coupling requires you to map ABSTRACTIONS to concrete types. Creating instances based on such maps is the core service offered by any DI CON-TAINER, but you must still define the map. In this example, you map the `IIngredient` interface to the concrete `SauceBéarnaise` class, which allows you to successfully resolve `IIngredient`:

```
var services = new ServiceCollection();

services.AddTransient<IIngredient, SauceBéarnaise>();

var container = services.BuildServiceProvider(true);

IServiceScope scope = container.CreateScope();

IIngredient sauce = scope.ServiceProvider
    .GetRequiredService<IIngredient>();
```

Maps a concrete type to a particular ABSTRACTION

Resolves SauceBéarnaise as an IIngredient

Here, the `AddTransient` method allows a concrete type to be mapped to a particular ABSTRACTION using the TRANSIENT LIFESTYLE. Because of the previous `AddTransient` call, `SauceBéarnaise` can now be resolved as `IIngredient`.

In many cases, the generic API is all you need. Still, there are situations where you'll need a more weakly typed way to resolve services. This is also possible.

RESOLVING WEAKLY TYPED SERVICES

Sometimes you can't use a generic API because you don't know the appropriate type at design time. All you have is a `Type` instance, but you'd still like to get an instance of that type. You saw an example of that in section 7.3, where we discussed ASP.NET Core MVC's `IControllerActivator` class. The relevant method is this one:

```
object Create(ControllerContext context);
```

As shown previously in listing 7.8, the `ControllerContext` captures the controller's `Type`, which you can extract using the `ControllerTypeInfo` property of the `ActionDescriptor` property:

```
Type controllerType = context.ActionDescriptor.ControllerTypeInfo.AsType();
```

Because you only have a `Type` instance, you can't use generics, but must resort to a weakly typed API. MS.DI offers a weakly typed overload of the `GetRequiredService` method that lets you implement the `Create` method:

```
Type controllerType = context.ActionDescriptor.ControllerTypeInfo.AsType();
return scope.ServiceProvider.GetRequiredService(controllerType);
```

The weakly typed overload of `GetRequiredService` lets you pass the `controllerType` variable directly to MS.DI. Typically, this means you have to cast the returned value to some ABSTRACTION, because the weakly typed `GetRequiredService` method returns `object`. In the case of `IControllerActivator`, however, this isn't required, because ASP.NET Core MVC doesn't require controllers to implement any interface or base class.

No matter which overload of `GetRequiredService` you use, MS.DI guarantees that it'll return an instance of the requested type or throw an exception if there are DEPENDENCIES that can't be satisfied. When all required DEPENDENCIES have been properly configured, MS.DI can AUTO-WIRE the requested type.

NOTE As an alternative to GetRequiredService, there's also a GetService method. GetRequiredService throws an exception when the requested type can't be resolved, where GetService returns null instead. You should prefer GetRequiredService when you expect an instance to be returned, which is almost always.

To be able to resolve the requested type, all loosely coupled DEPENDENCIES must have been previously configured. Let's investigate the ways that you can configure MS.DI.

15.1.2 *Configuring the* ServiceCollection

As we discussed in section 12.2, you can configure a DI CONTAINER in several conceptually different ways. Figure 12.5 reviewed the options: configuration files, CONFIGURATION AS CODE, and AUTO-REGISTRATION. Figure 15.2 shows these options again.

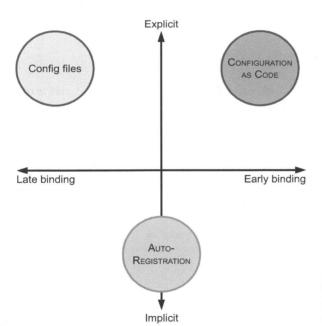

Figure 15.2 The most common ways to configure a DI CONTAINER shown against dimensions of explicitness and the degree of binding

WARNING MS.DI is designed around CONFIGURATION AS CODE and contains no API that supports either configuration files or AUTO-REGISTRATION.

Although there's no AUTO-REGISTRATION API, to some extent, you can implement assembly scanning with the help of .NET's LINQ and reflection APIs. Before we discuss this, we'll start with a discussion of MS.DI's CONFIGURATION AS CODE API.

CONFIGURING THE `ServiceCollection` USING CONFIGURATION AS CODE

In section 15.1.1, you saw a brief glimpse of MS.DI's strongly typed configuration API. Here, we'll examine it in greater detail.

All configuration in MS.DI uses the API exposed by the `ServiceCollection` class, although most of the methods are extension methods. One of the most commonly used methods is the `AddTransient` method that you've already seen:

```
services.AddTransient<IIngredient, SauceBéarnaise>();
```

Registering `SauceBéarnaise` as `IIngredient` hides the concrete class so that you can no longer resolve `SauceBéarnaise` with this registration. But you can fix this by replacing the registration with the following:

```
services.AddTransient<SauceBéarnaise>();
services.AddTransient<IIngredient>(
    c => c.GetRequiredService<SauceBéarnaise>());
```

◄──── **Registers a delegate that calls back into the container to resolve the previously registered concrete type**

Instead of making the registration for `IIngredient` using the AUTO-WIRING overload of `AddTransient`, you register a code block that, when called, forwards the call to the registration of the concrete `SauceBéarnaise`.

Torn LIFESTYLES

In this section, we've shown how you can call `AddTransient` multiple times to register a component as multiple service types. The following example shows this once more:

```
services.AddTransient<SauceBéarnaise>();
services.AddTransient<IIngredient>(
    c => c.GetRequiredService<SauceBéarnaise>());
```

You might be tempted, however, to think this is equivalent to the following code:

```
services.AddTransient<SauceBéarnaise>();
services.AddTransient<IIngredient, SauceBéarnaise>();
```

The former example, however, isn't equivalent to the latter. This becomes apparent when you change the LIFESTYLE from TRANSIENT to, for instance, SINGLETON.

BAD
CODE

```
services.AddSingleton<SauceBéarnaise>();
services.AddSingleton<IIngredient, SauceBéarnaise>();
```

Although you might expect there to only be one `SauceBéarnaise` instance for the lifetime of the container, splitting up the registration causes MS.DI to create a separate instance per `AddSingleton` call. The LIFESTYLE of `SauceBéarnaise` is therefore considered to be *torn*.

WARNING Each call to one of the AddScoped and AddSingleton methods results in its own unique cache. Having multiple Add... calls can, therefore, result in multiple instances per scope or per container. To prevent this, register a delegate that resolves the concrete instance.

In real applications, you always have more than one ABSTRACTION to map, so you must configure multiple mappings. This is done with multiple calls to one of the Add... methods:

```
services.AddTransient<IIngredient, SauceBéarnaise>();
services.AddTransient<ICourse, Course>();
```

This maps IIngredient to SauceBéarnaise, and ICourse to Course. There's no overlap of types, so it should be pretty evident what's going on. But you can also register the same ABSTRACTION several times:

```
services.AddTransient<IIngredient, SauceBéarnaise>();
services.AddTransient<IIngredient, Steak>();
```

Here, you register IIngredient twice. If you resolve IIngredient, you get an instance of Steak. The last registration wins, but previous registrations aren't forgotten. MS.DI can handle multiple configurations for the same ABSTRACTION, but we'll get back to this topic in section 15.4.

Although there are more-advanced options available for configuring MS.DI, you can configure an entire application with the methods shown here. But to save yourself from too much explicit maintenance of container configuration, you could instead consider a more convention-based approach using AUTO-REGISTRATION.

CONFIGURING ServiceCollection USING AUTO-REGISTRATION

In many cases, registrations will be similar. Such registrations are tedious to maintain, and explicitly registering each and every component might not be the most productive approach, as we discussed in section 12.3.3.

Consider a library that contains many IIngredient implementations. You can configure each class individually, but it'll result in an ever-changing list of Type instances supplied to the Add... methods. What's worse is that every time you add a new IIngredient implementation, you must also explicitly register it with the container if you want it to be available. It would be more productive to state that all implementations of IIngredient found in a given assembly should be registered.

As stated previously, MS.DI contains no AUTO-REGISTRATION API. This means you have to do it yourself. This is possible to some degree, and in this section, we'll show how with a simple example but delay more detailed discussions of the possibilities and limitations until section 15.4. Let's take a look how you can register a sequence of IIngredient registrations:

```
Assembly ingredientsAssembly = typeof(Steak).Assembly;

var ingredientTypes =
    from type in ingredientsAssembly.GetTypes()
    where !type.IsAbstract
    where typeof(IIngredient).IsAssignableFrom(type)
    select type;

foreach (var type in ingredientTypes)
{
    services.AddTransient(typeof(IIngredient), type);
}
```

⌐ **Convention-based scan**

◄── **Registers each type based on the IIngredient interface**

The previous example unconditionally configures all implementations of the
IIngredient interface, but you can provide filters that enable you to select only
a subset. Here's a convention-based scan where you add only classes whose name
starts with *Sauce*:

```
Assembly ingredientsAssembly = typeof(Steak).Assembly;

var ingredientTypes =
    from type in ingredientsAssembly.GetTypes()
    where !type.IsAbstract
    where typeof(IIngredient).IsAssignableFrom(type)
    where type.Name.StartsWith("Sauce")   ◄──
    select type;

foreach (var type in ingredientTypes)
{
    services.AddTransient(typeof(IIngredient), type);
}
```

Removes classes whose names don't start with *Sauce*

Apart from selecting the correct types from an assembly, another part of AUTO-
REGISTRATION is defining the correct mapping. In the previous examples, you used the
AddTransient method with a specific interface to register all selected types against that
interface.

But sometimes you'll want to use different conventions. Let's say that instead of
interfaces, you use abstract base classes, and you want to register all types in an assembly
where the name ends with *Policy* by their base type:

```
Assembly policiesAssembly = typeof(DiscountPolicy).Assembly;

var policyTypes =
    from type in policiesAssembly.GetTypes()   ◄──
    where type.Name.EndsWith("Policy")   ◄──
    select type;

foreach (var type in policyTypes)
{
    services.AddTransient(type.BaseType, type);
}
```

Gets all types in the assembly

Filters by the Policy suffix

◄── **Registers each policy component by its base class**

Even though MS.DI contains no convention-based API, by making use of existing .NET framework APIs, convention-based registrations are possible. This becomes a different ball game when it comes to generics, as we'll discuss next.

AUTO-REGISTRATION OF GENERIC ABSTRACTIONS

During the course of chapter 10, you refactored the big, obnoxious `IProductService` interface to the `ICommandService<TCommand>` interface of listing 10.12. Here's that ABSTRACTION again:

```
public interface ICommandService<TCommand>
{
    void Execute(TCommand command);
}
```

As discussed in chapter 10, every command Parameter Object represents a use case, and there'll be a single implementation per use case. The `AdjustInventoryService` of listing 10.8 was given as an example. It implemented the "adjust inventory" use case. The following listing shows this class again.

Listing 15.2   The `AdjustInventoryService` from chapter 10

```
public class AdjustInventoryService : ICommandService<AdjustInventory>
{
    private readonly IInventoryRepository repository;

    public AdjustInventoryService(IInventoryRepository repository)
    {
        this.repository = repository;
    }

    public void Execute(AdjustInventory command)
    {
        var productId = command.ProductId;

        ...
    }
}
```

Any reasonably complex system will easily implement hundreds of use cases, and this is an ideal candidate for using AUTO-REGISTRATION. But because of the lack of AUTO-REGISTRATION support by MS.DI, you'll have to write a fair amount of code to get this running. The next listing provides an example of this.

Listing 15.3   AUTO-REGISTRATION of `ICommandService<TCommand>` implementations

```
Assembly assembly = typeof(AdjustInventoryService).Assembly;

var mappings =
    from type in assembly.GetTypes()            Selects concrete types
    where !type.IsAbstract          ◄─────┐
    where !type.IsGenericType       ◄─────── Selects non-generic types
```

```
from i in type.GetInterfaces()
where i.IsGenericType
where i.GetGenericTypeDefinition()
    == typeof(ICommandService<>)
select new { service = i, type };
```

> Selects types implementing
> **ICommandService< TCommand >**

```
foreach (var mapping in mappings)
{
    services.AddTransient(
        mapping.service,
        mapping.type);
}
```

> **Registers the type by its interface**

As in the previous listings, you make full use of .NET's LINQ and Reflection APIs to allow selecting classes from the supplied assembly. Using the supplied open-generic interface, you iterate through the list of assembly types, and register all types that implement a closed-generic version of `ICommandService<TCommand>`. What this means, for instance, is that `AdjustInventoryService` is registered because it implements `ICommandService<AdjustInventory>`, which is a closed-generic version of `ICommandService<TCommand>`.

> **WARNING** The code in listing 15.3 presents many shortcomings. For instance, in case you accidentally implement the same closed-generic interface on multiple classes, the registration will fail silently. The code will happily register all implementations. In case a command service is requested, where multiple implementations for that type exist, the last registration is resolved. One major problem, however, is that it's undetermined which registration is last, and this could even change after an application restart![1]

This section introduced the MS.DI DI CONTAINER and demonstrated these fundamental mechanics: how to configure a `ServiceCollection`, and, subsequently, how to use the constructed `ServiceProvider` to resolve services. Resolving services is done with a single call to the `GetRequiredService` method, so the complexity involves configuring the container. The API primarily supports CONFIGURATION AS CODE, although to some extend AUTO-REGISTRATION can be built on top of it. As you'll see later, however, the lack of support for AUTO-REGISTRATION will lead to quite complex and hard-to-maintain code. Until now, we've only looked at the most basic API, but there's another area we have yet to cover—how to manage component lifetime.

15.2   *Managing lifetime*

In chapter 8, we discussed LIFETIME MANAGEMENT, including the most common conceptual lifetime styles such as TRANSIENT, SINGLETON, and SCOPED. MS.DI supports these three LIFESTYLES and lets you configure the lifetime of all services. The LIFESTYLES shown in table 15.2 are available as part of the API.

---

[1]   The ordering of the list of types returned by `Assembly.GetType()` is undefined. This can change when the application is recompiled or even when the application is restarted.

Table 15.2 Microsoft.Extensions.DependencyInjection LIFESTYLES

Microsoft name	Pattern name	Comments
Transient	TRANSIENT	Instances are tracked by the container and disposed of.
Singleton	SINGLETON	Instances are disposed of when the container is disposed of.
Scoped	SCOPED	Instances are reused within the same `IServiceScope`. Instances are tracked for the lifetime of the scope and are disposed of when the scope is disposed of.

MS.DI's implementation of TRANSIENT and SINGLETON are equivalent to the general LIFESTYLES described in chapter 8, so we won't spend much time on them in this chapter. Instead, in this section, you'll see how you can define LIFESTYLES for components in code. By the end of this section, you should be able to use MS.DI's LIFESTYLES in your own application. Let's start by reviewing how to configure instance scopes for components.

15.2.1 Configuring LIFESTYLES

In this section, we'll review how to manage LIFESTYLES with MS.DI. A LIFESTYLE is configured as part of registering components. It's as easy as this:

```
services.AddSingleton<SauceBéarnaise>();
```

This configures the concrete `SauceBéarnaise` class as a SINGLETON so that the same instance is returned each time `SauceBéarnaise` is requested. If you want to map an ABSTRACTION to a concrete class with a specific LIFESTYLE, you can use the `AddSingleton` overload with two generic arguments:

```
services.AddSingleton<IIngredient, SauceBéarnaise>();
```

Compared to other DI CONTAINERS, there aren't many options in MS.DI when it comes to configuring LIFESTYLES for components. It's done in a rather declarative fashion. Although configuration is typically easy, you mustn't forget that some LIFESTYLES involve long-lived objects that use resources as long as they're around.

15.2.2 Releasing components

As discussed in section 8.2.2, it's important to release objects when you're done with them. Similar to Autofac and Simple Injector, MS.DI has no explicit `Release` method, but instead uses a concept called *scopes*. A scope can be regarded as a request-specific cache. As figure 15.3 illustrates, it defines a boundary where components can be reused.

An `IServiceScope` defines a cache that you can use for a particular duration or purpose; the most obvious example is a web request. When a SCOPED component is requested from an `IServiceScope`, you always receive the same instance. The difference from true SINGLETONS is that if you query a second scope, you'll get another instance.

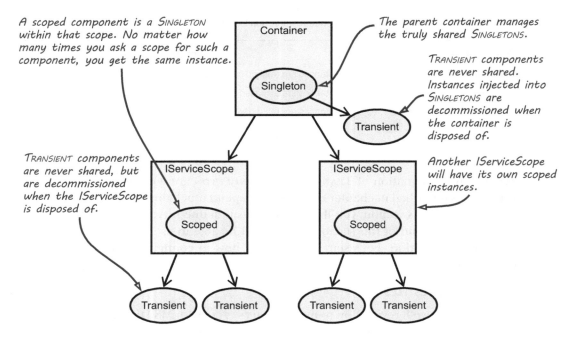

Figure 15.3   Microsoft.Extensions.DependencyInjection's scopes act as containers that can share components for a limited duration or purpose.

One of the important features of scopes is that they let you properly release components when the scope completes. You create a new scope with the `CreateScope` method of a particular `IServiceProvider` implementation, and release all appropriate components by invoking its `Dispose` method:

```
using (IServiceScope scope = container.CreateScope())      ◀── Creates a scope from
{                                                               the root container
    IMeal meal = scope.ServiceProvider
        .GetRequiredService<IMeal>();      ◀── Resolves a meal from the
                                               newly created scope

    meal.Consume();      ◀── Consumes the meal

}      ◀── Releases the meal by ending the using block
```

A new scope is created from the container by invoking the `CreateScope` method. The return value implements `IDisposable`, so you can wrap it in a `using` block. Because `IServiceScope` contains a `ServiceProvider` property that implements the same interface that the container itself implements, you can use the scope to resolve components in exactly the same way as with the container itself.

When you're done with the scope, you can dispose of it. With a `using` block, this happens automatically when you exit that block, but you can also choose to explicitly dispose of it by invoking the `Dispose` method. When you dispose of the scope, you also release all the components that were created by the scope; here, it means that you release the meal object graph.

Note that DEPENDENCIES of a component are always resolved at or below the component's scope. For example, if you need a TRANSIENT DEPENDENCY injected into a SINGLETON, that TRANSIENT DEPENDENCY will come from the root container, even if you're resolving the SINGLETON from a nested scope. This tracks the TRANSIENT within the root container and prevents it from being disposed of when the scope gets disposed of. The SINGLETON consumer would otherwise break, because it's kept alive in the root container while depending on a component that was disposed of.

> **IMPORTANT** With MS.DI, a TRANSIENT component is a component that's expected to live as long as the consumer it's injected into. That's why MS.DI allows injecting TRANSIENTS into SINGLETONS, although injection of SCOPED instances into SINGLETONS is blocked.[2] Although injecting a TRANSIENT into a SINGLETON might be exactly the desired behavior, more often it's not. You need to take extra care to check that TRANSIENTS don't become accidental CAPTIVE DEPENDENCIES.

Earlier in this section, you saw how to configure components as SINGLETONS or TRANSIENTS. Configuring a component to have a SCOPED LIFESTYLE is done in a similar way:

```
services.AddScoped<IIngredient, SauceBéarnaise>();
```

Similar to the `AddTransient` and `AddSingleton` methods, you can use the `AddScoped` method to state that the component's lifetime should follow the scope that created the instance.

> **WARNING** MS.DI tracks most components—even disposable TRANSIENTS. This will cause problems when you resolve from the root container instead of a scope. When resolving from the root container, new instances are still created on each call to `GetService`, but those disposable TRANSIENTS are kept alive in order to allow them to be disposed of when the container is disposed of. Because the root container won't be disposed of until the application stops, this causes memory leaks, so it's important to remember to resolve all components from a scope and dispose of the scope after use.

Due to their nature, SINGLETONS are never released for the lifetime of the container itself. Still, you can release even those components if you don't need the container any longer. This is done by disposing of the container itself:

```
container.Dispose();
```

In practice, this isn't nearly as important as disposing of a scope, because the lifetime of a container tends to correlate closely with the lifetime of the application it supports. You normally keep the container around as long as the application runs, so you'd only dispose of it when the application shuts down. In this case, memory would be reclaimed by the operating system.

---

[2] This happens when you enable scope validation, as we discussed in section 15.1.1.

This completes our tour of LIFETIME MANAGEMENT with MS.DI. Components can be configured with mixed LIFESTYLES, and this is true even when you register multiple implementations of the same ABSTRACTION. Until now, you've allowed the container to wire DEPENDENCIES by implicitly assuming that all components use CONSTRUCTOR INJECTION. But this isn't always the case. In the next section, we'll review how to deal with classes that must be instantiated in special ways.

15.3 Registering difficult APIs

Until now, we've considered how you can configure components that use CONSTRUCTOR INJECTION. One of the many benefits of CONSTRUCTOR INJECTION is that DI CONTAINERS such as MS.DI can easily understand how to compose and create all classes in a DEPENDENCY graph. This becomes less clear when APIs are less well behaved.

In this section, you'll see how to deal with primitive constructor arguments and static factories. These all require your special attention. Let's start by looking at classes that take primitive types, such as strings or integers, as constructor arguments.

15.3.1 Configuring primitive DEPENDENCIES

As long as you inject ABSTRACTIONS into consumers, all is well. But it becomes more difficult when a constructor depends on a primitive type, such as a string, a number, or an enum. This is particularly the case for data access implementations that take a connection string as constructor parameter, but it's a more general issue that applies to all strings and numbers.

Conceptually, it doesn't always make sense to register a string or number as a component in a container. Using generic type constraints, MS.DI even blocks the registration of value types like numbers and enums from its generic API. With the non-generic API, on the other hand, this is still possible. Consider as an example this constructor:

```
public ChiliConCarne(Spiciness spiciness)
```

In this example, Spiciness is an enum:

```
public enum Spiciness { Mild, Medium, Hot }
```

> **TIP** As a rule of thumb, enums are code smells and should be refactored to polymorphic classes.[3] But they serve us well for this example.

If you want all consumers of Spiciness to use the same value, you can register Spiciness and ChiliConCarne independently of each other:

```
services.AddSingleton(
    typeof(Spiciness), Spiciness.Medium);

services.AddTransient<ICourse, ChiliConCarne>();
```

Uses the non-generic AddSingleton overload that accepts a precreated object; in this case, the value of the enum

AUTO-WIRES ChiliConCarne with Spiciness

---

[3]   See Martin Fowler et al, *Refactoring: Improving the Design of Existing Code* (Addison-Wesley, 1999), 82.

When you subsequently resolve `ChiliConCarne`, it'll have a `Medium Spiciness`, as will all other components with a DEPENDENCY on `Spiciness`. If you'd rather control the relationship between `ChiliConCarne` and `Spiciness` on a finer level, you can use a code block, which is something we get back to in a moment in section 15.3.3.

The option described here uses AUTO-WIRING to provide a concrete value to a component. A more convenient solution, however, is to extract the primitive DEPENDENCIES into Parameter Objects.

15.3.2 *Extracting primitive DEPENDENCIES to Parameter Objects*

In section 10.3.3, we discussed how the introduction of Parameter Objects allowed mitigating the OPEN/CLOSED PRINCIPLE violation that `IProductService` caused. Parameter Objects, however, are also a great tool to mitigate ambiguity. For example, the `Spiciness` of a course could be described in more general terms as a flavoring. Flavoring might include other properties, such as saltiness, so you can wrap `Spiciness` and the saltiness in a `Flavoring` class:

```
public class Flavoring
{
    public readonly Spiciness Spiciness;
    public readonly bool ExtraSalty;

    public Flavoring(Spiciness spiciness, bool extraSalty)
    {
        this.Spiciness = spiciness;
        this.ExtraSalty = extraSalty;
    }
}
```

As we mentioned in section 10.3.3, it's perfectly fine for Parameter Objects to have one parameter. The goal is to remove ambiguity, and not just on the technical level. Such a Parameter Object's name might do a better job describing what your code does on a functional level, as the `Flavoring` class so elegantly does. With the introduction of the `Flavoring` Parameter Object, it now becomes possible to AUTO-WIRE any `ICourse` implementation that requires some flavoring without introducing ambiguity:

```
var flavoring = new Flavoring(Spiciness.Medium, extraSalty: true);
services.AddSingleton<Flavoring>(flavoring);

container.AddTransient<ICourse, ChiliConCarne>();
```

This code creates a single instance of the `Flavoring` class. `Flavoring` becomes a configuration object for courses. Because there'll only be one `Flavoring` instance, you can register it in MS.DI using the `AddSingleton<T>` overload that accepts a precreated instance.

Extracting primitive DEPENDENCIES into Parameter Objects should be your preference over the previously discussed option, because Parameter Objects remove ambiguity, at both the functional and technical levels. It does, however, require a change to a component's constructor, which might not always be feasible. In this case, registering a delegate is your second-best pick.

15.3.3 *Registering objects with code blocks*

Another option for creating a component with a primitive value is to use one of the Add... methods, which let you supply a delegate that creates the component:

```
services.AddTransient<ICourse>(c => new ChiliConCarne(Spiciness.Hot));
```

You already saw this AddTransient method overload previously, when we discussed torn LIFESTYLES in section 15.1.2. The ChiliConCarne constructor is invoked with a hot Spiciness every time the ICourse service is resolved. The following example shows the definition of this AddTransient<TService> extension method:

```
public static IServiceCollection AddTransient<TService>(
    this IServiceCollection services,
    Func<IServiceProvider, TService> implementationFactory)
    where TService : class;
```

As you can see, this AddTransient method accepts a parameter of type Func<IService-Provider, TService>. With respect to the previous registration, when an ICourse is resolved, MS.DI will call the supplied delegate and supply it with the IServiceProvider belonging to the current IServiceScope. With it, your code block can resolve instances that originate from the same IServiceScope. We'll demonstrate this in the next section.

When it comes to the ChiliConCarne class, you have a choice between AUTO-WIRING or using a code block. But other classes are more restrictive: they can't be instantiated through a public constructor. Instead, you must use some sort of factory to create instances of the type. This is always troublesome for DI CONTAINERS, because, by default, they look after public constructors. Consider this example constructor for the public JunkFood class:

```
internal JunkFood(string name)
```

Even though the JunkFood class might be public, the constructor is internal. In this example, instances of JunkFood should instead be created through the static Junk-FoodFactory class:

```
public static class JunkFoodFactory
{
    public static JunkFood Create(string name)
    {
        return new JunkFood(name);
    }
}
```

From MS.DI's perspective, this is a problematic API, because there are no unambiguous and well-established conventions around static factories. It needs help—and you can give that help by providing a code block it can execute to create the instance:

```
services.AddTransient<IMeal>(c => JunkFoodFactory.Create("chicken meal"));
```

This time, you use the AddTransient method to create the component by invoking a static factory within the code block. JunkFoodFactory.Create will be invoked every time IMeal is resolved, and the result will be returned.

If you have to write the code to create the instance, how is this in any way better than invoking the code directly? By using a code block inside an `AddTransient` method call, you still gain something:

- *You map from `IMeal` to `JunkFood`.* This allows consuming classes to stay loosely coupled.
- *LIFESTYLES can still be configured.* Although the code block will be invoked to create the instance, it may not be invoked every time the instance is requested. It is by default, but if you change it to a SINGLETON, the code block will only be invoked once, and the result cached and reused thereafter.

In this section, you've seen how you can use MS.DI to deal with more-difficult creational APIs. Up until this point, the code examples have been fairly straightforward. This will quickly change when you start to work with multiple components, so let's now turn our attention in that direction.

15.4 Working with multiple components

As alluded to in section 12.1.2, DI CONTAINERS thrive on distinctness but have a hard time with ambiguity. When using CONSTRUCTOR INJECTION, a single constructor is preferred over overloaded constructors, because it's evident which constructor to use when there's no choice. This is also the case when mapping from ABSTRACTIONS to concrete types. If you attempt to map multiple concrete types to the same ABSTRACTION, you introduce ambiguity.

Despite the undesirable qualities of ambiguity, you often need to work with multiple implementations of a single ABSTRACTION. This can be the case in these situations:

- Different concrete types are used for different consumers.
- DEPENDENCIES are sequences.
- Decorators or Composites are in use.

In this section, we'll look at each of these cases and see how you can address each with MS.DI. When we're done, you should have a good feel for what you can do with MS.DI and where the boundaries lie when multiple implementations of the same ABSTRACTION are in play. Let's first see how you can provide more fine-grained control than AUTO-WIRING provides.

15.4.1 Selecting among multiple candidates

AUTO-WIRING is convenient and powerful but provides little control. As long as all ABSTRACTIONS are distinctly mapped to concrete types, you have no problems. But as soon as you introduce more implementations of the same interface, ambiguity rears its ugly head. Let's first recap how MS.DI deals with multiple registrations of the same ABSTRACTION.

CONFIGURING MULTIPLE IMPLEMENTATIONS OF THE SAME SERVICE

As you saw in section 15.1.2, you can register multiple implementations of the same interface:

```
services.AddTransient<IIngredient, SauceBéarnaise>();
services.AddTransient<IIngredient, Steak>();
```

This example registers both the Steak and SauceBéarnaise classes as the IIngredient service. The last registration wins, so if you resolve IIngredient with GetRequiredService<IIngredient>(), you'll get a Steak instance.

You can also ask the container to resolve all IIngredient components. MS.DI has a dedicated method to do that, called GetServices. Here's an example:

```
IEnumerable<IIngredient> ingredients =
    scope.ServiceProvider.GetServices<IIngredient>();
```
◄———— **Gets a sequence with all registered ingredients**

Under the hood, GetServices delegates to GetRequiredService, while requesting an IEnumerable<IIngredient>. You can also ask the container to resolve all IIngredient components using GetRequiredService instead:

```
IEnumerable<IIngredient> ingredients = scope.ServiceProvider
    .GetRequiredService<IEnumerable<IIngredient>>();
```

Notice that you use the normal GetRequiredService method, but that you request IEnumerable<IIngredient>. The container interprets this as a convention and gives you all the IIngredient components it has.

When there are multiple implementations of a certain ABSTRACTION, there'll often be a consumer that depends on a sequence. Sometimes, however, components need to work with a fixed set or a subset of DEPENDENCIES of the same ABSTRACTION, which is what we'll discuss next.

REMOVING AMBIGUITY USING CODE BLOCKS

As useful as AUTO-WIRING is, sometimes you need to override the normal behavior to provide fine-grained control over which DEPENDENCIES go where, but it may also be that you need to address an ambiguous API. As an example, consider this constructor:

```
public ThreeCourseMeal(ICourse entrée, ICourse mainCourse, ICourse dessert)
```

In this case, you have three identically typed DEPENDENCIES, each of which represents a different concept. In most cases, you want to map each of the DEPENDENCIES to a separate type.

As stated previously, when compared to both Autofac and Simple Injector, MS.DI is limited in functionality. Where Autofac provides keyed registrations, and Simple Injector provides conditional registrations to deal with this kind of ambiguity, MS.DI falls short in this respect. There isn't any built-in functionality to do this. To wire up such an ambiguous API with MS.DI, you have to revert to using a code block.

Listing 15.4 Wiring `ThreeCourseMeal` by resolving courses in a code block

Registers IMeal using a lambda expression

```
services.AddTransient<IMeal>(c => new ThreeCourseMeal(
    entrée: c.GetRequiredService<Rillettes>(),
    mainCourse: c.GetRequiredService<CordonBleu>(),
    dessert: c.GetRequiredService<CrèmeBrûlée>())));
```

Injects the three constructor arguments by requesting them from the container

This registration reverts from AUTO-WIRING and constructs the `ThreeCourseMeal` using a delegate instead. Fortunately, the three `ICourse` implementations themselves are still AUTO-WIRED. To bring AUTO-WIRING back for the `ThreeCourseMeal`, you make use of MS.DI's `ActivatorUtilities` class.

REMOVING AMBIGUITY USING `ActivatorUtilities`

The lack of AUTO-WIRING of `ThreeCourseMeal` isn't that problematic in this example because, in this case, you override all constructor arguments. This could be different if `ThreeCourseMeal` contained more DEPENDENCIES:

```
public ThreeCourseMeal(
    ICourse entrée,
    ICourse mainCourse,
    ICourse dessert,
    ...        More DEPENDENCIES
    )
```

MS.DI contains a utility class called `ActivatorUtilities` that allows AUTO-WIRING a class's DEPENDENCIES, while overriding other DEPENDENCIES by explicitly supplying their values. Using `ActivatorUtilities`, you can rewrite the previous registration.

Listing 15.5 Wiring `ThreeCourseMeal` using `ActivatorUtilities`

Supplies the IServiceProvider

```
services.AddTransient<IMeal>(c =>
    ActivatorUtilities.CreateInstance<ThreeCourseMeal>(
        c,
        new object[]
        {
            c.GetRequiredService<Rillettes>(),
            c.GetRequiredService<CordonBleu>(),
            c.GetRequiredService<MousseAuChocolat>()
        }));
```

Requests a ThreeCourseMeal to be created

Supplies the three courses to override as an object array

This example makes use of the `ActivatorUtilities`'s `CreateInstance<T>` method, defined as follows:

```
public static T CreateInstance<T>(
    IServiceProvider provider,
    params object[] parameters);
```

The `CreateInstance<T>` method creates a new instance of the supplied `T`. It goes through the supplied `parameters` array and matches each parameter to a compatible constructor parameter. Then it resolves the remaining, unmatched constructor parameters with the supplied `IServiceProvider`.

Because all three resolved courses implement `ICourse`, there's still ambiguity in the call. `CreateInstance<T>` resolves this ambiguity by applying the supplied `parameters` from left to right. This means that because `Rillettes` is the first element in the `parameters` array, it'll be applied to the first compatible parameter of the `ThreeCourseMeal` constructor. This is the entrée parameter of type `ICourse`.

NOTE In case you overspecify the parameters, for example, by providing a fourth `ICourse` value, `CreateInstance<T>` throws an exception, because there isn't a matching parameter for the overspecified parameter.

When compared to listing 15.4, there's a big downside to listing 15.5. Listing 15.4 is verified by the compiler. Any refactoring to the constructor would either allow that code to stay working or fail with a compile error.

The opposite is true with listing 15.5. If the three `ICourse` constructor parameters are rearranged, code will keep compiling, and `ActivatorUtilities` would even be able to construct a new `ThreeCourseMeal`. But unless listing 15.5 is changed according to that rearrangement, the courses are injected in an incorrect order, which will likely cause the application to behave incorrectly. Unfortunately, no refactoring tool will signal that the registration must be changed too.

Even the related registrations of Autofac and Simple Injector (listings 13.7 and 14.9) do a better job of preventing errors. Although neither listing is type-safe, because both listings match on exact parameter names, a change to the `ThreeCourseMeal` would at least cause an exception when the class is resolved. This is always better than failing silently, which is what could happen in the case of listing 15.5.

Overriding AUTO-WIRING by explicitly mapping parameters to components is a universally applicable solution. Where you use named registrations with Autofac and conditional registrations with Simple Injector, with MS.DI, you override parameters by passing in manually resolved concrete types. This can be brittle if you have many types to manage. A better solution is to design your own API to get rid of that ambiguity. It often leads to a better overall design.

In the next section, you'll see how to use the less ambiguous and more flexible approach where you allow any number of courses in a meal. To this end, you must learn how MS.DI deals with sequences.

15.4.2 *Wiring sequences*

In section 6.1.1, we discussed how CONSTRUCTOR INJECTION acts as a warning system for SINGLE RESPONSIBILITY PRINCIPLE violations. The lesson then was that instead of viewing Constructor Over-injection as a weakness of the Constructor Injection pattern, you should rather rejoice that it makes problematic design so obvious.

When it comes to DI Containers and ambiguity, we see a similar relationship. DI Containers generally don't deal with ambiguity in a graceful manner. Although you can make a DI Container deal with it, it can seem awkward. This is often an indication that you could improve the design of your code.

In this section, we'll look at an example that demonstrates how you can refactor away from ambiguity. It'll also show how MS.DI deals with sequences.

REFACTORING TO A BETTER COURSE BY REMOVING AMBIGUITY

In section 15.4.1, you saw how the `ThreeCourseMeal` and its inherent ambiguity forced you to either abandon Auto-Wiring or make use of the rather verbose call to `Activator-Utilities`. A simple generalization moves toward an implementation of `IMeal` that takes an arbitrary number of `ICourse` instances instead of exactly three, as was the case with the `ThreeCourseMeal` class:

```
public Meal(IEnumerable<ICourse> courses)
```

Notice that, instead of requiring three distinct `ICourse` instances in the constructor, the single dependency on an `IEnumerable<ICourse>` instance lets you provide any number of courses to the `Meal` class—from zero to ... a lot! This solves the issue with ambiguity, because there's now only a single Dependency. In addition, it also improves the API and implementation by providing a single, general-purpose class that can model different types of meal: from a simple meal with a single course to an elaborate 12-course dinner.

In this section, we'll look at how you can configure MS.DI to wire up `Meal` instances with appropriate `ICourse` Dependencies. When we're done, you should have a good idea of the options available when you need to configure instances with sequences of Dependencies.

AUTO-WIRING SEQUENCES

MS.DI understands sequences, so if you want to use all registered components of a given service, Auto-Wiring just works. As an example, you can configure the `IMeal` service and its courses like this:

```
services.AddTransient<ICourse, Rillettes>();
services.AddTransient<ICourse, CordonBleu>();
services.AddTransient<ICourse, MousseAuChocolat>();

services.AddTransient<IMeal, Meal>();
```

Notice that this is a completely standard mapping from Abstractions to concrete types. MS.DI automatically understands the `Meal` constructor and determines that the correct course of action is to resolve all `ICourse` components. When you resolve `IMeal`, you get a `Meal` instance with the `ICourse` components `Rillettes`, `CordonBleu`, and `MousseAuChocolat`.

MS.DI automatically handles sequences, and unless you specify otherwise, it does what you'd expect it to do: it resolves a sequence of DEPENDENCIES to all registered components of that type. Only when you need to explicitly pick only some components from a larger set do you need to do more. Let's see how you can do that.

PICKING ONLY SOME COMPONENTS FROM A LARGER SET

MS.DI's default strategy of injecting all components is often the correct policy, but as figure 15.4 shows, there may be cases where you want to pick only some registered components from the larger set of all registered components.

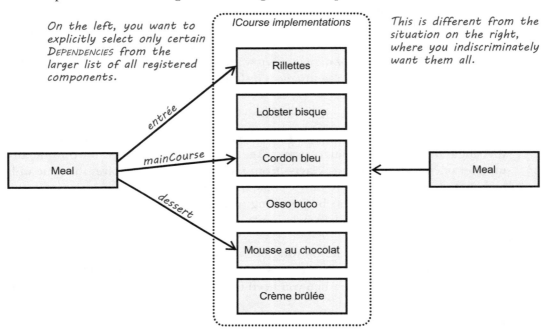

Figure 15.4   Picking components from a larger set of all registered components

> **NOTE**   The need to inject a subset of a complete collection isn't a common scenario, but it does demonstrate how to solve some more-complex needs that you might encounter.

When you previously let MS.DI AUTO-WIRE all configured instances, it corresponded to the situation depicted on the right side of the figure. If you want to register a component as shown on the left side, you must explicitly define which components should be used. In order to achieve this, you can use the AddTransient method that accepts a delegate. This time around, you're dealing with the Meal constructor, which only takes a single parameter.

> **Listing 15.6 Injecting an `ICourse` subset into `Meal`**

```
services.AddScoped<Rillettes>();
services.AddTransient<LobsterBisque>();
services.AddScoped<CordonBleu>();
services.AddScoped<OssoBuco>();
services.AddSingleton<MousseAuChocolat>();
services.AddTransient<CrèmeBrûlée>();


services.AddTransient<ICourse>(
    c => c.GetRequiredService<Rillettes>());
services.AddTransient<ICourse(
    c => c.GetRequiredService<LobsterBisque>());
services.AddTransient<ICourse>(
    c => c.GetRequiredService<CordonBleu>());
services.AddTransient<ICourse>(
    c => c.GetRequiredService<OssoBuco>());
services.AddTransient<ICourse>(
    c => c.GetRequiredService<MousseAuChocolat>());
services.AddTransient<ICourse(
    c => c.GetRequiredService<CrèmeBrûlée>());


services.AddTransient<IMeal>(c => new Meal(
    new ICourse[]
    {
        c.GetRequiredService<Rillettes>(),
        c.GetRequiredService<CordonBleu>(),
        c.GetRequiredService<MousseAuChocolat>()
    }));
```

Registers all courses by their concrete type, instead of their interface. In this case, multiple LIFESTYLES are used.

Registers all courses by their ICourse interface, which allows each to be resolved as an IEnumerable<ICourse>. You prevent torn LIFESTYLES by registering delegates.

Resolves three specific courses by their concrete type and injects them into the Meal constructor

MS.DI natively understands sequences; unless you need to explicitly pick only some components from all services of a given type, MS.DI automatically does the right thing. AUTO-WIRING works not only with single instances, but also for sequences, and the container maps a sequence to all configured instances of the corresponding type. A perhaps less intuitive use of having multiple instances of the same ABSTRACTION is the Decorators design pattern, which we'll discuss next.

15.4.3 *Wiring Decorators*

In section 9.1.1, we discussed how the Decorator design pattern is useful when implementing CROSS-CUTTING CONCERNS. By definition, Decorators introduce multiple types of the same ABSTRACTION. At the very least, you have two implementations of an ABSTRACTION: the Decorator itself and the decorated type. If you stack the Decorators, you can have even more. This is another example of having multiple registrations of the same service. Unlike the previous sections, these registrations aren't conceptually equal, but rather DEPENDENCIES of each other.

DECORATING NON-GENERIC ABSTRACTIONS

MS.DI has no built-in support for Decorators, and this is one of the areas where the limitations of MS.DI can hinder productivity. Nonetheless, we'll show how you can, to some degree, work around these limitations.

You can hack around this omission by, again, making use of the `ActivatorUtil-ities` class. The following example shows how to use this class to apply `Breading` to `VealCutlet`:

```
services.AddTransient<IIngredient>(c =>
    ActivatorUtilities.CreateInstance<Breading>(
        c,
        ActivatorUtilities
            .CreateInstance<VealCutlet>(c)));
```

Registers a code block that calls CreateInstance to construct a Breading Decorator using Auto-Wiring

By supplying a VealCutlet instance to the params array, injects Breading with VealCutlet. Creates VealCutlet using standard AUTO-WIRING.

As you learned in chapter 9, you get veal cordon bleu when you slit open a pocket in the veal cutlet and add ham, cheese, and garlic into the pocket before breading the cutlet. The following example shows how to add a `HamCheeseGarlic` Decorator in between `VealCutlet` and the `Breading` Decorator:

```
services.AddTransient<IIngredient>(c =>
    ActivatorUtilities.CreateInstance<Breading>(
        c,
        ActivatorUtilities
            .CreateInstance<HamCheeseGarlic>(        ◄———  Adds a new Decorator
            c,
            ActivatorUtilities
                .CreateInstance<VealCutlet>(c))));
```

By making `HamCheeseGarlic` become a DEPENDENCY of `Breading`, and `VealCutlet` a DEPENDENCY of `HamCheeseGarlic`, the `HamCheeseGarlic` Decorator becomes the middle class in the object graph. This results in an object graph equal to the following PURE DI version:

```
new Breading(
    new HamCheeseGarlic(
        new VealCutlet()));
```

VealCutlet is wrapped by HamCheeseGarlic, which is wrapped by Breading.

As you might guess, chaining Decorators with MS.DI is cumbersome and verbose. Let's add insult to injury by taking a look at what happens if you try to apply Decorators to generic ABSTRACTIONS.

DECORATING GENERIC ABSTRACTIONS

During the course of chapter 10, we defined multiple generic Decorators that could be applied to any `ICommandService<TCommand>` implementation. In the remainder of this chapter, we'll set our ingredients and courses aside, and we'll take a look at how to register these generic Decorators using MS.DI. The following listing demonstrates how to register all `ICommandService<TCommand>` implementations with the three Decorators presented in section 10.3.

Listing 15.7 Decorating generic AUTO-REGISTERED ABSTRACTIONS

Scans the given assembly for non-generic ICommandService<TCommand> implementations

```
Assembly assembly = typeof(AdjustInventoryService).Assembly;

var mappings =
    from type in assembly.GetTypes()
    where !type.IsAbstract
    where !type.IsGenericType
    from i in type.GetInterfaces()
    where i.IsGenericType
    where i.GetGenericTypeDefinition()
        == typeof(ICommandService<>)
    select new { service = i, implementation = type };

foreach (var mapping in mappings)
{
    Type commandType =
        mapping.service.GetGenericArguments()[0];

    Type secureDecoratoryType =
        typeof(SecureCommandServiceDecorator<>)
            .MakeGenericType(commandType);
    Type transactionDecoratorType =
        typeof(TransactionCommandServiceDecorator<>)
            .MakeGenericType(commandType);
    Type auditingDecoratorType =
        typeof(AuditingCommandServiceDecorator<>)
            .MakeGenericType(commandType);

    services.AddTransient(mapping.service, c =>
        ActivatorUtilities.CreateInstance(
            c,
            secureDecoratoryType,
            ActivatorUtilities.CreateInstance(
                c,
                transactionDecoratorType,
                ActivatorUtilities.CreateInstance(
                    c,
                    auditingDecoratorType,
                    ActivatorUtilities.CreateInstance(
                        c,
                        mapping.implementation)))));
}
```

Extracts the concrete TCommand type from the closed ICommandService<TCommand> ABSTRACTION

Uses the extracted commandType to build closed generic implementations of the Decorators that need to be applied

Adds a delegate registration for the closed ICommandService<TCommand> ABSTRACTION. This delegate calls ActivatorUtilities's CreateInstance method multiple times to AUTO-WIRE all Decorators and the scanned implementation as innermost component.

The result of the configuration of listing 15.7 is figure 15.5, which we discussed previously in section 10.3.4.

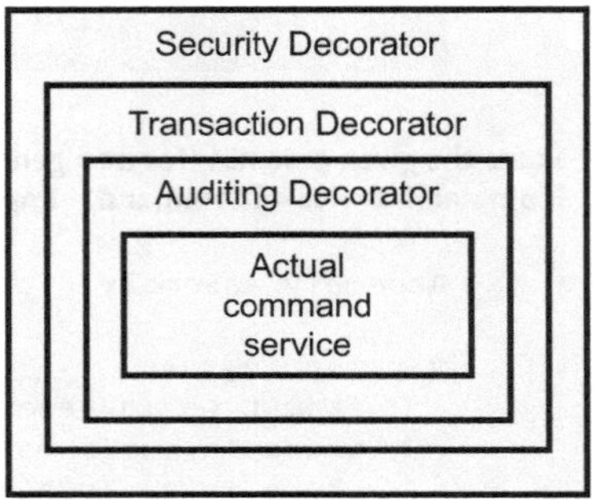

In case you think that listing 15.7 looks rather complicated, unfortunately, this is just the beginning. That listing presents many shortcomings, some of which are difficult to work around. These include the following:

Figure 15.5   Enriching a real command service with transaction, auditing, and security aspects

- Creation of closed-generic Decorator types can become difficult when either of the generic type arguments of the Decorator don't exactly match that of the ABSTRACTION.[4]
- It's impossible to add open-generic implementations that get Decorators applied without being forced to explicitly make the registration for each closed-generic ABSTRACTION.
- Applying Decorators conditionally, for instance, based on generic type arguments, gets complicated.
- With an alternative LIFESTYLE, it becomes complex to prevent Torn LIFESTYLES in case an implementation implements multiple interfaces.
- It's hard to differentiate LIFESTYLES; all Decorators in the chain get the same LIFESTYLE.
- Adding correct release behavior is challenging; instances created using `ActivatorUtilities.CreateInstance` will not automatically get tracked for disposal. This means that only the outer-most decorator will get tracked by MS.DI, even when its decoratees implement `IDisposable`.

You could try working through these limitations one-by-one and suggest improvements to listing 15.7, but you'd effectively be developing a new DI CONTAINER on top of MS.DI, which is something we discourage. This wouldn't be productive. Good alternatives, such as Autofac and Simple Injector, are a better pick for this scenario.[5]

Although consumers that rely on sequences of DEPENDENCIES can be the most intuitive use of multiple instances of the same ABSTRACTION, Decorators are another good example. But there's a third and perhaps a bit surprising case where multiple instances come into play, which is the Composite design pattern.

15.4.4   *Wiring Composites*

During the course of this book, we discussed the Composite design pattern on several occasions. In section 6.1.2, for instance, you created a `CompositeNotificationService`

---

[4]   As an example, imagine a `CachingDecorator<TRequest, TResponse>` that implements an `IHandler<TRequest, ReadOnlyCollection<TResponse>>`.

[5]   As listings 13.10 and 14.11 demonstrated, both Autofac and Simple Injector allowed this scenario to be completed in a few lines of code.

(listing 6.4) that both implemented INotificationService and wrapped a sequence of INotificationService implementations.

WIRING NON-GENERIC COMPOSITES

Let's take a look at how you can register Composites, such as the CompositeNotification-Service of chapter 6 in MS.DI. The following listing shows this class again.

> **Listing 15.8 The `CompositeNotificationService` Composite from chapter 6**

```
public class CompositeNotificationService : INotificationService
{
    private readonly IEnumerable<INotificationService> services;

    public CompositeNotificationService(
        IEnumerable<INotificationService> services)
    {
        this.services = services;
    }

    public void OrderApproved(Order order)
    {
        foreach (INotificationService service in this.services)
        {
            service.OrderApproved(order);
        }
    }
}
```

Registering a Composite requires it to be added as a default registration, while injecting it with a sequence of resolved instances:

```
services.AddTransient<OrderApprovedReceiptSender>();
services.AddTransient<AccountingNotifier>();
services.AddTransient<OrderFulfillment>();

services.AddTransient<INotificationService>(c =>
    new CompositeNotificationService(
        new INotificationService[]
        {
            c.GetRequiredService<OrderApprovedReceiptSender>(),
            c.GetRequiredService<AccountingNotifier>(),
            c.GetRequiredService<OrderFulfillment>(),
        }));
```

In this example, three INotificationService implementations are registered by their concrete type using the AUTO-WIRING API of MS.DI. The CompositeNotificationService, on the other hand, is registered using a delegate. Inside the delegate, the Composite is newed up manually and injected with an array of INotificationService instances. By specifying the concrete types, the previously made registrations are resolved.

Because the number of notification services will likely grow over time, you can reduce the burden on your COMPOSITION ROOT by applying AUTO-REGISTRATION. Because

MS.DI lacks any features in this respect, as we discussed previously, you need to scan the assemblies yourself.

Listing 15.9   Registering `CompositeNotificationService`

```
Assembly assembly = typeof(OrderFulfillment).Assembly;

Type[] types = (
    from type in assembly.GetTypes()
    where !type.IsAbstract
    where typeof(INotificationService).IsAssignableFrom(type)
    select type)
    .ToArray();          ◄───────────── | Materializes the results of
                                         | the query into an array
foreach (Type type in types)
{
    services.AddTransient(type);
}

services.AddTransient<INotificationService>(c =>
    new CompositeNotificationService(
        types.Select(t =>
            (INotificationService)c.GetRequiredService(t))
        .ToArray()));
```

Compared to the Decorator example of listing 15.7, listing 15.9 looks reasonably simple. The assembly is scanned for `INotificationService` implementations, and each found type is appended to the `services` collection. The array of types is used by the `CompositeNotificationService` registration. The Composite is injected with a sequence of `INotificationService` instances that are resolved by iterating through the array of types.

> **NOTE** In listing 15.9, the resulting types are materialized into an array. This prevents the `Select` statement inside the Composite registration from iterating over all the types of `OrderFulfillment`'s assembly over and over again on each resolve, which would easily drain your application's performance if the number of types in the assembly is large.

You might be getting used to the level of complexity and verbosity that you need when dealing with MS.DI, but unfortunately, we're not done yet. Our LINQ query will register any non-generic implementation that implements `INotificationService`. When you try to run the previous code, depending on which assembly your Composite is located, MS.DI might throw the following exception:

Exception of type 'System.StackOverflowException' was thrown.

Ouch! Stack overflow exceptions are really painful, because they abort the running process and are hard to debug. Besides, this generic exception gives no detailed information about what caused the stack overflow. Instead, you want MS.DI to throw a descriptive exception explaining the cycle, as both Autofac and Simple Injector do.

NOTE While writing this chapter, we found that exception messages thrown by MS.DI are often generic or confusing, which makes troubleshooting problems harder than with most of the other popular DI CONTAINERS. Most mature DI CONTAINERS have pretty clear exception messages.

This stack overflow exception is caused by a cyclic DEPENDENCY in Composite-NotificationService. The Composite is picked up by the LINQ query and resolved as part of the sequence. This results in the Composite being dependent on itself. This is an object graph that's impossible for MS.DI, or any DI CONTAINER for that matter, to construct. CompositeNotificationService became a part of the sequence because our LINQ query found all non-generic INotificationService implementations, which includes the Composite.

There are multiple ways around this. The simplest solution is to move the Composite to a different assembly; for instance, the assembly containing the COMPOSITION ROOT. This prevents the LINQ query from selecting the type. Another option is to filter CompositeNotificationService out of the list:

```
Type[] types = (
    from type in assembly.GetTypes()
    where !type.IsAbstract
    where typeof(INotificationService)          Filters the Composite
        .IsAssignableFrom(type)
    where type != typeof(CompositeNotificationService)   ◀──
    select type)
    .ToArray();
```

Composite classes, however, aren't the only classes that might require removal. You'll have to do the same for any Decorator. This isn't particularly difficult, but because there typically will be more Decorator implementations, you might be better off querying the type information to find out whether the type represents a Decorator or not. Here's how you can filter out Decorators as well:

```
Type[] types = (
    from type in assembly.GetTypes()
    where !type.IsAbstract
    where typeof(INotificationService).IsAssignableFrom(type)
    where type != typeof(CompositeNotificationService)
    where type => !IsDecoratorFor<INotificationService>(type)
    select type)
    .ToArray();
```

And the following code shows the IsDecoratorFor method:

```
private static bool IsDecoratorFor<T>(Type type)
{
    return typeof(T).IsAssignableFrom(type) &&
        type.GetConstructors()[0].GetParameters()
            .Any(p => p.ParameterType == typeof(T));
}
```

The `IsDecoratorFor` method expects a type to have only a single constructor. A type is considered to be a Decorator when it both implements the given T ABSTRACTION and when its constructor also requires a T.

WIRING GENERIC COMPOSITES

In section 15.4.3, you saw how to register generic Decorators. In this section, we'll take a look at how you can register Composites for generic ABSTRACTIONS.

In section 6.1.3, you specified the `CompositeEventHandler<TEvent>` class (listing 6.12) as a Composite implementation over a sequence of `IEventHandler<TEvent>` implementations. Let's see if you can register the Composite with its wrapped event handler implementations. To pull this off in MS.DI, you'll have to get creative, because you have to work around a few unfortunate limitations.

We found that the easiest way to hide event handler implementations behind a Composite is by not registering those implementations at all, and instead moving the construction of the handlers to the Composite. This isn't pretty, but it gets the job done. In order to hide handlers behind a Composite, you have to rewrite the `CompositeEventHandler<TEvent>` implementation of listing 6.12 to that in listing 15.10.

Listing 15.10   MS.DI–compatible `CompositeEventHandler<TEvent>` implementation

```
public class CompositeSettings
{
    public Type[] AllHandlerTypes { get; set; }        Parameter Object that allows
}                                                      injecting the complete list of event
                                                       handlers into the Composite
public class CompositeEventHandler<TEvent>
    : IEventHandler<TEvent>
{
    private readonly IServiceProvider provider;
    private readonly CompositeSettings settings;

    public CompositeEventHandler(
        IServiceProvider provider,
        CompositeSettings settings)          The Composite depends on both the Parameter
    {                                        Object and IServiceProvider. IServiceProvider
        this.provider = provider;            allows it to resolve handlers.
        this.settings = settings;
    }

    public void Handle(TEvent e)
    {
        foreach (var handler in this.GetHandlers())     Iterates through the list of handlers
        {                                               and invokes them one by one
            handler.Handle(e);
        }
    }
}
```

```
IEnumerable<IEventHandler<TEvent>> GetHandlers()
{
    return
        from type in this.settings.AllHandlerTypes
        where typeof(IEventHandler<TEvent>)
            .IsAssignableFrom(type)
        select (IEventHandler<TEvent>)
            ActivatorUtilities.CreateInstance(          ⎤ AUTO-WIRES the selected type
                this.provider, type);                   ⎦
}
}
```

Selects only the types that implement the given interface. In case you're calling a CompositeEventHandler<OrderApproved> handler, only those types that implement IEventHandler<OrderApproved> will be selected.

Compared to the original implementation of listing 6.12, this Composite implementation is more complex. It also takes a hard dependency on MS.DI itself by making use of its `IServiceProvider` and `ActivatorUtilities`. In view of this dependency, this Composite certainly belongs inside the COMPOSITION ROOT, because the rest of the application should stay oblivious to the use of a DI CONTAINER.

Instead of depending on an `IEventHandler<TEvent>` sequence, the Composite depends on a Parameter Object that contains all handler types, which includes types that can't be cast to the specific closed-generic `IEventHandler<TEvent>` of the Composite. Because of this, the Composite takes on part of the job that the DI CONTAINER is supposed to do. It filters out all incompatible types by calling `typeof(IEventHandler<TEvent>).IsAssignableFrom(type)`. This leaves you with a registration of the Composite and the scanning of all event handlers.

Listing 15.11   Registering `CompositeEventHandler<TEvent>`

```
var handlerTypes =
    from type in assembly.GetTypes()
    where !type.IsAbstract
    where !type.IsGenericType                          ⎤ Scans the assembly for all concrete,
    let serviceTypes = type.GetInterfaces()            ⎥ non-generic classes that implement
        .Where(i => i.IsGenericType &&                 ⎥ IEventHandler<TEvent>
            i.GetGenericTypeDefinition()               ⎦
                == typeof(IEventHandler<>))
    where serviceTypes.Any()
    select type;

services.AddSingleton(new CompositeSettings            ⎤ Registers the Parameter Object
{                                                      ⎥ that allows passing the list of
    AllHandlerTypes = handlerTypes.ToArray()           ⎦ types into the Composite
});

services.AddTransient(
    typeof(IEventHandler<>),                           ⎤ Registers the Composite
    typeof(CompositeEventHandler<>));                  ⎦
```

Together with the fat Composite implementation, this last listing effectively implements the Composite pattern in combination with MS.DI.

> **TIP** In case you want to apply Decorators to individual event handlers, the trick is to mix the code of listing 15.7 into the `GetHandlers` method of listing 15.10. In other words, the Composite becomes responsible for the creation of the object graph, including the Decorators.

Even though we've managed to work around some of the limitations of MS.DI, you might be less lucky in other cases. For instance, you might run out of luck if the sequence of elements consists of both non-generic and generic implementations, when generic implementations contain generic type constraints or when Decorators need to be conditional.

We do admit that this is an unpleasant solution. We preferred writing less code to show you how to apply MS.DI to the patterns presented in this book, but not all is peaches and cream, unfortunately. That's why, in our day-to-day development jobs, we prefer PURE DI or one of the mature DI CONTAINERS, such as Autofac and Simple Injector.

No matter which DI CONTAINER you select, or even if you prefer PURE DI, we hope that this book has conveyed one important point—DI doesn't rely on a particular technology, such as a particular DI CONTAINER. An application can, and should, be designed using the DI-friendly patterns and practices presented in this book. When you succeed in doing that, selection of a DI CONTAINER becomes of less importance. A DI CONTAINER is a tool that composes your application, but ideally, you should be able to replace one container with another without rewriting any part of your application other than the COMPOSITION ROOT.

Summary

- The Microsoft.Extensions.DependencyInjection (MS.DI) DI CONTAINER has a limited set of features. A comprehensive API that addresses AUTO-REGISTRATION, Decorators, and Composites is missing. This makes it less suited for development of applications that are designed around the principles and patterns presented in this book.
- MS.DI enforces a strict separation of concerns between configuring and consuming a container. You configure components using a `ServiceCollection` instance, but a `ServiceCollection` can't resolve components. When you're done configuring a `ServiceCollection`, you use it to build a `ServiceProvider` that you can use to resolve components.
- With MS.DI, resolving from the root container directly is a bad practice. This will easily lead to memory leaks or concurrency bugs. Instead, you should always resolve from an `IServiceScope`.
- MS.DI supports the three standard LIFESTYLES: TRANSIENT, SINGLETON, and SCOPED.

glossary

Here are brief definitions of selected terms, patterns, and other concepts discussed in this book. Each definition includes a reference to the chapter or section where the term is discussed in greater detail.

- ABSTRACTION—A unifying term that encompasses both interfaces and (abstract) base classes. See chapter 1.
- AMBIENT CONTEXT—A DI anti-pattern that supplies application code outside the COMPOSITION ROOT with global access to a VOLATILE DEPENDENCY or its behavior by the use of static class members. See section 5.3.
- ASPECT-ORIENTED PROGRAMMING (AOP)—An approach to software that aims to reduce boilerplate code required for implementing CROSS-CUTTING CONCERNS and other coding patterns. It does this by implementing such patterns in a single place and applying them to a code base either declaratively or based on convention, without modifying the code itself. See chapter 10.
- AUTO-REGISTRATION—The ability to automatically register components based on a certain convention in a DI CONTAINER by scanning one or more assemblies for implementations of desired ABSTRACTIONS. See section 12.2.3.
- AUTO-WIRING—The ability to automatically compose an object graph from maps between ABSTRACTIONS and concrete types by making use of type information supplied by the compiler and the Common Language Runtime. See section 12.1.2.

- CAPTIVE DEPENDENCY—A DEPENDENCY that's inadvertently kept alive for too long, because its consumer was given a lifetime that exceeds the DEPENDENCY's expected lifetime. See section 8.4.1.
- COMMAND-QUERY SEPARATION—The idea that each method should either return a result, but not change the observable state of the system, or change the state, but not produce any value. See section 10.3.3.
- COMPOSER—A unifying term that encompasses any object or method that composes DEPENDENCIES. See chapter 8.
- COMPOSITION ROOT—A central place in an application where the entire application is composed from its constituent modules. See section 4.1.
- CONFIGURATION AS CODE—Allows a DI CONTAINER's configuration to be stored as source code. Each mapping between an ABSTRACTION and a particular implementation is expressed explicitly and directly in code. See section 12.2.2.
- CONSTRAINED CONSTRUCTION—A DI anti-pattern that forces all implementations of a certain ABSTRACTION to require their constructors to have an identical signature. See section 5.4.
- CONSTRUCTOR INJECTION—A DI pattern where DEPENDENCIES are statically defined as a list of parameters to the class's constructor. See section 4.2.
- CONTROL FREAK—A DI anti-pattern where you depend on a VOLATILE DEPENDENCY in any place other than a COMPOSITION ROOT. It's the opposite of INVERSION OF CONTROL. See section 5.1.
- CROSS-CUTTING CONCERN—An aspect of a program that affects a larger part of the application. It's often a non-functional requirement. Typical examples include logging, auditing, access control, and validation. See chapter 9.
- DEPENDENCY—In principle, any reference that a module holds to another module. When a module references another module, it depends on it. Informally, the term DEPENDENCY is often used instead of the more formal VOLATILE DEPENDENCY. See chapter 1.
- DEPENDENCY INVERSION PRINCIPLE—This principle states that higher-level modules in your applications shouldn't depend on lower-level modules; instead, both types should depend on ABSTRACTIONS. The *D* in SOLID. See section 3.1.2. See also SOLID.
- DEPENDENCY LIFETIME—See OBJECT LIFETIME.
- DI CONTAINER—A software library that provides DI functionality and automates many of the tasks involved in OBJECT COMPOSITION, INTERCEPTION, and LIFETIME MANAGEMENT. It's an engine that resolves and manages object graphs. See chapter 12.
- ENTITY—A domain object with an inherent, long-term identity. See section 3.1.2.
- FOREIGN DEFAULT—A default implementation of a VOLATILE DEPENDENCY that's defined in a different module than the consumer. See section 5.1.3.

- INTERCEPTION—The ability to intercept calls between two collaborating components in such a way that you can enrich or change the behavior of the DEPENDENCY without the need to change the two collaborators themselves. See chapter 9.

- INTERFACE SEGREGATION PRINCIPLE—This principles states that no client should be forced to depend on methods it doesn't use. The *I* in SOLID. See section 6.2.1. See also SOLID.

- INVERSION OF CONTROL—This concept lets a framework control the lifetime of objects instead of directly controlling them. See chapter 1.

- LEAKY ABSTRACTION—Even though an ABSTRACTION is defined, the implementation details show through and thus lock the ABSTRACTION to the implementation. See section 6.2.1.

- LIFESTYLE—A formalized way of describing the intended lifetime of a DEPENDENCY. See chapter 8.

- LIFETIME MANAGEMENT—See OBJECT LIFETIME.

- LISKOV SUBSTITUTION PRINCIPLE—A software design principle that states that a consumer should be able to use any implementation of an ABSTRACTION without changing the correctness of the system. The *L* in SOLID. See section 10.2.3. See also SOLID.

- LOCAL DEFAULT—A default implementation of an ABSTRACTION that's defined in the same assembly as the consumer. See section 4.2.2.

- METHOD INJECTION—A DI pattern where DEPENDENCIES are injected into the consumer as method parameters. See section 4.3.

- OBJECT COMPOSITION—The concept of composing applications from disparate modules. See chapter 7.

- OBJECT LIFETIME—Generally speaking, this term covers how any object is created and deallocated. In DI context, this term covers the lifetime of DEPENDENCIES. See chapter 8.

- OPEN/CLOSED PRINCIPLE—This principle states that classes should be open for extensibility, but closed for modification. The *O* in SOLID. See section 4.4.2. See also SOLID.

- PROPERTY INJECTION—A DI pattern where DEPENDENCIES are injected into the consumer via writable properties. See section 4.4.

- PURE DI—The practice of applying DI without a DI CONTAINER. See part 3.

- SCOPED LIFESTYLE—A LIFESTYLE where there's a single instance within a well-defined scope or request, and instances aren't shared across scopes. See section 8.3.3.

- SEAM—A place in application code where ABSTRACTIONS are used to separate modules. See chapter 1.

- SERVICE LOCATOR—A DI anti-pattern that supplies application components outside the COMPOSITION ROOT with access to an unbounded set of VOLATILE DEPENDENCIES. See section 5.2.

- SETTER INJECTION—See PROPERTY INJECTION.
- SINGLE RESPONSIBILITY PRINCIPLE—This principle states that a class should have only a single responsibility. The *S* in SOLID. See section 2.1.3. See also SOLID.
- SINGLETON LIFESTYLE—A LIFESTYLE where a single instance is reused for all consumers within the scope of a single COMPOSER. See section 8.3.1.
- SOLID—An acronym that stands for five fundamental design principles: SINGLE RESPONSIBILITY PRINCIPLE, OPEN/CLOSED PRINCIPLE, LISKOV SUBSTITUTION PRINCIPLE, INTERFACE SEGREGATION PRINCIPLE, and DEPENDENCY INVERSION PRINCIPLE. See chapter 10.
- STABLE DEPENDENCY—A DEPENDENCY that can be referenced without any detrimental effects. The opposite of a VOLATILE DEPENDENCY. See section 1.3.1.
- TEMPORAL COUPLING—Code smell that occurs when there's an implicit relationship between two or more members of a class, requiring clients to invoke one member before the other. See section 4.3.2.
- TESTABILITY—The degree to which an application is susceptible to automated unit tests. See chapter 1.
- TRANSIENT LIFESTYLE—A LIFESTYLE where all consumers get their own instance of a DEPENDENCY. See section 8.3.2.
- VOLATILE DEPENDENCY—A DEPENDENCY that involves side effects that can be undesirable at times. This may include modules that don't yet exist or that have adverse requirements on its runtime environment. These are the DEPENDENCIES that are addressed by DI. See section 1.3.2.

resources

In print

- Boike, David. *Learning NServiceBus*, 2nd Ed. (Packt Publishing, 2015)
- Brown, William J., et al. *AntiPatterns: Refactoring Software, Architectures, and Projects in Crisis* (Wiley Computer Publishing, 1998)
- Chatterjee, Ayan. *Building Apps for the Universal Windows Platform* (Apress, 2017)
- Cwalina, Krzysztof and Brad Abrams, *Framework Design Guidelines: Conventions, Idioms, and Patterns for Reusable .NET Libraries*, 2nd Ed. (Addison-Wesley, 2009)
- Evans, Eric. *Domain-Driven Design: Tackling Complexity in the Heart of Software* (Addison-Wesley, 2004)
- Feathers, Michael C. *Working Effectively with Legacy Code* (Prentice Hall, 2004)
- Fowler, Martin, et al. *Refactoring: Improving the Design of Existing Code* (Addison-Wesley, 1999)
- Fowler, Martin. *Patterns of Enterprise Application Architecture* (Addison-Wesley, 2002)
- Gamma, Erich, et al. *Design Patterns: Elements of Reusable Object-Oriented Software* (Addison-Wesley, 1994)
- Groves, Matthew D. *AOP in .NET* (Manning, 2013)
- Howard, Michael and David LeBlanc. *Writing Secure Code*, 2nd Ed. (Microsoft Press, 2003)
- Hunt, Andy and Dave Thomas. *The Pragmatic Programmer* (Addison-Wesley, 2000)
- Lock, Andrew. *ASP.NET Core in Action* (Manning, 2018)
- Meyer, Bertrand. *Object-Oriented Software Construction* (ISE Inc., 1988)

- Martin, Robert C., et al. *Pattern Languages of Program Design 3* (Addison-Wesley, 1998)
- Martin, Robert C. *Agile Software Development, Principles, Patterns, and Practices* (Prentice Hall, 2003)
- Martin, Robert C. *Clean Code* (Prentice Hall, 2009)
- Meszaros, Gerard. *xUnit Test Patterns: Refactoring Test Code* (Addison-Wesley, 2007)
- Nygard, Michael T. *Release It! Design and Deploy Production-Ready Software* (Pragmatic Bookshelf, 2007)
- Osherove, Roy. *The Art of Unit Testing*, 2nd Ed. (Manning, 2013)
- Smith, Jon. *Entity Framework Core in Action* (Manning, 2018)

Online

- Atwood, Jeff. "The problem with logging" (2008), https://blog.codinghorror.com/the-problem-with-logging/
- Deursen van, Steven. "Meanwhile, on the query side of my architecture" (2011), https://www.cuttingedge.it/blogs/steven/pivot/entry.php?id=92
- Deursen van, Steven, and Peter Parker. "What's wrong with the ASP.NET Core DI abstraction?" (2016), https://simpleinjector.org/blog/2016/06/
- Deursen van, Steven, et al. "Implementing Row based security" (2014), https://github.com/dotnetjunkie/solidservices/issues/4
- Deursen van, Steven, et al. "Logger wrapper best practice" (2011), https://stackoverflow.com/questions/5646820/logger-wrapper-best-practice
- Fowler, Martin. "Domain Event" (2005), https://martinfowler.com/eaaDev/DomainEvent.html
- Fowler, Martin. "Event Sourcing" (2005), https://martinfowler.com/eaaDev/EventSourcing.html
- Fowler, Martin. "Introduce Parameter Object" (1999), https://refactoring.com/catalog/introduceParameterObject.html
- Fowler, Martin. "Inversion of Control Containers and the Dependency Injection pattern" (2004), https://martinfowler.com/articles/injection.html
- Fowler, Martin. "InversionOfControl" (2005), https://martinfowler.com/bliki/InversionOfControl.html
- Gorman, Jason. "Reused Abstractions Principle (RAP)" (2010), http://www.codemanship.co.uk/parlezuml/blog/?postid=934
- Heintz, John. "The Outbox pattern" (2014), http://gistlabs.com/2014/05/the-outbox/
- Lippert, Eric. "Immutability in C# Part One: Kinds of Immutability" (2007), https://blogs.msdn.microsoft.com/ericlippert/2007/11/13/immutability-in-c-part-one-kinds-of-immutability/

- Munsch, John, et al. "How to explain Dependency Injection to a 5-year old" (2009), https://stackoverflow.com/questions/1638919/
- Palermo, Jeffrey. "Constructor over-injection smell—follow up" (2010), https://jeffreypalermo.com/2010/01/constructor-over-injection-smell-ndash-follow-up/
- Seemann, Mark. "Interfaces are not abstractions" (2010), https://blog.ploeh.dk/2010/12/02/Interfacesarenotabstractions/
- Seemann, Mark. "Passive attributes" (2014), https://blog.ploeh.dk/2014/06/13/passive-attributes/
- Seemann, Mark. "Pure DI" (2014), https://blog.ploeh.dk/2014/06/10/pure-di/
- Seemann, Mark. "Service Locator 2 Released" (2007), https://blogs.msdn.microsoft.com/ploeh/2007/03/15/service-locator-2-released/
- Seemann, Mark. "The Register Resolve Release pattern" (2010), https://blog.ploeh.dk/2010/09/29/TheRegisterResolveReleasepattern/
- Smith, Josh. "Patterns: WPF Apps With The Model-View-ViewModel Design Pattern" (2009), https://msdn.microsoft.com/en-us/magazine/dd419663.aspx

Other resources

- Autofac, https://autofac.org
- Common Service Locator, https://github.com/unitycontainer/commonservicelocator
- Common.Logging, https://github.com/net-commons/common-logging
- JSON.NET, https://www.newtonsoft.com/json
- log4net, https://logging.apache.org/log4net/
- Microsoft.Extensions.DependencyInjection, https://github.com/aspnet/DependencyInjection
- PostSharp, https://www.postsharp.net/
- Simple Injector, https://simpleinjector.org

index

A

abstract classes vs. interfaces   68–69
Abstract Factory pattern   7, 130–131, 191–194
  abusing   180–194
    to overcome lifetime problems   180–187
    to select Dependencies based on runtime
      data   187–194
Abstractions   4, 65, 67
  decorating   457–458
  generic
    applying transaction handling using   326–327
    Auto-Registration of   436–437, 475–476
    Auto-Registration using
      AsClosedTypesOf   401–402
    decorating   458–459, 490–492
    decorating with
      RegisterGenericDecorator   421–422
    fixing LSP using   324–326
    mapping to concrete types   396–397, 430–431,
      469–470
  non-generic
    decorating   489–490
    decorating with RegisterDecorator   420–421
abstract keyword   69
ActionDescriptor property   397, 431
Activator class   156
Activator.CreateInstance   156
ActivatorUtilities class   485–486, 487, 490, 497
Adapter design pattern   12, 72
AddProductCommand property   224
AddProduct method   224

AddScoped method   378, 473, 479
AddSingleton method   231, 378, 473, 479
AddSingleton<T>() method   175
AddTransient method   378, 472, 479, 482
AdjustInventory command   321, 324
AdjustInventoryService   323, 335, 402, 436, 475
AdjustInventoryViewModel   321
Administrator role   331
ADO.NET Data Services   46
AlertUser method   298
Ambient Context anti-pattern   353
  accessing time through   147–148
  logging through   149–153
  negative effects of   150–152
  refactoring toward DI   152–153
ambient scopes   443–444
ambiguity, removing
  refactoring by   417–418, 455, 487
  using ActivatorUtilities   485–486
  using code blocks   484–485
  using conditional registrations   453–454
AOP (Aspect-Oriented Programming)   31, 302
  overview of   302–305
  SOLID as driver for   308–337
    adding Cross-Cutting Concerns   327–336
    analysis of IProductService from perspective of
      SOLID   311–313
    applying SOLID principles to improve
      design   314–327
    implementing product-related features using
      IProductService   309–310

AOP (Aspect-Oriented Programming) *(continued)*
SOLID principles   305–308
DIP (Dependency Inversion Principle)   308
Interception and   308
ISP (Interface Segregation Principle)   307–308
LSP (Liskov Substitution Principle)   307
OCP (Open/Closed Principle)   306–307
SRP (Single Responsibility Principle)   306
tool-based
compile-time weaving   348–355
dynamic Interception   342–348
APIs (application programming interfaces),
registering   409–412, 447–451, 480–483
configuring primitive Dependencies   409–411,
448–449, 480–481
extracting primitive Dependencies to Parameter
Objects   449–450, 481
registering objects with code blocks   411–412,
450–451, 482–483
App class   227
ApplyDiscountFor method   104, 108
Apply method   108
AsClosedTypesOf   401–402
As method   397, 414
aspect attributes   332, 350
ASP.NET Core framework
IUserContextAdapter specific to   71–73
MVC applications, composing   228–234
constructing custom middleware components
with Pure DI   233–234
creating custom controller activators   230–232
using custom controller activators in   230–231
ASP.NET Core web application   87
AspNetUserContextAdapter class   73, 158, 160,
197, 205, 244, 260, 367, 370, 375
ASP.NET Web Forms   98, 213
Assert.Equal method   24
Assert.Fail method   312
asynchronous application models   276–278
async keyword   233
AsyncScopedLifestyle   444
attribute parameter   111
auditing   288
implementing aspects   328–331
implementing audit trail   203
implementing using Decorators   287–290
composing
AuditingUserRepositoryDecorator   290
for user repository   288–289

AuditingCommand-
ServiceDecorator<TCommand>   330
AuditingUserRepositoryDecorator class   289–290,
306, 307, 327
authorization   334
Autofac container   380
configuring ContainerBuilder   398–404
Lifetime Management   404–409
configuring instance scopes   405–406
releasing components   406–409
overview of   394–404
registering difficult APIs   409–412
configuring primitive Dependencies   409–411
registering objects with code blocks   411–412
resolving objects   395–398
working with multiple components   412–425
selecting among multiple candidates   413–417
wiring Composites   422–425
wiring Decorators   420–422
wiring sequences   417–420
Autofac.Core.KeyedService   425
Auto-Registration   361, 376, 379, 383, 474
configuring containers with   434–436
configuring ServiceCollection with   473–475
of generic Abstractions   401–402, 436–437,
475–476
to configure ContainerBuilder   400–401
to configure DI Containers by convention
379–385
AutoWireContainer   366, 371
Auto-Wiring   363, 370, 410, 413, 415, 417, 430, 453,
489
DI Containers that support   364–371
sequences   418, 455, 487–488
await keyword   233
Azure   18, 46
AzureProductRepository class   132
Azure Table data access layer   46
Azure Table Service   76

B

BCL (Base Class Library)   17, 26, 44, 65
BeginLifetimeScope method   407
BeginScope method   442
big object graphs   98
Binding markup extension   225
Bitmap   108

BuildServiceProvider 469
bus factor 386

C

caching 291
CalculateRoute 191
Captive Dependencies 110, 266–269, 446–447
Castle Dynamic Proxy 344–346
  applying Interceptor inside Composition Root
    using Pure DI 345–346
  implementing Circuit Breaker Interceptor
    344–345
Castle.DynamicProxy.IInterceptor interface 344
Castle.DynamicProxy.IInvocation 347
Chain of Responsibility pattern 287
CircuitBreakerAttribute 353
CircuitBreaker class 295
CircuitBreakerInterceptor 347
  applying inside Composition Root using Pure
    DI 345–346
  implementing 344–345
CircuitBreakerInterceptor 347
Circuit Breaker pattern 293–294
  creating for IProductRepository 294–295
  implementations of 295–297
  intercepting with 292–297
CircuitBreakerProductRepositoryDecorator
    class 294, 296, 303, 308, 342
client applications 7
Closed state 295
CLR (Common Language Runtime) 57, 348, 363
code blocks
  registering objects with 411–412, 450–451,
    482–483
  removing ambiguity with 484–485
code cohesion 40
code smells 118, 127, 164
  abusing Abstract Factory 180–194
    to overcome lifetime problems 180–187
    to select Dependencies based on runtime
      data 187–194
  fixing Dependency cycles 194–206
    caused by SRP violations 195–198
    common strategies for 204
    refactoring from SRP violations to
      resolve 200–204
    with Property Injection 204–206

large number of Dependencies 190
  Leaky Abstraction 182–183
cohesion 40, 306
collaborators 15
Collection.Create method 457
Collection.Register method 434, 440
Command-Query Separation (CQS) 315
commands 315
CommerceContext class 38, 48, 50, 70, 74, 251,
    290, 367
CommerceContext.DbContext 203
CommerceControllerActivator class 90, 232, 244,
    252, 257
Commerce.Web assembly 375
Common Language Runtime (CLR) 57, 348, 363
Common Service Locator (CSL) 139
compile time
  coupling caused by compile-time weaving
    354–355
  loss of support with dynamic Interception 347
compile-time support 347
compile-time weaving 348–355
  analysis of 351–355
  applying transaction aspect using 349–351
  aspects are DI-unfriendly 352–354
  causes coupling at compile time 354–355
  unsuitable for use on Volatile Dependencies 355
component elements 404
ComponentNotRegisteredException 396
components
  in Autofac, multiple
    selecting among multiple candidates 413–417
    wiring Composites 422–425
    wiring Decorators 420–422
    wiring sequences 417–420
  in MS.DI, multiple 483–498
    selecting among multiple candidates 483–486
    wiring Composites 492–498
    wiring Decorators 489–492
    wiring sequences 486–489
  in Simple Injector, multiple 451–464
    selecting among multiple candidates 452–454
    sequences are streams 462–464
    wiring Composites 459–462
    wiring Decorators 457–459
    wiring sequences 454–457
  interaction between 74–75

components *(continued)*
  named   416–417
  releasing   406–409, 440–443, 477–480
  selecting from larger set   418–420, 455–457, 488–489
composability
  evaluating   45–47
    building new data access layers   46
    building new UIs   45–46
  missing, analysis of   47–50
    data access interface analysis   48–50
    dependency graph analysis   47–48
Composer class   242, 264
Composite design pattern   12, 170
CompositeEventHandler<TEvent> class   424, 461, 496
CompositeLogger   275
CompositeNotificationService   172, 177, 422–423, 459, 492–493
Composite pattern
  generic, wiring   424–425, 461–462, 496–498
  non-generic, wiring   422–424, 459–461, 493–496
  wiring   422–425, 459–462, 492–498
composite wrapping   177
Composition Root pattern   60, 68, 85–94
  applying Interceptor inside   345–346
  composing applications in   73–74
  DI Containers in   88–89
  explosion of dependencies with   92–94
  implementing in UWP applications   226–228
  implementing using Pure DI   89–91
  of UpdateCurrency program   215–216
  overview of   87–88
concrete classes   69
Concrete Factory   130
concrete types   396–397, 430–431, 469–470
concurrency bugs, by tying instances to lifetime of threads   275–278
  asynchronous application models cause multi-threading issues   276–278
  thread lifetime is often unclear   276
conditional registrations   453–454
configuration
  ContainerBuilder   398–404
    Auto-Registration of generic Abstractions using AsClosedTypesOf   401–402
    using Auto-Registration   400–401
    using Configuration as Code   398–400
    using configuration files   403–404

containers   432–438
  Auto-Registration of generic Abstractions   436–437
  using Auto-Registration   434–436
  using Configuration as Code   433–434
  using configuration files   437–438
DI Containers   372–385
  by convention using Auto-Registration   379–385
  mixing and matching approaches to   385
  using Configuration as Code   377–379
  using configuration files   373–376
instance scopes   405–406
  configuration files   406
  with code   405–406
Lifestyles   439–440, 477
multiple implementations of same service   413–414, 452–453, 484
primitive Dependencies   409–411, 448–449, 480–481
ServiceCollection   471–476
  Auto-Registration of generic Abstractions   475–476
  using Auto-Registration   473–475
  using Configuration as Code   472–473
Configuration as Code   377
  configuring ContainerBuilder with   398–400
  configuring containers with   433–434
  configuring DI Containers with   377–379
  configuring ServiceCollection with   472–473
configuration files
  configuring ContainerBuilder with   403–404
  configuring containers with   437–438
  configuring DI Containers with   373–376
  configuring instance scopes with   406
connectionString parameter   367
console applications, composing   213–218
  building Composition Root of UpdateCurrency program   215–216
  composing object graphs in CreateCurrencyParser   216
  layering in UpdateCurrency   217–218
  updating currencies with UpdateCurrency program   214
Console class   17
ConsoleMessageWriter class   16, 18, 20, 25, 30
ConsoleWriter class   20

Constrained Construction anti-pattern 19, 98, 154–161
    analysis of 156–161
    late binding ProductRepository 154–156
    negative effects of 157
    refactoring toward DI 157–161
Constructor Chaining 134
Constructor Injection pattern 16, 24, 54, 60, 64, 91, 94–103
    adding currency conversions to featured products 100–102
    known use of 99
    overview of 95–96
    when to use 97–99
Constructor Over-injection code smell 164–180
    recognizing 165–168
    refactoring from
        to domain events 173–180
        to Facade Services 168–173
ConstructorResolutionBehavior property 119
ContainerBuilder, configuring 398–404
    Auto-Registration of generic Abstractions using AsClosedTypesOf 401–402
    using Auto-Registration 400–401
    using Configuration as Code 398–400
    using configuration files 403–404
Container class 433
ContainerOptions class 119
containers
    configuring 432–438
        Auto-Registration of generic Abstractions 436–437
        using Auto-Registration 434–436
        using Configuration as Code 433–434
        using configuration files 437–438
    detecting Captive Dependencies 446–447
    diagnosing for lifetime problems 444–447
        letting container detect Captive Dependencies 446–447
        suppressing warnings on individual registrations 447
Content property 225
context parameter 111
Control Freak anti-pattern 88, 97, 127–137, 185
    analysis of 135–137
    negative effects of 136
    refactoring toward DI 136–137

    through factories 129–134
        Abstract Factory 130–131
        Concrete Factory 129–130
        Static Factory 131–134
    through newing up Dependencies 128
    through overloaded constructors 134–135
controller activators, custom
    creating 230–232
    using in ASP.NET Core 230–231
Controller class 42
controllers 42, 231, 362
ControllerTypeInfo property 397, 431
controllerType variable 397, 431, 470
converter field 102
ConvertTo method 112
coupling at compile time 354–355
CQS (Command-Query Separation) 315
CreateCurrencyParser method 216, 276
CreateHomeController method 252
CreateInstance method 156
CreateInstance<T> method 486
Create method 90, 183, 186, 230, 243
CreateNew method 366
CreatePage method 228
CreateRateDisplayer method 264
CreateScope method 478
create, update, and delete (CUD) operations 299
Cross-Cutting Concerns 12, 28, 31, 49, 150, 282, 348
    adding 327–336
        composing object graphs using generic Decorators 335–336
        implementing auditing aspects 328–331
        implementing security aspects 331–334
    implementing 290–300
        intercepting with Circuit Breaker 292–297
        preventing unauthorized access to sensitive functionality using Decorators 298–300
        reporting exceptions using Decorator pattern 297–298
        with ICommandService 321–323
cross-sellings 310
CSL (Common Service Locator) 139
CUD (create, update, and delete) operations 299
currencies, updating 214
Currency class 217

currency conversions
    adding to featured products   100–102
    adding to Product Entity   112–113
CurrencyMonitoring program   262
CurrencyParser class   216
Currency property   102
CurrencyRateDisplayer class   262, 264
Current property   146
CurrentUser property   197
CustomerServices class   107

D

Danish krone symbol   58
data access interface   48–50
data access layers   46, 50, 53, 70–71, 77
data access library   47
database engines   5
DataContext property   221, 225
data layers   36–39
DataTemplate   225
Data Transfer Objects (DTOs)   58, 182
DateTime method   146
DbContext.ChangeTracker property   203
DbContext class   37, 251, 262–266
DbContextOptionsBuilder   38
DbContext.SaveChanges method   203
DbSet<T> class   175
DDD (Domain-Driven Design)   105
DDOS (Distributed Denial of Service)   292
Decorator pattern   284–287
    generic   335–336
    implementing auditing using   287–290
        composing
            AuditingUserRepositoryDecorator   290
        for user repository   288–289
    preventing unauthorized access to sensitive
        functionality using   298–300
    reporting exceptions using   297–298
    wiring   420–422, 457–459, 489–492
        decorating Abstractions   457–458
        decorating generic Abstractions   458–459,
            490–492
        decorating generic Abstractions with
            RegisterGenericDecorator   421–422
        decorating non-generic Abstractions   489–490
        decorating non-generic Abstractions with
            RegisterDecorator   420–421
defaultAssembly attribute   375, 404

Delete method   248, 303
Dependencies   85
    Captive   266–269, 446–447
    consumers of   105–108
    cyclic, fixing   194–206
        caused by SRP violations   195–198
        common strategies for   204
        refactoring from SRP violations to
            resolve   200–204
        with Property Injection   204–206
    disposable   245–255
        consuming   246–249
        managing   250–255
    injected   108–109
    injecting into MainViewModel   221–225
    lifecycles of   239–242
    named   414–416
    newing up   128
    primitive
        configuring   409–411, 448–449, 480–481
        extracting to Parameter Objects   449–450, 481
    releasing   250, 254–255
    selecting based on runtime data   187–194
        analysis of code smell   190
        refactoring from Abstract Factory to
            Adapter   191–194
    Stable   26
    Volatile   26–27
    with Composition Root   92–94
dependency graphs
    analyzing   75–78
    evaluating   44–45
    for analysis of missing composability   47–48
Dependency Inversion Principle (DIP)   67, 305
Dependency Lifetime, managing   238–245
    Lifetime Management   238–242
    managing lifetime with Pure DI   242–245
Dependency property   114
deployment artifact   87
diagnosing containers for lifetime problems   444–447
    letting container detect Captive
        Dependencies   446–447
    suppressing warnings on individual
        registrations   447
diagnostic warnings   447
DI Containers   8, 26, 77, 85, 261
    configuring   372–385
        by convention using Auto-Registration   379–385

DI Containers *(continued)*
    mixing and matching approaches to 385
    using Configuration as Code 377–379
    with configuration files 373–376
  in Composition Root 88–89
  overview of 361–371
    Auto-Wiring 363–364
    Resolve API 361–363
  resolving controllers with 362
  resolving object graphs with 362–363
  supporting Auto-Wiring 364–371
  when to use 385–391
    Pure DI gives shorter feedback cycle 388–389
    third-party libraries involve costs and risks 386–388
Dictionary<TKey, TValue> class 175
DI (Dependency Injection)
  advantages of 17–24
    extensibility 19–20
    late binding 18–19
    maintainability 21
    parallel development 20–21
    testability 21–23
    unit testing logic 23–24
  compile-time weaving aspects are unfriendly to 352–354
  myths about 5–8
    Abstract Factory 7
    DI Containers 8
    late binding 5–6
    unit testing 6
  purpose of 8–14
  refactoring from Ambient Context toward 152–153
  refactoring from Constrained Construction toward 157–161
  refactoring from Control Freak toward 136–137
  refactoring from Service Locator toward 145
  scope 27–32
    Interception 30–31
    Object Composition 29
    Object Lifetime 30
    three dimensions of 31–32
DIP (Dependency Inversion Principle) 67–68, 305
DiscountedProduct class 60
DisplayRates method 265
disposable Dependencies 245–255
  consuming 246–249
  managing 250–255

disposables, ephemeral 247–249
disposable Transients 479
Dispose method 442
Distributed Denial of Service (DDOS) 292
Domain-Driven Design (DDD) 105
domain events 173–180
domain layers 36, 39–42
domain models, independent, building 61–69
  Dependency Inversion Principle 67–68
  interfaces vs. abstract classes 68–69
DoSomething method 110
DRY (Don't Repeat Yourself) principle 117, 306, 342
DTOs (Data Transfer Objects) 58, 182
dynamic Interception 342–348
  analysis of 346–348
  aspects are strongly coupled to tooling 347
  does not fix underlying design problems 348
  not universally applicable 347–348
  with Castle Dynamic Proxy 344–346
    applying Interceptor inside Composition Root using Pure DI 345–346
    implementing Circuit Breaker Interceptor 344–345

E

e-commerce applications, rebuilding 53–74
  building data access layers 70–71
  building independent domain models 61–69
  building maintainable UIs 56–61
  composing applications in Composition Root 73–74
  implementing ASP.NET Core-specific IUserContext Adapter 71–73
EditProductCommand property 225
EditProduct method 224
EditProductViewModel 248
EndpointAddress 109
EndpointAddressBuilder 109
Entity 63
Entity Framework Core 38, 70
enum 188
ephemeral disposables 248
Equal method 24
error handling 140, 291
ErrorHandlingProductRepositoryDecorator class 298
event handlers 424
exceptions, reporting 297–298

Exclaim method   16, 24
executables   87
Execute method   323
extensibility   17, 19–20, 48, 118–120

F

Facade Services   168–173
factories, Control Freak through   129–134
   Abstract Factory   130–131
   Concrete Factory   129–130
   Static Factory   131–134
fault tolerance   291, 328
fear, uncertainty, and doubt (FUD)   4
FeaturedProductsViewModel class   57
feedback cycles   388–389
finally statement   254
Fixture Teardown   144
folding   84
Foreign Default   97, 134
FormalGreeter   286
FUD (fear, uncertainty, and doubt)   4

G

general-purpose library   77
Generic Subdomain   361
generic type constraints   431
GetAllInstances method   462
GetAll method   295
GetAttributeAdapter   111
GetById method   289
GetByName method   199, 201
GetCurrentScope method   444
GetCurrentTime method   148
GetFeaturedProducts method   47, 60, 64, 74, 102,
   112, 113, 128, 142, 185, 270
GetInstance method   430, 462
GetLogger method   151
GetRequiredService method   470, 476, 484
GetRoute method   188
GetService method   140, 144, 471
GetTypesToRegister method   435
GetWelcomeMessage method   148
GoBack method   224
God Class   166
God Objects   69
Greet method   285

GridView, XAML   225
Guard Clauses   16, 59, 119, 140, 167
Guard method   295

H

Half-Open state   295
Handle method   176
HasTierPrices property   318
Hello DI!   14–24, 28
   collaborators   15
   implementing application logic   15–17
HomeController class   42, 56, 95, 138, 181, 232, 367
HttpContext   40
HttpContextAccessor   72
HttpContext.Response.RegisterForDispose
   method   230, 254

I

IApplicationContext   108
IAttributeAdapter method   111
IAuditTrailAppender interface   195, 198, 200, 206,
   288, 306
IBillingSystem   166
ICircuitBreaker interface   295, 303, 353
ICommandService interface   319, 321–323, 326,
   382, 401, 436, 475
IComponentContext interface   420
IConstructorResolutionBehavior interface   119, 450
IControllerActivator interface   90, 229, 397, 431
ICurrencyConverter.Exchange method   112
ICurrencyConverter interface   101, 112, 113, 214
ICustomerRepository interface   108
IDisposable interface   30, 184, 239, 245
IEnumerable<T> interface   175, 273–275
IEventHandler<TEvent> interface   175
IExchangeRateProvider interface   216
IGreeter interface   285
IHttpContext interface   182
IIdentity   20
IImageEffectAddIn   109
IInventoryManagement   166, 168
IInvocation interface   345
ILifestyleSelectionBehavior   440
IL (Intermediate Language)   348
ILocationService   166, 168
IMessageService   166

IMessageWriter interface 16, 18, 19, 20, 25
IMessageWriter.Write method 24
implementation attribute 438
implementations, splitting 315–317
INavigationService.NavigateTo method 222
independent domain models, building 61–69
    Dependency Inversion Principle 67–68
    interfaces vs. abstract classes 68–69
Index method 42, 44
Index view markup 43
Initialize method 109–110, 222
injected streams 463
INotificationService 170, 173, 179, 422, 459, 492
INotifyPropertyChanged interface 222
Insert method 303
InsertProduct command 318
inside-out technique 55
InstancePerDependency 446
instance-scope attribute 406
instance scopes, configuring 405–406
    configuration files 406
    with code 405–406
Interception 30–31, 62
    dynamic 342–348
        analysis of 346–348
        aspects are strongly coupled to tooling 347
        does not fix underlying design problems 348
        not universally applicable 347–348
        with Castle Dynamic Proxy 344–346
    implementing Cross-Cutting Concerns 290–300
        intercepting with Circuit Breaker 292–297
        preventing unauthorized access to sensitive functionality using Decorators 298–300
        reporting exceptions using Decorator pattern 297–298
    overview of 283–290
        Decorator design pattern 284–287
        implementing auditing using Decorator 287–290
Intercept method 87, 345
interfaces 6
    abstract classes vs. 68–69
    splitting 315–317
Intermediate Language (IL) 348
InvalidOperationException 469
InventoryController 322

Invoke method 233
IoC (Inversion of Control) 29, 77
I/O operations 347
IOrderFulfillment interface 168
IOrderRepository interface 166, 246
IPrincipal interface 65, 67
IProductCommandServices interface 315, 336
IProductManagementService interface 249
IProductQueryServices interface 336
IProductRepositoryFactory interface 130, 158, 183, 186
IProductRepository interface 62, 70, 76, 128, 130, 132, 154, 158, 183, 257, 294–295, 298, 346, 367, 369, 381
IProductService interface 59, 310, 348, 367, 436, 475
    analysis from perspective of SOLID 311–313
    implementing product-related features using 309–310
    violates ISP 311–312
    violates OCP 312–313
    violates SRP 312
IRouteAlgorithmFactory interface 189, 191
IRouteAlgorithm interface 188, 191
IRouteCalculator interface 191
isCustomerPreferred parameter 41
IsDecoratorFor method 424, 496
IServiceCollection 89
IServiceProvider 497
IServiceScope 469, 477, 482
ISP (Interface Segregation Principle) 187, 305
    fixing by splitting interfaces and implementations 315–317
    IProductService violates 311–312
ItemClickCommand 225
ITimeProvider interface 146, 196, 329
ITypeDescriptorContext 111
IUIControlFactory interface 7
IUpdateProductReviewTotalsService 318
IUserByNameRetriever 201
IUserContext Adapter 71–73
IUserContext interface 65, 67, 71, 101, 158, 183, 198, 200, 367
IUserRepository 200, 288, 306
IValidationAttributeAdapterProvider interface 111
IViewModel interface 223
IVoucherRedemptionService 107

J

JIT (Just-In-Time) compiler   348
justification argument   447

K

KeyedService class   425
KeyNotFoundException   141
key-value database   46

L

lambda expression   369
late binding   17, 5–18, 29, 48, 154–156, 377
layering in UpdateCurrency   217–218
LazyAuditTrailAppender   206
Lazy<T>   269–273
LazyUserContextProxy   272
Leaky Abstractions
    as parameterless factory methods   183–184
    code smells   182–183
    IEnumerable<T> as   273–275
    Lazy<T> as   269–273
    to leak Lifestyle choices to consumers   269–275
legacy applications   22
libraries
    resuable   69
    third-party   386–388
lifecycles of Dependencies   240
Lifestyles
    bad choices   266–278
        Captive Dependencies   266–269
        causing concurrency bugs by tying instances to lifetime of threads   275–278
        using Leaky Abstractions to leak Lifestyle choices to consumers   269–275
    configuring   439–440, 477
    patterns   255–266
        Scoped Lifestyle   260–266
        Singleton Lifestyle   256–258
        Transient Lifestyle   259–260
Lifestyle.Singleton and Lifestyle.Transient   442
Lifetime Management   30, 184, 404–409, 438–447, 476–480
    ambient scopes   443–444
    configuring instance scopes   405–406
        with code   405–406
        with configuration files   406

configuring Lifestyles   439–440, 477
diagnosing containers for lifetime problems   444–447
    letting container detect Captive Dependencies   446–447
    suppressing warnings on individual registrations   447
overview of   238–242
    adding complexity to Dependency lifecycles   240–242
    simple Dependency lifecycle   239–240
releasing components   406–409, 440–443, 477–480
lifetime scopes   406
LINQ query   495
Liskov Substitution Principle   11, 22, 30, 241, 284
    analyzing accidental violations   323–324
    fixing using generic Abstraction   324–326
Local Default   97, 101, 114
Locator class   140, 143
Locator.Reset() method   144
logging   77, 103, 149, 328, 331
LoggingMiddleware class   233
logic
    implementing application logic   15–17
    unit testing   23–24
logical artifacts   87
LogManager.GetLogger method   151
Log method   275
long-running applications   262–266
loose coupling   5, 26, 284
loosely coupled code
    analyzing loosely coupled implementations   74–78
        analyzing dependency graphs   75–78
        interaction between components   74–75
    rebuilding e-commerce applications   53–74
        building data access layers   70–71
        building independent domain models   61–69
        building maintainable UIs   56–61
        composing applications in Composition Root   73–74
        implementing ASP.NET Core-specific IUserContext Adapter   71–73
LSP (Liskov Substitution Principle)
    analyzing accidental violations   323–324
    fixing using generic Abstraction   324–326

M

Main method 15, 28, 87, 89, 213
maintainability 17, 21, 49
MainViewModel class 222, 224
    injecting Dependencies into 221–225
    wiring up 225
MakePreferred method 106
mapping Abstractions to concrete types 396–397,
    469–470
messages, intercepting 23
messageWriter application 19
messaging 179
method calls
    varying Dependency consumer on each 105–108
    varying injected Dependency on each 108–109
MethodExecutionTag property 351
Method Injection pattern 54, 104–113
    adding currency conversions to Product
        Entity 112–113
    known use of 111–112
    overview of 104–105
    when to use 105–110
        Temporal Coupling code smell 109–110
        varying Dependency consumer on each
            method call 105–108
        varying injected Dependency on each method
            call 108–109
Microsoft Azure 46
Microsoft Distributed Transaction Coordinator
    (MSDTC) 322
Microsoft.Extensions.DependencyInjection 378
middleware 233–234
Model property 57, 225
MS.DI (Microsoft.Extensions.DependencyInjection)
    Lifetime Management 476–480
        configuring Lifestyles 477
        releasing components 477–480
    overview of 467–476
        configuring ServiceCollection 471–476
        resolving objects 468–471
    registering difficult APIs 480–483
        configuring primitive Dependencies 480–481
        extracting primitive Dependencies to
            Parameter Objects 481
        registering objects with code blocks 482–483
    working with multiple components 483–498
        selecting among multiple candidates 483–486

wiring Composites 492–498
wiring Decorators 489–492
wiring sequences 486–489
MSDTC (Microsoft Distributed Transaction
    Coordinator) 322
multi-threading 276–278
MVC (Model View Controller) applications, for ASP.
    NET Core 228–234
    constructing custom middleware components
        with Pure DI 233–234
    creating custom controller activators 230–232
MVVM (Model-View-ViewModel) 218, 220
MyApp.Services.Products namespace 323

N

Named method 414
Navigate method 225
NavigateTo method 222
.NET Core console application; net core 87
.NET events; net events 204
new keyword 50, 127, 135
NewProductViewModel 224
n-layer application 35, 60
no operation 117
NuGet packages 441
null argument 96
Null Object pattern 102, 117
NullReferenceException 11, 115, 293, 353
null value 141

O

Object Composition 28–29, 91, 212, 385
object graphs 73, 98
    composing in CreateCurrencyParser 216
    composing using generic Decorators 335–336
    resolving with DI Containers 362–363
Object Lifetime 30
    bad Lifestyle choices 266–278
        Captive Dependencies 266–269
        causing concurrency bugs by tying instances to
            lifetime of threads 275–278
        using Leaky Abstractions to leak Lifestyle
            choices to consumers 269–275
    disposable Dependencies 245–255
        consuming 246–249
        managing 250–255
    Lifestyle patterns 255–266

Object Lifetime *(continued)*
    Scoped Lifestyle   260–266
    Singleton Lifestyle   256–258
    Transient Lifestyle   259–260
    managing Dependency Lifetime   238–245
        Lifetime Management, overview of   238–242
        managing lifetime with Pure DI   242–245
objects
    Abstractions to concrete types   430–431
    resolving   395–398, 429–432, 468–471
        mapping Abstractions to concrete
            types   396–397, 430–431, 469–470
        resolving weakly typed services   397–398,
            431–432, 470–471
        with code blocks, registering   411–412, 450–451,
            482–483
OCP (Open/Closed Principle)
    fixing using Parameter Objects   317–321
    IProductService violates   312–313
OnLaunched method   219
OnMethodBoundaryAspect   350
OnSuccess method   351
Open/Closed Principle   14, 21, 116, 200, 297, 410
Open state   295
optional method arguments   222
Options property   119
OrderAccepted event   179
OrderApproved class   174
OrderCancelled class   174
OrderFulfillment class   175
OrderService class   167–168, 246
outside-in technique   54
overloaded constructors   134–135

P

parallel development   17, 20–21, 49
parameterless factory methods   183–184
Parameter Objects   318, 450
    extracting primitive Dependencies
        to   449–450, 481
    fixing OCP using   317–321
passive attributes   332
patterns, choosing   120–122
performance monitoring   328
PermittedRoleAttribute   333
persistence ignorance   70
per-thread Lifestyle   266
POCOs (Plain Old CLR Objects)   57, 220

Policy suffix   401
PostSharp tool   350
PowerShell   213
predicate value   454
price value parameter   105
primitive Dependencies
    configuring   409–411, 480–481
    extracting to Parameter Objects   481
private readonly field   152
Proceed method   345
Product class   37, 50, 63, 70
Product Entity   112–113
product-management rich clients, wiring
        up   219–225
    injecting Dependencies into
        MainViewModel   221–225
    wiring up MainViewModel   225
productRepository   239
ProductRepository   74, 154–156
ProductRepositoryFactory class   132
ProductRepositoryStub   142
ProductService class   41, 47, 64, 73, 86, 101, 112,
        128, 134, 140–142, 143, 239, 244, 260, 272
ProductViewModel class   57
Program class   87, 213, 264
Property Injection pattern   94, 102, 114–120, 204
    as extensibility model of reusable
        library   118–120
    breaking Dependency cycles with   204–206
    known uses of   118
    overview of   114–115
    when to use   115–118
public keyword   69
Pure DI   15, 89, 145, 216, 376
    applying Interceptor inside Composition Root
        using   345–346
    constructing custom middleware components
        with   233–234
    implementing with Composition Root   89–91
    managing lifetime with   242–245
    shorter feedback cycle with   388–389

R

readonly field   145
readonly keyword   245
reads, separating from writes   314–315
RedeemVoucher method   106

refactoring
    by removing ambiguity 417–418, 455, 487
    from Abstract Factory to Adapter 191–194
    from Ambient Context toward DI 152–153
    from Constrained Construction toward
        DI 157–161
    from Constructor Over-injection to domain
        events 173–180
    from Constructor Over-injection to Facade
        Services 168–173
    from Control Freak toward DI 136–137
    from Service Locator toward DI 145
    from SRP violations to resolve Dependency
        cycles 200–204
RegisterAssemblyTypes method 400, 401, 421, 423
RegisterConditional method 453
RegisterDecorator 383, 420–421, 457, 461
registered components 456
RegisterGenericDecorator 420–422, 424
Register method 141, 366, 411
Register Resolve Release pattern 373
RegisterType method 397
registrations
    conditional 453–454
    difficult APIs 409–412, 447–451, 480–483
        configuring primitive Dependencies 409–411,
            448–449, 480–481
        extracting primitive Dependencies to
            Parameter Objects 449–450, 481
        named Dependencies 414–416
        objects with code blocks 411–412, 450–451,
            482–483
        suppressing warnings on individual 447
Release method 230, 254
releasing components 406–409, 440–443, 477–480
reliable messaging 179
Repository pattern
    resolving multiple 259–260
    thread-safe in-memory 257–258
repository variable 128, 242
Reset method 141
Resolve API 361–363
ResolvedParameter class 415
Resolve method 89, 362, 368
Resolve<T> method 397
resolving 394–404
    objects 395–398, 429–432, 468–471
    weakly typed services 397–398, 431–432, 470–471

reusable libraries 69, 118–120
role-based security 334
RouteCalculator class 192, 243
RouteController 188, 191, 232
RouteType 188
row-based security 334
runtime data, selecting Dependencies based
      on 187–194
    analysis of code smell 190
    refactoring from Abstract Factory to
        Adapter 191–194

S

Salutation class 16, 19, 23–24
scoped DbContext 262–266
Scoped Dependencies 261, 278
Scoped Lifestyle pattern 260–266
    composing long-running applications using a
        ScopedDbContext 262–266
    when to use 262
scopes, ambient 443–444
Seams 25, 213, 218
SecureMessageWriter class 20, 30, 287
SecureProductRepositoryDecorator 299, 308, 331
security 19, 291, 328, 331–334
sensitive functionality 298–300
separation of concerns 40, 50
sequences
    Auto-Wiring 418, 455, 487–488
    streams as 462–464
    wiring 417–420, 454–457, 486–489
        refactoring by removing ambiguity 417–418,
            455, 487
        selecting components from larger
            set 418–420, 455–457, 488–489
ServiceCollection, configuring 471–476
    Auto-Registration of generic
        Abstractions 475–476
    using Auto-Registration 473–475
    using Configuration as Code 472–473
Service Locator anti-pattern 7, 88, 138–145, 353
    analysis of 142–145
    negative effects of 142–145
    ProductService using 140–142
    refactoring toward DI 145
ServiceProvider property 468, 478
services, weakly typed 397–398, 431–432, 470–471

SimpleDecorator class   285
Simple Injector
  Lifetime Management   438–447
    ambient scopes   443–444
    configuring Lifestyles   439–440
    diagnosing containers for lifetime
      problems   444–447
    releasing components   440–443
  overview of   428–438
    configuring containers   432–438
    resolving objects   429–432
  registering difficult APIs   447–451
    configuring primitive Dependencies   448–449
    extracting primitive Dependencies to
      Parameter Objects   449–450
    registering objects with code blocks   450–451
  working with multiple components   451–464
    selecting among multiple candidates   452–454
    sequences are streams   462–464
    wiring Composites   459–462
    wiring Decorators   457–459
    wiring sequences   454–457
SimpleInjector.Containe   430
SingleInstance method   405
Singleton Dependencies   261
Singleton Lifestyle pattern   242, 256–258, 439
  using thread-safe in-memory Repository
    257–258
  when to use   256
Singletons   245
Site property   118
SOLID
  analysis of IProductService from perspective
    of   311–313
    concluding analysis of IProductService   313
    IProductService violates ISP   311–312
    IProductService violates OCP   312–313
    IProductService violates SRP   312
  applying principles to improve design   314–327
    analyzing the accidental LSP
      violations   323–324
    applying transaction handling using generic
      Abstraction   326–327
    fixing ISP and SRP by splitting interfaces and
      implementations   315–317
    fixing LSP using generic Abstraction   324–326
    fixing OCP using Parameter Objects   317–321

  implementing Cross-Cutting Concerns with
    ICommandService   321–323
  separating reads from writes   314–315
  as driver for AOP   308–337
    adding Cross-Cutting Concerns   327–336
    analysis of IProductService from perspective of
      SOLID   311–313
    applying SOLID principles to improve
      design   314–327
    implementing product-related features using
      IProductService   309–310
  principles for   305–308
    DIP (Dependency Inversion Principle)   308
    Interception and   308
    ISP (Interface Segregation Principle)
      307–308
    LSP (Liskov Substitution Principle)   307
    OCP (Open/Closed Principle)   306–307
    SRP (Single Responsibility Principle)   306
split classes   204
splitting
  implementations   315–317
  interfaces   315–317
SpyMessageWriter   24
SqlAuditTrailAppender   196, 198, 205
SqlExchangeRateProvider   216, 276
SqlProductRepository   66, 73, 128, 132, 134, 158,
    185, 239, 243, 283, 350, 367, 370, 381
SqlProductRepositoryFactory   158, 159, 160
SqlProductRepositoryProxy   186
SqlUserByNameRetriever   201
SqlUserRepository class   197, 199, 202, 205, 260
SRP (Single Responsibility Principle)   21, 28, 31,
    40, 50, 165
  fixing by splitting interfaces and
    implementations   315–317
  IProductService violates   312
  violations of
    Dependency cycles caused by   195–198
    refactoring from   200–204
Stable Dependencies   26
StackOverflowExceptions   200, 371
Startup class   89, 230, 233, 245
Startup.ConfigureServices method   90
stateless service   259
Static Factory   131–134
string argument   154

SummaryText property   57
SuppressDiagnosticWarning   447
SUT (System Under Test)   22
System.Activator class   366
System.ComponentModel.DataAnnotations   328
System.ComponentModel.Design.IDesigner   111
System.ComponentModel namespace   111
System.Data.SqlClient.SqlDataReader   462
System.DateTime.Now   27
System.IO.StreamReader class   99
System.IO.StreamWriter class   99
System.Lazy<T> class   269
System.Random   27
System.Security.Cryptography.
     RandomNumberGenerator   27
System.Security.Principal.WindowsIdentity class   20
System.Timers.Timer class   265
System.Transactions.TransactionScope class   322
System Under Test (SUT)   22
System.Windows.Input.ICommand   221
System.Xml assembly   25

T

Table Storage Service   46
TCommand argument   382
TDD (Test-Driven Development)   6, 56, 182
Temporal Coupling code smell   109–110
testability   17, 21–23, 49, 182
Test Doubles   22, 24
Test-Driven Development (TDD)   6, 56, 182
testing   6–23, 6–24
TEvent type   175
text messages, intercepting   23
third-party add-ins   5
third-party libraries   386–388
ThreadPool.QueueUserWorkItem   276
threads   260
    lifetime is often unclear   276
    tying instances to lifetime of   275–278
thread-safe in-memory Repository   257–258
three-layer diagram   35
tightly coupled code
    analysis of missing composability   47–50
        data access interface analysis   48–50
        dependency graph analysis   47–48

building tightly coupled applications   35–44
    creating data layers   36–39
    creating domain layers   39–42
    creating UI layers   42–44
evaluating tightly coupled applications   44–47
    evaluating composability   45–47
    evaluating dependency graphs   44–45
TimeProvider class   148
TimeSpan   156
TitledGreeterDecorator class   286
ToEndpointAddress method   109
Torn Lifestyles   388, 399
TrackDisposable method   252, 254
transaction aspect, applying using compile-time
        weaving   349–351
TransactionAttribute   350
TransactionCommandServiceDecorator class   321
transaction handling, applying using
        Abstraction   326–327
TransactionScope class   322, 351, 444
Transient Lifestyle pattern   259–260, 439
    resolving multiple Repositories   259–260
    when to use   259
Transients, disposible   408, 479
transitivity   93
try statement   254
Type instance   19
type parameters   175, 362

U

UI Layer   36
UIs (user interfaces)
    building   45–46
    creating layers   42–44
    maintainable, building   56–61
UI (user interface) toolkits   7
unauthorized access to sensitive functionality
        298–300
uninterrupted power supply (UPS)   11
UnitPrice property   225
unit testing   6–24
UpdateCurrencyCommand   217
UpdateCurrency program   262
    building Composition Root of   215–216
    layering in   217–218
    updating currencies with   214

UpdateHasDiscountsApplied   312
UpdateHasTierPricesProperty command   310,
    312, 318
UpdateProductReviewTotals   324
UpdateProductReviewTotalsService   323
updating currencies   214
UPS (uninterrupted power supply)   11
Uri property   109
Use extension method   233
userContext variable   198
user interface (UI) toolkits   7
UserMailAddressChanged even   203
User property   39, 43
user repository   288–289
userRepository variable   198
UserService class   199
using statement   249
uto-Registered Abstractions   458
UWP (Universal Windows Programming)
    applications   87
  composing   218–228
  implementing Composition Root in   226–228

V

Validate method   247
validateScopes   469
validation   291, 328
ValidationAttribute   111
valueAccessor delegate   415
Value property   270
violations
  of LSP, accidental   323–324
  of SRP
    Dependency cycle caused by   195–198
    refactoring from to resolve Dependency
      Cycle   200–204
Virtual Proxy   205, 272
Visual Studio   5
Volatile Dependencies   26–27, 51, 53, 127, 355

W

warnings, suppressing   447
WcfProductRepository class   249, 294, 297
WCF (Windows Communication Foundation)   247

web-based UI   76
WelcomeMessageGenerator   152
whenDone action   222
Where method   401
Windows Communication Foundation (WCF)   247
Windows Presentation Foundation (WPF)   45
wiring
  Composites   422–425, 459–462, 492–498
    generic   424–425, 461–462, 496–498
    non-generic   422–424, 459–461, 493–496
  Decorators   420–422, 457–459, 489–492
    decorating Abstractions   457–458
    decorating generic Abstractions   458–459,
      490–492
    decorating generic Abstractions with
      RegisterGenericDecorator   421–422
    decorating non-generic Abstractions   489–490
    decorating non-generic Abstractions with
      RegisterDecorator   420–421
  MainViewModel   225
  product-management rich clients   219–225
  sequences   417–420, 454–457, 486–489
    Auto-Wiring sequences   418, 455, 487–488
    refactoring by removing ambiguity   417–418,
      455, 487
    selecting components from larger
      set   418–420, 455–457, 488–489
WithParameter method   412, 415, 419, 425
WPF applications   87
WPF-based UI   76
wrapping, composite   177
Write method   16, 20
writer instance   14
writes, separating from reads   314–315
WrittenMessage property   24

X

XmlProductRepository   156
XmlReader argument   156
XmlWriter   24

Y

YAGNI principle   55

C# in Depth, Fourth Edition
by Jon Skeet

ISBN: 9781617294532
528 pages
$49.99
March 2019

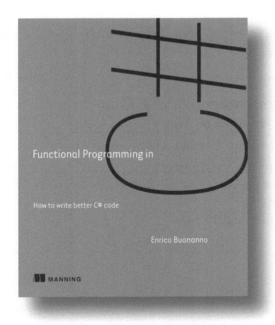

Functional Programming in C#
How to write better C# code
by Enrico Buonanno

ISBN: 9781617293955
408 pages
$44.99
August 2017

MORE TITLES FROM MANNING

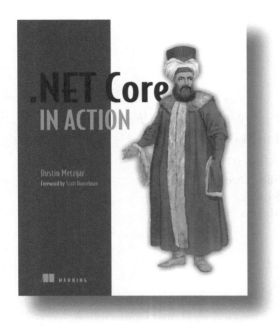

.NET Core in Action
by Dustin Metzgar

ISBN: 9781617294273
288 pages
$44.99
July 2018

Microservices in .NET Core
with examples in Nancy
by Christian Horsdal Gammelgaard

ISBN: 9781617293375
344 pages
$49.99
January 2017

MORE TITLES FROM MANNING

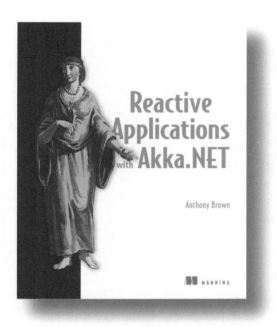

Reactive Applications with Akka.NET
by Anthony Brown

    ISBN: 9781617292989
    150 pages
    $44.99
    February 2019

Concurrency in .NET
Modern patterns of concurrent and parallel
programming
by Riccardo Terrell

    ISBN: 9781617292996
    568 pages
    $59.99
    June 2018

For ordering information go to www.manning.com

MORE TITLES FROM MANNING

Learn Azure in a Month of Lunches
by Iain Foulds

ISBN: 9781617295171
384 pages
$44.99
August 2018

Learn Windows PowerShell in a Month of Lunches, Third Edition
by Don Jones and Jeffery Hicks

ISBN: 9781617294167
384 pages
$44.99
December 2016

For ordering information go to www.manning.com